THE RISALE-I NUR COLLECTION

The
WORDS

The Reconstruction of Islamic Belief and Thought

BEDİÜZZAMAN SAİD NURSİ

Translated by
Hüseyin Akarsu

TUGHRA
BOOKS
New Jersey

Published by Tughra Books
335 Clifton Ave
Clifton, NJ 07011

www.tughrabooks.com

Library of Congress Cataloging-in-Publication Data

Nursi, Said, 1877-1960.
  [Sozler. English]
The Words : the reconstruction of Islamic belief and thought / Bediuzzaman Said
Nursi; [translated by Huseyin Akarsu].
     p. cm.
  Includes bibliographical references and index.
  ISBN 1-932099-16-6
  1. Nurculuk--Doctrines. 2. Islam--Essence, genius, nature. 3. Islam--Appreciation.
I. Title.
BP252.N8613 2005
297.8'3--dc21

2002012564

The
WORDS

Table of Contents

THE TWENTY-SIXTH WORD

THE TWENTY-SEVENTH WORD

THE TWENTY-EIGHTH WORD

THE TWENTY-NINTH WORD

Bediüzzaman Said Nursi
and the Risale-i Nur

EDIUZZAMAN SAID NURSI'S (1877–1960) ACHIEVEMENTS, PERSONALITY, character, and continuing influence make him an important twentieth-century Muslim figure. A most effective and profound representative of Islam's intellectual, moral, and spiritual strengths, he spent most of his life overflowing with love and ardor for Islam, pursuing a wise and measured activism based on sound reasoning, and following the Qur'an and the Prophetic example. Much has been said and written about the lofty ideal he pursued and his deep familiarity with the world and his times, as well as his simplicity, austerity, tenderness, loyalty, chastity, modesty, and contentedness.

Though outwardly simple, many of his ideas and activities were wholly original. He embraced humanity; opposed unbelief, injustice, and [religious] deviation; and struggled against tyranny—even at the cost of his life. His deep belief and feeling, when combined with his wise and rational ideas and problem-solving methods, produced an example of love, ardor, and feeling. His balanced thought, acts, and methods of acting made him a far-sighted man who assessed and judged surrounding conditions and solved problems.

Many contemporaries explicitly or tacitly acknowledged him as the most important thinker and writer of twentieth-century Turkey, or even of the Muslim world. Despite this and his leadership of a new Islamic intellectual, social, and political revival, he remained a humble servant of God. His life exemplified his understanding of humility: Desire for fame is the same as show and ostentation, a "poisonous honey" extinguishing the heart's spiritual liveliness.

Born in a small mountain village in eastern Anatolia, Said Nursi voiced the sighs and laments of the whole Muslim world, as well as its belief, hopes, and aspirations. He said:

> I can bear my own sorrows, but the sorrows arising from the calamities visiting Islam and Muslims have crushed me. I feel each blow delivered to the Muslim world as delivered first to my own heart. That is why I have been so shaken.... During my life of over 80 years, I have tasted no worldly pleasure. I have spent my life on battlefields, in prisons or other places of suffering. They have treated me like a criminal, banishing me from one town to another, keeping me under constant surveillance. There has been no persecution I have not tasted, no oppression I have not suffered. I neither care for Paradise nor fear Hell. If I see my nation's belief secured, I will not even care about burning in Hell, for while my body is burning my heart will be as if in a rose garden. (*Tarihçe-i Hayat* [Biography], Nesil, Istanbul: 1996, vol 2, p. 2206)

Said Nursi lived during a global crisis: Materialism was triumphant, communism was popular, and Muslims were being urged to reject Islam. Shocked by the West's scientific and military victories and influenced by modern thought, Muslims were discarding their roots and sometimes their belief. Many intellectuals left the Straight Path and pursued Western ideas. Said Nursi, however, pointed people to the source of belief and inculcated in them a strong hope for an overall revival. His writings showed Islam's truth and opposed the growing deviation. Relying on God and his firm conviction in Islam's truth, and driven by his belief in the Muslim world's bright future, he defended Islam and sought to raise a new generation that would realize his hopes.

At a time when science and philosophy were used to produce young atheists and nihilism was popular; when such things were done in the name of civilization, modernization, and contemporary thinking; and when resisters were persecuted, Said Nursi worked for a people's revival, infusing them with modern and traditional education as well as spiritual training.

Said Nursi diagnosed the Muslim world's long-standing "diseases" and offered the most effective cures. Basing his activity on the Qur'an and Sunna (the Prophet's traditions), as well as the Islamic tradition and natural phenomena (considered signs of Divine Existence and Unity), he concentrated, respectively, on proving the pillars of Islam; the necessity of belief, worship, morality, and good conduct; and socio-economic issues facing contemporary Muslims.

Said Nursi's times and prescribed cures

Said Nursi lived during a time of transition—the Ottoman State's dying years and the Turkish Republic's formative years. He traveled widely, seeing first-hand the ignorance, poverty, and internal conflict prevailing in Anatolia and the larger Muslim world. In 1911, in the Umayyad Mosque (Damascus) to about 10,000 people, including a hundred high-ranking scholars, he analyzed why the Muslim world was stuck in the "Middle Ages": growing despair, the loss of truthfulness in social and political spheres; the love of belligerency and ignorance of the bonds proper among believers; pervasive despotism; and ego-centricity. He offered his cure—hope, truthfulness and trustworthiness, mutual love, consultation, solidarity, and freedom in accordance with Islam—and stressed the following:

> History shows us that the Muslims have progressed to the extent of their adherence to the truths of Islam and have derived their power from the strength of these truths, while they have declined to the extent of their weakness in following them. The reverse of this reality is true for other religions. Their followers have progressed to the extent of their weakness in adherence to their religions and suffered revolutions and decline in proportion to their attachment.
>
> We Muslims, who are the students of the Qur'an, follow proof and accept the truths of belief with our reason, intellect, and heart. Unlike some members of other religions, we do not abandon proof and blindly imitate religious leaders. Therefore, in the future, when reason, sciences, and knowledge will dominate, it will be the Qur'an, the decrees and propositions of which are all confirmed by reason, that will certainly rule. (from "The Sermon of Damascus", *Gleams of Truth: Prescriptions for a Healthy Social Life*, (trans.), Tughra Books, New Jersey, pp. 124, 125)

If our actions display the perfection of Islamic moral qualities and the truths of belief, followers of other religions will enter Islam in whole communities. Even some entire regions and states will take refuge in Islam.

During his time and our own, ignorance of God and the Prophet, upon him be peace and blessings, heedlessness of religious commands, indifference to the Islamic dynamics of prosperity in both worlds, and ignorance of modern scientific knowledge were leading causes of Muslim backwardness. He stated that Muslims could escape this backwardness only through modern scientific and religious knowledge as well as systematic thought, and could protect themselves against deviation only by acquiring true knowledge.

Ignorance was a source of Muslim poverty, internal conflict, and other problems. Ignorance of Islam's truth, when added to ignorance of science and technology, resulted in vast uncultivated plains and the Muslims' natural wealth flowing to foreigners. Although the Qur'an demands unity, Muslims remained divided even as their lands were being invaded and their people humiliated.

At the same time, those Muslim intellectuals to whom the masses looked for leadership and salvation were attracted by the violent storm of denial blowing from Europe. Emerging in the previous century from a human-centered worldview rooted in scientism, rationalism, and positivism, as well as from the contradictions between modern science and an anti-science Church, this storm gradually robbed Europe of most of its belief in Christianity. As a result, Revelation was forced to yield to human reason.

This process, unparalleled in history, shook the "building" of an Islam that was already old and decayed in many hearts and minds (individual and communal). Said Nursi believed that this "building" could be protected by presenting Islam's essentials and their branches to the faculties and reason of modern people. According to him, the Muslim world, so clearly beached on the oceans of modernity, would sail freely again only by undergoing a successful, comprehensive renewal in all fields of Islam.

How Muslims came to be dominated

Said Nursi explained the Ottoman collapse and subsequent Western domination of the Muslim world in the following terms in his *Sunuhat* (Occurrences to the Herat) and *Lemeat* (Gleams of Truth):

> The calamity was the calamity of all humankind. The common cause, inclusive of all humankind, was the misguided thinking that arose from materialism—bestial freedom, the despotism of carnal desires and fancies. Our share in it resulted from our neglect and abandonment of the pillars of Islam. For the Creator the All-Exalted wanted one hour out of the twenty-four.
>
> He ordered us, willed that we, for our good, assign one hour for the five daily Prayers. But out of laziness we gave them up, neglected them in heedlessness. So we received the following punishment: He made us perform Prayers of a sort during these last five years through a constant, twenty-four hour drill and hardship, keeping us ceaseless-

ly moving and striving. He also demanded of us one month a year for fasting, but we pitied our carnal souls, so in atonement He compelled us to fast for five years. He wanted us to pay as *Zakah* either a fortieth or a tenth of the property He gave us, but out of miserliness we did wrong: we mixed the unlawful with our property, and did not give the *Zakah* voluntarily. So He had our accumulated *Zakah* taken from us, and saved us from what was unlawful in our property. The deed causes the punishment of its kind. The punishment is of the same as the deed. The neglect of the *Hajj* and its wisdom drew not calamity, but Divine Wrath, and the punishment it incurred was not atonement for our sins but an increase in our sins. It was the neglect of the elevated Islamic policy, which exists in the *Hajj* and brings unity of views through mutual acquaintance and cooperation through mutual assistance, and it was neglect of the vast social benefits contained in the *Hajj* which have prepared the ground for the enemy to employ millions of Muslims against Islam... Instead of hastening to the *Hajj* eagerly, which is pure good, millions of Muslims have been made to make long journeys under the enemy flag, which is pure evil. Ponder on this and take heed! (*Gleams of Truth*, pp. 47, 48)

Said Nursi also writes:

Friend! A questioner once asked: "As 'The truth prevails' is the truth, why are the unbelievers triumphant over Muslims and force or might is triumphant over right?"

I replied: Consider these four points and your difficulty will be resolved:

The first point is this. Every means to every truth and right may not be true and rightful at all times. Similarly, not every means of every falsehood has to be false. The result is a means which (falsehood employs and) is true prevailing over a false means (which truth or right uses). In which case, a truth is overcome by falsehood. But this has occurred temporarily and indirectly, not essentially or permanently. However, the final triumph is always that of the truth. (It should also not be forgotten that) force possesses a truth, and there is a purpose and meaning in its creation.

The second point is this: While it is obligatory that all attributes of all Muslims are Muslim, in reality this may not always be so. Similarly, not all the attributes of all unbelievers have to be connected to unbelieving or arise from their unbelief. In the same way, all the attributes of all sinful transgressors may not be sinful, nor do they need always arise from sinfulness.

This means that an unbeliever's Muslim attribute prevails over a Muslim's irreligious at-tribute. Indirectly and due to the means, the unbeliever can prevail over the believer. Furthermore, in this world the right of life is all-embracing. Life—that meaningful manifestation of the universal Mercy—has an instance of wisdom, which unbelief cannot impede.

The third point is this: two of the All-Majestic One's Attributes of perfection give rise to two sets of laws. One is the Shari'a of life or of the creation and operation of the universe, which proceeds from the Attribute of Will; and the other, the well-known Shari'a, which proceeds from the Attribute of Speech. Just as the commands or laws of the well-known Shari'a are obeyed or disobeyed, so too do people obey or disobey the Shari'a of life. The reward and punishment for the former is received mostly in the Hereafter, while the penalties and rewards of the latter are suffered mostly in this world. For example, the reward of patience is success, while the penalty for laziness is privation; and the reward of labor is wealth. The reward of steadfastness is triumph. The punishment of poison is illness and the reward of its antidote is health. Sometimes the commands of both Shari'as are in force in a single thing; it has aspects pertaining to each. That means, obedience to the rules of life is a truth, and obedience prevails, while disobedience to it is a false attitude. If a truth has been the means to a falsehood, when it prevails it will be the true means to a falsehood. This is an example of truth being defeated by a falsehood owing to the means. It is not the defeat of the truth itself by falsehood. In consequence, "The truth prevails" means: "The truth is triumphant essentially or in it-self." Also, the end or consequence is intended.

The fourth point is this: a truth has remained in potential or it is powerless, or adulterated or contaminated. It needs to be developed or given fresh strength. In order to improve and brighten it, falsehood is temporarily allowed to attack it, so that however much pure gold of truth is needed will emerge unadulterated. Even if in the beginning falsehood is victorious in this world, it cannot win the war. "The final (happy) outcome is in favor of the God-revering, pious," will strike it a blow! So falsehood is defeated. The truth of "The truth prevails" inflicts punishment on it. See: the truth is triumphant. (*Gleams of Truth*, pp. 69-70)

Belief, knowledge of God, and worship

Said Nursi completed the normal madrasa (traditional religious school) education when he was fourteen. Long dissatisfied with the existing education system, he soon developed comprehensive proposals for reform based on joining traditional religious with modern secular sciences and establishing universities in major Anatolian cities. Although he twice received funds for his university and saw its foundations laid in 1913, the consequences of WWI and the vicissitudes of the time prevented its completion.

Unlike traditional religious scholars, Said Nursi studied natural and social science, mathematics, and philosophy. During WWI, he was captured and held by the Russians for 2 years. After his escape and return to Istanbul, he began expounding Islam's pillars. But new and irreversible events in Anatolia led to a secular regime, and anti-Islamic trends and attitudes among intellectuals and the young (due to a deliberately positivist—even materialist—system of education) were growing. These factors forced him to focus on the essentials of belief and worship and the Qur'an's main purposes: explaining and proving Divine Existence and Unity, Prophethood, Resurrection, and the need for worship and justice. He explains in various places of his *The Words*, *The Letters*, and *Lahikalar* (Addenda):

> Creation's highest aim and most sublime result is belief in God. The most exalted rank of humanity is knowledge of God. The most radiant happiness and sweetest bounty for jinn and humanity is love of God contained within knowledge of Him; the spirit's purest joy and the heart's purest delight is spiritual ecstasy contained within love of God. All true happiness, pure joy, sweet bounties, and unclouded pleasure are contained within the knowledge and love of God.
>
> Belief is not restricted to a brief affirmation based on imitation; rather, it has degrees and stages of development. It is like a seed growing into a fully grown, fruit-bearing tree; like the sun's image in a mirror or in a drop of water to its images on the sea's surface and to the sun itself. Belief contains so many truths pertaining to God's Names and the realities contained in the universe that the most perfect science, knowledge, and virtue is belief and knowledge of God originating in a belief based on argument and investigation. While belief based on imitation can be refuted through doubt and questions raised by modern thought, belief based on argument and investigation has as many degrees and grades of manifestation as the number of Divine Names. Those who attain certainty of belief coming from direct observation of the truths on which belief is based study the universe as a kind of Qur'an.
>
> The Qur'an, the universe, and humanity are three kinds of manifestations of one truth. The Qur'an, issuing from the Divine Attribute of Speech, may be regarded as the written or composed universe. The universe, originating in the Divine Attributes of Power and Will, may be considered as the created Qur'an. Since the universe is the Qur'an's counterpart and, in one respect, the collection of Divine laws of cre-

ation, sciences that study the universe must be compatible with Islam. Therefore now (when science prevails) and in the future (the age of knowledge), true belief should be based on argument and investigation; on continual reflection on God's "signs" in the universe; and on natural, social, historical, and psychological phenomena. Belief is not something based on blind imitation; rather, it should appeal to both the intellect or reason and the heart, for it combines reason's acceptance and affirmation with the heart's experience and submission.

There is another degree of belief: certainty coming from direct experience of its truths. This depends on regular worship and reflection. Those with such belief can challenge the world. So, our first and foremost duty is to acquire such belief and, in complete sincerity and purely for God's sake, spread it to others. A *hadith* relates that it is better for you if one embraces belief through you than for you to possess the world.

In short, Said Nursi argues that belief consists of acquiring Islam in its entirety.

An outline of Said Nursi's life after 1925

When a revolt broke out in southeastern Turkey in 1925, Said Nursi and many others were sent into internal exile although he never participated in the revolt. At first, he lived a wretched, isolated life in Barla, a mountainous village in southwestern Turkey. However, he found true consolation in the Omnipresence of God and in complete submission to Him.

The basic works of the *Risale-i Nur* Collection (Epistles of Light), *The Words* and *The Letters*, were written in Barla and multiplied by hand-writing. Hand-made copies soon circulated throughout Turkey, and read widely. In 1935, Said Nursi was tried in Eskişehir Criminal Court. Although he always opposed revolt and breaches of the public peace and order, and stressed that one person's rights could not be violated even for society's sake, he was accused of working to destroy the public order. When asked his opinion of the Republic, he replied: "My biography, which you have in your hands, proves that I was a religious republican before any of you were born." He was held in prison for eleven months before acquittal.

Following his release, he had to live in Kastamonu. He stayed on the top floor of the police station, and later was settled in a house immediately opposite it. He lived in Kastamonu for seven years, and wrote a major part of the *Risale-i Nur* there. During this period, both he and his students [from

Kastamonu and elsewhere] faced constant pressure from the authorities. This gradually increased, and culminated in widespread arrests, the Denizli trials, and imprisonment in 1943-44. Said Nursi was accused of forming a Sufi order and organizing a political society. Although acquitted, he spent nine months in solitary confinement in a tiny, dark, damp cell under the most appalling conditions.

After his release, Said Nursi was sent to Emirdağ (in Afyon province). In 1948 a new case was opened against him in Afyon Criminal Court. The Appeals Court quashed this court's arbitrary ruling, and Said Nursi and his students were acquitted. Following this, he stayed for brief periods in Emirdağ, Isparta, Afyon, Istanbul, and elsewhere. In 1952 he was tried once more, this time for his publication of *Guide for Youth*. He was acquitted.

On his death in Urfa on March 23, 1960, which may well have been the Night of Power in Ramadan, the coroner fixed his estate as a turban, a gown, and 20 lira. The real legacy of this hero of Islam was the 6,000-page *Risale-i Nur* Collection, which have been translated into many foreign languages and have had a wide circulation throughout the world.

The Risale-i Nur

To comprehend this work's quality and main characteristic, the following experience of Dr. Colin Turner of Durham University, UK, is worth quoting at length. He writes:

> As someone born and raised in Britain, I am often asked what we as Muslims have to offer to the West. But before I answer, I should like to ask a question myself: Are we Muslims because we believe in God Almighty, or do we believe in God because we are Muslims?
>
> The question occurred to me during a march through the streets of London, over a decade ago, to protest against the Russian occupation of Afghanistan. I'd made a formal conversion to Islam several years prior to this, and it wasn't my first demonstration. There were banners and placards and much shouting and chanting. Towards the end of the demonstration I was approached by a young man who introduced himself as someone interested in Islam. "Excuse me," he said, "but what is the meaning of *la ilaha illa Allah?*"
>
> Without a moment's hesitation I answered, "There is no god but Allah."

"I'm not asking you to translate it," he said, "I'm asking you to tell me what it really means." There was a long awkward silence as it dawned on me that I was unable to answer him.

You are no doubt thinking, What kind of Muslim is it that does not know the real meaning of *la ilaha illa Allah*? To this I would have to say: a typical one. That evening I pondered my ignorance. Being in the majority didn't help; it simply made me more depressed.

Islam simply made sense, in a way that nothing else ever had. It had rules of government; it had an economic system; it had regulations concerning every facet of day-to-day existence. It was egalitarian and addressed to all races, and it was clear and easy to understand. Oh, and it has a God, One God, in whom I had always vaguely believed. That was that. I said *la ilaha illa Allah* and I was part of the community. For the first time in my life I belonged.

New converts are invariably enthusiastic to know as much as possible about their religion in the shortest possible time. In the few years that followed, my library grew rapidly. There was so much to learn, and so many books ready to teach. Books on the history of Islam, the economic system of Islam, the concept of government in Islam; countless manuals of Islamic jurisprudence, and, best of all, books on Islam and revolution, on how Muslims were to rise up and establish Islamic governments, Islamic republics. When I returned to Britain in early '79 from my trip to the Middle East to learn the meaning of la ilaha illa Allah, I was ready to introduce Islam to the West.

It was to these books that I turned for an answer to the question: What is the meaning of *la ilaha illa Allah*? Again I was disappointed. The books were about Islam, not about Allah. They covered every subject you could possibly imagine except for the one which really mattered. I put the question to the imam at the university mosque. He made an excuse and left. Then a brother who had overheard my impertinent question to the imam came over and said: "I have a tafsir of *la ilaha illa Allah*. If you like, we could read it together." I imagined that it would be ten or twenty pages at the most. It turned out to have over 5,000 pages, in several books. It was the *Risale-i Nur* by Said Nursi.[*]

Said Nursi saw that modern unbelief did not originate from ignorance, but from science and philosophy. Paradoxically, the Muslims' neglect of science and technology caused them to fall behind the West economically and militarily. But the same science and technology that enabled the West to achieve

---

[*] Quoted from Dr. Turner's paper presented at the 1991 conference on Said Nursi, held in Istanbul.

global military and economic superiority caused Western people to lose their belief and traditional moral and spiritual values, and fall into pessimism, unhappiness, and spiritual crisis. This was natural, because although the Divine laws of nature (the subject matter of science) are the counterpart of the Divine Scripture or religion, they were separated from each other in the West. Secular morality and economic self-interest then replaced religious and other traditional values. Said Nursi viewed nature as the collection of Divine signs. Thus science and religion could not be in conflict, for they are two (apparently) different expressions of the same truth. Minds should be enlightened with science, and hearts need to be illumined with religion.

Initially, Said Nursi based his defense of the religious truths on arguments derived from modern Western philosophy.** Later on, he saw that this way degraded Islam and that its essentials could not be reached by the principles of human philosophy. He then returned to the Qur'an almost exclusively. He writes:

> Thinkers accept the principles of human philosophy and the Western way of thinking, and depend on them in their struggle with Europe. I also filled my brain with the philosophical and the Islamic sciences, thinking that the philosophical sciences would lead to spiritual progress and enlightenment, and believing that European thought and philosophy could reinforce and strengthen Islam's truths. By grafting the shoots of philosophy, which we supposed were deep-rooted, onto Islam's trunk, we imagined that Islam could be strengthened. However, I abandoned this way, as it is a very hard, an improbable way to overcome anti-Islamic trends, and degrades Islam to some extent. Islam's essentials are too deep for the principles of philosophy to reach.

In arguing with Islam's opponents, in resisting and overcoming modern (materialistic) trends of thought, the Qur'an was enough:

> While there is a permanent miracle like the Qur'an, my mind considers it unnecessary to search for further proof. While there is an evidence of truth like the Qur'an, would it be heavy for my heart to silence those who deny? (The Twenty-fifth Word)

Although lacking in positive rational argument, unbelief and atheism derived from science and philosophy are harder to deal with and remove than

---

** The religious truths are defined as Divine Existence and Unity, Resurrection, Prophethood, the Qur'an's Divine origin, the Unseen World and its inhabitants or immaterial dimensions of existence, the need for worship and morality, humanity's ontological character, and so on. (Tr.)

unbelief derived from ignorance. Creating the universe and establishing its parts' relations clearly require an absolute, all-encompassing knowledge, will, and power. Nature cannot be its own creator: It is a design, not a designer; that which is printed, not a printer; a passive object, not an active agent; a collection of Divine laws, not the lawgiver. Similarly causes or the law of causality—having only a nominal existence without knowledge, will, and power—cannot create anything. If we ask those who attribute creation to causality or causes what makes a flower, they first should tell us how water, soil, and sunlight know what to do, how they do it, and how they enable a flower to grow.

The *Risale-i Nur* removes the veil of "sorcery" that materialist science has laid over creation. In the words of Dr. Turner:

> The *Risale-i Nur* affirms that anyone who sincerely wishes to look upon the created world as it is, and not as he wishes or imagines to be, must inevitably come to the conclusion of *la ilaha illa Allah*, for he will see order and harmony, beauty and equilibrium, justice and mercy, lordship, sustenance and munificence. And at the same time he will realize that those attributes are pointing not to the created beings themselves but to a Reality in which all of these attributes exist in perfection and absoluteness. He will see that the created world is thus a book of names, an index, which seek to tell about its Owner.
>
> The *Risale-i Nur* takes the interpretation of *la ilaha illa Allah* even further. The notion that it examines is that of causality, the cornerstone of materialism and the pillar upon which modern science has been constructed. Belief in causality gives rise to statements such as: It is natural; Nature created it; It happened by chance; and so on. With reasoned arguments, the *Risale-i Nur* explodes the myth of causality and demonstrates that those who adhere to this belief are looking at the cosmos not as it actually is or how it appears to be, but how they would like to think it is.
>
> The *Risale-i Nur* demonstrates that all beings on all levels are interrelated, interconnected, and interdependent, like concentric or intersecting circles. It shows that beings come into existence as though from nowhere, and that during their brief lives, each with its own particular purpose, goal, and mission, act as mirrors in which various Divine Attributes and countless configurations of Divine Names are displayed. Consider this: When you stand by a river, you see countless images of the Sun reflecting in the floating bubbles on it. When those bubbles enter into a tunnel, the images are no longer seen. However, other bubbles coming to the point where you stand will also show the same reflections, and when they also go into the

tunnel, the reflections will disappear. This evidently demonstrates that those images do not belong to the bubbles themselves: bubbles cannot own them. Rather, by reflecting its images, the bubbles show the Sun's existence, and through their disappearance in the tunnel they demonstrate their transience vis-à-vis the permanence of the Sun. It is just like this that through their coming into life, impotence, and contingence, their total dependence on factors other than themselves, beings demonstrate beyond doubt that they owe their existence to the One Who necessarily exists, creates, and has power over all things, and that through their transience and death they show the permanence of that One.

The materialists, however, see things differently—they do not see different things. They ask us to believe that this cosmos, whose innate order and harmony they do not deny, is ultimately the work of chance. Of chaos and disorder, of sheer accident. They then ask us to believe that this cosmos is sustained by the mechanistic interplay of causes—whatever they may be, and not even the materialists know for sure—causes which are themselves created, impotent, ignorant, transient, and purposeless, but which somehow contrive, through laws which appeared out of nowhere, to produce the orderly works of art of symphonies of harmony and equilibrium that we see and hear around us.

The *Risale-i Nur* destroys these myths and superstitions. Given that all things are interconnected, it reiterates, whatever it is that brings existence to the seed of a flower must also be responsible for the flower itself, as well as for the apparent causes of the flower's existence such as air, water, sunlight, and earth; and given their interdependence, whatever brings into existence the flower must also be responsible for the tree; and given the fact that they are interrelated, whatever brings into existence the tree must also be responsible for the forest, and so on. Thus to be able to create a single atom, one must also be able to create the whole cosmos. That is surely a tall order for a cause which is blind, impotent, transient, dependent, and devoid of knowledge of our purpose.

The attribution of creative power to nature or natural laws is no more than a personal opinion reached not as the result of an objective, scientific investigation. Similarly, denial of the Creator of the cosmos, who has placed apparent causes there as veils to cover His hand of power, is not an act of reason but an act of will. In short, causality is a crude and cunning device with which man distributes the property of the Creator among the created in order that he might set himself up as absolute owner and ruler of all that he has, and all that he is.

Inspired by the verse *la ilaha illa Allah*, the *Risale-i Nur* shows that the signs of God, these mirrors of His Names and Attributes, are revealed to us constantly in new and ever-changing forms and configurations, eliciting acknowledgment, acceptance, submission, love, and worship. The *Risale-i Nur* shows that there is a distinct process involved in becoming Muslim in the true sense of the word: contemplation to knowledge, knowledge to affirmation, affirmation to belief or conviction, and from conviction to submission. And since each new moment, each new day, sees the revelation of fresh aspects of Divine truth, this process is a continuous one. The external practices of Islam, the formal acts of worship, also contribute to this process. Belief is therefore subject to increase or decrease, or strengthening or weakening, depending on the continuance of the process. Thus it is the reality of belief that deserves most of our attention; from there the realities of Islam will follow on inevitably.

The *Risale-i Nur* also concentrates on the ontological character of man. Each of us is born in total ignorance; the desire to know ourselves and our world is an innate one. Thus "Who am I? Where did I come from? What is this place in which I find myself? What is my duty here? Who is responsible for bringing me into existence? What is that which life and death ask of us?"—these are questions which each of us answers in his own way, either through direct observation or through blind acceptance of the answers suggested by others. And how one lives one's life, the criterion by which one acts in this world, depends totally on the nature of those answers. According to the *Risale-i Nur*, all the answers given to these questions, by which each of us determines his own way of living and worldview, are given by either the Divine Revelation manifested in the form of Divine Religions or the ego of everyone. History records the conflicts between these two flows of human life or these two main branches of the tree of humanity, namely religion and human ego. Rejecting to follow the Divine Revelation, ego claims self-ownership in haughtiness, appropriating for itself whatever is given to it by the Creator, and attributing to itself all the accomplishments God Almighty confers on it. This, however, results in the abjection, wretchedness, and unhappiness of man. This branch of humanity has so far yielded the fruits of Pharaohs, Nimrods, Neros, and other tyrants and those who, having given in to their carnal desires, have themselves gone astray and misled others. Opposite to this branch is the branch on which the Prophets, saints, and other examples of virtuousness have grown. This branch lies in one's being conscious of one's servanthood, whose power lies in acknowledgment of one's inherent weakness before God Almighty's absolute Power, and whose wealth lies in admission of one's inherent poverty before His Riches. It also requires deep devotion and worship in absolute thankfulness, together with continuous reflection on His signs in the universe, and a never-ending enthusiasm in preaching His religion. The *Risale-i Nur* is no less than a guided tour of the cosmos, as well as of man's inner world, and the traveler is one who is seeking answers to the questions above, and indeed finds them.

Dr. Turner continues:

> The secular, self-aborted society of the West is designed on all levels to blind and stupefy. To mask the fact that the religion of the self has failed to live up to its promises; that the secular trinity of "unlimited progress, absolute freedom, and unrestricted happiness" is as meaningless as [another sacred] Trinity discarded centuries ago. To cover up the fact that economic and scientific progress, which has secular humanism as its underlying ethos, has turned the West into a spiritual wasteland and ravaged generation after generation. Yet there are those who are beginning to awake, to realize the illusion under which they have been living. It is to these that the disease of ego must be pointed out. One suffering from cancer cannot be cured by giving him a new coat. Yet it is not only modern Western man suffering from this disease; it is common to almost all [people] in the world. What is needed is a correct diagnosis, radical surgery, and constant back-up treatment. The *Risale-i Nur* provides all of these.
>
> The *Risale-i Nur* envisages a revolution, a revolution of the mind, of the heart, of the soul and the spirit. It is designed to lead Muslims from belief by imitation to belief through investigation, study of nature and man's inner self and reflection on them, and worship, and through further intellectual enlightenment. It also aims to lead unbelievers from worship of the self to worship of God Almighty.

According to Dr. Turner, the *Risale-i Nur* is the only self-contained, comprehensive Islamic work that sees the cosmos as it actually is, presents the reality of belief as it truly is, interprets the Qur'an as the Prophet intended, diagnoses the real and very dangerous diseases that afflict modern men and women, and offers a cure. The *Risale-i Nur* also covers almost everything related to the essentials of belief, worship, and morality, and provides the necessary criteria for understanding Islam and the Qur'an in this world. Such a work, which reflects the light of the Qur'an and illuminates the cosmos and humanity's inner world, cannot be ignored.

Foreword

HE *WORDS* REPRESENTS A 10-YEAR EFFORT BY SAID NURSI TO SPREAD the essential truths of Islam especially pertaining to Islamic thought and belief while enduring strict surveillance and occasional imprisonment based upon unproven charges. During this time of hardship, Said Nursi, his disciples, and Turkish Muslims trying to live a religious life were passing through a harsh time. Faced with the erection of the Republic of Turkey upon the ruins of the Ottoman State, as well as the replacement of centuries of Islamic traditions with European imports in the legal, official, education, and personal spheres, Said Nursi exerted all of his intellectual and literary talents to ensure that the Turkish people and society would not slip out of the sphere of Islam altogether.

An active participant in the social arena, Said Nursi gradually eschewed such activism on the grounds that politics divides Muslims against each other and weakens them in an already hostile environment. Marking this choice by referring to himself as the "New Said" in his writings, he spent the rest of his life explaining Islam's truths in modern and scientific terminology to counteract the newly emerging anti-religious trends.

Why Said Nursi wrote The Words

As always, his first and foremost concern is to prove God's Existence and Unity, bodily Resurrection, the Day of Judgment, and the validity of the Qur'an and Muhammad's Prophethood with a holistic view of life, nature and religion, and by being able to present the physical truths with the sociological ones and those pertaining to the spiritual life of people. He is also based on what the West considers "rational" thought, meaning science, observation, and logic. He chose this path after realizing the futility of approaching new generations who were being educated according to the Western paradigm that considers religion irrational and hostile to real knowledge, progress, and development. Thus, unlike many religious leaders, he learned how to discuss with such people within the scientific context that formed their worldview.

His next major concern is to show that religious and scientific knowledge are not contradictory and mutually exclusive. In all of his writings we notice the same approach: direct observation of events in nature and what can be inferred or stated from such study, beginning with a hypothesis and seeking to support it by using scientific logic and reasoning to counter the arguments of those opposed to it, and testing the hypothesis in the real world to see if it is accurate or needs to be refined. However, while doing that, he never neglects showing the counterpart in human conscience and heart of what he finds in nature. For him humanity, nature or the universe and the Qur'an are three books containing the same meaning, pointing to the same cardinal truth - God's Existence and Unity - but made up of three different material. Is this not the exact approach used by scientists seeking to understand the multifaceted aspects of creation?

A synopsis of the main ideas

This volume contains 33 Words written by Said Nursi to instruct people who wish to draw closer to God through acquiring a degree of understanding of how He has unveiled Himself through the universe, humanity and the Qur'an, and Prophet Muhammad.

After briefly mentioning various matters such as the meaning of *basmala*—In the Name of God, the All-Merciful, the All-Compassionate—the meaning and importance of five daily prayers, where human happiness lies, the importance of belief and worship, etc. that are discussed at great length later on, in the Tenth Word Said Nursi confronts us with an issue that all of us will face on our own and shorn of all our illusions: the Resurrection of humanity on the Day of Judgment. How could this be otherwise, when the Qur'an and the Prophet tell us repeatedly that this life is no more than a testing arena in which we are to strive to realize our full potential: to reflect the Divine Name or Attribute that we were created to reflect. But his approach is wholly original.

There are no calls for blind belief and unreasoning acceptance; rather, he uses the very laws of nature so loved by scientists to make his points. For example:

> There are thousands of suitable analogies for rebuilding and resurrecting human bodies on the Day of Resurrection. Consider, for example, the way in which trees, which are far more numerous than people, are restored with all their leaves perfectly and almost identically to those of the preceding year within a few days after the beginning of each spring. Consider the way in which the leaves, blossoms and fruits of the trees are re-created just like those of the preceding spring with extreme rapidity. Consider the sudden awakening, unfolding and coming to life of countless seeds, kernels and roots, which are the origin of spring growth. Consider the way in which trees, resembling standing skeletons, suddenly begin to show signs of "resurrection after death" at a single command. Consider the amazing reanimation of countless small creatures, especially the resurrection of different species of fly—particularly of those which, continuously cleaning their faces, eyes, and wings, remind us of our ritual ablution and cleanliness, and caress our faces—during a few days despite being far more numerous than all humans. (pp. 125-126)

In The Twelfth Word and elsewhere, he analyzes a subject that continues to bedevil all religion-based civilizations and cultures: how to approach the modern secular and/or atheistic philosophical assumptions underpinning the modern era? He returns to this topic over and over again in all of his writings. His analysis, based upon history and his observations of the times in which he was living, is so attuned to social reality that we can only say: "But of course! How obvious." He writes:

> Philosophy considers force or might to be the point of support in social life, and the realization of self-interest is its goal. It holds that the principle of life is conflict. The unifying bonds between the members of a community and communities are race and aggressive nationalism; and the fruits philosophy offers are the gratification of carnal desires and the continuous increase of human needs. However, force calls for aggression, seeking self-interest causes fighting over material resources, and conflict brings strife. Racism feeds by swallowing others, thereby paving the way for aggression. This is why humanity has lost happiness.
>
> As for the Qur'anic wisdom, it accepts right, not might, as the point of support in social life. Its goal is virtue and God's approval, not the realization of self-interests. Its principle of life is mutual assistance, not conflict. The only community bonds it accepts are those of religion, profession, and country. Its final aims are controlling carnal desires and

> urging the soul to sublime matters, satisfying our exalted feelings so that
> we will strive for human perfection and true humanity. Right calls for
> unity, virtues bring solidarity, and mutual assistance means hastening
> to help one another. Religion secures brotherhood, sisterhood, and
> cohesion. Restraining our carnal soul and desires and urging the soul to
> perfection brings happiness in this world and the next. (pp. 147-148)

Of special interest to his audience are the sections on God, the Qur'an, and Prophet Muhammad. God is not depicted as a nebulous presence "somewhere out there," a fierce figure waiting to punish us, an undiscriminating figure who bases His decisions upon our sweetened words instead of our concerted efforts, or who lost interest in His creation and, going somewhere else, left us to our own devices.

Said Nursi depicts God as a living Presence within our lives. Why else, he asks repeatedly, was the Qur'an revealed in such a way that any person, regardless of education, sophistication, or era, can find in it whatever he or she needs? Even more, God has made it easy for us to make our will conform to the Divine Will by sending Prophets and Messengers, none of whom were divine or a semi-divine, to show us how to live in a way that will earn His good pleasure. And, since all of them were fully human, we can aspire toward an ever-more perfect imitation of them and understanding of their teachings. All of these points are brought out beautifully in a simple story found in The Eleventh Word:

> A king had a vast treasury of precious stones and buried treasuries
> known only to him. He was well-versed in all industries, and had a vast
> knowledge of all artistic and scientific disciplines and countless fine
> arts. As anyone with perfect beauty and perfection tend to see and
> show themselves, that glorious king wanted to open up an exhibition
> and display his kingdom's magnificence, his wealth's splendor and
> extent, and the wonderful products of his artistry and skill. He so
> desired in order to behold his beauty and perfection with his own dis-
> cerning eye and through the eyes of others.
>
> And so he began to build a very large, magnificent palace.
> Dividing it into many apartments and rooms, he decorated it with his
> finest and most beautiful works of art, and embellished it with his pre-
> cious stones. Designing it according to his artistic and scientific prin-
> ciples and disciplines, he furnished it with the miraculous products of
> his knowledge. Finally, he set up therein tables containing most deli-
> cious specific foods and drinks, and specified an appropriate table for
> each tribe of his subjects. He provided them so elaborately, generous-

ly, and artistically that it was as though each table had come into existence through the works of at least a hundred separate skills.

Then, the king invited all his subjects in his dominion to feast and behold the spectacle. Having taught a supreme commander he had appointed why he had built such a palace and the uses and meanings of its contents, he sent him to inform the guests about the maker of the palace—the king—and explain why he had built it, the rules they had to obey, and about the palace's architecture, decorations, furniture, and ornaments. The supreme commander also had the duty of describing in what ways those contents of the palace demonstrate the king's skills and perfections, and how the guests could please him.

This supreme teacher had many assistants, each of which was deputed for a certain department, while he himself stood among his students in the largest department, addressing all guests or spectators as follows:

"O people! Our lord, who owns this palace, wants to make himself known to you by building it. In return, know and recognize him properly. He also wants to make himself lovable to you through these ornaments. In return, appreciate his artistry and works, thereby making yourselves loved by him. He demonstrates his love for you through these favorings of his, so love him by obeying him. His offerings display his care and compassion for you, so thank him by showing your respect for him. Through these works of his perfection, he wants to show his beauty and grace. In return, exhibit a great desire to see him and secure his attention. By setting his special, inimitable stamp on everything you see, he demonstrates that he is unique, absolutely independent and without partner, that this palace and its contents are his work and belong to him exclusively. So, acknowledge his uniqueness, absolute independence, and lack of partner."

The supreme commander or teacher continued his address. Then the audience separated into two groups.

THE FIRST GROUP: Since they were sensible and aware of themselves, on seeing the palace's wonders, they concluded that nothing could be purposeless. They asked the supreme teacher about the king's purposes and demands from them. They attentively listened to the answer of the teacher, accepted his instructions, and acted in a way to please the king. In return, the king, pleased with their conduct and manners, invited them to a far larger and indescribably more beautiful palace, wherein he set out to entertain them permanently in a way worthy of a generous king and fitting for such obedient, well-mannered subjects.

THE SECOND GROUP: They were morally corrupt, and devoid of sound reasoning. Defeated by their carnal souls, they took notice of nothing apart from the delicious foods. They closed their eyes to all the virtues and did not heed the directives of the supreme teacher and the warnings of his students. They concentrated only on eating and sleeping. Drinking of the forbidden beverages, which had been prepared for certain other purposes, they became drunk and bothered all other guests. They broke the glorious king's rules. So, his soldiers put them in prison appropriate for such ill-mannered people. (p. 133-135)

See how easily Said Nursi deals with such difficult topics as how God and humanity relate to each other, the reason for creation, the role of Prophets and Messengers, Divine Revelation, the types of humanity, what God expects of us, and death and the afterlife—several paragraphs understandable to everyone, instead of thick books accessible only to the elite. No wonder his writings find new readers every day not only in Turkey but throughout the world by means of its translations into many languages.

Said Nursi gives advice for living "the good life," a topic of great interest to philosophers and theologians of every religion, and even of no religion. His advice is simple and practical, so that maximum benefit may be derived: Do everything in God's name, for it will provide you with an inexhaustible source of energy and blessing; submit to God's Will and find contentment; realize that this life is transient and strive for the eternal life of the Hereafter; each five prescribed daily prayer corresponds to a stage in a person's life and is the vehicle for seeking God's aid; and that the path of belief is the only logical choice.

In The Seventeenth Word, Said Nursi explains how our outer states are related to the inner stages through which we pass while on our way back to God. For example, is the onset of old age anything more than His gentle reminder that youth, health, beauty, and so on are only temporary and that now it is time to start contemplating what death means? Are the misfortunes that we suffer something other than opportunities to submit to His testing with patience and trust, thereby deepening our relationship with Him? In other words:

Alas! We have been deceived. We thought that this worldly life is constant, and thus lost it thoroughly. Indeed, this passing life is but a sleep that passed like a dream. This life, having no foundation, flies like the wind. Those who rely on themselves and think they will live forever certainly will die. They race toward death, and this world, humanity's home, falls into the darkness of annihilation. Ambitions are time-bounded, but pains endure in the spirit. (p. 228)

Such advice resonates with people of all revealed religions, for each true and uncorrupted Message brings the same news: Your life here is only temporary, so use it well to prepare the best possible life for yourself after you die and are brought back to the Source from whence you originally came.

The Twentieth Word contains a penetrating analysis of the Qur'an's miraculous eloquence and how it refers to modern scientific discoveries. While repeatedly making the point that the Qur'an is not a scientific textbook, Said Nursi points out that the Qur'an relates the miracles of Prophets and Messengers, besides many other reasons, to hint at future scientific discoveries. For example, the Qur'an alludes to trains (85:4-8, 36:41-42), electricity (24:35), aircraft (34:12), tools for tapping underground water (2:60), and other matters. It also points to future discoveries, among them finding a cure for each illness (3:49), teleportation (27:40), and understanding the languages of animals (27:16, 38:19). By determining which Divine Name dominates a particular field of scientific inquiry, great discoveries can be made and the resulting knowledge can be used for the benefit of humanity.

In the Twenty-third Word, Said Nursi deals with belief, unbelief, and the role of prayer in one's life. Is his view, a person's destiny can be fulfilled only by belief, for: *Surely We have created humanity of the best stature as the perfect pattern of creation; then We reduced it to the lowest of the low, save those who believe and do good, rihgteous deeds* (95:4-5) states that we are to strive to live up to our status as beings of the best pattern. In the absence of our belief in God, which is a fundamental part of our human make-up (*fitra*), such an attainment is impossible and reduces us to living lives of futility and unbelief.

Belief serves many beneficial purposes. For example, it removes our ignorance as to our true identity (God's vicegerent on the earth) and purpose (to reflect the Divine Names and Attributes), informs us of our true status in this world (spending a very short time in this guest-house on the way to our eternal and real life in the Hereafter), and shows us that our ego is neither self-originated nor self-existent, but rather a measure given to us by our Creator to use in an attempt to better understand Him.

As Said Nursi writes:

> Thus the essential and intrinsic duty of our existence is to seek perfection through learning and to proclaim our worship of and servanthood to God through prayer and supplication. It is to seek answers for such essential questions as: "Through whose compassion is my life so wisely administered? Through whose generosity am I being so affectionately trained? Through whose favors and benevolence am I being so solicitously nourished?" It is to pray and petition the Provider of Needs in humble awareness of our needs, even a thou-

sandth of which we cannot satisfy on our own. In short, it is flying
to the highest rank of being worshipful servants of God on the wings
of consciousness of our innate impotence and poverty. (p. 332)

Belief also provides us with the best tool to help us reach this goal: prayer
in all of its verbal and action-related aspects.

While explaining the reason for human happiness and misery, Said Nursi
advises us to overcome our tendency to indulge our senses in the things of this
world instead of the Hereafter:

> Our essence is equipped by Power with great potential and is inscribed
> by Destiny with important programs. If we use our potential and fac-
> ulties in this narrow world under the soil of worldly life to satisfy the
> fancies of our carnal, evil-commanding soul, we will, like a rotten seed,
> decay and decompose for an insignificant pleasure in a short life
> amidst hardships and troubles. Thus we will depart from this world
> with a heavy spiritual burden on our unfortunate souls.
>
> But if we germinate the seed of our potential under the "soil of
> worship" with the "water of Islam" and the "light of belief" according
> to the Qur'an's decrees, and use our faculties for their true purposes, we
> will grow into eternal, majestic trees whose branches extend into the
> Intermediate World and the World of Representations or Immaterial
> Forms, and which will be favored with countless bounties and yield
> innumerable fruits of perfection in the next world and Paradise. We
> will, in fact, become the blessed, luminous fruit of the Tree of
> Creation. (p. 338)

When we understand that our suffering arises from the temporary nature
of all things, even ourselves, we begin to see that they are only indications of
what awaits us in the Hereafter. Our realization that everything here soon will
vanish "without saying good-bye" breaks our attachment to them and so closes
a major source of our own self-inflicted suffering. This opens up the door to
another and even greater realization: that the blessings of Paradise are eternal
and therefore will cause us only endless joy.

In The Twenty-fourth Word, Said Nursi discusses why different Prophets
and Messengers were sent to humanity, and why saints and other people of high
spiritual attainment seemed to stress certain aspects of religion at the expense
of other aspects. According to him, such discrepancies are caused by what
Names and Attributes they reflect as well as their audience's level of understanding. For example, Prophet Muhammad was sent to a polytheistic people
who revered eloquence. Said Nursi also emphasizes that in the future reason,

logic, science, and eloquence will be more influential in human life. Thus, the Qur'an, as the last Book sent by God to embrace all humanity until the end of time, emphasizes God's Oneness and Unity and is considered a unique master-piece of Arabic eloquence that can never be equaled or surpassed, as Said Nursi illustrates throughout all of his writings.

Moses, sent to a people who had been enslaved so long that they had lost all sense of self-identity, brought a Divine law designed to turn his people once again to the path of righteousness. And Jesus, sent to a people lost in second-ary matters of law at the expense of its spiritual aspect and meaning and more important rules, and having great respect for medicine, spent his time explain-ing the law's true meaning, as opposed to its literal one, and healing people in order to reflect God's Love, Compassion, and Mercy. It is the same with saints and people of great spiritual attainment, for each of them reflects the Divine Names and Attributes according to their own personalities and inclinations in a way to lead their people closer to God. Thus the appearance of many ways leading to God is essentially one way, for differences appear only in matters of secondary importance.

After giving his definition of the Qur'an in the Twenty-fifth Word, Said Nursi relates many examples of the Qur'an's miraculousness in such areas as eloquence, which was highly prized by the Prophet's contemporaries. For example, he derives the following from the five short sentences making up *Suratu'l-Ikhlas*:

> This short *sura* has six sentences, three positive and three negative, which prove and establish six aspects of Divine Unity and reject and negate six types of associating partners with God. Each sentence has two meanings: one *a priori* (functioning as a cause or proof) and the other *a posteriori* (functioning as an effect or result). That means that the *sura* contains thirty-six *suras*, each made up of six sentences. One is either a premise or a proposition, and the others are arguments for it. (p. 393)

Said Nursi writes that its miraculousness also can be seen in its compre-hensiveness (e.g., 78:7, 21:30, 36:38, 2:5), which allows all people to draw clos-er to their Creator based as much as their level of understanding; its concise and all-inclusive manner of expressing the most elevated and complex truths as well as universal principles through a couple of words or phrases (e.g., 30:22, 12:45-46, 40:36); the information it gives of past and future events, such spiritual realities as the Unseen Divine truths, and the Hereafter's realities; and its freshness, which allows all generations to find answers to their questions.

This last characteristic is especially relevant, for the underlying principles of social life never change. According to Said Nursi:

> As for the Qur'anic wisdom, it accepts right, not might, as the point of support in social life. Its goal is virtue and God's approval, not the realization of self-interests. Its principle of life is mutual assistance, not conflict. The only community bonds it accepts are those of religion, profession, and country. Its final aims are controlling carnal desires and urging the soul to sublime matters, satisfying our exalted feelings so that we will strive for human perfection and true humanity. Right calls for unity, virtues bring solidarity, and mutual assistance means hastening to help one another. Religion secures brotherhood, sisterhood, and cohesion. Restraining our carnal soul and desires and urging the soul to perfection brings happiness in this world and the next.. (pp. 426-427)

Modern civilization teaches and values the exact opposite of all of these, which explains why there is so much strife, hatred, and injustice in the world today. This is a major theme in all of his writings, for the world in which he lived was being moved away from its religious foundations so that it could be reconstructed on alien and secular values and understandings.

He provides other signs of the Qur'an's miraculousness, such as its overall harmony, even though it was revealed over 23 years in a wide variety of circumstances; how it emphasizes and summarizes certain points by ending the verses with certain Divine Names or Attributes; using a particular event to summarize a universal principle; and how it warns people against certain actions or views only to end with words of encouragement to abandon their ways and to seek God's forgiveness, which is always forthcoming in the case of sincere repentance, and specific words of guidance to lead them out of the swamps of darkness, sin, ignorance, and denial into the glorious light and clarity of God's Presence. In the appendices, Said Nursi shows why the Qur'an's supposed stylistic weaknesses (e.g., reiteration, over-emphasis on certain points, abrupt jumps from Islam's secondary principles and social laws to elevated and universal truths) are really aspects of its miraculousness.

The Twenty-sixth Word, on Divine Destiny and Decree and human free will, attracts the attention of all those who say that Islam teaches fatalism and predestination and thereby deprives the individual of choice, personal responsibility, accountability, and the freedom to act. Said Nursi refutes all such arguments:

Although our free will cannot cause something to happen, Almighty God, the absolutely Wise One, uses it to bring His will into effect and guides us in whatever direction we wish. He in effect says: "My servant! Whichever way you wish to take with your will, I will take you there. There-fore, the responsibility is yours!" For example, if a child riding on your shoulder asks you to take him up a high mountain, and you do so, he might catch a cold. How could he blame you for that cold, as he was the one who asked to go there? In fact, you might even punish him because of his choice. In a like manner, Almighty God, the Most Just of Judges, never coerces His servants into doing something, and so His Will considers our free will in our actions. (p. 487)

In the Addendum, he describes the way he has derived from the Qur'an (based on 53:32, 59:19, 4:79, and 28:88) to work one's way back to God, as one that "depends upon our perception and confession of helplessness and poverty before God's Might and Riches, and upon affection and reflection" (p. 494) and how it differs from all other paths.

Said Nursi devotes The Thirtieth Word to the ego and the movement of atoms. In the first part, he explains that the ego is the trust from which other members of creation shrank from bearing and which humanity agreed to bear (33:72). He writes:

The All-Wise Maker has entrusted each human being with selfhood having clues and samples to urge and enable him or her to recognize the truths about His Lordship's attributes and essential characteristics. Selfhood is the measure or means of comparison that makes Lordship's attributes and Divinity's characteristics known. A measure or means of comparison does not have to have actual existence, for its posited or supposed existence can serve as a measure, just like hypothetical lines in geometry. (p. 554)

Humanity was given this measure so that it could distinguish between light and dark, good and evil, belief and unbelief, and so on, all of which gives us just a slight indication of God's Names and Attributes. This is a trust, for it is quite easy to take the ego as a self-existent and self-originating entity, instead of realizing that it has only nominal existence and is meant to give us a better understanding of God's Names and Attributes. Those who fall under its seduc-tive spell (e.g., materialist philosophers, secularists, atheists, polytheists, nature worshippers, and all who deny God's Unity and Existence) gradually deify it and commit one of the greatest sins: *associating partners with God* (31:13).

As for atoms, they are no more than tools used by the Creator to display His Existence and Unity. How, Said Nursi asks, could this be otherwise, given that no atom can decide when to move, where to go, which other atom to join with or break from, or what it will do once it enters an animate or inanimate object. Having such knowledge would require the atom to know how to move among other atoms to its intended destination, how to enter that body, exactly where to go and what to do—a whole series of clearly preposterous assumptions. Given that, the only other alternative is that God directs each atom as He sees fit and in order to achieve specific purposes.

In the Thirty-second Word, Said Nursi discusses the role of love in creation:

> Due to His love for His Own Beauty, He loves His beloved, who mirrors that Beauty. Due to His love for His Own Names, He loves His beloved, who manifests those Names in a most comprehensive way, as well as all other Prophets. Due to His love for His Art, He loves His beloved, who displays that Art, and those who are like him (the other Prophets). Due to His love for His creatures, He loves His beloved, who welcomes those creatures with due appreciation and applause, saying: "What wonders God has willed! God bless them! How beautifully they have been created!" and those who follow him. Due to His love for the beauties of His creatures, He loves His beloved, who is the most comprehensive embodiment of all those beauties and all moral virtues shared by them, and his followers. (p. 636)

God created humanity out of His sacred Love to make Himself known, sent Prophets and Messengers out of love so that we could obtain some knowledge of Him, created the universe out of love in such a way that we could survive and actually prosper, and created eternal life in Paradise out of love so that we could reach our full potential and exist forever in a state of bliss with those whom we loved while on the earth.

We exist because of God's Sacred Love, know the way back to Him because all Prophets and Messengers sent to humanity performed their duties out of their sincere love for Him, and interact with all people and creation on the basis of our love for them as fellow creatures created by the same God, One and Eternal. And so the great "circle of virtue," in which we occupy a central position, is formed and continues to travel through time toward the Day of Judgment. In short: "The essence of the universe is love. All creatures move with the motive of love. All laws of attraction, rapture, and gravity originate in love" (p. 637).

Conclusion

Many people who write on religion spend their lives authoring academic tomes or theological treatises that are so abstract or divorced from the reader's life. Others offer simplistic and "feel-good" explanations that they are worse than useless and in fact might actually do great harm.

Said Nursi, however, makes the same points just as eloquently through simple parables and allegories from which everyone can benefit. Even more importantly, his solutions and explanations fit right into real life, regardless of our level of mental, spiritual, or cultural development. In that respect, he follows the style of the Qur'an, the final Divine Revelation addressed to every person, regardless of his or her particular era, culture, language, age, or level of intelligence. He also explains the most complicated matters of theology, answers many questions occupying the minds of modern people, and deduces many precious criteria to understand Islam with its basic principles, to think rightly and live a good life to please God and to serve all creation.

Although written during the second quarter of the twentieth century, the views expressed in this volume have not been rendered obsolete. As human nature does not change, all of us still have to answer the basic questions that make us human: Why am I here? Who created me? What path should I follow in life? What happens after I die? What is expected of me? Said Nursi answers these and other questions according to the precepts of Western logic and rationalism. There is no appeal to blind faith, religious tradition and authority, or the speculations and theories of earlier theologians and philosophers. Everything is based solely on the Qur'an and his own observations of nature and human life.

A final note: Every effort has been made in this book to allay the misperception that Islam is a male-dominated religion and for men only. This view has been popularized in the media and in academia. We would like to point out that no religion can be blamed for the misunderstandings of its followers. Islam teaches that Adam and Eve were created, sinned, and forgiven equally; that men and women are equal in God's eyes; and that they are equal as regards their responsibilities and duties toward God and others. As God states in the Qur'an: *I shall not allow to go to waste the deed of any doer among you, whether male or female. You are one from the other* (3:195). However, in the interest of textual fidelity, most of the time only men are mentioned.

— The Editor

The
First Word

The First Word

Brother! You asked for advice, so listen to a few truths contained in the following parables in the successive nine Words. Since you are a soldier, I will express them in military terms.

The worth of Bismillah

In the Name of God, the All-Merciful, the All-Compassionate.

And from Him do we seek help. All praise be to God, the Lord of all worlds, and blessings and peace be upon our master Muhammad, his Family,[1] and Companions.[2]

ISMILLAH (IN THE NAME OF GOD) IS THE START OF ALL GOOD things, so we will start with it. This blessed phrase is a mark of Islam, one constantly recited by all creatures through their tongues of disposition. If you want to perceive its inexhaustible source of strength and blessing, consider the following parable:

Travelers in Arabian deserts must travel under a tribal chief's name and protection, or else they will be bothered by bandits and unable to acquire what they need for the journey. Two people, one humble and the

---

[1] The Prophet's Family: The Prophet, Ali, Fatima, Hasan, and Husayn. These people are known as the *Ahlu'l-Bayt*, the Family (or People) of the House. (Tr.)

[2] The Companions: Those who gathered around the Prophet to receive instruction and follow his example as closely as possible. They are considered the Muslim nation's elite and vanguard and are given the highest respect and admiration after the Prophets. (Tr.)

other arrogant, set out on a journey. The humble one obtained the name of a tribal chief; the arrogant one did not. The former traveled everywhere in safety. Whenever he met a bandit, he said: "I'm travelling in the name of such-and-such tribal chief," and so was left alone. He was treated with respect in every tent he entered. In contrast, the arrogant one suffered disaster and constant fear, for he had to struggle and beg for every need. He became base and vile.

O arrogant soul! You are that traveler, and this world is the desert. Your weakness and poverty are endless, and the enemies and privations to which you are exposed are beyond number. Given this, invoke the name of the Eternal Owner and the Everlasting Ruler of this world, for only this can deliver you from such begging and fear.

Bismillah is a blessed treasure. It transforms your boundless weakness and poverty, by binding you to the All-Powerful and Merciful One's infinite Power and Mercy, into the most heeded intercessor at His Exalted Court. When you say *bismillah*, you act in His name. You are like a soldier acting in the state's name, fearing no one, doing all things in the name of the law and the state, and persisting against all odds.

How does everything recite *bismillah* through its very mode of existence? For example: A stranger arriving in a city can order its people to gather at a certain place to work on a certain task. If this order is obeyed, the stranger obviously is acting in the name of the ruler's strength and authority, not his own. In the same way, everything acts in the name of God, the All-Mighty. Small seeds and grains carry huge trees on their heads and raise weights as heavy as mountains. Each tree says *bismillah* and, filling its hands with fruit from Mercy's treasury, offers them to us on a tray. Each garden, a cooking pot from the Divine Power's kitchen where countless varieties of delicious foods are prepared, says *bismillah*.

All blessed animals (e.g., cows, camels, sheep, and goats) say *bismillah* and become fountains of milk from Mercy's abundance. They offer us, in the All-Providing's name, a most delicate and pure food like the water of life. Every plant and blade of grass, every root and stem, says *bismillah*. All plant, tree, and grass roots and fibers, soft as silk, say *bismillah* and pierce hard stones and soil. Mentioning His Name, the Name of the All-Merciful, subjects everything to them.

A tree's branches spread in the sky, and its roots spread unhindered among stones and soil. It generates underground spontaneously, and its delicate green leaves hold moisture despite intense heat. These realities vex the naturalist. It jabs a finger into the naturalist's unseeing eye and says: "You put so much trust in the power of hardness and heat, yet they obey the Divine Command. That is why each soft fiber of the plant's roots, like Moses' staff, obeys: *And We said: 'O Moses, strike the rock with your staff!'* (2:60) and penetrates the rock. Every delicate, paper-thin leaf, like one of Abraham's limbs, recites: *O fire, be coolness and peace!* (21:69) in defiance of the intense heat.

All things inwardly say *bismillah* and deliver God's bounties to us in His name. Thus we also should say *bismillah*, give and take in His name, and accept nothing from those who do not give in God's name.

QUESTION: We pay people for whatever they bring us, even though they are only "tray-bearers." What payment does God, their true Owner, ask of us?

ANSWER: That true Bestower of all precious bounties and goods we enjoy requires three things: remembrance, thanksgiving, and reflection. Saying *bismillah* at the beginning is a manner of remembrance, and saying *al-hamdu lillah* (All praise and gratitude are for God) at their end is a manner of thanksgiving. Reflection means always being mindful and thinking of the precious and ingenious bounties we receive as miracles of the Eternally Besought One's Power and as gifts from His Mercy.

If you kissed the hand of someone who brought you a precious gift without recognizing the true sender (the king), you would be making a great mistake. Praising and loving the apparent bestower of bounty, while forgetting the true Bestower of Bounty, is far worse. O soul! If you wish to avoid such stupidity, give and receive in God's name. Begin and act, to the very end, in His name. This is the kernel of the matter.

The second station of the Fourteenth Gleam

About the six of the innumerable mysteries of: *In the Name of God, the All-Merciful, the All-Compassionate*.

NOTE: A bright light from the *Basmala* concerning Divine Mercy touched my dimmed mind from afar. I wanted to capture and record it as notes in 20 to 30 sections of "Mysteries." Alas, I have not been able to do this yet, and my 20 to 30 have been brought down to 6. Even though addressed particularly to myself, I refer it for the approval of my exacting brothers with the hope that it may benefit those with whom

I am associated spiritually and whose souls are wiser than mine. The argument addresses the heart rather than the mind, and regards the inner experience and pleasure rather than being rational proofs.

In the Name of God, the All-Merciful, the All-Compassionate.

[The Queen] said: "Chieftains, here delivered to me is a letter worthy of respect. It is from Solomon, and is: In the Name of God, the All-Merciful, the All-Compassionate." (27:29-30)

FIRST MYSTERY: Three stamps of Lordship are impressed upon the face of the universe, the earth, and humanity. They are one within the other, and each carries a pattern of the others:

DIVINITY: We see this in how all entities in the universe help and cooperate with each other, and in their general interconnectedness and reciprocity. The referent is *In the Name of God*.

DIVINE MERCIFULNESS: We see this in the resemblance, proportion, orderliness, harmony, grace and mercy in disposing, raising, and administering plants and animals. The referent is *the All-Merciful*, in *In the Name of God, the All-Merciful*.

DIVINE COMPASSION: We see this in the subtleties of kindness, fine points of affection, and rays of compassion on the face of the human comprehensive nature. The referent is *the All-Compassionate*, in *In the Name of God, the All-Merciful, the All-Compassionate*.

Thus, the *basmala* is the sacred title of Divine Absolute Oneness' three stamps. They form a luminous line on the page of the universe, a robust stay, and a golden thread. Revealed from above us, its tip rests upon humanity, a miniature of the universe and its fruit. The *basmala* links the world to the Divine Throne, and is a stairway for us to rise to the throne of true humanity.

SECOND MYSTERY: Divine Unity is evident in the boundless multiplicity of individualized creatures. So as not to overwhelm our minds all at once, the Qur'an, being a miracle of exposition, constantly reiterates the manifestation of Divine Absolute Oneness[3] within Unity—the manifestation of a Divine Name on all beings.

Consider this analogy: The sun encompasses innumerable things in its light. But to hold the totality of its light in our minds, we would need a vast

---

[3] Divine Oneness: God's Oneness manifested by the concentration of His Names on one entity (Tr.)

conceptual and perceptual power. So lest the sun be forgotten, all shining objects reflect its properties (light and heat) as best they can and so manifest its being the sun, and those properties (heat, light, and the color spectrum) encompass the objects that the sun is facing.

Similarly—*to God applies the most sublime attribute*—just as God's Oneness, His being Eternally Besought, and His Divine Names are manifested in everything, particularly in living things and especially in our mirror-like nature, each Divine Name related to creatures encompasses all creatures through Divine Unity. Thus the Qur'an constantly draws our attention to the stamp of Divine Oneness within Divine Unity, lest our minds be overwhelmed by Unity and our hearts become heedless of the Pure and Holy Essence. So, it is the *basmala* which indicates the three important aspects of the stamp of Divine Absolute Oneness or Uniqueness.

THIRD MYSTERY: Divine Mercy causes the universe to rejoice. It gives the spark of light and life to dark entities, and nurtures and raises up creatures struggling with their endless need. It causes the universe to be directed toward humanity, just as a tree is directed toward its fruit, and to hasten to our assistance. It fills and lights up boundless space, an otherwise void and empty world, making it rejoice. For transient humanity, Divine Mercy also appoints eternity and the rank of the creature addressed and beloved of the One, Eternal before and after eternity. Since Divine Mercy is so powerful a truth, so inviting, mild, helpful, and worthy of love, say: *In the Name of God, the All-Merciful, the All-Compassionate*, and cling to this truth, and be saved from endless desolation and need. Draw near to the King of eternity, and become the one He addresses, befriends, and loves through the rays and intercession of that Mercy.

Why do all entities gather around humanity with purpose and foresight, and hasten to meet our needs with perfect orderliness and grace? Do they recognize us and so run to help us—as irrational as it is, in many respects, impossible for it requires that we, who have no power, should have the power of the mightiest, absolute sovereign? Or does this help reach us via the recognition of One Absolutely Powerful behind the veil of the visible universe? In other words, the One, All-Knowing and All-Compassionate, knows and has mercy on us, and puts all the entities of the universal out our service.

Consider this: How could the All-Majestic One, Who causes all entities to turn toward you with their hands outstretched to help you, not know and see you? He knows you and teaches you through His Mercy that He knows you . So know Him, and reverently show that you do. Understand with conviction that Divine Mercy, existing together with Wisdom, Knowledge, Grace, and Power, subjects the universe to your service, even though you are a slight, transient, wholly feeble, powerless, and needy creature. Most certainly, such Mercy requires total and sincere gratitude as well as honest and ardent reverence. So say: *In the Name of God, the All-Merciful, the All-Compassionate*, which expresses and interprets such feelings. Make it the means of admission to His Mercy, and an intercessor at the Court of the All-Merciful.

The presence and actuality of Divine Mercy is as clear as the sun. Just as a center-patterned tapestry is woven by positioning and sequencing the warp and weft and then gathered to the center, so also the luminous threads extending from the manifestations of Divine Names throughout the universe weave a seal of such compassion, a tapestry of such kindness, a pattern of such grace within the stamp of Mercy, that it is impressed upon the mind more brilliantly than the sun.

The Gracious All-Merciful One, Who causes everything to serve life; Who demonstrates His Compassion in the self-sacrifice, the extraordinary sweetness of compassion, of motherhood in plants and animals; Who subjects animate life to humanity and thereby displays our importance and status as the finest and loveliest weave from the Divine Lordship as well as His Mercy's brilliance—that One has, due to His absolute lack of need, made His Mercy an acceptable intercessor for His animate creatures and humanity. So, if you are truly human, say: *In the Name of God, the All-Merciful, the All-Compassionate*, and find that intercessor.

Nothing but Divine Mercy brings to life, nurtures, and administers all plant and animal species. It neither overlooks nor confuses one with another, but raises each at the right time and with perfect order, wisdom, and grace. It impresses the seal of Divine Oneness upon the earth's surface. Just as this Mercy's existence is as certain as the existence of the earth's creatures, each creature also is a proof of its actual manifestation or being a reality.

The seal of Mercy and Divine Oneness is impressed upon the earth and upon humanity's nature. The mercy stamped upon us is not less than the compassion and mercy stamped upon the universe. Our nature is comprehensive, as we are the weave's center and the Divine Names' focal point.

How could the One Who gives you this face, Who impresses upon it the stamp of Mercy and the seal of Oneness, leave you to your own devices?

How could He consider you of no account, have no regard for your actions, and so make all creation, which is directed toward you, futile and wasteful? How could He make the Tree of Creation worthless and rotten with decayed fruit? Would He cause His perfect, indisputable Mercy to be denied when it is as obvious as the sun, and His Wisdom, which is as clear as light?

You can ascend to the throne of that Mercy by *In the Name of God, the All-Merciful, the All-Compassionate*. Grasp its importance by looking at the beginning of each Qur'anic *sura* (chapter), all worthwhile books and good actions. A most decisive argument for this phrase's worth is the comment of the foremost Islamic scholars like Imam ash-Shafi'i[4]: "Although the *basmala* is a single verse, it was revealed 114 times in the Qur'an."

FOURTH MYSTERY: In the face of Divine Unity manifested within the boundless multiplicity of individualized creatures, declaring, *You alone do we worship* (1:5) is not enough for everyone, for our minds wander from Reality. We would have to possess so comprehensive a heart as the earth to observe the One in His Oneness behind the unity within the totality of individualized entities, that we could say: *You alone do We worship, and from You alone do We seek help* (1:5). Thus, the seal of Divine Oneness must be apparent on each individualized entity and species, and a seal of Divine Oneness should exist within the stamp of Divine Mercifulness, so that everyone at every level can turn to the Pure and Holy One and, by saying: *You alone do we worship, and from You alone do we seek help* (1:5), address Him directly.

It is for this mighty truth that the wise Qur'an abruptly juxtaposes individualized detail with totality, small with large, particular with general. To prevent the mind from wandering and the heart from drowning, to allow the spirit to find its True Object of Worship directly, it mentions our creation and speaking, and the fine details of the favors and wisdom in our features, while mentioning the creation of the heavens and the earth. This truth is miraculously shown in *And among His signs is the creation of the heavens and the earth, and the varieties in your languages and in your colors* (30:22).

There are stamps of various kinds and degrees in the universe showing that it is God Almighty Who has created, sustains, and directs is. Although

---

[4] Imam ash-Shafi'i (d. 820): Muslim legal scholar, founder of the Shafi'i legal school. He developed a new synthesis of Islamic legal thought. Most of the ideas were already familiar, but he structured them in a new way. He mainly dealt with what the sources of Islamic law were and how they could be applied by the law to contemporary events. His *ar-Risala* entitles him to be called the "father of Muslim jurisprudence." (Ed.)

these stamps, existing in concentric circles of different size, display a unity behind multiplicity of innumerable creatures, it is still a unity within multiplicity and, therefore, cannot enable worshippers to address God directly. Thus the stamp of Divine Oneness must be on everything, that is, through the concentrated manifestation of God's Names on it, each thing and species should display that it is God Who has created, sustains, and directs it, so that multiplicity may not detract minds from seeing the Pure and Holy One in everything in the universe, and a way be opened up to the hearts to enable them to turn to and address Him directly.

Also, a most entrancing design, radiant light, agreeable sweetness, pleasing beauty, and powerful truth have been placed upon the stamp of Divine Oneness to draw our attention and hearts to it. Mercy's vigor and power draw sentient beings' attention to It, and enable them to attain to the seal of Oneness, to concentrate on the One of the Absolute Oneness, and thereby to address Him directly, declaring: *You alone do we worship, and from You alone do We seek help* (1:5).

Thus *In the Name of God, the All-Merciful, the All-Compassionate*, being the index of the Chapter of Opening (*Suratu'l-Fatiha*) and an epitome of the Qur'an, is the sign and interpreter of this mighty truth. Whoever equips him/herself with it can travel through the levels of Divine Mercy; whoever causes it to speak can learn the mysteries of Divine Mercy and see the lights of Divine Compassion and Pity.

FIFTH MYSTERY: There is a *hadith* (Prophetic Tradition)[5] to the effect that God created humanity in the form of the All-Merciful One. Its extravagant interpretation by some Sufis does not accord with the fundamentals of belief.[6] Some ecstatic Sufis assert that our spiritual nature is "in the form of the All-Merciful." Immersed in their contemplative and spiritual trances, they might be excused for expressing mistaken views. If others consider such views acceptable, they are in error.

The Pure and Holy God, Who orders and administers the universe as easily as if it were a palace or a house, Who turns galaxies as if they were particles and sends them travelling through space with wisdom and grace, Who dispatches the minutest particles as if they were obedient officials, has

---

[5] *Hadith*, as a term, stands for "what was transmitted on the Prophet's authority, his deeds, sayings, and tacit approvals." (Tr.)

[6] Sufism is a spiritual Islamic belief and practice in which Muslims seek to find Divine love and knowledge through the ways particular to it. Its adherents are known, in the West, as Sufis. (Ed.)

no equal or match, no partner or opposite. According to: *There is nothing like to Him, and He is the All-Hearing, the All-Seeing* (42:11), He has no form, likeness, or peer. Nothing resembles or is similar to Him. On the other hand, according to: *And to Him applies the most sublime attribute in the heavens and the earth, and He is Exalted in Might, the All-Wise* (30:27), humanity can conceive of His acts, Attributes, and Names via allegory and comparison. Thus the Tradition's intended meaning is: "Humanity's form, in its totality, reflects the Divine Name the All-Merciful."

This Divine Name is evident via the lights of all Names manifested in the universe, and on the earth through innumerable evidences of God's absolute Lordship. In the same way, the All-Merciful is also manifested fully in our comprehensive form, which is a miniature form of the universe.

A further indication may be derived from the following analogy: Animate creation and humanity are loci of evidences of the Necessarily Existent One, proofs and mirrors to the All-Merciful, All-Compassionate. These proofs are so certain, clear, and evident that just as we might say that a mirror reflecting the sun "has the form of (or is like) the sun" (emphasizing the brilliant evidence of the sun's light), we also might say: "Humanity has the All-Merciful One's form," stressing our being a clear evidence of, and perfect connection with, the All-Merciful. Therefore, the more moderate and balanced believers in the Unity of Being said: "There is no existent but He," expressing the evidence's clarity and the connection's perfection.

> O God, O All-Merciful, All-Compassionate. Through the truth of *In the Name of God, the All-Merciful, the All-Compassionate*, have mercy on us as befits Your being the All-Compassionate. Open to our understanding the mysteries of this phrase, as befits Your being the All-Merciful. Amin.

SIXTH MYSTERY: O unhappy humanity laboring under limitless impotence and unending need! Understand Mercy's value as a means and an intercessor. It is the means to a Majestic Sovereign in Whose army vast galaxies and minute particles serve together in perfect obedience and harmony. That Majestic Sovereign of Eternity is the Absolutely Wealthy and Self-Sufficient One, having no need and being in need of nothing and no one at all. Everything is under His authority and direction, obedient before His Glory and Grandeur, awed and prostrate before His Majesty. O human, Mercy uplifts you to the Presence of that Absolutely Wealth, Independent, and Eternal Sovereign Who befriends you and addresses you as His well-loved servant.

Yet just as its light gives you the sun's reflection through your mirror although you cannot draw close to it, so also the Light of His Mercy makes the Pure and Holy One, the Sun of Eternity, close to us although we are infinitely far from Him. So, O human! Whoever finds this Mercy finds an eternal treasure of unfailing light. This Mercy can be reached through the Sunna of the most noble Prophet,[7] its most brilliant exemplar and representative, its most eloquent voice and herald, who the Qur'an hails as "a mercy for all the worlds." He can be reached by calling the blessings of God upon him, for the intent of this prayer is mercy. As a prayer of mercy for the living embodiment of Divine Mercy, it reaches the "mercy to all the worlds." So use this prayer to reach him, and make him the means by which you can reach the Mercy of the All-Merciful. All Muslims repeatedly say this prayer for the "mercy to all the worlds," which is synonymous with mercy. Doing so is a dazzling demonstration of how precious a gift Mercy is, and how broad is its sphere.

In conclusion, Prophet Muhammad, upon him be peace and blessings, is both the most precious jewel in Mercy's treasury and Its door-keeper. The first and foremost key to It is *In the Name of God, the All-Merciful, the Al-Compassionate*, and the easiest key to use is praying for or calling God's blessings and peace on the Prophet.

> O God! For the sake of the mysteries of *In the Name of God, the All-Merciful, the All-Compassionate*, bestow blessings and peace on the one You sent as a mercy to all the worlds as befits Your Mercy and the honor due to him, and on his Family and Companions. Grant us mercy so that we are free of need for the mercy of any, among your creatures, other than You. Amin.

> All-Glorified You are! We have no knowledge save what You have taught us. Surely You are the All-Knowing, the All-Wise.

---

[7] The *Sunna* is the record of the Messenger's every act, word, and confirmation as the second source of Islamic legislation and life (the Qur'an is the first one). In addition to establishing new principles and rules, the Sunna expounds the erudition in the Qur'an by expanding upon what is mentioned only briefly in it, specifies what is unconditional, and enables generalizations from what is specifically stated and particularizations from what is generally stated. (Ed.)

The
Second Word

The Second Word

The way to contentment

In the Name of God, the All-Merciful, the All-Compassionate.

Those who believe in the Unseen (2:2)

IF YOU WISH TO UNDERSTAND HOW TO ENJOY GREAT CONTENTMENT and blessing through belief, and how to experience fulfillment and ease, consider the following parable: Two people travel for both pleasure and business. The first one is conceited and pessimistic, and so ends up in what he considers a most wicked country. He sees himself surrounded by poor and hopeless people tormented by bullies and living ruined lives. He sees the same grievous, painful situation wherever he goes, as if the whole country were a house of mourning. In order not to feel this painful situation, he finds no other way out than becoming drunk. Everyone seems to him to be an enemy and foreigner. He has awful visions of corpses and orphans, and his soul is plunged into torment.

The second person, a God-serving, decent, and fair-minded man, goes to a country that he considers quite excellent. Seeing a universal festival, he finds joy and happiness in every corner, and a house for remembering God overflowing with rapture. Everyone is a loving friend, even a relative, to him. He sees the celebrations of a general discharge from duties accompanied by cries of good wishes and thanks. Hearing a drum and a band for enlisting soldiers with happy calls of "God is the All-Great" and "There is no deity but God," he becomes happy at his own joy and that of others. He enjoys a comfortable trade and thanks God.

When he returns after some while, he meets the other man, understands his situation and says: "You've become crazy. The bad and ugly things you see come from and reflect your inner world. You imagine laughter to be weeping, and discharge from duties to be sack and pillage. Come to your senses and clean your heart, so that this inauspicious veil will be raised from your eyes and you may see the truth. This is an orderly, prosperous, and civilized country with a powerful, compassionate, and just ruler. So things cannot be as you see or think." The man comes to his senses and is full of regret: "Yes, I've really gone crazy because of all those intoxicants. Thank you. May God be pleased with you for rescuing me from such a hellish state."

O my soul! The first person represents an unbeliever or a heedless sinner who sees this world as a place of general mourning, all living things as weeping orphans due to the pain of separation and decay, people and animals as lonely and uncivilized creatures cut down by death, and great masses (mountains and oceans) as terrible corpses without souls. His unbelief and misguidance breed great anxieties that torture him.

The second person believes in and affirms God Almighty. He sees the world as a place where people glorify, praise and exalt Him, a practice arena for people and animals, and an examination hall for people and jinn. Animals and humanity are demobilized so that after death believers can travel in spiritual enjoyment to the other world—for this world needs a new generation to populate and work in it.

All animals and people enter this world for a reason. All living things are as soldiers or officials, happy with their appointed task. The sound we hear is their praise and glorifying as they begin, or their pleasure while working, or their thanksgiving as they finish. Believers see all things as obedient servants, friendly officials, a lovable book of their All-Munificent Master and All-Compassionate Owner.

Many more such beautiful, sublime, and pleasurable truths arise from belief. This is because belief bears the seed of what is, in effect, a Tuba tree of Paradise, whereas unbelief contains the seed of a Zaqqum tree of Hell. Safety and well-being are found only in Islam (submission to God) and belief. Therefore, always thank God, saying: "Praise be to God for Islam and perfect belief."

The
Third Word

The Third Word

Choosing the right way

In the Name of God, the All-Merciful, the All-Compassionate.

O you people, worship... (2:21)

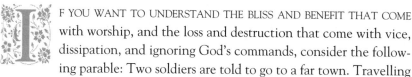F YOU WANT TO UNDERSTAND THE BLISS AND BENEFIT THAT COME with worship, and the loss and destruction that come with vice, dissipation, and ignoring God's commands, consider the following parable: Two soldiers are told to go to a far town. Travelling together, they come to a fork and meet a wise person who tells them: "The road on the right is risk-free, and nine out of ten travelers meet with great advantage but no difficulty. The road on the left offers no benefit, and nine out of ten travelers suffer great loss. Both roads are the same length. But there is one difference: Those who take the left road, which has no rules or someone in charge, travel without equipment or arms, and so appear comfortable and at ease. Those who take the right road, which is under military order, carry their own food, and a heavy weapon in case of attack."

One soldier takes the right fork. Shouldering his heavy load, his heart and soul are simultaneously freed of any burdensome debt and fear. Travelling in peace, he reaches his destination, where he receives a reward worthy of an honest soldier who fully performs his duties. The other soldier takes the left fork. Carrying nothing heavy, his heart and soul nevertheless suffer from innumerable dangers and anxieties. He is constantly fearful and in need. When he reaches the destined town, he is treated as a rebel and fugitive.

Now, my undisciplined and carnal soul, pay attention. The first soldier represents an obedient servant of God; the second soldier represents rebels and those who follow their own desire. The road is the lifeline coming from the world of souls, passing through this world and the grave, and continuing toward the Hereafter.

The heavy load and weapon are worship and piety. Worship seems to be a strenuous demand, but in reality gives indescribable peace and comfort. Those who pray recite *ashhadu an la ilaha illa'llah* (I bear witness that there is no deity but God),[8] the Creator and the All-Providing. Only He can give harm and benefit. He is the All-Wise Who does nothing useless, the All-Compassionate Whose mercy and bounty are abundant. Having belief, the believing soldier sees in every event a door to the wealth of God's Mercy and knocks on it via prayer and supplication. Realizing that his Lord and Sustainer controls everything, he takes refuge in Him. Putting his trust in and fully submitting to God, he resists evil. His belief gives him complete confidence.

As with every good action, courage arises from belief in and loyal devotion to God. As with every bad action, cowardice arises from misguidance. If the earth were to explode, those servants of God with truly illuminated hearts would not frightened—they might even consider it a marvel of the Eternally Besought One's Power. A rationalist but unbelieving philosopher might tremble at the sight of a comet, lest it should strike the earth. (This was how some Americans reacted to the recent sighting of Halley's comet.)

Our ability to meet our endless demands is negligible. We are threatened with afflictions that our own strength cannot withstand. Our strength is limited to what we can reach, yet our wishes and demands, suffering and sorrow, are as wide as our imagination.

Anyone not wholly blind to the truth understands that our best option is to submit to God, to worship, believe, and have confidence in Him. A safe road is preferable to a dangerous one, even one with a very low probability of safe passage. The way of belief leads one safely to endless bliss with near certainty; the way of unbelief and transgression, meanwhile, is not profitable

---

[8]   The Islamic profession of faith. Anyone who says it is considered a Muslim, and is entitled to all the rights and benefits, as well as regulations and duties, of Islam. (Ed.)

and has a near certainty of endless loss.[9] Even its travelers agree on this truth, as do countless experts and people of insight and observation.

In conclusion, just like the other world's bliss, happiness in this world depends upon submitting to God and being His devoted servant. So always praise Him, saying: "Praise be to God for obedience and success in His way," and thank Him that we are Muslims.

---

[9] The author uses the term *near certainty*, as opposed to *absolute certainty*, out of respect for God's absolutely free will. God cannot be made or regarded as obliged to put believers in Paradise and unbelievers in Hell, for He does whatever He wills. But as He promised that He would reward those who believe and do good deeds with eternal bliss in Paradise, and punish those who do not believe in Hell, He will fulfill His promise. (Tr.)

The
Fourth Word

The Fourth Word

The Prescribed Prayers' value

In the Name of God, the All-Merciful, the All-Compassionate.

The Prescribed Prayers are the pillar of the Religion.

IF YOU WANT TO FULLY UNDERSTAND THE IMPORTANCE AND VALUE of the Prescribed Prayers, and with what little expense they are gained, and how crazy and at what great loss is the person who neglects them, consider the following parable: A ruler gives each of his two servants twenty-four gold coins and sends them to settle on one of his beautiful farms that is two months' travel away. He tells them: "Use this money to buy your ticket, your supplies, and what you will need after you arrive. After traveling for a day, you will reach a transit station. You can proceed from there either by car or by train or by ship or by plane. You can choose one according to your capital."

The servants leave. One spends only a little money before reaching the station. He uses his money so wisely that his master increases it a thousandfold. The other servant gambles away twenty-three of the twenty-four coins before reaching the station. The first servant advises the second one: "Use this coin to buy your ticket, or else you'll have to walk and suffer hunger. Our master is generous. Maybe he'll forgive you. Maybe you can take a plane, so we can reach the farm in a day. If not, you'll have to go on foot and endure two months of hunger and loneliness while crossing the desert." If he ignores his friend's advice, ad instead of buying a ticket, which is like the key to a treasury, spends his remaining one coin on passing pleasures, anyone can understand how foolish and senseless he is.

Now, those of you who do not pray, as well as you, my soul that is not inclined toward Prayer. The ruler is our Lord, our Creator. One servant represents religious people who pray with fervor; the other represents people who do not like to pray. The twenty-four coins are the twenty-four hours of a day. The farm is Paradise, the transit station is the grave, and the journey is human life from birth to the grave, and therefrom to eternal life. People cover the part of the journey from the grave at different times according to their deeds and reverence for and obedience to God. Some of the truly devout pass in a day a thousand years like lightning, while others pass, like imagination, fifty thousand years. The Qur'an alludes to this truth in 22:47 and 70:4.[10]

The ticket is the prescribed Prayers, all of which can be prayed in an hour. What a great loss one suffers who spends 23 hours a day on this brief worldly life and does not reserve the remaining hour for the prescribed Prayers, and to what extent he wrongs himself; how unreasonably he behaves. Would not anyone who considers himself to be sensible understand how contrary to reason and wisdom and how far from sensibility it will be, if, considering it reasonable, one uses half of his money for a lottery being played by a thousand people and in which the possibility of winning is one in a thousand, but he does not spend one 24th of it on an eternal, inexhaustible treasure where the possibility of winning has been confirmed to be at ninety-nine out of a hundred?

Prayer comforts the soul, the heart, and the mind, and is not burdensome and trying for the body. Furthermore, if we regularly pray, correct, sincere intention transforms our daily deeds and conduct into worship. Thus our short lifetime is spent for the sake of eternal life in the other world, and our transient life gains a kind of permanence.

---

[10]   ... A day with your Lord is like 1,000 years in your reckoning (32:5), and ... The angels and the spirit ascend to Him in a day, the measure of which is 50,000 years (of your normal worldly years) (70:4), respectively. (Tr.)

The
Fifth Word

The Fifth Word

The right training for believers

In the Name of God, the All-Merciful, the All-Compassionate.

Surely God is with those Who refrain from disobeying Him in awe
of Him and who do good deeds (as if they saw Him). (16:128)

F YOU WANT TO SEE WHAT A TRULY HUMAN DUTY AND WHAT A
natural, proper result of the creation of humanity it is to perform
the Prescribed Prayers and avoid major sins, consider the following parable: During a war, two privates find themselves in a regiment, one well-trained and conscientious, and the other a recruit and a
slave to his carnal self. The well-trained, conscientous one attends training
exercises and struggles against the enemy, without ever worrying about rations and allowances, because he knows it is the government's duty to sup-
ply the necessary military equipment, food, and when necessary, medical
care. All he has to do is training for war and fighting for the country.
However, he also helps out by supplying food and working in the kitchen.
When asked what he is doing, he responds: "Some of the state's chores." He
does not say he is working for his living. But the other soldier does not train
or fight, for: "It's none of my business. It's a government matter." He cares
only about his livelihood, and so deserts his regiment and goes to the marketplace to do shopping.

His well-trained friend advises him: "Brother, you're supposed to be
training to fight for the country. That's why you're here. The government

will meet your needs, because that's its duty. You can't meet all your needs regardless of time or place. As we're in a state of war, you might be accused of desertion or rebellion and be punished. There are two duties, one is the government's, and the others is ours. The government meets our needs, for which we also work to certain extent. Our duty is to prepare for fighting and to fight when necessary, with which the government helps us greatly." Imagine what trouble the second soldier will be in if he ignores his friend's words.

O my indolent soul! The turbulent battlefield represents our tumultuous worldly life. The army divided into regiments represents humanity divided into nations. That particular regiment stands for the Muslim community in this century. One soldier is a devout and pious Muslim who knows what he is asked to do and so does the obligatory religious duties and avoids major sins, and struggles against his self and Satan in order not to commit other sins. The other soldier is a sinful loser who is so obsessed with working for his livelihood as to accuse the true Bestower of provision, and so does not perform his religiously obligatory duties and commits many sins recklessly for the sake of earning his life. Training represents the duties of worship, including especially the Prescribed Prayers. The war stands for struggling against the carnal, evil-commanding soul and its lusts, and against the satans among the jinn and humanity, in order to be able to keep distant from sins and despicable morals, and to save the heart and spirit from eternal perdition. As for the duties: The first is giving life and maintaining it; while the other is worshipping and beseeching the One Who gives and maintains life, and trusting in Him.

Only He Who gives life, a most brilliant miracle of the Eternally Besought One's Art and a wonder of the Lord's Wisdom, sustains life with provision. Do you need convincing? The weakest and simplest animals are the best fed; like fish and worms in fruit. The least capable and most vulnerable creatures, such as babies or new-born animals, get the best food. It is enough to compare fish with foxes, the new-born with wild beasts, and trees with animals, in order to understand that the procurement of fundemantal, lawful food depends on neediness and impotence, rather than power and will.

So, those who ignore the Prescribed Prayers to pursue their livelihood are like the soldier who neglects his exercises, deserts the front for fear of hunger, and wanders around the marketplace. However, seeking one's rations from the kitchen of the All-Munificent Provider's Mercy after praying, and not burdening others is fine and proper. This too is a kind of worship.

Furthermore, our nature and spiritual being demonstrate that we are created to worship God. For in respect of our physical power and capability necessary for our worldly life, we cannot compete even with sparrows. But in respect of our knowledge necessary for our spiritual life and Hereafter, and of understanding our neediness, and supplication and worship, we are the king and commander of all animate creatures.

O my soul. If you consider this world your major goal and work for it, you will remain only a soldier with no more control over your affairs than a sparrow. But if you make the life of the Hereafter your aim, and make this life of the world the means of it and a field to be sown for it, and act accordingly, you will become the ruler of the animal kingdom, a beloved, supplicant servant of God Almighty, and His favored and honored guest in this world. You can choose either option. So ask for guidance and success on His way from the Most Merciful of the Merciful.

The
Sixth Word

The Sixth Word

The supreme transaction

In the Name of God, the All-Merciful, the All-Compassionate.

God has bought from the believers their selves and their possessions in exchange for Paradise. (9:111)

IF YOU WANT TO UNDERSTAND HOW PROFITABLE A TRANSACTION, how honorable a rank, it is to sell one's soul and property to God and to be His slave and soldier, listen to the following parable: Once a king entrusted two servants with one estate each, including all necessary workshops, machinery, horses, weapons, and other equipment. But as it was wartime, when everything is in flux, this merciful and compassionate king sent his noblest officer to them with the following message:

> Sell me the entrusted property so that I may keep it for you. Don't let it be destroyed in vain. After the war is over, I'll return it to you in better shape than it was before. Furthermore, I'll pay a great, higher price for it as if it was your own property. The machinery and tools will be used in my name at my workbench. Both the price and the fee for their use will be increased, maybe a thousandfold. I'll give all the profit to you. You are weak and poor, and can't pay for these great tasks. Let me take care of the expenses and equipment, and give you the income and profit. You can use it until demobilization. Consider these five advantages of this transaction.
>
> If you don't sell the property to me, consider this. As you see, no one is able to preserve what he possesses. You too will lose what you now hold. It will go in vain, and you will miss out on the high price

I offer you. All the delicate, precious tools and fine scales that are ready to be used will lose their value, since there are no metals worthy of their use. You'll have to find some way to administer and preserve them. Moreover, you'll be punished for betraying your trust. So consider the five ways you will lose.

By selling your property to me, you will become my soldier and act in my name. Far from being a mere recruit or irregular, you will be an honored and free officer of an exalted monarch.

After the two men had listened to this gracious decree, one said: "I'm honored and happy to sell. Thank you so much." The other was as proud, arrogant, selfish, and dissipated as Pharaoh. As if he would stay on that estate forever, he ignored the earthquakes and tumults and said: "No! Who is this king? I won't sell my property or diminish my comfort." After a while, the first man reached such a high rank that everyone envied his position. He had the king's favor and lived happily in the king's palace. The other one fell so low that everyone pitied him but realized that he deserved his position. As a result of his mistake, he forfeited his happiness and property, and suffered punishment and torment.

Now, O soul full of caprice, consider the truth displayed here. The king is the Monarch, Eternal before and after eternity, your Lord and Creator. That which He has entrusted to you represent your body, spirit, and heart, and so on, as well as your outer and inner senses such as sight, taste, intelligence, imagination. The noblest officer is the Messenger; the compassionate decree is the Qur'an, which states: *God has bought from the believers their selves and their possessions in exchange for Paradise* (9:111). The surging battlefield is the tempestuous surface of the world in flux, and causes everyone to reflect:

"Everything will leave our hands, perish, and be lost. Is there no way to make it eternal, to preserve it?" While engaged in such thoughts, the heavenly voice of the Qur'an is heard:

"There is a beautiful and easy way that offers five advantages or profits." What is this way?

To sell the trust to its real Owner. The resulting five profits are:

FIRST PROFIT: The transient property becomes everlasting. This waning life, when given to the Eternal and Self-Subsistent Being of Majesty and spent for His sake, is transmuted into permanence and gives everlasting fruits. The moments of one's present life apparently vanish and rot, as do kernels and seeds. But then the flowers of happiness open and bloom in the Realm of Eternity, and each presents a luminous, lovely scene in the Intermediate Realm of the grave.

SECOND PROFIT: The price to be paid is Paradise.

THIRD PROFIT: The value of each bodily limb and sense is increased a thousandfold. For example, if you use your intelligence for the sake of your carnal soul, it becomes such an ill-omened, destructive, and debilitating instrument that it burdens you with sad sorrows of the past and terrifying fears of the future. This is why sinful people frequently resort to drunkenness or other frivolous pleasures. But if you sell your intelligence to its true Owner and use it on His behalf, it becomes like a mysterious key unlocking the infinite treasure-houses of compassion and wisdom-filled vaults, and elevates you to the rank of a pious and righteous guide deserving eternal happiness.

The eye is a window through which the spirit looks at this world. If you use it on behalf of your carnal soul, without selling it to God Almighty, by gazing at transient, impermanent beauties and spectacles, it panders to lust and other carnal desires. But if you sell it to its All-Seeing Maker and use it on His behalf and within His limits, it rises to the rank of a reader of the Great Book of the Universe,[11] a witness of the miracles of His creation, a blessed bee sucking on the blossoms of Mercy in the garden of this world.

Taste is another of the senses. If you do not sell it to your All-Wise Originator, but use it on behalf of your carnal soul and for the sake of your tongue or stomach, it sinks and declines to the level of a gatekeeper at the stomach's stable, a watchman at its factory. But if you sell it to the All-Munificent Provider, the sense of taste rises to the rank of a skilled overseer at Divine Compassion's treasure-houses, a grateful inspector in the kitchens of the Eternally Besought One's Power.

O intelligence, be careful! Think of what is an instrument of destruction and what is a key to all being. O eye! See the difference between an abominable panderer and a learned overseer of the Divine Library! O

---

[11] The universe, man and the Qur'an are three books which make the Creator known to us. The universe and man are created books which have issued from God's Attributes of Power and Will and are the collections of the manifestations of God's Names, while the Qur'an is their revealed counterpart. These three books interpret each other. Like the Qur'an, by studying the universe and man or himself, man acquires knowledge of God and draws close to Him. (Tr.)

tongue! Taste well the difference between a stable doorkeeper or a factory watchman and the trustee of the treasure house of God's Mercy!

When you compare all other instruments, faculties, and limbs to these, you understand that believers acquire a nature worthy of Paradise and unbelievers a nature conforming to Hell. Each attains its respective value. Due to their belief, believers use what the Creator has entrusted to them on His behalf and within His limits. Unbelievers betray the trust and use it for the sake of the carnal soul.

FOURTH PROFIT: Man is helpless but exposed to misfortune; he is indigent but has uncountable needs; and he is impotent, but the burden of life is very heavy. If he does not rely on the All-Powerful One of Majesty, trust in and submit to Him with full confidence, his conscience will always be troubled. He finds himself caught in vain torments, pains and regrets, all of which suffocate him. They either intoxicate him or turn him into a beast.

FIFTH PROFIT: Those who unveil the true nature of things and experience the truth agree that the reward for worshipping and glorifying God performed by your limbs, senses, and faculties will be given at the time of greatest need, in the form of Paradise's fruits.

If you refuse this transaction with its five-fold profit, in addition to being deprived of its profit, you suffer the following five-fold loss:

FIRST LOSS: Your beloved property and offspring, your adored carnal soul and its desires, and your foolishly loved youth and life all will vanish, burdening you with their sins and pains.

SECOND LOSS: You will be punished for betraying the trust, for you have wronged yourself by using the most precious tools on the most worthless objects.

THIRD LOSS: By debasing your precious faculties to a level much inferior to animals, you have insulted and transgressed against God's Wisdom.

FOURTH LOSS: In your helplessness and poverty, you will shoulder life's heavy burden and continually groan under the blows of transience and separation.

FIFTH LOSS: You convert the All-Merciful's fair gifts, such as the intellect, the heart, the eye, the tongue, meant to be used for laying the foundations of everlasting life and happiness in the Hereafter, into an ugly form, fit to open the gates of Hell before you.

We should make this bargain. Why do many people not want to make it? Is it so difficult? By no means! The resulting burdens are not hard. The limits of the religiously permissible enjoyment are broad and adequate for your desire, and so you do not need to indulge in what is forbidden. The duties imposed by God are light and few. To be His servant and soldier is an honor beyond description.

Your duty is to act and embark on all things in God's name, like a soldier, to receive and give on God's behalf, and to obey His permission and law. If you sin, seek His forgiveness by saying: "O Lord, forgive our sins and accept us as your servants. Enable us to remain faithful to Your trust until the time of restitution arrives. Amin." And petition Him.

The
Seventh Word

The Seventh Word

The door to human happiness

F YOU WANT TO UNDERSTAND HOW PRECIOUS A KEY TO REVEAL THE enigmatic riddle of the universe and open the door to happiness for the human spirit it is to belive in God and the Hereafter; and to understand how invaluable medicines for all ailments they are to patiently rely on your Creator and ask and pray to your Provider in gratitude, and seek refuge in Him; and also to understandhow important, valuable and splendid a ticket for your journey to eternity, a light for the grave, and a provision for the next life they are to heed the Qur'an, abide by its laws, to perform the Prescribed Prayers, and to refrain from major sins[12]— if you want to understand all these, consider the following parable: Once a soldier in the middle of a battlefield and testing, in the arena of gain or loss, found himself in frightening circumstances. He was wounded on his right and left sides. Behind him was a lion ready to tear him apart, and ahead of him stood a gallows on which his friends and comrades were being hanged; it was awaiting him too. Before him lay a long road, which he had to travel. As the unfortunate soldier was pondering in despair, a wise, pious person appeared on his

---

[12] The major sins consist of associating partners with God; disrespecting one's parents; consuming the property of others, especially of orphans; engaging in usury; retreating when the army advances; slandering chaste women; committing crimes with a prescribed punishment (e.g., theft, fornication, adultery, murder); engaging in prohibited acts despite the Qur'an's or the Traditions' threat of a severe punishment for doing so in the next life; and deeds cursed by the Prophet. (Tr.)

right and said: "Don't despair. I'll give you two talismans and teach you them. If you use them properly, the lion will become an obedient horse for you, and the gallows will become like a swing for your enjoyment. I'll also give you two medicines that will heal your wounds and make them smell like roses. Furthermore, I'll give you a ticket that allows you to travel the distance of years in one day. Try them and see if my words are true." The soldier did so a bit, and found his words true. I, this unfortunate Said, affirm it too. For I also tried them a bit and saw they were absolutely true.

Suddenly, a devilish, cunning man appeared on his left with ornate finery, pictures, fantasies and intoxicants, saying: "Hey, come on, friend! Let's enjoy ourselves, listen to music, look at these pictures of beautiful women, and eat and drink these delicious things." He asked the soldier what he was mumbling. The soldier replied: "A sacred invocation," to which the man said: "Leave these complicated issues. Let's not ruin our comfort. What's that in your hands?" The soldier replied: "Medicine." The man snorted: "Throw it away. There's nothing wrong with you. What's that paper with five seals upon it?" When the soldier said it was a ticket and a rations card, the man said: "Tear them up! How can you think of going anywhere on such a beautiful spring day?" This is how that devilish man tried to lead the soldier astray. The soldier eventually has been tempted a bit to follow, for he is human and thus subject to deception.

To his right, the soldier suddenly hears a thunder-like voice: "Wake up! Don't be deceived. Say to that devil: 'If you can kill the lion, do so. If you can remove the gallows, do so. If you can heal my wounds, do so. If you can arrange it so that I will not travel this road before me, do so. Do these things, and then we can enjoy ourselves. If you cannot, be quiet!'"

Thus, O my soul, which laughed in its youth and now weeps at its laughter! The soldier represents you and every other human being. The lion is our appointed hour of death, while the gallows stand for our continual separation from friends. The two wounds are our infinite and troublesome impotence and our grievous and boundless poverty. The travel is the long journey of testing passing through the World of Spirits, our life as an embryo, our youth, old age, the grave, the Place of Resurrection and Supreme Gathering, and the *Sirat* (the "Bridge" which leads to Hell or Heaven). The two talismans are belief in God and the Hereafter.

Understand: *Belief in God and the Hereafter*. Through this sacred talisman death (the lion) becomes like an obedient horse to take believers from the dungeon of the world to the gardens of Paradise, to the presence of the All-Merciful One. It is because of this that the pious and learned, those who have a true understanding of death, are not afraid of dying and actually wish to die even before their appointed time. The passage of time, punctuated by separation from friends (because of death, represented by gallows), is transformed by belief into a means to watch with perfect pleasure the perpetually renewed and always colorful embroideries of God's wonderful acts, His Power's miracles, and His Compassion's manifestations. Its like is this: Since the "mirrors" reflecting the colors in the sunlight and the scenes of a film are varied and replaced, the resulting views are even more beautiful.

As for the medicines: one is patience and trusting in God, relying on His Power, and having confidence in His Wisdom. What is there to fear when, realizing our helplessness, we rely upon the Owner of the command, *Be, and it is* (36:82)[13]? Even when confronted with a most frightening situation and a great calamity, he says: *Surely, to God do we belong, and to Him is our return* (2:156), and places his trust in his All-Compassionate Lord with utmost serenity. Those who have true knowledge of God are content to realize their helplessness before God and put their hope in His judgment. There is pleasure in the fear of God. If a one-year old were asked what is the most pleasant thing he or she knows, the reply would be: "Taking refuge in my mother's warm embrace, conscious of my weakness and helplessness—from her sweetest slap." As a mother's compassion is only a small spark from God's Compassion, people of perfection take great pleasure in their helplessness and fear of God. Forsaking what is in their power, they take refuge in God and make their fear and helplessness a means of intercession before Him.

The other medicine is petitioning God with thanksgiving and contentment, and relying upon the Munificent All-Provider's mercy. How could the guests of an All-Munificent Provider, Who has made the earth's surface as a table and the spring for flowers to put on that table, regard their own poverty and helplessness before God as unbearable! Their poverty and need become their appetite, and so they try to increase their poverty. This is why spiritually perfect people are proud of their poverty. However, do not misunderstand this! It means to be aware of one's poverty before God and to entreat Him, not to parade poverty before the people and assume the air of a beggar.

---

[13] *When He wills a thing to be, He but says to it "Be!" and (in the selfsame instant,) it is.* (36:82). (Tr.)

The ticket to eternity comprises the Prescribed Prayers, observing the other obligations, and avoiding the major sins. All people of discernment and learning agree that the only way to get a light, some provisions, and a vehicle for the long journey to eternity is to abide by the Qur'an's commands and prohibitions. Science, philosophy, and craftsmanship alone are not worth much, for they only light the road as far as the grave.

O my indolent soul! How easy and light it is to perform the five daily Prayers and renouncing the seven major sins, and how important and great their results are1 If you understand the truth here, you will say to the devilish one who tries to seduce you into vice and dissipation: "If you have the means to abolish death, impotence, and poverty, and close the door on the grave, then tell us and let's heed it. Otherwise, be still! In the greatest mosque of the universe, the Qur'an reads the universe, so let's listen to it. Let's become filled with its light and act according to its guidance. Let's read it regularly! It is its right to speak and what it says is true. The Qur'an is the truth, coming from the Ultimate Truth. It guides to the truth, spreading its light everywhere."

O God, illuminate our hearts with the light of belief and the Qur'an. Enrich us with the perception and offering of our poverty before You. Don't impoverish us with indifference toward You. We have given up our power and strength for Your sake and taken refuge in Your Power and Might, so make us among those who place their trust in You. Do not leave us to ourselves. Preserve us with Your preserving. Have mercy on us and all believing men and women.

Bestow blessings and peace upon our master Muhammad, Your servant and Prophet, Your chosen one and intimate friend—the beauty of Your Kingdom, the foremost of Your creation, the focus of Your affection, and the sun of Your guidance; the tongue of Your proofs, the embodiment of Your Mercy, the light of Your creation, and the glory of Your creatures; the lamp of Your Oneness among the multiplicity of Your creatures; the discloser of the mystery of Your creation; the herald of Your Lordship's Kingdom; the preacher of what pleases You; the proclaimer of Your Names' Treasures; the teacher of Your servants; the interpreter of Your signs; the mirror of Your Lordship's Beauty; the means of witnessing You and bearing witness to You; Your beloved one and Messenger whom You sent as a mercy to the worlds—and upon his Family and Companions, his fellow Prophets and Messengers, Your angels brought near to You, and Your righteous servants. Amin.

The
Eighth Word

The Eighth Word

The necessity of religion

In the Name of God, the All-Merciful, the All-Compassionate.

God, there is no god but He, the Ever-Living, the Self-Subsistent. (2:255)

The religion with God is Islam. (3:19)

IF YOU WANT TO PERCEIVE THE TRUE NATURE OF THE WORLD AND human spirit within it, and the religion's nature and its value for humanity; if you want to perceive how the absence of the True Religion makes this world the darkest dungeon and the unbeliever the most unfortunate creature, and why belief in God's Existence and Unity, as well as reliance upon Him, opens the universe's secret sign and saves our souls from darkness—if you want to perceive all these, consider the following parable:

Two brothers travel together. Coming to a fork in the road, they see a wise old man and ask him which way to take. He tells them: "The way to the right requires observance of certain laws but this observance brings a certain security and happiness, while the road to the left promises a certain kind of freedom but within this freedom lie certain danger and distress. Now, the choice is yours!"

The well-disciplined, well-mannered brother, relying on God, takes the right way and accepts dependence on law and order.

The other brother, who is immoral and a layabout, takes the left way for the sake of freedom. He seems comfortable, but in fact feels no inner tranquillity. Reaching a desert, he suddenly hears the terrible sound of a beast that is about to attack him. He runs away and, seeing a waterless well 60 meters deep, jumps into it. Halfway down, he grabs a tree growing out of the wall to break his fall. The tree has two roots, both of which are being gnawed away by two rats, one white and the other black. Looking up, he sees the beast waiting for him. Looking down, he sees a horrible dragon almost at his feet, its large mouth open to receive him. Looking at the wall, he notices that it is covered with laboring insects. Looking again at the tree, he notices that although it is only a fig tree, it miraculously has many different fruits growing on it, such as walnuts and pomegranates.

Hanging in the well, he does not understand all that has happened. Unable to reason, he cannot imagine that all of these things are not there by chance, and that they must have some significant meaning. He cannot grasp that there must be one who causes all these things to happen that way. Although inwardly distressed, and despite his spirit's and heart's complaints, his carnal, evil-commanding soul pretends everything is fine and so ignores their weeping. Pretending that he is enjoying himself in a garden, he starts eating all kinds of fruits—for free. But some of them are poisonous and will harm him.

In a *hadith qudsi*,[14] God says: "I will treat My servants in the way they think of Me."[15] This man sees everything happening to him as having no meaning, and thus that is the way it is for him. So he is and will be treated in the way he thinks and sees. He neither dies nor lives well, but merely persists in an agony of suspense.

Recalling the other, well-disciplined, wise brother, let us see his situtatuion. Since he is well-mannered and has a good character, he always thinks of the good, affirms and observes the law, and feels secure and free. Finding beautiful flowers and fruits together with certain ruined and ugly things in a garden, he focuses on what is good and beautiful. His brother cannot, for he has concerned himself with what is ruined and ugly and finds no ease in such a garden. The wise brother lives according to: "Look on the good side of everything," and so is generally happy with everything.

---

[14] *Hadith Qudsi*: This is a specific category of sayings from the Prophet. The wording is the Prophet's, but the meaning belongs to God directly. (Tr.)

[15] al-Bukhari, "Tawhid" 15, 35; *Muslim*, "Dhikr" 2, 19, *at-Tirmidhi*, "Zuhd" 51.

On his way he too reaches a desert, just as his brother did, and a beast shows up. He too is afraid but not as much as his brother, because he contemplates that there must be an owner and ruler of the desert and that the beast must be in his service and under his command. He also jumps down a well and, halfway down, catches hold of some tree branches. Noticing two rats gnawing at the tree's two roots, as well as the dragon below and the beast above, he finds himself in a strange situation. But unlike his brother, since he has a good character, which causes him to think positively and see the good side of everything, he infers that everything must have been arranged by someone and constitute a sign. Thinking that he is being watched and examined, he understands that he is being directed and guided as a test and for a purpose. His curiosity aroused, he asks: "Who wants to make me know him and guides me to a certain point along such a strange way?" This curiosity arouses in him a love for the sign's owner, which makes him want to understand the sign, what the events mean, and to acquire good qualities to please its owner.

He realizes that the tree is a fig tree, although it bears many kinds of fruit. He is no longer afraid, for he realizes that it is a sample catalogue of the unseen owner's fruits that he has prepared in his garden for his guests. Otherwise, one tree would not bear so many different fruits. He starts to pray earnestly and, as a result, the key to the secret is inspired in him. He declares: "O owner of this scene and events, I am in your hands. I take refuge in you and am at your service. I desire your approval and knowledge of you." The wall opens, revealing a door (the dragon's mouth) leading onto a wonderful, pleasant garden. Both the dragon and the beast become two servants inviting him in. The beast changes into a horse on which he rides.

And so, my lazy soul and imaginary friend! Let's compare their positions and see how good brings good and evil brings evil. The brother who took the left way of self-trust and self-willed freedom is about to fall into the dragon's mouth, trembling with fear. He is always anxious, lonely, and in despair, and considers himself a prisoner facing the attacks of wild beasts. He adds to his distress by eating apparently delicious but actually poisonous fruits that are only samples; they are not meant to be eaten for their own sake, but to persuade people to seek the originals and become customers of them. He changes his day into darkness. He wrongs himself, changing his situation into a hell-like one, so that he neither deserves pity nor has the right to complain.

In contrast, the brother who took the right way is in a fruitful garden and surrounded by servants. He studies every different and beautiful incident in awe, with a pleasant fear, and a lovely quest for knowledge. In hope and with yearning, he sees himself as an honored guest enjoying himself with his generous host's strange and beautiful servants. He does not eat up the fig tree's fruits; rather, he samples them and, understanding reality, postpones his pleasure and enjoys the anticipation.

The first brother is like one who denies his favored situation at a banquet in a summer garden surrounded by friends, and instead, becoming drunk, imagines himself among wild beasts in winter and complains thereof. Wronging himself and insulting his friends, he deserves no mercy. The other brother, who accepts trustingly what is given and observes the law, sees and accepts reality, which for him is beautiful. Having perceived the beauty of the reality, he respects the perfection of the owner of the reality, and therefore deserves his mercy. Thus can we attain a partial understanding of: *Whatever good befalls you is from God, and whatever ill befalls you is from yourself* (4:79).

Reflecting upon the brothers, we see that one's carnal, evil-commanding soul prepared a hell-like situation for him, corresponding to his own attitude of reality, whereas the other's potential goodness, positive intention, and good nature led him to a very favored and happy situation. Now, I say to my own soul as well as to the one who is listening to this story together with my soul: If you want to be the fortunate brother in the parable, not the unfortunate one, listen to the Qur'an, obey its decrees, follow its guidance.

The gist of the parable is as follows: One brother is a believing spirit, a righteous heart; the other is an unbelieving spirit, a vice, transgressing heart. The right way is that of the Qur'an and belief; the left way is that of unbelief and rebellion. The garden is the transient human social life, which has both good and evil, clean and polluted aspects. A sensible person "takes what is clear and pleasant, leaves what is turbid and distressing," and proceeds with a tranquil heart. The desert is the earth, the beast is death, the well is our life, and 60 meters is our average lifespan of 60 years.

The tree in the well is life, the two rats gnawing on its roots are day and night, and the dragon is the grave's opening. For a believer, it is no more than a door opening onto the Garden. The insects are the troubles we face, and in reality are God's gentle warnings that prevent believers from becoming heedless. The fruits are the bounties of this world presented as samples from the blessings of the Hereafter, inviting customers toward the fruits of Paradise. The tree with various fruits shows the unique stamp of Divine Power, the peculiar seal of Divine Lordship, and the inimitable signature of the Divine Sovereignty, Whose unique virtue is "to create everything out of one thing" and "to change everything into one thing"; to make various plants and fruits from the same soil; to create all living things from one drop of water; and to nourish and sustain all living things in the same manner but through different foods. Creating everything out of one thing and changing everything into one thing is a sign, a mark, peculiar to the Creator of everything, Who has power over everything. The sign shows the secret will of God in creating. It is opened with belief, and its key is: "O God, there is no deity but God; God, there is no deity but He, the All-Living, the Self-Subsistent."

For one brother, for the people of the Qur'an and belief, the dragon's mouth (the grave) changes into a door opening onto the gardens of eternity in Paradise from the dungeon of the world and the arena of testing, onto the mercy of the All-Merciful from the troubles of the worldly life. For the other, as for all people of misguidance and rebellion, it is the door to a narrow, suffocating place of torment. The beast changing into an obedient servant, a disciplined and trained horse means that for unbelievers death is a painful separation from loved ones, an imprisonment after leaving their deceiving, worldly paradise. For believers, it is a means of reunion with dead friends and companions. It is like going to their eternal home of happiness, a formal invitation to pass into the eternal gardens, an occasion to receive the wage to be bestowed by the All- Compassionate and Merciful One's generosity for services rendered to Him, and a kind of retirement from the burden of life.

In sum, those who pursue this transient life place themselves in hell, even though they stay in what appears—to them—as a paradise on the earth. Those who seek the eternal life find peace and happiness in both worlds. Despite all troubles they may suffer in the world, they show patience and thank God, as they see the world as the waiting room for Paradise.

> O God, make us among the people of happiness, salvation, the Qur'an, and belief! Amin. O God, bestow peace and blessings upon our master Muhammad, and upon his Family and Companions, to the number of all letters contained in the Qur'an, reflected by the permission of the All-Merciful in the sound waves of each word recited by Qur'anic reciters from its first revelation to the end of time. Have mercy on us and our parents, and on all believers to the number of those words, through Your Mercy, O Most Merciful of the Merciful. Amin. All praise and gratitude are for God, the Lord of all the worlds.

The
Ninth Word

The Ninth Word

The different Prayer times

In the Name of God, the All-Merciful, the All-Compassionate.

So glorify God when you enter the evening and when you enter the morning—And (proclaim that) all praise and gratitude in the heavens and on the earth are for Him—and in the afternoon, and when you enter the noon time. (30:17-18)

OU ASK ME, BROTHER, WHY THE DAILY PRAYERS MUST BE PRAYED AT specific five times. I will give just one of the many wise reasons for this. Each Prayer time marks the start of a significant turning point, a mirror to the Divine disposal of power as well as the universal Divine bounties therein. We are therefore ordered to pray at those specific times to give more adoration and glory to the All-Powerful One of Majesty, and to give more thanks for the bounties accumulated between any two periods. To comprehend this subtle and profound meaning a little better, consider these five points together with my own soul:

FIRST POINT: Prayer stands for praising, glorifying, and thanking God Almighty. We glorify Him by saying *Subhanallah* (All-Glorified is God) by word and action in awareness of His Majesty. We exalt and magnify Him by saying *Allahu akbar* (God is the All-Great) through word and action in awareness of His Perfection. We offer thanks to Him by saying *Al-hamdu lillah* (All praise and gratitude are for God) with our heart, tongue, and body, in awareness of His Grace. That is to say, the heart of Prayer consists of glorification, exaltation, praise, and thanksgiving. Thus, these three seeds are present in all words and actions that constitute Prayer. Further, following each Prayer, they are repeated 33 times each to confirm and complete the Prayer's objectives. The meaning of Prayer is pronounced consecutively with these concise utterances.

SECOND POINT: The meaning of worship is this: We are God's servants. Aware of our defects, weakness, and poverty in the Divine Court, we prostrate in love and awe before His Lordship's perfection, His Divine Power on Which every creature relies, and His Divine Mercy. Just as His Lordship's sovereignty demands devotion and obedience, His Holiness requires us to see our defects and seek His forgiveness, and by saying "All-Glorified is God," to proclaim that He has no defect and is absolutely free from the false ideas and imputations of the people of misguidance, and that He is beyond all failings of His creatures.

Also, His perfect Power as the Lord requires that, realizing our weakness and the helplessness of all creatures, we proclaim: "God is the All-Great" in admiration and amazement before the majesty of the works of the Eternally Besought One's Power. Bowing humbly, we are to seek refuge in Him and place our trust in Him. Also, His Mercy's boundless treasury demands that we declare our need and those of all creatures by praying and asking for His help, and that we proclaim His blessings through praise and gratitude by uttering "All praise and gratitude are for God." In short, the Prayer's words and actions comprise all these meanings, and so were ordered and arranged by God.

THIRD POINT: Each person is a miniature of the universe. In the same way, the Qur'an's first sura (chapter), Suratu'l-Fatiha, is an illuminated miniature of the whole Book, and Prayer is a bright index involving all ways of worship, a sacred map hinting at the diverse kinds of worship practiced by all living beings.

FOURTH POINT: Just like the second-hand, minute-hand, hour-hand, and day-hand of a clock which tells the weeks, the alternations of day and night, which are like the seconds of this world—a vast clock of God Almighty— and the years which tell its minutes, and the stages of human life-span which tell the hours, and the epochs of the world's life-span which tell the days look to one another, are examples of one another, resemble one another, and recall one another. For example:

The time for *fajr* (before sunrise) corresponds to spring's birth, the moment when sperm takes refuge in the mother's womb, and to the first of the six consecutive days during which the heavens and earth were created. It recalls how God disposes His Power and acts in such times and events.

The time for *zuhr* (just past midday) may be likened or corresponds to the middle of summer, the completion of adolescence, and to the period of humanity's creation in the world's lifetime. It also points to God's manifestations of mercy and profusion of blessings in those events and times.

The time for *'asr* (afternoon) resembles autumn, old age, and the happy time of the Last Prophet, upon him be peace and blessings. It calls to mind the Divine acts and the All-Merciful's favors in them.

The time for *maghrib* (sunset) reminds us of many creatures' decline at the end of autumn and also of our own death. It thus forewarns us of the world's destruction at the Resurrection's beginning, teaches us how to understand the manifestation of God's Majesty, and wakes us from a deep sleep of neglect.

The time for *'isha* (nightfall) calls to mind the world of darkness veiling all daytime objects with its black shroud, and winter covering the dead earth's surface with its white shroud. It also brings to mind the remaining works of the dead being forgotten, and points to this testing arena's inevitable, complete decline. Thus *'isha* proclaims the awesome acts of the All-Overwhelming One of Majesty.

Night reminds us of winter, the grave, the Intermediate World, and how much our spirit needs the All-Merciful's Mercy. The late-night *tahajjud* Prayer reminds and warns us of how necessary this Prayer's light will be in the grave's darkness. By recalling the True Bestower's infinite bounties granted during these revolutions, it proclaims how worthy He is of praise and thanks.

The next morning points to the morning following the Resurrection. Just as morning follows night and spring comes after winter, so the morning of the Resurrection or "spring" follows the intermediate life.

Each appointed Prayer time is the beginning of a vital turning point and a reminder of greater revolutions or turning points in the universe's life. Through the awesome daily disposals of the Eternally Besought One's Power, the Prayer times remind us of the Divine Power's miracles and the Divine Mercy's gifts regardless of time or place. So the Prescribed Prayers, which are an innate duty, the basis of worship, and an unquestionable obligation, are most appropriate and fitted for these times.

FIFTH POINT: By nature we are weak, yet everything involves, affects, and saddens us. We have no power, yet are afflicted by calamities and enemies. We are extremely poor, yet have many needs. We are indolent and incapable, yet the burden of life is very heavy. Being human, we are connected with the rest of the world, yet what we love and are familiar with disappears, and the resulting grief causes us pain. Our mentality and senses inspire us toward glorious objectives and eternal gains, but we are unable, impatient, powerless, and have only a short lifetime.

Given all of this, it will self-evidently be understood how essential a support for human spirit it is to present a petition through Prayer and supplication to the Court of an All-Powerful One of Majesty, an All-Compassionate One of Grace, at the time of *fajr*, and to seek help and success from Him. Such support is direly necessary to bear and endure the troubles and burdens waiting for us during daytime.

Zuhr (noon) is the period of time when the day is at its zenith, and starts to move forward to complete its course. People take a break from their activities. The spirit needs a pause from the heedlessness and insensibility caused by hard work, and Divine bounties are fully manifest. So, praying at this time is good, necessary, agreeable, and proper. This Prayer gives relief from the pressures of daily life and heedlessness. We stand humbly in the presence of the Real Bestower of blessings, express gratitude, and pray for His help. We bow to demonstrate our helplessness before His Glory and Might, and prostrate to proclaim our wonder, love, and humility before His everlasting Perfection and matchless Grace.

'*Asr* (afternoon) resembles and recalls the sad season of autumn, the mournful state of old age, and the distressing period at the end of time. The day's tasks are brought toward completion, and the Divine bounties received that day (e.g., health, safety, and good service in His way) have accumulated to form a great total. It is also the time when the sun fades away, proving that everything is impermanent. We, who long for eternity, are created for it and show reverence for favors received, also are saddened by separations. So we stand up, perform *wudu'* (ablution), and pray. Thus praying '*asr* is an exalted duty, an appropriate service, a reasonable way of paying a debt of gratitude, and an agreeable pleasure. We acquire peace of mind and find true consolation and ease of spirit by supplicating at the Eternal Court of the Everlasting, the Eternally Self-Subsistent One, and seeking refuge in His infinite Mercy, offering thanks and praise for His endless bounties, bowing humbly before His Lordship's Might and Glory, and prostrating humbly before His Eternal Divinity.

Evening reminds us of winter's beginning, the sad farewells of elegant summer and autumn creatures, and our sorrowful separation from loved ones through death. It also recalls the time when the lamp of the earth— the sun—will be extinguished, and the earth's inhabitants will emigrate to the other world following this one's destruction. It is a severe warning for those who adore transient, ephemeral beloveds, each of whom will die.

By its nature, the human spirit longs for an Eternal Beauty. During the evening Prayer, it turns toward the Eternal Being, Who does all these mighty works and commands huge heavenly bodies. It refuses to rely on anything finite and, standing in the presence of the Everlasting One, cries *Allahu akbar* (God is the All-Great). Then, by saying *Al-hamdu lillah*, we praise Him in awareness of His faultless Perfection, matchless Beauty and Grace, and infinite Mercy. Afterwards, by declaring: *You alone do we worship, and from You alone do We seek help* (1:5), we offer our worship of, and seek help from, His unassisted Lordship, unpartnered Divinity, and unshared Sovereignty. Bowing before His infinite Greatness, limitless Power, and perfect Honor and Glory, we demonstrate, with the rest of creation, our weakness and helplessness, humility and poverty by saying: "All-Glorified is my Lord, the All-Supreme." Prostrating in awareness of the undying Beauty and Grace of His Essence, His unchanging sacred Attributes, and His constant everlasting Perfection, we proclaim, through detachment from all other than Him, our love and servanthood in wonder and self-abasement. Finding an All-Beautiful Permanent, an All-Compassionate Eternal One to Whom we say: "All-Glorified is my Lord, the All-Exalted," we declare our All-Exalted Lord free of any decline or fault.

Then we sit reverently and offer all creatures' praises and glorifications to the Eternal, All-Powerful, and All-Majestic One. We also ask God to bestow peace and blessings on His holy Messenger in order to renew our allegiance to him, proclaim our obedience to His commands, and renew and strengthen our belief. By viewing the universe's wise order, we testify to the Creator's Oneness and Muhammad's Messengership, herald of the sovereignty of God's Lordship, proclaimer of what pleases Him, and interpreter of the Book of the Universe's signs or verses.

Given this, how can we be truly human if we do not realize what an agreeable duty, a valuable and pleasurable service, a fine and beautiful worship, a serious matter, a significant conversation with the Creator, and a source of permanent happiness in this transient guest-house it is to perform the evening Prayer?

The time of 'isha (nightfall), when night covers the earth, reminds us of the mighty disposals of the All-Majestic Powerful One's Lordship as the Changer of Night and Day. It calls to our mind the Divine activities of the All-Wise One of Perfection as the Subduer of the sun and the moon, observed in His turning the white page of day into the black page of night, and in His changing summer's beautifully colored script into winter's frigid white page. It recalls His acts as the Creator of life and death in sending the dead entity's remaining works to another world. It reminds us of the Creator of the heavens and earth's majestic control and graceful manifestations in the total destruction of this narrow, mortal, and lowly world and the unfolding of the broad, eternal, and majestic world of the Hereafter. It also warns that only the One Who so easily turns day into night, winter into summer, and this world into the other world can be the universe's Owner and true Master and is alone worthy to be worshipped and truly loved.

At nightfall our spirits, infinitely helpless and weak, infinitely poor and needy, tossed to and fro by circumstances and whirling onward into a dark and unknown future, perform the 'isha Prayer. In a manner recalling Abraham's proclamation, *I love not those that set* (6:76), we seek refuge at the Court of the All-Living, the Ever-Worshipped, the Eternal Beloved One. From our transient life in this dark, fleeting world and dark future, we beseech the Enduring, All-Permanent One. For a moment of everlasting conversation, a few seconds of immortal life, we seek the All-Merciful and Compassionate's favors. We ask for the light of His guidance that will illuminate our world and our future, and bind up the pain from the decline of all creatures and friends.

We forget the world, which has left us for the night, and pour out our heart's grief at the Court of Mercy. Before death-like sleep comes, after which anything can happen, we perform our "last" duty of worship. To close our day's activities on a favorable note, we pray and enter the presence of the Eternal Beloved and Worshipped One rather than that of the mortal ones we loved all day; the presence of the All-Powerful and Munificent One rather than that of the impotent creatures from which we begged all day; the presence of All-Compassionate Protector in the hope of being saved from the evil of the harmful creatures before which we trembled all day.

We start the Prayer with *Suratu'l-Fatiha*, thus extolling and praising the Lord of the worlds, Perfect and Self-Sufficient, Compassionate and All-

Munificent, instead of flattering and feeling indebted to flawed, needy creatures. We move on to *You alone do We worship* (1:5). That is, despite our
insignificance and being alone, through our connection with the Owner of
the Day of Judgment, the Eternal Sovereign, we attain the status of an
indulged guest and important officer in the universe. By saying *You alone do
we worship and from You alone do we seek help* (1:5), we offer Him the worship of the huge congregation of all creatures and seek His assistance for
them. Saying *Guide us to the Straight Path* (1: 6), we ask to be guided to the
radiant, straight path leading to the eternal happiness.

Saying *God is the All-Great*, we bow down and contemplate the Grandeur
of the All-Majestic One. Like the plants and animals, that have now gone to
sleep, the hidden suns and waking stars are like soldiers subject to His command, and His lamps and servants in this guesthouse of the world.

We think of all creatures' universal prostration. That is, like the creatures that sleep at night, when all creation living in a certain year or age is
discharged from the duty of worship by the command of *"Be!" and it is* like
a well-ordered army of obedient soldiers, and is sent to the World of the
Unseen, it prostrates on the rug of death in perfect orderliness saying, "God
is the All-Great." They are resurrected in the spring by an arousing, life-giving trumpet-blast from the command of *Be! and it is*, and rise up to serve
their Master. Insignificant humanity makes the same declaration in the
presence of the All-Merciful One of Perfection, the All-Compassionate One
of Grace, in wonder-struck love, eternity-tinged humility, and dignified self-
effacement. We then prostrate and achieve a sort of Ascension.

Thus each Prescribed Prayer time points to a mighty revolution, is a
sign to the Lord's tremendous activity, and a token of the universal Divine
bounties. And so this matter is a result of perfect wisdom.

> All-Glorified are You. We have no knowledge save what You have
> taught us. Surely You are the All-Knowing, the All-Wise.
>
> O God! Bestow blessings and peace upon the one whom You
> sent as a teacher to Your servants to instruct them in knowledge of
> You and worship of You and to make known the treasures of Your
> Names; as the interpreter of the signs or verses of Your Book of the
> Universe; to serve as a mirror, through his worship, to the Grace of
> Your Lordship; and upon his Family and Companions. Have mercy
> on us and all believers. Amin. For the sake of Your Mercy, O Most
> Merciful of the Merciful.

The
Tenth Word

The Tenth Word

The Resurrection and the Hereafter

[NOTE: I use metaphors and parables to ease comprehension and show how rational, proper, consistent, and coherent are the truths of Islam. The inner meanings are contained in the truths concluding them. Each story is like an allusion pointing to these truths. So, in this sense, they are not fictions but, rather, undoubted truths.]

In the Name of God, the All-Merciful, the All-Compassionate.

Look upon the imprints of God's Mercy, how He revives the earth after its death. He it is Who will revive the dead [in a similar way]. He has full power over everything. (30:50)

 F YOU WISH TO HEAR ABOUT THE RESURRECTION AND THE Hereafter in simple everyday language and style, consider the following parable together with my soul: Two people went to a Paradise-like land (this world). They saw all doors opened and shops unlocked, as if the people did not care about protecting their possessions. The first one took whatever he wanted and, following his desire, committed every kind of injustice and indecency. The people did almost nothing to stop him.

His friend said to him: "What are you doing? You'll be punished, and you'll get me into trouble too! This property is collectively owned, for these people are soldiers or government servants. They're working as civilians now, and so aren't interfering so much with you. But the order is strict. The

king has installed phones, and his officers are everywhere. Go and seek forgiveness!" The foolish, obstinate man replied: "No, this property belongs to
some charity or other and has no owner. Everyone can use it as he or she
pleases. Why shouldn't I use these fine things? I won't believe unless I see
with my own eyes." He also spoke, as might a philosopher, a lot of sophistry.

A debate ensued. When the obstinate one asked: "Who is the king? I
don't know him," his friend said: "Every village must have a headman,
every needle a manufacturer and craftsperson, and every letter a writer.
How could such an extremely well-ordered land have no ruler? How could
such wealth have no owner, when a train filled with precious and artful
gifts arrives hourly, as if coming from the Realm of the Unseen?[16] It
unloads here and goes on. All those announcements and proclamations, all
the seals and stamps found on those goods, all coins and flags waving
throughout the kingdom—how could they have no owner? It seems you
have acquired some training in a foreign culture, for you can read the foreign, but not the Islamic, script. You also refuse to ask those who can read
it. Come now, let me read the supreme decree to you."

The obstinate one retorted: "Even if there is a king, I'm using so little
of his wealth that he can't possibly be hurt by this. What will it diminish in
his treasury? I see no prison here, so why should I worry about being punished?" His friend replied: "Be serious! This land is a maneuvering ground,
an exhibition of the king's wonderful royal arts, a temporary hospice. Can't
you see that a caravan arrives daily as another one departs and vanishes?
The land is constantly filled and emptied. Soon it will be changed. Its people will be transported to another, and eternal, land where they will be
rewarded or punished for their service."

The foolish, obstinate one stated: "I don't believe it. How can this
land perish and move to another place?" His faithful friend answered: "Let
me show you, O obstinate and rebellious one, some of the innumerable
proofs that what I've told you is true."

Twelve pictures

FIRST PICTURE: Could such a magnificent kingdom not have a system
of reward for those who obey and of punishment for those who rebel? As

---

[16] *The train indicates a year, as each spring is a carload* of provisions coming from the Unseen.

reward and punishment are virtually non-existent here, there must be a Supreme Tribunal somewhere else.

SECOND PICTURE: Look at this organization and administration. Everyone, including the poorest and the weakest, receives the most appropriate and perfect sustenance. The sick who have no one to care after receive the best care. Notice the royal and delicious foods, dishes, jeweled decorations, embroidered clothes, magnificent feasts. Everyone takes their duties seriously, except for rebels like you, and do not transgress their bounds. The greatest people are engaged in modest and most obedient service, and work in an attitude of fear and awe.

Given this, the ruler must have great generosity and an all-embracing compassion, great dignity, and the most exalted honor and high state. Generosity requires liberality, compassion cannot be dispensed without beneficence, and dignity, honor and high state require that the discourteous be chastised. But not even a minute part of what that compassion and high state require is visible here. The oppressor remains powerful and the oppressed humiliated. As they both depart and migrate from this realm, their affairs must be left to a Supreme Tribunal.

THIRD PICTURE: All affairs are managed with lofty wisdom and order; transactions are effected with true justice and balance. A wise polity requires that seekers of the state's protecting wing receive favor. Justice demands that subjects' rights be preserved so that the government's dignity and the state's authority and splendor are maintained. But only a minute part of that is fulfilled here (in human kingdom). Disobedient people like you often leave this realm unpunished. Their affairs must be left to a Supreme Tribunal.

FOURTH PICTURE: Look at the innumerable and peerless jewels that are displayed here, these incomparable dishes laid out like a banquet. The ruler must have an inexhaustible treasury and infinite generosity, both of which deserve and require a bountiful and eternal display of all objects of desire as well as the eternal nature of those enjoying the feast, so that they will not suffer pain due to death or separation until eternity. For just as pain's end brings pleasure, pleasure's end brings pain.

Look at these displays and listen to the announcements. Heralds proclaim the miracle-working monarch's fine and delicate arts. They show his perfections, declare his matchless and invisible beauty, and tell of his hidden beauty's subtle manifestations. Given this, he must have an amazing beauty and perfection. This hidden perfection requires those who will appreciate and admire it, who will gaze on it and exclaim: "What wonders God has willed!" thus displaying it and making it known. As for concealed and matchless beauty, it wills to see and be seen, to contemplate itself in many mirrors and via the contemplations of ecstatic spectators and amazed admirers. It wills to see and contemplate itself eternally, and to be contemplated without cease. It wills permanent existence for those who gaze upon it in awe and joy, for eternal beauty cannot be content with transient admirers. This is because admirers destined to perish without hope of return will find their love changed into enmity whenever they imagine their death. Such admiration and respect will lean toward contempt, for we are enemies of what we do not know and cannot reach. However, we leave this guest-house quickly and vanish, after having seen, for only a moment, a dim light or shadow of that perfection and beauty. As this sight does not satisfy us, we know that we are moving toward an eternal realm of seeing.

FIFTH PICTURE: Given the above, that peerless being also has infinite mercy and affection. He quickly sends aid to every afflicted or unfortunate one. He answers every request and petition affectionately, even the lowliest subject's lowliest need. If, for example, the foot of a herdsman's sheep should hurt, he provides medicine or sends a veterinarian.

Come on, let's go to a great meeting being held in that peninsula. All nobles of the land have assembled there. A most noble commander, one bearing an exalted decoration, is petitioning the compassionate king for certain things. Everyone is saying after him: "Yes, yes, we ask for the same." They agree with and affirm his words. Now, listen to what that noble commander, who is best loved by the king, is saying:

> Our king, you who nurture us with your bounty, show us the origin and true form of these examples and shadows you have shown us. Draw us close to your seat of rule. Don't let us perish in these deserts, but rather admit us to your presence. Have mercy on us. Feed us there on the true form of the exquisite bounty that you have caused us to taste here. Don't afflict us with despair and banishment, or leave your yearning, thankful, and obedient subjects to their own devices. Don't cause us to be annihilated.

Having heard what he says, could such a merciful and powerful king, who fulfills his lowliest subject's lowliest desire, deny the request of his most beloved and noble commander's finest and highest aim? Moreover, what the commander asks for is the request of the whole humanity; it is what the king is pleased with, and its fulfillment is required by his compassion, and justice.

Giving what the commander asks for is as easy for the king as creating these transient places of enjoyment. Having expended so much on this transient place, which lasts only five or six days, to show the samples of his treasures, perfections, and skills, he will certainly display their originals at his seat of rule in such a manner, and open before us such spectacles, that our intellects will be astonished. This means, those sent to this field of trial will not be left to their own devices; rather, palaces of bliss or dungeons of punishment await them.

SIXTH PICTURE: Come now, look! All these imposing trains, planes, machines, warehouses, and exhibitions show that a majestic king exists and governs behind a veil.[17] Such a sovereign requires subjects worthy of himself. But his subjects are gathered in a guesthouse that is filled and emptied daily. Moreover, his subjects now are gathered on a testing ground for maneuvers, a ground that is changed hourly. Again, his subjects stay in an exhibition hall for a few minutes to behold examples of his beneficence, priceless products of his miraculous art. But the exhibition alters each moment. Whatever leaves does not return, and whatever comes is destined to go. All of this proves that there are permanent palaces and lasting abodes, as well as gardens and treasuries full of the pure and exalted originals of the samples, beyond what we see here. This is why we exert our-

---

[17] When an army is told to "take up your weapons and fix your bayonets," according to the rules of war while on maneuver, it resembles a forest of oaks. When a garrison's soldiers are commanded on a festive day to wear their parade uniforms and medals, the army resembles an ornate garden full of flowers of every color. This is how it is with all of the earth's species of unfeeling plants and trees that, like angels, jinn, humanity, and animals, are only one of the infinitely various armies of the Eternal King, when they receive the order Be! And it is in the struggle for life's maintenance, and the command "Take up your weapons and equipment to defend yourselves and maintain your lives!" At that time, all those plants and trees fix their bayonets, in the form of trees and plants with thorns, and resemble a splendid army standing on the parade or battle ground.

Each spring day and week is like a festive day for each vegetable species. Each species presents itself to the Eternal King's watching and witnessing gaze, with the jeweled decorations He has bestowed on them, as if on parade to display the precious gifts He has given them. It is as if they were obeying His command to "wear the garments produced by Divine Artistry and put on the decorations (flowers and fruit) made by His Creativity." At such a time, the face of the earth represents a garrison on a magnificent parade on a splendid festive day that is brilliant with the soldiers' uniforms and jeweled decorations. Such a purposeful and well-arranged equipment and decoration demonstrates, to all who are not blind, that they occur only due to the command of a king with infinite power and unlimited wisdom.

selves here for their sake. We work here, and he will reward us there with a form and degree of happiness suited to our capacity.

SEVENTH PICTURE: Let's walk and see what is going on. Everywhere you see cameras taking pictures and scribes recording everything, no matter how insignificant or ordinary. Now look up at the tall mountain; there you see a supreme camera installed, devoted to the service of the king.[18] The king must have ordered that all transactions and deeds performed in his kingdom be recorded. One day, he will use these records to call his subjects to account.

Would such a wise and preserving being not record his greatest subjects' deeds—the most significant of the deeds in his kingdom? Would he not call everyone to account in order to reward or punish them? After all, those subjects do things that offend his glory, are contrary to his pride, and are unacceptable to his compassion. They remain unpunished in this world, and so must be called before a Supreme Tribunal (somewhere else).

EIGHTH PICTURE: Let me read the king's decrees to you. He makes the following promises and threats many times: "I will take you from your present abode and bring you to the realm of my absolute rule so that I may bestow happiness on the obedient and imprison the disobedient. I will destroy that temporary abode and establish a different realm containing eternal palaces and dungeons." He does what he promises with great ease, and these promises are very important for his subjects. His dignity and power do not allow him to break his promise.

So reflect, O confused one. While you assent to your lying imagination, distressed intellect, and deceiving soul, you deny the words of one who never needs to break his promise, whose high stature allows no deception, and to whose trustworthiness all visible deeds bear witness. You certainly deserve a great punishment, for you are like a traveler who closes his eyes to the sunlight and, instead, turns to his imagination for light. You want to illuminate your awesomely dark path with the light of your brain,

---

[18] Some of the meanings depicted here will be presented in the Seventh Truth: The supreme camera devoted to the king's service indicates the Supreme Preserved Tablet. This Tablet's reality and existence is proved in The Twenty-sixth Word as follows: A little portfolio suggests the existence of a great ledger; a little document points to the existence of a great register; and little drops or leakages point to the existence of a great water source. Thus our memories, a tree's fruits, a fruit's seeds and kernels are like a little portfolio or a miniature preserved tablet, or each is like a drop proceeding from the Pen that inscribes the Supreme Preserved Tablet. They all point to, indicate, and prove the existence of a Supreme Memory, a Great Register, a Supreme Preserved Tablet.

although it is no more than a glowworm. The king fulfills all his promises, an act that is easy for him and necessary for creation as well as for himself and his kingdom. Thus, there is a Supreme Tribunal and a lofty happiness.

NINTH PICTURE: Look at some among the managers of these offices and group leaders.[19] Each has a private phone to communicate personally with the king. Sometimes they go directly to his presence. All of them say that the king has prepared a magnificent and awesome place for reward and punishment. His promises are emphatic, and his threats are stern. His pride and dignity do not allow him to suffer the humiliation inherent in breaking a promise.

The bearers of this report, all of whom confirm each other, unanimously report that the seat and headquarters of the lofty kingdom, some of whose traces are visible here, are located in another realm far from here. The buildings here are temporary and soon will be exchanged for eternal palaces. This world will change, for that magnificent and unfading kingdom, the splendor of which is apparent from its works, cannot be founded or based on something transient, impermanent, unstable, insignificant, changing, defective, and imperfect. It can be based only on matters worthy of it, and which are eternal, stable, permanent, and glorious. Thus there is another realm toward which we are heading.

TENTH PICTURE: Today is the vernal equinox.[20] Certain changes will take place, and wonderful things will happen. On this fine spring day, let's go for a walk on the green plain adorned with beautiful flowers. Other people also are heading for it. Some magic must be at work, for ruins suddenly have become buildings again, and this once-empty plain resembles a populous city. It shows a different scene every hour, just like a movie screen, and assumes a different shape. Note the perfect order among these complex, swiftly changing and numerous scenes, and that each item is put in its proper place. The imaginary movie scenes cannot be as well-ordered as this, and

---

[19] The indicated meanings can be found in the Eight Truth. For example, we use *office managers* and *group leaders* for Prophets and saints, and *phone* for a link and relation with God that goes forth from the heart, and is Revelation's mirror and inspiration's receptacle. The heart is like the telephone's ear-piece.

[20] These aspects are explained in the Ninth Truth. The equinox represents the beginning of spring, while the green fields full of flowers represent the earth in spring. The changing scenes stand for the creatures, beings, and things, and the provisions of humanity and animals, which an All-Majestic, All-Powerful Maker, an All-Wise, All-Gracious Creator, changes in utmost order, renews with utmost compassion, and sends one after the other, from the beginning of spring to the end of summer.

millions of skilled magicians could not possess such artistry. Given this, the invisible king must have performed even greater miracles.

O obstinate one! You ask how this vast kingdom can be destroyed and re-established somewhere else. Are you blind to the numerous changes and revolutions that occur hourly, just like the transfer from one realm to another that you deny? This gathering in and scattering forth indicate that a certain purpose is concealed within these visible and swift joinings and separations, these compoundings and dissolvings. It is as if ten years of effort is devoted to a joining together destined to last no longer than an hour. How can such circumstances be ends in themselves? They are no more than parables indicating or imitating something beyond themselves. That exalted being brings them about in miraculous fashion, so that they are copied and their results are recorded and preserved, just as what happens on the testing ground for maneuvers is recorded (Sixth Picture). This implies that an infinitely vast gathering place will be built, and the proceedings therein will be based on what happens here. Furthermore, the results of what occurs here will be shown permanently at some supreme exposition. All transient and fluctuating phenomena seen here will yield the fruit of eternal and immutable form. Thus all variations observed in this world are for the sake of a supreme happiness, a lofty tribunal, and for exalted aims as yet unknown to us.

ELEVENTH PICTURE: So, my obstinate friend, let's travel through time and see what miraculous works this king has accomplished in other places. We can see similar marvels regardless of where we go, although they differ with respect to art and form. But the order and harmony betokening manifest wisdom, indications of evident favoring, signs of lofty justice, and fruits of comprehensive mercy still are seen in these transient stations, impermanent spheres, and passing scenes. Even those with limited insight understand that there can be, or imagined, no wisdom more perfect than his, no providence more beautiful than his, no compassion more comprehensive than his, and no justice more glorious than his.

If, supposing the impossible and as you deny, there were no permanent abodes, lofty places, fixed stations, and permanently resident and contented populations in his kingdom—especially while this impermanent realm is not proper for the full manifestation of his wisdom, favoring, mercy, and justice— then we would have to deny the wisdom, provision, mercy, and justice, which we observe (in the life of especially unconscious creatures). This would be as idiotic as denying the sun, whose light we clearly see at midday.

We would also have to regard the source of these wise measures, generous acts, and merciful gifts—all of which are clearly visible—as a trickster or a tyrant. This would mean truths changing into their opposites, which all rational beings say it is impossible. The only exception to this rule are Sophists, for they deny everything. Thus there is another realm that contains a supreme tribunal, a lofty place of justice, and an exalted place of reward. There, all this favoring, wisdom, mercy, and justice will be manifested fully.

TWELFTH PICTURE: Let's visit the chiefs and officers of these groups, check out their equipment, and see whether it was given so they could survive for a while here or to use it as a means to obtain a permanent life of bliss in another realm. As we cannot do this with everyone, let's look at that officer's identity card and register.

We see that his rank, salary, duty, supplies, and instructions are recorded. His rank is not for just a few days. In fact, it might have been given to him for a prolonged period. It says on his card: "You will receive so much salary on such-and-such a day from the royal treasury." But the date in question is far in the future, after this realm has been vacated. Similarly, the duty mentioned on his card is not meant for this temporary realm alone, but rather for the sake of earning permanent happiness in the proximity of the king. His supplies are not meant to ensure his survival here for a few days; they can be only for the sake of a long and happy life. The instructions explain that he is destined for a different place and that he is working for another realm.

Look at these registers. They explain how to use and dispose of the equipment. If there were no exalted and eternal realm, such a register of categorical instructions and an identity card with clear information would be meaningless. That respected officer, noble commander, and honored chief would be lower than anybody else, for he would be the most wretched, unfortunate, abased, afflicted, indigent, and weak person. Apply the same principle to everything. Whatever you see testifies to another and eternal world.

This temporary world is like a field, a training ground, a market that will be replaced by a supreme tribunal and ultimate happiness. If you deny this, you must deny all officers' identity cards, equipment, and instructions, as well as the country's order, its government, and whatever the government does. If you do so, how can you be considered a true human being or even a conscious being?

The proof for this transfer of creation from one realm to another is not restricted to these Twelve Pictures. Countless other indications and proofs show that this impermanent, changing kingdom will be transferred to a permanent, immutable realm. Innumerable signs and evidences show that we will leave this temporary hospice and be sent to the eternal seat of the rule of all creation. I will discuss one proof that is stronger than all Twelve Pictures taken together.

In the midst of the great assembly visible in the distance, the same noble commander we saw earlier is making an announcement. Let's go and listen. He is conveying an imperial edict, hung high over there. He says: "Prepare yourselves. You will go to another and permanent realm, a realm that will make this one seem like a dungeon. You will go to the seat of our king's rule, and receive his compassion and bounty, if you heed and obey this edict. If you rebel and disobey it, you will be cast into awesome dungeons."

Such is the message he conveys. This decree bears a miraculous seal that cannot be imitated. Only obstinate, rebellious people like you do not understand that this is from the king. Moreover, the noble commander bears such bright decorations that everyone, except blind people, understands that he is the truthful conveyor of the king's orders. Is it then possible to object to the this transient realm being changed into a permanent one, which the noble commander claims with all his strength based on the supreme edict, unless you deny all that we have seen. So, my friend, what have you got to say for yourself?

My friend replied: "What can I say? What can contradict all of this? Who can doubt the existence of the sun at midday? I only can say: 'Praise be to God! A hundred thousand thanks that I have been saved from the dominance of vain fancy my carnal soul, and delivered from an eternal prison. I believe that there is an abode of happiness in the proximity of the king, one that is separate from this confused and impermanent hospice. We are bound to go there."

Our parable indicating the truth of the Resurrection and the Hereafter is concluded. Now, with God's grace, we will pass on to the most exalted truth. We will set forth twelve interrelated truths corresponding to the Twelve Pictures discussed above.

Four indications and twelve truths

FIRST INDICATION: The two people mentioned above correspond to three other pairs:

- My instinct-driven soul and the heart [the seat of spiritual intellect].

- Students of philosophy and students of the wise Qur'an.
- Unbelievers and the community of believers [Muslims].

The worst error and misguidance of the strict-driven soul, students of philosophy, and unbelievers lies in not recognizing God. Whereas the believer in our parable said: "There can be no letter without a scribe, no law without a legislator." We say as follows: How can a book, particularly one in whose every word another book is written with a miniature pen, and in each letter of which a magnificent ode is composed with a fine pen, lack an author? This universe likewise must have its Author, for it is such a book that each of its pages includes many other books, every word of its contains a book, and every letter, an ode. The earth's surface is one of its pages, which comprises innumerable other books. Every tree is a word, every fruit a letter, and every seed a dot containing an elaborate tree's index. Such a book could have been inscribed only by the mighty pen of a Majestic One, Who is qualified by the Attributes of Majesty and Grace, and Who has infinite Power and Wisdom. So, affirming the statement of the believer in the parable flows necessarily from observing this world, unless one is sunk in delusion.

Also, a house must have an architect, particularly one displaying such astounding artistry, design, and subtle ornament. There is more art in one of its stones than in a whole palace. How could it not have an architect? Its rooms are reshaped and altered hourly, as easily and orderly as changing clothes, or shifting one scene to another on a movie screen. In addition, numerous little rooms are continually created in each scene.

In like manner, the universe's very existence requires an infinitely wise, all-knowing, and all-powerful maker, for it is a palace whose lamps are the sun and the moon, whose candles are the stars. Time is like a suspended rope upon which the All-Majestic Maker threads a new world annually. He renews the world's form or appearance daily with absolute orderliness and wisdom. He makes the earth's surface a bountiful spread that, adorned each spring with countless plant and animal species, is filled with uncountable varieties of generous gifts. Despite their vast abundance and being intermingled, each creature is distinctly individualized. Is it then possible to miss the existence of the Maker of such a palace?

How can you deny the sun's existence at noon on a cloudless day, when its presence is reflected in every bubble on the surface of the sea, and in all transparent objects on the earth? To do so means you believe that each bubble and transparent object contains a miniature, real, and existent sun; that each minute particle contains a massive sun, although that particle has room enough only for itself. Similarly, it would be greater lunacy not to affirm the existence of the All-Majestic Creator with His Attributes of perfection while witnessing this orderly universe, which continually changes in systematic, purposive ways and is ceaselessly renewed in an orderly manner. Denying Him means believing that every existent thing has absolute divinity.

For example, an atom of air easily enters and works in a flower, a fruit, or a leaf. The denial of this atom being employed by someone other comes to mean that it knows the structure and form of all objects it penetrates and affects. It must have an all-encompassing power and knowledge. Or, a soil atom enables countless different seeds to grow. If it is not acting under command, it must have the means and instruments appropriate to all trees and plants, or it must have such knowledge and power that it knows the structure and all forms of each plant and fashions those forms? This also is true for all other levels and realms of creation. From this you can understand that there are numerous clear evidences of God's Unity in all things. To create everything from one thing, and to make everything into one thing, is peculiar only to the Creator of all. Pay heed: *There is nothing but it glorifies Him with praise* (17:44). If you reject God, the One and Unique, you must accept as many gods as there are created beings.

SECOND INDICATION: Our parable mentioned a most noble commander. We pointed out that those who see his decorations and medals must know that he is the king's favored servant who acts according to the king's commands. This commander is God's Most Noble Messenger. The All-Holy, the Creator of so beautiful a universe, must send a noble Messenger, just as the sun must emit light. The sun cannot exist without emitting light, and Divinity cannot be without revealing itself by sending Prophets.

Could an absolute, perfect beauty not will to present itself through one who will demonstrate and display it? Could a perfectly beautiful artistry not will to make itself known through one who will draw our attention to it? Could the universal dominion of an all-embracing Lordship not will to make known its being One and the Eternally Besought to all levels of multiplicity and particularity through an envoy ennobled by his double authority? That is, the universality of that his worship makes him the Realm of Multiplicity's envoy to the Divine Court, and his nearness to God and his being entrusted with His Message make him the Divine Court's envoy to that realm.

Could the One of infinite essential Beauty not will to behold, and have others behold, in numerous mirrors, His Beauty's aspects and His Grace's dimensions? Could He not do so by means of a beloved Messenger, who both makes himself loved by Him through his worship, and holds up a mirror to Him, making Him beloved by His creatures and demonstrating the beauty of His Names.

Could the Owner of treasuries filled with extraordinary miracles and priceless goods not will to show His hidden perfections to an appreciative humanity via an expert master "jeweler," an eloquent describer? Could the One Who has adorned the universe with His artifacts that display His Names' perfections and so made it resemble a palace decorated with every variety of subtle, miraculous artistry not appoint a teacher and guide who will make those perfections known and teach people how to live in such a palace?

Could the Owner of the universe not resolve, by means of a messenger, our bewilderment over why there is constant change in the universe, and answer the questions in everyone's mind: What is our origin? Where are we headed? What is our purpose [here]? Could the All-Majestic Maker, Who makes Himself known to conscious beings through His fair creation and loved through His precious gifts, not send a messenger to convey to them what His Will demands from them in exchange? Could He create us with a disposition to suffer from multiplicity (this world and its charms) alongside an ability to engage in universal worship, without simultaneously wanting us to turn away from multiplicity and toward Unity by means of a teacher and guide?

Prophethood has many other functions, each of which is a decisive argument that Divinity necessarily implies Messengership. Has there ever been a person more worthy and qualified to fulfill these functions, more fitted to the rank of Messenger, more suited to the task of conveying God's Message, than Prophet Muhammad, upon him be peace and blessings? No. He is the master of Messengers, the foremost of Prophets, the leader of purified scholars, the nearest to God of those who have drawn near to Him, the most perfect of creatures, and the master of those who guide to righteousness.

Apart from the countless indications of his Prophethood, including his almost one thousand miracles such as splitting the moon with a gesture of his finger and the flowing of water from his hands, which have been unanimously confirmed by all scholars, the supreme miracle of the glorious Qur'an—an ocean of truths and a miraculous book in forty different aspects—alone establishes his Prophethood. Since we have discussed these aspects elsewhere in some other treatises, particularly The 25th Word, we limit our discussion here.

THIRD INDICATION: It should not be thought that we are too insignificant for this vast world to be replaced with a new one so that we may be brought to account for our deeds. For by virtue of its comprehensive nature, humanity is the master of all creatures and has been endowed with the capacity to herald God's Dominion and offer Him universal worship. Given this, we are the most important being in creation.

Nor should it be asked how such a transient being can deserve eternal punishment. For unbelief is an insult to the whole existence as it seeks to make creation, which is invaluable and exalted as a letter of God, meaningless and pointless. It also means the rejection of the manifestations, imprints, and inscriptions of God's Holy Names, which are evident in all that is, and the denial of the infinite proofs showing the truth of God. In short, unbelief is a crime of infinite proportions deserving infinite punishment.

FOURTH INDICATION: The parable in the Twelve Pictures argued that a king who had the attributes discussed had and controlled a realm like this transient world necessarily must have another, an eternal realm where the majesty and sublimity of his being king are properly displayed. So, it is inconceivable that the Eternal Creator of this transient world would not create an eternal realm; that the Everlasting Maker of this beautiful but mutable universe would not create another permanent and everlasting one; that the All-Wise, All-Powerful, All-Compassionate Creator of this world, which is an arena of trial and exhibition, would not create the Hereafter, in which His purposes for creation will be manifested wholly.

The way into this truth consists of twelve gates that can be unlocked via twelve truths. We begin with the shortest and simplest one.

FIRST TRUTH: *The gate of Lordship and Sovereignty, the manifestation of His Name the Lord.* Would the Glory of God's being the Lord and Divine Sovereign create this temporary universe to display His perfections, with such noble aims and purposes, without also establishing a reward for believers who, by belief and worship, seek to satisfy them? Should He not punish those misguided people who scornfully reject His purposes?

SECOND TRUTH: *The gate of Munificence and Mercy, the manifestations of His Names the All-Munificent and the All-Compassionate.* Would the Lord of this world, Who demonstrates infinite munificence, mercy, dignity, and glory through His works, recompense according to His Munificence and Mercy and punish according to His Dignity and Glory?

Consider the following: All animate beings are given some form of appropriate sustenance.[21] Indeed, the weakest and most powerless receive the best sustenance; every troubled one finds its remedy almost on hand. Such bountiful largesse given with such noble magnanimity betokens a giving hand of Infinite Munificence. During spring, for instance, all trees are dressed in silk-like finery, covered with blossoms and fruits as if bejeweled, and made to offer many varieties of the choicest fruits on their branches, stretched forward like a servant's arms. We receive sweet and wholesome honey from a stinging honeybee, dress in the finest and softest cloth woven by a handless silkworm, and find a great treasure of Mercy stored for us in tiny seeds. Who but One having the most perfect Munificence, the finest and most subtle Mercy, can do such things?

Except for humanity [and jinn] and certain wild animals, all creatures—from the sun, the moon, and the earth down to the minutest ones—perform their tasks with complete exactitude, do not overstep their bounds, and are perfectly obedient in an atmosphere of solemn awe. This shows that they function by the command of One having Supreme Majesty and Authority. Similarly, the way all mothers in the vegetable, animal, and human realms support their helpless infants by tenderly and compassionately nurturing their growth with milk shows the all-embracing Mercy.[22]

Since the Lord and Ruler of this world has such infinite Munificence and Mercy, and such infinite Majesty and Dignity, for sure, His Munificence requires infinite giving, His Mercy requires favoring worthy of Itself, and His Majesty and Dignity require chastising those who disrespect them. As only a minute fraction of such Attributes are established and

---

[21] All allowed nourishment is obtained through neediness. The decisive argument for this is how powerless infants enjoy the best livelihood, while strong, wild beasts suffer all kinds of want; how unintelligent fish grow fat, while cunning foxes and monkeys grow thin, in quest of their livelihood. There appears to be an inverse relationship between sustenance received on the one hand, and force and will on the other. The more one relies on force and will, the greater difficulty he or she will have in obtaining sustenance.

[22] A hungry lion can prefer its offspring to itself and let it eat the meat that normally it would have eaten. A timid hen can challenge a dog to protect its chicks. A fig tree contents itself with mud while feeding its offspring (its fruit) on pure "milk." Thus they obey the One of Infinite Mercy, Munificence, and Solicitousness. Likewise, the fact that unconscious plants and beasts act in the most purposive and conscious manner shows irrefutably that One All-Knowing and All-Wise has set them to their tasks, and that they act in His Name.

manifested in this impermanent world and passing life, there must be a blessed realm that can fulfill these duties. Denying such a realm means denying the Mercy so evident to us, which would be like denying the sun whose existence lightens every day. Death without resurrection would turn compassion into torment, love into the affliction of separation, blessing into a vengeful curse, reason into an instrument of wretchedness, and pleasure into pain. Such events would mean the vanishing of Divine Mercy, which is absolutely impossible and inconceivable.

There also must be a realm of punishment suitable for the Almighty's Majesty and Dignity. This world's oppressors generally die with their oppressive power intact, while the oppressed die still subjected to humiliation. Such wrongs necessarily are deferred to a supreme tribunal; they are never ignored. Indeed, punishment is sometimes enacted even in this world. The torments endured by earlier disobedient and rebellious peoples show that we cannot escape whatever correction God Almighty's Glory and Majesty chooses to apply.

Why should humanity refuse to recognize Him and respond to Him in belief, for we have the highest duty in creation and so are blessed with the most important capacities? In addition, our Lord and Sustainer reveals Himself through His orderly works. Why should humanity not respond to Him by making ourselves beloved of God through worship, for He makes Himself loved by us for the numerous, adorned gifts of His Mercy? Why should humanity not respond to Him with reverent thanks and praise, for He shows His Love and Mercy to us through the gifts of His Grace?

Does it make sense that we should remain unrecompensed and unanswerable, that the All-Majestic One of Dignity and Glory should not prepare a realm of requital for us? Does it make sense[23] that the All-Merciful and the All-Compassionate One would not prepare a realm of permanent reward and bliss for believers who respond to His making Himself known

---

[23] In this and other arguments, such interrogative words and phrases as *could*, *would*, *is it conceivable*, and *does it make sense* are reiterated to point to a very significant truth: Misguidance and unbelief often arise from the habit of imagining things to be impossible or beyond sense and then denying them. In our discussion of the Resurrection, we argued emphatically that the real impossibility, absurdity, and irrationality come along the path of unbelief and misguidance, whereas real possibility, facility, and rationality are characteristics of the broad highway of belief (Islam). In sum, materialist and naturalist philosophers veer into unbelief by regarding possibilities as impossible, whereas The Tenth Word, by using such words as mentioned above, points to where the impossibility really is.

by recognizing Him in belief, to His making Himself beloved by loving Him in worship, and to His Mercy by offering reverent thanks and praise?

THIRD TRUTH: *The gate of Wisdom and Justice, the manifestations of His Names the All-Wise and All-Just.* Would the Majestic Being, Who manifests the sovereignty of His being Lord in the universe's order, purposiveness, justice, and balance, not show His favor to believers who seek the protection of His being their Lord and Sovereign, who believe in His Wisdom and Justice, and act in conformity with them through worship? Would He not chastise those who, denying His Wisdom and Justice, rebel against Him? Since only a minute amount of His Wisdom and Justice with respect to humanity is established in this impermanent world, they must be deferred. Most of the misguided die unpunished, and most of the guided die unrewarded. Such affairs certainly are deferred to a supreme tribunal, an ultimate contentment.

The One Who administers this world does so in accordance with an infinite wisdom. We can see this in how all things are used and benefit others. Have you not seen how many wise purposes are served by each human limb, bone, and vein, as well as by every brain cell and every cell atom in your body? Indeed, the purposes every limb of a tree serves are as numerous as its fruits. All this confirms that everything is arranged in accordance with infinite wisdom. A further proof is the absolute orderliness in which everything is fashioned.

The miniaturization of the whole, exact program of a flower's growth in a tiny seed, as well as the Pen of Destiny's making a large tree's seed the index of its life-history and all its parts, show that an absolute wisdom moves that Pen. The perfection of subtle artistry in all things proves an infinitely Wise Artist's impress. Including an index of the whole universe within a small human body, as well as the keys to Mercy's treasuries and mirrors to reflect all Divine Names, further shows the wisdom within that infinitely subtle artistry. Could this Wisdom, Which so permeates the workings of Lordship, not want to favor those who eternally seek refuge in that Lordship's protection and who offer obedience in belief?

Do you need convincing that everything is done with justice and balance? The fact that all things are given being and form, and then placed according to a precise equilibrium and measure, is enough proof for you. The fact that everything is given its due according to its capacity, that is, everything receives whatever it needs for its existence and maintenance in the most fitting form shows the hand of an infinite justice. Also, every petition and plea offered in the tongue of disposition, of natural need, or absolute necessity, also demonstrates infinite justice and wisdom.

Is it then conceivable that the Justice and Wisdom Which hasten to meet the pettiest need of the smallest of creation would not provide the greatest need (immortality) of creation's most important member (humanity)? Is it conceivable that they would fail to respond to our greatest plea and cry for help, and that they would preserve the dignity of God's being Lord by rewarding His servants? However, we cannot experience the true essence of this Justice in this transient world in a short life. Thus the affair is deferred to a supreme tribunal.

The true justice requires that we be rewarded and punished not according to our apparent insignificance, but according to the greatness of our wrong, the significance of our true nature, and the importance of our function. Since this transient world cannot manifest such an amount of wisdom and justice in respect of humanity, which is created for eternity, there must be an eternal Hell and an everlasting Paradise of that All-Majestic One of Grace and All-Gracious One of Majesty to befit His Justice and Wisdom.

FOURTH TRUTH: *The gate of Generosity and Beauty, the manifestation of the Names the All-Generous and the All-Beautiful.* Would unlimited generosity and liberality, inexhaustible riches and treasures, unequalled eternal beauty and grace, as well as everlasting perfection, not demand the existence of grateful supplicants, along with amazed and yearning onlookers, destined to dwell permanently in an abode of blissful repose? Adorning the world with so many beautiful objects, making the sun and moon its lamps, filling the planet's surface with the finest varieties of sustenance and making it into an overflowing feast of plenty, and making fruit-bearing trees into dishes and renewing them several times each season— all of this shows the existence of an unlimited generosity and liberality.

Such inexhaustible treasures of Mercy require an everlasting abode of blissful repose that contains all desirable objects. They also require that those who enjoy it should dwell there eternally, without suffering the pain of cessation and separation. For the end of pain is a sort of pleasure, and the end of pleasure is a sort of pain. As unlimited generosity cannot allow such a thing, it requires the existence of an eternal paradise and of supplicants to abide therein eternally. Unlimited generosity and liberality desire to bestow infinite bounty and kindness, which require infinite gratitude. Thus, those who are to receive this bounty and give continual thanks in turn must live forever. A slight contentment, spoiled by its brevity or cessation, is incompatible with unlimited generosity and liberality.

Also, reflect upon the world's different regions, how each exhibits God's handiwork and proclaims His being Lord in the diversity of all plants and animals.[24] Listen to the Prophets and saints who proclaim His Lordship's beauties. See how they point to the All-Majestic Maker's flawless perfections and demonstrate His miraculous arts, thereby inviting our admiration.

The Maker of this world has very important, amazing, and hidden perfections, which He wills to display via His miraculous arts. Hidden perfections long to be known by those who will gaze upon it with admiration and appreciation. Eternal perfection requires eternal manifestation, which in turn requires the eternal existence of those who will appreciate and admire it. The value of perfection diminishes in the view of its admirer if the latter is not eternal.[25]

Those brilliant, beautiful, artistic, and adorned creatures that cover the face of the universe demonstrate the dimensions of an unequaled transcendent Grace and point to the subtle aspects of a hidden Beauty, just as sunlight testifies to the sun's existence.[26] Every manifestation of that transcendent Beauty, that holy Grace, points to the existence of innumerable unseen treasures in each of God's Names. So exalted, peerless, and hidden a Beauty wills to behold Itself in a mirror, to see Its degrees and measures reflected in animate beings, and to become manifest so that It may look upon Itself through the eyes of others. In short, Beauty wills to see Itself both in mirrors of different colors and through the eyes of Its yearning lovers and dazzled admirers. So, since Divine Beauty and Grace are eternal and everlasting, they require the everlasting existence of their lovers and admirers, for Eternal Beauty can never be content with transient admirers. The love of an admir-

---

[24] A brilliantly shaped and dazzlingly adorned flower, and a most artfully wrought jewel-like fruit on a twig as fine as wire and attached to a tree as rigid as bone—such things proclaim the fine artistry of a most skilled, wise, and miraculous Fashioner to all animate beings. The same is true of the animal and vegetable realms.

[25] A celebrated beauty once rejected a common man who had become infatuated with her. To console himself, the man said: "How ugly she is!" and so denied her beauty. A bear once stood beneath a vine trellis and longed to eat the grapes upon it. Unable to reach the grapes or to climb the trellis, it said to itself, by way of consolation: "The grapes must be sour," and went on its way growling.

[26] While all beings that act as mirrors for Divine Beauty continually depart and disappear, others succeed them, manifesting in their forms and features the same Beauty. This shows that such Beauty does not belong to them; rather, the visible instances of beauty are the signs and indications of a transcendent, holy Beauty.

er condemned to permanent separation will turn to hatred once the thought of separation takes hold. Admiration yields to an ill opinion, and respect yields to contempt. For selfish people may be enemies of what they do not know, are be opposed to what lies beyond their reach. A finite love responds to a beauty that deserves infinite admiration with tacit hostility, hatred, and rejection. This is a profound reason for why unbelievers hate God.

So unlimited generosity and liberality, unequalled beauty and absolute perfection require the existence of supplicants and admirers with eternal longing and gratitude. But this temporary world's inhabitants depart having tasted that generosity only long enough to whet their appetites. Seeing only a dim shadow of beauty and perfection's light, they are not fully content. Thus we can be sure that we are traveling to a place of eternal joy where we will be fully content. In short, just as this world and its creatures prove the All-Majestic Creator's Existence, His holy Attributes and Names point to and necessitate the Hereafter's existence.

FIFTH TRUTH: *The gate of Compassion and the Prophet's worship and servanthood, the manifestation of the Names the Answerer of Prayer and the All-Compassionate.* Is it conceivable that a Lord of infinite compassion and mercy, Who most compassionately fulfills the least need of His lowliest creatures in the most unexpected fashion, Who answers the faintest cry of help of His most obscure creature, and Who responds to all petitions, would ignore the greatest petition of His foremost servant, his most beloved creature, by not granting his most exalted prayer? The tender solicitude manifested in nurturing weak, young animals show that the Sovereign Lord of the universe exercises His being Lord with infinite mercy. Is it conceivable that such compassion and mercy in the exercise of Lordship would refuse the prayer of the most virtuous and beautiful of all creation?[27] This truth is explained in The Nineteenth Word, but we reiterate the argument here.

We mentioned in the parable a meeting held in a certain land, at which a most noble commander spoke. To discover this parable's truth, imagine

---

[27] Namely, the Prophet, who has ruled for fourteen centuries over billions of subjects, who daily renew their allegiance to him, continually bear witness to his perfections, and obey his commands. His spiritual temperament has shaped one-half of the globe and one-fourth of humanity. He is the beloved of their hearts, the guide of their souls, and the greatest servant of the Lord of the worlds. Since most of the realms of created beings applaud the duty and role entrusted to him through each bearing the fruit of his miracles, he is the most beloved creature of the Creator of all. Further, the desire for permanence and continuance implanted in our nature, which lifts us from the lowest to the highest rank, is the greatest desire and petition, and is presented to the Provider of all needs by His greatest servant.

that we go back to the Arabian peninsula during the blessed age of the Prophet, and visit and watch him perform his duties and worship. Just as through his Messengership and guidance he is the means for the attainment of eternal happiness, he is also the reason for that happiness' creation—the creation of Paradise—through his worship and prayer.

See how he is praying for eternal happiness with such perfect supplication and sublime worship. It is as if the peninsula, indeed the whole world, were praying and supplicating with him, for his worship contains his community's worship, as well as the essentials of all other Prophets' worship, for they all obeyed the same One Lord. He offers his supreme prayer and supplications amid so many beings that it is as if all illustrious and perfect people, from the time of Adam to the present, were following him in prayer and saying "Amin" to his petition.[28] He is petitioning for so universal a need—immortality—that all inhabitants of creation share in it and silently affirm: "Accept his prayer, O Lord, because we also desire it." He pleads for everlasting happiness so plaintively, with such yearning and longing, that creation is moved to tears and shares in his plea.

See he prays for such a goal and purpose that it raises all creatures from the abyss of utter annihilation, worthless and aimless futility, to the summit of worth, exalted purpose, eternal permanence, and being a missive of the Eternally Besought One. His petition is so noble, an asking for mercy so sweet, that it is as if he inspired all beings, the heavens, and the Divine Throne to hear and echo his words with ecstatic cries of "Amin, O Lord, Amin!"[29]

---

[28] From the Prophet's first petition until now, all invocations upon him of peace and blessings resemble a continual "Amin" after his prayer, a universal participation. Also, each such invocation during one's Prayers, and the prayer of the followers of the Shafi'i school for him after the second call to worship during the Prescribed Prayers, is a powerful and universal "Amin" to his plea for eternal happiness. The eternity and everlasting happiness so strongly desired by humanity, in accord with its essential nature, is desired for them by the Prophet, upon him be peace and blessings, and the illustrious segment of humanity says after him: "Amin!" Could such a universal petition not be granted?

[29] Could the Master of this world, all of Whose acts are self-evidently based on His absolute Awareness, Knowledge, and Wisdom, be unaware and uninformed of his foremost creature's deeds and prayers, remain indifferent to them, or consider them unimportant? Being aware and not indifferent, could the All-Powerful and All-Merciful Sovereign of the world not accept his prayers? The light of Muhammad, upon him be peace and blessings, has changed the world's form. The true essence of humanity and of all beings in the universe became apparent through that light; namely, that each is a missive of the Eternally Besought One

He asks for eternal happiness from such an All-Hearing, All-Munificent Powerful One, such an All-Seeing, All-Compassionate Knowing One, that He visibly sees, hears, accepts, and pities the most hidden wish and least desire of His most obscure creature. He answers all pleas and bestows His favors in so wise, insightful and compassionate way that no one can doubt that the one who does these is the One All-Hearing and All-Seeing, All-Munificent and All-Compassionate.

For what is the pride of all being petitioning? He is humanity's fountain of honor, the unique individual who stands on this earth with all humanity behind him and with his hands opened toward God's Throne and prays. In reality, his worship and servanthood to God includes the worship of all humankind and is the essence of it. He asks for eternal happiness for himself and all believers, for eternity and Paradise. He petitions through and with all sacred Divine Names, Whose beauty is reflected in all created beings. Surely you see that he is seeking intercession from those Names. Even if there were not innumerable other reasons and causes for it, a single prayer of his would suffice for creating Paradise, a task as easy for the All-Merciful's Power as creating spring.

How could creating Paradise be difficult for One All-Powerful, Who each spring makes the earth's surface a vast field of revival and brings forth countless resurrections? Just as the Prophet's being the Messenger was the reason for establishing this realm of trial—*But for you, I would not have created the worlds* is an indication of this—his worship was the cause for establishing the abode of eternal happiness.

Would the perfect artistry and unequalled beauty of God's being Lord, manifested in creation's amazing orderliness and comprehensive mercy, refuse the Prophet's prayer and thereby allow extreme ugliness, pitilessness, and discord? Would the All-Sustaining Lord hear and grant the most insignificant desire but refuse the greatest and most important desire as worthless? No, He would not! Such Beauty could never countenance such ugliness and thereby

---

proclaiming the Divine Names; a valued, meaningful being with God-given functions and destined for eternity. Were it not for that light, beings would be condemned to utter annihilation; without worth, meaning, or use; bewildered effects of blind chance and lost in the blackness of illusion. That is why just as humanity says "Amin" to the Prophet's prayer, all other beings from the earth's surface to the Divine Throne, from underground to above the stars, take pride in his light and proclaim their connection with him. The very spirit of the Prophet's worship and servanthood is prayer. All of the universe's motions and workings are in essence prayer, just as, for example, a seed's growth until it becomes a tree is a form of prayer to its Creator.

make Itself ugly. Just as the Prophet opened this world's gates by being God's Messenger, he opens the Hereafter's gates by worshipping Him.

> Upon him be the blessings of the All-Merciful One, to the extent of that which fills this world and the abode of Gardens—Paradise. O God, bestow blessings and peace on Your servant and Messenger, that beloved one who is the master of both realms, the pride of all worlds, the source of life in both worlds, the means for attaining happiness here and in the Hereafter, one who combines Prophethood and Messengership in himself, who preached the principles of a happy life in this world and the next, who is the Messenger sent to both humanity and jinn—on him, his Family, all his Companions, as well as his fellow Prophets and Messengers. Amin.

SIXTH TRUTH: *The gate of Majesty and Eternity, the manifestation of the Names the All-Majestic and the All-Permanent.* Is it conceivable that the majesty in His being the Lord, to Whose command all beings from suns and trees to atoms are subdued like obedient soldiers, should focus entirely upon the transient beings in this temporary world, and not create a permanent sphere of majesty and an exalted abode of Lordship? The majestic operations like the change of seasons, the awesome, speedy motions of gigantic planets, the amazing instances of subjugation such as making the earth our cradle and the sun our lamp, and such vast transformations as reviving and adorning a dry, dead earth—all of these show that a sublime Lordship rules with a splendid sovereignty behind the veil of what is seen.

That infinite, glorious sovereignty of Lordship requires subjects worthy of itself, as well as a fitting vehicle for its manifestation. But humanity, the world's most important inhabitant and blessed with the most comprehensive functions, is gathered to stay here only for a limited while and is in a pitiable state. The world is filled and emptied daily, as well as transformed hourly, and we stay only temporarily to be tested in service. All of the Sovereign's subjects are like would-be buyers who come for a while to view samples of the precious gifts bestowed by the All-Majestic Maker, His miraculous works of art in the showcase of this world. They soon leave, while the spectacle changes every minute. Whoever departs never returns, and whoever comes eventually departs. Such a reality argues that behind and beyond this world and its activities is a permanent, eternal abode that fully manifests God's everlasting Sovereignty—everlasting palaces and mansions, and gardens and treasure houses stocked with the pure and perfect originals of the forms and copies we see here. We strive here for what awaits us there. We labor here and are rewarded there. Bliss awaits all, provided that they are not among the losers, and is enjoyed according to each person's capacity. Indeed, an Eternal Sovereignty cannot focus exclusively upon a realm whose transience makes it wretched.

Consider this analogy: While travelling, you see a caravanserai built by a great person for those coming to visit him. Decorated at the greatest expense, it delights and instructs the guests during their night's stay. But they see only a little of those decorations, and only for a very short time. Having briefly tasted the joys of what is offered, they continue on their journey unsatisfied. However, each guest photographs the objects in the caravanserai, while the great person's servants record every guest's conduct and preserve the record. The guests notice that most of the wonderful decorations are replaced daily with fresh ones for newly arriving guests.

Having seen all this, will you doubt that the person who built this caravanserai must have permanent exalted dwellings, inexhaustible and precious treasures, and an uninterrupted flow of unlimited generosity? He shows his generosity in the caravanserai to arouse his guests' appetite for what he keeps in his immediate presence, and to awaken their desire for the gifts prepared for them.

If you reflect upon this world with an unclouded concentration, you will understand the Nine Principles explained below:

- *First principle*: This world (the caravanserai) neither exists nor assumed this shape by itself. Rather, it is a well-constructed hostelry, wisely designed to receive the caravan of beings that constantly arrive, stay for a while, and then leave.

- *Second principle*: We are guests here, invited to the Abode of Peace by our All-Generous Lord.

- *Third principle*: You will understand that this world's adornments are not merely for the sake of enjoyment. As they are temporary, like your life being short, they give pain upon separation; they give you a taste, rouse your appetite, but never satisfy you. So, they are here only to instruct in wisdom,[30] to arouse gratitude, and to encourage us to seek the permanent originals of which they are copies. In short, they are for exalted goals far beyond themselves.

---

[30] The lifespan of all worldly things is short, whereas their worth and the subtleties in their fashioning are most exalted and beautiful. This implies that everything is only a sample to draw the viewer's gaze to its authentic original. Given this, we may say that this world's diverse adornments are samples of Paradise's bounties, made ready by the All-Merciful and All-Compassionate for His beloved servants.

- *Fourth principle*: The world's adornments are like samples and forms of the blessings stored in Paradise by the All-Merciful's Mercy for people of belief.[31]
- *Fifth principle*: All transient things were created not to go into annihilation after a brief appearance but to exist briefly to acquire their requisite forms so that they can be recorded, their images taken, their meanings understood, and their consequences preserved. This is so that, for example, everlasting spectacles might be wrought from them for the people of eternity, and serve many other purposes in the Realm of Permanence.

---

[31] Everything exists for many purposes, and numerous effects result from it. These purposes and effects are not, as the misguided suppose, related only to this world and to their own selves; rather, they relate to these three categories:

The first and the most exalted pertains to the Creator, namely, to present to the Pre-Eternal Witness' view the splendidly adorned wonders He has attached to each thing, as if for a military parade. The most fleeting existence suffices for the realization of this purpose. Indeed, the mere potentiality for existence suffices. This purpose is fully realized, for example, by fragile creatures that swiftly perish, and by seeds and kernels, each a masterpiece, that never flower or bear fruit. Their existence is never tainted by vanity and futility. This means, the primary purpose of all things is to display, by their very being, the miracles of their Maker's Power and works of His Art, presenting them to His view.

The second category pertains to conscious beings. Every thing is like a truth-bearing missive, or artistic poem, or a wise word of the All-Majestic Maker offered to angels and jinn, humanity and animals, inviting them to "read" them. Every thing is an object for the contemplation and instruction of every conscious being that looks upon it.

The third category relates to the things' themselves, and consists of such minor effects as the experience of pleasure and joy, of abiding with some degree of permanence and comfort. If we consider the functions of a steersman employed on a royal yacht, we see that only 1% of those functions actually relate to the steersman (e.g., his wages); the other 99% relate to the king who owns the yacht. A similar proportion obtains between the things' purposes related to its self and worldly existence and those related to its Maker.

Given this multiplicity of purposes, we can explain the ultimate correlation between Divine Wisdom and economy, as well as Divine Liberality and Generosity (which are in reality unlimited), even though they seem to contradict each other. In one respect, liberality and generosity predominate and the Name the All-Generous is manifested. For example, fruits and grains are beyond reckoning and manifest this Name. But in the universal purposes things are made to serve, the Name the All-Wise is manifested. It may be said that a fruit of a tree has as many purposes as the number of the fruits. These purposes can be divided into the three categories just mentioned.

These universal purposes demonstrate an infinite wisdom and economy. Infinite wisdom and infinite generosity are thus correlated, despite their apparent opposition. For example, one purpose for raising an army is to maintain order. The troops already available may be enough to achieve this. However, the whole army may be barely enough for such other purposes as protecting national frontiers and repelling enemies. Wisdom and multiplicity are thus correlated, just as the purpose of a government's existence never contradicts its splendor.

Things are created for eternity not for utter annihilation. Apparent annihilation marks a completion of duty and a release from service, for while every transient thing progresses to annihilation in one aspect, it remains eternally in numerous other aspects. Consider a flower, a word of God's Power. It smiles upon us for a while and then hides behind the veil of annihilation. Like a spoken word which goes but entrusts its thousands of copies to ears, and whose meaning remains in the minds of those who heard it, the flower disappears, but it leaves its visible form in the memory of those who saw it and its inner essence in its seeds. It is as if each memory and seed were a device to record the flower's adornment or a means for its perpetuation.

As this is true for such a simple living entity, we can see how much closer we are attached to eternity, given that we are life's highest form and have an imperishable soul. Again, from the fact that the laws, which resemble spirit in one respect and according to which flowering and fruit-bearing plants are formed,[32] and the representations of their forms are preserved and perpetuated in the most orderly manner in tiny seeds through all tempestuous changes [of weather, seasons, and the like], we can understand easily how closely human spirit is attached and related to eternity. The spirit, which gives each person a most exalted and comprehensive nature, is like a conscious and luminous law issuing from the Divine Command and clothed in external, sensible existence.

- *Sixth principle:* We have not been left to wander at will, like a loosely tethered animal pasturing where it pleases. Our deeds are "photographed" and recorded, with their consequences being preserved for the Day when we will have to account for them.

- *Seventh principle:* The wholesale death of spring and summer creatures during autumn is not an annihilation, but a dismissal after the duty's completion, an emptying that makes way for new creatures to come next spring and assume their functions.[33] It is a Divine warning to

---

[32] These laws have the same meaning for the life and existence of plants as a spirit has for the individual human being. (Tr.)

[33] It is fitting that a tree's leaves, flowers, and fruits, which are Mercy's treasures of sustenance, depart when they have grown old and their duties ended. Otherwise the gate open to those to follow would be closed and the expansion of mercy and the services to be performed by newcomers be blocked. In addition, they themselves become wretched due to their old age. Similarly, spring is like a fruit-bearing tree indicating the vast Plain of Resurrection. In every age the world of humanity is like a tree full of lessons; the earth is a tree of Power full of wonders; the world is another, amazing tree whose fruits are sent ahead to the market of the Hereafter.

rouse conscious beings from their forgetfulness, to shake them out of the torpor that causes them to neglect their duty to give thanks.

- *Eighth principle*: This transient world's Eternal Maker has an eternal world toward which He urges and impels His servants.
- *Ninth principle*: In that world, One so Merciful will give His chosen servants gifts that are so far beyond our knowledge that we cannot imagine them. In this we believe.

SEVENTH TRUTH: *The gate of Recording and Preservation, the manifestation of the Names the All-Preserving and the All-Watchful.* Is it conceivable that an attribute of preservation, which preserves within absolute orderliness and equilibrium everything that exists, and sifts their consequences to call to account, would allow the acts of His noble vicegerent, who bears the Supreme Trust, to go unrecorded, unsifted and unaccounted, unweighed in the balance of justice, unpunished or unrewarded fittingly, even though his acts relate so closely to God's universal Lordship?[34] No, it is not.

The Being Who administers this cosmos preserves all things in an order and balance, which manifest His Knowledge and Wisdom, Will and Power. For we see that everything is created in perfect proportions, and all its subsequent individual forms are fashioned in perfect, pleasing, symmetrical orderliness. Moreover, the All-Preserving of Majesty preserves many forms of things that perish after finishing their duties, in people's memories, which are like a Supreme Preserved Tablet, and in mirrors belonging to the Realm of Ideal Forms.[35] He inscribes a compact life-history in a seed (that life's issue and outcome). Thus He causes all things to be preserved in mirrors corresponding to outer and inner worlds. Human memories, a tree's fruit, a fruit's kernel, a flower's seed—all manifest the law of preservation's universality and inclusiveness.

Have you not seen how the records of the deeds of all spring flowers and fruits, laws of their formation, and images of their forms are all inscribed within minute seeds and there preserved? The following spring, those records are opened—a bringing to account appropriate to them—and another vast world of spring emerges with absolute orderliness and wisdom. This shows the powerful and comprehensive exercise of the Divine

---

[34] God's vicegerency means that humanity is the "means" God "uses" to execute His commands on the earth and that we rule it according to His laws. The Supreme Trust is our selfhood or essential nature, which has been equipped, relatively, with all manifestations of Divine Names and Attributes, particularly with will-power. Also, see The Thirtieth Word. (Tr.)

[35] See footnote 18. (Tr.)

Attribute of Preservation. Considering that the issue of such transient, commonplace, and insignificant things is preserved, how could our deeds, which from the viewpoint of universal Lordship yield important fruit in the Unseen world, the Hereafter, and the World of Spirits, not be preserved and recorded as a matter of high significance?

This comprehensive preserving shows us what great care the Master of creation devotes to the orderliness of everything that occurs under His Rule. He is also absolutely attentive to the task of His Sovereignty and His Lordship's authority. Therefore He records, or causes to be recorded, the least event and smallest service and preserves everything's form in numerous records. This Attribute of Preservation indicates that the records of our deeds will be laid open and, as the deeds of the noblest and the most honored and significant of creation, closely scrutinized and weighed.

Ennobled with God's vicegerency and Trust, we are witnesses to the universality of His being Lord and proclaim His Unity in this Realm of Multiplicity. Thus we act as controllers of and witnesses to the worship of most beings. How can then we be consigned to an endless sleep in the grave, never to be roused and questioned about what we did? Without a doubt, we will travel to the Plain of Resurrection or Supreme Gathering and be tried at the Supreme Tribunal.

How can we flee and hide in nothingness under the ground from the All-Powerful One of Majesty, the miracles of Whose Power in the past—all past events—bear decisive witness to the fact that He can do whatever He wills in the future and Who every year creates spring and winter, which resemble the Resurrection?[36] Since we are not called to account and

---

[36] The past consists of happenings. Every day, year, and century that came into being is a line, a page, and a book inscribed by the Pen of Destiny. Divine Power inscribes Its miraculous works in it in perfect wisdom and orderliness. While the future, from now until the Resurrection, Paradise, and eternity, consists entirely of contingencies. Comparing these two, we understand with certainty that the Being Who created yesterday and its creatures can create tomorrow and its creatures. As past wonders are the miraculous works of a Powerful and Majestic One, they affirm that He can create the future and its contingencies and show His wonders.

The One Who is supposed to create an apple certainly must be able to create all apples and bring spring into being. One who cannot create spring cannot create a single apple, for they are made at the same workbench. Each apple is a miniature example of a tree, a garden, or a cosmos. Its seed carries within itself the tree's life-history, and displays such perfect artistry that it is a miracle created by the One Who can do anything. Likewise, the One Who creates today can create the Day of Resurrection, and only He Who is able to create the Resurrection can create spring. The One Who threads and displays all past events on the ribbon of time in perfect wisdom and order can attach another universe to the ribbon

judged in this world suited to that Power, we must proceed to a Supreme Tribunal and happiness in another.

EIGHTH TRUTH: *The gate of Promise and Threat, the manifestation of the Names the Beautiful and the Majestic.* Would the Maker of this world, Who has Absolute Knowledge and Absolute Power, not fulfill the oft-repeated promise and threat affirmed by all Prophets, truth seekers, and saints? Not doing so would display impotence or ignorance. His Power can realize His promise and threat as easily as He brings back in spring the innumerable beings of the spring before, some identical (the roots of trees and grass) and some similar (leaves and fruits). Our need for everything, and the requirement of His being Sovereign and Lord, means that He will fulfill His promise. Not doing so would contradict His Power's dignity and authority as well as His Knowledge's comprehensiveness.

If you deny such facts, in reality you are following your own lying fancy, capricious intellect, and deceiving soul. You call Him a liar, though He never breaks His promise, for His Glory and Dignity make this impossible for Him. Moreover, His truthfulness is attested to by everything you see. Despite your insignificance, your error is infinite and thus deserving of a great and eternal punishment. The fact that according to certain Traditions, a tooth of some people of Hell will be as large as a mountain points to this truth.[37] Those who deny resemble travelers who close their eyes to sunlight and turn to the light of their own fantasies, although it is no stronger than a glowworm's, to light the awful road ahead. The Almighty will certainly do what He promises; all of the creatures are His truthful words, and all events in the universe, His eloquent signs. So He will establish a Supreme Tribunal and bestow supreme happiness.

NINTH TRUTH: *The gate of reviving and causing death, the manifestation of the Names the All-Living and the Self-Subsistent, and the All-Reviving and the One Who Causes To Die.* God revives this vast earth when it is dead and dry, thereby displaying His Power via resurrecting countless species of creation, each as extraordinary as the promised resurrection of humanity. He shows His all-embracing Knowledge in these creatures' infinite distinctions and differentiations within their complex intermingling. Also, He turns His ser-

---

of the future and display them there. In several treatises of *The Words*, we proved that the One Who can create one thing can create everything. Also, if everything's creation is attributed to a Single Being, their creation becomes as easy as creating one thing. But if creation is attributed to multiple agents or causes, the creation of one thing is as hard as creating everything and therefore it borders on the impossible.

[37] *Muslim,* "Jannah" 44; *at-Tirmidhi,* "Sıfatu Jahannam" 3.

vants' attention toward eternal happiness by promising their resurrection in His heavenly decrees, and displays the splendor of His Lordship by causing all His creatures to help and cooperate with each other and directing them within the orbit of His Command and Will. Furthermore, He shows the value His gives to us by creating us as the Tree of Creation's most comprehensive, subtle, worthiest, and most valued, fruit; by addressing us directly; and by subjugating all things to us. So, Could an All-Powerful and Compassionate, the All-Knowing and Wise, One Who does all these, not (or be unable to) bring about the Resurrection? Could He not institute His Supreme Court and create Paradise and Hell? Such ideas are inconceivable.

Indeed, the Almighty Disposer of this world's affairs continually creates on this finite, transient earth numerous signs, examples, and indications of the Supreme Gathering and the Plain of Resurrection. Each spring we see countless animal and plant species resurrected in a few days. All tree and plant roots, as well as certain animals, are revived and restored exactly as they were. Other animals are re-created in nearly identical forms. Seeds that appear so alike quickly grow into distinct and differentiated entities, after being brought to full vigor with extraordinary rapidity and ease, in absolute orderliness and harmony. How could anything be difficult for the One Who does this? How could He create the heavens and the earth in 6 days and yet be unable to resurrect humanity with a single blast?

Suppose a gifted writer could rewrite in an hour countless books whose letters were confused or effaced on a sheet of paper without error or omission, fully and in the best style. If someone then told you that he could rewrite in a minute from memory a book which he had written and had fallen into water, how could you say that he could not do so? Or think of a king who, to show his power or warn or for recreation, removes mountains with a command, turns his kingdom about, and transforms the sea into dry land. Then you see that a great boulder blocks the path of guests going to his reception. If someone says that the king will remove the boulder with a command, would you say that he could not do so? Or imagine someone assembles a great army in a day, and you are told that he will re-assemble it in battalions by a trumpet blast after dismissing them to rest, would you respond with disbelief? If you did, your error would be enormous.

Now, see how the Eternal Designer closes winter's white page and opens spring's and summer's green pages before our eyes. With the Pen of Power and Destiny, He inscribes infinite species on the page of the earth in a most beautiful style. They are all intermingled but he inscribes them without confusion and error, giving each its distinct form. Inscribing one does not hinder the inscription of another. Is it reasonable to ask concerning the All-Wise and All-Preserving, Who compacts a great tree's being into a dot-sized seed, how He preserves the spirits of those who die; how the All-Powerful One, Who spins the earth like a pebble in a sling, will remove the earth from the path of His guests travelling to the Hereafter?

Is it reasonable to ask concerning the All-Majestic One, Who installs the atoms of all living beings in their respective bodies with perfect orderliness with the command of *Be! and it is*, and thus creates disciplined, well-organized armies—is it reasonable to ask how He can re-assemble these atoms and bodily members, which have already known each other in perfectly organized battalions of bodies, after they have dispersed?

You see with your own eyes the numerous designs made by God as signs, similitudes, and analogies of the Resurrection. He displays them in every era, the alternation of day and night, even in the coming and going of clouds. If you imagine yourself a thousand years in the past and then compare past and future, you will see as many examples and analogies of the Resurrection as there are centuries and days past. If, after this, you still consider bodily Resurrection improbable and unacceptable to reason, there is something seriously wrong with your powers of reasoning.

Concerning this truth, the Supreme Decree says: *Look upon the imprints of God's Mercy, how He revives the earth after its death. He it is Who will revive the dead [in a similar way]. He has full power over everything* (30:50). In short, there is nothing which makes the Resurrection impossible, and there is much necessitates it.

The glorious and eternal Lordship, the all-mighty and all-embracing Sovereignty, of the One Who gives life and death to this wide and wonderful earth as if it were a single organism; Who has made it as a pleasing cradle and handsome craft for humanity and animals; Who has made the sun a lamp that gives it both its light and heat; Who has made the planets transports for His angels—such Lordship and Sovereignty cannot be confined to a mutable, transitory, unstable, slight, and imperfect world. Thus there is another realm, one worthy of Him, immutable, permanent, stable, great, and perfect. He causes us to work for this realm and summons us to it. Those who have penetrated from outward appearances to truth, who have been ennobled by proximity to the Divine Presence, all spiritual "poles" endowed with light-filled hearts, and those with enlightened minds, testify that He will transfer us to that other kingdom. They teach us that

He has prepared a reward and a requital for us there, and that He gives us His firm promises and stern warnings thereof.

Breaking a promise is base humiliation and therefore irreconcilable with His Sanctity's glory. Failure to carry out a threat can arise either from forgiveness or impotence (ignorance). Unbelief is an unforgivable crime.[38] The All-Powerful is exempt from and far above all impotence. All who teach this and bear witness to it are all agreed on this fundamental, even though they follow different paths of thought and approach. Their testimony has the authority of learned consensus. Each of them is a guiding light of humanity, the cherished one of a people and the object of their veneration. In importance, each is an expert and authority on this matter. In any art or science, two experts are preferred to thousands of non-experts, and two positive affirmers are preferred to thousands of negators in a report's transmission. For example, the testimony of two competent men that they have sighted the crescent moon marking the beginning of Ramadan nullifies the negation of thousands of deniers.

In short, this world contains no truer report, firmer claim, or more evident truth than this. The world is a field, and the Resurrection is a threshing-floor, a harvesting-ground for grain that will be stored in Paradise or Hell.

TENTH TRUTH: *The gate of Wisdom, Grace, Mercy, and Justice, the manifestation of the Names the All-Wise, the All-Munificent, the All-Just, and the All-Merciful.* The Majestic Owner of all existence displays such manifest wisdom, evident grace, overwhelming justice, and comprehensive mercy in this impermanent world, transitory testing ground, and unstable display hall of the earth. Is it conceivable that He would not have permanent abodes with immortal inhabitants residing in everlasting stations in His visible and invisible, corporeal and incorporeal realms ad so He would allow that all these realities of wisdom, grace, mercy, and justice to decline into nothingness?

Would the All-Wise choose us to receive His direct and universal address; make us a comprehensive mirror to Himself; let us taste, measure, and

---

[38] Unbelief is an insult to the whole creation as it degrades it, alleging it to be with no meaning and worth. It is also a disrespect to the Divine Names because it denies their manifestations in the mirrors of creatures. It also rejects the witness borne to the Unity of God by all beings, and so gives them the lies. Therefore, unbelief so corrupts our potentialities that we cannot reform and become unreceptive to good. It is also an act of absolute injustice, a transgression against the rights of God's Names and creation. The defense of those rights, and an unbeliever's irredeemable state, require that unbelief be unpardonable. The Divine declaration, *Associating partners with God is truly a tremendous wrong* (31:13), expresses this.

get to know the contents of His treasuries of Mercy; make Himself known to us with all His Names; love us and make Himself beloved by us—and then not send us to an eternal realm, an abode of permanent bliss, and make us happy therein? Would He lay on every being, even a seed, a burden as heavy as a tree, charge it with duties as numerous as flowers, and appoint to it beneficial consequences as numerous as fruits, while assigning to them purposes that are relevant only here? Why would He restrict His purpose to this worldly life, something less valuable than a grain of a mustard seed? Would it not be more reasonable for Him to make beings in this world as seeds for the immaterial world of meanings and essences, where the true meanings of everything here will be manifested, and as a tillage for the Hereafter, where they will yield their true and worthy produce? Would He really allow such significant parades and performances (as we witness) to be purposeless, void, and futile? Why would He not employ them for the sake of eternity in the Eternal, Immaterial World of Meanings and Essences, so that they might reveal their true purposes and fitting results there?

Is it conceivable that by causing things to contradict their own nature by not building the eternal realm, He would show Himself to be characterized by the opposites of wisdom, munificence, justice and mercy—which are among His essential Attributes? How could He deny the true essences of all beings that indicate His Wisdom, Munificence, Justice, and Mercy, and rebut all things' testimony to Him? Could reason agree that He would charge our heads and all the senses and faculties in it with innumerable duties, and then give us only a worldly reward worth less than a hair, and so act absurdly, in a way to contradict His true Justice and true Wisdom?

God shows Himself to be absolutely All-Wise in attaching infinite purposes and benefits to every living being, to each of its members, to each creature. Given this, is it conceivable that by not bestowing on us meeting with Him and eternal happiness in an eternal realm—which are the greatest of purposes, and the most significant and necessary of beneficial results, and which make wisdom, blessings, and mercy into what they are, and are the origin and goal of all purposes, blessings, instances of mercy and beneficial results, He would allow all His acts to be marked by pointlessness? That He would cause Himself to resemble a builder who built a palace consisting of stones bearing thousands of designs, corners holding thousands of adornments, and parts providing thousands of valuable tools and instruments—but forgot to cover it with a roof, so that everything therein rotted and became use-

less. God forbid such a thought! From absolute Goodness comes forth only goodness, and from the absolutely Beautiful One comes forth only beauty, an nothing in vain or purposeless comes forth from the absolutely Wise One.

Whoever travels back to history in mind sees stages, places, exhibitions,
and worlds, as many as the years that have passed and each like this present
world. Although different from each other in form and quality, they resemble each other in their perfect arrangement, exquisiteness, and how they display the Maker's Power and Wisdom. In those impermanent halting-places,
transient arenas, and fleeting places of exhibition, we see well-arranged
works of manifest wisdom, signs of evident favoring, indications of overwhelming justice, and fruits of comprehensive mercy. Those with any perception understand that there cannot be a more perfect wisdom, gracious
favoring, glorious justice, and comprehensive mercy.

If there were no permanent abodes, elevated places, everlasting residences,
eternal mansions, eternal residents, blissful servants in the Eternal Sovereign's
realm, Who does all those things and continuously changes those hostelries
and their guests, we would have to reject the true essences of Wisdom, Justice,
Favoring, and Mercy—which are universal, substantial and as manifest as the
four universal elements, namely light, air, water, and soil. For this fleeting
world and its contents cannot manifest their true essences fully. Therefore, if
there were no other place wherein they could be manifested fully, we would
have to deny the wisdom apparent in what we see, the favoring we observe
manifested on us and all other things, the justice[39] indicated by its signs that
appear so effectively, and the mercy we witness everywhere. We also would
have to regard the One Who is the unique source of all wise processes, munificent deeds, and merciful gifts that we see in the universe, as a foolish trickster
and a pitiless tyrant. God forbid that this should be so; it is a totally inconceiv-

---

[39] There are two forms of justice, one positive and the other negative. The positive one consists
in giving the right to the one who deserves it. [Except for the injustices we commit in the realm
where our free wills have a part], this form of justice is clearly observed throughout the world.
For, as discussed in the Third Truth, the All-Majestic Originator gives in definite measures and
according to definite criteria everything that is asked for in the tongues of natural need and
absolute necessity. In other words, He meets all the requirements of everything's life and existence. Therefore, this form of justice is as certain as existence and life.

The negative form of justice involves punishing the unjust, and so giving the wrongdoers their due via requital and chastisement. Even though this form is not manifested fully
here, countless signs suggest its existence. For example, the blows of punishment striking
the rebellious peoples from 'Ad and Thamud in the past to those of the present age show
that a very exalted justice dominates the world.

able reversal of the truth. Even Sophists who deny the existence of everything, including their own selves, would not readily contemplate such a proposition.

In short, the world's universal fusions of life and swift separations of death, imposing gatherings and rapid dispersions, splendid parades, performances, and mighty manifestations are irreconcilable with their negligible results and insignificant, temporary purposes in this fleeting world. [If there were no Hereafter], this would mean giving a great mountain a purpose as insignificant as a small stone. This is utterly unreasonable and pointless.

Such a large disparity between beings and those affairs on the one hand, and the purposes they serve in this world on the other, testifies that they basically work on behalf of the Immaterial World of Meanings, where their true meanings and results will be manifested fully. They relate to the Sacred Divine Names. Implanted in this world's soil, they flourish in the World of Ideal Forms or Representations. According to our capacity, we sow and are sown here to harvest in the Hereafter. If you look at the aspects of things pertaining to the Divine Names and the Hereafter, you will see that each seed (a miracle of Power) has aims as vast as a tree, that each blossom[40] (a word of Divine Wisdom) has as many meanings as a tree's blossoms. Each fruit, a marvel of Divine Art and a composition of Divine Mercy, has as many purposes as a tree's fruits. Serving us as foods is only one of its countless purposes. After it fulfills that service and expresses its meaning, it dies and is "buried" in our stomachs.

Seeing that these transient things yield everlasting fruits in another place, where they leave permanent forms of themselves, express eternal meanings of different aspects, and constantly glorify God, we can attain true humanity by approaching things from these aspects and thereby find a way to eternity through this ephemeral world. Since this is true, all these creatures that move between life and death, that are first integrated and gathered together and then dispersed and dissolved, must serve some other purposes.

This state of affairs resembles arrangements made for imitation and representation. Brief gatherings and dispersions are arranged, at great expense, so that pictures can be taken and shown later continuously on screens. Similarly, one reason for our brief individual and social lives is that pictures may be taken and the results of our deeds recorded and preserved. They then will be judged

---

[40] I choose examples chiefly among seeds, flowers, and fruits because they are the most marvelous and delicate miracles of Divine Power. Despite this, since misguided naturalists and scientists cannot "read" the subtle designs inscribed in them by the Pen of the Divine Destiny and Power, they have drowned in them and fallen into the swamp of naturalism.

in a vast place of gathering and shown in a great place of exhibition, so that all may understand that they have the potential to yield supreme happiness. The Prophet expressed this: "This world is the tillage for the Hereafter."

Since the world exists, and since Wisdom, Favoring, Mercy, and Justice prevail therein with their imprints, the Hereafter also exists. Since all worldly things are mainly turned toward that world, they are headed for it. To deny the Hereafter amounts to denying this world and its contents. Just as the appointed hour and the grave await us, so do Paradise and Hell anxiously await our arrival.

ELEVENTH TRUTH: *The gate of humanity, the manifestation of the Name the Ultimate Truth.* Could the Almighty Truth, the only One worthy of worship, make us the most important servant to His absolute, universal Lordship, and then deny us the Eternal Abode for which we are fitted and longing? Could He make us a most comprehensive mirror in which to manifest His Names, choose us as the most thoughtful one to address, and then deny us the Eternal Abode?

Could He create us as His Power's most beautiful miracle and in the fairest form, so that we might receive His Greatest Name's manifestation as well as the greatest manifestations of all His Names, and then deny us the Eternal Abode? Could He create us as investigators equipped, more than any other creature, with measuring instruments and systems to assess and perceive the contents of Divine Mercy's treasuries, and then deny us the Eternal Abode? Could He make us more needy of His infinite bounties than all other beings, more afflicted by mortality and most desirous of eternity, and then deny us the Eternal Abode?

Could He create us as the most delicate and destitute animate being, the most wretched and susceptible to pain in worldly life but the most developed in capacity and structure, and then deny us the Eternal Abode? How could the Almighty Truth create us with all such qualities and then not send us to the Eternal Abode, for which we are fitted and longing? Could He so nullify our essence, act so totally contrary to His being the Absolute Truth, and commit an injustice that truth must condemn as ugly?

Could the All-Just Ruler, the absolutely Compassionate One, give us the potential to bear the Supreme Trust, from which the heavens and mountains shrank, and then deny us eternal happiness? Could He enable us to measure and know, with our slight and partial measures and accomplishments, our Creator's all-encompassing Attributes, universal acts, and infinite manifestations, and then deny us eternal happiness? Could He create us as the most delicate, vulnerable, impotent, and weakest beings, task us with ordering the earth's vegetable and animal life and let us interfere with their forms of worship and glorification of God, and then deny us eternal happiness?

Could He cause us to represent His universal operations on a miniature scale, thereby declaring through us His glorious Lordship throughout the universe in word and deed, and then deny us eternal happiness? Could He prefer us over His angels and give us the rank of vicegerent,[41] and then deny us eternal happiness, which is the purpose, result, and fruit of all these duties? Could He reduce us to being the most wretched, ill-fortuned, suffering, and humiliated creature, and make reason or intellect, a gift of His Wisdom and a most blessed and light-diffusing means of finding happiness, a tool of torment for us? As a result, could He be act totally contrary to His absolute Wisdom and Mercy? No, never!

Remember that in the parable we looked at an officer's identity card and register. We saw that his rank, duty, salary, instructions, and supplies meant for a permanent realm and he exerted himself for its sake. Like this, as all exacting scholars and purified ones able to unveil hidden truths agree, all the faculties in the registers of our hearts, and the senses and capacities in the notebooks of our intellect have been given to us to obtain eternal happiness. For example, if the faculty of imagination (a servant of the intellect forming conceptions) were told that it would live for a million years amidst royal pomp and pleasure and then undergo eternal annihilation, it would heave a deep sigh of sorrow, unless deceived by vain fancy and the carnal soul.

This means that the greatest temporary worldly pleasure cannot satisfy our smallest faculty. So, as our character and disposition—ambitions extending to eternity, thoughts embracing all creation, and desires felt for all varieties of eternal happiness—show, we were created for and will proceed to eternity. This world is like a waiting room for the Hereafter.

TWELFTH TRUTH: *The gate of Messengership and Revelation, the manifestation of In the Name of God, the All-Merciful, the All-Compassionate.* Could groundless fancies, wandering doubts, and illusions, all weaker than a gnat's wing,

---

[41] God Almighty has distinguished us with knowledge, speech, and free will. Although He allows us to act on our own according to our free will, He wants us to rule here according to His Commandments so that the world might be integrated with other parts of the universe in peace, harmony, and tranquility, and so that we can find the happiness in both worlds for which we long. Being vicegerent means having the authority to rule on Earth in His name, but with the responsibility of following His Commandments sent through His Prophets. (Tr.)

close the path to the Hereafter and the gate to Paradise? These have been opened by thousands of decisive Qur'anic verses, miraculous in forty ways, and the noble Messenger of God, relying on the power of his almost a thousand established miracles. This is the same Messenger whose words are affirmed by all Prophets, based on their miracles; whose claim is confirmed by saints, based on their visions and spiritual experiences and discoveries; and whose truthfulness is testified to by all purified, exacting scholars relying on their investigations.

These twelve truths show that the Resurrection is a firmly rooted truth that cannot be shaken. God Almighty established it as a requirement of His Names and Attributes; His Messenger affirms it with the strength of his miracles and the proofs of his Prophethood; the Qur'an proves it with its truths and verses; and the universe testifies to it with all its phenomena and purposeful events taking place therein. How could the Resurrection, upon which the Necessarily Existent Being and creation (except unbelievers) agree, and whose truth is as mighty and firmly rooted as mountains, be shaken by doubts feebler than a hair and satanic whisperings?

These are not the only arguments for the Resurrection, for the Qur'an alone, which instructs us in these Twelve Truths, points to thousands of other aspects of this issue. And each aspect is a clear sign that our Creator will transfer us from this transient abode to an eternal one. Also, the Divine Names requiring the Resurrection are not limited to those mentioned: All-Wise, All-Munificent, All-Compassionate, All-Just, and All-Recording and Preserving. In reality, all Divine Names manifested in the universe's ordering and administration require the Resurrection.

The "natural" phenomena pointing to the Resurrection are not restricted to those we have discussed. Most things in the universe have aspects and properties resembling curtains opening to the right and the left. One aspect testifies to the Maker, and the other indicates the Resurrection. For example, while our creation in the fairest form demonstrates the Maker, together with the comprehensive abilities lodged in that fairest form, our rapid decline points to the Resurrection.

If we look at the same aspect in two ways, we sometimes notice that it indicates both the Maker and the Resurrection. For example, the wise ordering and arrangement, gracious decoration, just balance and measurement, and merciful favoring seen in most things show that they proceed from the hand of the Power of an All-Wise, All-Munificent, All-Just and All-

Compassionate Maker. But despite the power and infinitude of these Names and their manifestations, if we look at the brief and insignificant life of those transient beings receiving their manifestations, the Hereafter appears. Thus, in the tongue of their being and life, all things recite and lead others to recite: "I believe in God and the Last Day."

Conclusion

The preceding Twelve Truths confirm, complement, and support each other. All together as if a single truth, they demonstrate the desired result. Can any doubt penetrate those twelve firm walls, each like steel or diamonds, and shake the belief in the Resurrection housed within them?

Your creation and your resurrection are as but a single soul (31:28) means that creating and resurrecting humanity or a single person are equally easy for the Divine Power. In *Nuqta* (Point), I elaborated this truth. Here, I will summarize it and present various comparisons.[42] For example, if the sun had free will and could manifest itself however it wished, as a light-giving object it could do so with the same ease in innumerable transparent objects or in one particle. Being transparent, the tiniest transparent thing equals the ocean's surface in containing the sun's image. By virtue of orderliness and its interrelated parts, a child can steer a battleship as easily as a toy boat. By virtue of obedience, a commander can order an army to move with the same "March!" issued to one soldier. Imagine a balance so sensitive that it can weigh two walnuts, and so large that it can weigh two suns. If two walnuts or suns of equal weight were placed in these pans, by virtue of balance or equilibrium, the same power that lifts one walnut to the heavens and lowers the other to the ground, would move the suns with the same ease.

In this lowly, imperfect, and transient world of contingency, by virtue of such qualities as *luminosity, transparency, orderliness* and *interrelatedness, obedience* and *balance* (or *equilibrium*), all things become equal, and numerous things appear as equal to one thing. Given this, and by virtue of the luminous manifestations of the Absolutely Powerful One's essential, infinite, and utterly perfect Power; the transparency of the inner dimension of things; the exact universal order dictated by Divine Wisdom and Destiny; the perfect obedience of things to His commands of creation; and because the existence or non-existence of all things is equally possible, little and

---

[42] This is included in *al-Mathnawi an-Nuri* (Seedbed of the Light), The Light, 2007. (Tr.)

much, small and great are equal in respect to His Power. And so He will resurrect us with one trumpet blast, as if we were one person.

Furthermore, a thing's degrees of strength and weakness are determined by the intervention of its opposite. Degrees of heat are determined by cold's intervention, degrees of beauty by ugliness' intervention, and degrees of illumination by darkness' intervention. But if a quality or property is essential to something, that is, if it originates directly from itself and is almost identical with itself, its opposite cannot intervene in it. If its opposite could intervene, this would mean that opposites of the same qualities would have to be united in a single thing—something clearly impossible.

The Absolutely Powerful One's Power is essential to His Divine Essence, originates from It directly, and is almost identical with It. Given this, and that It is also absolutely perfect, It cannot have an opposite to intervene in It. Hence the Lord of Majesty creates spring as easily as He creates a flower, and will resurrect and assemble humanity with the same ease as He resurrects one person. If material causes had to create just one flower, on the other hand, it would be as difficult for them as to create an entire spring.

All that we have explained so far is derived from the radiation of the wise Qur'an. So, let us listen to more of what it has to say:

> For God is the final, conclusive argument. (6:149)

> Look upon the imprints of God's Mercy, how He revives the earth after its death. He it is Who will revive the dead [in the same way]. He has full power over everything. (30:50)

> He has coined for Us a comparison,having forgotten his own origin and creation, saying: "Who will revive these bones when they have rotted away?" Say: "He Who produced them in the first instance will revive them. He has full knowledge of all creation." (36:78)

> O humankind, keep from disobedience to your Lord in piety. The violent convulsion of the Last Hour is an awesome thing. The day you see it, every suckling woman will forget her suckling-babe, and every pregnant one will drop her burden. You will see humans as drunk, yet they are not drunk. Dreadful will be the doom of God. (22:1-2)

> God, there is no deity but He. Surely He will gather you all to a Day of Judgment about which there is no doubt. Who is more true than God in the words [He speaks] and the news [He gives]? (4:87)

> The pious, purified will be in bliss and blessings. The wicked will be in blazing Fire. (82:13-14)

When the earth quakes with a violent quaking destined for it and throws up its burdens, and human cries out: "What is the matter with it?" That day it will proclaim its tidings because Your Lord has inspired it. That day humans will come forth in scattered groups to be shown their deeds. Whoever does an atom's weight of good will see it, whoever does an atom's weight of evil will see it. (99:1-8)

The sudden, mighty strike! What is the sudden, mighty strike? Would that you knew what the sudden, mighty strike is! The day whereon humans will be like moths scattered about, and the mountains will be like carded wool. Then the one whose scales are heavy [in faith and good deeds] will be in a pleasing life. But the one whose scales are light will have his home in a bottomless pit. What enables you to perceive what it is? It is a raging Fire! (101:1-11)

To God belongs the unseen of the heavens and the earth. The affair of the Hour is as the twinkling of an eye, or even quicker. God has full power over everything. (16:77)

Listening to these and other similar verses, we should say: "We so believe and affirm."

I believe in God, His angels, His Books, His Messengers, the Last Day, and Destiny in that whatever comes as good or evil [is recorded in His Knowledge and created by Him]. Resurrection is true, Paradise is true, the Fire is true, intercession [on the Last Day] is true, and *Munkar* and *Nakir* are true.[43] God will resurrect those in the graves. I bear witness that there is no deity but God, and I bear witness that Muhammad is the Messenger of God.

O God, bestow blessings on the most graceful, noble and dignified, perfect and beautiful fruit of Your Mercy, which has blossomed throughout the universe like a blessed tree; on him whom You sent as a mercy for all worlds, and as a means for us to attain to the most adorned, fairest, brightest, and most exalted fruit of that "tree" extending into the Hereafter, that is, into Paradise. O God, save us and our parents from the Fire, and take us and our parents into Paradise with the purified, pious ones, for the sake of Your chosen Prophet. Amin.

O brother (or sister) who are studying this treatise with an open mind, do not ask: "Why can't I immediately understand this Tenth Word in all its details?" Do not become bored if you cannot understand it right away. Even such a master of philosophy as Ibn Sina (Avicenna) judged that the

---

[43] *Munkar* and *Nakir* are the two angels who interrogate the dead in the Intermediate Realm (between this and the next) about their beliefs and deeds in this world. (Ed.)

Resurrection could not be understood through rational criteria; we must believe in it. Also, scholars consider it one of the revealed truths requiring belief and one that cannot be established through reason. Therefore, it is difficult for human reason to grasp such a profound and exalted issue in one attempt. Thanks to the All-Merciful Creator's Mercy and the wise Qur'an's radiation, I hope that this Tenth Word, if studied carefully and repeatedly, will convince your reason of the Resurrection's truth and help secure belief in it.

One difficulty that human reason encounters here is that since the Resurrection and Supreme Gathering will occur through the manifestation of God's Greatest Name, this event can be established rationally only by demonstrating His acts through His Greatest Name's manifestation and the universal manifestations of other Names, as if proving the coming of next spring. We tried to follow this approach in this Word.

Addendum

In the Name of God, the All-Merciful, the All-Compassionate.

So glorify God when you enter the evening and when you enter the morning—and (proclaim that) all praise and gratitude in the heavens and on the earth are for Him—and in the afternoon, and when you enter the noon time. He brings forth the living out of the dead, and brings the dead out of the living, and revives the earth after its death. It is in this way that you will be brought forth from the dead. And among His signs is that He created you from earth; then you have grown into a human population scattered widely. And among His signs is that He has created for you, from your selves, mates, that you may incline towards them and find rest in them, and He has engendered love and tenderness between you. Surely in this are signs for people who reflect. And among His signs is the creation of the heavens and the earth, and the diversity of your languages and colors. Surely in this are signs indeed for people who know. And among His signs is your sleeping at night and in the day, and your seeking (livelihoods) out of His bounty. Surely in this are signs for people who pay heed. And among His signs is His displaying before you the lightning, giving rise to both fear and hopeful expectation, and that He sends down water from the sky, and revives with it the earth after its death. Surely in this are signs for people who reason. And among His signs is that the heaven and the earth stand firm by His Command. In the end, when He calls you forth from the earth, then (at once) you will come forth. To Him belongs all that is in the heavens and on the earth. All are obedient to Him in humble service. He it is Who originates creation and then reproduces it, and will bring it back:

and that is most easy for Him. Whatever attribute of sublimity there is in the heavens and the earth, it is His in the highest degree, and He is the All-Glorious and Mighty, the All-Wise. (30:17-27)

One most significant argument included in these sublime heavenly verses, which point to one pole of belief, in these exalted sacred proofs that establish the Resurrection's reality, is here set forth. It is a subtle instance of Divine grace that, at the end of *Muhakemat* ("The Reasonings"), which I wrote about 30 years ago to set down the principles of Qur'anic commentary, came the words: "A Second of Two Other General Proofs: This explains two of the proofs of the Resurrection, which the Qur'an indicates. In the Name of God, the All-Merciful, the All-Compassionate." And there it stopped.

Praise and thanks as numerous as the proofs and indications of the Resurrection to my All-Compassionate Creator that 30 years later on, I have been enabled to resume that task. About 9 or 10 years ago, God granted me The Tenth and Twenty-ninth Words, two works containing numerous strong proofs and interpretations of the Divine Decree—*Look upon the imprints of God's Mercy, how He revives the soil after its death. Surely He will revive the dead [in the same way], and He has full power over everything.* The Tenth and Twenty-ninth Words silenced those who denied the Resurrection. Now, a decade or so later, He has granted to me the interpretation of the supreme verses quoted above, unassailable fortresses of belief in the Resurrection. That interpretation consists of some parts.

Part One: Introduction

[This introduction consists of two points that briefly expound one of the many spiritual benefits of belief in the Resurrection and one of its vital comprehensive results. They also show how that belief is essential for human life, particularly social life, and summarize one of its many comprehensive proofs. Also included is an explanation of how evident and indubitable a matter is belief in the Resurrection.]

FIRST POINT: We will relate only four of the many arguments for belief in the Hereafter as the very basis and bedrock of human social and individual life, and the foundation of all happiness and achievement.

FIRST ARGUMENT: Children are one-third of humanity. They cannot endure death, which must seem to them an awful tragedy, except via the idea of Paradise, which spiritually strengthens their weak, fragile natures. It gives them the hope to live joyfully, despite the vulnerability of their nature, which can so readily burst into tears. Keeping Paradise in mind, they may say: "My little sister or friend has died and become a bird in Paradise. She is playing there and enjoying a better life." If they could not do this, their awareness of the deaths of those around them would overwhelm them; crush their powers of resistance and inner strength; cause their eyes and all inner faculties, heart, mind, and spirit to weep; and destroy them or transform them into distraught and crazed animals.

SECOND ARGUMENT: The elderly make up another one-third of humanity. They can endure death only by believing in the afterlife, which consoles them somewhat for the imminent extinction of this life to which they are so attached, for their exclusion from their lovely world. Only the hope of eternal life allows them to counter the pain and despair which the anticipation of death and separation give rise to in their child-like, fragile temperament and spirit. Without such a hope, our venerable elders who are so worthy of compassion, our aged parents who need a serene and steady heart, would become so distraught in spirit and distressed at heart that their world would seem to be a dark prison, their lives a heavy burden of torment.

THIRD ARGUMENT: Young people are the mainspring and foundation of social life. Only the thought of Hell enables them to control the stormy energy of feelings and passions, their tempestuous, evil-commanding souls, from destructiveness and oppression, and divert them into serving the collective interest. Without this fear, and drunk on the energy of youth, they would follow the principle of "might makes right" and give free rein to their passions. This would turn the world into a hell for the weak and powerless, and lower human life to the level of beasts.

FOURTH ARGUMENT: The family is the inclusive core of our worldly life, our most fundamental resource, and the paradise, home, and castle of our worldly happiness. Each person's home is his or her own miniature world. The vitality and happiness of our homes and families depend upon sincere and devoted respect, true kindness, and self-denying compassion. All of this, in turn, depends upon eternal friendship and companionship, an immortal bond, as well as the belief that feelings and relations between parents and children, brothers and sisters, and husbands and wives will be everlasting.

For example, a man can say: "My wife will be my eternal companion in an eternal world. Even if she is now old and not as beautiful as before, her eternal beauty will show itself in the Hereafter. For the sake of that companionship in eternity, I sacrifice and show her compassion in this world." Thus he can regard his aged wife with love, care, and compassion, as if she were a gorgeous *houri*. A companionship that ends in permanent separation after a few hours of bodily togetherness can only be slight, transient, and insecure. It would produce only a superficial love and respect based on physical charm and sexual instinct. Other interests and powerful emotions eventually would arise and, defeating that respect and concern, turn a worldly paradise into a worldly hell.

Thus, one of the numerous benefits of belief in the Resurrection relates to our social life. If the related aspects and benefits are deduced via analogy with these four, it will be clear that the Resurrection's reality and truth is as certain as our own existence and universal need. It will be even more evident than the argument that food must exist because our stomachs require it. If the Resurrection's reality and truth, and all the consequences thereof, are subtracted from the human state, the meaning of being human—so exalted, vital, and important within creation—is lowered to that of a carcass fed upon by microbes. Let those concerned with humanity's orderly life, morals, and society focus on this matter. If the Resurrection is denied, with what will they fill the resulting void and cure the deep wounds?

SECOND POINT: Among innumerable proofs of the reality of the Resurrection, we set out, in a compressed and succinct form, the support offered by the other pillars of belief. All miracles affirming Muhammad as Messenger, upon him be peace and blessings, all proofs of his Prophethood, and all evidence of his truthfulness bear witness to and establish the Resurrection's reality and truth. For after the Unity of God Almighty, all the claims that exalted person set forth during his life focused on the Resurrection. Indeed, the miracles and proofs attesting to all Prophets, and urging humanity to attest to them, bear witness to the same truth. Similarly, the requirement for Muslims to believe in God's Books, which makes completely clear the testimony to His Messengers, bears witness to this truth. It is as follows: All their miracles, proofs, and truths establishing the Qur'an's truth likewise establish and prove the Resurrection's reality and truth. About one-third of the Qur'an deals with the Hereafter, most of its short *suras* begin with powerful verses evoking it, and it proclaims this truth explicitly or implicitly in hundreds of verses, thereby proving it. For example:

When the sun is folded up. (81:1)

O humankind, keep from disobedience to your Lord in piety; the violent convulsion of the Last Hour is an awesome thing. . (22:1)

When the earth quakes with a violent quaking destined for it. (99:1)

When the heaven is cleft open. (82:1)

When the heaven is split asunder. (84:1)

What are they asking each other about? (78:1)

Has the account of the overwhelming event come to you? (88:1)

Just as the initial verses of about 20 *suras* state that the Resurrection's truth is a most important and essential reality of creation, many other verses affirm and provide other evidence of the same truth. How can you even consider not believing in the Resurrection? Would it be as impossible and absurd as the denial of the sun and the claim of the non-existence of the universe that one would consider belief in the Resurrection false, which emerges like the sun from innumerable arguments and testimonies of a Book, even a verse of which has yielded numerous fruits in Islamic and cosmic sciences?

A sovereign sometimes sends his army into battle merely to prove the truth of one of his statements. Is it, then, even conceivable to contradict the truth of that most solemn and dignified sovereign's innumerable words, promises, and threats? Is it possible that they should be false? This glorious sovereign (the Qur'an) has ruled, administered, and educated countless spirits, intellects, hearts and souls according to perfect righteousness and truth for more than 13 centuries. While one indication from it suffices to prove the Resurrection's truth, it proves and demonstrates it with thousands of explicit proofs. So, what else can we say than that those who continue to deny this truth are worthy of and deserve punishment in Hellfire?

Furthermore, all Divine Pages or Scrolls and Sacred Books other than the Qur'an, each of which was addressed to a specific age and time, accept the truth of the Resurrection, which the Qur'an, addressing all times, explains and establishes in detail and with explicit arguments. Even their brief and sometimes allusive explanations affirm it so powerfully that they constitute a thousandfold signature of what the Qur'an teaches.

We include an argument drawn from the *Treatise on Supplication*. This brief argument, including the testimony of belief in the Last Day by the other pillars of belief, mainly belief in God's Messengers and Books, is forceful and may suffice to end all doubt. In this supplication, we say:

O All-Compassionate Lord. I have understood from the instruction of Your noblest Messenger, upon him be peace and blessings, and the teaching of the wise Qur'an that all the Divine Books and Prophets, primarily the Qur'an and Your noblest Messenger, unanimously assert and testify that the manifestations of all Your Names of Majesty and Grace, Whose exemplary manifestations are observed throughout the universe, will continue to manifest themselves in eternity in a more splendid way; that Your gifts, the compassionate manifestations and specimens of which are experienced in this fleeting world, will endure in a more brilliant fashion in the Abode of Eternal Bliss; and that those who are fond of them and who discern them in this brief worldly life with pleasure and seek them in love will accompany them to and through all eternity.

Also, based on the countless proofs of their Prophethood, including their hundreds of evident miracles, and on the promises and threats that You reiterated in all the heavenly Pages or Scrolls and sacred Books; and relying on the dignity of Your Majesty and the dominion of Your Lordship, and on Your sacred Attributes and essential Qualities of Yours such as Power, Mercy, Beneficence, Wisdom, Majesty and Grace, Which require the Hereafter; and through their spiritual unveilings and observations, together with their convictions at the degree of certainty of knowledge and certainty of vision or observation, all of the Prophets with luminous spirits, including first and foremost God's noblest Messenger, upon him be peace and blessings, the saints with illuminated hearts and the pure, saintly scholars with enlightened intellect—all of these give jinn and humankind the glad tidings of eternal happiness for the people of guidance, and warn that there is Hell for the misguided, while being the first to believe in the rewards and punishments to come.

O All-Powerful, O All-Wise! O All-Merciful and All-Compassion-ate; O All-Munificent One Who is absolutely True to His promises! O All-Overwhelming One of Majesty with Dignity, Grandeur, and Majesty! Failure to bring about the Resurrection would mean contradicting so many truthful friends of Yours. It would mean breaking Your vehemently repeated threats and promises, negating Your sacred Attributes and essential Qualities, and negating the definite requirements of the dominion of Your Lordship; it would mean rejecting the prayers and petitions for the Hereafter of Your innumerable servants whom You love, and who make themselves loved by You by confirming and obeying You. Undoubtedly You are exalted far above such a failure!

You are also exalted far above confirming the people of unbelief and misguidance in their rejection of the Resurrection, who through unbelief and disobedience, and by contradicting You in Your promises, insult Your Grandeur, attack the dignity of Your Majesty, offend the honor of Your Divinity and disparage your Lordship's Compassion. I declare Your infinite Justice, Grace and Mercy to be absolutely free of such limitless ugliness and evil. We believe with all our power that these numerous truthful Messengers of Yours and hundreds of thousands of Prophets, pure, saintly scholars, and saints, who are heralds of Your dominion, are absolutely true in their testimony to Your eternal treasures of Mercy and Benevolence, and the extraordinarily exquisite manifestations of Your All-Beautiful Names in the world of permanence with certainty based on knowledge, and certainty based on vision, and certainty based on experience. They also believe and teach others by Your command that the greatest ray of Your Name, the Ultimate Truth, which is the origin, sun and preserver of all truths, is this greatest truth of Resurrection.

O Lord, for the sake of their instruction and teaching, grant to us and our brothers and sisters perfected belief and a fair ending to our life, and that we may have some share of their intercession. Amin.

All arguments and evidences establishing the truth of the Qur'an and all other Divine Books, as well as the miracles and proofs that establish the Prophethood of the beloved of God—Prophet Muhammad—and of all other Prophets, point to the Hereafter's reality, which has the greatest place—next to God's Existence and Unity—in their claim or cause.

Similarly, most arguments and evidences for the Necessarily Existent Being's Existence and Unity implicitly affirm the existence and opening out of the Abode of Happiness, the Realm of Eternity where God's Lordship and Divinity will be fully manifested. For both the Existence of the Necessarily Existent Being and most of His Names and all His Attributes and essential Qualities, like Lordship, Divinity, Grace, Wisdom, and Justice, necessitate an eternal realm with utmost certainty and demand the Resurrection and Last Judgment for dispensing absolutely just punishment and reward.

Since God eternally exists, He must have an eternal abode where His Divine Sovereignty will eternally dominate. Since we see that a most magnificent, purposively wise, and caring absolute Lordship exists throughout the universe and animate creation, there must certainly be an eternal realm of happiness to which admission is granted, so that the majesty of that Lordship is not extinguished, Its wisdom not turned into pointlessness, and Its caring not destroyed by betrayal.

Since these visible and infinite bounties, blessings, kindnesses, and instances of generosity and mercy show to alert minds and hearts that an All-Merciful and All-Compassionate Being exists beyond the veil of the Unseen, there must be an eternal life in an eternal world, for only that which will show that His Bounty does not mock, His Benevolence does not deceive, His

Favoring does not create enmity, His Mercy does not torment, and His Generosity does not betray. In addition, it is only eternity in an eternal realm which makes all bounties and blessings assume their true and perfect forms.

Since each spring we see a Pen of Power tirelessly inscribe uncountable interleaved books on the narrow page of the earth without allowing any error, and the Owner of that Pen has promised repeatedly in all His Decrees: "I will write and have you read a beautiful, imperishable book in a place far more spacious than this, and in a fashion far easier than this cramped and intermingled book of spring that is written on such a narrow page," certainly its origin has been written already, and will be set down in writing with all its marginalia on the Day of Resurrection. The records of all people's deeds will also be included in that book.

Since by virtue of the multiplicity of its inhabitants and of its being the abode, origin, workshop, and place of display and resurrection of countless constantly changing forms, the earth is given great importance as the universe's heart, center, choice, core, ultimate end, and very reason for its creation, and despite its small size, the heavenly Decrees hold it equal to the vast heavens, saying, *the Lord of the heavens and the earth...*

And since there is humanity—we are dominant throughout the earth. We have dominion over most of its creatures, subordinate and gather around ourselves almost all animate beings, and order, display, and ornament created objects according to our need and desire. We catalogue and classify everything in all its wonderful variety, each species in its own place, and in such a way that all people and jinn gaze at it, all dwellers of the heavens and the universe regard it with appreciation, and even the Lord of the universe bestows His appreciative glance upon it. Thus we gain great importance and value and show through our art and science that we are the reason for the universe's existence, the supreme fruit of creation and serve as God's vicegerents on the earth. Since we demonstrate and arrange the Maker's miraculous works here, we are given a respite and granted success despite our rebellion, ingratitude and unbelief and our punishment is postponed.

Since despite being endowed with such qualities, we nevertheless are extremely weak and impotent and have innumerable needs and subject to innumerable pains. However, there is a most powerful, wise, and caring Ruler Who has made the planet a storehouse stocked with every kind of mineral and food we need and with all the merchandise we desire, and Who provides for us in a way altogether beyond our power and will.

Since the Lord Who possesses these qualities, loves us and makes Himself our beloved. He is Eternal and has eternal worlds. He does all things with justice and wisdom. But this Eternal Ruler's majesty of dominion and eternality of sovereignty cannot be contained in the transient life of this fleeting, temporary world. Furthermore, the enormity of human injustice and rebellion as well as its members' betrayal, denial, and unbelief toward their Benefactor and Provider, which are hostile to and contradict the universe's just balance and harmonious beauty, generally go unpunished in this world. The cruel and the treacherous live easily, while the oppressed and downcast live in wretchedness. But the whole nature and being of Absolute Justice, signs of which are seen throughout the universe, are totally at odds and irreconcilable with the idea that the cruel and treacherous—who die just like the oppressed and the desperate—should never be resurrected [to account for their cruelty in a supreme tribunal].

Since the Owner of the universe has chosen the earth from the universe and humanity from the earth, giving both a high rank and significance. Out of humanity, He has chosen the Prophets, saints, and pure, saintly scholars, true human beings who conform to His purposes as the Lord of creation and make themselves loved by Him through belief and submission. He has taken them as friends and objects of His address, and ennobles them with miracles and Divine support and punishes their opponents with heavenly blows. Out of these people, He has chosen their leader and fulcrum: Muhammad, upon him be peace and blessings. For long centuries He has illumined with his light the half of the globe and one-fifth of humanity. As if creation were created for his sake, all of its high purposes become manifest through him, his Religion, and the Qur'an he brought. Although he deserved and was worthy to infinitely receive an infinite reward for the infinite value of the services he rendered—services that usually would take thousands of years to perform— he was granted a brief life of sixty-three years spent in hardship and struggle. How could we believe that he would not be resurrected, together with all his peers—the other Prophets—and Companions? Or that he should not, even now, be alive in the spirit? Or that they should die and disappear into eternal extinction? The entire universe and the truth on which it is based demand his being again, demand his life from the Owner of all that is.

Since it has been established in The 7th Ray, The Supreme Sign, with thirty-three conclusive proofs that the universe is a Single Being's handicraft. That Being's Oneness and Unity give rise to all His Perfections and cause creation to obey Him absolutely. By means of a new life, that of the Hereafter, those Perfections remain defect-free;[44] His Absolute Justice is not deformed into absolute treachery, His universal Wisdom into foolish pointlessness, His all-inclusive Mercy into frivolous tormenting, and His exalted Power being confounded with impotence.

Out of hundreds of realities which belief in God gives rise, these eight ones described in the paragraphs beginning with "since" demonstrate, the Resurrection will occur. Only after the abodes of reward and punishment open their gates will the earth's significance and centrality, and our true significance and value, be truly accomplished; and the All-Wise Ruler's Justice, Wisdom, Mercy, and Sovereignty, Who is the Creator and Lord of our planet and of us, will be manifested eternally with all their perfections. All true friends and ardent lovers of the Eternal Lord will be delivered from eternal annihilation, and the nearest and dearest of them will be rewarded for the sacred services with which have made the entire universe pleased and indebted. And the Eternal Sovereign's Perfections will affirm themselves to be without defect, His Power without incompetency, and His Justice without oppressiveness. In sum, the Hereafter exists because God exists.

Just as the above-mentioned three pillars of faith—belief in God, belief in Prophethood, and belief in Divine Books—bear witness to the Resurrection, along with all the evidences testifying to their truth, so also the remaining two pillars of faith—belief in His angels and in Destiny, whatever good or evil happens to us being included in it without excluding human free will and created by God Almighty—require the Resurrection and bear witness to the World of Eternity. It is as follows:

All arguments, testimonies, and conversations held with them, which prove that angels exist and serve God, also attest indirectly to the existence of the World of Spirits, the Unseen, the Hereafter, and the Abode of Bliss (Paradise) and Hell, which in the future will be peopled by humanity and jinn. For angels can see and enter those worlds by God's leave. All angels nearest to the Divine Throne and who communicate with humanity, such as Gabriel, report their existence and travels therein. Just as we accept America's existence (which we have never actually seen) from the reports of returning travelers, so do we believe in the existence of the Realm of Eternity, the Hereafter, Paradise and Hell, from the angels' reports, which have the authority of numerous undisputed narrations.

---

[44] The Divine Perfections will be manifested without veil in the Hereafter. The defects referred to are such things as injustice, hardship, cruelty, and all disparities that humanity, having free will, suffers and causes others to suffer. (Ed.)

All arguments contained in The Twenty-sixth Word (about Divine Decree and Destiny), which establish belief in Destiny, attest indirectly to the Resurrection, to the publishing in another world of our recorded deeds (in this world), and their weighing in the Supreme Balance. For the events in the existence of all things are impressed before our eyes and recorded, and the life history of every animate being is inscribed in its memory, its seed, and other tablet-like forms; the deeds of every being endowed with spirit, especially humanity, are registered on preserved tablets. So, such an all-embracing Determination, wise and purposive ordaining, detailed and minutely exact recording and inscribing can exist only to enable the giving of a permanent reward or punishment at the Supreme Judgment after a universal tribunal. Otherwise, such a comprehensive, meticulous recording and registering would have no purpose or meaning, and would be contrary to sense and reality. Moreover, if there were no Resurrection, all exactly established meanings inscribed by the Pen of Divine Destiny in the Book of the Universe would be annihilated. This would be tantamount to denying the universe's existence.

In short, then, the five pillars of faith and their proofs point to and require, bear witness to and necessitate, the Resurrection and that the Realm of the Hereafter be opened out. Thus, the truth of the Resurrection has such vast and unshakable supports and proofs worthy of its sublimity, and about one-third of the Qur'an is devoted to it. The Qur'an makes it— next to belief in God—the bedrock of all of its truths, and constructs everything on this basis.

Part two

> Look upon imprints of God's Mercy, how He revives the earth after its death. Surely He it is Who will revive the dead [in the same way], and He has full power over everything. (30:50)

This verse contains nine convincing arguments for the Resurrection. The first, concerning life and will be expounded upon below, is very clear and pointed to in:

> Glory be to God, when you enter evening and when you enter morning. All praise is to Him in the heavens and on the earth and at nightfall and when you enter noon. He brings forth the living from the dead and the dead from the living, and revives the earth after its death. So you will be brought forth. (30:17–19)

It was also stated among the properties of life that life relates to the six pillars of belief and that it offers proof for them.

Indeed, since the most important result and fruit of the universe and the purpose of its creation is life, certainly that elevated reality cannot be restricted to this fleeting, brief, deficient, painful worldly life. The aim and result of the Tree of Life, and its fruit that is worthy of its tremendousness is the eternal life or the life of the Hereafter; it is the life in the realm of eternal, perfect happiness, the very stones, trees, and earth of which are alive. Or else, the tree of life, equipped with numerous significant members, would be without fruit, benefit, purpose, or any reality for conscious beings, including, in particular, humanity. Humanity, which in respect of its capital and faculties is, say, twenty times greater than a sparrow, and which is the most exalted and important creature in the universe, would fall twenty times lower than a sparrow with regard to the happiness of life, and become the most unhappy, the most debased of wretches. Furthermore, through preoccupation with the pains of the past and fears of the future, reason, the most precious of bounties, would continuously wound the human heart; because it muddies a single pleasure with nine pains, it would become the most calamitous affliction. So, the claim that there is no eternal life is a manifold falsehood. As a result, the life of this world, which every spring displays before our eyes hundreds of thousands of examples of the Resurrection, proves decisively the pillar of belief in the Hereafter.

Is it at all possible that the All-Powerful Disposer of Affairs, Who prepares with wisdom, grace, and mercy in your body, garden and country all the things and members that are necessary for your life, and makes them reach you just in time, Who knows and hears even the particular prayer for food offered by your stomach through its desire for maintenance, and Who shows that He accepts its prayer by gratifying it with innumerable delicious foods—is it at all possible that He does not see you or know you, or that He does not prepare all that is necessary for eternal life, humanity's greatest goal, or that He does not accept humanity's most urgent, important, general, and most necessary and proper prayers for eternity by not constructing the Hereafter and creating Paradise, or that He does not hold humanity, the ruler and result of the earth, as important as the stomach, that He ignores its most powerful, general prayer, which reverberates from the ground to the Divine Throne, thus causing His perfect Wisdom and endless Mercy to be denied? God forbid, a hundred thousand times, God forbid!

And is it at all possible that He should hear the most secret voice of the tiniest living creature, heed its plea, answer its need, nourish it with perfect care and concern, and cause even His large creatures to serve it, but should not hear the thunderous voice of the greatest, most valuable, immortal, and most delicate "life?" Is it possible that He does not take into consideration its extremely important plea and prayer for eternity? Is it possible that He should equip and maintain a mere soldier with the greatest care while ignoring a magnificent, obedient army? Is it possible that He should see an atom and not see the sun? Is it possible that He should hear the buzzing of a mosquito and not hear the roar of thunder? God forbid! A hundred thousand times, God forbid!

And could reason in any way accept that an All-Powerful and All-Wise One Who is infinitely merciful, loving, and affectionate, and Who greatly loves His own Art and makes Himself much loved and loves greatly those who love Him, would condemn to eternal non-existence both the life, which loves Him more than anything else and is lovable and loved and by nature adores its Maker, and the spirit, the essence and substance of life; thus making that beloved friend of His resentful of Himself for all eternity, and wounding it in such terrible fashion that He both denies and causes to be denied the essence and meaning of His Mercy and the light of His Love? A hundred thousand times, God forbid! The absolute Grace and Beauty Which adorns the universe with its manifestation and the absolute Mercy Which makes happy all creatures are most certainly free of such infinite ugliness; they are absolutely exalted above such complete wrong and mercilessness.

Conclusion: Since there is life in this world, certainly those who understand the mystery of life and do not misuse their lives will be favored with eternal life in the abode of eternal permanence and everlasting Paradise. In this we believe!

Transparent objects on the earth shine with the sun's reflections, and bubbles on the surface of the sea and rivers glisten and die away with gleams of the sun's light, while the bubbles that follow on after them act again as mirrors that reflect miniature suns. This obviously shows that those gleams, those reflected suns in transparent objects and bubbles are the reflected images of a single sun high above. They sing the sun's existence with a myriad of voices, and point to it with their fingers of light.

In just the same way, through the all-comprehensive manifestation of the All-Living and Self-Subsistent One's Name of the Giver of Life, the living creatures shine on the earth and in the sea through Divine Power, and then in order to make way for those to follow, utter, "O Living One!", disappearing under the veil of the Unseen, thus indicating and testifying to the eternal Life and necessary Existence of the eternally All-Living and Self-

Subsistent One. Likewise, all the evidence that bears witness to the Divine Knowledge Which the order of the universe manifests, and all the proofs that demonstrate the Divine Power Which controls the entire universe, all the realities that establish the Divine Will Which directs the universe, all the signs and miracles which prove the Prophetic missions as the channels of the Divine Speech and Revelations, and all the evidence that testifies to the seven Attributes of God Almighty[45]—all these unanimously indicate and bear witness to the Life of the All-Living, Self-Subsistent One. For something having sight is certain to have life; hearing is a sign of life; speaking indicates the existence of life; and will or free choice demonstrates life. Thus, all-encompassing Attributes such as absolute Power, all-inclusive Will, and all-embracing Knowledge, the existence of Which is evidently demonstrated by their work in the universe, together with all the evidence that establishes their existence, bear witness to the necessary existence of the All-Living, Self-Subsistent One and testify to His perpetual Life, Which illuminates the whole universe with just one of Its shadows, giving life to the entire realm of the Hereafter with all its particles with just one manifestation.

Life also relates to belief in the angels, and proves this belief indirectly. As the most important result in the universe is life; as living creatures are the most widely spread and most abundantly created beings because of their value, and they enliven the guesthouse of the earth with their coming and going in caravans; as the earth has been filled with so many varieties of living creatures and is continually being emptied and refilled owing to the Divine purposes for their constant renewal and multiplication; as even the rotting and corrupt substances become the media of the creation of numerous kinds of creatures, allowing the earth to become a place through which innumerable microorganisms swarm; and as consciousness and intelligence,

---

[45] God has three kinds of Attributes: the Essential Attributes of the "Essence," Affirmative Attributes, and Negative Attributes. His Affirmative Attributes refer to the assertion of His absolute Unity and to what God is; His Negative Attributes refer to the negation or what God is not. The Essential Attributes of the Essence are Existence, Having no beginning, Permanence, Dissimilarity to the Created, Oneness, and Self-Subsistence. The Affirmative Attributes are Life, Knowledge, Power, Will, Speech, Seeing, Hearing, and, according to some theologians, Creation. The Negative Attributes can be explained as follows: God cannot be described by any physical or anthropomorphic terms. He does not consist of body, color, and size. No person or thing can see Him, imagine, or conceive Him. He cannot be presented in the terms of substance or contingency of matter or form, localized in any part of space, confined to any part of time, or aligned and counted with any being. Nothing can be co-existent or co-extensive with Him. He never begets nor is begotten. And so on. (Tr.)

which are the purest extracts of life distilled from life, and spirit, its most sub-tle and stable essence, are created in great abundance on the earth, with the result that the earth is revived with life, intelligence, consciousness, and spir-its—because of all these it is not possible that the heavens, which are more refined and more spacious than the earth, should be left without life and con-sciousness. It is due to the meaning and purpose of life that there must be liv-ing, conscious beings who inhabit the heavens, suns, and stars particular to each, and so show them to be alive, and who display the result of the creation of the heavens, and receive Divine addresses. These beings are the angels.

The essential nature of life also relates to the pillar of belief in the Prophets, and proves it indirectly. Indeed, since the universe has been cre-ated to yield life; and since life is the greatest manifestation of the Eternal All-Living and Self-Subsistent One, as well as the most perfect embroidery of His and His most beautiful work of Art; and since the everlasting life demonstrates itself and is known through the sending of the Messengers and the revelation of the Divine Scriptures; and since speech shows that the one who speaks is alive—all these illustrate that it is the Prophets and the Divine Scriptures that were revealed to or sent through them that have made known the speeches of the One Who speaks, orders, and prohibits from beyond the realm of the Unseen veiled by the corporeal universe. Just as the life in the universe most certainly testifies to the necessary Existence of the Eternally Living One, so too does it also relate to pillars of the send-ing of the Prophets and the revelation of the Scriptures, which are rays, manifestations, and communications of that eternal life, and so too does it prove them allusively. In particular, the Messengership of Muhammad, upon him be peace and blessings, and the revelation of the Qur'an—since they are like the "spirit" and intelligence of life—can be said to be as certainly true as the existence of life.

Indeed, just as life is a pure extract distilled from the universe, just as con-sciousness and sense perception are extracts distilled from life, and intelli-gence is an extract distilled from consciousness and sense perception, and spir-it is the pure essence of life—indeed, it is life itself stable and autonomous—so too is the physical and spiritual life of Muhammad, upon him be peace and blessings, the most refined extract distilled from the life and spirit of the uni-verse. The Messengership of Muhammad, upon him be peace and blessings, is the purest extract distilled from the sense perception, consciousness, and intelligence of the universe. Indeed, as testified to by his works, accomplishments, and legacy, the physical and spiritual life of Muhammad, upon him be peace and blessings, the very life of the universe's life, and his Messengership are the light and very consciousness of the universe's consciousness. And the revelation of the Qur'an, as borne witness to by its ever-alive truths, is the spirit of the universe's life and the intelligence of its consciousness.

If the light of Muhammad's Messengership, upon him be peace and blessings, one day leaves the universe, the universe will die; and if the Qur'an leaves it, the universe will go mad and the earth will lose its reason and strike its then unconscious head on a planet, causing the destruction of the world.

Life also relates to the pillar of belief in Divine Destiny and proves it allusively. This is because, as life is the light of the physical, visible world throughout which it permeates, and as it is the result of the aim of existence, and since it is the most comprehensive mirror to the Creator of the universe and the most perfect epitome and index of the acts of Divine Lordship, and—if we may say so—is like some sort of program for these acts, then certainly, life necessitates that the creatures in the worlds of the seen and Unseen, that is, in the past and in the future, should exist and be identified in an order, known, and predisposed to obey the rules of God Almighty's creation and operation in the universe.

The original seed of a tree and its roots, as well as the seeds of its fruit, are all alive, just like the tree is itself as a whole entity; indeed, they follow the laws of life more subtle than those of the tree. Similarly, the seeds and roots left by the last autumn, as well as the seeds and roots that will be left to future springs after this spring has ended—they all have life, just like spring, and are subject to the laws of life. In just the same way, all the branches and twigs of the tree of the universe each has a past and a future. They have a chain of existence that consists of their past and future states and stages. The various, multiple existences and states of each species and each member of each species, which are contained in Divine Knowledge, form a chain of existences pertaining to or recorded in that Knowledge. Just like their external existence, their existence in Divine Knowledge bears a ray of immaterial life from the universal, all-encompassing life. All the states and stages of their material life occur according to these tablets of Divine Destiny, which are all alive.

The fact that the world of spirits, one form of the World of the Unseen, is full of spirits, which are life itself or the essences or substances of life, certainly requires that the past and future—which are another form and second section of the World of the Unseen[46]—should also be favored with some sort of life. Furthermore, the perfect order and the meaningful arrangement things display and their stages of life and fruits demonstrate that they have some sort of immaterial life in Divine Knowledge. So, life, which is a light from the Sun of the Eternal Life, cannot be restricted to the visible or physical world, this present time, or the observed, external existence. Rather, each world receives a manifestation from that light in accordance with its capacity, and the universe is alive and illuminated through it with all its worlds. Otherwise, as the misguided imagine, with the exception of this apparent, temporary (physical) life, each world would have been a vast and terrible corpse, a dark ruin.

Thus, the pillar of "belief in Divine Destiny and Decree" is understood in a broad sense through life and is established by it. That is, the orderliness of the visible world with whatever is in it and the results it produces manifest its life and vitality. Similarly, belonging to the World of the Unseen, the creatures of both the past and the future (which clearly indicate orderliness in their arriving in and departing from the world and through their worldly lives) have an immaterial living existence and an immaterial presence in God Almighty's Knowledge. The trace of this life and presence is manifested and observed by means of the Tablet of Destiny and Decree and through all the stages of their worldly lives.

Part three

QUESTION: The repeated declarations of the Qur'an, *It is but a single blast* (36: 53) and *The matter of the Hour is but the twinkling of an eye, or even quicker* (16:77) show that the Supreme Resurrection will happen in an instant. Our limited understanding needs a tangible analogy to enable us to concur with and accept such a unique, miraculous event.

---

[46] The original word corresponding to what we translate as "the Unseen" or "the world of the Unseen" is *ghayb*: that which we absolutely or relatively cannot penetrate with our five senses, or is absolutely or relatively invisible and unknown to us. That which is absolutely unknown to us is the" absolute Unseen," while that which we can acquire some knowledge about is the "relative Unseen." Like the World of Spirits that we cannot see, and the nature of which we cannot know through our senses, past and future are also unknown to us unless we somehow obtain knowledge of them. Past and future, being the two branches of time, is the "realm" where the World of the Absolutely Unseen manifests itself in the visible world, and may be regarded as its second form. (Tr.)

ANSWER: There are three matters concerning the Resurrection: spirits will return to their bodies; bodies will be reanimated; and bodies will be rebuilt and resurrected.

THE FIRST MATTER: An example for the spirits returning to their bodies: Imagine the soldiers of a highly disciplined army. Having dispersed in all directions in order to rest, they can be summoned back together with one loud bugle blast. The Archangel Israfil's[47] Trumpet is certainly no less powerful than a bugle. In addition, our spirits—each of which responded with "Yes, You are!" to the question "Am I not your Lord?" which came from the direction of pre-eternity when they were in the world of atoms— are more obedient, disciplined and submissive than any soldiers. The Thirtieth Word has demonstrated convincingly that not only the spirits but all atoms are the armies of the All-Glorified One, each being a dutiful soldier.

THE SECOND MATTER: An example for the bodies being reanimated: For a celebration in a great city, uncountable lamps may be turned on instantly by flicking a switch in the city's power station. It also would be possible to light an infinite number of lamps throughout the world from a single power station, if one existed. If a creation of God such as electricity, a servant and a candle-holder in this transient realm, can manifest this property on account of its Creator's training and discipline, the Resurrection is surely able to occur in the twinkling of an eye and within the framework of Divine Wisdom's orderly laws, which are represented and demonstrated by thousands of His light-giving servants such as electricity.

THE THIRD MATTER: There are thousands of suitable analogies for rebuilding and resurrecting human bodies on the Day of Resurrection. Consider, for example, the way in which trees, which are far more numerous than people, are restored with all their leaves perfectly and almost identically to those of the preceding year within a few days after the beginning of each spring. Consider the way in which the leaves, blossoms and fruits of the trees are re-created just like those of the preceding spring with extreme rapidity. Consider the sudden awakening, unfolding and coming to life of countless seeds, kernels and roots, which are the origin of spring growth. Consider the way in which trees, resembling standing skeletons, suddenly begin to show signs of "resurrection after death" at a single command. Consider the amazing reanimation of countless small creatures, especially the resurrection of different species of fly—particu-

---

[47] *Israfil* is the archangel who will blow the *Sur* (Trumpet) just before the destruction of the universe and the Resurrection, to which the Qur'an alludes in 39:68. (Tr.)

larly of those which, continuously cleaning their faces, eyes, and wings, remind us of our ritual ablution and cleanliness, and caress our faces—during a few days despite being far more numerous than all humans.

This world is the realm of Wisdom;[48] the Hereafter is the abode of Power. So, in accordance with the requirements of Divine Names such as the All-Wise, the All-Arranging, the All-Disposing, and the All-Nurturing, creation in the world is gradual and extends over a certain period of time. This is required by His Wisdom as the Lord. But given that Power and Mercy are more evident than Wisdom in the Hereafter, creation in that realm is instantaneous and free from anything related to matter, space, time and duration. In order to show that what takes a day or a year to do here will be accomplished within an instant in the Hereafter, the Qur'an decrees: *The matter of the Hour is but the twinkling of and eye, even quicker* (16:77). If you seek firmer confirmation that the Resurrection will come just as surely as the next spring, study the Tenth and the Twenty-ninth Words.

THE FOURTH MATTER: As for the destruction of this world: if a meteorite or asteroid were to collide with this planet by the command of God, our dwelling place would be destroyed instantly, just as a palace that took ten years to build could be destroyed in a minute.

Part four

> He said: "Who will revive to these bones when they are rotted away?" Say: "He Who produced them in the first instance will revive them." He has full knowledge of all creation. (36:78)

Recall the analogy used in the third comparison in the Ninth Truth of The Tenth Word. In sum: Someone assembles a huge army within one day before your eyes. If you were told that that one could reassemble and reorder with a blow of bugle a battalion whose members had dispersed for rest, and you replied that he could not, you would be regarded as crazy.

Similarly, the All-Powerful and All-Knowing, by His command *Be! and it is*, created all animate beings' atoms and subtle bodily constituents out of nothing. He then recorded and assigned them to their places, as if they were an army, with perfect orderliness and balance. During every spring, He creates countless different species and groups of animate crea-

---

[48] This world is the Realm of Wisdom, where things happen according to certain purposes and deliberation, in conformity with certain laws, and in which God usually acts from behind the veil of cause and effect. The Hereafter is the Abode of Power, in which God will act without any such veils. (Tr.)

tures, each of which resembles an army. Surely He can re-gather, with a blast on Israfil's trumpet, all the fundamental atoms and original components that enjoyed mutual acquaintance through their collective submission to the body's order—an order that exceeds that of any battalion. If you consider this improbable, are you not irrational?

In some of its verses, the Qur'an tells us what wonders God Almighty has performed here to convince our hearts of the wonderful acts He will accomplish in the Hereafter, and to prepare our minds to confirm them. Or it describes the amazing deeds He will perform in the future and the Hereafter by analogies with what we see here. One example is: *Has man not considered that We have created him from (so slight a beginning as) a drop of (seminal) fluid? Yet, he turns into an open, fierce adversary* (36:77), and the subsequent verses to the end of the sura.

The wise Qur'an establishes the Resurrection in seven or eight different ways. It first directs our attention to our own origin: "You see how you progressed—from a sperm drop to a blood clot suspended on the womb's wall, from a suspended blood clot to a formless lump of flesh, and from a formless lump of flesh to a human form through several other stages. How can you, then, deny your second creation? It is just the same as the first, or even easier [for God to accomplish]."

Also, God Almighty refers to certain great bounties He has granted to us: *He Who has made for you fire from the green tree* (36:80). He means: "Does the One Who has bestowed such bounty upon you leave you free to behave as you wish and then enter the grave to sleep permanently without rising again?" He also means: "You see how dead or dried trees come to life again and grow green. Yet you deem it unlikely that wood-like bones will be revived? Further, is He Who created the heavens and the earth unable to create and re-create humanity, the fruit of the heavens and the earth? Does One Who governs a huge tree attach no importance to its fruit and leave it to others? Do you think He will leave humanity, the result of the Tree of Creation, to it own devices or to others, and thereby allow that Tree of Creation, all parts of which have been kneaded with wisdom, to go to waste?"

God also says: "The One Who will restore you to life at the Resurrection is the One before Whom the whole universe is like an obedient soldier. It bows its head submissively before the command of *'Be!' and it is.* Creating spring is as easy for Him as creating a flower. It is He for Whose Power creating all animals is as easy as creating a single fly. No one should defy or challenge His Power by asking: "Who will give life to these bones?"

In: *So, All-Glorified is He in Whose Hand is the absolute dominion of all things, and to Him you are being brought back* (36:83), the Qur'an signifies: The All-Mighty controls everything and has the keys to everything. He alternates night and day, and winter and summer, as easily as turning the pages of a book. He is such an All-Powerful One of Majesty that, like closing one house and opening another, He closes this world and opens the next. Given this: *To Him you will be brought back* (36:83). He will revive you, take you to the Plain of Resurrection, and judge you in His majestic Presence.

Such verses prepare our minds and hearts to accept the Resurrection, because they show how it resembles several common things in our lives. Also, the Qur'an sometimes mentions God's acts in the Hereafter in a way calling attention to their worldly parallels, so that no room is left for doubt and denial. Examples are found in the *suras* beginning with: *When the sun is folded up* (81:1); *When the heaven is cleft open* (82:1); and *When the heaven is split asunder* (84:1). In these *suras*, the All-Mighty describes the world's destruction and the vast revolutions and the Lordly deeds during the Resurrection in such a manner that we see similar events in the world, i.e., during spring and autumn, and so can have some understanding of the awesome events being described. As even a brief analysis of these three *suras* would bee too lengthy, I will point out only one verse as an example: *When the scrolls (of the deeds of every person) are laid open* (81:10).

This verse states that at the time of the Resurrection, everyone's deeds will be revealed on a written page. At first glance, this appears rather strange and incomprehensible. But as the sura indicates, in addition to many other examples in spring's general renewal of the events to occur during the Resurrection, the "laying of the scrolls open" has also a very clear parallel. Every fruit-bearing tree and flowering plant has its properties, functions, and deeds. It performs the kind of worship particular to it according to how it manifests Divine Names. Thus, all of its deeds (its life-cycle from germination to blossoming and yielding fruits) are recorded or inscribed in its each seed that will emerge next spring in another plot of soil. As with the tongue of shape and form, the trees or flowering plants [growing from seeds buried the previous autumn] eloquently point to the original tree's or flowering plant's life and deeds, they also spread out or lay open the pages of their deeds through their branches, twigs, leaves, blossoms, and fruits. Thus the One Who does this work before our eyes as manifestations of His Names the All-Wise, the All-Preserving, the All-Arranging, the All-Upbringing, and All-Subtle, is He Who says: *When the scrolls (of the deeds of every person) are laid open.*

You can pursue other issues of the Resurrection through this analogy. I will mention another example to help you: *When the sun is folded up* (81:1). Besides the brilliant metaphor in *folded up* (meaning "rolled" or "wrapped up"), the verse alludes to several related events:

First: The All-Mighty drew aside the veils of non-being, then of ether and the heavens, to bring forth from His Mercy's treasury and show the world a jewel-like lamp—the sun—to lighten that world. After closing the world, He will wrap that jewel again in its veils and remove it.

Second: The sun may be considered an official charged with diffusing light and alternately winding light and darkness around the earth's head. Every evening, it is ordered to gather up its commodity (light) and be concealed. Sometimes the sun does only a little business, because a cloud veils it or the moon might form a veil that prevents it from carrying out its task completely. Just as it so closes its account book to certain extent for a short, fixed time due to such reasons, at some [future] time, this official will resign from its post. Even if there were no reason for such a dismissal, the two spots on its face—now small and liable to grow—may grow to the point that the sun will take back, by its Lord's command, the light that it wraps around the earth's head. God will wrap that light around the sun's own head, saying: "Come, you have no more duty toward the earth. Now, go to Hell and burn those who worshipped you and thus mocked with disloyalty an obedient official like you." With its dark, scarred face, the sun announces the decree: *When the sun is folded up* (81: 1).

Part five

A *hadith* says that one hundred and twenty-four thousand Prophets,[49] who are the most eminent and distinguished among humanity, have been sent. All of these Prophets, based on Divine Revelation and their own spiritual observation, unanimously and in complete agreement gave news that the Hereafter does exist, that human beings will be sent there, and that the Creator will bring it as He promised. In addition, one hundred and twenty-four million saints, with spiritual illumination, discovery, and observation have confirmed the reports of the Prophets with the degree of certainty aris-

---

[49] Ahmad ibn Hanbal, *al-Musnad*, 5:265; Ibn Hibban, *as-Sahih*, 2:77. (Tr.)

ing from knowledge, and testified to the existence of the Hereafter. Also, all the Names of the All-Wise Maker, through their manifestations in this world, show the absolutely necessary existence of and necessitate an everlasting realm. For example, the Eternal Power, Which every spring restores to life innumerable corpses of dead trees on the face of the earth with the command of "Be! and it is," and Which revives hundreds of thousands of species of plants and animals as samples of the resurrection of the dead, most clearly necessitates the existence of the Hereafter. Likewise, the infinite, Eternal Wisdom, Which allows nothing to be in vain or purposeless, and the Eternal Mercy and Perpetual Favor, Which, with perfect compassion and in an extremely wonderful fashion, provide the sustenance of all living beings that are in need of it, and for a brief time in spring allow them to display their manifold varieties of adornment and decoration, require the Hereafter. Furthermore, the human being is the most perfect fruit of the universe and its Creator's most beloved creature, and of all beings the human is the most closely and deeply connected and concerned with the other beings in the universe. The intense, unshakeable, and constant love of eternity and ambition for permanence that are innate in human nature prove the existence of a permanent realm, an everlasting abode of happiness that will follow this transient world, so decisively that they necessitate the acceptance of the Hereafter with the same certainty that we accept the existence of this world.[50]

Since one of the most important things the wise Qur'an teaches us is belief in the Hereafter, and since this belief is so powerful and it provides such hope and solace that if a single person were overwhelmed by old age a hundred thousand times over, the consolation arising from this belief would be sufficient to face it, then surely we who are elderly should say, "All praise be to God for perfect belief," and love our old age.

---

[50] It may be realized from the following comparison how easy it is to report an already existing thing or clear fact and how hard it is to deny it. If someone says: "Somewhere on this earth is a wonderful garden that provides "canned" milk" in the form of fruit, and others dispute this, the first person only has to show the garden or some of its produce. Deniers, however, must inspect and display the whole world to justify their negation. Similarly, the testimony of two truthful witnesses (such as Prophets or saints) establishes Paradise's existence, even if we ignore the many signs and indications demonstrated by others who assert its existence. Deniers must examine, explore, and sift the infinite cosmos and travel throughout infinite and eternal time before they can prove Paradise's non-existence. Therefore, my elderly brothers and sisters, understand how secure and sound it is to believe in the Hereafter.

The
Eleventh Word

The Eleventh Word

The Divine purposes for creating humanity and the world and the truth of the Prescribed Prayers

In the Name of God, the All-Merciful, the All-Compassionate.

By the sun and its brightness, and the moon as it follows it, and the day as it reveals it, and the night as it enshrouds it, and the heaven and Him Who built it, and the earth and Him Who spread it, and the soul and Him Who has formed it to perfection. (91:1-7)

F, O BROTHER (SISTER), YOU WANT TO UNDERSTAND SOMETHING OF the Divine purposes for creating humanity and the universe, and why the five daily Prayers are obligatory, consider this parable together with my own soul: A king had a vast treasury of precious stones and buried treasures known only to him. He was well-versed in all industries, and had a vast knowledge of all artistic and scientific disciplines and countless fine arts. As anyone with perfect beauty and perfection tend to see and show themselves, that glorious king wanted to open up an exhibition and display his kingdom's magnificence, his wealth's splendor and extent, and the wonderful products of his artistry and skill. He so desired in order to behold his beauty and perfection with his own discerning eye and through the eyes of others.

And so he began to build a very large, magnificent palace. Dividing it into many apartments and rooms, he decorated it with his finest and most beautiful works of art, and embellished it with his precious stones. Designing it according to his artistic and scientific principles and disciplines, he furnished it with the miraculous products of his knowledge. Finally, he set up therein tables containing most delicious specific foods and drinks, and specified an appropriate table for each tribe of his subjects. He provided them so elaborately, generously, and artistically that it was as though each table had come into existence through the works of at least a hundred separate skills.

Then, the king invited all his subjects in his dominion to feast and behold the spectacle. Having taught a supreme commander he had appointed why he had built such a palace and the uses and meanings of its contents, he sent him to inform the guests about the maker of the palace—the king—and explain why he had built it, the rules they had to obey, and about the palace's architecture, decorations, furniture, and ornaments. The supreme commander also had the duty of describing in what ways those contents of the palace demonstrate the king's skills and perfections, and how the guests could please him.

This supreme teacher had many assistants, each of which was deputed for a certain department, while he himself stood among his students in the largest department, addressing all guests or spectators as follows:

> O people! Our lord, who owns this palace, wants to make himself known to you by building it. In return, know and recognize him properly. He also wants to make himself lovable to you through these ornaments. In return, appreciate his artistry and works, thereby making yourselves loved by him. He demonstrates his love for you through these favorings of his, so love him by obeying him. His offerings display his care and compassion for you, so thank him by showing your respect for him. Through these works of his perfection, he wants to show his beauty and grace. In return, exhibit a great desire to see him and secure his attention. By setting his special, inimitable stamp on everything you see, he demonstrates that he is unique, absolutely independent and without partner, that this palace and its contents are his work and belong to him exclusively. So, acknowledge his uniqueness, absolute independence, and lack of partner.

The supreme commander or teacher continued his address. Then the audience separated into two groups.

THE FIRST GROUP: Since they were sensible and aware of themselves, on seeing the palace's wonders, they concluded that nothing could be purposeless. They asked the supreme teacher about the king's purposes and demands from them. They attentively listened to the answer of the teacher, accepted his instructions, and acted in a way to please the king. In return, the king, pleased with their conduct and manners, invited them to a far larger and indescribably more beautiful palace, wherein he set out to entertain them permanently in a way worthy of a generous king and fitting for such obedient, well-mannered subjects.

THE SECOND GROUP: They were morally corrupt, and devoid of sound reasoning. Defeated by their carnal souls, they took notice of nothing apart from the delicious foods. They closed their eyes to all the virtues and did not heed the directives of the supreme teacher and the warnings of his students. They concentrated only on eating and sleeping. Drinking of the forbidden beverages, which had been prepared for certain other purposes, they became drunk and bothered all other guests. They broke the glorious king's rules. So, his soldiers put them in prison appropriate for such ill-mannered people.

O friend, who listens to this story together with me! You have certainly understood for what purposes the glorious king built the palace. The realization of these purposes depends on the following two things:

The first is the existence of the supreme teacher, for if he did not exist, those purposes would be as nothing, just in the same way that an incomprehensible book without a teacher to explain it is only a pack of sheets.

The second is that the people should heed the instructions of the teacher. This means, the teacher is absolutely necessary for the existence of the palace, and the people's obedience is the reason for maintaining it. So, it can be said that but for the teacher, the glorious king would not have built the palace, and that when the people totally ignore the teacher's instructions, the palace will be destroyed and changed.

O friend! Now, let us the reality which the parable conveys. The palace is this world, whose roof is the heavens illuminated with smiling stars, whose floor is the earth embellished with numerous kinds of flowers. The king is the All-Holy One, the King of all eternity, Whom the seven firmaments and the earth, along with all their contents, glorify and extol in tongues particular to each. He is such a Powerful King that He created the heavens and the earth in six days.[51] "Seated" on His Throne of Lordship[52], He alternates day and

---

[51] Like the Bible, the Qur'an mentions that God created the universe in six days. However, the Qur'an never mentions mornings and evenings, and presents "day" as a relative period whose measure is changeable. See 22:47, 32:5, and 70:4: (Tr.)

[52] The original word translated as "Lord" is *Rabb*. It denotes God as One Who brings up, trains, educates, sustains, and administers His creatures. Note: It must not be confused with the Christian understanding of "Lord," namely, Jesus Christ. (Tr.)

night like a white and a black thread, inscribing His signs on the vast sheet of the universe. He is One, All-Majestic and Powerful, to Whom the sun, the moon, and the stars are all subjugated.

The palace's departments or rooms are the thousands of worlds, each designed, furnished, and decorated in a specific way. The finest and most beautiful works of art are the miracles of Divine Power, which we see throughout the world; the foods are the wonderful fruits of Divine Mercy that we see here, especially in summer; and the kitchen is the surface of the earth, with its fire being the sun's heat an the fire in the earth's center. The precious stones are manifestations of the Divine Sacred Names, and the embellishments are the well-ordered, finely made beings and perfectly proportioned inscriptions of the Pen of the Power that adorn this world and point to the Names of the Majestic All-Powerful One.

The supreme commander or teacher is our master Prophet Muhammad, upon him be peace and blessings. His assistants are all other Prophets, upon them be peace, and his students are all saints and pure, saintly scholars. The servants are angels, and the invited guests are jinn and humanity, and the animals created to serve humanity. The first group of people are believers, students of the Qur'an that interprets the verses of the Book of the Universe. The second group are the people of unbelief and rebellion, "deaf and dumb" misguided people who, obeying their carnal souls and Satan, accept only the worldly life and so place themselves below animals.

The first group, comprising the happy, godly people, listened to the teacher's message of intellectual enlightenment and spiritual well-being, the path of prosperity in both worlds. That teacher is a both worshipping servant who, in regard to servanthood, describes his Master and makes Him known to people, and is an envoy of his community in the court of Almighty God; and a Messenger who, in regard to Messengership, communicates his Master's commandments to humanity and jinn via the Qur'an.

The happy people heeded the Messenger and the Qur'an, and so found themselves in elevated stations and invested with many subtle and pleasing duties of the Prescribed Prayer, the index of all varieties of worship:

- **First:** They saw the Divine works and, seeing themselves in the station of objective observers of the Kingdom of Divine Lordship's wonders, said "God is the All-Great," thus glorifying and extolling Him.
- **Second:** Seeing themselves in the station of announcing the Divine Sacred Names' precious manifestations, they esteemed Him as the

All-Holy and praised Him, declaring: "All-Glorified is God. All praise and gratitude are for God."

- **Third:** In the station of tasting and perceiving with their outer and inner senses the bounties stored in Divine Mercy's treasuries, they began fulfilling the duty of thanking and praising Him.
- **Fourth:** In the station of weighing and coming to know the jewels in the Divine Names' treasuries with the scales of their mental and spiritual faculties, they set out to fulfill the duty of praising Him and declaring Him to be free of all fault and defect.
- **Fifth:** In the station of studying the Master's Messages written on the lines of Destiny by the Pen of His Power, they contemplated and commended Him.
- **Sixth:** In the station of observing the subtle beauties and delicacies in the creation of things, as well as in the art of creation and declaring God to be free of all fault and defect, they set out to fulfill their duty of loving and yearning for their Majestic All-Originating and Gracious Maker.

Therefore, after doing all duties of worship in the stations mentioned above by observing the universe and its contents as God's works of Art and so addressing God indirectly, they rose to the station of contemplating the All-Wise Maker's deeds and the way He acts, they were amazed by the realization of how the All-Majestic Creator makes Himself known to conscious beings through the miracles of His art. In direct response, they proclaimed in His presence: "All-Glorified are You. We are unable to know You as the duty of knowing You requires. What makes You known are Your miracles displayed in Your creatures."

Then, In response to the All-Merciful making Himself loved through the lovely fruits of His Mercy, they proclaimed in love and ecstasy: *You alone do we worship, and from You alone do we seek help* (1:5). Afterward, in response to the Real Giver of Bounties exhibiting His Care and Compassion through His decorous gifts, they thanked and praised Him, saying: "All-Glorified are You, and all praise and gratitude are for You." In other words: "How can we thank you as You deserve thanking? You are so worthy of thanks and praise that all Your favors in the universe praise You in the tongue of their disposition. All Your bounties arranged and exhibited in the world's market and on the earth's face declare Your praise and commendation. The beautiful, well-proportioned fruits and produce of Your Mercy and

Graciousness bear witness to Your Generosity and Munificence, and thank You before the eyes of all creatures."

Then, in response to His displaying His Grace, Majesty, Perfection, and Grandeur in the "mirrors" of creatures constantly recruited and renewed, they declared: "God is the All-Great," and bowed before Him in perception of His Grandeur and their own impotence. Afterward, they prostrated in humility and with wonder and love. Before the All-Wealthy One's display of His Wealth's abundance and His Mercy's comprehensiveness, they showed their poverty and need by praying: *From You alone do we seek help* (1:5).

Then, in response to the All-Majestic Maker's exhibition of His Art's subtleties and wonders through animate beings, they showed their appreciation by saying: "What (wonders) God has willed," and their commendation by saying: "How beautifully they have been made." Continuing to observe, they said: "God bless them. How wonderfully they have been made," and testified to Him by proclaiming their belief. In full admiration, they called everyone to witness the same: "Come and see! Hasten to (the way to) prosperity!"

In response to the Eternal King's declaration of His Lordship's Kingdom and His Oneness' manifestation throughout the universe, they believed in and confirmed His Unity, and showed their obedience and submission by saying: "We have heard and obeyed." To the manifestation of the Lord of the Worlds' Divinity, they responded with worship by declaring their impotence embedded in weakness, their poverty embedded in need, and with the Prescribed Prayer, which is the essence of worship.

While in that huge mosque of the world, they devoted themselves to these and similar duties of worship and so assumed the best pattern of creation. Above all other creatures, they became God's trustworthy vicegerents, equipped with the blessing of belief and trustworthiness.[53] After this abode of trial and testing, their Munificent Lord invited them to eternal happiness to recompense their belief and to the Abode of Peace to reward their devotion to Islam. There, out of His Mercy, He bestowed on them dazzling bounties beyond description and imagination, and eternity and everlasting life. For the observing and reflecting lovers of an eternal, abiding beauty will certainly go to eternity. Such is the end and final station of the students of the Qur'an. May Almighty God include us among them. Amin!

---

[53] God's vicegerency is defined as humanity being the "means" used by God to execute His commands on the earth and ruling on it according to His laws. (Tr.)

As for the members of the second group, those sinful and wicked ones, when they entered the palace of this world at the age of discretion, they rejected all the evidence of Divine Oneness and were ungrateful for all bounties. So, they insulted all creatures by accusing them of being worthless, and rejected and denied the Divine Names' manifestations. In sum, they committed an infinite crime in a short time and deserved eternal punishment.

We have been given this capital of life and human faculties to spend on the duties mentioned above. Given this, our duty is not restricted to living an easy life (according to the requisites of modern corrupt civilization) and gratifying our carnal desires. Nor are our delicate senses and abilities, sensitive faculties and organs, well-ordered members and systems, and inquisitive senses and feelings included in the "machine" of our life (our body) to satisfy the base, carnal soul's low desires. Rather, they were included therein and made a part of our nature for two reasons: First, to make us feel all varieties of the bounties bestowed by the Real Giver of Bounties, and to urge us to be grateful. So, feel them and be grateful to Him. Second, to make known and urge us to experience all manifestations of each Divine Sacred Name seen in the universe. So experience and know them, and believe. If we can realize these aims, we can gain human perfection and become true human beings.

As shown in the following parable, we were not given our human faculties only to earn our worldly sustenance: A master gave a servant 20 gold coins and told him to buy a suit of a particular cloth. The servant bought and then wore a fine suit made from the best quality of cloth. The master gave another servant 1,000 gold coins, put a written list in his pocket, and sent him to do some trade. Obviously 1,000 gold coins were not to be used for clothes. So if the second servant does not read the list, but rather chooses to imitate the other servant by buying a suit with the money given to him, and, moreover, receives a suit of the worst possible quality, will his master not reprimand and punish him severely for his stupidity?

O my carnal soul and my friend! You are not sent here to spend the capital of your life and your vital potentials on material pleasures and this transient life. If you do, you will fall to the lowest ranks, although you are far superior with regard to "capital" than the most developed animal.

O my heedless soul! If you would like some understanding of your life's aim and nature, its form and how it performs its duty, and the perfect happiness in your life, then look! The aims of your life can be summed up in the following nine matters:

The first: It is weighing on the scales of your body's senses the bounties stored in Divine Mercy's treasuries and offering universal thanks .

The second: It is opening with the keys of all instruments placed in your nature the hidden treasuries of the Divine Sacred Names and recognizing the All- Holy One through those Names.

The third is consciously displaying through your life before all creation- in this place of exhibition the amazing arts that the Divine Names have attached to you and their subtle manifestations in your being.

The fourth is proclaiming your worship and servanthood to the Court of your Creator's Lordship, verbally and through the tongue of your disposition.

The fifth: In the manner of a soldier who, appearing before the king on ceremonial occasions with the decorations received from him, displays the marks of the king's favor, you must adorn yourself consciously with the "jewels" of subtle human senses and faculties embedded in your being through the Divine Names' manifestations and present yourself before the Eternal Witness.

The sixth: Other living beings worship and glorify their Creator by consciously or unconsciously obeying the laws He established for their lives. This is the main purpose for their creation and life. Thus you should consciously observe their obedience to Him, their worship and glorification of Him, and reflect on and testify to their worship and glorification.

The seventh: Using your defective attributes (e.g., partial knowledge, power, and will) as units of measurement, recognize the Majestic Creator's absolute Attributes and sacred Qualities. For example, you have built this beautiful and well-ordered house by using your partial knowledge, will, and power. So, you should know that the Maker of this palace of the universe is powerful, knowledgeable, wise, and capable to the degree it is greater than your house.

The eighth: You should perceive how each being proclaims in its own language the Creator's Oneness and the Maker's Lordship.

The ninth: From your impotence and weakness, poverty and need you should try to infer the degrees of the Divine Power's and Richness' manifestations. Just as food's pleasures and varieties are understood or distinguished according to your hunger and need, so you should understand the degrees of the manifestations of infinite Divine Power and Richness through your infinite impotence and poverty.

Briefly, those are the aims of your life, the nature of which can be summarized as follows: It is an index of wonders originating in the Divine Names, a measure to consider the Divine Attributes, a unit to know the worlds in the universe, a catalogue of the macrocosm, a map of the universe and its fruit or compressed form, a set of keys with which to open Divine Power's hidden treasures, and a most excellent pattern of the Divine perfections reflected in creatures and manifested through time.

As for the form of your life and how it performs its duty: Your life is an inscribed word, a wisdom-displaying word written by the Pen of Power. Observed and sensed, it points to the Divine Beautiful Names. What gives your life its meaning and specifies its function is that it is a mirror manifesting Divine Oneness and God's being the Eternally Besought One. Through its comprehensiveness as the focal point for all Divine Names manifested in the world, it functions as a mirror that reflects God's being the Eternally Besought One. As for the perfection of your life in happiness, it is to perceive and love the lights of the Eternal Sun pictured in the mirror of your life, to display ardor for Him as a conscious being, to be enraptured with love of Him, and to establish His Light's reflection in the center of your heart. As a result of all this, a *hadith qudsi*[54] expresses your highest rank in creation by saying: "(God said): I am not contained in the heavens and the earth, but I am contained in the believer's heart."

So, my selfhood! While your life was given to you to realize such sublime aims, and it contains such priceless treasures, how can you even think of wasting it on gratifying fleeting carnal desires and seeking transient worldly pleasures? So as not to waste it, reflect on the oaths and the truths in the verses below, to which the above parable refers, and act accordingly:

> By the sun and its brightness, and the moon as it follows it, and the day as it reveals it, and the night as it enshrouds it, and the heaven and Him Who built it, and the earth and Him Who spread it, and the soul and Him Who has formed it to perfection and inspired it (with conscience) of what is wrong for it and what is right for it. He is indeed prosperous who has grown it in purity, and he has indeed failed who corrupts it. (91:1-10)

> O God! Bestow blessings and peace on the sun of the sky of Messengership, on the moon of the constellation of Prophethood, and on his Family and Companions, who are the stars of guidance. Have mercy upon us and all believers. Amin! Amin! Amin!

---

[54] A *hadith qudsi* is a Prophetic saying whose meaning is directly inspired in the Prophet's heart or revealed to him by God. (Tr.)

The
Twelfth Word

The Twelfth Word

A brief comparison between the Qur'an's wisdom and human philosophy and scientism

In the Name of God, the All-Merciful, the All-Compassionate.

Whoever has been given the Wisdom, certainly has been given much good. (2:269)

[NOTE: This Word presents a brief comparison between the Qur'an's sacred wisdom and human philosophy, a concise summary of the Qur'anic instruction and training for humanity's personal and social life, and an indication of the Qur'an's superiority to all other Divine Words and all human speeches.]

Four fundamentals

 IRST FUNDAMENTAL: Look at certain differences between the Qur'anic wisdom and human philosophy through the telescope of the following parable: A religious, skillful, and renowned ruler wanted to make a copy of the Qur'an as beautifully as required by its sacred meanings and miraculous wording in order to adorn its wonderful words in a worthy fashion. So, he wrote it in a truly wonderful fashion with all kinds of precious jewels. To point out the variety of its truths, he wrote some of its letters in diamonds and emeralds, others in pearls and agate, brilliants and coral, and gold and silver. He adorned and decorated it in such a way that everyone, lettered or unlettered, was full of admiration and astonishment. That copy of the Qur'an became a most precious artwork for the people of truth, for its outer beauty indicated its brilliant inner beauty and striking adornment.

The ruler showed this Qur'an to a foreign [non-Muslim] philosopher and a Muslim scholar. Seeking to test and reward them, he told each one to write about it. The two men complied. The philosopher discussed the letters' shapes, decorations, and interrelationships, and the jewels' properties and methods of use. He said nothing of its meaning, for he saw it only as an ornamented object and was unaware that it was an invaluable book with depths of meaning. As he was well-informed about engineering and chemistry, could describe things, and knew a great deal about jewelry but nothing about Arabic, he wrote his book accordingly. But the truth-loving Muslim scholar, understanding that it was the wise Qur'an, the Book clear in itself and clearly showing all truth, ignored its outward ornamentation and the letters' decorations and, instead, described the sacred truths and secret lights behind the veil of decorations, for they are far more valuable and worthy of respect, more useful and comprehensive.

Both men presented their books to the glorious ruler, who began with the philosopher's book. Seeing that he had worked very hard, the ruler nevertheless refused his book and expelled him from his presence. Why? Because he had written nothing of the bejeweled Qur'an's true wisdom, understood none of its meanings, and showed his disrespect for it by thinking that this source of truths consists of meaningless decoration. Looking through second book, and seeing that the truth-loving scholar had written a very beautiful and useful interpretation, a wise and illuminating composition, he congratulated him. It was pure wisdom, and its author was a true scholar, a genuine sage. As a reward, the scholar was given 10 gold coins from the ruler's inexhaustible treasury for each letter of his book.

The meaning is as follows: The embellished Qur'an is this artistically fashioned universe; the ruler is the Eternal Sovereign. The first man represents the line of philosophy and philosophers; the second man represents the way of the Qur'an and its students. Indeed, the wise Qur'an is the most exalted expounder and a most eloquent translator of this universe (a macro-Qur'an). It is the Criterion that instructs jinn and humanity in the truths of creation—Divine laws regarding creation and the universe's operation—inscribed by the Pen of Power on the sheets of the universe and pages of time. It looks upon creatures, each a meaningful letter, as bearing the meaning of another (on account of their Maker) and says: "How beautifully they have been made, how meaningfully they point to the Maker's Beauty and Grace." Thus it shows the universe's real beauty.

Philosophy, focused on the design and decorations of creation's "letters," has lost its way. While it ought to look upon this macro-book's letters as bearing the meaning of another (on account of God), it looks upon them as signifying themselves (on account of themselves) and says: "How beautiful they are," not "How beautifully they have been made." Thus philosophers insult creation and cause it to complain of themselves. In truth, materialistic philosophy is falsehood, an insult to creation.

SECOND FUNDAMENTAL: A comparison between the Qur'an's moral training in one's personal life and that of philosophy: A sincere student of philosophy is a Pharaoh-like tyrant;[55] he is a contemptible tyrant who bows in adoration before the meanest thing, if he perceives it to be in his interest. That irreligious student is obstinate and refractory; but he is so wretched that he accepts endless degradation for one pleasure. He is unbending but so mean as to kiss the feet of devilish people for a base advantage. He is also conceited and domineering, but, unable to find any point of support in his heart, he is an utterly impotent and vainglorious tyrant. That student is a self-centered egoist who only strives to gratify his material and carnal desires; a sneaky egotist who pursues the realization of his personal interests in certain national interests.

However, a sincere student of the Qur'an is a worshipping servant of God, but he does not degrade himself by bowing in worship before even the greatest of the created. He is a dignified servant who does not take even a supreme benefit like Paradise as the aim of his worship. He is modest, mild and gentle, yet he does not lower himself voluntarily before anybody other than his Originator, unless He allows him to do so. He is also aware of his innate weakness and need, but he is independent due to the other-worldly wealth that his Munificent Owner has stored up in him; and he is powerful because he relies on his Master's infinite Power. He acts and strives purely for God's sake and good pleasure, and to be equipped with virtue. The training given by the Qur'an and philosophy may be understood through the above comparison.

THIRD FUNDAMENTAL: The Moral training of the Qur'an and philosophy in human social life: Philosophy considers force or might to be the point of support in social life, and the realization of self-interest is its goal. It holds

---

[55] Pharaoh is a title given to the kings of ancient Egypt, and signifies any tyrant one. (Tr.)

that the principle of life is conflict. The unifying bonds between the members of a community and communities are race and aggressive nationalism; and the fruits philosophy offers are the gratification of carnal desires and the continuous increase of human needs. However, force calls for aggression, seeking self-interest causes fighting over material resources, and conflict brings strife. Racism feeds by swallowing others, thereby paving the way for aggression. This is why humanity has lost happiness.

As for the Qur'anic wisdom, it accepts right, not might, as the point of support in social life. Its goal is virtue and God's approval, not the realization of self-interests. Its principle of life is mutual assistance, not conflict. The only community bonds it accepts are those of religion, profession, and country. Its final aims are controlling carnal desires and urging the soul to sublime matters, satisfying our exalted feelings so that we will strive for human perfection and true humanity. Right calls for unity, virtues bring solidarity, and mutual assistance means hastening to help one another. Religion secures brotherhood, sisterhood, and cohesion. Restraining our carnal soul and desires and urging the soul to perfection brings happiness in this world and the next.

FOURTH FUNDAMENTAL: If you want to understand why the Qur'an is superior to all other Divine Words and all human speech, consider the following two comparisons:

The first: A king has two forms of speech and address. He either speaks on his private phone to a common subject regarding a minor matter or private need, or, in his capacity or position as the supreme sovereign, supreme head of the religious office, and supreme ruler, conveys his orders in the form of an exalted decree manifesting his majesty by means of an envoy or high official.

The second: A person holds a mirror toward the sun. According to the mirror's capacity, he receives the sun's seven-colored light and thereby establishes a connection with it. When he directs this light-filled mirror toward his dark house or roof-covered garden, he benefits from the sun only according to the mirror's ability to reflect it. Another person opens broad windows in his house or roof-covered garden, thus exposing them to the benefits of direct and continuous sunlight. In gratitude, he says: "O fine sun, beauty of the world and skies, who gilds the earth with your light and makes flowers smile. You have furnished my house and garden with your heat and light, just as you have done for the skies, the earth, and flowers." The first person cannot say such things, for he has to be content with his mirror's reflections of the sun's light and heat.

Consider the Qur'an in the light of these two comparisons. See its miraculousness and understand its holiness. The Qur'an declares: *If all the trees on the earth were pens, and all the sea (were ink), with seven more seas added thereto, the words of God would not be exhausted in the writing* (31:27).

The reason why the Qur'an holds the greatest rank among God's infinite words is this: Having come from God's Supreme Throne, originated in His Greatest Name, and issued from each Name's most comprehensive rank,[56] the Qur'an is God's Word on account of God's being the Lord of the Worlds, and His decree on account of His having the title of Deity of all creatures. It is a discourse in the Name of the Creator of the heavens and the earth; a speech and conversation in regard to His absolute Lordship; an eternal sermon on behalf of the All-Glorified One's universal Sovereignty. It is also a register of the All-Merciful One's favors from the viewpoint of His all-embracing Mercy; a collection of messages or communications that sometimes begin with ciphers in respect of His Divinity's sublime majesty; and a a wisdom-infusing holy Scripture that, having descended from the Divine Greatest Name's all-comprehensive realm, looks over and surveys the circle surrounded by His Supreme Throne.

This is why the title "the Word of God" has been and will always be given to the Qur'an. As for other Divine words, some of them are speeches coming as particular manifestations of a particular aspect of Divine Mercy, Sovereignty, and Lordship under a particular title and with a particular regard. They vary in degree with respect to particularity and universality. Most inspiration is of this kind and infinitely varies in degrees. For example, in ascending order, God sends the most particular and simple inspiration to animals. It increases in importance as it is sent to ordinary people, ordinary angels, saints, and greater angels, respectively. This is why a saint who supplicates without mediation directly through the telephone of his heart "connected to God" says: "My heart reports to me from my Lord." He does not say: "It reports to me from the Lord of the Worlds." They can say: "My heart is a mirror, a Throne, of my Lord," but not: "My heart is the Throne of the Lord of the Worlds," for saints receive the Divine address only according to their capacity and to how many of the "70,000" veils separating humanity and God they have removed.

---

[56] For example, the manifestations of the All-Coloring and the All-Decorating in spring are not at the same level as in winter. (Tr.)

A king's decree issued in his capacity as the supreme sovereign is higher and more exalted than his conversation with a commoner. We receive far more benefit from direct exposure to the sun than we do from its reflection. The Qur'an is superior to all other speeches and books in the same way. Next come the other Divine Books and Scrolls, which are superior in different degrees to all other speech and books, for they are based on Revelation. If all non-Qur'anic but nevertheless fine words, epigrams, and wise sayings that have issued from humanity and jinn were collected, they could not equal the Qur'an.

If you want to have some understanding of how the Qur'an has originated in God's Greatest Name and in the greatest level of every Name, consider the universal, sublime statements of *Ayatu'l-Kursi* (2: 255) and the following verses:

> God, there is no deity but He; the All-Living, the Self-Subsisting (by Whom all subsist). Slumber does not seize Him, nor sleep. His is all that is in the heavens and all that is on the earth. Who is there that will intercede with Him save by His leave? He knows what lies before them and what lies after them (what lies in their future and in their past, what is known to them and what is hidden from them); and they do not comprehend anything of His Knowledge save what He wills. His Seat (of dominion) embraces the heavens and the earth, and the preserving of them does not weary Him; He is the All-Exalted, the Supreme. (2:255)

> With Him are the keys of the Unseen. (6:59)

> O God, Master of all dominion. (3:26)

> He covers the day with the night, each pursuing the other urgently, with the sun, the moon, and the stars obedient to His command. (7:54)

> "O earth, swallow up your water, o sky, cease (your rain)!" (11:44)

> The seven heavens and the earth, and all within them glorify Him. (17:44)

> Your creation and your resurrection are as but as a single soul. (31:28)

> We offered the Trust to the heavens and the earth and the mountains. (33:72)

> On the Day when We will roll up the heaven as written scrolls are rolled for books. (21:104)

They have no true measure of God, such as His being God requires, and the whole earth will be in His grasp on the Day of Resurrection. (39:67)

If We had sent down this Qur'an upon a mountain, you would certainly see it humbled, splitting asunder for awe of God. (59: 21)

Also, meditate upon the initial verses of those *suras* beginning with *al-hamdu li-llah* (All praise and gratitude are for God) or *sabbaha* or *yusabbihu* (glorifies Him), so that you may see certain rays of this mighty fact. Look at the openings of those *suras* beginning with *Alif Lam Mim, Alif Lam Ra,* and *Ha Mim,* so that you may have some understanding of the Qur'an's importance in the sight of God Almighty.

If you understand the significant kernel of this fourth fundamental, you may understand that Revelation mostly came to Prophets via an angel, while inspiration is mostly without mediation. You may also understand why even the greatest of saints cannot attain the level of any Prophet. Again, you may have some glimpse of the Qur'an's grandeur, sacred glory, and the mystery of its miraculousness' sublimity. You may also understand the necessity of Prophet Muhammad's Ascension, that is, how and why he ascended to the heavens, reached the *Lote-tree of the furthest limit* and to *The distance between two bow strings, or less,*[57] and there supplicated the All-Majestic One, Who is closer to us than our jugular vein (50:16), and returned in the twinkling of an eye. Just as splitting the moon was a miracle of Messengership demonstrating his Prophethood to the jinn and humanity, the Ascension was a miracle of his worship and servanthood to God demonstrating to spirits and angels that he is the Beloved of God.

O God, bestow blessings and peace upon him and his Family as befits Your Mercy and his value and dignity Amin!.

---

[57] *The Lote-tree of the furhest limit* signifies the furthest limit to which a mortal, however great, can reach. *The distance between two bow strings, or less* signifies the nearness Prophet Muhammad attained in the Ascension to the Almighty, which is unattainable by any other mortal. (Tr.)

The
Thirteenth Word

The Thirteenth Word

The fruits of the Qur'an's wisdom and modern scientific thought and philosophy

In the Name of God, the All-Merciful, the All-Compassionate.

We send down [stage by stage], of the Qur'an, that which is a healing and a mercy for the believers. (17:82)

We have not taught him poetry; it is not seemly for him. (36:69)

F YOU WANT TO COMPARE THE FRUITS OF THE QUR'AN'S WISDOM and modern scientific thought and philosophy, as well as their instructions, teaching, and degrees of knowledge, consider this: With its profound explanations, the Qur'an of miraculous exposition rends the veils of familiarity and habit over all creatures and events, which are considered ordinary but are miracles of Divine Power. Revealing these astonishing wonders [of Divine creation] to conscious beings and attracting their gaze to them opens up an inexhaustible treasury of knowledge.

Philosophy conceals the Power's extraordinary miracles within veils of familiarity and overlooks them in ignorance and indifference. It calls attention to aberrations that, outside creation's order and thus deviated from their perfect true natures, are no longer extraordinary. It offers such things to conscious beings as objects of wise instruction. For example, philosophy considers our creation commonplace, although we are a most comprehensive miracle of Divine Power, and looks at us indifferently. But it is amazed by a three-legged or two-headed person, who is no longer within creation's perfection, and considers it an object of amazing instruction. It sees the regular sustenance of all infants and young from the Unseen's treasury, a most subtle and universal miracle of Mercy, as ordinary and draws a veil of ingratitude over it. But when it sees an insect left alone under water and isolated from its fellows, yet feeding upon a green leaf, it tries to make fishermen weep for it because of the favor and grace manifested in it.

Reflect on the noble Qur'an's wealth and riches with respect to its wisdom and knowledge of God, and on philosophy's poverty and bankruptcy with regard to learning, instruction, and knowledge of the Maker, and take a lesson.

It is because of this, because the wise Qur'an encompasses infinite brilliant and exalted truths, it is free from and high above the fancies of poetry. Another reason why the Qur'an of miraculous exposition is not in strict verse despite its perfect order and arrangement and its expounding of the Book of the Universe's artistic beauty and order with its well-ordered styles is that free from the constraints of poetry, it allows each of its verses to be a sort of center to many of its verses and thus there is a connection among all verses within an encompassing context. It is as if each verse has an eye looking to most other verses and a face turned toward them.

Thus there are thousands of Qur'ans within the Qur'an, each being adopted by a different path or school in Islam. For example, and as described in The Twenty-fifth Word, *Suratu'l-Ikhlas* contains a treasury of knowledge of Divine Unity provided by thirty-six *Suratu'l-Ikhlas*es, each one formed of a combination of six sentences and each having many aspects. This is comparable to the way each star, apparently at random, extends as if from a center a line of connection to every other star in the surrounding area. Such a network also indicates the hidden relation between all creatures. It is as if, like the stars of Qur'anic verses, each star has an eye looking to and a face turned toward all stars. Reflect on the perfect order in apparent disorder, and take a lesson. Understand one meaning of: *We have not taught him poetry; it is not seemly for him* (36:69).

Understand also from the meaning of *it is not seemly for him* that poetry tends to adorn insignificant and dull facts with grand, shining images and fancies to make them attractive. But the Qur'anic truths are so great and elevated, so brilliant and splendid, that even the greatest and most brilliant poetic imaginings appear dull and insignificant. For example, innumerable truths like: *On the day when We will roll up the heaven as written scrolls are rolled for books* (21:104); *He covers the day with night, each pursuing the other urgent-*

ly (7:54); and *It is but one single blast, and see, they are all arraigned before Us* (36:53) testify to this.

If you want to see and appreciate how each star-like Qur'anic verse removes the darkness of unbelief by spreading the light of miraculousness and guidance, imagine yourself in pre-Islamic Arabia. Everything in that time of ignorance and desert of savagery was enveloped in the veil of lifeless nature amidst the darkness of ignorance and heedlessness. Suddenly, you hear from the Qur'an's sublime tongue such verses as: *All that is in the heavens and all that is on the earth glorifies God, the Absolute Sovereign, the All-Holy and All-Pure, the All-Glorious and Mighty, the All-Wise* (62:1). See how those creatures, considered lifeless and unfeeling, spring to life in the audience's minds at the sound of *glorifies*, how they awaken, spring up, and begin to extol God by praising His Names! At the sound of, *The seven heavens and the earth glorify Him* (17:44), the dark heaven appears to those who hear it as a mouth, with each star being a wisdom displaying word and a truth-radiating light; and the earth as a head, with the land and sea each a tongue, and all animals and plants words of glorification.

If you consider these verses from a modern viewpoint, if you look at it through a superficial veil of familiarity, after the darkness of the ignorance of the pre-Islamic age has long been changed into the "already known" by the Qur'an's "sun" and Islam's light, you cannot see what sort of darkness each verse removes in a sweet melody of miraculousness, and so cannot appreciate this aspect of its miraculousness.

If you want to see one of the Qur'an's highest degrees of miraculousness, consider the following parable: Imagine an extremely vast and spreading tree hidden behind a veil of the Unseen. You know that just as between the members of a human body, there has to be and is a harmony and balance between various parts of a tree—between its branches, leaves, flowers, and fruits— and each part has its proper form and shape according to the tree's nature. If someone draws an exact replica of that hidden tree, correctly displaying all its parts, relationships, and proportions without seeing it, no one can doubt that the artist sees and depicts the hidden tree with an eye penetrating the Unseen.

In the same way, the Qur'an's explanations on the reality of things, namely, the reality of the Tree of Creation stretching from the beginning of creation to eternity, from the earth to the Divine Throne,[58] from parti-

---

[58] The nature of the Divine Throne (Arabic: *'Arsh*) is unknown to us. Elsewhere, Said Nursi writes that the Divine Throne is a composition of the Divine Names the First, the Last, The All-Outward, and the All-Inward. He also writes that the earth is the Throne of Life (*'Arshul-Hayah*), and water is the Throne of Mercy (*'Arshur-Rahmah*). (Tr.)

cles to the sun, maintain the proportion between all parts to such a degree, and give each part and fruit such a suitable form that all exacting and truth-seeking scholars have concluded: "What wonders God has willed. May God bless it. Only you, O wise Qur'an, solve the mystery of creation."

The highest comparison is (and must be put forth) for God—let us represent His Names and Attributes, as well as His Lordship's acts and qualities, as a tree of light so vast and great that it stretches through eternity. It encompasses the whole universe and includes Divine acts in an infinitely vast sphere stretching from: *He intervenes between a person and his heart* (8:24), *Surely God is the Splitter of the seed-grain and the date-stone* (6:95), and: *It is He Who fashions you in the wombs as He wills* (3:6) to: *And the heavens rolled up in His Right Hand* (39:67), *and He has created the heavens and the earth in six days* (7:54), and: *He made the sun and the moon subservient to His command* (13:2). The wise Qur'an describes this radiant reality, the truths of those Names, Attributes, Qualities, and acts in all of their ramifications and results in so harmonious, fitting, and appropriate a way that all who have penetrated the reality of things and discovered the hidden truths, as well as all sages journeying in the Realm of the Inner Dimension of Existence, have declared: "All-Glorified is God. How right, how conformable with reality, how beautiful, and how fitting."

Take the six pillars of belief[59], which relate to both the Sphere of Contingency (the Realm of Creation) and the Sphere of Necessity (the Realm of Divine Existence), and may be regarded as a branch of these two mighty "trees." The Qur'an describes these six pillars of belief with all their elements and furthest fruits and flowers such proportionately, observes their harmony to such a degree, and presents them in such a balanced and well-measured way that we are amazed and scarcely able to grasp its beauty. It also observes the perfect relationship, complete balance, and amazing harmony among the five pillars of Islam, which form a twig of the branch of belief, down to the finest details, most insignificant points of conduct, furthest aims, most profound wisdom, and most particular fruits. With its perfect order and balance, as well as its due proportion and soundness, the supreme Shari'a, which originated from the comprehensive Qur'an's decisive statements, different aspects or dimensions of wording and meaning, indications, and allu-

---

[59] The six pillars of belief are: belief in God, belief in angels, belief in God's Books, belief in God's Messengers, belief in the Hereafter, and belief in Divine Destiny and Decree The five pillars of Islam are: Confession of the pillars of belief, performing the Prescribed Prayers, paying the Prescribed Alms, Fasting during Ramadan, Pilgrimage to Makka. (Tr.)

sions, is an irrefutable and decisive proof, and just and undeniable witness for this.

Given this, the Qur'an's explanations could not have issued from any human being's knowledge, especially from that of an unlettered person. Rather, its explanations rest on an all-comprehensive knowledge and is the Word of One Who sees all things together like a single thing, Who simultaneously observes all truths between two eternities. The verse: *All praise and gratitude are for God, Who has sent down unto His servant the Book, and has allowed no crookedness therein* (18:1) expresses this reality.

> O God, O One Who sent down the Qur'an. For its sake, and for the sake of the one to whom You sent it down, illumine our hearts with the light of belief and the Qur'an. Amin, O One from Whom help is sought.

Second station

> In the Name of God, the All-Merciful, the Al-Compassionate.

> [NOTE: A conversation held with young people surrounded by temptation but still able to judge what is happening around them.]

Some young people, seeking to counter modern amusements and fancies and so save themselves from punishment in the Hereafter, sought help from the *Risale-i Nur*. In its name, I told them what follows:

The grave is there, no one can deny it. Whether they want or not, everyone will enter it. It is represented in three ways, there is not the forth:

For believers, it is the door to a more beautiful world. For those who admit the next life but live a misguided, dissipated life, it is the door to solitary imprisonment that will separate them from their loved ones. Since they believe and confirm but do not live according to their belief, that is exactly how they will be punished. For unbelievers and the misguided who do not believe in the Hereafter, it is the door to eternal execution. Since they believe death to be an execution without resurrection, they will be punished eternally.

Death may come at any time without differentiating between young and old; its appointed hour is unknown. Such an awesomely threatening reality makes it our greatest, most urgent matter to search for a way to avoid eternal punishment and imprisonment, for a way to change the grave into a door opening onto a permanent world of light and eternal happiness.

Death will be experienced in these three ways, as has been reported by 124,000 truthful reporters—the Prophets, in whose hands are signs of truthfulness (miracles). Their reports have been confirmed by millions of saints relying on their discernment, vision, and intuition. Also, innumerable truth-seeking scholars have proved it rationally with their decisive proofs at the level of "certainty based on knowledge." All groups agree that only belief in and obedience to God can save one from eternal punishment and imprisonment, and make the grave a way to eternal happiness.

If only one reliable reporter warns that a particular way carries a one percent risk of death, people will be so afraid that they will avoid it. But countless truthful, authoritative reporters—Prophets, saints, and truth-seeking scholars—have provided proof of their truth and warn us that misguidance and dissipation carry a hundred percent risk of death followed by eternal punishment. In contrast, belief and worship change the grave into a door opening onto an eternal treasury, a palace of lasting happiness. If we, especially those of us claiming to be Muslims, do not truly believe and worship in the face of such a mighty warning, how will we overcome our anxieties while waiting to die, even if we were given the rule of the whole world and enjoyed all its pleasures?

Seeing old age, illness, misfortune, and numerous instances of death everywhere reopens our pain and reminds us of death. Even if the misguided and the dissolute appear to enjoy all kinds of pleasure and delight, they most certainly are in a hellish state of spiritual torment. However, a profound stupor of heedlessness makes them temporarily insensible to it.

Obedient believers experience the grave as the door to an eternal treasury and endless happiness. Since the "belief coupon" they have causes them to have a priceless ticket from the allocations of eternal Divine Destiny, they expect the call "come and collect your ticket" with profound pleasure and spiritual delight. If this pleasure could assume the material form of a seed, it would grow into a private paradise. But those who abandon this great delight and pleasure to indulge the drives of youth, who choose temporary and illicit pleasures, which resemble poisonous honey causing limitless pains, fall far below the status of animals.

They are not like Western unbelievers, who may recognize another Prophet even if they deny their own; who may yet recognize God even if they deny all Prophets; or who may have some good qualities, which are means to certain perfections, even if they do not recognize God. Muslims, however, know the Prophets, God, and all perfections because of Prophet

Muhammad, upon him be peace and blessings, and so those Muslims who abandon the Prophet's instruction and break with his line cannot recognize any other Prophet or find support in their souls to preserve any human perfection. For Prophet Muhammad is the last and greatest Prophet; superior to all with respect to his mission, miracles, and accomplishments; and came with a universal religion and Message for all time and peoples. Muslims who abandon this Pride of humankind's principles of training and the rules his religion will most certainly be unable to find any light or achieve any perfection. They will be condemned to absolute loss and decline.

So, those of you who are addicted to worldly pleasure, and in anxiety at the future, struggle to secure it and your lives, if you want pleasure and delight, happiness and ease in this world, be content with what is religiously lawful. It is sufficient for your enjoyment. You must have understood by now that each forbidden pleasure contains many pains. If the dissolute were shown their future—their states in fifty years from now—in the way past events are shown in the movie theater, they would be horrified and disgusted with themselves. Those who wish to be eternally happy in both worlds should follow the Prophet's instruction on the firm ground of belief.

A warning and lesson to a group of unhappy young people

One day several bright young people came to me. They were seeking an effective deterrent to the dangers arising from modern worldly life, youth, and animal desires. I spoke to them as I had spoken to a group of young people who had previously sought help from the *Risale-i Nur*:

Your youth will definitely disappear. If you do not remain within the bounds of what is religiously lawful, it will be lost and, rather than pleasure, it will bring you suffering and calamities here, in the grave, and in the Hereafter. But if you adhere to Islamic discipline and spend it chastely, uprightly and in worship in gratitude to the blessings of youth, in effect, your youth will remain perpetually and be the cause of gaining eternal youth.

A life without belief, or with belief rendered ineffective by rebelliousness, only produces pain, sorrow, and grief that far exceed the superficial, fleeting enjoyment and resulting pleasure. This is because humanity has intelligence and, unlike animals, is connected to the past, present, and future, and derives both pain and pleasure from them. Whereas animals have no intelligence and therefore neither sorrows to arise from the past nor fears and anxieties concerning the future spoil their present pleasure. But such sorrows and anxieties plague the misguided and heedless, marring their pleasure and diluting it with pain. If this pleasure is illicit, it becomes like poisonous honey.

Given this, we are far lower than animals when it comes to life's enjoyments. In fact, the lives of misguided, heedless people consists only of the day in which they find themselves, as is the case with their entire existence and world. According to their misguided belief, that which is past no longer exists. But their intellect, which connects them to the past and the future, produces only darkness, and their lack of belief in eternal life makes the future non-existent for them. It is this non-existence that makes separations eternal and continually darkens their lives. In contrast, a life built upon belief results in the past and the future being illuminated and acquiring existence through the light of belief. Such a life also provides exalted spiritual pleasures and lights of existence for their spirits and hearts.

This is the reality of life. If you want to enjoy life, animate it with belief, adorn it with religious obligations, and maintain it by avoiding sins.

As for the fearsome reality of death, which is demonstrated by deaths everywhere and always, the following parable will suffice: Imagine that we are facing a gallows. Beside it is a lottery office selling tickets for truly high prizes. Each of us, willingly or not, will be invited there. Since our appointed hour is unknown, they will call us any time, saying: "Come to the gallows for execution!" or "You have won a huge prize! Come and collect it!"

While we are waiting, a woman and a man approach us. The woman is scantily clad, beautiful, and alluring. She holds in her hand some apparently very delicious, but in fact poisonous, sweets and offers them to us. The man, who is honest and solemn, comes up behind her and says: "I have brought you a talisman, a lesson. If you study it and don't eat the sweets, you will be saved from the gallows, and you will receive the winning ticket with this talisman. You see that those who eat the sweets inevitably mount the gallows, and further, they suffer dreadful stomach pains from the poison of the sweets until they mount them. Those who receive the ticket also mount the gallows, but millions of witnesses testify that instead of being hanged, they use the gallows as a step to enter the prize arena easily. So, look from the windows! The highest officials, the high-ranking persons connected with this business, proclaim: "Just as you see clearly those people mounting the gallows, so be certain that those who have the talisman will receive the ticket for the prize."

Thus, the dissolute, religiously forbidden pleasures of youth are like poisonous sweets. Since they cause people to lose their belief, their ticket to an eternal treasury and a document for everlasting happiness, those who follow them are subject to be hanged on the gallows and suffer the tribulations of the grave, which is the door to eternal darkness for them. As the hour of death is unknown, the executioner may come at any time without differentiating between young and old. But if you abandon religiously forbidden pleasures and acquire the Qur'anic talisman (belief and performing religious obligations), 124,000 Prophets and innumerable saints unanimously inform us that you will receive the ticket for the treasury of eternal happiness from the extraordinary lottery of Destiny. They also show its signs and proofs.

In short, youth passes. Wasting it results in infinite misfortune and pain in both worlds. If you want to understand how many of such youths end up in hospitals with mental and physical diseases, mainly because of their abuse, in prisons or hostels for the destitute due to their excesses, and in bars because of the distress provoked by their spiritual unease, go and ask at those places. As you will hear from the mute eloquence of hospitals' tongue the the moans and groans of those who pursued youth's appetites, so will you hear from prisons the regretful sighs of unhappy people imprisoned mainly for illicit actions due to their "youthful excesses." You will also understand that most torments of the grave are due to a misspent youth, as related by saints who can discern the life of the grave (the Intermediate Realm), and affirmed by all scholars of truth.

Further, consult the elderly and the sick. Most of them will answer you with grief and regret: "Alas! We wasted our youths in frivolity. Be careful not to do as we did!" Those who do not control the illicit passions of five to ten years' youth bring upon themselves grief and sorrow in this world, torment and harm in the Intermediate Realm, and the severe punishment of Hell in the Hereafter. Although they might be in a most pitiable situation, since they freely chose to pursue such a path, they are not worthy of pity. For one who is freely resigned to harm is not worthy of pity. May Almighty God save all of us from the alluring temptations of this age and preserve us against them. Amin.

A footnote

In His Name, All-Glorified is He.

Prisoners are in great need of the *Risale-i Nur*'s consolation; especially those who suffered the blow of youth and spend the prime of their lives in prison need the *Risale-i Nur* as much as they need bread. Youths are driven by emotion rather than reason. Emotion and desire are blind; they cannot see consequences and prefer an ounce of immediate pleasure to tons of future pleasure. They kill for a minute's satisfaction of revenge, and then suffer uncountable hours of painful imprisonment. One hour of dissolute pleasure spent raping a woman may destroy a lifetime's contentment through the fear of prison and enemies.

Young people meet many pitfalls that cause them to transform life's sweetness into a most bitter and remorse-laden existence. In particular, a huge and mighty state to the north is misusing its youths' passions and shaking this century with its storms. For it has made lawful for its blind-emotion driven young people the beautiful daughters and wives of upright, innocent people. By allowing men and women to go together to public baths, it encourages immorality. It also allows the vagabond and the poor to use freely, even plunder, the property of the rich. Everyone trembles in the face of this calamity.

During this age, all Muslim youths must act heroically and respond to this two-pronged attack with "sharp swords" like the Risale-i Nur's "Fruits (of Belief)" and "A Guide for Youth." Otherwise, those unfortunate youths will destroy their future, their happiness in both worlds, their eternal afterlife, and transform both into torment and suffering. They will wind up in hospitals due to their abused energy and dissipation, in prisons due to their excesses, and be full of regret when they are old. But if they protect themselves with Qur'anic training and the Islamic truths, some of which the Risale-i Nur expounds, they will become truly heroic youths, perfect human beings, prosperous Muslims, and in some ways masters over the rest of animate beings.

If young people in prisons spend just one hour a day on the five Prescribed Prayers, and while imprisonment prevents the perpetration of many sins, avoid other painful sins and seek God's forgiveness for the crime that led them to their present state, both their own future and their relatives, nation, and country will benefit. In addition, the Qur'an of miraculous exposition and all other revealed Scriptures give the certain, glad tidings that their fleeting ten to fifteen years of youth will gain them an eternal, brilliant youth. If young people act in gratitude for the delightful blessing of youth by following the Straight Path in obedience to God, the blessing increases and becomes eternal and even more pleasurable. If they do not, they are pursued by calamity, pain, and grief. Their lives become nightmarish and then disappear. They live aimlessly, and so harm both their relatives and their nation and country.

If those who have been imprisoned unjustly perform the Prescribed Prayers will find that each hour spent behind bars equals one day of worship. Their cells will become like a place of retreat for them, and they themselves may be considered among the pious people of old times who retreated to caves to devote themselves to worship. If they are poor or aged or ill and seek to learn the truths of belief, will find that each hour spent in prison will equal twenty hours of worship, provided they seek God's forgiveness for the crime they committed and perform the religious obligations. The prison will resemble a rest house, a place of friendliness owing to those who compassionately care after them, and a place of training, and education. Staying in prison may even bring them greater happiness than they could find on the outside, for there they would be perplexed and assaulted by sin. If they receive proper education while in prison, former murderers or revenge-seekers would be released as repentant, mature, and well-behaved people who can benefit their nation. Those who saw the Denizli prisoners attain this rank quickly through the moral instruction of the *Risale-i Nur* remarked: If, instead of fifteen years of imprisonment, they receive a fifteen-week instruction from the *Risale-i Nur*, this will reform them much better.

Since death does not die and the appointed hour is unknown, it may come at any time; since the grave cannot be closed, and people enter it in successive convoys; and since the Qur'an declares that believers experience death as a discharge from worldly duties and that belief saves them from eternal punishment, while unbelievers experience death as an execution leading to everlasting torment and unending separation from their loved ones and all other creatures, for sure, the happiest people are those who thank God in patience and, benefiting from their time in prison, take the necessary moral and religious teaching to serve the Qur'an and belief on the Straight Path.

O addicts of enjoyment and pleasure! I am now seventy-five years old. I have come to know with utmost certainty from thousands of experiences and proofs that true enjoyment, pure pleasure, grief-free joy, and happiness are found only in belief and the sphere of its truths. One worldly pleasure yields many pains, as if delivering ten slaps for a single grape, and thus mars the pleasure of life.

O you unfortunate people suffering imprisonment! Since you are mourning here and your life is bitter, benefit from your time in prison so that you may not mourn in the Hereafter and so that your eternal life may be sweet. Just as an hour's watch under severe battle conditions sometimes equals a year of worship, the hardship of each hour spent worshipping in prison multiplies and changes hardship into mercy.

෨෧ ෨෧

In His Name, All-Glorified is He.

Upon you be peace and God's mercy and blessing!

My dear, truthful brothers and sisters!

I will offer an effective solace for prisoners and for those who kindly help them and supervise their food, which comes from outside.

FIRST POINT: Each day spent in prison may gain as much reward as ten days of worship, and with regard to their fruits, may transform these transient hours into enduring hours, and a few years of punishment may be the means of being saved from millions of years of eternal imprisonment. Imprisoned believers can gain this most significant and valuable advantage by praying five times a day, asking God's forgiveness for the sins that led to their imprisonment, and thanking God in patience. Prison is an obstacle to certain sins; it prevents them.

SECOND POINT: As pleasure's disappearance causes pain, so pain's disappearance gives pleasure. When thinking of past happy and enjoyable days, everyone feels regret and longing and utters a sigh of grief. When recalling past calamitous and painful days, everyone feels pleasure because they are gone, thanks God that such days are past and have left their reward, and sighs with relief. This means, an hour's temporary pain leaves an immaterial pleasure in the spirit, while an hour's pleasure leaves pain.

This is reality. Past hours of misfortune and their pain have disappeared, and the imagined distress of the future has not yet come. Since pain does not come from something inexistent, it is foolish to think now of past and future pains—pains that do not exist—and to be impatient, ignore one's faulty self, and to act as though complaining about God. This would be like continually eating and drinking today because you fear hunger or thirst tomorrow. So, do not waste your patience on the past and future. Rather, use it to deal with present pain, for that will cause the existing pain to decrease tenfold.

This is not a complaint: During this third period of my imprisonment in the "school of Prophet Joseph," a few days of the material and spiritual affliction and illness the like of which I had not experienced before, especially my despair and distress at being unable to serve the Qur'an, crushed me. However, after the Divine Favor showed me this truth, I accepted my distressing illness and imprisonment. Since it is a great profit for a poor man like me, who waits at the door of the grave, to turn an hour of possible heedlessness into ten hours of worship, I thanked God.

THIRD POINT: There is great reward in compassionately attending prisoners, providing their food, and soothing their spiritual wounds. Helping their food coming from outside reach them causes a spiritual reward equivalent to giving that food as alms to be added to the helpers' records of good deeds, even to those of the guards. If the prisoners are old, sick, poor, or without support or protection, the reward of such alms-giving multiplies. To gain this valuable benefit, however, one must perform the Prescribed Prayers so that their help should be purely for God's sake. In addition, one should hasten to help prisoners with sincerity, compassion, and cheerfulness, and in such manner that they do not feel themselves placed under obligation to you.

࿇ ࿇

In His Name, All-Glorified is He.

There is not a thing but it glorifies Him with praise.

Upon you be peace and His mercy and blessing everlastingly!

My friends in prison and brothers and sisters in religion!

I will explain a truth that will save you from torment here and in the Hereafter. Imagine that someone killed your sibling or relative. One minute of satisfaction derived from revenge will cause uncountable minutes of distress and imprisonment, and the fear of retaliation and the anxiety of always being pursued will drive all pleasure and enjoyment out of life. Thus you will suffer both fear and vexation. The only solution is the reconciliation which the Qur'an and right, truth, humanity, and Muslimness encourage.

Right, truth, and mutual advantage require reconciliation. As each one's death comes at its fixed time, the victim would not have lived any longer anyway. God's decree was executed via the murderer. Unless they are reconciled, both parties will continue to suffer from fear and vindictiveness. This is why Islam says that a believer should not be angry or hold a grudge against another believer for more than three days.

If the murder was not the result of a grudge or enmity, and a hypocritical one instigated it, the parties must make peace without delay so that this minor disaster will not grow and persist. If they do so, and the murderer repents and prays continually for the victim, both parties gain and become like siblings. In compensation for a lost family member, they gain several new ones. Submitting to the Divine Destiny and Decree, they abandon enmity. Especially if they have taken part in the *Risale-i Nur*'s teachings, individual and collective peace and brotherhood in the *Risale-i Nur*'s circle require that they put aside all grudges.

In Denizli prison, all prisoners who had been enemies became brothers via the *Risale-i Nur*. This was one of the reasons for our acquittal. Even the irreligious criminals said about us: "How wonderful! How blessed they are!" All prisoners began going out for fresh air. However, I have seen here that a hundred men suffer because of one man, and do not go out to enjoy the fresh air together. Believers with sound consciences do not harm other believers because of some insignificant and minor error or advantage. If they make a mistake and cause harm, they should repent immediately.

ॐ ॐ

In His Name, All-Glorified is He.

There is not a thing but it glorifies Him with praise.

Upon you be peace and God's mercy and blessing.

My dear new brothers and old prisoners!

I am convinced that Divine Favor placed us among you for a specific purpose relating to you: The *Risale-i Nur*, with its consolation and the truths of belief, is meant to save you from imprisonment's distress and a great deal of the worldly harm thereof. It is also meant to save your life, which otherwise would be wasted in grief and sorrow, to save you from moaning in both worlds.

If this is so, you obviously should be brothers to each other, after the example of the Denizli prisoners and the *Risale-i Nur* students. You see that guardians search through everything—food, bread, and so on—coming to you from the outside, so that you cannot use a slipped-in knife to attack each other. Besides, the guards who faithfully serve you suffer much trouble. You are not allowed to go outside together for fresh air because they think that you may attack each other like wild beasts.

Now, you new friends who are by nature heroic and courageous, you should display an example of spiritual valor and tell the prison's administrative board: "Even if we were given guns and revolvers, instead of knives, and ordered to use them, we would not hurt our unfortunate friends who suffer as we do. We are determined to forgive them and not to offend them, regardless of our former reasons for hostility, for these are requirements of belief and Islamic brotherhood, in our interests, and commanded by the Qur'an.

By this means and attitude, you may transform this prison into a blessed place of study.

An important matter

I will explain briefly a comprehensive truth that occurred to my heart on *Laylatu'l-Qadr* (the Night of Power and Destiny).[60] The Second World War was a display of extreme tyranny and injustice that entailed ruthless destruction. Countless innocent people were ruined due to one criminal. The defeated were led to awesome despair, while the victors worried about keeping their supremacy. Many suffer ghastly pangs of conscience because they could not repair the destruction they caused. The war showed just how transitory worldly life is, how deceitful modern civilization's frivolities are. The war gravely and extensively damaged human nature's essence and exalted potential. In some places, heedlessness, misguidance, and gross naturalism have been smashed by the Qur'an's diamond sword, while it has unveiled the extreme ugliness and cruelty of the true face of world politics, the most extensive, suffocating, and deceiving reflection of heedlessness and misguidance.

All this proves that since the worldly life, of which humanity is enamored, is ugly and transitory, human true, conscious nature will search with all its strength for eternal life, for which it truly yearns and loves. Signs have already appeared in the North, the West, and the United States. The Qur'an of miraculous exposition, which has had countless students for over thirteen centuries, every truth of which has been confirmed by innumerable truthful scholars, and which has remained alive in the minds of millions of its memorizers with all its holiness, teaches and proclaims the eternal life, explicitly or implicitly, in many of its powerful, striking, and reiterated verses. It instructs people in its particular tongues and, in a way unmatched by any other book, conveys the good news of eternal life and everlasting happiness, healing all our wounds. Given this, and provided that humanity does not lose its ability to reason or suffer complete physical or spiritual destruction, the vast masses and

---

[60] *Laylatu'l-Qadr*, to which the Qur'an refers in 97:1-5, is the most sacred night of the year. According to the majority of scholars, it is the 27th night of Ramadan. The Qur'an says concerning it: *Laylatu'l-Qadr is better than a thousand months. The angels and the Spirit descend in it by the permission of their Lord with His decrees for every affair—being a pure mercy and security, being until the rise of the dawn.* (97:3-5) (Tr.)

great states will search out the Qur'an of miraculous exposition. Having perceived its truths, they will become devoted to it heart and soul, just as some famous preachers in Sweden, Norway, Finland, and England, and a significant community in the United States in quest of the true religion, have shown an inclination to accept it. This will take place because the Qur'an has no equal, and nothing can take the place of this greatest miracle.

We also may say that among many other useful books and compilations, the *Risale-i Nur* has performed a service like a diamond sword in the hand of this Greatest Miracle, and that it silences even its most stubborn enemies. Having originated in the Qur'an, the *Risale-i Nur* explains and offers the Qur'anic truths in a way that enlightens the mind, soul, and feelings. It heals those wounded by modern trends, and defeats heretics and their anti-Qur'an propaganda. Many of its treatises, such as "The Treatise of Nature," "The Staff of Moses," and "The Fruits of Belief," have smashed naturalism and scientific materialism, the most formidable fortification of misguidance. They have banished heedlessness in its most dense, suffocating, and extensive dimensions, all of which evolved under the broad veil of scientism, by demonstrating the light of Divine Unity in a most radiant fashion.

Each science speaks of God in its own tongue

[NOTE: The following is a brief indication to one of the thousands of the universal proofs of the pillar of belief in God, many of which, together with explanations, are in the *Risale-i Nur*.]

In Kastamonu, some high-school students came to me and asked: "Tell us about our Creator, for our teachers do not speak of Him." I replied as follows:

Each science you study continuously speaks of God, the Creator, and makes Him known in its own tongue. So, listen to them, not your teachers.

For example, a well-equipped, well-designed pharmacy which has many medicines and pills composed of different precisely measured components certainly indicates an extremely skillful and learned pharmacist. In the same way, to the extent that it is bigger and more perfect than this pharmacy, the pharmacy of the earth, which has countless life-giving cures and medicaments implanted within all plant and animal species, shows and makes known even to blind eyes, through the science of medicine, the All-Wise One of Majesty, Who is the Pharmacist of the largest pharmacy on the earth.

Another example: A wonderful factory which weaves thousands of different cloths from a simple material undoubtedly makes known a manufacturer and skillful mechanical engineer. Likewise, to the extent that it is bigger and more perfect than this factory, with its countless parts, each having hundreds of thousands of machines, this traveling machinery or factory of the Lord which we call the earth shows and make known its Manufacturer and Owner through the science of engineering.

A store or shop that serves as a well-organized storage place for numerous varieties of provisions brought from all sides shows that it has a wonderful proprietor, preparer, and distributor of provisions and foodstuffs. In the same way, this All-Merciful One's food-store known as the earth; this vessel of the All-Glorified, which annually traverses a wide orbit and, while passing through seasons, fills spring, like a huge wagon, with uncountable different provisions and brings them to innumerable living creatures which it houses and whose sustenance was exhausted during winter; this depot or shop of the Lord, which holds vast varieties of goods, equipment, and conserved food— to whatever degree it is bigger and more perfect than the store mentioned, it makes known, through the measure of the science of economics which you study, its Owner, Manager, and Organizer, and makes Him loved.

To take another example: Imagine an army of tribes and nations, each one requiring unique provisions, weapons, uniforms, drills, and demobilization. If its miracle-working commander meets all their needs on his own, without forgetting and confusing any of them, surely the army and camp will point to him and make him loved and appreciated. In the same way, every spring a single Commander-in-Chief provides a newly recruited army of countless animal and plant species with uniforms, rations, weapons, training, and demobilizations in a perfect and regular fashion. He forgets nothing and does not become confused. To the extent that they are vaster and more perfect the human army and its camp, this Divine army of spring and its camp make known, through military science, to the attentive and sensible, the Ruler of the earth, its Lord, Administrator, and All-Holy Commander, generating admiration and acclaim, and makes Him loved, praised, and glorified.

Imagine a magnificent city illuminated by millions of mobile and fixed electric lamps with an inexhaustible fuel and power source. This makes known a wonder-working artisan and an extraordinarily talented electrician who manages the electricity, makes the lamps, establishes the power source, and brings the fuel. Such a person is admired, congratulated, and loved by others. In just the same way, some lamps (stars and planets) in this palace of the world's roof, in this city of the universe, are far larger than the earth and move with amazing speed. Still they move in a very delicate order without colliding with each other, and are not extinguished, or run out of fuel. The science of astronomy, which you study, say that our sun, a lamp and stove in the All-Merciful One's guest-house, is several billion years old and a million times larger than the earth. To keep burning, each day it needs as much oil as the seas of the earth, as much coal as its mountains, or as many logs and wood as ten earths.

So, such lamps point with their finger of light to an infinite Power and Sovereignty that, in turn, illuminates the sun and other similar stars without oil, wood, or coal. It does not allow them to be extinguished and makes them travel with great speed without colliding with each other. However much greater in size and more perfect in management from the lamps in the example are these lamps of the palace of the world in the magnificent city of the universe, through the science of electricity and through the testimony of those radiant stars, they make known the Sovereign, Illuminator, Director, and Maker of the biggest exhibition of the universe, and make Him loved, glorified, and adored.

Imagine a marvelous book. A different book is finely written within each line, and a *sura* is inscribed in each word with a fine pen. This book is most meaningful and expressive, and all of its subjects corroborate each other. Such a book shows without doubt and as clearly as daylight that it is the product of a particular artist or author possessed of extraordinary perfections, arts, and skills. It makes him appreciated with such phrases as: "What wonders God has willed!" and "May God bless him!"

The same is true of the "macro-book" of the universe. We see a pen at work, inscribing on the earth's face, one of its sheets, countless plant and animal species, which are like hundreds of thousands of volumes. They are inscribed all together, one within the other, without error or confusion and so perfectly and finely that an ode is compressed in a word like tree, and a book's complete index in a seed-sized point. To the extent that this infinitely meaningful compendium of the universe, this macro-Qur'an of the cosmos, in each word of which are numerous instances of wisdom, is greater and more perfect and meaningful than the book in the example, through the extensive measure and telescopic vision of the science of nature that you study, and the sciences of reading and writing that you practice at school, it makes known its Inscriber and Author with His infinite Perfections. In the meaning of "God is the All-Great," it makes Him known. In the glorification of "All-Glorified is God," it describes Him. Through praises like "All praise and gratitude are for God," it makes Him loved.

Like those mentioned, through its extensive measure, particular mirror, far-reaching view, and searching and instructing perspectives, each of the sciences makes the Majestic Creator of the universe known by His Names, and makes known His Attributes and Perfections. It is in order to teach this decisive proof explained, which is a magnificent and brilliant proof of Divine Oneness, that the Qur'an of miraculous exposition frequently describes our Creator through such phrases as "the Lord of the heavens and the earth" and "He has created the heavens and the earth."

This is what I told the students, who accepted and affirmed it, saying: "Endless thanks be to God; we have received a true, sacred lesson. May God be pleased with you." I added:

Each of us is a living machine subject to many sorrows and capable of knowing many pleasures. Although wholly impotent, we have infinite physical and spiritual enemies. Although wholly destitute, we have infinite outer and inner needs and suffer continual blows of decay and separation. Yet if, through belief and worship, we can establish connection to the Sovereign of Majesty, we find a point of support against all of our enemies and a source of help for all of our needs. Everyone takes pride in the honor and rank of his master to whom he is attached. So, if one establishes connection to the infinitely Powerful and Compassionate Sovereign through belief, enters His service through worship, and (in doing so) changes the announcement of their execution at the appointed hour of death into welcome discharge papers—you can understand by comparison the degree of the contentment, thankfulness, and pride they will feel.

I repeat to the calamity-stricken prisoners what I said to the schoolboys: Those who recognize and obey Him are prosperous even if they are in prison, while those who forget Him are wretched and imprisoned even if they live in palaces. Once a wronged but fortunate [due to his belief and being martyred] man said to the wretched wrongdoers who were executing him: "I am not being executed; rather, I am being discharged from my duties and going to eternal happiness. Moreover, as I can see you even now condemned to eternal punishment, I am taking complete revenge on you." He then said: "There is no deity but God," and died happily.

> All-Glorified are You. We have no knowledge save what You have taught us. Surely You are the All-Knowing, the All-Wise.

᪐ ᪑

He: A point of Divine Unity

In His Name, All-Glorified is He.

There is nothing but it glorifies Him with His praise.

My dear and faithful brothers and sisters!

While reflecting on air during a mental journey, a subtle point related to Divine Unity suddenly became clear to me in the word *He* in "There is no deity but He" and "Say: He is God." I saw that the way of belief is so easy as to be necessary, and that the way of misguidance and associating partners with God is so hard as to be inconceivable. I will explain this comprehensive matter briefly.

A handful of soil serves as a flowerbed for hundreds of flowers. If this process is attributed to nature or causality, each handful must contain hundreds of minute machines or factories [to produce the flowers] and an immaterial factory [to determine and govern their lives in place of Divine Knowledge and Destiny]. Or, each atom of dust must know how to make each flower's different characteristics and living elements. Thus each atom would have infinite knowledge and power, which are unique to God.

Similarly, each air molecule (a conductor of Divine Will and Command), each shift of air making the sound *He*, must have minute centers, exchanges, receivers, and transmitters of all human means of communication so that each air molecule can perform those countless acts at the same time. Or, each atom or molecule must have all the relevant faculties and capacities of all who speak or communicate through means of communication, know their languages, and transmit their words to other atoms at the same time. Thus, there are as many impossibilities and inconceivabilities in the way of naturalists and materialists as atoms of air.

If attributed to the Majestic Maker, however, all air atoms become soldiers under His Command. Through their Creator's permission and Power, and due to their connection to and reliance on Him, they perform innumerable universal duties as easily as if they were doing only one duty of one atom. They perform them instantly and with the ease of uttering *He* and the movement of air. Air becomes a "page" for the Pen of Power's endless, wonderful, orderly inscriptions. Its atoms become the Pen's ribs, and their duties, the points inscribed by the Pen, Which works with the same ease as the movement of a single atom.

While observing and studying the world of air during my reflection on "There is no deity but He" and "Say: He is God," I saw this truth clearly and in detail. I realized with a certainty based on knowledge that just as the word "He" has a brilliant proof of Divine Unity manifested by the whole universe, so is there in its meaning and indications a radiant manifestation of Divine Oneness displayed by each individual thing. Since that proof contains a powerful indication to the identity of the One to Whom the indefinite, third-person, singular pronoun *He* refers, I also came to know that both the Qur'an of miraculous exposition and those who regularly mention God with His Names frequently repeat this sacred word to express Divine Unity.

If several points are jumbled around one on a piece of paper, it is almost impossible to distinguish that point. If you do several jobs simultaneously, you will be confused. If a living creature is loaded with many burdens at once, it will be crushed. If you listen to or say many words simultaneously, they become confused and muddled. However, although thousands of points, letters, and words are deposited in each air molecule—even in each atom—they are conveyed without confusion or irregularity. Also, the air performs all its duties simultaneously and without confusion. Each air molecule or atom bears heavy burdens without lagging behind or displaying any weakness. Also, countless words enter ears and come up to mouths with perfect order. In performing all of its extraordinary duties, each atom and air molecule says in the tongue of its being and functioning, in ecstasy and perfect freedom, and through its testimony: "There is no deity but He" and "Say: He is God, the One." All of them travel among air-clashing waves like lightning and thunderstorms in perfect order and harmony, without one task of them hindering the other.

Given this, either each atom or air molecule necessarily has infinite wisdom, knowledge, will, power, and all qualities needed to dominate all other atoms so that it can perform those functions—which is so absurd and inconceivable that even Satan could imagine it—or, from a position of certainty based on knowledge, clear observation, and personal experience, air functions as a changing "page" for the Pen of Power and Destiny, used by the All-Majestic One with infinite knowledge and wisdom, and as a signboard (a kind of Tablet of Effacement and Confirmation) reflecting a changeable copy of the Divine decrees preserved on the Supreme Preserved Tablet.

In addition to showing a manifestation of Divine Oneness and the impossibility of misguided assertions in its duty of transmitting sound, the element of air simultaneously performs other duties (e.g., transmitting such subtle forces as electricity and light, attraction and repulsion), and carries to all plants and animals the substances essential for their life (e.g., for respiration and pollination) with perfect order. Thus, it decisively proves that it is an important means of conveying the decrees of Divine Will, and random chance, blind force, deaf nature, confused and aimless causality, or powerless, lifeless, and unknowing matter have no part in the fulfillment of its duties. I understood that each atom and air molecule proclaims in the tongue of its being and functioning: "There is no deity but God" and "Say: He is God, the One." Just as I witnessed these wonders in the physical aspect of air with the key of *He*, so air itself became a key, like *He*, to the World of Ideal Forms or Representations and the World of Meaning.

The
Fourteenth Word

The Fourteenth Word

Important explanations to understand the truths of the Qur'an and the Prophetic Traditions

In the Name of God, the All-Merciful, the All-Compassionate.

Alif Lam Ra. A Book whose Revelations in verses have been made firm, and arranged in sequence and distinctly detailed. It is from One All-Wise, All-Aware. (11:1)

[NOTE: To help those hearts which suffer from the lack of submission and obedience in order to be able to reach some of the elevated truths of the Qur'an and the Hadith, its true interpreter, I will point out several comparisons of those truths and conclude with a lesson and a mystery of Divine favor. Since the comparisons of Doomsday and the Resurrection, which are among those truths, are found in The Tenth Word (particularly in the Ninth Truth), I will not repeat them here. Here, as examples of other truths, I will mention only five matters.]

Five matters

 IRST MATTER: THE QUR'AN STATES: (GOD) HAS CREATED THE *heavens and the earth in six days* (7:54). A Qur'anic day corresponds to a long period, such as 1,000 or 50,000 human years.[61] This implies that the human and animal kingdoms will last "six days." To be convinced of this Qur'anic truth, consider and reflect on the travelling, passing worlds that the All-Majestic Creator creates each day,

---

[61] *A day with your Lord is like a thousand years in your reckoning* (22:47). *A day the measure of which is fifty thousand years (of your normal worldly years).* (70:4) (Tr.)

year, and century. It is as though these worlds are all guest like humans. By the All-Majestic One's command, they are filled and emptied each season.

SECOND MATTER: Consider the following verses:

> Not a thing, fresh or withered, wet or dry, but it is in a Manifest Book. (6:59)

> Everything We have written down and kept in a Manifest Record. (36:12)

> Not so much as the weight of an atom in heaven and earth escapes Him, neither is anything smaller than that, or greater, but it is in a Manifest Book. (34:3)

These verses state that all things, as well as their life cycles, were recorded before their worldly existence; that they are recorded during their worldly existence; and that these recorded instances of their worldly existence are left behind after they die. To have a firm conviction of this great truth, observe how the All-Majestic Inscriber encapsulates and preserves the indexes of the existence of the innumerable well-ordered creatures He recruits each season, particularly in spring, in their seeds and roots, as well as of their life-histories and the principles according to which they act.

Consider how He records and preserves all things after they die in their fruits and seeds that resemble chips of wood and bones, in perfect order with the Pen of His Destiny. It is as if each spring is attached, like a flower, to the earth's face in an extremely well-ordered and well-balanced fashion by the hand of One All-Beautiful and Gracious and All-Majestic, and then plucked. This reality manifests a reflection of the Supreme Preserved Tablet, a page upon which the Pen of Divine Destiny prerecorded everything, as well as an index of the Master's art. And yet the misguided call this inscription of creation, this design of art, this passive mold of wisdom "nature" and consider it the originator or creator of itself. The extent of their mistake is infinite.

THIRD MATTER: There are groups of angels. Some bear God's Throne, while others superintend the movements of heavenly bodies, as well as the lives and deeds of the earth's inhabitants, and present to the Divine Court the praises and glorifications that these inhabitants perform in the tongue of their being and disposition. Other groups glorify and worship God comprehensively.

To grasp the Prophet's description of some of these groups—that they glorify God each with its forty thousand tongues in each of its forty thousand heads, and do so in forty thousand different ways—consider the following verses: *The seven heavens and the earth and all within them glorify Him* (17:44); *We subdued the mountains to glorify (their Lord) along with him* [David] (38:18); and: *We offered the Trust to the heavens and the earth and the mountains* (33:72).

The All-Majestic One states that even the greatest and most universal of creatures glorifies Him according to its universality and greatness. Just as the heaven's words of glorification are the suns, moons, and stars, so animals, plants, and trees are words of praise of the earth, a flying object glorifying and praising. That is, each tree and star performs a specific form of glorification, while the earth and each of its parts, each mountain and valley, the land and the sea, and the firmament's spheres and heaven's constellations all perform a universal form of glorification. The earth, which possesses thousands of heads in each of which are countless tongues has an angel appointed for it who translates and displays its flowers of glorification and fruits of praise in the World of Ideal Forms, and who represents and proclaims them in the World of Spirits.

If many things come together to form a collectivity, a collective personality comes into being. If such a collectivity forms a strong union, it will have a sort of collective spirit to represent it, as well as an appointed angel to perform its duty of glorification. Consider, for example, the plane tree in front of my room. It is a comprehensive word of the tongue of that mountain in the mouth of Barla. See how many twigs are on the three heads of its trunk's three main branches. Study how many hundreds of words (well-ordered and well-proportioned fruits) it has and how many letters (well-designed winged seeds) there are in each fruit. Hear and see how eloquently this tree praises and glorifies its Majestic Maker, the Owner of the command of *"Be!" and it is*. Wisdom requires the angel appointed for it represents its glorification with numerous tongues in spiritual worlds.

FOURTH MATTER: Consider the exalted truth expressed by verses like:

> When He wills a thing to be, He but says to it: "Be!" and it is. (36:82)

> The affair of the Hour is but the twinkling of an eye. (16:77)

> We are nearer to him than his jugular vein. (50:16)

> The angels and the Spirit ascend to Him in a day the measure of which is fifty thousand years. (70:4)

The Absolutely Powerful One creates things with such ease, speed, and lack of physical contact that it appears as if He creates with a mere command. Although the All-Powerful Maker is infinitely near to creatures, they are infinitely far from Him. Despite His infinite grandeur, He includes even the tiniest thing in the importance He attaches to designing and fashioning creation, as well as in artistic beauty. The perfect order and absolute easy observed in things coming into existence and formations in the world testify to these Qur'anic truths. The following comparison also illustrates them.

The highest comparison is (and must be put forth) for God—the sun, in its capacity as a dense, solid mirror for the Divine Name of Light, is infinitely near to all transparent and shiny things; it is even nearer to them than their own selves and affects them in many ways, such as through its light, heat, image, and reflection. By contrast, those transparent things are millions of miles away from it, have no effect on it, and cannot claim nearness to it. Also, every transparent object which reflects an image of the sun according to its capacity, shape and color shows that it is as though the sun were present it it. In addition, the extent of the sun's luminosity increases the capacity and comprehensiveness of its penetration. Due to the greatness of its luminosity, nothing can hide or escape from it. In other words, being a luminous object, the sun's immensity and grandeur does not cause it to exclude things from the sphere of its comprehension; rather, it includes everything down to the smallest.

The sun manifests itself in all such things with such ease and speed, and over so comprehensive an area, that if it had free will, we would have to suppose that it did all these things through a mere command. An atom and a planet are equal before its manifestation, and it gives heat and light to an ocean's surface and the finest particle with perfect order and in accordance with each thing's capacity. Thus we see that the sun, which is no more than a light-giving "bubble" in the "ocean" of the heavens, a small solid mirror reflecting the manifestation to the Absolutely Powerful One's Name of Light, displays examples of the truths expressed in the verses above. So, we believe with complete certainty, as though witnessing it, that the All-Majestic One, the Light of Lights, the Illuminator of Light, the Determiner of Light, and in comparison to Whose Knowledge and Power the sun's light and heat are as impenetrable as soil, is all-present, all-seeing, and infinitely near to all things through His Knowledge and Power. Also, all things are infinitely far from Him, and creating is so easy for Him that He seems to do it with a mere command. In addition, everything is included in the sphere of His Power, and He encompasses all things in His greatness.

FIFTH MATTER: The Eternal Monarch's greatness of Lordship and His Divinity's grandeur encompass a limitless area of disposal stretching from:

They have no true judgment of God , such as His being God requires, and the whole earth will be in His grasp on the Day of Resurrection, and the heavens will be rolled up in His "Right Hand" (39:67), to: *Know that surely God comes between a person and his heart* (8:24); from: *God is the Creator of all things, and He is the Guardian over all things* (39:62), to: *God knows what they keep secret and what they disclose* (2:77); from: *He has created the heavens and the earth* (7:54), to: *He creates you and all that you do* (37:96); and from: *This is how God wills; only whatever He wills is, and there is no power save with God* (18:39), to: *You cannot will unless God wills* (76:30).

Given this, why does the Qur'an contain severe criticisms and awesome threats directed toward humanity, which is infinitely weak and powerless, destitute and needy, and which has only partial free will and no power to create? To acquire a conviction of this profound and exalted truth, consider the following two comparisons:

FIRST COMPARISON: Imagine a splendid garden containing innumerable fruit-bearing trees and flowering plants. Many servants are charged with attending it, but only one is entrusted with opening the water canal's valve so that the water can spread throughout the garden and benefit everything therein. If that one is lazy and does not open the valve, the garden cannot grow, and it even might begin to wither. Thus, apart from the Creator's art, the Monarch's royal supervision, and the humble service of light, air, and soil, all other servants have the right to complain about him, for his laziness renders their duties useless or causes them to harm.

SECOND COMPARISON: An ordinary man's neglect of his duty on a mighty royal ship harms the crew's work and even makes some of their work worthless. So, the ship's owner will complain bitterly about him in the name of the others. He cannot excuse himself by saying: "I am just an ordinary person. I don't deserve such severity because of my insignificant neglect." For one single instance of non-existence can result in many instances of non-existence, while the existence of something is restricted to itself. In other words, while the existence of something depends upon the existence of all its necessary conditions, causes, and necessary parts, its non-existence is possible through the non-existence of one condition or component. That is why "destroying is much easier than fixing" is a universally accepted principle.

Unbelief and misguidance, as well as rebellion and disobedience, mean denial and rejection, abandonment and non-acceptance. Although they superficially appear to have the marks of positive existence, in reality they are extinction and non-existence. Thus their negative effects are contagious. Just as they damage the results of other beings' acts, they also draw a veil over the manifestations of the Divine Names' beauties.

The Monarch of creatures criticizes rebellious humanity in the name of all those who have the right to lodge innumerable complaints against humanity. His doing so is perfect wisdom, and rebellious humanity deserves His severe and awesome threats.

Conclusion

In the Name of God, the All-Merciful, the All-Compassionate.

The worldly life is but a transient enjoyment of delusion. (3:185)

[NOTE: A severe, warning lesson for my heedless soul.]

O my wretched soul, sunk in heedlessness, which sees this life as sweet and, oblivious of the Hereafter, seeks it alone. You resemble an ostrich that, seeing the hunter and unable to escape by flying away, sticks its head in the sand so that the hunter may not see it. However, its huge body remains in the open, so of course the hunter can see it. Only the ostrich's eyes are closed in the sand, and so it cannot see the hunter.

O my soul! Consider the following comparison and understand how focusing only on this world changes a great pleasure into a grievous pain:

Imagine that there are two people in this village (Barla). Ninety-nine out of every hundred of one's friends have moved to Istanbul, where they are living happily. He will shortly join them, and so longs for and thinks of Istanbul. When he is told he can go there, he will be overjoyed and go happily. The second person, facing the same situation, thinks that some of his friends have perished and that the others have gone where they do not see and cannot be seen. Imagining that they have gone to utter misery, he seeks consolation in his only remaining friend, who is about to get ready. He wants to compensate for the heavy pangs of separation through that friend.

O my soul! God's Beloved above all, Prophet Muhammad, upon him be peace and blessings, and all your friends are on the other side of the grave. One or two remain here, but they also will go there. So do not fear death or the grave, or avert your attention from death. Look at it bravely and listen to what it seeks. Laugh in its face and see what it wants. And be sure that you are not like the second person.

O my soul! Do not say: "Times have changed. This age is different, for everyone is plunged into this world and adores this life. Everyone is openly committed to the struggle for livelihood." For death does not change. Separation does not end and become eternal union or companionship. Our intrinsic impotence and poverty do not change; rather, they increase. Our journey (through this world) is not cut; rather, it becomes faster.

Do not say: "I am like everyone else." Everyone befriends you only as far as the grave. The consolation of everyone suffering the same misfortune cannot help you on the other side. Neither imagine that you are free and independent. Look at this temporary world with the eye of wisdom. See that everything has an order and purpose. How can you be left to yourself, for this would place you outside the order and cause you to be without purpose. All those events like earthquakes are not playthings of chance.

You see the earth's extremely well-designed and finely embroidered clothes, which it is dressed in one over and within the other, and all plant and animal species are adorned and decked out from top to bottom with important purposes and instances of wisdom. It is turned like an ecstatic Mevlevi dervish in perfect order and for exalted aims. So how can you suppose its vital, death-bringing events, like the recent earthquake,[62] which may be understood as the earth's shaking off the weight of certain forms of human heedlessness of which it does not approve—especially in believers—to be without purpose and the result of chance? How can you, by showing the grievous losses of those affected by such events as unrecompensed and as having gone for nothing, throw them into a dreadful despair? People who do so are committing a great error and a great wrong.

Such events happen at the command of One All-Wise and All-Compassionate so that what the believers lose via such events might become just as worthy of reward as alms and thereby gain permanence. This loss is also an atonement for those sins arising from ingratitude for Divine bounties.

A day will come when this subjugated earth will see our works, which are the adornments of its face, tainted by associating partners with God and without the necessary gratitude. It will disapprove of them and, when the Creator commands, will wipe them off its face and cleanse it. At God's command, it will pour those who associate partners with God into Hell and say to the thankful: "Come and enter Paradise."

---

[62] It refers to the 1935 earthquake in Izmir, Turkey.

Addendum

> In the Name of God, the All-Merciful, the All-Compassionate.
>
> When the earth quakes with a violent quaking destined for it; and the earth yields up its burdens, and humanity cries out, "What is the matter with it?" On that day, she will recount all its tidings, as your Lord has inspired her to do so. (99:1-5)

This *sura* states explicitly that the earth moves and quakes at a command, on receiving inspiration. Sometimes it trembles.

> [NOTE: The following comprises my brief answers to seven questions asked in connection with the recent earthquake.]

FIRST QUESTION: More stressful than the recent earthquake's material disaster is that the fear of its recurrence and the ensuing despair destroy the nightly rest of most people in most areas. What is the reason for this terrible torment?

ANSWER: They were broadcasting obscene songs (some sung by girls) over the radio in a sort of drunken rapture during the *tarawih* Prayers throughout this blessed center of Islam.[63]

SECOND QUESTION: Why are Muslims, instead of unbelievers, afflicted with such heavenly blows?

ANSWER: Major cases and crimes are tried and judged in large centers, while minor ones are decided in small centers. God's wisdom requires that most of the punishment destined for unbelievers be postponed to the Last, Supreme Judgment, and that believers be partly punished in this world.[64]

THIRD QUESTION: Why does this disaster, which arose from the wrongdoing of particular people, encompass almost all people in the area?

ANSWER: Since the general disaster results from the majority's wrongdoing, most people must have participated in the minority's sinful actions by giving them direct or indirect support, or in some other way.

FOURTH QUESTION: Since this disaster is the result of wrongdoing and atonement for sins, why did innocent and faultless people suffer? Why does Divine Justice allow this?

---

[63] *Tarawih*: Supererogatory Prayer performed during Ramadan after the night Prayer. (Tr.)

[64] Those (like the communist Russians) who abandoned an abrogated and corrupted religion do not incur Divine wrath (in the world) to the extent of those who betray a true and eternal religion that will never be abrogated. Thus the earth shows its anger toward believers and leaves the others (alone) at present.

ANSWER: Since this matter deals with Divine Destiny, I refer you to the "Treatise on Destiny and Human Free Will." Here, I say only: *Beware of a trial that will surely not smite exclusively those among you who are engaged in wrongdoing* (8:25). This means that this world is a field of trial and testing, a place of responsibility and struggle. Testing and responsibility require a veiling of the truth in certain matters so that, through competition and struggle, some rise to the highest rank while others fall to the lowest level. If the innocent were not touched by such disasters, everyone would submit in the same way. This would close the door of spiritual progress through struggle, and render our responsibility and testing meaningless.

If Divine Wisdom requires that the wronged and wrong-doer suffer through the same disaster, what is the share of the former in Divine Mercy and Justice? For the wronged person, there is a kind of mercy behind the wrath and anger shown in the disaster. Just as an innocent person's lost property becomes like alms he gives to the poor and thereby gains permanence, his death in the disaster may be regarded as a kind of martyrdom through which he earns an eternal life of happiness. Thus, such people gain a great and perpetual profit from a relatively small and temporary difficulty and torment, and the earthquake becomes an instance of Divine Mercy within wrath for them.

FIFTH QUESTION: Why does the All-Just, All-Compassionate, All-Powerful, and All-Wise not give specific punishments for specific wrongs, and uses a mighty element (like the earth) for punishment? Can this be reconciled with His Mercy's grace and His Power's inclusiveness?

ANSWER: The All-Powerful One of Majesty gives many duties to each element in creation, and causes each duty to produce many effects. Even though one effect of an element's duties may be ugly, evil, or calamitous, its other effects may be good or beautiful. If that one ugly or evil effect prevented the element from performing its other duties, many instances of good also would be prevented. Since not doing a necessary good is evil, instances of evil would be committed as the number of the good effects. Leaving many instances of good undone to avoid one evil is extremely ugly, contrary to wisdom and reality, and a fault. However, Divine Power, Wisdom, and Truth are free of fault. As certain faults constitute a rebellion comprehensive enough to rouse the earth and other elements to anger, and constitute an insulting infringement of the rights of numerous creatures, sometimes a mighty element is commanded to reprimand the rebellious, as part of its universal duty, so that the incident's extraordinary ugliness can be seen by all. In such cases, this is perfect wisdom and justice, and for the wronged it is perfect mercy.

SIXTH QUESTION: The heedless say that the earthquake results from a subterranean fault in the rock strata, and consider it a natural and purposeless chance event. They do not recognize non-material causes and results, and so are unaware of the truth and learn nothing from this event. Does their allegation contain any truth?

ANSWER: No. It contains only misguidance. Each year the earth is dressed in and changes innumerable embroidered well-designed clothes. Flies are only one of the millions of species adorning the earth. Consider a fly's wing from among numerous organs or parts of its body. The intention, will, purpose, and wisdom it manifests show that, let alone the acts, movement, and states of the huge earth, which is the cradle, matrix and protector of numberless conscious beings, nothing on it and connected with it, whether particular or universal, is ignored by Divine Will and Wisdom and left to its own devices. However, as His Wisdom requires, the Absolutely Powerful One veils His acts with apparent causes. When He wills an earthquake, He may order the rock strata to move. Even if the apparent cause of an earthquake is this movement, both this movement and resulting earthquake still occur by Divine Command and in accordance with His Wisdom.

Consider this: Someone shoots and kills someone else. If only the bullet's movement is considered and the murderer is disregarded, the victim's rights are violated and the result is utter foolishness and injustice. Similarly, disregarding the Lord's command, will, and wisdom concerning any movement or occurrence connected with the earth, a docile official of the All-Powerful One of Majesty, a vessel or aircraft of His, and attributing it to nature or cause and effect, is a serious error and utter foolishness.

AN ADDITION: Misguided people and materialists seek to maintain their way and to counter the believers' awakening in such ways or show such degree of obduracy that it makes people regret their humanity. Our awesome and wrongful rebellion, recently and to a certain degree, has assumed a general form, and this rouses the universe and certain universal elements to anger. So, in order to warn people to give up their awesome, wrongful rebellion and concerning their duty in the universe and toward God as the Lord of the whole creation, and in order to awaken them to recognize the universe's Sovereign, whom they tend not to recognize, the Creator of the heavens and the earth sends various calamities to our way. Not on account of a particular manifestation of His Lordship, but of a universal manifestation as the Lord of the whole creation, He makes us endure such widespread and terrible calamities as earthquakes, storms, floods, and world wars, and so demonstrates most clearly His Wisdom, Power, Justice, Self-Subsistence, Will, and Sovereignty.

Although this is the truth, certain misguided people respond to such universal signs of Divine Lordship and Divine reprimands by saying: "Nature does this. It results from a fault in the rock strata, and is just the result of chance. It is the sun's heat clashing with electricity that stopped all machinery in America for five hours. This also caused Kastamonu's atmosphere to turn red and assume the appearance of a conflagration."

Due to their misguidance and obstinate atheism and materialism, they do not know that natural causes are only so many occasions and veils. If their understanding were true, a huge pine tree would require a village full of factories and looms just to grow from a seed. However, by attributing the tree to its seed and certain apparent causes, materialist unbelievers deny the Maker's numerous miracles displayed in that tree and reduce to nothing a comprehensive act of the Creator's Lordship performed through Will and Wisdom. Sometimes they attach a "scientific" name to a most profound, unknowable, and significant reality that has countless purposes in each of its innumerable aspects. They think that doing so means that its entire nature has been understood and explained. But in reality, they only have made it commonplace and stripped it of all purpose, wisdom, and meaning.

They attribute a particular and purposeful act of the Master to a law of nature, although such laws are only expressions of one aspect of the Universal Will, Encompassing Choice and the Universal Sovereignty. By such an attribution they sever the connection between an act of the Master (an event) and Divine Will and purpose, and thus they limit it to chance and nature. This sheer ignorance is like attributing a battlefield victory to military regulations and discipline, while ignoring the purposeful, intentional actions and practices of the soldiers, commander, king, and government.

Or, it is like this: A wonder-working person produces a hundred pounds of various foodstuffs and a hundred yards of diverse cloths from a fingernail-sized wood chip. Someone comes over and, pointing to the wood chip, says that all these things have come into being out of it naturally and by chance. Thus the maker's wonderful arts and skills are reduced to nothing.

SEVENTH QUESTION: How do we know that this earthquake was aimed at Muslims in Turkey? Why were the areas of Erzincan and Izmir the most affected?

ANSWER: It took place at night during a hard and very cold winter, and was restricted to the region insulting Ramadan. Since people have not taken the necessary lesson, it continues mildly to arouse the neglectful. These signs, together with some others, show that the earthquake is aimed at believers and warns them to perform the Prayers and other acts of worship, and the earth itself is trembling.

There are two reasons why it shook places like Erzincan more than others: First, as their faults were few and slight, they were forgiven without being left to the Supreme Tribunal in the Hereafter. Second, considering that the strong and truthful defenders of belief and Islam were few or utterly defeated in those places, the enemies of Islam established an effective center of activity. Thus, punishment must have been visited on them first.

None save God knows the Unseen.

All-Glorified are You. We have no knowledge save what You have taught us. Surely You are the All-Knowing, the All-Wise.

The
Fifteenth Word

The Fifteenth Word

The clash between angels and devils in the heavens

In the Name of God, the All-Merciful, the All-Compassionate.

Indeed, We have adorned the lowest (world's) heaven with lamps, and We have made (out of) them missiles to drive away devils. (67:5)

Let's climb a seven-step stairway to understand this verse.

Seven steps

FIRST STEP: JUST AS THE EARTH HAS ITS OWN INHABITANTS, reality and wisdom require that the heavens have theirs. In Islam, such beings are called angels and spirit beings.

Reality requires it to be so, for despite its small size and relative insignificance, the earth is filled with, emptied of, and replenished with living and conscious beings. Thus the well-decorated castle-like heavens having magnificent towers must have conscious and percipient beings.

Like humanity and jinn, those beings observe the world, study the Book of the Universe, and herald the Divine Lordship's sovereignty. For the universe's Master has embellished and ornamented it with infinite decorations, beauties, and inscriptions, all of which require the existence of contemplative and appreciative eyes to observe and be delighted. Beauty requires a lover, and food is given to the hungry. Humanity and jinn perform only a minute portion of this boundless duty, glorious viewing, and comprehensive worship. Therefore, these infinite and diverse duties and acts of worship require the existence of countless angels and spirit beings.

Prophetic Traditions suggest, and the wisdom in the universe's order indicates, that certain kinds of angels use moving bodies, from planets to drops of rain, to tour and view the visible, material world.[65] In addition, certain kinds of animal bodies, from the "green birds" of Paradise[66] to flies, serve as "aircraft" for one kind of spirits. Spirits who enter such bodies by God's command view the physical miracles of creation through those beings' senses. The Creator, Who continuously creates subtle life and enlightened, percipient beings from dense soil and turbid water, must have created innumerable conscious beings from light, even from darkness, which are worthier of a life and spirit.

SECOND STEP: the earth and the heavens are like two countries, under one government, that conduct important relations and transactions. For example, things necessary for the earth like light, heat, blessings, and forms of mercy (like rain) are sent from the heavens. Also, as all Revealed religions confirm and as all saintly scholars who unveil creation's secret truths based on what they have witnessed agree, angels and spirit beings descend to the earth from the heavens. Thus we may deduce that there is a way for the earth's inhabitants to ascend to the heavens.

Just as people can travel to the heavens through their mind, vision, and imagination, so, freed from or purified of their carnal and material being's gross heaviness, the spirits of Prophets and saints travel in such realms by God's leave; the spirits of ordinary believing people do so after death. Since those who are "lightened" and have acquired "subtlety" and spiritual refinement travel there, certain inhabitants of the earth and the air may go to the heavens if they are clothed in an "ideal" body, energetic envelope, or immaterial body or form, and are light and subtle like spirits.

THIRD STEP: The heavens' silence and tranquility, order and serene regularity, and vastness and radiance show that their inhabitants differ from those of the earth: They obey God and do not quarrel or dispute among themselves, for they are innocent, their realm is vast, their nature is pure, and their stations are fixed. This differs from the earth, where opposites exist side by side, evil is mixed with good, and disputes arise, and the result is conflict and suffering. Conscious beings are tested and set to compete, which results in progress or regress. This is so for the following reason:

Humanity is the fruit of the Tree of Creation. The fruit of something is its furthest, most delicate and important part. Thus we are the fruit of the universe; a most comprehensive, wonderful, impotent, weak, and subtle mir-

---

[65] at-Tirmidhi, "Zuhd" 9; Ibn Maja, "Zuhd" 19. (Tr.)
[66] Muslim, "'Imara" 121; Abu Dawud, "Jihad" 25. (Tr.)

acle of Power. Given this, the earth, despite its small size and insignificance when compared with the heavens, is the universe's heart and center with respect to the meaning and art it contains, for it is our cradle and dwelling place. Moreover, it is the place where God's miracles of Art are exhibited and the manifestations of Divine Names are concentrated. It reflects God's infinite activity as the Lord (Master, Sustainer, Trainer, and Ruler) of all beings. It also is the center and pivot of the endless Divine creativity displayed in infinite liberality, especially in the numerous small plant and animal species, as well as the place where samples of creatures of the broadest worlds of the Hereafter are shown in small scale. It is the speedily operating workshop for eternal textiles, the fast-changing place of copies of eternal scenes, and the narrow, temporary field and tillage rapidly producing seeds for permanent gardens (in the Hereafter).

It is because of this greatness of the earth with respect to its meaning and its importance in regard to art, the wise Qur'an puts it on a par with the heavens, although it is like a tiny fruit of a huge tree when compared with the heavens. It places the earth in one pan of a pair of scales and the heavens in the other, and repeatedly mentions them together, saying, the "Lord of the heavens and the earth."[67]

The rapid and constant changes and transformations on the earth require that its inhabitants undergo corresponding changes. As this bounded earth is the object of Divine Power's countless miracles, the faculties of humanity and jinn are essentially unrestricted, thereby allowing infinite progress and regress. A great field of trial and testing has opened for everyone, from Prophets and saints to Nimrods and devils. Thus the endless evil of Pharaoh-like devils will make them attack the heavens and its inhabitants.

---

[67] The earth may be regarded as equal to the heavens, for it may be argued that "a constant spring is greater than a lake with no inlet." Likewise, a bushel, used to measure grain, may be seen to be in balance with a hill-sized amount of grain that has been measured with it and heaped somewhere. It is exactly the same with the earth: God Almighty created it to exhibit the works of His Art and manifest His Power, as a garden where His Mercy flowers and as a field to cultivate the seeds of Paradise. It functions as a measure to fill and empty the universe of countless worlds of creation, and resembles a spring flowing into the "seas" of the past and the World of the Unseen. Consider the "shirts" woven of creatures in countless forms that the earth changes each year, and the ever-renewed worlds with which the earth is filled each time and then pours into the past into the world of the Unseen. Consider all of these as present before your eyes, and then compare the earth with the somewhat monotonous and plain heavens. You will see that even if the earth does not weigh more than the heavens, it certainly does not weigh less. From this, you may understand the meaning of *the Lord of the heavens and the earth*.

FOURTH STEP: The All-Majestic One, the Master, Administrator, and Creator of all worlds, has many Titles and Beautiful Names that issue various decrees and perform different tasks. For example, the Title or Name requiring the angels to help the Companions fight the unbelievers also requires battle between angels and devils, and struggle between the heavens' good and the earth's evil inhabitants. Certainly the All-Powerful One of Majesty, Who holds the unbelievers' souls within His Power's grasp, does not eradicate them with a command or trumpet blast. Having the Title of the Lord of the whole creation, and as the requirements of His Names the All-Wise and Administrator, He opens a field of testing and contest.

Consider this: A king has many names and titles with respect to the different areas of his rule. For example, in the department of justice he is known as Just Ruler, in the armed forces as Supreme Commander, in the office of religious affairs as Caliph (or Supreme Head of the Church), and in the civil service as Ruler. His obedient subjects call him Gracious Sovereign, while the rebellious call him Overwhelming Ruler.

That exalted king, who enjoys absolute sovereignty, does not order rebels to be executed; rather, as a requirement of his title Just Ruler, they are sent to court. Similarly, he does not reward honest, capable officials by personally admitting or directly phoning them. Instead, under his titles relating to the majesty of sovereignty and expedients of government, he opens a field of competition to show how much the officials deserve the reward, and commands his ministers to invite the people to watch. He organizes a welcoming ceremony and, after a magnificent royal testing, publicly rewards and proclaims the winners' worthiness.

Thus—*The highest comparison is (and must be put forth) for God*—the Eternal King has numerous Beautiful Names. Through the manifestations of His Majesty and His Grace, He has many Titles and Qualities essential to His Divine Being. Whichever Title and Name requires the existence of light and darkness, summer and winter, and Paradise and Hell, also require that the law of contest should be universal, like the laws of generation and mutual assistance. From the contest of angelic inspirations and satanic whisperings around the heart to the contest between angels and devils in the vast realm of the heavens, they require that law to be all-embracing.

FIFTH STEP: Beings travel between the earth and the heavens, and important necessities for the former are sent from the latter. Given that pure spirits travel to the heavens, evil spirits attempt to do likewise, as they are physically light and subtle. But they are driven off, for they are by nature evil and unclean. There must certainly be in the visible, material world a sign of this important interaction and contest. For the wisdom of Divine Lordship's sovereignty requires that it should place a sign on His important disposals in the invisible realm for conscious beings, particularly for humanity, whose most important duty is observing, witnessing, supervising, and acting as a herald to, those disposals; in the same way that He has made rain a sign for us to explain, in physical terms, His countless miracles in spring. He has made apparent (natural) causes point to His Art's wonders, so that He may attract the attentive gaze of the inhabitants of the heavens and the earth to witness that amazing exhibition. He displays the vast heavens as a castle, a city arrayed with towers on which sentries are posted, so that the inhabitants of the heavens and the earth may reflect on His Lordship's majesty.

Since wisdom requires the announcement of this elevated contest, there will be a sign for it. Accordingly, other than shooting stars , no atmospheric or "heavenly" event seems appropriate to this announcement. These stellar events are perfectly suitable for repulsing devils; they resemble missiles and signal rockets fired from the formidable bastions of high castles, and, unlike other "heavenly" events, no other function is known for such events. Moreover, this function has been widely known since the time of Adam and witnessed by those who know the reality of things and events.

SIXTH STEP: Since humanity and jinn are potentially inclined to and capable of endless evil and dispute, they recognize no bounds to opposition, rebellion, and transgression. Thus the wise Qur'an restrains them with such miraculous eloquence, sublime and clear styles, and exalted and evident comparisons and parables that the universe trembles. For example, listen to the awesome warning, fearsome threat, and severe restraining in:

> O company of jinn and humanity! If you are able to penetrate and pass beyond the spheres of the heavens and the earth, then penetrate and pass beyond (them). You will not penetrate and pass beyond them save with an authority. Which then of the blessings of your Lord do you deny? There will be sent on you a flash of fire, and smoke, and no help will you have. (55:33-36)

This suggests: "If you, humanity and jinn, can ignore My Commands, pass beyond My Kingdom's bounds, if you are able to." With such miraculous eloquence, it breaks their conceited opposition, and shows how helpless and wretched they are in relation to the immense grandeur of the sovereignty of God's Lordship. Such verses, as well as: *We have made them missiles for the devils* (67:5), in effect say:

> O humanity and jinn, conceited and refractory despite your abjection, and disobedient and obdurate despite your destitution and weakness. How dare you rebel against the commands of so glorious a King that the stars, moons, and suns obey His commands like orderlies at the service of an officer. You oppose such a Majestic Ruler that He commands soldiers so awesome and obedient that were your devils to stand against them, they would stone them to death with mountain-sized cannon balls. Your ingratitude causes you to revolt in the realm of such a Majestic Sovereign that He has such servants and troops that, it is not insignificant impotent creatures like you, but if were each infidel enemies the size of mountains or the earth, they could hurl at you mountain-sized or even the earth-sized stars, blazing projectiles, and flames of fire and smoke, and rout you. If necessary, they could throw the earth in your face and rain down the earth-sized stars like cannon balls on you.

The Qur'an concentrates on certain important points not because of the enemies' strength but to display Divine Majesty and exhibit the enemies' wickedness. Sometimes it mobilizes the greatest and most powerful causes or means against the least and weakest thing to show the perfect order, infinite justice, boundless knowledge, and power of wisdom [displayed in it, the universe, and the human social system it builds]. By doing so, the Qur'an also seeks to prevent injustice and aggression. For example:

> If you support each other against him [the Prophet], truly God is his Guardian, and Gabriel and the righteous among the believers, and furthermore, the angels, are his supporters. (66:4)

What great respect it expresses for the Prophet, and how considerate it is for his wives' rights. This emphasis is only to express the great respect for the Prophet, the importance of two weak beings' (the women) complaints, and to remind others to observe their rights in a way to arouse compassion for them.

SEVENTH STEP: There are many kinds of stars. Everything that shines in the sky can be called a star. The All-Majestic Creator, the All-Gracious Maker, created them as jewels in the sky, shining fruits of a vast tree, or floating fishes in an infinite ocean. He made them places of excursion, mounts, or dwelling places for angels. One sort of small stars was created to drive off and kill devils. Thus, firing shooting stars to repulse devils may mean:

- A sign that the law of contest also exists in the heavens.

- The heavens contain watchful guards and obedient inhabitants, Divine forces, who do not like earthly evil-doers mixing with and eavesdropping on them.

- Spying devils, representatives of the filth and wickedness on the earth, try to dirty the clean and pure realm of the heavens inhabited by pure beings, and spy on their talk in the name of evil spirits.[68] Shooting stars drive them from the heavens' doors.

So, those of you who shut your eyes to the Qur'an's sun and rely on your mind's dim light, open your eyes and climb these seven steps. In the light of the Qur'an's miraculousness, as bright as daylight, see the meaning of the verse cited at the beginning. Taking stars of truth from the heavens of that verse, hurl them at the devils in your minds and kill them. We too should do the same and say: "My Lord, I seek refuge in You from the evil suggestions of Satan."

God's is the perfect proof and the decisive wisdom.

All-Glorified are You. We have no knowledge save what You have taught us. Surely You are the All-Knowing, the All-Wise.

Addendum

In His Name, All-Glorified is He.

There is nothing that does not glorify Him with praise.

In the Name of God, the All-Merciful, the All-Compassionate.

If a provocation from Satan should provoke you, seek refuge in God. Surely He it is Who is the All-Hearing, the All-Knowing. (7:200)

The Qur'an's argument against Satan and his party

This topic comprises a rational, objective discussion with Satan to refute one of his deceptive arguments. In the discussion, he and the transgressors finally are silenced and overcome.

One day eleven years ago during Ramadan, I was listening to a Qur'anic recitation in Istanbul's Bayazid Mosque. Suddenly, I felt as if an invisible person were telling me: "You regard the Qur'an as highly exalted and radiant. Study it objectively—suppose it to be a man's word, and see if it is really so exalted and radiant." I was taken in for a brief moment, and

---

[68] Disbelieving jinn and their human companions trying to mislead people, especially through sorcery, mediumship, and soothsaying. (Ed.)

fancied that the Qur'an was a human work. However, perceiving that the speaker was Satan, who wanted to show me the Qur'an devoid of its lights and lead me astray, I sought help from the Qur'an and immediately felt a light in my heart. This encouraged me to argue:

> O Satan! Objective reasoning means impartial judgment, but the "impartial" judgment used by you and your disciples means siding with the Qur'an's opponents and following temporary unbelief. For supposing the Qur'an to be a human work and arguing as if it were is to take the part of the opposing side; it is to side with unbelief or falsehood.

When he retorted: "Then accept it as neither the Word of God nor the work of a human being," I replied:

> I cannot justify such a position. For if two people argue about an item, it is deposited with a third person, provided that the two parties are in reasonable proximity to each other. If they are not, the property is left with the one who already holds it until the dispute is settled. It is not left somewhere between them.
>
> The Qur'an is a priceless item; there is an infinite distance between its owner (God) and its claimant (humanity). It cannot be left between these two sides, nor can be a meeting point, for they are opposites like existence and non-existence. Thus, it should be left in the "hands" of God. {Also, since its Revelation, billions of people have accepted it as God's Word.] Therefore, if the opposing side can refute all the arguments proving it to be God's Word and prove that it is the work of a human being, it can claim ownership of it. Who would dare to remove that brilliant Qur'an from the Greatest Throne of God, onto which it is fixed with thousands of "nails" of decisive proofs?
>
> Despite you, O Satan, the people of truth and justice deal with the issue by just reasoning and strengthen their belief in the Qur'an through even the smallest decisive proof. Those who are deceived by you and your disciples find it very difficult to move from unbelief's darkness to belief's light, for it requires a proof as strong as all these "nails," once it has been cast to the ground by supposing it to be the work of a human being. Thus many people are deceived into that false pretence of "objective" reasoning and ultimately lose their belief.

But Satan insisted: "The Qur'an resembles human speech, for it follows a human style or conversation. If it were the Word of God, it should be extraordinary in all aspects. As His artistry cannot be likened to what is human, His Word likewise should not resemble human speech." I replied:

> Our Prophet, upon him be peace and blessings, was a human being. All of his acts and attitudes, except for his miracles and states of

Prophethood, originated in his humanity. Like all other human beings, he was subject to and dependent upon God's laws of life. He suffered from cold, felt pain, and so on. He was not extraordinary in all his acts and attitudes so that he could set an example to humanity through his conduct. If he had been extraordinary in all his acts and manners, he could not have an absolute guide in every aspect of life or *a mercy for all* through all his states.

In the same way, the wise Qur'an leads conscious beings, directs humanity and jinn, guides people of perfection, and instructs truth-seeking people. Thus it must follow the style of human speech and conversation. Humanity and jinn take their supplications and prayers from it, talk about their affairs in its terms, and derive their principles of good conduct from it. In short, every believer adopts it as the authorized reference for all their affairs. If, by contrast, it had been like the Word of God heard by Moses on Mount Sinai, no one could have borne it or used it as a reference. Moses, one of the five greatest Messengers of God, could endure to hear only a few pieces of that Word and asked: "Is this Your speech?" God answered: "I have the power of all tongues and languages."

Satan continued: "As many people discuss, in religion's name, almost the same subjects as those in the Qur'an, a human being could have written it," and I replied, through the Qur'an's light:

FIRST: Religious people speak the truth out of their love of religion and in the name of God's commandments. They do not lie against or imitate God and do not speak on His behalf for fear of the Qur'anic threat: *Who is more in wrong than the one who lies against God?* (39:32).

SECOND: No one can imitate God and speak on his behalf. People can imitate only those of nearly the same level. Only those of the same species can take each other's form. Only those of nearly the same level can pretend to each other's level. However it is very difficult, even in that case, for them to deceive people for long, as their pretensions and false display eventually unmask them to perceptive people. If, on the other hand, counterfeiters are greatly inferior to those they try to imitate (e.g., an ordinary person claiming Ibn Sina's (Avicenna) knowledge, or a shepherd pretending to be a king), they would open themselves to ridicule.

Could a firefly make itself appear as a star for 1,000 years, or a fly make itself appear as a peacock for a year? Could a private pretend to be a famous marshal and occupy his chair for a long time without giving himself away? Could a deceitful unbeliever sustain for a lifetime, before discerning people, a false display of a most pious person's loyalty, truthfulness, and conviction? If these "ifs" are inconceivable or unacceptable to any intelligent person, considering the Qur'an a human work would mean seeing that Manifest Book, which has been like a star of truths or a sun of perfections radiating the lights of truths in the sky of the Muslim world for centuries, as a collection of falsehoods invented by a counterfeiter. It would mean his Companions of thirty-three years, as well as all who have followed him during the next fourteen centuries, were unaware of his real identity. This is beyond belief.

O Satan, you cannot deceive sensible people in such a way, even if you were far more advanced in your devilish craft. You only can deceive people into looking at the Qur'an and the Prophet from a very great distance and seeing those star-like objects as fireflies.

THIRD: Calling the Qur'an a human work means that a most bright, true, and comprehensive criterion of the human world, miraculous of exposition and bringer of well-being to the world, is the product of an illiterate man's mind. Moreover, his pretence and counterfeiting have appeared as earnestness, sincerity, and purity of intention for fourteen centuries to even great intellects and exalted geniuses. It is a most inconceivable allegation.

Further, accepting it would mean that a most illustrious and virtuous being who spent his entire life displaying and preaching conviction, truthfulness, trustworthiness, sincerity, earnestness, and uprightness in all his states, words, and actions, as well as raising many truthful persons, was a mean and discreditable rascal, wholly insincere, and the foremost in unbelief. Even Satan would be ashamed to conceive of such a great lie.

There is no third alternative. If the Qur'an were a human work, it would be so debased that it could be a source only of superstition. The rank of him who brought it also would be degraded from being a source of perfection to the greatest cheat. Thus, he could not be God's Messenger, for one who lies in His name is the worst of people. Such a supposition is as inconceivable as continuously seeing a fly to be a peacock and observing a peacock's attributes in a fly. No normal person could regard such suppositions as possible.

FOURTH: The Community of Muhammad, the Muslim community, has proved to be the greatest and most magnificent people of history. The Qur'an has enabled them to conquer this world and the next; has equipped them materially and spiritually; and has instructed and educated them in all rational, moral, and spiritual matters according to the particular level of each. It has purified them and used each bodily member, sense, and faculty in its most proper place.

The Prophet, who brought the Qur'an from God, used his life to exemplify His laws in all his attitudes and actions. He instructed us via his actions and sincere practice of the principles of truth as long as he lived. He showed and established the ways of true guidance and well-being via his sincere and reasonable sayings. In addition, as his life and good conduct testify, he is the most knowledgeable of God and the most fearful of His punishment. He has established his splendid rule of perfection over half the globe and one-fifth of humanity. He truly became, through his well-known manners and actions as a Prophet, statesman, commander, spiritual and intellectual guide, father, husband, friend, and so on, the pride of humanity and of creation.

So, if you consider the Qur'an a human work, it would be no more than a worthless fabrication of a liar who did not recognize or fear God. For there is no middle, meeting point between these two alternatives. No intelligent person, O Satan, could be deceived by such an inconceivable supposition, not even if you were far more powerful in your devilish tricks.

Satan retorted: "How can I fail to deceive? I already have deceived most people, including the foremost in rational thought, and led them to deny both the Qur'an and Muhammad." I said:

FIRST: When looked at from a great distance, the largest thing can look like a tiny particle; a star can be considered a candle.

SECOND: When considered superficially and in a way vulnerable to distraction and illusion, an inconceivable thing can appear conceivable. Once an old man scanned the horizon to catch sight of the new moon of the month of Ramadan. A white hair from his eyebrow curved over his eye and came into his line of sight. Deceived by that illusion, he said: "I have seen the moon." Because he concentrated on the moon and his hair appeared to him without his will and intention, he took the hair for the moon.

THIRD: Denial differs from non-confirmation, which is a kind of indifference and lack of judgment. Thus, many inconceivable things may exist unintentionally in non-confirmation. Denial is a judgment and means confirming non-existence that usually is reached through reasoning. A devil like you deprives people of sound judgment and leads them to denial. You use heedlessness, deviation, sophistry, obstinacy, demagogy, arrogant superiority, conceit, seduction, and custom to cause people to see falsehood as truth and the inconceivable as conceivable. Thus you have led many people (human in appearance but perhaps not in essence) into unbelief, which requires accepting many inconceivable things.

FOURTH: The Qur'an is a book of pure truths and matchless value, which guides saints and scholars of truth and purity, who shine in the sky of humanity like stars. It teaches and invites to truth and love of the truth, truthfulness and loyalty, trustworthiness and reliability. It secures happiness in both worlds through Islam's pillars of beliefs and fundamental principles. The Prophet is a most trustworthy being, the foremost and firmest in belief and conviction. This is testified to by Islam and its law, which he preached and showed by his acknowledged piety and sincere worship manifested throughout his life, as required by his laudable virtues, and confirmed by all people of truth and perfection.

Given this, considering the Qur'an a human work would mean that it is a collection of fallacies and lies, and that the Prophet is an unreliable, unbelieving liar with no fear of God. This supposition is the most dangerous kind of unbelief, deviation, and wrong-doing. Even devils and Sophists would be ashamed to conceive of such things.

In short: It was mentioned in the 18th Sign of the 19th Letter that those whose power of hearing allow them to appreciate the Qur'an's miraculousness acknowledge that it is not of the same kind and degree as all other books they have heard. Thus it is either inferior or superior to all other books. As not even a devil would assert the former, we must accept that it is superior and therefore a miracle. That being the case, based on the two decisive proofs of dichotomy and *reductio ad absurdum*, we openly declare:

O Satan and your disciples. The Qur'an is either God's Word manifested through His Supreme Throne and Supreme or Greatest Name, or, God forbid such a thought, the fabrication of an unbeliever who does not recognize or fear God. Even you, O Satan, could never say that this second alternative is true. Thus the Qur'an is, of necessity and undoubtedly, the Word of the Creator of the universe, given that there is no third alternative, as explained above.

Likewise Muhammad is either a Messenger of God, as well as the most perfect Messenger and superior to all other creatures, or, God forbid such a supposition, a man of unbelief and the lowest nature, since he lied against God and neither recognized Him nor His punishment.[69] Not even European philosophers or hypocrites of other lands, in whom you place great trust, have alleged—nor will able to allege—such a thing, O Satan, because no one will heed and accept such an allegation. So, even the most corrupt philosophers and unscrupulous hypocrites in whom you trust, say: "Muhammad was a very wise man and of exemplary good conduct."

---

[69] Since the Qur'an mentions such a supposition to refute the unbelievers' unbelief and bad language, I felt justified in mentioning it, though fearfully and with aversion, only as a most impossible supposition to show how groundless and false are such assertions.

Finally, there are only two alternatives. As the second alternative with respect to both the Qur'an and Prophet Muhammad is absolutely inconceivable and unacceptable, the Qur'an is self-evidently and of necessity God's Word and Muhammad, upon him be peace and blessings, His Messenger; he is the most perfect Messenger, and superior to all other creatures. This is true whether you or your followers like it or not. Upon him be blessings and peace to the number of angels, human beings, and jinn.

Satan's second, insignificant objection

While I was reciting:

> Not a word he utters, but by him is an observer ready. And the stupor of death comes in truth; that is what you were trying to escape. And the Trumpet is blown; that is the Day of the Threat. And every soul comes, along with it a driver and a witness. "You were heedless of this. Now We have removed from you your covering, and so your sight today is piercing." And his comrade (the witness) says: "This is (his record of deeds) that I keep ready with me." (The sentence is pronounced): "Cast, you two, into Hell every rebel ingrate." (50:18-24)

Satan said: "You find the Qur'an's eloquence primarily in its fluent style and intelligible expression. Yet, where is the fluency and coherence in these verses? There are great gaps, for they jump from the throes of death to the world's destruction, from the blowing of the Trumpet to the end of the Reckoning and therefrom to throwing the sinful into Hell. There are many other examples of this in the Qur'an."

I made the following points in reply:

> A most fundamental element of the Qur'an's miraculousness is its eloquence and precision. It contains so many instances of this that observant critics have been filled with wonder and admiration. For example, eloquent people have prostrated before: *And it was said: "O earth, swallow up your water, o sky, cease (your rain)!" And the water was made to subside. And the commandment was fulfilled, and the Ark settled in al-Judi, and it was said: "Away with the people of the evildoers"* (11:44), which tells of the Flood's might so precisely and miraculously within a few short sentences.
>
> In: *Thamud denied in their arrogant rebellion, when the most wretched of them rushed forward; then the Messenger of God said to them: "The She-Camel of God; observe her turn in drinking." But they denied him, and hamstrung her, so their Lord doomed them for their sin, and leveled them. He fears not the issue thereof* (91:11-15), the Qur'an recounts

precisely and clearly the people of Thamud's story and fate in a most comprehensible way.

In: *And Dhu'n-Nun, when he departed in anger and was convinced that We would never straiten him: then he called out in the layers of darkness: "There is no deity but You. All-Glorified are You. Surely I have been one of the wrongdoers"* (21:87), much remains unsaid between *We would never straiten him* and *he called out in the layers of darkness.* Those few words retell the chief points of Prophet Yunus' (Jonah) story in a way that neither diminishes comprehensibility nor mars eloquence. What is not stated directly is left to the person's understanding.

Also in *Sura Yusuf*, seven or eight sentences are omitted between *so send me forth* (end of verse 45) and *Yusuf (Joseph), O you truthful one* (beginning of verse 46). This neither affects comprehensibility nor mars the Qur'an's eloquence.

The Qur'an contains many more instances of miraculous precision. The precise description given in the verses in question from *Sura Qaf* make them even more beautiful and miraculous. Pointing to the unbelievers' future, which is so long that a day of it is equal to 50,000 earthly years, they draw attention to the fearful events that will befall them. They bring before our minds the whole span of those upheavals like a flash of lightening, thereby compressing that extremely long time into one page or one single picture so that we can ponder it. Referring the unmentioned events to the imagining faculty of the listener or reader, they achieve a sublime fluency. *When the Qur'an is recited, give ear to it and pay heed, that you may be shown mercy* (7:204).

I asked Satan if he had more objections. He replied: "I don't oppose those truths. But many foolish people follow me. Many devils in human form assist me. Many philosophers are just as conceited as Pharaoh. I teach them things that contribute to their pride and selfishness. They will prevent the publication of your Words, and so I'll never yield to you."

All-Glorified are to You. We have no knowledge save what You have taught us. Surely You are the All-Knowing, the All-Wise.

The
Sixteenth Word

The Sixteenth Word

The Divine Essence, Unity, and Acts

In the Name of God, the All-Merciful, the All-Compassionate.

When He wills a thing to be, He but says to it: "Be," and it is. So All-Glorified is He in Whose hand is the absolute dominion of all things, and to Him you are being brought back. (36:82–3)

[NOTE: This Word was written to enlighten my blind soul by pointing out four rays from the light of the above verses. The rays dispel darkness and give conviction and certainty.]

Four rays

IRST RAY: O MY IGNORANT SOUL! YOU MENTION THE FOLLOWING Qur'anic truths: the Divine Being is One, despite His Acts' universality; the Divine Person is One, yet His Lordship's acts (e.g., sustaining, upbringing, and administering) are universal and unassisted; He is One, yet His control is all-embracing and unshared; He is not contained in space, yet is omnipresent; He is close to all beings despite His infinite transcendence; and He is One, yet dominates everything simultaneously. The Qur'an is wise, so it does not impose non-reason on reason. Reason sees an apparent contradiction between these "truths." I want an explanation that will cause reason to submit.

The Answer: Relying on the Qur'an's enlightenment, I say that the Divine Name of Light has solved many of my difficulties and will solve this one. Choosing the method of comparison, which clarifies the mind and enlightens the heart, I say as Imam Rabbani did:

I am neither of the night nor a worshipper of the night;
I am a servant of the sun, therefore I give tidings of the sun.

Since comparison is a most brilliant mirror to the Qur'an's miraculousness, I will use it to explain this truth. A being may gain universality via mirrors. While being only one individual, it may become like a universal thing with general functions. For example, the sun is one being, but is made so universal by all transparent objects that it fills the earth with its reflections and images. Although its heat, light, and the seven colors in its light encompass whatever they confront, each transparent thing contains the sun's heat, light, seven colors, and image, making its pure heart a throne for the sun. The sun is manifested in all objects with all its attributes (unity), and so encompasses all things confronting it; yet it is manifested in one object with all or many of its attributes simultaneously (oneness), and so is present, with many of its attributes, in each item.

We have passed from comparison to discussion of a thing's reflection or presence somewhere through some sort of manifestation of its being. Out of the many types of possible reflection, I will discuss three:

THE FIRST: *REFLECTIONS OF DENSE, MATERIAL OBJECTS:* Such reflections are other than the thing reflected, and so have a different identity. They are also lifeless, having no quality other than their lifeless appearance. For example, if you enter a store full of mirrors, one Said will become thousands of Saids, but only the one living Said is Said—the others are dead.

THE SECOND: *REFLECTIONS OF MATERIAL, LIGHT-GIVING OBJECTS:* Such reflections are neither identical with nor other than the original. While not of the same nature as the original, they have most of its features and may be considered as living. For example, the sun is reflected in countless objects. Each reflection either contains its heat or light, together with its light's seven colors. If the sun were conscious, with its heat as its power, its light as its knowledge, and its seven colors as its seven attributes, it would be present in everything simultaneously, and able to rule over or make contact with each one freely and without one hindering the other. It also would be able to meet with all of us via our mirrors. While we are distant from it, it would be nearer to us than ourselves.

THE THIRD: *REFLECTIONS OF PURE SPIRITS CREATED FROM LIGHT AND HAVING THEIR ORIGINAL PURITY:* Such reflections are living and identifiable with the original. However, since they reflect or manifest themselves according to the receptive object's or mirror's capacity, the reflections are not wholly of the same nature as the original. For example, Gabriel could be with the Prophet in the form of Dihya (a Companion), prostrating in the Divine Presence before God's Most Exalted Throne, and be in innumerable other places relaying the Divine Commands simultaneously. Performing one duty does not block another. In the same way Prophet Muhammad, upon him be peace and blessings, whose essence is light and whose identity is of light, hears each member of his community in this world call blessings upon him simultaneously. On the Day of Judgment, he will meet with all purified people at the same time. In fact, some saints who have acquired a high degree of purity and refinement (*abdal*: substitutes) are seen in many places and doing many things simultaneously. Just as glass and water reflect material objects, so do air, ether, and certain beings of the World of Ideas or Immaterial Forms reflect and transport such beings with the speed of light and imagination. This allows them to travel in thousands of pure realms and refined abodes at the same time.

Helpless and subjugated items like the sun, and creatures like matter-restricted spirit beings, can be present in many places at once because they are either light-giving creatures or created of light. Despite being particulars bounded by certain conditions, they become like absolute universals. With their limited power of choice, they can do many things at once.

The All-Holy, All-Pure Being is wholly transcendent and free of matter, far above and exempt from any restriction and the darkness of density and compactness. All lights and luminous beings, whether light-giving or created of light, are dense shadows of His Names' sacred lights. All existence and life, as well as the World of Spirits and the World of Ideas or Immaterial Forms, are semi-transparent mirrors of His Beauty. His Attributes are all-embracing, and His essential Qualities are universal. What could escape or hide from His manifestation with all His Attributes, particularly His universal Will, absolute Power, and all-encompassing Knowledge? What could be difficult for Him? Who could be distant from Him? Who could draw close to Him without acquiring universality?

The sun's unrestricted light and immaterial reflection makes it nearer to you than your eye's pupil, while your being bounded by certain conditions keeps you far from it. To draw near, you must transcend many restrictions and rise above many universal levels. Simply, in terms of spiritual transcendence, you have to become as large as the earth and rise as far as the moon. Only then could you directly approach, to a degree, the sun in its essential identity and meet with it without veil. In the same way, the All-Majestic One of Grace, the All-Gracious One of Perfection, is infinitely near to you, while you are infinitely far from Him. If you have enough power of heart and sublimity of mind, try to see certain other realities in the other aspects of the comparison.

SECOND RAY: O my senseless soul. You say that such verses as: *When He wills a thing to be, He but says to it: "Be," and it is* (36:82); and: *It is but one single blast, and see, they are all arraigned before Us* (36:53); show that things happen instantaneously and through a command. However, such other verses as: *This is the pattern of God, Who has perfected everything* (27:88); and: *He Who makes excellent everything that He creates* (32:7), say that a thing's existence is gradual, that it comes about through a vast power on the basis of knowledge, and that it is a fine art depending on wisdom. How can these be reconciled?

The Answer: Relying on the enlightenment of the Qur'an, I say:

FIRSTLY: There is no contradiction here, for some things happen instantaneously like repeating the original, and others are gradual as in the original creation.

SECONDLY: The infinitely perfect order and firmness and solidity, and extremely delicate and fine artistry and perfect creation vis-à-vis the ease, speed, multiplicity, and liberality observed in the universe, testify to the truths contained in such verses. Therefore, such a discussion is unnecessary Instead, we should discuss the wisdom in them. So, consider the following comparison:

A tailor makes something with much difficulty, as well as with great artistry and skill, and then fashions a model. After that, a copy can be made quickly and easily. Sometimes it becomes so easy that it seems to result from one command, and acquires such a perfect order that it seems to be the result of one touch.

In the same way, after originally making this world and all its contents, the All-Wise Maker, All-Knowing Designer, destined a measure and proportion (like a model) for everything. Making each century a model, the Eternal Designer clothes it with a new world bejeweled with His Power's miracles. Making each year a measure, He sews a new system artistically fastened with His Mercy's wonders. Making each day a line, He inscribes on it recruited and renewed creatures adorned with His Wisdom's subtleties.

The Absolutely Powerful One also makes the earth, each mountain and plain, each garden and orchard, and each tree a model. He continuously sets up new systems on the earth and creates new worlds. Removing a world, He replaces it with a new, perfect one. Season after season, He displays His Power's miracles and His Mercy's gifts in all gardens and orchards, wherein He inscribes a new wisdom-displaying book and sets up a fresh kitchen of His Mercy. He clothes each in an ever-renewed garment full of art. He dresses all trees in garments of brocade every spring, adorns them with fresh jewels, and fills their hands with gifts of His Mercy.

Thus, the One Who does these things with an infinitely fine art and perfect order, Who varies the moving worlds following each other along the string of time with innumerable instances of wisdom and favor, and with perfection of power and art, is infinitely Powerful and Wise, All-Seeing and All-Knowing. Chance cannot interfere. By declaring: *When He wills a thing to be, He but says to it: "Be," and it is* (36:82); and: *The matter of the Hour is but the twinkling of an eye, or even quicker* (16: 77), the All-Majestic Being proclaims His Power's perfection and the ease with which His Power can destroy the universe and raise the dead. To express the ease in His creation, He declares in the Qur'an that He does everything via a mere command, for His command of creation consists in Power and Will, all things are subjugated and obedient to His command, and He creates without physical contact or gradualism.

In conclusion, some verses proclaim the extremely fine artistry and infinite perfection of wisdom in beings, especially at the start of their creation; others describe the extreme ease, speed, and infinite obedience, especially in repeating and renewing created beings.

THIRD RAY: O my transgressing soul, full of doubts and subject to evil suggestions. You say that such verses as: *In His hand is the absolute dominion of all things* (36:83); *No moving creature is there but He holds it by its forelock* (11:56); and: *We are nearer to him than his jugular vein* (50:16), show that God is infinitely near to us. On the other hand, such verses as: *To Him you are being brought back* (36:83) and: *The angels and the Spirit ascend to Him in a day the measure of which is fifty thousand years* (70:4), as well as the *hadith*: "God Almighty is beyond seventy thousand veils" and such truths as those contained in the Prophet's Ascension, show that we are infinitely far from

Him. I want an explanation which will make this profound mystery understandable.

The Answer: O my soul, consider the following: At the end of the "First Ray," I said that due to its unrestricted light and immaterial reflection, the sun is nearer to you than your eye's pupil, your spirit's window and mirror. However, because you are bounded by certain conditions and imprisoned within matter's walls, you are very far from it. You can make contact with it only through some of its reflections and shadows, meet with it through its particular manifestations, and draw close to its colors (attributes) and rays and images (a grouping of its names).

If you seek direct contact, you must transcend numerous restrictions and rise above many universal levels. Simply, in terms of spiritual transcendence, only after becoming as large as the earth, expanding in spirit like the air, rising as far as the moon, and directly confronting the sun as the full moon does, could you claim to meet with the sun in person and without any veil, and draw near to it to some degree. In the same way, the All-Majestic One of Perfection, the Peerlessly Beautiful One, the Necessarily Existent One, the Creator of All Things, the Eternal Sun, the Monarch with no beginning and end, is nearer to you than yourself, although you are infinitely far from Him. If you have enough power (of heart and sublimity of mind), try to see certain other realities in the other aspects of the comparison.

SECONDLY: A king has many names or ranks, one being Commander-in-Chief. With this rank, he enjoys full authority in all military offices and ranks from the office of Field Marshall to that of Corporal. A private acknowledges a corporal as his superior, and through him is in touch with one connected to the Commander-in-Chief. If he wishes direct contact with the Commander-in-Chief, he must rise higher in the ranks. This means that the king is extremely close to the soldier in many different ways (e.g., through his name, rule, law, knowledge, and so on). If he is purified spiritually, he may oversee every soldier simultaneously without being seen. Nothing can block him. But many ranks and veils block the private from the king's presence. Sometimes, however, the king admits a private to his presence out of his compassion, and favors him with his grace.

In almost the same way—*The highest comparison is (and must be put forth) for God*—the All-Majestic One, the Lord of the command *Be! and it is*, for Whom the suns and stars are like obedient soldiers, is nearer to all things than themselves, while all things are infinitely far from Him. If you wish to enter His Presence of Grandeur directly, you would have to pass through seventy thousand veils of darkness and light (i.e., material and physical veils as well as those of the Divine Names and Attributes), transcend thousands of particular and universal degrees of each Name's manifestation, rise through the most elevated levels of His Attributes, and ascend as high as His Greatest Throne, which is favored with His Greatest Name's manifestation. If God does not favor you by drawing you to Himself, you would have to strive and journey spiritually for thousands of years.

For example, if you want to draw near to Him through His Name of Creator, you must connect with Him first on account of His being your creator, and then on account of His being the Creator of all human beings, then His being the Creator of all living creatures, and then the Creator of all beings. Otherwise, you will remain in shadow and only find a particular manifestation.

A NOTE: As the king in the above example is relatively impotent, he uses such intermediaries as field marshals and generals to execute his commands. But the Absolutely Powerful One, in Whose hand is the absolute dominion of all things, needs no intermediaries. The intermediaries [like angels and natural causes] are only appearances, veils to His Dignity and Grandeur, and heralds and observers of His Lordship's sovereignty in worship, amazement, helplessness, and want. They are not His assistants, and cannot be partners in His Lordship's sovereignty.

FOURTH RAY: So, O my lazy soul. The reality of the Prayer (a kind of Ascension) is like a soldier being admitted to the royal presence as a pure favor; it is being admitted to the Presence of the All-Majestic One of Grace, the All-Gracious One of Majesty, the True Object of Worship, as an instance of pure mercy.

Declaring "God is the All-Great," this world and the next are left behind in spirit and imagination, or by intention. Transcending matter's restriction, you rise to a universal rank of worship or a shadow or form of it. Being honored with admission to the Divine Presence, you are favored (according to your capacity) with the most exalted attainment of addressing God directly: *You alone do we worship* (1:5). Through repeating "God is the All-Great" in its acts, the Prayer is a sign of attaining higher spiritual ranks, of rising from being an insignificant, particular being to a universal one. It is a concise title to the perfections of God's Grandeur, which are beyond our knowledge. It is as if each "God is the All-Great" shows the attainment of a new degree on the way to Ascension. To attain to even a shadow or a ray of the Prayer's reality in spirit, intention, or imagination is a great happiness.

This is why "God is the All-Great" is frequently repeated during the Hajj (pilgrimage to Makka), for Hajj is the kind of worship at a most comprehensive level for every pilgrim. For example, like a general, a private can participate in a special occasion like a festive or celebration day held by the king, and can receive his favors. Similarly, like a saint who has left behind many ranks, a pilgrim, however ordinary a person he is, turns toward his Lord as the Mighty Lord of the whole earth. He is honored with universal worship.

The Hajj is the key that opens up many degrees of the Divine universal Lordship's manifestation, and the telescope through which many horizons of Divine Grandeur are observed. Its acts or rites cause both the spheres of servanthood and worship on the part of humanity and the levels of Divine Magnificence to expand more and more in pilgrims' hearts and imagination. The awe and amazement, and feelings of majesty in front of Divine Lordship that ensue from all these experiences can be quietened only by repeating: "God is the All-Great," it is only with this proclamation that such degrees of manifestations to humanity can be announced.

After the Hajj, this sublime, universal meaning is found in different degrees in the religious festival (*'Id*) Prayers, and the Prayers for rain, during solar and lunar eclipses, and in congregational ones. That is why Islam's public symbols and rites, including the *sunna* ones, are so important.

> All-Glorified is He Who has placed His treasuries between *Kaf* and *Nun*.[70] All-Glorified is He in Whose hand is the absolute dominion of everything, and to Him You are being brought back.
>
> All-Glorified are You. We have no knowledge save what You have taught us. Surely You are the All-Knowing, the All-Wise
>
> Our Lord, take us not to task if we forget or make mistakes.
>
> Our Lord, do not let our hearts to swerve after You have guided us, and bestow upon us mercy from Your Presence. Surely You are the All-Bestowing.

---

[70] *Kaf* and *Nun* are the letters forming *Kun*, meaning *Be!*, which symbolizes God's creation of things. (Tr.)

Bestow blessings and peace upon Your most noble Messenger, favored with the manifestation of Your Greatest Name, and upon his Family, his Companions, all brothers and sisters in religion, and followers. Amin, O Most Merciful of the Merciful!

Addendum

The All-Powerful and All-Knowing One, the All-Wise Maker, shows through the system and order exhibited by His practices, which have taken on the form of laws, His Power and Wisdom and that chance has no part in His works. By making occasional exceptions to those laws (the wonders in His practices), changes in outward forms, differences in individual characteristics, and changes in sending His favors (the coming of rain, for example), He demonstrates His Will and free Choice, and shows that He does whatever He wills and is not restricted. By thus rending the veil of monotony and showing that everything is in constant need of and obedient to His Lordship, He dispels heedlessness and turns humanity and jinn from (natural) causes to Himself as the Creator of causes. This basic principle is evident in the Qur'anic explanations.

For example, in most places some trees yield fruits one year, that is, they are given to them from Mercy's treasury, and they offer them to us. Then the following year even though all apparent causes are present, they do not take them and offer them. Also, the coming of rain is so changeable that it is included in "the five things of the Unseen known only to God," for life and mercy have the most important position in existence. As the source of life and pure mercy, and being the water of life and mercy, rain cannot depend on a law-inducing monotony, for this leads to heedlessness and veils the Divine hand. Rather, the All-Mighty One of Majesty, the True Bestower of Bounties and the Giver of Life, and the All-Merciful and All-Compassionate, directly controls rain and makes it immune to natural causes. Thus He all the time keeps the doors of prayer and thanksgiving open.

Again, for example, giving sustenance and creating every body with a particular countenance are works of special favor, and their occurring in unexpected ways show the Lord's Will and Independence. You may compare other Divine acts (e.g., free disposal of wind and subjugation of the clouds) with these examples.

The
Seventeenth Word

The Seventeenth Word

The meaning of worldly life, and remedies for worldly misfortune

In the Name of God, the All-Merciful, the All-Compassionate.

We have made all that is on the earth an ornament for it that We may test them: which of them is best in conduct. Yet, We surely reduce all that is on it a barren dust-heap. (18:7-8)

The present, worldly life is but a play and pastime. (6:32)

[NOTE: This Word consists of two exalted Stations and an Addendum of signal importance.]

Two stations

 IRST STATION: THE ALL-COMPASSIONATE CREATOR, ALL-Munificent Provider, All-Wise Maker shapes this world as a festival, a place of celebration for spirits and spirit beings. He has decorated it with His Names' most wonderful inscriptions, and clothes each spirit in a body equipped with suitable and appropriate senses so that it may benefit from the innumerable good things and bounties therein. He gives each spirit a corporeal body and sends it to this spectacle once.

He divides the festival, which in terms of time and space is very extensive, into centuries, years, seasons, and days, and into certain parts. Each one is an exalted festival during which all animate beings and plants parade.

Especially in spring and summer, the earth's surface is a vast series of festivals for small creatures, an arena so glittering and attractive that it draws the gaze of angels and the heavens' other inhabitants, and spirit beings in the higher abodes. For those who think and reflect, it is an arena for reflection so wonderful that we cannot describe it appropriately.

However, the displays of the Divine Names the All-Merciful and the Giver of Life in this Divine festival are counterbalanced by the Names the All-Overwhelming and All-Crushing, and the One Who Causes to Die via death and separation. This does not seem to be in line with the all-embracing Mercy expressed in: *My Mercy encompasses all things* (7:156). Nevertheless it is so in several ways, one of which is as follows:

After each group has completed its turn of parade and the desired results have been obtained, the All-Munificent Maker, the All-Compassionate Creator, causes most of them, by His Compassion, to feel weariness and distaste for the world. He grants them a desire for rest and a longing to emigrate to another world. Thus, when they are to be discharged from life's duties, He arouses in them an enthusiastic inclination to return to their original home.

The All-Merciful One bestows martyrdom on soldiers who die in the course of duty (defending their sacred values), and rewards the cattle sacrificed for His sake with an eternal corporeal existence in the Hereafter, and with the rank of being mount for their owner on the Bridge[71]—like Buraq.[72] Therefore, it is not far from His infinite Mercy that other animate beings who die and suffer while performing their God-given duties, in accord with their nature and obedience to the Divine commands, should receive a spiritual reward and wage according to their capacities from His Mercy's inexhaustible treasures. So, they should not be resentful of their departure from this world; rather, they should be pleased. *Only God knows the Unseen.*

Humanity, being the most honored of animate beings, is the greatest beneficiary of these festivals and the most enamored of and immersed in the world. So, when death approaches, God, out of His Mercy, gives each person a mood whereby he or she feels distaste with this world and longs to go to the eternal world. Whoever is not lost in misguidance benefits from this mood and dies with a tranquil heart. I will give five of the many reasons leading to this mood:

[71] See ad-Daylami, *al-Musnad*, 1:85. (Tr.)

[72] The heavenly mount that bore the Prophet through the heavens during his Ascension. (Tr.)

ONE: Due to old age, the All-Merciful One shows the stamp of transience and decline on that which is beautiful and tempting in this world, as well as the bitter meaning they have. By causing us to become dissatisfied with the world, He causes us to seek a permanent beloved.

TWO: Ninety-nine percent of our friends have died and gone to the other world. By engendering within us a longing for the same place through that heart-felt attachment, He enables us to meet death with joy.

THREE: By causing us to feel our inherent infinite weakness and impotence and thereby to understand the great weight of our life's burdens and responsibilities, He implants within us a great wish for rest and a sincere longing to go to another world.

FOUR: He shows believers through the light of belief that death is a change of abode, not an eternal execution; that the grave is the door to illuminated worlds, not the mouth of a dark well; and that for all its glitter this world is like a dungeon when compared to the Hereafter. Therefore, to leave this dungeon for the gardens of Paradise, and pass from the troublesome turmoil of bodily life to the world of rest and the realm where spirits soar, and to slip free of the distressing noise of creatures and go to the All-Merciful's Presence is a journey and a happiness to be desired most earnestly.

FIVE: By revealing to those who give ear to the Qur'an the knowledge of truth it contains, as well as the world's true nature through the light of truth, He explains that love for and attachment to this world are meaningless, for:

- The world is a book of the Eternally Besought One. Its letters and words point to Another's Essence, Names, and Attributes. So learn and adopt its meaning, abandon its decorations, and go.

- The world is a tillage; sow it, harvest your crop, and preserve it. Throw away the chaff, and give it no importance.

- The world is a collection of mirrors that continuously pass on, one after the other. Know the One Who is manifest in them, see His lights, understand the manifestations of the Names appearing in them, and love the One they signify. End your attachment for those fragments of glass, which are doomed to be broken and perish.

- The world is a moving place of trade. Do your business and leave. Do not tire yourself by uselessly pursuing caravans that leave you behind.

- The world is a temporary place of recreation. Study it to learn what you need to know. Ignore its apparent, ugly face, but pay attention to its hidden, beautiful face, which looks to the Eternal All-Gracious One. Go for a pleasant and beneficial visit and then come back. When the scenes displaying those fine views and beautiful things disappear, do not cry like a child, and do not be anxious.

- The world is a guest-house. Eat and drink within the limits set by the All-Munificent Host Who has built it, and offer thanks. Act and behave in accordance with His Law. Then leave and go away without looking back. Do not interfere in it; nor busy yourself in vain with things that leave you and do not concern you.

He shows the world's real character through such plain truths, and makes death less painful. Indeed, He makes death desirable to those awake to truth, and shows that everything He does has a trace of His Mercy. The Qur'an's verses also point to other particular reasons.

Woe to him who has no share of these five reasons or realities!

SECOND STATION

O helpless one, stop wailing over misfortune and trust God,
For know this wailing is an error that causes trouble after trouble;
If you have found Him Who makes you suffer, then know
this suffering is a gift bringing peace and happiness.

So, stop wailing and thank God, like nightingales: their touching
songs on roses are in fact heartfelt thanks offered for all flowers.
But if you do not find Him, know that the whole world
is a place of suffering, misfortune, and loss.

Why wail over a small misfortune
when you bear a worldwide responsibility,
Come, put your trust in God and smile at the face of misfortune
so that it may also smile, for as it smiles, it lessens and changes.

Know, O selfish one: happiness in this world lies in forsaking it.
If you know and seek God, this is enough, for then
all things will be for you even if you abandon them.

If you are selfish, this is total loss, for
whatever you do, all things will be against you.
So, in either case, forsake the world.

Forsaking the world means considering it God's property and
dealing with it with His permission, in His name...
The only profitable business here is to make your mortal life eternal.

If you seek your selfhood, it is rotten and without foundation.
If you seek the outer world, upon it is
the stamp of decline and transience.
Nothing is worth purchasing in this market of rotten goods.
So pass on... Beyond it, the sound goods are all lined up...

A fruit of the black mulberry

(NOTE: In the blessed mulberry tree, the Old Said spoke the following with the tongue of the New Said.)

I am addressing not Ziya Pasha, but those enamored of Europe.
It is not my selfhood speaking, but my heart speaking
on behalf of the Qur'an's students.

What is said in the previous Words is the truth.
Beware. Don't go astray; don't exceed it.
Don't incline toward the ideas of Westerners, for they are misguided.
Don't adopt them, or they'll make you regret it.

You see their most enlightened and smartest people
exclaim in bewilderment: "Alas, I am perplexed.
Of whom and to whom can I complain?"

The Qur'an leads me to speak, and I speak—I won't hold back.
I complain to Him, to His Grace of whatever befalls me
by His leave; I am not confused like you.

I cry out to the Truth—God; I don't exceed the bounds, as you do.
While on the earth, I shout my cause to the heavens.
I don't run away, as you do.

The Qur'an's cause is light upon light; I don't desert it, as you do.
The Qur'an is pure truth and wisdom, I'll prove it.
I count as nothing the philosophy opposing it.

In the Criterion—the Qur'an—are diamond-like truths.
I accept them with all my heart; I don't sell them, as you do.
I travel from creation to the Creator; I don't deviate, as you do.

I fly over the thorny paths; I don't tread them, as you do.
From the earth to the Divine Throne, I offer thanks.
I don't neglect to do so, as you do.

I look on death as a friend; I'm not afraid, as you are.
I'll enter the grave smiling; I'm not frightened, as you are.

I don't see it as a monster's mouth, a beast's den,
a passage to nothingness, as you do.
It reunites me with my friends. I'm not vexed by the grave, as you are.

It is the door of mercy, the door of light and truth.
I'm not discomforted by it; I won't withdraw.
Saying: "In the Name of God," I'll knock at the door.
I'll not look back or feel terror.

Saying: "All praise and gratitude are for God,"
I'll lie down and find ease.
I'll not suffer trouble or remain in solitude.

On hearing the call to the Resurrection,
I'll rise up saying: "God is the All-Great."[73]
I won't hang back from the Supreme Gathering
or that most vast place of prostration.

I'll feel no distress, thanks to Divine favor,
the Qur'an's light, and the radiance of belief.
Not stopping, I'll hasten and fly
to the shade of the All-Merciful's Throne.
God willing, I won't be confused, as you are.

A supplication

O Lord. Heedlessly not trusting in You, but relying on my own power and will, I looked in all six directions for a cure to my pain. I found none. However, it occurred to me: "Isn't it enough for you that you have pains as cure?"

In heedlessness I looked to the past on my right to find solace. But yesterday appeared in the form of my father's grave, and the past as the huge tomb of my forefathers. Instead of consolation, it filled me with horror.*

*Belief shows that huge, terrifying tomb to be a familiar and illuminated meeting place for the gathering of friends.

I looked to the future on the left, but found no cure. Rather, tomorrow appeared in the form of my grave, and the future as the large tomb of my contemporaries and future generations. Instead of giving me relief, It scared me.*

*Belief and the peace it provides show that frightful large tomb to be a feast of the All-Merciful in delightful palaces of bliss.

---

[73] I'll hear the call of the Archangel Israfil on the dawn of the Resurrection, and declaring "God is the All-Great," will rise up. I will not hang back from the "most comprehensive Prayer" and the Supreme Gathering.

As no good appeared from the left either, I looked at the present. I saw it like a coffin carrying my desperately struggling corpse.*

*Belief shows that coffin to be a place of business and a glittering guest-house.

Finding no cure in that direction either, I raised my head and looked at the top of the tree of my life. I saw that its single fruit was my corpse, looking down at me.*

*Belief shows that this fruit is not a corpse. In reality, it shows that the spirit, which is to be favored with eternal happiness in an eternal life, has left its worn-out home to travel among the stars.

Despairing of that direction too, I lowered my head and saw that the dust of my bones had mixed with the dust of my first creation. This only increased my pain.*

*Belief shows that dust to be the door to Mercy and the curtain over the windows of the hall of Paradise.

Turning away, I looked behind and saw a temporary world with no foundation revolving in valleys of nothingness and the darkness of non-existence. Giving no cure, it added more gloom and terror to my pain.*

*Belief shows that world to be the missives of the Eternally Besought One and sheets of Divine inscriptions. Having completed their duties and expressed their meanings, they leave their results behind for a new existence.

Since I saw no good from that direction either, I looked in front and saw the door of my grave standing open at the end. Behind it was the highway leading to eternity, which caught my eyes from afar.*

*Belief shows the grave to be the door to the world of light. As that way leads to eternal happiness, it cures my pain.

While looking in these six directions, I felt only horror and desolation. Apart from an insignificant free will, I have nothing with which to resist or oppose them.*

*Belief gives a document for relying on an Infinite Power in place of our willpower, which is like matter's smallest indivisible part. Indeed, belief itself is such a document.

Human free will lacks power, and its range is short and itself is inaccurate. Apart from serving as a tool to achieve human deeds [which God creates], it cannot do or create anything.*

*Belief causes the willpower to be used in God's name and makes it sufficient against whatever it faces. It is like a soldier who uses his insignificant power on the state's behalf being able to do far greater things than he could do on his own.

It can neither penetrate the past nor discern the future, and is of no benefit in regard to my ambitions and pains in regard to them.*

*Since belief takes its reins from the hand of the animal body and gives them to
the heart and the spirit, it can penetrate the past and the future, for the heart's and
spirit's sphere of life is broad.

Human willpower is active only in the brief present time and the passing present instant. I have infinite needs and an innate weakness. I am destitute and helpless. I am in a wretched state due to the terror and loneliness
coming from the six directions. And yet infinite desire and ambition,
inscribed on the page of my being by the Pen of Power, is embedded in my
nature. Indeed, samples of everything in the universe are contained in my
being. I am connected with all of them, and I work for them.

The sphere of need is as extensive as sight, and extends as far as the
imagination. I need whatever I do not have, and so my need is limitless. Yet
my power extends only as far as I can reach. Thus my wants and needs are
infinite, while my capital is minute and insignificant. So, what does that
insignificant willpower signify when confronted with such need? I have to
search for another solution.

The solution is not to rely on our willpower, but to submit to the
Divine Will and seek refuge in His Power by trusting in Him. "O Lord.
Since this is the way of salvation, I give up my free will on Your way and
abandon my ego.

I do this so that Your Grace may help and support me out of compassion for my impotence and weakness, that Your Mercy may take pity on me
because of my want and need, and that It may be a support for me and open
its door to me."

Whoever finds the boundless sea of Mercy does not rely on his own
free will, which is no more than a drop of water seen in a mirage. He does
not abandon Mercy and resort to his will.

Alas! We have been deceived. We thought that this worldly life is constant, and thus lost it thoroughly. Indeed, this passing life is but a sleep that
passed like a dream. This life, having no foundation, flies like the wind. Those
who rely on themselves and think they will live forever certainly will die. They
race toward death, and this world, humanity's home, falls into the darkness of
annihilation. Ambitions are time-bounded, but pains endure in the spirit.

Since this is the reality, come, my wretched soul that is fond of living
and wants a long life, that loves the world and has boundless ambition and

pain. Awaken and come to your senses. Consider that while the firefly relies on its own dim light and always remains in night's boundless darkness, the honeybee finds the sun of daytime and observes its friends (flowers) gilded with sunlight because it does not rely on itself. In the same way, if you rely on yourself, and your being and self-confidence, you will be like the firefly. But if you dedicate yourself, your transient being and body on the way of the Creator Who gave it to you, you will find, like the honeybee, an endless life of being. Dedicate it, for your being and your body is no more than a Divine trust to you.

Moreover, it is the Creator's property; it is He Who gave it to you. So use it for His sake unhesitatingly and without placing Him under obligation so that it will gain permanence. For a negation negated is an affirmation. Thus if our non-being is negated (in favor of Being), our being finds true existence. The All-Munificent Creator buys His own property from you. In return, He gives you a high price like Paradise, looks after it for you, and increases its value. He will return it to you in a perfected and permanent form. So, my soul, do not wait. Do this business, which is profitable in five respects. As well as being saved from five losses, make a fivefold profit in one transaction.[74]

∾ ∾

In the Name of God, the All-Merciful, the All-Compassionate.

But when it set, he said: "I love not those that set." (6:76)

This verse on the universe's decay, uttered by Prophet Abraham, upon him be peace, made me weep.

The eyes of my heart wept bitter tears for it. Each tear was so bitterly sad that it caused others to fall, as though the tears themselves were weeping. Those tears make up the lines that follow. They are like a commentary on the words of a wise Prophet contained in God's Word—the Qur'an.

A beloved who disappears is not beautiful, for one doomed to decline cannot be truly beautiful. It is not, and should not be, loved in the heart, for the heart is created for eternal love and is a mirror of the Eternally Besought One.

A desired one doomed to set an disappear is unworthy of the heart's attachment or the mind's preoccupation. It cannot be the object of desire, and is unworthy of being missed with grief. So why should the heart adore and be attached to it?

---

[74] Refer to The Sixth Word for the five profits or advantages and five losses. (Tr.)

One sought who is lost in decay and death—I do not desire such a one. For I am mortal and therefore do not seek or desire anything mortal.

One worshipped who is buried in death—I do not invoke or seek refuge with such a one. For I am infinitely needy and impotent. That which is powerless cannot cure my endless pain or solve my infinitely deep wounds. How can anything subject to decay be an object of worship?

A mind obsessed with appearances wails upon seeing that which it adores in the world decay and die, while the spirit, which seeks an eternal beloved, also wails, saying: "I love not those that set."

I do not want or desire separation, for I cannot endure it.

Meetings followed immediately by bitter separation are not worthy of thought or longing. For just as the disappearance of pleasure is pain, imagining it is also pain. The works of lovers, that is, the works of poetry on metaphorical love (love for the opposite sex), are lamentations caused by the pain arising from imagining this disappearance. If you condensed their spirit, this lament would flow from each.

Thus, it is due to the pain coming from such meetings and painful metaphorical loves that my heart cries out, like Abraham: "I love not those that set."

If you desire permanence in this transient world, permanence is born out of transience an annihilation. Annihilate your evil-commanding soul so that you may gain permanence.

Free yourself of bad morals, the basis of worldly adoration, and realize self-annihilation. Sacrifice in the sphere of your possession and control for the True Beloved' sake. See the end of beings, which marks extinction. For the way leading from this world to permanence passes through self-annihilation.

The human mind, absorbed in causality, laments the upheavals caused by the world's decay. The conscience, desiring true existence, wails like Abraham: "I love not those that set." It severs its connection with metaphorical beloveds and decaying beings, and attaches itself to the Truly Existent One, the Eternal Beloved.

O my base soul. This world and all beings are mortal. However, you can find two ways to the All-Permanent Being in each mortal thing, and discern two gleams or mysteries of the manifestations of the Undying Beloved's Grace—if you sacrifice your mortal being.

The act of bestowing is discerned and the All-Merciful's favor is perceived in each bounty. If you discern this act through what is bestowed, you will find the All-Bestowing One. Each work of the Eternally Besought One points out the All-Majestic Maker's Names like a missive. If you understand the meaning through the inscription, the Names will lead you to the One called by those Names.[75] Since it is possible to find the kernel, the essence, of these transient things, obtain it. Discard their meaningless shells into the flood of mortality.

Every item that exists is a word of embodied meaning and shows many of the All-Majestic Maker's Names. Since beings are words of Divine Power, understand their meanings and place them in your heart. Fearlessly cast the letters left without meaning into the wind of transience and forget about them.

The worldly mind, preoccupied with appearances and whose capital consists only of knowledge of the material world, cries out in bewilderment and frustration, as its chains of thought end in nothingness and non-existence. It seeks a true way leading to truth. Since the spirit has withdrawn from what sets and is mortal and the heart has abandoned the deceiving beloveds, and since the conscience has turned away from transitory beings, you, my wretched soul, must seek help in: "I love not those that set," and be saved.

See how well Mawlana Jami', who was intoxicated with the "wine" of love as if created from love, expressed it in order to turn faces from multiplicity to unity—the parenthetical additions belong to me:

> Want only One (the rest are not worth wanting).
> Call One (the others do not come to your assistance).
> Seek One (the others are not worth seeking)
> See and follow One (the others are not seen all the time; they
> become invisible behind the veil of mortality)
> Know One (knowledge other than that does not add to
> your knowledge of Him is useless)
> Mention One (words not concerning Him may be regarded as useless).

O Jami', I admit that you spoke the truth. The True Beloved, True Sought One, True Desired One, and True Object of Worship is He alone. In the mighty circle of remembering and reciting God's Names, this universe and its inhabitants declare, in various tongues and tones: "There is no deity but God," and testify to Divine Oneness. It salves the wound caused by those that set, and points to the Undying Beloved.

---

[75] For example, through its coming into existence, beauty, shape, proportions, color, and the function it does, a flower displays the Divine Names the Maker, the All-Beautiful, the All-Shaping, the All-Just, the All-Coloring, and the All-Wise, respectively; and the Names point out the One Who has them. (Tr.)

(NOTE: About 25 years ago on Yuşa Tepesi in Beykoz, Istanbul, when I had decided to renounce the world, several important friends came to call me back to the world and my former position. I told them to leave me till the following morning so I could seek Divine guidance. That morning the following two "Tables," occurred to me. They resemble verse, but they are not. I have not changed them for the sake of that blessed memory. They are included here for they are appropriate.)

First table

(A depiction of the true spirit of the heedless people's world.)

Do not invite me to the world,
I came and found it evil and mortal.

Heedlessness was a veil;
I saw the light of truth concealed.

All things, the whole of creation—
I saw were mortal and full of harm.

Existence, indeed I put it on.
Alas! It was non-existence; I suffered much.

As for life, I experienced it;
I saw it was torment within torment.

Intellect became pure retribution;
I saw permanence to be tribulation.

Life was like a wind, it passed in whims;
I saw perfection to be pure loss.

Actions were only for show;
I saw ambition to be pure pain.

Union was in fact separation;
I saw the cure to be the ailment.

These lights became darkness;
I saw these friends to be orphans.

These voices were announcements of death;
I saw the living to be dead.

Knowledge changed into whim;
I saw in science thousands of ailments.

Pleasure became unmixed pain;
I saw existence to be compounded non-existence.

I have found the True Beloved;
Ah, I suffered much pain because of separation.

Second table

(This table describes the true spirit of the world of the people of guidance and peace.)

Heedlessness has disappeared;
I have seen the light of truth to be manifest.

Existence is a proof of Divine Being.
See, life is the mirror reflecting The Truth.

Intellect has become the key to treasuries.
See, mortality is the door to eternity.

The spark of self-attainment has died.
But see, there is the sun of grace and beauty.

Separation has become true union;
See, pain is pure pleasure.

Life has become pure action.
See, eternity is pure life.

Darkness is a thin membrane enclosing light.
See, there is true life in death.

All things have become familiar.
See, all sounds are the mentioning of God.

All the particles in creation:
See, each glorifies God and calls Him by His Names.

I have found poverty to be a treasury of wealth.
See, in impotence lies perfect power.

If you have found God,
See, all things are yours.

If you are a slave of the Owner of all things,
See His property is yours.

If you are egotist and claim self-ownership,
See, it is endless trial and tribulation.

It is infinite torment, taste it,
See, it is an unbearable calamity.

If you are truly a slave of God, devoted to Him,
See, it is an infinite delight.

Taste its uncountable rewards,
See the boundless bliss; experience it.

෨෨ ෧

(NOTE: After an afternoon Prayer during Ramadan 25 years ago, I recited 'Abdu'l-Qadir al-Jilani's composition of the Divine Names in verse. I wanted to write a supplication using the Divine Names, but could write only the following. I wanted to write a supplication similar to that of my blessed master. But alas, I have no ability to write in verse and so could not complete it. It is included here, for it is appropriate.)

He, the All-Permanent One

The Absolutely Wise in His decrees, we are under His decree;
He is the All-Wise and All-Just; His is the earth and the heavens.

The All-Knowing of the secrets and all that is hidden in His Kingdom;
He is the All-Powerful, the Self-Subsistent; His is all from the Supreme Throne to the ground.

The All-Subtle in skills and inscriptions in His making and artistry;
He is the All-Originating, the All-Loving; His is the beauty and the splendor.

The All-Majestic in His manifestations and acts in His creation;
He is the All-Sovereign, the All-Holy and Pure; His is the might and glory, and the grandeur.

The Originator of beings; we are among the inscriptions of His Art;
He is the All-Constant, the All-Permanent One; His is the dominion and permanence.

The All-Munificent Bestower of favors; we are among the caravans of His guests;
He is the All-Providing, the All-Sufficer; His is the praise and glorification.

The All-Beautiful Granter of gifts; we are among the weavings of His Knowledge;
He is the Creator, the All-Faithful; His is the generosity and the favoring.

The Hearer of the complaints and prayers from His creatures;
He is the All-Pitying, the All-Healing; His is the thanks and the praise.

The Forgiver of the faults and sins of His servants;
He is the All-Forgiving, the All-Compassionate; His is forgiveness and approval.

O my soul! Like my heart weep, cry out and say:

I am mortal, so I do not want the mortal.

I am impotent, so I do not desire the impotent.

I surrendered my spirit to the All-Merciful, so I desire none else.

I want only one who will remain my friend forever.

I am but an insignificant particle, but I desire an everlasting sun.

I am nothing in essence, but I wish for the whole of creation.

జ్ఞ ఆ

A fruit of the pine, cedar, juniper, and wild poplar trees in the uplands of Barla

During my exile, while watching from a mountain top the awe-inspiring forms of the pine, cedar, and juniper trees and the tremendous spectacle they made, a gentle breeze blew. The scene was transformed into a magnificent, delightful, and noisy display of dancing, a rapturous performance of praising and glorifying God. My enjoyment changed into watching for instruction and listening for wisdom. I recalled these Kurdish lines of Ahmed-i Jizri:

Everyone has hastened to gaze at Your Beauty;
they are putting on airs due to Your Beauty.

To express the meanings of the instruction it derived from the scene, my heart wept as follows:

O Lord, all living creatures hasten from everywhere to gaze on
You, on Your Beauty.

From every corner they emerge and look on the face of the earth,
which is a work of Your Art.

Emerging from above and below, they cry out like heralds.

Those herald-like trees dance in pleasure at the beauty of Your inscriptions.

Filled with delight at Your Art's perfection, they are joyful and
sing sweet melodies.

It is as if the sweetness of their melodies fills them with renewed
joy and makes them sway coyly.

At last they have started dancing and are seeking ecstasy.

It is through the work of Divine Mercy that all living creatures receive
instruction in the glorification and Prayer particular to each.

After receiving instruction, each tree stands on a high rock and raises its
head toward the Divine Throne.

Each, like Shahbaz-i Kalender,[76] stretches out hundreds of hands to the
Divine Court and assumes an imposing position of worship.

They make their twigs curl like dancing love-locks, and arouse fine
ardor and exalted pleasures in those who are watching.

As if the most sensitive strings were touched, they sing love songs at a
high pitch, and make even the dead hear their eternal tunes arising
from the sweet sorrow caused by touching.

A meaning comes to mind: They recall the weeping caused by the
painful fading of metaphorical love and deeply touching sighs.

They make audible the melancholy songs that lovers sing at their
beloveds' grave.

They seem to make the eternal tunes and sorrowful voices heard
by the dead, who no longer hear worldly voices and words.

The spirit understands from this that things respond with glorification to the manifestation of the Majestic Maker's Names; they
perform a graceful chant.

The heart reads the meaning of Divine Unity in this exalted,
miraculous spectacle from these trees, each of which is like an
embodied Qur'anic verse .

In other words, there is so wonderful an order, art, and wisdom
in their creation that if all "natural causes" were conscious agents
able to do whatever they wished, they could not imitate them
even if they joined all their forces.

On seeing this, the soul thinks that the earth is revolving in a
clamorous tumult of separation and seeks an enduring pleasure. It
has received the meaning: "You will find it by abandoning your
adoration of the world."

From such chanting of animals, plants, trees and air, the mind discerns a
most meaningful order of creation, inscriptions of wisdom, and treasury of
secret truths. It concludes that everything glorifies the All-Majestic Maker.

---

[76] Shahbaz-i Kalender: A famous hero who, through the guidance of 'Abdul-Qadir al-Jilani,
took refuge at the Divine Court and achieved the rank of sainthood.

The desirous soul receives such pleasure from the murmuring air and whispering leaves that it forgets mundane pleasures, the basis of its life, and seeks to realize self-annihilation in this pleasure of truth.

The imagination beholds the scene as if angels appointed for trees were embodied in each tree, from whose branches hang many flutes.

It is as though the Eternal Monarch clothed these angels in trees for a magnificent parade accompanied with the sounds of countless flutes. So the trees show themselves to be conscious and meaningful.

The flutes' tunes are pure and touching, as if issuing from an elevated heavenly orchestra.

The mind does not hear the sorrowful wails of separation that all lovers, including primarily Mawlana Jalalud-Din ar-Rumi, hear;

Rather, it hears the grateful thanks offered to the All-Living, Self-Subsistent One for His Mercy, and praises for His sustaining.

Since the trees are bodies and their leaves are tongues, a breeze makes each tree to recite with its thousands of tongues: "He, He (meaning God)." As the glorification and praise of their lives, they proclaim their Maker to be the All-Living and Self-Subsistent.

All things form a universal circle to proclaim God's Unity: "There is no deity but God," and perform their duties.

In the tongue of disposition, they often declare "O Ultimate Truth," and ask for their vital needs from His treasury of Mercy. Through the tongue of being favored with life, they continuously recite His Name: "O All-Living One."

O All-Living, O Self-Subsistent! For the sake of Your Names, the All-Living and Self-Subsistent, endow this wretched heart with life, and show this confused mind the right direction. Amin.

(NOTE: Once at night in a high spot on Çamdağı near Barla, I was looking at the heavens when the following lines suddenly occurred to me. I imagined I heard the stars' speaking in the tongue of their disposition. Since I do not know the rules of versification, I wrote them as they occurred to me.)

Discourse of the stars

Listen to the stars and heed their beautiful sermons.
See what Wisdom has written in these luminous missives of It.

They are all delivering this discourse with the tongue of truth:
"Each of us is a radiant proof for the majestic Sovereignty of an All-
Powerful One of Glory.

We are light-diffusing witnesses to the Existence of the Maker,
and also to His Unity and Power.

We are His subtle miracles gilding the face of the skies,
for the angels to make excursions on.

We are the innumerable discerning eyes of the heavens
directed to Paradise, and overseeing the earth.[77]

We are the exquisite fruits attached to the heavenly branch of the
Tree of Creation; and to the twigs of the Milky Way,
attached by the hand of wisdom of the All-Gracious One of Majesty.

For the inhabitants of the heavens, we are travelling mosques,
revolving houses and exalted homes,
light-diffusing lamps, mighty ships, and planes.

We are miracles of the Power of the All-Powerful One of
Perfection, the All-Wise One of Majesty.
Each of us is a wonder of His creative Art, a rarity of His
Wisdom, a marvel of His creation, a world of light.

To the people who are truly human, we present countless
proofs in countless tongues;
The eyes of the materialists, may they be blind, never see our faces,
nor do their ears hear our speech; we are signs that speak the truth.

On us is the same stamp and seal. We obey and glorify our Lord,
and mention Him in worship.
We are ecstatic lovers in the widest circle of the Milky Way,
the circle reciting our Lord's Names.

---

[77] It is as if the stars, which can be considered as the eyes of heavenly bodies, were watching the intricate works of creation on the earth and then turning toward Paradise to observe the permanent forms of those works, just as the angels observe the miracles of Divine Power exhibited on the earth, the land sown with the seeds of the flowers of Paradise.

The
Eighteenth Word

The Eighteenth Word

- ➤ *Putting the carnal self in its place*
- ➤ *Whatever God creates is good*
- ➤ *Love of God requires following the Prophet*

In the Name of God, the All-Merciful, the All-Compassionate.

Do not reckon those who rejoice in what they have thus contrived and love to be praised for what they have not achieved—do not reckon them secure from punishment; rather, there is a painful punishment for them. (3:188)

Three points

FIRST POINT: A CHASTENING SLAP FOR MY EVIL-COMMANDING soul. O foolish soul delighted with self-pride, enamored with fame, fond of praise, and peerless in egotism. If it is a just claim that a tiny seed is the agent of all the fruit on a fig tree, or it is a dry branch of the vine which produces bunches of grapes on it, and that those who benefit from them must respect and praise the branch and the seed, you might have the right to be proud and conceited about the gifts given to you. But in reality, you deserve only to be chided constantly because you are not like the seed and the branch even. Since you have free will, you reduce these gifts' value through your pride, damage them through your conceit, nullify them through your ingratitude, and usurp them by appropriating them to yourself. Your duty is being thankful to God, instead of taking pride in yourself. What is fit for you is not fame, but humility and feeling shame (for your deficiencies). Your right is not praise, but repentance and seeking forgiveness, and your perfection lies not in self-centeredness but in attributing every good to God.

O my soul, you in my body resemble nature in the world. Both of you were created to receive good and be the thing to which evil is referred. You are not the agent and the origin, but rather the recipient and the means, the ground or the scene. You are effective only when you cause an evil by refusing to accept the good coming from the Absolute Good. You and natural causes were created as veils, so that apparently ugly things, the beauty of which is not visible, should be attributed to you, and so that you should be the means of the All-Holy Divine Essence being acknowledged as free of defect. But you have assumed an attitude completely contrary to your duty of creation. Although due to your incapacity you to change good into evil, you act as though you were a partner to your Creator. That means those who so adore themselves and nature are extremely foolish and serious wrongdoers.

Do not say: "I am an object of manifestation. One who receives and manifests beauty becomes beautiful." For that beauty has not assumed a perpetual form in you, and so you can reflect it for only a short time. Do not say: "Among people, I was chosen. All of these results, all the works I have produced, are shown through me. That means I have some merit." No! Rather, they were given to you first because you are more bankrupt and needy of them, and more afflicted with shortcomings, than anyone else.

SECOND POINT: This point explains one meaning of: *(He) who makes excellent everything that He creates* (32:7). Even the things that appear to be the ugliest included, everything has an aspect of true beauty, and is either beautiful in itself (beautiful by itself) or beautiful on account of its results (beautiful through others). Some occurrences are apparently ugly and confused but, beneath that apparent veil, there are most radiant instances of beauty and order.

For example, beneath the veil of spring's stormy rains and muddy soil are smiles of innumerable beautiful flowers and well-ordered plants. Behind the veils of autumn's harsh destruction and mournful separations are amiable small animals (friends of delicate, shy flowers) being discharged from their duties and preserved from winter's blows and torments, which manifest instances of Divine Majesty. Under the veil of winter, the way is prepared for a new and beautiful spring. Beneath the veil of storms, earthquakes, plagues, and similar events are numerous hidden "immaterial flowers" that unfold. Seeds of many potentialities that have remained undeveloped sprout and flourish due to such apparently ugly events. It is as if upheavals, revolutions, and general changes function as "immaterial" rain.

However, being superficial and self-centered observers inclined to judge by outward appearances, we consider only the external and consider such events ugly, reason according to the result we desire and so consider them evil. But in reality, if one of the aims in things and events relates to us, many others are directly connected with their Maker's Names. For example, we may consider thorny plants and trees harmful and meaningless, even though these great miracles of the Creator's Power are "well-equipped, heroic guards" of plants and trees. God's causing hawks to harry sparrows is apparently incompatible with Mercy. But such things cause sparrows to develop their potentialities. We might consider snow to be cold and unpleasant, but under those veils are such warm purposes and sweet results that they are indescribable.

As our judgments are based on outward appearance and our own interest, we suppose that many things that are perfectly polite and compatible with well-mannered behavior are contrary to good manners. For example, in our view, the discussion of our private parts is shameful. But this veil of shame only relates to us. Whereas from the perspectives of creation, art, and their aims and purposes, and when considered with the eye of wisdom, they are perfectly correct. Some expressions of the Qur'an, the source of good manners and right conduct, should be viewed from these perspectives. Likewise, beneath the faces of apparently ugly and useless creatures and events are many beautiful and purposeful instances of art, as well as aspects of beauty concerning their creation. They are connected with their Maker. Many beautiful veils which conceal instances of wisdom, and many apparent instances of disorder and confusion are, in reality, the most well-arranged examples of sacred Divine composition.

THIRD POINT: "*If you love God, follow me so that God may love you* (3:31)." Since the universe contains an observable beauty of art, it certainly requires Muhammad's Messengership, for such beauty demonstrates that its Fashioner wills to make beautiful and to adorn. This shows that the Maker has a sublime love and sacred inclination toward the perfections of His Art He displays in His creatures. This love and inclination must primarily be directed toward and concentrated on humanity, the most enlightened and perfect being, the conscious fruit of the Tree of Creation. A tree's fruit is its most comprehensive and furthest part. The person with the most comprehensive view and universal consciousness can be a most elevated and brilliant individual. Such a person will meet with and be addressed by the All-Beautiful Maker, and will use his universal consciousness and comprehensive view to worship his Maker, appreciate His Art, and give thanks for His bounties.

Here two spheres appear. One is a most magnificent sphere of Lordship and a most finely fashioned, bejeweled tablet of Art. The other is a most enlightened and "flower-adorned" sphere of worshipful servanthood, and the broadest and most comprehensive tablet of reflection, appreciation, thankfulness, and belief. This second sphere acts with all its strength in the name of the first sphere. See how closely this second sphere's leader—Prophet Muhammad—is connected with the Maker, how he serves the purposes of the Maker's artistry, and how beloved and esteemed He is in His eyes.

Could the Bounteous Fashioner of these fine creatures, Who loves His Art and even considers all the tastes of their mouths, remain indifferent to His most beautiful creature? This most beautiful being, who through his worship in an outpouring of appreciation and admiration causes the Divine Throne and the earth to reverberate and, in a chant of thanks and exaltation, brings the land and the sea to ecstasy, is constantly turned toward Him. Would He not speak to him and want to make him His Messenger, to be imitated by others in his praiseworthy conduct? It is impossible that He would not speak to him and not make him His Messenger.

Surely, the religion with God is Islam. (3:19)

Muhammad is the Messenger of God. Those who are with him... (48:29)

ॐ ॐ

Tears of a weeping soul at daybreak far from home

The breeze of Divine manifestations blows at daybreak;
Wake up, O my eyes, at daybreak.
Seek help from the Court of God.
Dawn is the time when the sinful seek forgiveness.
Awake, O my heart, at daybreak,
Repent and seek forgiveness from the Court of God.

Daybreak is a kind of resurrection. Every being is awake and glorifying God. When, O my foolish soul, will you awake from the sleep of heedlessness? You are in the afternoon period of your life and heading for the grave. Perform the prescribed Prayer and supplicate to Him like a plaintive flute, saying: "O Lord. I repent and am ashamed of my innumerable sins. I am wretched and abased, tearful and restless with life. I am exiled and lonely, weak and impotent, old and ill, and I have no choices at all. I beg for Your Mercy and forgiveness, and cry for help from Your Court, O God."

The
Nineteenth Word

The Nineteenth Word

Muhammad's Messengership and his matchless character

In the Name of God, the All-Merciful, the All-Compassionate.

I have not praised Muhammad with my words;
Rather, my words are praiseworthy because of him.

This Word consists of 14 droplets. It is the attributes of Prophet Muhammad, upon him be peace and blessings, which have made this Word beautiful.

Fourteen droplets

 IRST DROPLET: THREE GREAT AND UNIVERSAL THINGS MAKE OUR Lord known to us: the Book of the Universe (explained elsewhere); Prophet Muhammad, upon him be peace and blessings, the Seal of the Prophets, who is the supreme sign in the Book of the Universe; and the glorious Qur'an. Now we must recognize and listen to the Seal of the Prophets, the second and articulate proof and announcer of God with all His Names and Attributes, His Existence and Unity.

Look at the universal personality of that proof: the earth's face is his mosque, Makka his *mihrab* (niche where he leads his community in the Prayer), and Madina his pulpit. Our Prophet, this illustrious proof, leads all believers and preaches to all people. He is the chief of Prophets, lord of saints, and leader in the remembrance of God of a circle comprising all Prophets and saints. With all Prophets as its roots and saints as its ever-fresh fruits, he is a radiant tree. All Prophets, with the support of their miracles, and all saints, depending on their wonders, confirm and corroborate his claims. For he declares: "There is no deity but God"; and all those illustrious ones forming the universal circle of God's remembrance and lined up in the past and the future repeat the same words in unison, as if to say: "You speak the truth." What illusion can dispute such an argument confirmed by such countless endorsements?

SECOND DROPLET: Just as this radiant proof of Divine Unity is affirmed by the unanimous consensus of all Prophets and saints, he is confirmed by hundreds of predictions in the revealed Scriptures (e.g., the Torah and the Gospels), thousands of indications of his Prophethood that appeared before his mission, famous reports of voices from the Unseen, the unanimous testimony of soothsayers, his hundreds of miracles (e.g., splitting the moon), and the truth of his Shari'a (the Law). Similarly, his laudable virtues that reached the utmost degree of perfection; his total confidence in his mission and most excellent qualities in relation to its fulfillment; and his extraordinary awe and consciousness of God, and his matchless worship, serenity, and firmness, all of which show his belief's strength and his total certainty and complete steadfastness. All of these show as clearly as daylight the truth of his claim and his utmost truthfulness in his cause.

THIRD DROPLET: Let's imagine that we visit him in the Arabian peninsula while he is performing his mission during the Age of Bliss. We see a person distinguished by the excellence of his character and beauty of his form. In his hand is a miraculous book, and on his tongue a truthful discourse. He is delivering an eternal sermon to humanity, jinn, and angels—indeed, to all beings. He solves and expounds the mystery of the world's creation; discovers and solves the intricate talisman that is the mystery of the universe; and provides convincing and satisfying answers to life's great and important questions: Who are you? What is your purpose? Where have you come from? Where are you going? What is your final destination?

FOURTH DROPLET: See! He spreads such a light of truth that, if you look at the universe without the light of his guidance, you see it as a place of general mourning, and beings as alien or even hostile to each other, and inanimate beings as ghastly corpses, and living creatures as orphans weeping under the blows of death and separation. Now see how through the light he spreads, this place of universal mourning has been transformed into a place of invocation where God's Names and praises are recited in joy and ecstasy. Alien and hostile beings have become friends, as well as brothers and sisters, and dumb, inanimate creatures familiar, obedient officials and docile servants. Weeping, complaining orphans are seen reciting God's Names and praises or offering thanks for being discharged from their duties.

FIFTH DROPLET: Through this light, all motions, variations, changes and transformations in the universe are no longer regarded as meaningless and futile playthings of chance; rather, they appear in their true form and function. Each is a missive of the universe's Master, a page inscribed with creation's signs, a mirror reflecting God's Names. The world itself is a book of the Eternally Besought One's Wisdom.

Without this light, humanity's boundless weakness and helplessness, poverty and neediness cause everyone to fall lower than the animals. Their intellects, by conveying grief, sorrow, and anxiety, make them more wretched. But when they are illumined with this light, they rise above all animals and creatures. Once their intellects are illumined, their poverty and helplessness become means of infinite wealth and power through dependence on God. Through entreaty, they become beloved "kings and queens" and, through complaints and petitions, God's favored servants entrusted with the honorable duty of improving the earth and ruling it in His name. If this light did not exist, the universe, humanity, and all things would be reduced to nothingness. Indeed, if such a person did not exist in such a wonderful universe, the universe's existence would not be necessary.

SIXTH DROPLET: That illustrious person announces and brings tidings of eternal happiness, unveils and proclaims God's infinite Mercy, observes and heralds the beauties of the Realm of the Lord's Sovereignty, and discloses and shows the Divine Names' treasuries. If you observe him as a devoted worshipper of God, you will see him to be a model of love, an embodiment of mercy, the pride of humanity, and the most illustrious fruit of the Tree of Creation. If you observe him as a Messenger, you will see him to be a proof of God, a lamp of truth, a sun of guidance, and the means of happiness. See how his light has lit up from east to west like dazzling lightning, and half of the globe and one-fifth of humanity have accepted the gift of his guidance and preserved it like their lives. So, why do our evil-commanding souls and devils not accept, with all its degrees, the essence of his mission: There is no deity but God?

SEVENTH DROPLET: Consider how he quickly eradicated his people's fanatic attachment to their evil and savage customs and immoral qualities, and how he equipped and adorned those disparate, wild, and unyielding peoples of the peninsula with all praiseworthy virtues, making them teachers and masters of the world, especially to the civilized nations. See, it was not an outward domination; rather, he conquered and subjugated minds, spirits, hearts, and souls. He became the beloved of hearts, the teacher of minds, the trainer of souls, and the ruler of spirits.

EIGHTH DROPLET: You know that a small habit like smoking in a small community can be removed permanently only by a powerful government and with great effort. But look! This person quickly removed numerous ingrained habits from large obsessed communities with little outward power and effort. In their place, he implanted and inculcated exalted qualities that became inherent in their being. Many more such miraculous accomplishments can be credited to him. To those who refuse to see the testimony of this blessed age, let them go to the present "civilized" Arabian peninsula with hundreds of philosophers, sociologists, psychologists and pedagogues, and strive for a hundred years. Would they be able to achieve in that period even one hundredth of what he achieved in a year?

NINTH DROPLET: An insignificant person in a small group cannot tell a small but shameful lie in an insignificant disputed matter without showing anxiety and disquiet enough for his or her enemies to remain unaware of it. Now consider this person. Under a supreme mission and a tremendous task, he was addressing the whole humanity and history. Threatened from all sides, he was in dire need of security. Then, can any contradiction be found in what he speaks fearlessly, with great ease and freedom, without hesitation or anxiety, with pure sincerity, great seriousness, and in an intense, elevated manner that irritates his enemies? Can there be any deception here? *What he speaks is nothing but Revelation revealed to him* (53:4). The truth cannot be deceptive, and one who sees it cannot be deceived. His path, which is pure truth, is free of deception. How could a fancy appear to one who sees the truth to be the truth, and deceive him?

TENTH DROPLET: See what curiosity-arousing, attractive, necessary, and awesome truths he shows and what matters he proves. You know that what incites people most is curiosity. Suppose someone told you: "If you give half of your life and property, someone will come from Mars or Jupiter to tell you about them, your future, and what will happen to you." If you have any curiosity at all, you would give them. But this person talks of a Monarch in

Whose realm the moon flies round a moth like a fly, the moth (the earth) flutters round a lamp, and the lamp (the sun) is merely one of thousands of lamps in one of thousands of guest-houses belonging to that Monarch. He also speaks truly of so wonderful a world and predicts such a revolution that if the earth was a bomb and exploded, it would not be all that strange.

Listen to the *suras* he recites, which begin with: *When the sun is folded up* (81:1), *When the heaven is cleft open* (82:1), and *The sudden, mighty strike* (101:1). Furthermore, he speaks truly of such a future that the future in this world is, in relation to it, like a trifling mirage. He informs us most solemnly of such happiness that all worldly happiness is like a flash of lightning in comparison to an eternal sun.

ELEVENTH DROPLET: Extraordinary wonders await us under the apparent veil of this wondrous and perplexing universe. So we need a wonderful and miracle-working being to communicate and explain these wonders to us. It is apparent from this person's conduct that he has seen and sees them, and tells us what he sees, and teaches us accurately what the One God of those heavens and the earth, Who nourishes us with His bounties, wants of us and what pleases Him. While we should therefore put everything else aside and run to this person who instructs us in such matters, what ails most people that they are so deaf, blind, and mad that they do not see, hear, or understand this truth?

TWELFTH DROPLET: As well as being an articulate proof, so true evidence of the Oneness of the Creator of all beings as the truth of His Oneness, this person is a decisive and clear proof of the resurrection of the dead and eternal happiness. Just as through his guidance he is the reason for eternal happiness coming about and the means of gaining it, so through his prayers and supplications he is the cause of its existence and the means of its creation.

See! He is making his petition during such a supreme, comprehensive Prayer (*Salah*) that it is as if the whole Arabian peninsula, even the whole the earth, joins in the service and, via his sublime prayer, makes its petitions. He is entreating amid so vast a congregation that it is as if all illustrious people of perfection, regardless of time, are following him and saying "Amin" to his supplications. He is imploring on behalf of so universal a need that not only the earth's inhabitants, but also those of the heavens and all beings, join his prayer and declare: "Yes, O Master, grant this, for we also desire it." He supplicates so needily and so touchingly, in such a loving, longing, and entreating fashion, that he brings the whole universe to tears and causes it to join in his prayer.

He also prays for such a goal and purpose that it elevates humanity and the world, even all of creation, from the lowest depth, humiliation, worthlessness, and uselessness to the highest rank of having value, permanence, and sublime duties. In a manner so elevated and help-seeking, so sweet and mercy-imploring, does he make his supplication and petition that it is as if all beings, the heavens, and the Divine Supreme Throne hear, and entering a state of ecstasy, are made to exclaim: "Amin, O God, Amin!"

See! He begs his needs from so Powerful a Being, All-Hearing and All-Generous, from so All-Knowing a Being, All-Seeing and All-Merciful, that He sees the most hidden living being's most secret need, and hears and accepts its pleas, and has mercy on that being. He provides its need, even though this being asks for it via the tongue of its particular disposition, and He gives it in so wise, seeing, and compassionate a form that it leaves no doubt that this provision and arrangement pertain only to an All-Hearing and All-Seeing One, One Most Generous and Most Merciful.

THIRTEENTH DROPLET: What does he want, this pride of humanity, this unique being and glory of all beings, who, standing on the earth with all eminent people behind him and with hands upraised, prays so intently? Listen. He is seeking eternal happiness and eternal life, to meet with God and enter Paradise. He wants all these through all the Sacred Divine Names, Which display their beauty and operations in the mirrors of all beings.

Even, were it not for the innumerable causes such as Mercy, Grace, Wisdom, and Justice for the fulfillment of that request, one of his prayers would have sufficed for building Paradise, which is as easy for Divine Power as creating spring. Just as his Messengership was the cause for opening this place of trial, so too his worship and servanthood to God is the cause for opening the next world.

Would the universe's perfect order, which causes the wise and reflective to say [to express the perfection and beauty of the universe]: "It is not possible for the universe to be more original and wonderful than it is," as well as the flawless beauty of art contained in His Mercy and the matchless beauty of His Lordship, —would these allow the ugliness, mercilessness, and disorder that the Owner of this order, beauty and mercy, Who hears and responds to the least significant, the least important desires and voices, refuses the most important and most necessary desires? God forbid! Such a beauty and mercy would not allow such an ugliness and themselves become ugly.

So, my friend, that is enough for now. Even if we stayed there for a hundred years, we would not comprehend fully even one-hundredth of this person's marvelous and remarkable acts, and never tire of watching him. So, let's look at each century during our return. See how each has bloomed fully via the flow of light it received from that Sun of Guidance. Each one has yielded thousands of such illustrious fruits as Abu Hanifa, ash-Shafi'i, Bayazid al-Bistami, 'Abdul-Qadir al-Jilani, Shah Naqshband, Imam Ghazzali, and Imam Rabbani. Postponing the details of our observations, we should invoke blessings on that worker of miracles and bringer of guidance, which refer to some of his certain miracles:

> Upon him who was sent the Wise Criterion of Truth (the Qur'an) by the All-Merciful and All-Compassionate One, from the Supreme Throne—our master Muhammad—upon him be peace and blessings thousands and thousands of times, to the number of the good deeds of his Community.
>
> Upon him whose Messengership was foretold by the Torah, the Gospels, and the Psalms; whose Prophethood was predicted by wonderful signs that appeared prior to his Prophethood, by the voices of jinn, saints, and soothsayers; and at whose gesture the moon split—our master Muhammad—peace and blessings thousands and thousands of times, to the number of the breaths of his Community.
>
> Upon him at whose beckoning came the trees; by whose prayer rain fell swiftly; whom the cloud shaded from the heat; with a dish of whose food hundreds of people were satisfied; from whose fingers water three times flowed out like the Spring of Kawthar; and to whom God made speak the lizard, gazelle, wolf, camel, mountain, rock, pole, and clod of soil; the one who made the Ascension (Mi'raj) and "whose eye did not waver"—our master and intercessor Muhammad—upon him be peace and blessings thousands and thousands of times, to the number of the letters (of the Qur'an) formed in the words represented with the All-Merciful's permission in the mirrors of the airwaves at the reciting of all the Qur'an's words by all reciters from the beginning of Revelation until the end of time. Forgive us and have mercy upon us, O God, for the sake of each of those blessings. Amin.

FOURTEENTH DROPLET: The wise Qur'an, the treasury of miracles and itself a supreme miracle, proves his Prophethood and God's Oneness so decisively that there is no need for further proof. Now we will give its definition and refer to one or two lights of its miraculousness that have been criticized.

The wise Qur'an, which makes our Master known to us, is the eternal translator of the great Book of the Universe; the discloser of the treasuries of the Divine Names hidden in the pages of the earth and the heavens; the key to the truths lying behind events; the treasury of the All-Merciful's favors and the eternal addresses coming from the Unseen beyond the veil of this visible world; the sun of Islam's spiritual and intellectual world, as well as its foundation and plan, and the map of the worlds of the Hereafter; the distinct expounder, lucid interpreter, articulate proof, and clear translator of Divine Essence, Attributes and essential Qualities; the educator, true wisdom, guide, and leader of the world of humanity; it is both a book of wisdom and law, and a book of prayer and worship, and a book of command and call to God, and a book of invocation and knowledge of God. It contains books for all of humanity's spiritual needs, and is like a sacred library offering booklets from which all saints, eminently truthful people, and all purified and discerning scholars have derived their own specific ways.

Consider the light of miraculousness in its reiterations, which are imagined to be a fault. Since the Qur'an is a book of invocation and prayer, a book of calls or invitations [to accept its eternal truths and gain eternal happiness], reiteration is a desirable and most necessary and beautiful instance of eloquence. The invocation of God requires reiteration to impress and enlighten hearts. Through repetition, prayer acquires and gives strength to hearts, and becomes ingrained therein. Commands and calls need restatement to be confirmed and enforced.

Not everyone can read the whole Qur'an whenever they want; usually they can read only one *sura* (chapter). This is why its most important purposes are reiterated in most of the longer chapters, each of which thereby can serve as a small Qur'an. Certain purposes and themes like Divine Unity, Resurrection, and the story of Moses are repeated so that no one is deprived of their benefits. Also, spiritual tastes and needs vary like bodily ones. We need some of them at every breath. Just as the body needs air, the spirit needs *Hu–Huwa* (He–God). We need some others every hour, like *Bismillah* (In the Name of God). And so on. The reiteration of verses therefore arises from the recurrence of needs. The Qur'an reiterates to point out those needs, to make them deeply felt, and to stir our desire to satisfy them.

Furthermore, in its role as a founder, the Qur'an is the basis of a manifest religion and the foundation of the Islamic world. It came to change human social life and answer the recurring questions and needs of various classes of human society. A founder uses repetition to affirm, and reiteration to emphasize. A new establishment requires confirmation and strengthening, and therefore repetition.

The Qur'an speaks of such important matters and subtle truths that reiteration in different contexts is necessary to impress their different aspects on people's minds and hearts. However, such repetitions are merely apparent, for in reality each verse has manifold meanings, numerous benefits, and many aspects and levels. In each place, the words or verses occur in a different way and context, for a different meaning, purpose, and benefit.

Also, the Qur'an mentions certain cosmological matters in a concise, allusive way. This method cannot be criticized, for it is another light of its miraculousness in its role as the guide of humanity.

Question: Why does the Qur'an not speak of beings in the same way as science and materialistic or naturalistic philosophy? It mentions some matters briefly, and others in an apparently simple and superficial way that everyone can understand them easily.

Answer: Scientism and materialistic philosophy have strayed from the path of truth. As the Qur'an is not a science book, why should it elaborate on cosmological matters? It mentions certain facts of creation to make known the Divine Essence, Attributes, and Names. It explains the meaning of the Book of the Universe to make known its Creator. Therefore it considers creation not for its own sake but for the sake of knowledge of its Creator. Science, which considers creation only for its own sake, usually addresses scientists. The Qur'an, however, addresses all humanity. Since it uses creation as evidence and proof to guide humanity, most of whom are common people, its evidence should be easily understandable. Guidance requires that unimportant things only be touched upon, and that subtle points be made understandable via parables. So as not to mislead people, it should not change what they consider obvious so that such information becomes useless or harmful.

For example, the Qur'an calls the sun "a moving lamp." It does not mention the sun for its own sake but because it is the "mainstay" of the order and the center of the universe's system, and order and system are two ways of learning about the Creator. By saying: *And the sun runs its course* (36:38), it suggests the well-ordered disposition of Divine Power in the revolutions of the seasons, day and night, and so implies the Maker's majesty. Whatever the reality of this *running* is does not harm the intended meaning, which is the observed order woven into the universe's structure.

The Qur'an also says: *And He has made the sun as a lamp* (71:16). By depicting the sun as a lamp, the Qur'an reminds people that the world is like a palace the contents of which are decorations, provisions, and other necessities prepared for humanity and other living creatures, with the sun being a lamp to illuminate it. Thus, it implies the Creator's Mercy and Bounty.

Now consider how science and materialistic philosophy deal with the sun: "The sun is an enormous mass of burning gases. It causes the planets, which have been flung off from it, to revolve around it. It is of such and such size and is of such and such qualities..." Such a description gives no perfection of knowledge to the spirit, but only a terrible dread and bewilderment. It also approaches the matter in a way different from that of the Qur'an.

From this comparison, you can judge the value of the merely scientific and philosophical way of thinking, which is outwardly splendid but inwardly hollow. So do not be taken in by the outward worth of scientific descriptions and disrespect the most miraculous style of the Qur'an.

> O God! Make of the Qur'an for us and for all who copy it a cure for all our sickness, a companion to us and to them in life and after death, a friend in the world, an intimate one in the grave, an intercessor on the Day of Judgment, a light on the (Bridge of) *Sirat*, a veil and a screen from Hellfire, a friend in Paradise, and a guide and a leader to all good deeds, by Your Grace, Generosity, Munificence, and Mercy, O Most Munificent of the Munificent and Most Merciful of the Merciful. Amin.
>
> O God! Bestow blessings and peace on him to whom You sent the wise Qur'an, the Criterion of Truth and Falsehood, and on all his Family and Companions. Amin.

The
Twentieth Word

The Twentieth Word

The Qur'an's miraculous eloquence and its references to modern scientific developments

Two stations

In the Name of God, the All-Merciful, the All-Compassionate.

IRST STATION: CONSIDER THE FOLLOWING VERSES:

When We said unto the angels: "Prostrate before Adam," they fell prostrate, but Iblis did not (though he received the same order). (2:34)

God commands you to sacrifice a cow. (2:67)

Yet after all this your hearts were hardened and become like rocks or even harder. (2:74)

Once, Satan suggested three things about these verses:

You say that the Qur'an is a miracle of infinite eloquence and guidance for everyone forever. So why does it persistently repeat, in a sort of historical manner, certain insignificant events like slaughtering a cow and even naming the longest *sura* (*al-Baqara* means "The Cow") after that event? Also, the angels' prostrating before Adam is a matter of the Unseen and reason cannot comprehend it. It may be accepted and affirmed only after one has attained a strong belief, and yet the Qur'an addresses all those who have reason or intellect and frequently warns: 'Will they not reason and understand?' Additionally, what kind of guidance is intended by describing so forcefully certain natural conditions of rocks that are only results of chance?

The following points occurred to me.

FIRST POINT: The wise Qur'an contains many particular events, each of which hides a universal principle and presents the tip of a general law. For example: *(He) taught Adam the names of all of them* (2:31) states that Adam was taught "the names" as a miracle to show his superiority over the angels in being favored with ruling the earth in God's name. Although this seems a small and particular event, it constitutes a tip of the following universal principle: Due to its comprehensive nature, humanity was taught (or given the potential to obtain) a great deal of information, many sciences concerning all aspects of the universe, and vast knowledge about the Creator's essential Qualities, Attributes and acts. All of this made humanity superior to the angels, the heavens, the earth, and the mountains, for only humanity could bear the Supreme Trust. It also made humanity the earth's ruler in God's name.

Likewise, the angels' prostration before Adam, in contrast with Satan's rejection, is a small, particular event in the Unseen. However, it is the tip of a most comprehensive and universally observed principle and suggests a most extensive truth: By mentioning their obedience and submission and Satan's haughty refusal, the Qur'an shows that most material beings in the universe and their spiritual representatives are subjugated to us and ever-ready to satisfy our needs and desires. In addition, it warns us about how terrible enemies and great obstacles on our path of progress toward perfection are evil beings and their immaterial representatives, as well as the earth's devilish inhabitants who corrupt our potential for perfection and seduce us into wrong paths. Thus, while narrating a particular event pertaining to a single individual (Adam), the Qur'an of miraculous exposition holds an elevated discourse with all creation and humanity.

SECOND POINT: Although part of the Sahara desert, the bounteous gifts of the blessed Nile have made Egypt a fertile, arable land. Such a blessed, paradise-like land being adjacent to the hellish Sahara caused farming and agriculture to be so established in the Egyptians' very nature that agriculture became sanctified and cows and bulls became objects of worship. In fact, the Egyptians of Prophet Moses' time actually worshipped cows and bulls, as can be seen by the Jews making a calf to worship years after the Exodus. The wise Qur'an explains by the account of a cow being slaughtered that through his Messengership, Prophet Moses, upon him be peace, eradicated this ingrained concept. Thus this apparently insignificant event points to a universal principle with an elevated miraculousness, and expounds upon it as a most essential lesson of wisdom for everyone at all times.

By analogy, certain minor incidents mentioned in the Qur'an as historical events are tips of universal principles. In *Lema'at*, under the title of "Gleams of miraculousness in the repetition of the story of Prophet Moses in the Qur'an" I used, as examples, the seven sentences of Moses' story to explain how each part of those particular sentences contains a significant universal principle.

THIRD POINT: Consider the following verse:

> Yet after all this your hearts were hardened and became like rocks, or even harder: For there are rocks from which rivers gush, and some from which, when they are cleft, water issues; and some which fall down for awe of God. God is not unaware of what you do. (2:74)

While reciting this verse, Satan the deceitful asked: "Why are certain natural conditions of rocks, which are known to everyone, mentioned as if they were among the most important issues?" In response, the following point issued from the enlightenment of the Qur'an: It is appropriate to do so, and there is a need for it. For it contains a profound truth, which has been simplified and summarized through the Qur'an's miraculous conciseness and bounty of guidance and enlightenment.

Conciseness is a foundation of the Qur'an's miraculousness, and bountiful enlightenment and beauty of explanation are parts of its guidance. These qualities require that universal truths and profound yet general principles be presented in simple terms to the broad masses that make up the majority of the Qur'an's audience. As most people are not deep thinkers, it requires that only their tips and simple forms should be shown. Also all events, each a Divine operation whose extraordinary character is veiled by familiarity, should be pointed out briefly.

Thus, because of this subtle reality, the Qur'an says in this verse:

> O Children of Israel and children of Adam! What has happened to you that your hearts have become harder and more lifeless than rocks? Look at those very hard, lifeless, large rocks formed in vast underground strata. See how obedient and submissive they are to Divine commands, how permeable and open they are to His Lordship's acts. This is so clear that the ease with which the Divine operations form trees can be seen with the same ease, order, and perfect wisdom underground. Water flows in well-arranged water chan-

nels and veins through those hard, deaf rocks without resistance, just like blood circulating in veins.[78] Just as tree and plant branches spread easily in the air, the roots' delicate veins spread underground with the same ease and lack of resistance from rocks.

The Qur'an points to this and teaches a comprehensive truth through that verse, and so by allusion says to the hard-hearted:

> O Children of Israel and children of Adam! You are weak and impotent, and yet you can make your hearts so hard that they resist the Divine Being's commands. Whereas huge strata of hard rocks perform their subtle tasks perfectly in darkness and in total submission to His commands. They act as a source of water and other means of life for all living creatures in such a way, and as means for their division and distribution with such wisdom and justice, that they are as malleable as wax or even air in the hand of Power of the All-Wise One of Majesty. Without resistance, they prostrate before His Power's vastness, for almost the same well-arranged occurrences and wise and gracious Divine operations that we see above ground take place underground.
>
> Moreover, Divine wisdom and favor are manifested there in a more wonderful and more wondrous manner than they are above ground. Consider how soft the hardest and most unfeeling huge rocks are toward God's commands and laws of creation and administration, and how unresisting and flexible they are to the pleasant waters, delicate roots, and silk-like veins that act according to His command. Like a lover, the rock smashes its heart at the touch of those delicate, beautiful things and becomes soft soil in their path.

Also, through the sentence in the verse *and there are some which fall down for awe of God*, the Qur'an displays the tip of a tremendous truth: When Prophet Moses, upon him be peace, asked for a vision of God while standing at the foot of a mountain, the mountain crumbled at the Divine manifestation and its rocks were scattered. Like this, through Divine Majesty's awesome manifestations like earthquakes and similar geological

---

[78] It is only fitting that the Qur'an should explain the three important tasks that the All-Majestic Creator entrusted to rock strata, the foundation of the magnificent, moving palace that we call the earth. The first task: Just as the earth acts, by the Lord's Power, as a "mother" to plants and raises them, so by the Divine Power do the rocks act as a "nurse" to the earth and "raise" it. The second task: They serve the orderly circulation of water in the earth's body, like the circulation of blood [in our bodies]. The third task: They act as a "treasurer" to the appearance and continuation, with well-ordered balance, of springs and rivers, sources and streams. Rocks "write" and scatter over the earth's face "evidences" of Divine Unity that they cause to flow, with all their strength, in "mouthfuls" in the form of water, which serves life.

events, rocks fall from summits, which are usually like huge monoliths formed of thickened fluid, and are shattered. Some of these crumble and become soil for the growth of plants; others remain as rocks and are scattered down to the valleys and plains.

They serve many purposes for the earth's inhabitants, as in their houses. In utter submission to Divine Power and Wisdom, and for certain hidden purposes and benefits, they stand ready to be used in accordance with the principles of Divine Wisdom. Not in vain, or because of accident or random chance, do they leave their positions at the summit out of awe of God and choose the lower places in humility, becoming the means of those significant benefits. Rather, such events occur by an All-Wise and All-Powerful One's wise operation, and there is a wise order in such seemingly chaotic events invisible to the superficial eye. This is demonstrated by the purposes and benefits for which these rocks are made to serve, as well as by the perfect order and fine artistry in the "garments" adorned and embossed with the jewels of fruits and flowers with which the "body" of the mountains down which they roll are clothed.

Thus, you have seen the value of the verse's three parts from the viewpoint of wisdom. See the Qur'an's fine manner of expression and miraculous eloquence, how through those three well-known and observed events mentioned in the three parts of a single verse, it shows the tips of the comprehensive and significant truths discussed above. Also, by reminding in the same three parts of three further events, each of which is a means of taking a lesson, it offers a fine guidance and restrains in a way that cannot be resisted.

For example, the verse's second part says: *and there are some from which, when they are cleft, water issues.* By referring to the rock cleft with "complete eagerness" when Prophet Moses struck it with his staff, and the subsequent pouring forth of twelve streams from twelve sources, it means:

> O Children of Israel! Large rocks soften and smash in the face of a single miracle of Moses. While they become tears out of awe or joy, how can you be so unjust and merciless as to remain obstinate and tearless when confronted with all of Moses' miracles? Are your eyes so dried and your hearts so hard?

In the third part, it says: *and there are some which fall down for awe of God.* By recalling the well-known event of the mountain crumbling and the rocks rolling down out of awe at the manifestation of Divine Majesty, which took place at Mount Sinai when Moses, upon him be peace, supplicated for a vision of God, it gives the following lesson:

> O People of Moses! You do not fear God, yet mountains formed of rocks crumble in awe of Him. You witness that He held Mount Sinai above you to receive your solemn promise of loyalty to Him, and that the mountain crumbled when Moses prayed for the Divine vision. Yet how is that you are so bold that you do not tremble out of fear of God, and you keep your hearts so hard and unfeeling?

In the first part, it says: *for there are rocks from which rivers gush.* By recalling such rivers as the Nile, the Tigris, and the Euphrates, which gush out of mountains, it points out how wonderfully and miraculously rocks are susceptible and subjugated to the Divine commands of creation. To awakened, attentive hearts, this means:

> The mountains cannot be the actual source of such mighty rivers, for even if they were formed completely of water, they could supply such a river for only a few months. Also rain, which penetrates only about a meter underground, cannot be sufficient income for that high expenditure. No ordinary reason, natural cause, or chance can explain these rivers' sources and flow. The All-Majestic Creator makes them flow forth in truly wonderful fashion from an unseen "treasury."

One Tradition refers to this: "Every minute a drop falls from Paradise into each of those three rivers. That is why they flow abundantly." Another Tradition states: "The source of these three rivers is in Paradise."[79] That is, as physical causes cannot produce their abundant flow, their sources must be in an unseen world, a hidden treasury of Mercy, so that the balance between incoming and outgoing water is maintained. By drawing attention to this meaning, the Qur'an gives the following instruction:

> O Children of Israel and children of Adam! Your hardness of heart and lack of feeling cause you to disobey the commandments of such a One of Majesty, and your heedlessness causes you to close your eyes to the light of knowledge of such an Everlasting Sun that by causing mighty rivers like the Nile to gush from the mouths of ordinary, solid rocks and turn Egypt into a paradise, He offers to the universe's heart and the earth's mind miracles of His Power and witnesses to His Oneness as strong and abundant as the gushing forth and flow of those mighty rivers, and makes them flow to the hearts and minds of

---

[79] al-Bukhari, "Ashriba" 12; Muslim, "Iman" 264; al-Baghdadi, *Tarikhu'l-Baghdad*, 1:55. (Tr.)

jinn and humanity. Further, it shows the All-Majestic Creator as the sunlight shows the sun that He makes some hard, unfeeling rocks the objects of the miracles of His Power in such wonderful fashion.[80] How is it then that you are so blind to the light of His knowledge and do not see the truth?

See how eloquently the Qur'an expresses these truths. Note the guidance of that eloquence. What hardness of heart and lack of feeling cannot be melted by its "heat?" If you have understood my words, see one guiding gleam of the Qur'an's miraculousness and thank God.

All-Glorified are You. We have no knowledge save what You have taught us. Surely You are the All-Knowing, the All-Wise.

O God, enable us to understand the mysteries of the Qur'an as You like and approve, and grant us success in the service of it. Amin, through Your Mercy, O Most Merciful of the Merciful.

O God, bestow blessings and peace upon the one to whom the wise Qur'an was sent, and upon his Family and Companions altogether.

SECOND STATION: (A gleam of the Qur'an's miraculousness, which shines through the Prophets' miracles.) Notice the two questions and their answers at the end.

In the name of God, the All-Merciful, the All-Compassionate.

Not a thing, fresh or withered, wet or dry, but it is in a Manifest Book. (6:59)

Several years ago in my *Isharatul-I'jaz* (Signs of Miraculousness),[81] I discussed in Arabic one meaning of this verse. Now two of my brothers-in-religion, whose wishes are important to me, have asked for a Turkish explana-

---

[80] One of the Nile's main branches rises in the mountains in central Africa, the Tigris' main branch rises in a cave in Turkey, and one of the Euphrates's main streams rises at the foothills of a mountain in Diyadin. It is scientifically established that mountains are rocks solidified from liquid matter. One of the Prophet's glorifications—*All-Glorified is He Who spread out soil on solidified liquid*—testifies that the earth's original formation is as follows: Some liquid matter solidified at Divine command and became rock, and then rock became soil. In other words, the liquid matter was too soft to settle on, and the rock was too hard to benefit from. Therefore, the All-Wise and Compassionate One spread soil over the rock and made it a place of habitation for living beings.

[81] *Isharatu'l-I'jaz* is a commentary on *Suratu'l-Fatiha* and the initial 32 verses of *Suratu'l-Baqara*.

tion of that discussion. Relying on Almighty God's help, and based on the Qur'an's enlightenment, I write what follows.

According to one interpretation, the Manifest Book is the Qur'an. This verse states that everything is found in it. This is true. However, we must realize that things are found at different levels. They are presented as seeds, nuclei, summaries, principles or signs, as well as explicitly or implicitly, allusively, vaguely or suggestively. Depending on the occasion, one form is preferred to best convey the Qur'an's purposes and meet the context's requirements. For example, progress in science and industry has resulted in airplanes, electricity, motorized transportation, and radio and telecommunication, and so on. Such things occupy a prominent position in our daily lives. As the Qur'an addresses humanity [at all times], it does not ignore these developments; rather, it points to them either through the Prophets' miracles or in connection with certain historical events. For example:

> Down with the makers of the trench of the fuel-fed fire. When they sat by it, and were themselves the witnesses of what they did to the believers. They ill-treated them for no other reason than that they believed in God, the All-Glorious and Mighty, the All-Praised One. (85:4-8)[82]

> ... in the loaded fleet. And We have created for them the like thereof, whereon they ride. (36:41-42)

Such verses point to trains, while the following verse, besides its many other meanings and connotations, alludes to electricity:

> God is the Light of the heavens and the earth. The parable of His Light is as a niche wherein is a lamp. The lamp is in a glass, and the glass is, as it were, a shining star kindled from a blessed olive tree, neither of the east nor the west, whose oil would almost glow forth (of itself) though no fire touched it: light upon light.[83] God guides to His Light whom He wills. (24:35)

Since many people have analyzed verses of the second type, those alluding to modern technology in connection with historical events, and since they require much care and detailed explanation, as well as being very

---

[82] These verses allude to trains, which offered great advantage to the unbelievers in bringing the Muslim world under their control.

[83] The phrases: *whose oil would almost glow forth (of itself) though no fire touched it: light upon light* makes the allusion clearer.

numerous, I will content myself with the two verses alluding to trains and electricity. Instead, I will discuss certain verses that point to modern scientific progress and technological wonders through Prophets' miracles.

Introduction

As God Almighty sent the Prophets to human communities as leaders of spiritual and moral progress, He has also endowed them with certain wonders and miracles and made them masters and forerunners of humanity's material progress. He commands people to follow them absolutely.

By relating the Prophets' spiritual and moral perfections, the Qur'an encourages people to benefit from them. By presenting their miracles, it urges people to achieve something similar through science. It may even be said that, like spiritual and moral attainments, material attainments and wonders were first given to humanity as gifts through Prophetic miracles. For example, Prophet Noah was the first to build ships, and Prophet Joseph was the first to build clocks. Thus the ship and clock were given first as Prophetic miracles. It is a meaningful indication of this reality that so many craft guilds take a Prophet as the "patron" or originator of their craft. For example, seamen take Noah, watchmakers take Joseph, and tailors take Enoch, upon them be peace.

Since truth-seeking scholars and the science of eloquence agree that each Qur'anic verse contains numerous aspects of guidance and instruction, it follows that the brilliant verses relating the Prophets' miracles should not be considered mere historical events. Rather, they comprise numerous indications of guidance. By relating these miracles, the Qur'an shows the ultimate goal of scientific and technological developments, and specifies their final aims, toward which it urges humanity. Just as the past is the field for the future's seeds and the mirror to its potential picture, so is the future the time to reap the past life's harvest and the mirror to the actual situation. Out of many examples, I will point out only a few.

The verse: *And to Solomon (We subjugated) the wind: its morning stride was a month's journey and the evening stride was a month's journey* (34:12), expresses the wind's subjugation to Prophet Solomon, upon him be peace: Prophet Solomon covered the distance of two months' walk in two strides by flying through the air. This suggests that humanity can and should strive to travel through the air. Almighty God also is saying: "One of My servants did not obey his carnal desires, and I mounted him on the air. If you give up laziness and benefit properly from certain of My laws in nature, which are titles of My practices, you too can mount it."

The verse: *When Moses asked for water for his people, We said: "Strike the rock with your staff." Then gushed forth therefrom twelve springs (so that) each tribe knew their drinking place"* (2:60), indicates that simple tools can unlock Mercy's underground treasuries. In places hard as rock, the water for life may be drawn with so simple a device as a staff. Through this meaning, the verse urges us to seek these treasures. Through this verse, God Almighty suggests: "One of My servants relied on Me, and so I gave him a staff that draws the water for life from wherever he wishes. If you rely on My laws of Mercy, you too can obtain such a device." Modern scientists have invented many devices to bring up subsurface water. The verse points to further goals, just as the previous one specified attainments far ahead of today's airplanes.

The verse: *I heal him who was born blind, and the leper, and I raise the dead by God's leave* (3:49), concerns a miracle of Jesus, upon him be peace. Just as the Qur'an explicitly encourages humankind to follow Jesus in his high morality, so through this miracle it alludes to and encourages the highest level of healing with which God endowed him. It suggests that even the most chronic ailments can be cured. Therefore, we should search for it. It is possible to give a temporary tinge of life to death. By the verse God Almighty means:

> I gave two gifts to one of My servants who renounced the world for My sake: the remedy for spiritual ailments, and the cure for physical sicknesses. Dead hearts were revived through the light of guidance, and sick people who were as though dead found health through his breath and cure. You can find the cure for all illnesses in My "pharmacy of wisdom" in nature, where I attached many important purposes to each thing. Work and find it.

Thus, this verse marks the final point of medical development far ahead of the present level and urges us toward it.

The verses: *We made iron supple for him [David]* (34:10); *We gave him [David] wisdom and sound judgment in speech and decision* (38:20); and *We caused the fount of copper to gush forth with him [Solomon]* (34:12), indicate that softening iron is one of God's greatest bounties, one through which He shows a great Prophet's virtue. Softening iron, smelting copper, and extracting minerals is the origin, source, and basis of all material industries. These verses state that softening iron and fining it like a thread and smelting copper are great favors granted to two great Prophets, who ruled according to God's commandments, and are the means to most general industries.

Since God endowed two Prophets, who were both spiritual and political leaders, with wise speech, craftsmanship, and industry, He urges people to speak wisely and encourages them toward craftsmanship and industry. By these verses, God Almighty suggests:

> O children of Adam! I gave such wisdom to the tongue and heart of a servant who obeyed My religious commandments to judge and distinguish between all things with perfect clarity and to discern the truth. I endowed him with such skill that he could cast iron into any mold and then use it as an important source of strength for his rule. Since this is possible and since iron has great significance for your social life, which requires it, such wisdom and skill will be bestowed on you if you obey My commands of creation, My laws of nature. Eventually you will attain it.

By softening iron and smelting copper, humanity has achieved great industrial progress and material power. These verses direct our attention toward this truth. Just as they warned earlier peoples who did not appreciate its importance, so they warn today's lazy people.

The verse: *One with whom was knowledge of the Book said: "I will bring it to you before your gaze returns to you (in the twinkling of an eye)." When Solomon saw it set in his presence...* (27:40), describes the wonderful event of bringing the Queen of Sheba's throne to Solomon's court. This suggests that things can be transported over long distances, either bodily or in their images. In fact, God Almighty bestowed this as a miracle upon Prophet Solomon, upon him be peace, who was honored with kingship as well as Divine Messengership, so that he could maintain his sinlessness and justice by being personally informed of all regions in his extensive realm, see his subjects' conditions, and hear of their troubles.

That means that if we rely on Almighty God and appeal to Him in the tongue of our potentials, as Solomon did in the tongue of his sinlessness, and if our acts conform to His laws in the universe and with what attracts His favor, the world may become like a town for us. The Queen's throne was in Yemen, yet it was seen in the region of Damascus either bodily or in image, as were the forms of the people around it, who were seen and heard.

This verse points to the transport of forms and transmission of sounds over long distances. In effect, it says: "O rulers! If you wish to realize perfect justice, try to see and know your realm in all its details, as Solomon did. Only by rising to such a level can a just ruler who cherishes his subjects be saved from being held accountable. Only in this manner may he realize perfect justice." God Almighty means:

> O humanity! I bestowed on one of My servants a vast realm. So that he might realize perfect justice throughout it, I allowed him to know whatever was happening therein. Since I have created every person with a capacity to be a vicegerent on the earth—to rule according to My commands and represent My justice there—I also have given him, as a requirement of My Wisdom, the potential to scan the earth's face and comprehend whatever is in it. If every person cannot reach this point, humanity as a species may realize it. If they do not achieve it physically, they can do it spiritually, like some saints. Therefore, you can benefit from this great blessing. Come on, let Me see you do it. Without ever neglecting your duties of worship, strive in such a way that you may turn the earth's face into a garden, every part of which you can see, and the sounds from every corner of which you can hear. Heed the decree of Mercy: *He has made the earth subservient to you, so walk in the paths thereof and eat of His provision. Unto Him is the resurrection* (67:15).

Thus the verse mentioned above marks the ultimate point in the transmission of images and sounds, which constitutes one of the latest and most significant developments in science and technology, and encourages humanity toward that furthest point.

The verses: *Others linked together in chains* (38:38), and: *Of the evil ones were some who dived for him, and did other work* (21:82), state that Prophet Solomon, upon him be peace, made the jinn, devils, and evil spirits obey him. He prevented their evil and used them for beneficial work. In other words: The jinn, who are conscious beings and the earth's most important inhabitants after humanity, may serve us and can be contacted. Devils also may be made to serve, either willingly or unwillingly. God Almighty made them obey a servant who obeyed His commands. God Almighty means:

> O humanity! I made jinn and devils, including their most evil ones, obey a servant who obeyed Me. If you submit yourself to My commands, most creatures, including jinn and devils, may be subjugated to you.

These verses mark the highest point in the occult or supernatural sciences dealing with paranormal events, which appear as a blend of art and science and out of our extraordinary material and spiritual sensitivity. They urge us not, as happens nowadays, to be subjugated to the jinn, devils, and evil spirits, who sometimes introduce themselves as the spirits of the dead, and to become their plaything and a laughing-stock, but to subjugate and employ them through the Qur'an, and be saved from their evil.

These verses, and others like: *Then We sent to her Our spirit and it assumed for her the form of a perfect man* (19:17), hint that spirit beings may assume visible forms and we can contact with spirits and the spirits of the dead. But the Qur'an is not alluding to modern necromancy, which some "civilized" people practice, for these, in reality, are evil spirits masquerading as the dead person. Rather, it is in the form known to certain saints, like Muhyid-Din ibnu'l-'Arabi, who could communicate with good spirits at will, make contact and form relations with them, and, by going to their abodes and drawing near to their atmosphere, benefit from their spirituality. The verses point to this and mark the final point of occult sciences.

The verses: *We subdued the hills to hymn the praises (of their Lord) with him at nightfall and after sunrise* (38:18); *O you mountains! Echo His psalms of praise, and you birds. And We made the iron supple for him* (34:10); and *We have been taught the language of birds* (26:17), which are about David's miracles, point out that Almighty God gave David's glorifications such strength and such a resonant and pleasing tone that they brought the mountains to ecstasy. Like a huge sound system, each mountain formed a circle around the chief reciter—David—and repeated his glorifications. This is a reality, for every mountain with caves can "speak" like a parrot. If you declare before a mountain: "All praise and gratitude are for God," the mountain will echo it back. Since God Almighty has granted this ability to mountains, it can be developed.

God endowed Prophet David, upon him be peace, with both Messengership and caliphate in an exceptional form. Thus He made this seed of ability flourish as such a miracle with that comprehensive Messengership and magnificent sovereignty that great mountains followed him like soldiers, students, or disciples. Under his direction and in his tongue, they glorified the All-Majestic Creator and repeated whatever he said.

At present, due to advancements in communication, a great commander can get a large army dispersed through the mountains to repeat his declaration "God is the All-Great" at the same time, and make the mountains speak and ring with the words. If an ordinary commander can do this, a magnificent commander of Almighty God can get them actually to utter and recite God's glorifications. Besides, each mountain has a collective personality and corporate identity, and offers glorifications and worship unique to itself. Just as each one glorifies in humanity's tongue via echoing, it also glorifies the All-Majestic Creator in its own particular tongue.

The verses: *We have been taught the tongues of birds* (27:16); and *The birds assembled* (38:19), point out that Almighty God bestowed on David and Solomon knowledge of the birds' languages and of the tongues of abilities (how they could be of benefit). Given this, and that the earth is a laden table of the All- Merciful set up in our honor, most animals and birds that benefit from this table may serve us. God uses such small animals as honeybees and silkworms, through the guidance of His special inspiration, to benefit humanity. By enabling us to use pigeons and make certain birds like parrots speak, He has added to the beauty of human civilization.

If we could discover how to use other birds and animals, many species might be employed for important tasks, just as domestic animals are. For example, if the languages of locust-destroying starlings were known and their movements could be controlled, they could be used against plagues of locusts. What a valuable free service this would be! Thus, the verses mentioned show the ultimate point in subjugating and benefiting from birds, and making such lifeless beings speak like a telephone or phonograph (or record players). By specifying the farthest aim in this field, the verses urge humanity toward it. By the same verses, God Almighty indicates:

> O humanity! So that his sinlessness as a Prophet and his justice as a sovereign might not be damaged, I subjugated to one of your fellow men, who was totally submitted to Me, the huge creatures in My Kingdom and made them speak. I put most of My troops and animals in his service. In the same way, since I have entrusted to each of you the Supreme Trust that the heavens, the earth, and the mountains shrank from bearing, and have endowed you with the potential to rule on the earth according to My commands,[84] you should yield to the One in Whose hand are the reins of all creatures. This will cause the creatures in His Kingdom to yield to you, so that you may use them in the name of the One Who holds their reins and rise to a position worthy of your potential.

Given this, rather than wasting your time with record players, musical instruments, playing with pigeons, making parrots speak, and so on, try for a most agreeable, elevated, and sacred amusement—that mountains may func-

---

[84] The Supreme Trust is our selfhood or human identity, which includes free will, knowledge, intellect, and speech. For an elaboration on this topic, consult The Thirtieth Word. (Tr.)

tion as a huge sound system for you as they did for David, that a breeze may cause the tunes of Divine praise and glorification to reach your ears from trees and plants, that mountains may manifest themselves as wonderful creatures reciting Divine glorifications in thousands of tongues, and that most birds may be each an intimate friend or an obedient servant, like Solomon's hoopoe. They may both entertain you and drive you with zeal toward the perfections and attainments of which you are capable, rather than causing you to fall from the position required by your humanity, as vain amusements do.

The verse: *We said: "O fire! Be coolness and peace for Abraham!"* (21:69), which is about one of Abraham's miracles, contains three subtle indications:

FIRST: Like every element in nature, fire performs a duty under a command; it does not act on its own and blindly. It did not burn Prophet Abraham, upon him be peace, for God commanded it not to do so.

SECOND: One type of heat burns through coldness. That is, it has an effect like burning. Through the phrase *Be peace!*, God Almighty ordered the cold: "Like heat, do not burn him."[85] It is simultaneously fire and cold. Science has discovered a fire called "white heat," which does not radiate its heat. Instead, by attracting the surrounding heat, it causes the surrounding area to become cold enough to freeze liquids and in effect burns them through its cold. The severest cold in winter is a category of fire which burns through its cold. Hell, which contains all degrees and sorts of fire, also must have this intense cold.

THIRD: Just as there is an immaterial substance like belief and an armor like Islam, which will remove and protect against the effects of Hellfire, there must be a physical substance that will protect against and prevent the effects of fire in the world. As is required by His Name the All-Wise, and since this world is the abode of Wisdom, [where everything occurs for a definite purpose and usually according to cause and effect], God Almighty acts behind the veil of cause and effect. Therefore, as the fire did not burn Abraham's body, it did not burn His clothes either. His clothes resisted fire. Thus the verse suggests:

> O nation of Abraham! Be like Abraham, so that your garments may be your guard against the fire, your greatest enemy, in both this world and the next. Coat your spirit with belief, and it will be your

---

[85] An interpreter of the Qur'an remarks: "If He had not said: *Be peace!*, it would have burned him with its coldness."

armor against Hellfire. Similarly, there are substances in the earth which God Almighty stored for you and will protect you from fire's evil. Search for them, extract them, and coat yourselves with them.

As an important step in his progress, humanity discovered a fire-resistant substance. But see how elevated, fine, and beautiful a garment this verse points to, which will be woven on the loom of purity of belief in and submission to God, and which will not be rent for all eternity.

The verse: *He taught Adam the names, all of them* (2:31), states that, as his greatest miracle in the cause of supreme vicegerency, Prophet Adam, upon him be peace, was taught the names. While other Prophets' miracles point to a particular wonder in the course of scientific and technological progress, the miracle of Adam, the father of all Prophets and the Opening of the Office of Prophethood, alludes almost explicitly to the ultimate points and final goals of human attainment and progress. By this verse, God Almighty suggests:

> O children of Adam! To prove his superiority over the angels as regards vicegerency, I taught Adam all the names.[86] Being his children and inheritors of his abilities, learn all the names and show that you are worthy of this superiority over all other creatures. For the way is open to you to rise to highest rank among all beings, and for vast creatures like the earth to be subjugated to you. Come on, step forward, hold on to My Names, and rise. But be careful! Adam was deceived by Satan once and for all, and temporarily fell to the earth from an abode like the Garden. So do not follow Satan in your progress, thereby making it the means of falling from the heavens of Divine Wisdom into the misguidance of attributing creativity to nature, or real effect to cause and effect in the creation and operation of nature. Raise your head and, studying My Beautiful Names, make science and your progress steps by which to ascend to the heavens. Then you may rise to My Names of Lordship, which are the essences and sources of your sciences and attainments, and through them look to your Lord with your hearts.

A significant point and important mystery

In describing all the attainments of learning, scientific progress, and wonders of technology with which we have been endowed due to our vast potential under the title of "the teaching of the names," the above verse alludes to a

---

[86] The Names taught to Prophet Adam, upon him be peace, are the names of things as the keys to human knowledge. They originate in Divine Names, each one the source of a branch of science. For example, medicine has its source in the Name the All-Healing, and engineering in the Names the All-Just and the All-Determining. (Tr.)

fine point: Each attainment, perfection, learning, progress, and science has an elevated reality based on a Divine Name. By being based on a Name, Which has a great variety of veils and manifests Itself in various ways and levels, that particular branch of science or art attains its perfection and becomes reality. Otherwise it remains imperfect, deficient, and shadowy.

For example, engineering's reality lies in the Divine Names the All-Just (One Who gives everything a certain measure and due proportions and creates everything just in its place) and the All-Determining. Its final aim is to discover those Names and observe and reflect their wise and majestic manifestations. Medicine is an art and a science. Its reality and final rank lie in the All-Wise's Name the All-Healing, and it reaches its perfection by finding out a cure for every illness by discovering the merciful manifestations of that Name in the earth, His vast "pharmacy."

The science which discusses the reality of entities can be a true science full of wisdom only by discerning the regulating, directing, administering, sustaining, and all-embracing manifestations of the Divine Name the All-Wise in things, and in their benefits and advantages, and by being based on that Name. Otherwise it either become superstition and nonsense or, like naturalistic philosophy, causes misguidance. You can compare other sciences and attainments with these three examples.

Thus, with this verse under discussion, the wise Qur'an points to the the furthest limits and final degrees of progress—from which we are still far removed—and urges us toward them. This verse is extremely rich and elaborate in meaning, but for now I will go no further.

The Qur'an is Prophet Muhammad's supreme miracle, the seal of the Office of Prophethood, the leader of Prophets, and the cause of pride of all beings, upon him be peace and blessings. When compared with his cause of Messengership, the miracles of all the other Prophets are like only one miracle. He was endowed in full with all the levels of all the names taught, in brief, to Adam. By raising his finger in a mood of majesty, the Prophet split the moon; by lowering his hand in a manifestation of grace, he made water flow from his ten fingers abundantly; and he was verified and corroborated by hundreds of miracles. Numerous verses like: Say: "If humanity and jinn banded together to produce the like of this Qur'an, they would never produce its like, not though they backed one another" (17:88), point out the Qur'an's— his supreme miracle—purity of explanation, eloquence of expression, comprehensive meanings, and sublime and sweet styles, which together constitute one of the most brilliant aspects of the miraculousness or inimitability of that eternal miracle. Thus, such verses attract humans and jinn to this aspect and provokes them. Stirring up the zeal of its friends and the obstinacy of its enemies, they encourage and stimulate them to produce something resembling it. They place that miracle before the eyes of creatures, as if reminding that humanity's only aim is to take it as our goal and guiding principle in life, and study it so that we can advance consciously and knowingly to the goal for our creation.

In brief, therefore, while the other Prophets' miracles point to a wonder of human arts or crafts and technology, Prophet Adam's miracle indicates a concise, summarized form of the basis of those crafts, as well as the indexes of sciences, branches of knowledge, and wonders and perfections, and urges us toward them. As for the Qur'an of miraculous exposition, the supreme miracle of Muhammad, upon him be peace and blessings, it is the object of all the Divine Names' manifestations in their fullness, shows fully the true goal of science and all branches of knowledge, as well as the perfections, attainments, and happiness of both worlds. It urges us toward them powerfully and in such a way that it means: "O people, the sublime aim in the creation of this universe is your response to Divine Lordship's manifestation (administering, directing, training, and sustaining) with universal worship. Your ultimate aim is to realize that worship through science, attainment, and perfections."

The Qur'an also hints at this: "At the end of time, humanity will pour into science and learning. People will derive all strength from science. Power and rule will pass to the hand of science and knowledge." By frequently emphasizing its eloquent and beautiful style, the Qur'an suggests: "At the end of time, eloquence and beauty of expression, the most brilliant sciences and branches of knowledge, will be most sought after in all their varieties. People will find that when it comes to making each other accept their opinions and exercise their rule, their most effective weapon will be eloquent expression; their most irresistible force will be fine oratory."

In short, most Qur'anic verses are keys to a treasury of perfections and a store of knowledge. If you want to ascend to the Qur'an's sky and reach the stars of its verses, make these 20 Words a 20-step stairway[87] and climb them. You will see what a brilliant, shining sun the Qur'an is. Notice how

---

[87] Rather, 33 Words (comprising *The Words*), 33 Letters (comprising *The Letters*), 31 Gleams (comprising *The Gleams*) and 13 Rays (comprising *The Rays*) are a 110-step stairway.

it radiates a pure light over the Divine truths and the truths of the contingent (created) realm. See what a brilliant light it spreads.

In conclusion, since the verses concerning the Prophets allude to contemporary technology's wonders and have a manner of expression that suggests their furthest limits, since each verse has numerous meanings, and since there are categorical commands to follow and obey the Prophets, the verses mentioned above must be pointing to the importance of human arts and sciences, in addition to their literal meanings, and urging us toward them.

Two important answers to two important questions

QUESTION: Since the Qur'an was sent for humanity, why does it not mention explicitly the wonders of civilization that we consider important? Why does it content itself with allusions, indications, or references?

ANSWER: The Qur'an does so because it discusses each topic according to its worth in the Qur'an's eyes. Its basic duty is to teach Divine Lordship's perfections, essential qualities, and acts, as well as servanthood's duties, status, and affairs. Given this, the wonders of human civilization merit only a slight indication or implicit reference or allusion.

For example, if an airplane[88] appealed to the Qur'an: "Give me the right to speak and a place in your verses," the aircrafts of Lordship's sphere (e.g., planets, the earth, the moon) would reply on the Qur'an's behalf: "You may have a place in proportion to your size." If a submarine asked for a place, submarines belonging to that sphere (e.g., heavenly bodies "swimming" in the vast "ocean" of the atmosphere and ether) would say: "Your place beside us is too small to be visible." If a shining, star-like electric light asked to be included, the electric lights of that sphere (e.g., lightning, shooting stars, and stars adorning the sky) would say: "You have a right to be mentioned and spoken of only in proportion to your light."

If the wonders of human civilization demanded a place with respect to the fineness of their art, a fly would reply: "Be quiet, for even one of my wings has more of a right than you do. If all of your fine arts and delicate instruments were joined together, they could not be as wonderful and as exquisite as the fine art and delicate members concentrated in my tiny body." The verse: *Surely those whom, apart from God, you deify and invoke*

---

[88] While discussing this serious subject, my pen involuntarily slipped into this light manner of writing, and I let it go. I hope this does not detract from the subject's seriousness.

will never be able to create (even) a fly, though they banded together to do it And if a fly snatches away anything from them, they never recover that from it. Powerless indeed is the seeker, and so is the sought (22:73), will silence you."

If those wonders appealed to the sphere of servanthood, they would receive a reply like the following:

> You have very little relationship with us, so you cannot enter our sphere. For our program is this: The world is a guest-house. Humanity is a guest with many duties. Each person will stay there for a short time. Being charged with preparing themselves for eternal life, they will give priority to their most urgent and important duties pertaining the eternal life. As you mostly seem to be designed in heedlessness and world-mindedness, as if the world were eternal, you have very little share in servanthood to and worship of God, which is founded upon love of truth and otherworldliness. However, if there are among you respected craftspeople, scientists, and inspired inventors, who, purely for the benefit of God's servants, serve the general interest and public ease and attainment of social life, which is a valuable sort of worship, the Qur'an's allusions and indications are sufficient for such sensitive people, who are a minority among their colleagues, to encourage them and honor their accomplishments.

QUESTION: You might ask: "After these discussions, I understand that the Qur'an contains, along with all other truths, indications of, as well as allusions to, modern civilization's most advanced wonders. Everything necessary for human happiness in both worlds is found in it, in proportion to its worth. But why does the Qur'an not mention them explicitly, so that even most stubborn unbelievers would have to believe and our minds would be eased?"

ANSWER: Religion is for examination, a test and trial offered by God to distinguish elevated and base spirits from each other. Just as raw materials are fired to separate diamonds from coal and gold from soil, Divine obligations test conscious beings so that the precious "ore" in the "mine" of human potential may be separated from the dross. Since the Qur'an was sent for humanity to be perfected through trial, it only alludes to future events pertaining to the world, which everyone will witness over time. It only opens the door to reason as much as needed to prove its argument. If it had mentioned such things explicitly, testing would be meaningless. They would be so clear, as if writing *There is no deity but God* on the face of the sky with stars, that everyone would be forced to believe. There would be no competition, and the testing and trial would mean nothing. A coal-like spirit would stay with and appear to be equal to a diamond-like spirit.[89]

In short, the Qur'an is wise and gives everything a position in proportion to its value. Thus, 1,300 years ago it saw the extent of human progress and its fruits, which were hidden in the darkness of the Unseen (the future), and showed them in a better form. This shows that the Qur'an is the Word of One Who sees at the same instant all time and all within it.

All that we have explained so far is only one gleam of the Qur'an's miraculousness, which shines on the "face" of the Prophets' miracles.

> O God! Enable us to understand the Qur'an's mysteries and make us successful in serving it at every instant and at all times.

> All-Glorified are You. We have no knowledge save what You have taught us. Surely You are the All-Knowing, the All-Wise.

> O God! Bestow blessings, peace, benedictions, and honor on our master and lord, Muhammad, Your servant and Prophet and Messenger, the unlettered Prophet, on his Family and Companions and wives and descendants; on all other Prophets and Messengers; on the angels near-stationed to You; and on the saints and the righteous. Bestow on them the most excellent of blessings, the purest peace, and the most abundant benedictions, to the number of the Qur'an's *suras*, verses, words, letters, meanings, indications, allusions, and references. Forgive us, have mercy on us, and be gracious to us, our God, our Creator, for the sake of each of those blessings, through Your Mercy, O Most Merciful of the Merciful. All praise and gratitude are for God, the Lord of the worlds. Amin.

---

[89] Abu Jahl the Accursed and Abu Bakr the Truthful would appear to be equal, and the purpose for testing people and accounting them responsible for their free acts would become meaningless.

The
Twenty-first Word

The Twenty-first Word

The five daily Prayers and cures for the wounds of the heart caused by involuntary thoughts and doubts

In the name of God, the All-Merciful, the All-Compassionate.

Surely the Prayer is a timed prescription for believers. (4:103)

Two Stations

IRST STATION: ONCE A WELL-KNOWN AND SOCIALLY IMPORTANT old man said to me: "Prayer is okay, but five times a day is too much; it bores and wearies." A long time after this, my carnal soul told me the same thing. I realized that its laziness had caused it to listen to this satanic idea. Understanding that those words had been spoken in the name of all carnal, evil-commanding souls, I told myself: "Since my soul orders evil, and one who does not reform his own soul cannot reform others, I will begin with my own soul." I said: "O soul! In response to such ignorant words said in the bed of indolence and the torpor of idleness, hear from me the following five warnings."

FIRST WARNING: O wretched soul! Is your life permanent? Do you have a document that you will live until next year or even tomorrow? Your weariness comes from your fancy that you will live forever. You complain as though you will remain here forever in eternal enjoyment. If only you understood that your life is short and passes in vain, you would understand that, far from causing boredom or weariness, spending one twenty-fourth of it on a fine, agreeable, easy, and gracious act of service which is the means to happiness in the real, eternal life actually arouses vigor and gives pleasure.

SECOND WARNING: O gluttonous soul! Every day you eat, drink and breathe; do these cause you boredom? They do not, because these needs recur and so give pleasure when satisfied. Thus the five daily Prayers should not bore you, for they attract and conduct the needs of your companions in the house of my body—the sustenance of my heart, the water of life of my spirit and the air of my spiritual intellect.

The food and strength of a heart exposed to endless grief and pain, and inclined to infinite pleasure and ambition, may be obtained by knocking on the One All-Compassionate and Munificent's door through supplication. Also, for a spirit connected with most beings and moving quickly to the other world amid cries of separation, the water of life may be imbibed by turning, through the five daily Prayers, toward the spring of the Everlasting Beloved, the All-Permanent Worshipped One, Who suffices and substitutes for everything.

Further, a conscious inward sense, a luminous and infinitely delicate faculty, and a subtle mirror to the Eternal Being, which by nature desires the eternity for which it was created, is most needy of "air," of relief and relaxation, so that it can deal successfully with the distressing, crushing, and suffocating conditions of worldly life. It can "breathe" only through the "window" of Prayer.

THIRD WARNING: O impatient soul! Is it at all sensible to think today of the hardship or difficulties of past worship and troubles of past calamities, and so be distressed, and to imagine the difficulties of future worship or service of Prayer, and the pain of future misfortune, and so display impatience? In being thus impatient you resemble a foolish commander who, although the enemy's right flank has joined his right flank and thus reinforced him, sends a significant force to the right flank only to weaken the center. Also, although no enemy forces are attacking the left flank, he sends a large contingent there and tells it to fire, thereby weakening his center more greatly. This encourages the enemy to attack the center and rout the troops.

Thus, you resemble this commander. For past troubles are now a mercy. Their pain has gone, while their pleasure remains. Hardships have changed into blessings, and trials and toils into rewards. So why should you be weary? Rather, feel a new eagerness and a fresh zeal, and make a serious effort to continue praying. Also, the future has not come yet, so why should you worry about it? This is as ridiculous as complaining now about future hunger and thirst, of thinking of them now and feeling bored and wearied. Since this is the reality, consider only today when it comes to matters of worship. Say: "I am spending one hour out of twenty-four on pleasant and elevated acts of service, the reward for which is great and whose trouble is little." Your bitter disappointment will change into a pleasurable endeavor.

O impatient soul! You are charged with three types of perseverance: in worship, in refraining from sin, and in the face of misfortune. If you are sensible enough, consider and follow the reality in the comparison in this third warning. Calling, "O All-Persevering One!" derive strength from these three types of perseverance. Using your God-given power of perseverance in the proper way will suffice for every difficulty and misfortune, so hold on to that power.

FOURTH WARNING: O foolish soul! Is this duty of worship so fruitless and its reward so little that you feel weary? Whereas if someone offers you money or threatens you, he would make you work until evening, and you would work without respite. So, are the five daily Prayers in vain while they are your weak heart's "food" in this guest-house of the world, sustenance and light in your grave (a station to eternal life), a document and warrant on the Day of Judgment, and a light and a mount on the Bridge, which everyone has to cross?

Is the Prayer's reward so little? If someone promised you a present of a hundred dollars, he would make you work for several days. Though he may go back on his word, you would trust him and work without respite. So if One Who never breaks His promise says that He will reward you with something like Paradise and a gift like eternal happiness, and employ you for a very short time in a most agreeable duty—if you leave that service undone or act reluctantly as if being forced and in a manner to accuse Him of His promise or belittle His gift, would you not deserve a severe reprimand and a terrible punishment? While you work without slacking at the most difficult jobs in this world out of your fear of imprisonment, does the fear of an eternal imprisonment like Hell not give you zeal for so light and pleasant an act of service as the Prayers?

FIFTH WARNING: O worldly minded soul! Are your sluggishness in worship and deficiency in the prescribed Prayers due to your many worldly preoccupations? Are you pressed for time on account of the struggle for livelihood? Were you created only for this world that you should spend all your time on it?

You know that you are superior to all animals in respect of you potential, but even a sparrow can do a better job than you when it comes to satisfying your daily needs. Why do you not understand from this that your duty as a human being is not to labor only for worldly aims like animals but to work for the real, everlasting life. Besides, most worldly concerns are trivial and useless matters from which you derive no benefit. Yet, leaving aside the most essential things, you spend your time acquiring useless information, as if you were going to live for thousands of years. For example, you waste your precious time on worthless things like learning what the rings around Saturn are like or how many chickens there are in the United States. Are you preparing a doctorate in astronomy or in livestock statistics?

If you say: "The essential requirements of earning a livelihood keep me from the Prayer and make me tired," my answer will be as follows: Suppose that you work for a daily wage of ten dollars, and someone comes and tells you: "Dig here for ten minutes, and you'll find a brilliant emerald worth $100." If you reply: "No, I won't come, because the boss will cut my wage by 20 cents, and so I will earn less," you can see how foolish that argument is.

In just the same way, you work in your orchard for your livelihood. If you abandon the prescribed Prayers, all the fruits of your work are limited to a worldly, insignificant, and unproductive livelihood. However, if you spend your rest periods praying, which is the means for your spirit to become lively and your heart to experience ease, you also will discover two mines which are important sources for both a productive worldly livelihood and your provisions for the Hereafter: First, through a sound intention, you will receive a share in the glorifications offered by your orchard's plants and trees. Second, whatever produce is eaten, by people or animals, will return to you like alms. But this will happen only if you work in the Real Provider's name and within His permission's sphere, and consider yourself a distribution official distributing His property among His creatures.

See what a great loss one who does not pray suffers, what significant wealth he loses, and he is deprived of the two mines that support one's efforts with high motives and actions with strong morale. As he ages, he will grow weary of gardening and saying: "What's all this to me? I'm leaving the world anyway, so why bother?" slides into idleness. But one who both prays and works for his livelihood says: "I will try harder to perform the obligatory worship and earn legitimately and honestly so that I may send more light to my grave and procure more provisions for my life in the Hereafter."

In short: O soul, yesterday has left you and you have no guarantee that you will be alive tomorrow. Your life consists of today. Set at least one hour aside for the mosque or the Prayer mat, a savings box and reserve fund for the Hereafter. Set this hour aside for your real future. Also know that each new day is the door to a new world. If you do not pray, your world of that day will go dark and wretched and will testify against you in the World of Immaterial Forms or Representations. Each day, everyone has a private world, the nature of which depends on one's heart and deeds, contained in this world. Just as a magnificent palace reflected in a mirror assumes the mirror's color and quality, just as an uneven mirror shows the finest things to be coarse, so do you change your own world's appearance through your heart, mind, deeds, and attitudes. You may cause it either to testify for or against you.

If you pray and turn toward the All-Majestic Maker, your private world will be illuminated suddenly. Prayer resembles a powerful electric light switched on by your intention to pray. It disperses your world's darkness and shows that the changes and movements in this confused, tumultuous world arise from, and for the purpose of, a wise order and a meaningful arrangement of Divine Power. It disperses over your heart a light from the light-filled verse: *God is the Light of the heavens and the earth* (24:35). And, illuminating your world on that day through its reflection, that light will cause your world to testify for you through its luminosity.

Never say: "My Prayers mean almost nothing when compared with the reality of what Prayer should be." For just as the date-palm stone encapsulates and contains the tree itself (the difference is only between the summary and the fully evolved or elaborated form), a great saint's Prayer is fully evolved while that of ordinary people like us (even if we are unaware of it) has a share in that Divine light, and a mystery in its truth. However, our perception of and illumination by that truth varies according to our degrees.

Just as there are many stages and degrees between a date-palm's stone and the fully grown tree, praying and benefiting from our Prayers are characterized by possibly even more numerous degrees and stages. However, the basis of that luminous truth is present in each degree or stage.

> O God! Bestow blessings and peace on him who said: "The prescribed Prayers are the pillar of religion," and on his Family and Companions.

SECOND STATION: This comprises five cures for five wounds of the heart.

> In the name of God, the All-Merciful, the All-Compassionate.

> O Lord, I take refuge in You from the evil suggestions of the satans, and I take refuge in You, O my Lord, lest they attend me. (23:97-98)

O you afflicted with involuntary evil thoughts and fancies, such things resemble a misfortune. The more you dwell on them, the more they grow. If you ignore them, they dwindle away; if you exaggerate them, they swell;

if you belittle them, they die down. If you fear them, they become grave and make you ill; if you do not fear them, they become slight and remain hidden. If you do not know their real nature, they persist and become established; if you recognize their nature, they disappear.

I will explain only five out of the many types or aspects of such oft-occurring evil thoughts. I hope that this explanation will benefit both of us, for such thoughts are attracted by ignorance and repulsed by knowledge. If you do not recognize them, they call on you; if you recognize them, they depart. The five aspects are as follows:

FIRST ASPECT—FIRST WOUND: Satan first casts a doubt into the heart. If the heart does not admit it, he offers a blasphemy and causes the mind to recall some unclean memories and pictures, some ugly scenes that resemble blasphemy. This causes the heart to despair. People experiencing such thoughts think that they are acting wrongfully toward their Lord and so feel great agitation and anxiety. To free themselves, they flee from the Divine presence and want to plunge into heedlessness and forgetfulness.

O fellow afflicted with such involuntary thoughts! Do not be alarmed, for such thoughts are imaginary and are not blasphemous. An involuntary fancy of unbelief is not unbelief, just as an involuntary fancy of blasphemy is not blasphemy. Logic dictates that a fancy is not an act of judgment, whereas blasphemy (a willful act) is. Such words do not come from your heart, for your heart is displeased with and regrets them. Rather, they come from "the tube of Satan," an inner faculty situated near the heart through which Satan whispers to it. The harm of involuntary evil fancies comes from imagining them to be harmful, for people think that a fancy not subject to judgment is reality. They ascribe Satan's work to their hearts by supposing that Satan's whisperings belong to their hearts, and thus think this is harmful and suffer harm. This is just what Satan wants.

SECOND ASPECT: Meanings arising in the heart are formless until they enter the imagination. The imagination, always under some prompting, weaves forms and leaves those forms to which it attaches importance on the way. Whatever meaning comes to the heart is clothed in, touched with, or veiled through these forms by the imagination. If the meanings are pure and clean, and the forms dirty and base, there is little contact between them; a pure meaning will not accept the base form as its dress. However, people suffering from involuntary evil thoughts confuse that little contact with being dressed, and exclaim: "How corrupted my heart is! This baseness and meanness will drive me out of religion." Satan takes advantage of this sentiment. The cure for this wound is as follows:

Just as your outward cleanliness, one of the conditions for the Prayer's correctness, is not affected or spoiled by the foulness in your intestines, sacred meanings or conceptions are not harmed by nearness to unclean forms. Suppose you are reflecting on God's signs in the universe or on the Qur'an's verses and suddenly feel ill, or want to eat or urinate. Your imagination will form whatever is needed to respond, and weave appropriate "lowly" forms. The meanings arising out of your (interrupted) reflections will pass by these forms. But there is no harm, soiling, error, or injury from this passage. If there is any fault, it lies in paying attention to the fact and imagining it to be harmful.

THIRD ASPECT: Hidden connections exist between things, and even "threads" of such connections exist among things you never expect to be connected. They are either there in fact, or your imagination makes them according to its preoccupation and tie things together with them. It is due to this connection that the sight of something sacred sometimes brings to mind an unclean thing. As the science of rhetoric puts it: "Opposition, which is the cause of remoteness in the outer world, is the cause of nearness in the imagination." In other words, an imagined connection brings the forms of two opposites together. The recollection happening through such a connection is called the *association of ideas.*

For example, while praying or reciting supplications before the Ka'ba in the Divine Presence, although you are reflecting on the signs of certain Divine truths, the association of ideas may take you to the furthest, lowest trifles. If such an involuntary association of ideas occurs to you frequently, do not be alarmed. Rather, when it passes, turn back. Do not condemn yourself or dwell on it to learn its nature, for this might cause it to grow stronger. When you show regret and consider it seriously, your weak recollection becomes a fixation and turns into a sickness of imagination. Do not be overdistressed—it is not a sickness of the heart. Such a recollection is mostly involuntary and especially common among sensitive, nervous people. Satan finds this a great field of activity. The cure for this wound is as follows:

The association of ideas is mostly involuntary, meaning that one is not responsible for it. Also, association includes proximity, not contact and combination. For this reason, the natures of ideas do not contaminate and harm each other. For example, Satan and the Angel of Inspiration are close to each other around the heart, and sinners and the pious live side by side. Such proximity is harmless. When unclean fancies enter among your pure thoughts due to the association of ideas, they are harmful only if intentional or when one imagines them to be harmful and becomes over-attentive to them. Sometimes the heart becomes tired or the mind entertains itself with anything that flits across it. Satan uses these to serve up unclean things.

FOURTH ASPECT: A kind of involuntary fancy arises from seeking a religious deed's best form. This can be better called a *scruple.* If people suppose it to be a true or pure piety, it becomes more vigorous and makes the resulting condition more severe. It can reach such a degree that, while searching for even better forms of the deed, such people fall into what is forbidden. Sometimes seeking after what is commended in worship causes people to neglect what is obligatory therein. Pausing over whether the act of worship was canonically acceptable or not, they repeat it. This state continues, and they soon fall into despair. Satan takes advantage of this state to wound these people. There are two cures for this wound.

First cure: Such a scruple may be right for the *Mu'tazilites,* who argue: "Deeds and things for which religion holds humanity responsible are either, of themselves and in regard to the Hereafter, good and therefore commanded, or bad and therefore prohibited." Thus, from the point of view of reality and the Hereafter, things are good or bad in their essence, and the Divine command and prohibition are dependent on this. Following this school of thought, a scruple arises in every act of worship: "Have I been able to perform this act in the good way that in essence it is?"

However, the *Ahlu's-Sunna wal-Jama'a* (people representing the great majority of Muslims who are believed to be on the right path) argue: "Almighty God orders a thing and it becomes good. He prohibits a thing and it becomes bad." So, whether a thing is good or bad depends on the Divine command and prohibition. Therefore, a thing is good or bad for people according to whether they have done something ordered or prohibited or whether they have done it in accordance with the rules established by the Shari'a. In addition, a thing is religiously good or bad not in respect to its apparent correctness and its apparent features, but with respect to the Hereafter.

For example, you performed *wudu'* (ritual ablution) or Prayer according to the rules of each. But there was a cause that of itself would invalidate them. However, you were completely unaware of it. Your ablution and Prayer are therefore sound and good. But the *Mu'tazilites* argue: "In essence they were bad and unsound. But they may be accepted due to your ignorance, which is an excuse." According to the *Ahlu's-Sunna wal-Jama'a*, you should not indulge in scruples about a deed you did in conformity with the rules of the Shari'a; do not worry about whether it was sound or not. Rather worry about if it was accepted; do not become proud and conceited.

Second cure: *There is no difficulty in religion.* Since the four Schools of Law are on the right path, and since realizing a fault, which leads to seeking forgiveness is preferable (particularly for those afflicted with scruples) to seeing deeds as good, as the latter leads to pride, it is better for such people to see their deeds as faulty and ask God's forgiveness rather than seeing them as good and becoming proud. Give up your scruples and say to Satan:

> This is merely a difficulty, for it is difficult to be aware of the exact truth and good in things. Excessive anxiety is contrary to the principles of *there is no difficulty in religion* and of *religion is ease*. As my deed conforms with the requirements of an established School of Law, it is sufficient. After that, in confession of my inadequacy, I take refuge with Divine Compassion. I humbly ask forgiveness for the duty of worship, which I cannot perform in a way worthy of it, and meekly supplicate that my defective deeds be accepted.

FIFTH ASPECT: Some suffer scruples in the form of [what they think are] doubts in matters of belief. Sometimes they confuse a passing fancy with a conceptualized idea, mistakenly considering this doubt to arise from themselves and therefore possibly harmful to their belief. They may think that such a doubt impairs their rational, conscious confirmation of the essentials of belief, or that thinking of something related to unbelief has made them unbelievers. That is, they confuse the use of reflection, study, and objective reasoning on the causes of unbelief with being contrary to belief. Frightened by these suppositions, which result from Satan's whispering, they believe that their hearts have become corrupted and their belief impaired. Unable to put these mostly involuntary states right by their free will, they give way to despair.

The cure is as follows: Imagining or reflecting on unbelief is not unbelief, and picturing or reflecting on misguidance is not misguidance. For imagination, conceptualization, picturing, and reflection are different from confirmation by reason and acceptance by heart; they are voluntary to certain degree. It is hard for the free will to control them so that we should be answerable for them.

Confirmation and acceptance are deliberate, for they depend on certain criteria and intentional reasoning. In addition, just as the former are not the same mental activities as confirmation and acceptance, neither are they the same as doubt and hesitation. However, they may pave the way to doubt if they are repeated unnecessarily and become established. If people continually support the opposing side on the pretext of objective reasoning or fairness, they may favor it involuntarily and thereby fall into danger. Gradually their state of mind becomes fixed and they become officious advocates of Satan or the enemy.

The most characteristic scruple here is that one confuses the theoretically possible with the reasonably likely. This violates a principle of reasoning in theology: A theoretical possibility does not negate certain knowledge of a present reality or contradict the demands of reason. For example, it is theoretically possible that the Black Sea could sink into the ground right now. However, we know and judge with certainty that that it has not done so. The theoretical possibility of its being otherwise causes no real doubt and does not impair our certainty about the present reality.

Theoretically, the sun might not set today or rise tomorrow. But this possibility does not impair our certainty or engender any real doubt. Such baseless suspicions arising from theoretical possibilities—for example, the death of this world and the resurrection of the dead in the Hereafter, which are among the truths of belief—do not impair the certainty of belief. Moreover, one of the established principles of the sciences of the methodology of Islamic law and the foundations of religion states that a possibility based on no evidence is not worth considering.

Question: What is the Divine purpose in letting involuntary evil thoughts and scruples pester us, for they cause harm and afflict believers?

Answer: If they are not carried to excess and allowed to overwhelm the person, essentially they are the cause of the vigilance and awareness that make people seek the truth and that which is better. They are also the means to seriousness, disperse indifference and repel carelessness and heedlessness. For this reason, the Absolutely Wise One put them in the hand of Satan as a whip of encouragement for us in this arena of testing, and Satan hits our heads with them. If they cause excessive hurt, we should complain to the All-Wise and All-Compassionate One and say: "I seek refuge with God from Satan, the accursed."

The
Twenty-second Word

The Twenty-second Word

Arguments for Divine Existence and Unity and how to acquire a firm conviction of Divine Unity

(This Word consists of two Stations)

In the name of God, the All-Merciful, the All-Compassionate.

God sets forth parables for humanity in order that they may bear (them) in mind and take lessons (through them). (14:25)

Such parables do We set forth for humanity so that they may reflect. (59:21)

First station

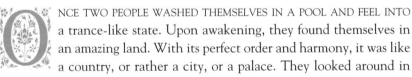NCE TWO PEOPLE WASHED THEMSELVES IN A POOL AND FEEL INTO a trance-like state. Upon awakening, they found themselves in an amazing land. With its perfect order and harmony, it was like a country, or rather a city, or a palace. They looked around in utmost amazement: from one point of view, it was a vast world; from another, a well-ordered country; from yet another, a splendid city. If it was looked from still another point of view, it was a palace though one it was in itself a magnificent world. They traveled and saw its creatures speaking a language they did not know. However, their gestures indicated that they were doing important work and carrying out significant duties.

One of them said: "This world must have an administrator, this well-ordered country a master, this splendid city an owner, and this skillfully made palace a master builder. We must try to know him, for it must be he who brought us here. If we do not, who will help us? What can we expect from those impotent creatures whose language we do not know and who ignore us? Moreover, one who has made a huge world in the form of a state, a city, or a palace and filled it with wonderful things, embellished it with every adornment, and decorated it with instructive miracles must have something he wants us and those who come here to do. We must know him and learn what he wants."

The other man objected: "I don't believe it, that there is such a being and he governs this world by himself." His friend replied: "If we do not recognize him and remain indifferent, we gain nothing and might face great harm. But if we try to recognize him, there is little hardship and the chance of great benefit. So, it is in no way reasonable to remain indifferent?" The other man insisted: "I find all my ease and enjoyment in not thinking of him. Besides, I am not to bother myself with things that make no sense to me. These are all confused things that are happening by chance or by themselves. They are none of my concern." His smart friend replied: "Such obstinacy will get us and many others in trouble. Sometimes a land is ruined because of one ill-mannered person."

The other person turned and said: "Either prove that what you say is true or leave me alone." At that, his friend said: "Since your obstinacy borders on insanity and will cause us to suffer a great calamity, I will show you twelve proofs that this palace-like world, this city-like state, has one master builder who administers it by himself and has no deficiency. He is invisible to us, but must see us and everything and also hear all voices. All his works seem miraculous. All these creatures whom we see but whose languages we do not understand must be his officials [working in his name].

Twelve proofs

FIRST PROOF: Look around! A hidden hand is working in everything, for something little and without strength like a seed is bearing loads weighing thousands of pounds.[90] Something without consciousness is doing much intelligent and purposive work.[91] As they therefore cannot be working on their own, a powerful, hidden one is causing them to work. If everything were happening on its own, all the work being done in this place must itself be a miracle, and everything a miracle-working marvel.

SECOND PROOF: Look at the adornments of these plains, fields, and residences! Each are marks pointing to that hidden one. Like a seal or stamp,

---

[90] This refers to seeds, which bear trees on their heads.

[91] This refers to delicate plants like grapevines, which cannot rise by themselves or bear the weight of fruits, and so throw their delicate arms around other plants or trees and wind themselves around and load themselves onto them.

each gives news of him. Look at what he produces from a few grams of cotton.[92] See how many rolls of cloth, linen, and flowered material have come out of it; how much sweet food and other delights are being made. If thousands of people clothed themselves from these or ate of those, there would still be enough. Again, look. He has taken a handful of iron, soil, water, coal, copper, silver, and gold and made some living creature.[93] Look and see. These sorts of work are particular to one that holds this land together with all its parts under his miraculous power and all-submissive to his will.

THIRD PROOF: Look at these priceless, moving works of art![94] Each has been fashioned as a miniature specimen of this huge palace. Whatever is in the palace is found in these tiny moving machines. Who but the builder of this amazing palace could include all of it in a tiny machine? Could chance or something purposeless have intervened in this box-sized machine that contains a whole world? However many artistically fashioned machines you see, each is like a seal of that hidden one, like a herald or a proclamation. In their language of being, they announce: "We are the works of art of one who can make this entire world as easily as he made us."

FOURTH PROOF: I will show you something even stranger. Look. All things in this land are changing. Each lifeless body and unfeeling "bone" has started to move toward certain purposes, as if each were ruling the others. Look at this machine beside us.[95] It is as though it were issuing commands and all the materials necessary for its adornment and functioning were running to it from distant places. Look over there. That seemingly lifeless body is as though beckoning, for it makes the biggest bodies serve it and work for it.[96] You may compare the rest with these.

---

[92] For example, an atom-sized poppy seed, an apricot stone that weighs a few grams, or a melon seed each produce from Mercy's treasury woven leaves more beautiful than broadcloth, flowers whiter or yellower than linen, fruits sweeter than sugar, and finer and more delicious than jams, and offer them to us.

[93] This refers to the creation of animal bodies from elements and living creatures from sperm.

[94] This refers to animals and human beings. Since an animal is a tiny index of the world, and humanity is a miniature of the universe, whatever is in the universe has a sample that is contained within each human being.

[95] This refers to fruit-bearing trees. As if bearing on their slender branches hundreds of looms and factories, they weave wonderful, richly adorned leaves, blossoms and fruits, and then cook these fruits and offer them to us. Such majestic trees like pines and cedars have set up their workbenches on hard, dry rock to work.

[96] This "body" signifies grains, seeds, and the eggs of flies. A fly leaves its eggs on an elm tree's leaves. Suddenly, the huge tree turns its leaves into a mother's womb, a cradle, a store full of honey-like food, as if it, although not fruit-bearing, produces animate fruit.

Everything seems to have subjugated to itself all creatures in the world. If you do not accept the hidden one's existence, you must attribute all his skills, arts, and perfections to the stones, soil, animals, and creatures resembling people to the things themselves. In place of one miracle-working being, millions of miracle-workers like him have to exist, both opposed to and similar to each other at the same time, and one within the other, without causing any confusion and spoiling the order. But we know that when two rulers intervene in an affair, the result is confusion. When a village has two headmen, a town two governors, or a country two kings, chaos arises. Given this, what would happen if there were an infinite number of absolute rulers in the same place and at the same time?

FIFTH PROOF: Look carefully at the palace's ornaments and the city's adornments! See this land's orderliness and reflect on this world's artistry. If the pen of a hidden one with infinite miracles and skills is not working, or if all these ornaments are attributed to unconscious causes, blind chance and deaf nature, then even every stone and every blade of grass here would have to be a miracle-working decorator and a wonderful inscriber able to write a thousand books in a letter, and to display infinitely different forms of artistry in a single ornament.

Look at the inscriptions in these stones.[97] Each contains the inscriptions of the whole palace, the laws for the city's order, and the programs for organizing the state. Given this, making the inscriptions a stone contains is as wonderful as making the state. So each inscription and instance of art is a proclamation of that hidden one and one of his seals. As a letter indicates its writer, and an artistic inscription makes its inscriber known, how can then an inscriber, a designer, or a decorator, who inscribes a huge book in a single letter and displays a thousand ornaments in a single one, not be known through his inscriptions and ornaments?

SIXTH PROOF: Come onto this vast plain![98] We will climb to the top of that huge mountain to see the surrounding area. We use these binocu-

---

[97] This refers to humanity, the fruit of the Tree of Creation, and to the fruit that bears the program of its tree and its index. For whatever the Pen of Divine Power has inscribed in the great Book of the Universe has been compressed in our creation. Whatever the Pen of Divine Destiny has written in a huge tree has been included in its fingernail-sized fruit.

[98] This signifies the earth's face in spring and summer, when innumerable individuals of countless species are brought into existence; they are "written" on the earth. They are recruited and may undergo changes without flaw and with perfect orderliness. Thousands of tables of the All-Merciful are laid out and then removed and replaced with fresh ones. All trees are like bearers of trays, and all gardens are like cauldrons.

lars, for curious things are happening in this land. Every hour things are happening that we never imagined.

Look! These mountains, plains, and towns are suddenly changing so that millions of new things can replace them with perfect orderliness, one within and after the other. The most curious transformations are occurring, just as though innumerable kinds of cloths are being woven inside and among others. See, familiar flowery things have been replaced in an orderly fashion with others of similar nature but different form. Everything is happening as if each plain and mountain is a page upon which infinite different books are being written without flaw or defect. It is utterly inconceivable that these things, which display infinite art, skill, and exactness, come about on their own. Rather, they show the artist who engenders them. The one who does all these things displays such miracles, for nothing is difficult for him. It is as easy for him to write a thousand books as to write one book.

Look around you! He puts everything in its proper place with such wisdom, pours his favor so generously on the needy and deserving, draws back and opens universal veils and doors so bountifully that all are satisfied, and lays out such munificent tables that a particular feast of bounties is given to each and every species of animate beings of this land. Indeed, each group and even each individual being is offered a table of bounties particular and suitable to it. Can there be anything more inconceivable than that any of these affairs could be attributable to chance, purposeless or vain, or have many hands behind it, and that their maker is powerful over everything, and everything is subjugated to him? So, my friend, what pretext can you find to persist in your denial?

SEVENTH PROOF: Come, friend! Let's turn to the mutual interrelations of this amazing palace-like world's parts. Look! Universal things are being done and general revolutions are taking place with such perfect orderliness that as if all rocks, soil, and trees in this palace were obeying this world's general rules and were free to do whatever they will. Things that are most distant come to each other's aid. Look at that strange caravan[99] coming from the unseen on mounts resembling trees, plants, and mountains. Each member is carrying trays of food on its head and bringing it to the animals waiting on this side. Look at the mighty electric lamp in that dome.[100] It not only provides light, but also cooks their food wonderfully; the food to be cooked is attached to a string[101]

---

[99] It refers to "caravans" of plants and trees bearing the sustenance of all animals.

[100] An allusion to the sun.

[101] The string and its attached food denote a tree's slender branches and the delicious fruits thereon.

by an unseen hand and held up before it. Also see these impotent, weak, defenseless little animals. Over their heads are small, spring-like "pumps" full of delicate sustenance.[102] They only have to press their mouths against these pumps to be fed.

In short, all things in this world, as if positioned face-to-face, help each other. As though seeing each other, they cooperate with each other. To perfect each other's work, they support each other and work together. The wonders in this world cannot be counted. You can approach them in the light of the examples cited. All of this decisively proves that everything is subjugated to the builder of that wonderful palace, the real owner of this world. Everything works on his behalf, like an obedient soldier carrying out his commands. Everything takes place by his power, moves by his command, and is arranged through his wisdom. Everything helps the others by his munificence, and everything is made to hasten to the aid of others through his compassion. O my friend, can you object to this?

EIGHTH PROOF: Come, O my friend who suppose yourself to be intelligent, as does my own selfhood! You do not want to recognize this magnificent palace's owner although everything points to him, shows him, and testifies to him. How can you deny such testimony? Given this, you have to deny the palace as well and say: "There is no world, no state." Deny your own existence, too, and disappear, or else come to your senses and listen to me.

In the palace are uniform elements and minerals that encompass the whole land.[103] It appears that everything is made from them. This means that whoever owns them owns everything made from them, for whoever owns the field owns its crops, and whoever owns the sea owns its contents. These textiles and decorated woven clothes are made from a single, similar basic thing. Obviously, the one who creates this thing both prepares it and makes it into yarn, for such a work does not allow the participation of others. Therefore, all of the things skillfully woven out of it are particular to him.

All types of such woven things are found throughout the land. They are being made all together, one inside or among others, in the same way and at the same instant. Therefore, they can be the work only of one person who

---

[102] The breasts of mothers.

[103] Elements and minerals denote the elements of air, water, light, and soil, which perform numerous systematic duties: By Divine permission, they hasten to help all needy beings, enter everywhere by Divine command and provide help, convey the necessities of life, and "suckle" living creatures. They also function as the source, origin, and cradle for the weaving and decoration of Divine artifacts.

does everything with one command. Otherwise such correspondence and conformity as regards time, fashion, and quality would be impossible. So, each skillfully made thing proclaims that hidden one and points to him. It is as if each kind of flowered cloth, skillfully made machine, and delicious morsel is a stamp, a seal, a sign of that miracle-working one, and proclaims in the language of its being: "Whoever owns me as a work of art also owns the boxes and shops in which I am found." Each decoration says: "Whoever embroidered me also wove the roll of cloth in which I am located." Each delicious morsel says: "Whoever cooked me also has the cooking pot in which I am located." Each machine says: "Whoever made me also makes all those like me that are found throughout the land. The one who raises us everywhere is also the same. As this same person owns the land and this palace, he also must own us." This is just as the real owner of, say a cartridge-belt or a button belonging to the state, has to own the factories in which they are made. If someone ignorantly claims ownership of it, it will be taken away. Such people will be punished for pretending to own the state's property.

In short, just as each element in this land has permeated throughout it, so can their owner only be the one who owns all the land. Since the artistry throughout this land is of the same nature and works of art resemble each other, displaying the same stamp, whatever has spread throughout the land is evidently the work of a single being's art. And, that one rules over everything. Thus there is a sign of oneness, a stamp of unity in this magnificent palace-like land. Some things are uniform, unique, and of the same nature, yet all-encompassing. Other things, though various and abundant, display a unity of grouping since they resemble each other and are found everywhere. Such unity demonstrates the one of unity. That means that this land's builder, host, and owner must be one and the same.

Look attentively! See how a thick string has appeared from behind the veil of the Unseen.[104] See how thousands of strings hang down from it. See their tips, to which have been attached diamonds, decorations, favors, and gifts. There is a gift particular to everyone. Can you be so foolish as not to recognize and thank the one who offers such wonderful favors and gifts from behind the veil of the Unseen? For if you do not recognize him, you must argue: "The strings themselves make and offer these diamonds and other gifts." In that case, you must attribute to each string the status and function

---

[104] The "thick string" is a fruit-bearing tree, the strings are its branches, and the diamond decorations, favors, and gifts are the various flowers and fruits hung thereon.

of a king [who has a miraculous power and knowledge to do whatever he wishes]. Whereas, before our very eyes an unseen hand is making the strings and attaching gifts to them! Given this, everything in this palace points to that miracle-working one rather than to itself. If you do not recognize him, by denying what is occurring in the palace, you show a determined ignorance of a kind to which a truly human being must not sink.

NINTH PROOF: Come, O friend! You neither recognize nor want to recognize the palace's owner because you deem his existence improbable. You deny because you cannot grasp his wonderful art and manner of acting. But how can all of these exquisite things, this wonderful existence, be explained without recognizing him? If we recognize him, all this palace and its abundant contents are as easy to understand as a single thing in it.

If we do not recognize him and if he did not exist, one thing would be as hard to explain as the whole palace, for everything is as skillfully made as the palace. Things would not be so abundant and economical. No one could have any of these things that we see. Look at the jar of conserve attached to that string.[105] If it had not been miraculously made in his hidden kitchen, we could not have bought it at any price. But now we buy it for a few cents.

Every kind of persistent difficulty and impossibility follows from not recognizing him. A tree is given life from one root, through one law, and in one center. Therefore, forming thousands of fruits is as easy as forming one fruit. If this depended on different, particular centers and roots and on separate, particular laws, each fruit would have been as hard to form as the tree. If an army's equipment is produced in one factory, through one law, and in one center, it is done as easily as equipping one soldier. But if each soldier's equipment is procured from many places, then equipping one soldier would require as many factories as needed for the whole army.

This is also true in this well-organized palace, splendid city, progressive state, and magnificent world. If the invention of all these things is attributed to one being, it is easy to account for their infinite abundance, availability, and munificence. Otherwise everything would be so costly and hard that the whole world would not be enough to buy a single thing.

TENTH PROOF: My friend, we have been here for fifteen days.[106] If we still do not know and recognize this world's ruler and rules, we deserve pun-

---

[105] The jar of conserve denotes Mercy's gifts (melons, watermelons, pomegranates, and coconuts like tins of milk), each of which is a conserve of Divine Power.

[106] An allusion to the age of 15, the age of responsibility.

ishment. We have no excuses, because for fifteen days we have not been interfered with, as though given respite. But neither have we been left to ourselves. We cannot wander about and cause disorder among creatures so delicate, well-balanced, subtle, skillfully made, and instructive as these. The majestic lord's punishment must be severe.

How majestic and powerful he must be to have arranged this huge world like a palace and turn it as though a light wheel. He administers this vast country like a house, missing nothing. Like filling a container and then emptying it, he continuously fills this palace, this city, this land with perfect orderliness and then empties it with perfect wisdom. Also, like setting up a table and then removing it, he lays out throughout the land, as though with an unseen hand, diverse tables with a great variety of foods one after the other, and then clears them away to bring new ones.[107] Seeing this and using your reason, you will understand that an infinite munificence is inherent in that awesome majesty.

Just as all these things testify to that unseen being's unity and sovereignty, so these revolutions and changes occurring one after the other bear witness to his permanence. How so? For the causes of things disappear along with them, whereas the things we attribute to causes are repeated after them. So nothing can be attributed to causes; everything takes place as the work of an undying one. For example, sparkling bubbles on a river's surface come and go, but new ones coming after them also sparkle. Therefore, what makes them sparkle is something constant standing high above the river and having permanent light. Similarly, the quick changes in this world and the things that replace the disappearing ones, assuming the same attributes, show that they are manifestations, inscriptions, mirrors, and works of art of a permanent and undying one.

ELEVENTH PROOF: Come, O friend! Now I will show you another decisive proof as powerful as the previous ten proofs put together. Let's board the ship and sail to that peninsula over there, for the keys to this mysterious world are there.[108] Moreover, everyone is looking to that peninsula, expect-

---

[107] The tables denote the earth's face in summer, during which hundreds of the All-Merciful's tables are prepared fresh and different in the kitchens of Mercy, and then are laid down and removed continuously. Every garden is a cooking pot, and every tree is a tray-bearer.

[108] The ship refers to history, the peninsula to the place of Age of Happiness, the age of the Prophet. Taking off the dress of modern civilization on the dark shore of this age, we sail on the ship of history over the sea of time, land on the Arabian peninsula in the Age of Happiness, and visit the Pride of Creation as he is carrying out his mission. We know that he is a proof of Divine Unity so brilliant that he illuminates the whole earth and the two faces of time (past and future), and disperses the darkness of unbelief and misguidance.

ing something and receiving orders from there. We have landed. Look at the huge meeting over there, as if all the country's important people have gathered. Look carefully, for this great community has a leader. Let's approach nearer to learn about him. See his brilliant decorations—more than a thousand.[109] How forcefully he speaks. How pleasant is his conversation. I have learned a little of what he says during these fifteen days, and you could learn the same from me. He is speaking about the country's glorious miracle-displaying sovereign, who has sent him to us. See, he is displaying such wonders that we have to admit that he is the special envoy of the sovereign.

Look carefully. Not only the peninsula's creatures are listening to him; he is making his voice heard in wonderful fashion by the whole country. Near and far, everyone is trying to listen to his discourse, even animals. Even the mountains are listening to the commandments he has brought so that they are stirring in their places. Those trees move to the place to which he points. He brings forth water wherever he wishes. He makes his fingers like an abundant spring and lets others drink from them.

Look, that important lamp in the palace's dome splits into two at his gesture.[110] That means this whole land and its inhabitants recognize that he is an envoy. As though understanding that he is the most eminent and true translator of an unseen miracle-displaying one, the herald of his sovereignty, the discloser of his talisman, and a trustworthy envoy communicating his commandments, they heed and obey him. All around him, those who are sensible affirm whatever he says. By submitting to his commands and answering his beckoning, everything in this land, even the mountains, the trees, and the huge light that illuminates everywhere, affirm him.[111]

---

[109] A thousand decorations signify the Prophet's miracles that, according to meticulous researchers, number around one thousand.

[110] The important lamp is the moon, which split into two at his gesture. As Mawlana Jami remarked: "That unlettered one who never wrote, wrote with the pen of his finger an *alif* [ا— the first letter of the Arabic alphabet] on the page of the skies, and made one forty into two fifties." In other words, before he split the moon, it resembled the Arabic letter *mim* (م), the mathematical value of which is forty. After splitting, it became two crescents resembling two *nuns* (ن), the value of which is fifty.

[111] The author refers to the mountains and trees answering the Prophet's call. See The Nineteenth Letter's ninth through twelfth signs in Said Nursi, *The Letters* (Turkey: The Light, Inc., 2007) (Tr.) The huge light is the sun. Once the Prophet was sleeping in 'Ali's arms, who did not wake him up out of deep love and respect for him. When the Prophet woke up, the sun was about to set, and 'Ali had not yet prayed the afternoon Prayer. Upon the Prophet's order, the earth revolved a little backwards and the sun appeared above the horizon so 'Ali could pray. This is one of the Prophet's famous miracles.

So, O friend, could there be any deception in the words of this most illustrious, magnificent, and serious of beings, who bears a thousand decorations from the king's royal treasury, about the miracle-displaying king and his attributes, and in the commands he communicates from him? He speaks with firmest conviction and is confirmed by all the country's notables. If you think they contain some deception, you must deny the existence and reality of this palace, those lamps, and this congregation. Your objections will be refuted by the proof's power.

TWELFTH PROOF: Come, O friend who must have come to your senses a little. I will show you further proof as strong as the sum of the previous eleven proofs. Look at this illustrious decree,[112] which has descended from above and which everyone looks upon with full attention out of amazement or veneration. That being with a thousand decorations is explaining its meaning. The decree's brilliant style attracts everyone's admiration, and speaks of matters so important and serious that everyone feels compelled to listen. It describes all the acts, attributes, and commands of the one who governs this land, who made this palace, and exhibits these wonders. There is a mighty seal on the decree, an inimitable seal on every line and sentence. The meanings, truths, commandments, and instances of wisdom it provides are in a style unique to him, which also functions like a stamp or seal.

In short, this supreme decree shows that supreme being as clearly as the sun, so that one who is not blind can "see" him. If you have come to your senses, friend, this is enough for now. Do you have more objections?

The stubborn man replied: "In the face of all these proofs I can only say: 'All praise and gratitude are for God,' for I have come to believe, in a way as bright as the sun and clear as daylight, that this land has a single Lord of Perfection, this world a single Owner of Majesty, and this palace a single Maker of Grace. May God be pleased with you for saving me from my former obstinacy and foolishness. Each proof was sufficient to demonstrate the truth. But since with each successive proof, clearer and finer, more pleasant, agreeable, and radiant levels of knowledge, scenes of recognition, and windows of love were opened and revealed, I waited and listened."

The parable indicating the mighty truth of Divine Unity and belief in God is completed. Through the grace of the All-Merciful, the enlighten-

---

[112] The illustrious decree refers to the Qur'an, and the seal to its miraculousness.

ment of the Qur'an, and the light of belief, I will now show, after an introduction, twelve gleams from the sun of Divine Unity, corresponding to the
twelve proofs in the parable. Success and guidance are from God alone.

Second station

In the name of God, the All-Merciful, the All-Compassionate.

God is the Creator of everything, and He is Guardian over everything;
unto Him belong the keys of the heavens and the earth. (39:62)

So All-Glorified is He, in Whose hand is the absolute dominion of
everything, and unto Whom you are being brought back. (36:83)

There is not a thing but its treasuries are with Us, and We send it
down but in a due and certain measure. (15:21)

No moving creature is there but He holds it by its forelock. Surely
my Lord is on a straight path. (11:56)

Introduction

In my "Qatra" (A Drop from the Ocean of Divine Unity's Proofs), which
discusses belief in God, the first and most important of the pillars of belief,
I briefly explained that every creature shows and bears witness to God's
Existence and Unity in fifty-five ways. In my "Nuqta," (A Point from the
Light of Knowledge of God)[113] I mentioned four universals out of the evi-
dences for Almighty God's Existence and Unity. In my around twelve
Arabic treatises, I discussed hundreds of decisive proofs for All-Mighty
God's Existence and Unity. Thus I will not discuss the matter here in great
depth, but only relate twelve gleams from the sun of belief in God. Once I
wrote about these in Arabic briefly.

Twelve gleams

FIRST GLEAM: The affirmation of Divine Unity is of two sorts. For
example, if an important, rich man's goods arrive in a market or a town,
their ownership can be known in two ways. One is a brief judgment: looking at the goods, an ordinary person concludes that only that rich man
could own so many items. However, if one with such brief conclusion
supervises them, much might be stolen or others might claim partial ownership. The second way is to read the label on every packet, recognize the

---

[113] *Qatra* and *Nuqta* are included in *Mathnawi* ("al-Mathnawi al-Nuri: Seedbed of the Light"),
The Light, 2007. (Tr.)

stamp on every roll, and know the seal on every bill, and so conclude that everything belongs to that person. Everything in effect points to him.

Similarly, there are two kinds of affirmation of Divine Unity. One is the believer's superficial and common affirmation: "God Almighty is One, without partner or like. This universe is His." The other is the true affirmation. By seeing His Power's stamp, His Lordship's seal, and His Pen's inscription on everything, one opens a window directly onto His light from everything. The person then confirms and believes, with almost the certainty coming from direct observation, that everything comes into existence by His Power's hand, that He has no partner or helper in His Divinity and Lordship and His absolute Sovereignty. Through this, one attains a degree of permanent awareness of the Divine Presence. I will now mention some "rays" to demonstrate that true, established affirmation of God's Unity.

NOTE: Divine Dignity and Grandeur require that material or natural causes should be a veil before the Power's operations. The real agent acting in the universe is the Eternally Besought One's Power. Divine Unity and Majesty, as well as God's absolute independence and transcendence, require this. The Eternal Sovereign's officials, all that conveys His commands (e.g., air, angels, or natural causes), are not executives through whom He exercises His Sovereignty, but heralds of His Sovereignty and, as with angels, observers and superintendents of His acts as Lord—Sustainer, Administrator, Upbringer, and Trainer—of the worlds. They exist because they make known the Power's dignity and Lordship's majesty, so that base and lowly things should not be attributed directly to Power.

Unlike a human king, who is essentially weak and destitute, God Almighty does not use officials to exercise His authority. Although everything seemingly occurs according to the principle of cause and effect, this is to preserve the Power's dignity in the superficial view of the mind.

Like a mirror, everything has two faces. One looks to the visible, material world, resembles the mirror's colored face, and may be a way to account for various "colors" and states. The other face is like the mirror's shining face and looks to and consists of the inner dimension of things, where Divine Power operates directly. In the apparent, material face of things, there may be states that are seemingly incompatible with the dignity and perfection of the Eternally Besought One's Power. In this face, Divine Power veils His operations behind cause and effect so that those states may be ascribed to causes. But in reality and with respect to the inner dimension of things, everything is beautiful and transparent. This dimension is fitting for the direct operation of Divine Power and that the Power should be associated with it. Whatever occurs in this dimension is not incompatible with Its dignity. Thus the function of causes is purely apparent and they have no effect in respect to this dimension.

Another reason for apparent causes is that people tend to judge superficially. They raise unjust complaints and baseless objections about things or happenings that they find disagreeable. Almighty God, Who is totally just, has put causes in this material dimension of existence as a veil between such things or happenings and Himself so that such comments should not be aimed at Him. The faults and mistakes that make things and events disagreeable essentially originate in people and things themselves.

Here is a meaningful illustration of this subtle point: Azrail, the Angel of Death, once said to God Almighty: "Your servants will complain about and resent me, for I take their souls." God Almighty told him in the tongue of wisdom: "I will put the veil of disasters and illnesses between you and my servants so that they will complain of them and not resent you." Thus illness is a veil to which people can attribute that which is disagreeable about death. However disagreeable in appearance, death in reality has many wise and beautiful aspects, and they are attributable to Azrail's duty. But Azrail is also an observer, a veil to Divine Power, so that people should attribute to him those aspects of death that their superficial reasoning cannot reconcile with Divine Mercy's perfection. Divine Dignity and Grandeur require that causes should be a veil before Divine Power's hand, while Divine Unity and Majesty demand that causes withdraw their hands from the true effect.

SECOND GLEAM: Look at this garden of the universe, this orchard of the earth. Notice the heavens' beautiful face, gilded with stars. You will see that each creature scattered and spread out in them bears a stamp unique to the Maker, the Creator of all things. Each species, "written" on the pages of night and day, spring and summer, and published by Divine Power's Pen, bears illustrious and inimitable seals, all of which belong to the All-Majestic Maker, the All-Beautiful Creator. I will mention only a few as examples.

Of the innumerable stamps, consider this one out of many He has placed on life: He makes everything out of one thing and one thing out of many things. He makes the countless members and systems of an animal's body out of fertilizing sperm-bearing fluid and also out of simple drinking water. To make everything out of one thing is surely the work of an Absolutely All-

Powerful One. Also, One Who transforms with perfect orderliness all substances contained in innumerable kinds of vegetable or animal food into particular bodies, weaving from them a unique skin for each and various bodily members, is surely an All-Powerful and Absolutely All-Knowing One.[114]

The Creator of life and death manipulates life in this workshop of the world according to His Wisdom in such manner and uses such a miraculous law issuing from the realm of His Creative Commands, that only one Who holds the whole universe in the grasp of His administrative Power and absolutely unconditioned authority could apply that law and enforce it. Thus, if you can reason and have a heart that "sees," you will understand that producing everything from one thing with perfect ease and order, and skillfully making many things into one thing with perfect harmony and orderliness, is a stamp unique to the Maker, the Creator of everything.

If you see that, together with weaving a hundred rolls of broadcloth and other materials like silk and linen from a single ounce of cotton, a wonder-working one also makes many foods from it like halva and pastries; and if you see that he skillfully makes gold out of iron and stone, honey and butter, water and soil, which he holds in his hand, you will conclude that he has a special art, a particular way of working, and that all earthly elements and substances are subjugated to his command and authority. Truly, the manifestation of the Divine Power and Wisdom in life is far more wonderful and amazing than this example. This is only one out of many stamps on life.

THIRD GLEAM: Look at the living creatures moving in this ever-moving universe, in these revolving bodies. You will see that the All-Living, Self-Subsistent One has placed many seals on each one. One of them is this: A living being, for example, a human being, is a miniature of the universe, a fruit of the Tree of Creation, and a seed of this world, for each human being comprises samples of most species of beings. It is as if each living being were a drop distilled from the universe with the most subtle and sensitive balance. So, to create a living being and be its Lord, one has to have full control over the universe.

If you are not lost in fancies and delusions, you will understand that to make a word of Power, for example, a honey-bee, a sort of small index of

---

[114] Countless beings eat the same kinds of food and are composed of the same elements, and yet each one has a unique face, fingerprints, character, ambitions, feelings, and so on. This is irrefutable proof of the Existence and Unity of an All-Knowing and All-Powerful Creator Who has absolute Will and can do whatever He pleases in whatever way He wills. (Tr.)

most things, to "write" on humanity (a page) most of the universe's features, to include in a tiny fig seed (a point) an entire fig tree's program, to exhibit in our heart (a letter) the works of all Divine Names manifested throughout the universe, to record in human memory, which is situated in lentil-sized place, enough "writings" to fill a library, and to include in it a detailed index of all events in the cosmos, is most certainly a stamp unique to the Creator of all things and the All-Majestic Lord of the universe.

Thus if one seal of Lordship on living beings displays its light and makes His signs read in such a fashion, if your were able to consider all those seals together, would you not proclaim: "All-Glorified is He Who is hidden by the intensity of His manifestation."

FOURTH GLEAM: Look carefully at the various multicolored beings floating in the heavens' "ocean" and scattered over the earth's face. Each one bears the Eternal Sun's inimitable signatures. Just as His seals on life and living beings are apparent, so are His signatures on His act of giving life. As comparisons make profound meanings more easily understood, I offer a suitable comparison. Consider the sun: From planets to drops of water, to fragments of glass and sparkling snowflakes, a signature from the sun's image and reflection, a radiant work (effect) particular to the sun, is apparent. If you do not accept the tiny suns apparent in these innumerable things as manifestations of the sun's reflection, you must be so foolish to accept that an actual sun exists in each drop of water, and in each fragment of glass and transparent object facing the sun.

Similarly, with respect to the giving of life from among the Eternal Sun's manifestations, He has placed such a signature on each living being that even if all causes came together and each one was a free agent able to do whatever it wills, they could not imitate that signature. Living beings (miracles of Divine Power) are each a focal point for the Divine Names' manifestations, which are like the Eternal Sun's rays. If, therefore, that amazing inscription of art, that curious composition of wisdom, that manifestation of the mystery of Oneness displayed by living beings is not attributed to the Single and Eternally Besought One, it means falling into total misguidance and superstition. For it would mean giving each living creature an infinite creative power, an all-embracing knowledge, and an absolute will by which to govern the universe. In short, each one would have all the eternal attributes unique to the Necessarily Existent One. As such, each atom of any item would have to be divine, for each atom, especially seeds, are given such a character or properties that they take up a position in exact accordance with the system of the beings of which they are parts. Atoms and seeds are even in a position related to the whole species to which the living being growing from it belongs, for a seed seems to act in such a way that it is planted exactly in the place suitable for the continuation of its species and to plant the species' flag.

We may even say that the seed takes up a position so that the living being can continue its transactions and relations with all the other creatures with which it is connected to receive its necessary sustenance. If, then, that seed or atom does not act under an Absolutely Powerful One's command and its connection with Him is severed, it would have to have an eye with which to see all things and a consciousness encompassing all things.

In short, if the sun's images or reflections in water drops, glass fragments, and multicolored flowers are not attributed to the sun, we must accept the existence of innumerable suns. This is an inconceivable superstition. Similarly, if everything that exists is not attributed to the Absolutely All-Powerful One, we must accept the existence of as many gods as atoms in the universe. Such an idea is clearly untenable.

In summary, then, each atom has three windows opening onto the Eternal Sun's light of Unity and Necessary Existence.

FIRST WINDOW: A soldier has relations with all levels of an army, duties in accordance with those relations, and actions in accordance with those duties and army regulations. It is the same with each atom in your body. For example, an atom in your eye's pupil has similar relations and duties with your eyes, head, powers of reproduction, attraction and repulsion; with your motor and sensory nerves, and veins and arteries, which circulate your blood and work your body; and with the rest of your body. This shows that each bodily atom is a work of an Eternal, All-Powerful One and operates under His command.

SECOND WINDOW: An air molecule may visit, enter, and work within any flower or fruit. If it were not subjugated to and working under an Absolutely All-Powerful One's command, it would have to know all systems and structures of all flowers and fruits and how they are formed, down to their peripheral lines. So, that molecule shows the rays of a light of Divine Unity like a sun. The same holds true for light, soil, and water. Science says that the original sources of things are hydrogen, oxygen, carbon, and nitrogen. All of these are the components of soil, air, water, and light.

THIRD WINDOW: Like the seminal fluids of animals, which have the same composition and nature, the seeds of all flowering and fruit-bearing plants, made up of carbon, nitrogen, hydrogen, and oxygen, have also the same composition and nature. The only basic difference is the program of their progenitor deposited in them by Divine Destiny. If we put different kinds of seeds in a pot filled with soil, which is composed of particular or certain elements, each plant will appear in its own wonderful form, shape, and amazing members. If the soil, air and water atoms were not subjugated to and under the command of One Who knows each thing with all its features, structures, lifecycles, and conditions of its life; One Who can endow everything with a suitable being and all that it needs; and to Whose Power everything is subjected without the least resistance, each soil atom would have to contain "immaterial factories" that determine all the plants' future forms and lives as well as a number of workshops equal to all flowering and fruit-bearing plants, so that each could be the origin for these various plants that differ in form, taste, color, and members. Or each plant would have to have an all-encompassing knowledge and be able to form itself. In other words, if a being's connection with Almighty God is severed, you must accept as many gods as the number of soil atoms. This is utterly untenable.

However, when you admit that the atoms are working under an All-Powerful and All-Knowing One's command, everything becomes very easy. An ordinary soldier, in the name of a powerful king and by relying and depending upon his power, can force a whole people to migrate, join two seas [by having them build a canal], or capture another king. Similarly, by the Eternal King's command and permission, a fly may kill a tyrant, an ant may destroy another tyrant's palace,[115] and a fig seed may bear the load of a fig tree.

Each atom contains two further true witnesses to the Maker's necessary Existence and Unity. Despite its absolute powerlessness, each atom performs many significant duties; despite its lifelessness, each atom acts in conformity with the universal order, which displays universal consciousness. Thus each atom testifies to the Absolutely All-Powerful One's necessary Existence through its impotence and to His Unity by acting in conformity with the order of the universe.

Each living being also contains two signs that He is the Unique One of absolute Unity and the Eternally Besought One. In each is a seal of Divine

---

[115] A fly, entering Nimrod's nose [a Mesopotamian king] and reaching his brain, caused him to die, and ants destroyed the palace of Pharaoh [Ancient Egypt's king].

Oneness and a stamp of His being the Eternally Besought One, for each living being reflects in the mirror of itself all the Divine Names manifested in most parts of the universe. Like a focal point, it reflects the supreme, most comprehensive manifestation of the All-Living, Self-Subsistent One. Since it reflects a display of the Oneness of the Divine Essence behind the veil of the Name the Giver of Life, it bears a stamp of Divine Oneness.

Again, since a living being is like a miniature of the universe and a fruit of the Tree of Creation, the easy satisfaction of its endless needs shows that God is the Eternally Besought One. That is, the being has such a Lord that He is concerned with it and always cares for it. Such concern and care is far more valuable for it than everything in the universe.

> [God's care] alone suffices a thing in place of everything,
> While all things cannot substitute for even a single instance of His regard.

This shows that the Lord of all beings needs nothing, that satisfying their needs does not diminish His Wealth, and that nothing is difficult for His Power. This is a sort of stamp of His being the Eternally Besought One. Through the tongue of life, every living being recites: *Say: "He—(He is) God, the Unique One of absolute Unity. God, the Eternally-Besought-of-All (Himself in no need of anything)"* (112:1-2).

There are other significant windows or openings. They have been discussed elsewhere. Seeing that each atom opens up three windows and two openings on the Necessarily Existent One's Oneness and that life opens two doors, understand how the levels of all beings radiate the light for knowing the All-Majestic One. From this you can understand the degrees of progress in knowledge of God and the degrees of awareness of His Omnipresence attained through it.

FIFTH GLEAM: One pen is enough to write a book by hand. To print it, however, as many metal "pens" as its letters must be arranged. Further, if most of the book is to be inscribed in an extremely fine script within certain letters, as *Sura Ya Sin* can (and has been) written within the initial two letters of *Ya* and *Sin*, smaller metal "pens" to the number of the book's letters are necessary. Similarly, if you accept that this Book of the Universe belongs to the One Who has written it with His Power's Pen, you follow a way so easy as to make the existence of the book necessary and inevitable. But if you attribute it to causality or nature, you follow a way so hard as to be impossible, and so riddled with superstition that even a most fanciful mind could not accept it.

Attributing existence no nature means that each soil atom, water drop, and air molecule contains millions of printing machines and innumerable immaterial factories [to substitute for Destiny in determining the forms and lives of all things in nature], so that nature could originate all flowering and fruit-bearing plants [and govern their lives]. Also, each air, water, and soil atom should be an all-encompassing knowledge and ability to do everything. For every piece of earth, water, and air can be the source of most plants. However, their formation and structure is so systematic, balanced and well-ordered, and their forms are so unique, that a specific factory or "printing machine" would be necessary for each one. Therefore, to be able to originate existence, nature would have to contain in each piece all the machines necessary for the existence of everything. So, attribution of existence to nature is such a superstition that even most superstitious people cannot accept it.

In short, every letter of a book points to itself only to the extent of being a letter and to only one aspect of its existence and meaning. However, it describes its writer and shows him in many ways—for example: "The one who wrote me has fine hand-writing or penmanship. His pen is red." Similarly, each letter of this vast Book of the Universe points to itself to the extent of its size and form, but describes the Eternal Designer's Names as elaborately as an ode, and testifies to Him and points to His Names with its "index fingers" as many as its qualities and states. Thus nobody, not even foolish Sophists who deny themselves and the universe, can deny the All-Majestic Maker.

SIXTH GLEAM: [Like the sun being reflected with its light and heat in each bubble on the surface of an ocean or each fragment of glass,] the All-Majestic Creator manifests certain of His Names on an individual creature or species of creatures and thus gives it its unique identity. So, each and every individual creature or species and each part of every creature bears the stamp of His absolute Oneness (Ahadiya). Also, [like she sun being reflected on the surface of the whole ocean or on the whole earth or the moon,] the Creator manifests certain or all of His Names on the wholes or universals or kingdoms of beings, and thus has numerous visible seals of His Unity (Wahidiya). Due to His Oneness and Unity, each and every individual being and each and every species and whole or universal, and the earth as a whole and the universe display unity, which demonstrates the Creator's absolute Unity (Wahda). Out of His innumerable stamps or seals, let's look at one placed on the earth's face in spring.

In spring, the Eternal Designer resurrects countless plant and animal species with complete differentiation and specification, and perfect orderliness and separation amid infinite intermingling and confusion. This is a stamp of Divine Unity as evident and brilliant as spring. One with a bit of consciousness will perceive that raising dead soil to life in spring, showing with perfect order countless samples of resurrection, and writing on the earth's page the individual members of countless species without fault or forgetting, mistake or deficiency, and in a most well-balanced and well-proportioned, well-ordered and perfect fashion, is a seal unique to One of Majesty, an All-Powerful One of Perfection, an All-Wise One of Grace and Beauty, One Who has infinite Power, all-encompassing Knowledge, and a Will able to govern the universe. The wise Qur'an declares: *Look upon the imprints of God's Mercy, how He revives the earth after its death. He it is Who will revive the dead [in a similar way]. He has full power over everything.* (30:50)

It will certainly be very easy for the Creative Power, Which displays countless examples of resurrection within a few days during the revival of the earth in spring, to revive the dead. For example, is it proper to ask a miracle-working one who, at a sign, raises up Mount Ararat if he can remove a huge rock blocking your way? Similarly, is it proper to say (in a manner implying doubt) to an All-Wise and Powerful One, an All-Munificent and Compassionate One, Who created the firmaments, the earth and the mountains in "six days" and continuously fills and empties them: "Can you remove this layer of soil over us that is blocking our way to Your banquet You have prepared and laid out in eternity? Can you level it and let us pass across it?"

Surely you have observed unity on the earth's face during summer and therefore witnessed the Unity of God. Now look! These most wise, insightful, and mighty operations on the earth's face during spring also bears a seal of unity and therefore displays God's Unity. For this activity is absolutely extensive, speedy, liberal or generous, and easy, and yet done in absolute orderliness and faultless differentiation, and exhibits a most perfect beauty of art and a most perfect form of creation. Thus only One with infinite knowledge and boundless power could own such a seal. That seal belongs to One Who, although nowhere, is all-present and all-seeing. Nothing is hidden from or difficult for Him. With respect to His Power, particles and stars are equal.

Once in a garden of the All-Compassionate One of Grace's munificence, I counted bunches (of grapes) hanging from a grapevine that was two-fingers thick. They were like one little pip among the "bunches" of His miracles. There were 155 bunches, and one bunch contained about 120 grapes. I thought: If this grape vine were a tap from which honeyed water flowed ceaselessly, only then would the water be enough, in this heat, for the bunches on which hang those hundreds of little "pumps" of mercy's sherbet. But this grapevine manages with only a little moisture, which it occasionally obtains. Therefore, the One Who does this must be powerful over all things. All-Glorified is He at Whose work minds are bewildered.

SEVENTH GLEAM: With a little care and effort, you can see the Eternally Besought One's seals on the earth's "page." When you raise your head to look at the great Book of the Universe, you will see on it a seal of Divine Unity as big and clear as itself. For like a factory's components or a palace's building blocks, or a well-organized city's part, all creatures support, aid, and work together—in perfect orderliness—to meet each other's needs. Joining efforts, they serve living beings. Cooperating, they obey an All-Wise Administrator toward a goal. They follow the rule of mutual assistance, which is in force throughout the universe. For example, the sun, the moon, night and day, winter and summer, and plants come to the aid of needy animals; animals hasten to the help of needy humans; nutritious substances rush to the assistance of delicate, helpless infants and fruits; and particles of food move to assist the cells of bodies. This clearly shows that they act through the power of a single, All-Munificent Upbringer and at the command of a single, All-Wise Administrator.

Such mutual support and assistance, answering of each other's needs, close cooperation, obedience, submission, and order testify that all creatures are administered through a single Administrator's organization and directed by a single Upbringer. Also, the universal providence and favor included in the universal wisdom, which is clearly apparent in the purposeful creation of things, as well as the comprehensive mercy evident from the providence and the universal sustenance required by that mercy to feed all living beings, form a seal of Divine Unity so brilliant that anyone with sight and thought will see and understand it.

A fabric of wisdom showing intention, consciousness, and will covers the universe; a fine net curtain of providence and favor showing grace, adornment, embellishment, and kindness is placed above it; over that is spread a robe of mercy radiating the will of being known and loved, of favoring with bounties and gifts enveloping the universe; and over that is laid a table of provision for maintaining all creatures, which shows Lordship's kindness, bestowal, benevolence, perfect caring, proper nurturing, grace, and favoring. All of this clearly shows an All-Gracious One Who is All-Wise, All-Munificent, All-Compassionate, and All-Providing.

Is everything in need of sustenance? Yes, indeed. Like an individual being needing food to live, all beings, especially living beings, whether universal or particular or wholes or parts, have many material and immaterial demands and needs that must be met if they are to continue living. Although they cannot obtain even the smallest need, we see that all their needs are met, in an unexpected way and from an unexpected source, with perfect order, at the appropriate time, in a suitable fashion, and with perfect wisdom. Does this not clearly show an All-Wise Nurturer of Majesty, an All-Compassionate Provider of Grace?

EIGHTH GLEAM: Seeds sown in a field show that the field and the seeds belong to the one who owns both. Likewise, life's fundamental elements (e.g., air, water, and soil), in which things are sown, are of similar, uncomplex nature and universal and omnipresent. Plants and animals, which are fruits of Mercy, miracles of Power, and words of Wisdom, also are of similar nature and found everywhere. This shows that they belong to and are under the command of a single miracle-displaying Maker. Every flower, fruit, and animal is a stamp, a seal, and a signature of that Maker. Regardless of location, each one proclaims in the tongue of its being: "The One Whose stamp I bear also made this location. The One Whose seal I carry also created this place as a missive. The One Whose signature I indicate also wove this land." Only the One Who holds all elements in His Power's grasp can own and sustain the least of creatures. Those who are not blind can see that only One Who exercises Lordship over all plants and animals can own, sustain, and govern the simplest one of them.

In the tongue of similarity to other individuals, each individual being says: "Only the one who owns my species can own me." In the tongue of spreading over the earth's face with other species, each species says: "Only the one who owns the earth's face can be our owner." In the tongue of being bound to the sun, with other planets, and of its mutual relations with the heavens, the earth says: "Only the one who owns the entire universe can own me."

Suppose apples were conscious and that someone told one of them, "You are my work of art," the apple would exclaim: "Be quiet! If you can form all apples on the earth; rather, if you have power over all fruit-bearing trees; rather, over all the gifts of the All-Merciful One proceeding from the treasury of Mercy in shiploads, only then can you claim to be my Lord!"

NINTH GLEAM: We have pointed out some of the seals, stamps, and signatures on particulars and parts, universals and wholes, as well as on the world, life, living beings, and on the giving of life. Now I will indicate one of the countless stamps on species.

Since a tree's countless fruits depend on one law of growth from one center, they are as easy and cheap to raise a single fruit. This means multiple centers would require for a single fruit as much hardship, expenditure, and equipment as for a whole tree, just as manufacturing the needed military equipment for one soldier would require all factories for a whole army. So, if creation were dependent upon multiple centers, there would arise as many difficulties as the number of individuals. The extraordinary ease seen in all species coming into existence is therefore the result of the facility arising from unity.

In short, the correspondence and similarity in basic members between a species' members and a genus' divisions proves that they are works of a single Maker; they are "inscribed" with the same Pen and bear the same seal. The absolute ease of their creation, which makes their existence almost inevitable, requires that they be the work of One Maker. Otherwise, the ensuing difficulties would doom that genus and that species to non-existence.

Given this, attributing everything to Almighty God makes all things are as easy as one thing; when attributed to "natural" causes, one thing becomes as difficult as all things. Thus the extraordinary economy and ease seen in the universe, as well as the endless abundance, clearly show the stamp of Unity. If these abundant and cheap fruits did not belong to the One of Unity, we could not buy a pomegranate even if we gave the world in exchange.

TENTH GLEAM: Just as life, which manifests Divine Grace, is an argument and proof for Divine Oneness (Ahadiya), even a sort of manifestation of Divine Unity, death, which manifests Divine Majesty, is an argument and proof for Divine Unity (Wahidiya).

Consider this—*The highest comparison is (and must be put forth) for God:* Bubbles on a mighty river reflect the sun's image and light, as do transparent objects glistening on the earth's face. Both testify to the sun's existence. Although the bubbles sometimes disappear (such as by passing under a bridge), successive troops of bubbles continue to show the sun's reflection and display its light. This proves that the little images of the sun, which appear, disappear, and then re-appear, point to an enduring, perpetual, single sun that continues to manifest itself from on high. Thus, just as through their appearance those sparkling bubbles demonstrate the sun's existence, so through their disappearance and extinction they display its continuation and unity.

Similarly, through their existence and life, these beings in continuous flux testify to the Necessarily Existent Being's necessary Existence and Oneness, while through their decay and death they bear witness to His eternity and permanence. The beautiful, delicate creatures that are renewed and recruited along with the alternation of day and night, summer and winter, and the passage of centuries and ages, show the Existence, Unity, and permanence of an elevated, everlasting One with a continuous display of beauty. Their decay and death, together with the apparent causes for their lives, show that (material or natural) causes are only veils. This proves that these arts, inscriptions, and manifestations are the constantly renewed arts, changing inscriptions, and moving mirrors of an All-Beautiful One of Majesty, all of Whose Names are sacred and beautiful. Also, they are His stamps that follow one after the other, and His seals that change through wisdom.

This Book of the Universe both instructs us in the signs of Divine Existence and Unity seen in the universe's creation and operation, and bears witness to all the All-Majestic One's Attributes of Perfection, Beauty, Grace, and Majesty. These signs also prove the essential Perfection of Divine Being, without fault and defect. For a work's perfection points to the perfection of the act lying in that work's origin. The act's perfection points to the name's perfection, which points to the attribute's perfection, which points to the essential capacity's perfection, which necessarily, intuitively, and evidently points to the perfection of the one with that essential capacity.

For example, a perfect palace's perfect design and adornments show the perfection of a master-builder's acts. The acts' perfection shows the perfection of the eminent builder's titles, which specify his rank. The titles' perfection show the perfection of the builder's attributes, which are the origin of the art. The perfection of the art and attributes show the perfection of the master's abilities and essential capacity. The perfection of those essential abilities and capacity show the perfection of the master's essential nature.

Similarly, the faultless works seen in the universe, about which the Qur'an asks: *Can you see any flaw?* (67:3), the art in the universe's well-ordered beings, points to an Effective, Powerful Agent's perfect acts. The acts' perfection point to the perfection of that All-Majestic Agent's Names. The Names' perfection points and testifies to the perfection of the

Attributes of the All-Majestic One known with the Names. The Attributes' perfection points and testifies to the perfection of the essential Character and Qualities of the Perfect One qualified by those Attributes. The perfection of the essential Character and Qualities point to the perfection of the One having such Character and Qualities with such certainty that all types of perfections observed throughout the universe are but signs of His Perfection, hints of His Majesty, and allusions to His Beauty in the forms of pale, weak shadows when compared to His Perfection.

ELEVENTH GLEAM AS RADIANT AS THE SUN: As shown in The Nineteenth Word, our master Muhammad the Trustworthy, upon him be peace and blessings, is the supreme sign of the great Book of the Universe, the "Greatest Name" of God manifested in that "Qur'an" of the cosmos, the seed and most illustrious fruit of the Tree of Creation, the sun of the palace of the world, the luminous full moon of the world of Islam, the herald of Divine Lordship's sovereignty, and the wise discoverer of creation's secret. He flies through the levels of truth on the wings of Messengership, which embraces all previous Prophets, and of Islam, which takes under its protection the world of Islam. With the support of all Prophets and Messengers, saints and truthful, truth-seeking scholars and purified ones, he attested to Divine Unity with all his strength and opened the way to the Divine Throne of Oneness. What fancy or doubt can divert belief in God, which he demonstrated, and close this way to Divine Unity, which he proved?

Since I described, to some extent, that clear proof and miracle-working being through fourteen droplets from the water of life of his knowledge in The Nineteenth Word, and through nineteen signs in The Nineteenth Letter (on his miracles), I conclude with calling God's blessing on him as testimony to his truthfulness.

> O God, bestow blessings on the one who leads to the necessity of Your Existence and Your Unity, and testifies to Your Majesty and Grace and Perfection; the truthful and confirmed witness, and the verified, articulate proof; the lord of Prophets and Messengers, the bearer of the meaning of their consensus, affirmation, and miracles; the leader of saints and fruitful ones, who has the meaning of their agreement, verifications, and wonder-working; and the one with evident miracles, clear wonders, and decisive proofs that corroborate and affirm him.
>
> [O God, bestow blessings on] the one with exalted virtues in his person, elevated morals in his duty, and lofty qualities in his Shari'a, perfect and free of all contradiction; the center where Divine

Revelation descended, as agreed upon by the One Who revealed, what was revealed, and the one who brought the Revelation to him; the traveler through the worlds of the Unseen and the inner dimensions of things; the observer of spirits, who conversed with angels; and the sample of all the perfections in creation, in regard to individuals, species, and genera (the Tree of Creation's most illustrious fruit).

[O God, bestow blessings on] the lamp of truth, the proof of reality, the embodiment of mercy, the model of love, the discoverer of the secret of creation, the herald of the sovereignty of Divine Lordship, the one who demonstrated through the sublimity of his spiritual personality that he was before the "eyes" of the Author of the World at the creation of the universe, and the one who brought a Shari'a that shows through the comprehensiveness and soundness of its principles that it is the order of the Composer of the world and established by the Creator of the universe.

The One Who composed the universe with this perfect order composed this religion [Islam] with its finest and most beautiful order. His Messenger is our master, master of the communities of the children of Adam; our guide to belief, the communities of believers, Muhammad ibn 'Abdullah ibn 'Abdul-Muttalib, upon him be the best of blessings and the most perfect peace as long as the earth and the heavens subsist. As the leader of all other witnesses and instructor of all human generations, this truthful and confirmed witness witnessed and announced with all his strength, utmost solemnity, utter steadfastness, strength of certainty, and perfection of belief: "I bear witness that there is no deity but God, the One. He has no partner."

TWELFTH GLEAM AS RADIANT AS THE SUN: This twelfth gleam is such an ocean of truths that all 22 Words are only 22 drops from it. It is such a source of light that they are only 22 rays from it. Each Word is only a ray from one of the stars of the verses shining in the heavens of the Qur'an. Each is a drop from the river of a verse flowing from that Ocean of the Distinguisher between Truth and Falsehood, a pearl from a verse, each of which is a chest of jewels in the greatest of treasuries: God's Book.

This Word of God is defined a little in the 14th droplet of The Nineteenth Word. Originating in the Greatest Name of God, it descended from the Supreme Divine Throne as the greatest manifestation of Divine Lordship. So elevated and comprehensive as to encompass and then even transcend time and bind the ground to the Supreme Divine Throne, it repeatedly declares with all its strength and its verses' absolute certainty:

"There is no deity but God." Making the universe testify to this, all of its contents sing in unison: "There is no deity but God."

If you look at the Qur'an with the eyes of a sound heart, you will see that its six sides are so brilliant and transparent that no darkness and misguidance, doubt and suspicion, or deception can penetrate it. Nor is there a fissure through which such things could infiltrate into the sphere of its purity. Above it is the stamp of miraculousness, beneath it proof and evidence, behind it its point of support—pure Divine Revelation, before it happiness in this world and the next, on its right questioning human reason about its truth and ensuring its confirmation, and on its left calling the human conscience to testify to its truth and securing its submission. In its inside is the pure guidance of the All-Merciful, and on its outside is the light of belief.

Its fruits, with the certainty depending on observation, are the purified and truth-loving scholars and saints, adorned with all human perfections and attainments. If you listen to that Tongue of the Unseen—the Qur'an—you will hear from its depths a most familiar and convincing, an infinitely solemn and elevated, heavenly voice furnished with proofs that declares repeatedly: "There is no deity but He." It states this with such absolute certainty depending on actual experience and complete conviction, that, concerning its truth, it gives you certainty of knowledge to the degree of the certainty coming from direct witnessing and observation.

In short, the Messenger and the Most Firm Criterion to distinguish between truth and falsehood (the Qur'an) are each a "sun." The former, the tongue of the visible, material world, along with the support of a thousand miracles and confirmation of all Prophets and purified scholars, points with the fingers of Islam and Messengership to the truth of "There is no deity but God" and shows it with all his strength. The latter, the tongue of the Unseen world, having forty aspects of miraculousness and confirmed by Divine signs of creation and the operation of the universe, points to the same truth with the fingers of right and guidance, and shows it in a most solemn manner. Thus that truth is clearer than the sun and more manifest than daylight.

O obstinate one immersed in misguidance, who attempts to deny and annul the Qur'an! How can you oppose these suns with your mind's dim lamp? How can you remain indifferent? Are you trying to extinguish them by blowing? Enough of your denying mind! How can you deny the words and claims spoken by the Qur'an and the Prophet in the Name of the Lord of the Worlds and Owner of the Universe? O you wretched one, more impotent that an fly! Who are you that you attempt to contradict the Majestic Owner of the universe?

Conclusion

O friend with an alert mind and an attentive heart. If you have understood this Word, take these twelve gleams in your hand so that you might obtain a lamp of truth as light-giving as thousands of electric lights. Hold fast to the Qur'anic verses descending from God's Supreme Throne. Climbing on the "mount" of Divine assistance, ascend to the heavens of truth. Rise to the "throne of Divine knowledge" and declare: "I bear witness that there is no deity but You. You are One, without partner."

Also declare: "There is no deity but God, One, having no partner; His is the dominion of all existence, and for Him is all praise and gratitude; He alone gives life and causes to die; He is living and dies not; in His hand is all good; and He has full power over everything."

> All-Glorified are You. We have no knowledge save what You have taught us. Surely You are the All-Knowing, the All-Wise.

> Our Lord, take us not to task if we forget or make mistakes. Our Lord, do not lay on us a burden like that which You laid on those before us. Our Lord, do not impose on us that which we cannot bear. Pardon us, forgive us, and have mercy on us. You are our Protector. Give us victory over the people of unbelief.

> Our Lord, do notlet our hearts swerve after You have guided us. Bestow upon us mercy from Your Presence. Surely You are the All-Bestowing. Our Lord, You are He who will gather humanity together on a Day of which there is no doubt. God never fails in His promise.

> O God, bestow blessings and peace on the one whom You sent as a mercy for all the worlds, and on his Family and Companions. Have mercy on us and his community, for the sake of Your Mercy, O Most Merciful of the Merciful. Amin.

> The conclusion of their call will be: "All praise and gratitude are for God, the Lord of the worlds."

The
Twenty-third Word

The Twenty-third Word

Virtues of belief and remarks on our happiness and misery

(This Word consists of two Chapters.)

In the Name of God, the All-Merciful, the All-Compassionate.

Surely We have created humanity of the best stature as the perfect pattern of creation; then We reduced it to the lowest of the low, save those who believe and do good, rihgteous deeds. (95:4-6)

First chapter

IN THE FOLLOWING FIVE POINTS, WE WILL EXPLAIN FIVE OUT OF THE thousands of virtues of belief.

FIRST POINT: We reach the highest degree of perfection and become worthy of Paradise through the light of belief. The darkness of unbelief reduces us to the lowest level so that we deserve Hell. For belief connects us to our All-Majestic Maker, so belief is a relation and connection. Thus our value derives from the Divine art and the Divine Names that are manifested in us through belief. Unbelief breaks this relation, thereby veiling the Divine art and reducing our value to that of a mere physical entity. Since matter is perishable and physical life is no more than a transient animal life, our value as a physical entity is virtually nothing. We will explain this through a parable.

The value of the iron (or any other material) from which a work of art is made differs from the value of the art expressed in it. Sometimes they may have the same value, or the art's worth may be far more than its material, or vice versa. An antique may fetch a million dollars, while its material is not even worth a few cents. If taken to the antiques market, it may be sold for its true value because of its art and the brilliant artist's name. If taken to a blacksmith, it would be sold only for the value of its iron.

Similarly, each person is a unique, priceless work of God Almighty's Art. We are His Power's most delicate and graceful miracles, beings created to manifest all His Names and inscriptions in the form of a miniature specimen of the universe. If we are illuminated with belief, these meaningful inscriptions become visible, and believers read them consciously. They manifest these inscriptions through their connection with their Maker; that is, the Divine art contained in each person is revealed through such affirmations as: "I am the work of the All-Majestic Maker, the creature and object of His Mercy and Munificence." As a result, and because we gain value in proportion to how well we reflect this art, we move from insignificance (in material terms) to beings ranked above all creatures. We communicate with God, are His guests on the earth, and are qualified for Paradise.

However, should unbelief, which means the severance of this connection, is ingrained in us, all of the Divine Names' manifestations are veiled by darkness and thus non-expressive. For if the Artist is unknown, how can the aspects expressing the worth of His Art be identified? Thus most meaningful instances of that sublime Art and elevated inscriptions are concealed. As regards the material aspects of our being, unbelievers attribute them to physical causes, nature and chance, thereby reducing them to plain glass instead of sparkling diamonds. They are no more significant than any other material entity, self-condemned to a transient and suffocating life, and no better than a most impotent, needy, and afflicted animal that eventually will become dust. Unbelief thus spoils our nature by changing our diamond into coal.

SECOND POINT: Belief is a light. Just as it illuminates human beings and reveals all the messages inscribed in their being by the Eternally Besought One, it also illuminates the universe and removes darkness from the past and future as well. We will explain this truth through what I experienced regarding the meaning of: *God is the Guardian of those who believe. He brings them out of the layers of darkness into the light* (2:257).

I saw myself standing on an awe-inspiring bridge set over a deep valley between two mountains. The world was completely dark. Looking to my right, I imagined I saw a huge tomb in darkness. Looking to my left, I felt as if I were seeing violent storms and calamities being prepared amid the tremendous waves of darkness. Looking down, I imagined I saw a very deep precipice. I had a torch in the face of this terrifying darkness. I used it and could see a little with its light. A dreadful scene appeared to me in its dim light. All along the bridge were such horrible dragons, lions, and monsters that I wished I had no torch. Whichever way I directed it, I got the same fright. "This torch brings me only trouble," I exclaimed, angrily throwing it away and breaking it. Suddenly darkness was replaced by light, as if I had switched on a huge light by breaking my torch. I saw everything in its true nature.

I discovered that the bridge was a highway on a smooth plain. The huge tomb was a green, beautiful garden in which illustrious persons were leading assemblies of worship, prayer, glorification, and discourse. The turbulent, stormy, frightening precipices on my left appeared as a banqueting hall, a shaded promenade, a beautiful resting place behind lovely mountains. The horrible monsters and dragons were actually camels, oxen, sheep, and goats. "Praise and thanks be to God for the light of belief," I said, and then awoke reciting: *God is the Guardian of those who believe. He brings them out of the layers of darkness into the light.*

Thus, the two mountains are this life's beginning and end, that is, this world and the world of grave (between death and Resurrection). The bridge is the lifespan, between the two phases of the past (on the right) and the future (on the left). The torch is our conceited ego that, relying on its own achievements, ignores Divine Revelation. The monsters were the worlds' events and creatures.

Those who have fallen into the darkness of misguidance and heedlessness because of their confidence in their egos resemble me in the former state—in the dim light of a torch. With their inadequate and misguided knowledge, they see the past as a huge tomb in the darkness of extinction and the future as a stormy scene of terror controlled by coincidence or chance. The torch also shows them events and creatures, which are in reality dutiful servants or officials of the All-Wise and All-Merciful fulfilling specific functions and serve good purposes, as harmful monsters. These are the people referred to in: *As to those who do not believe, their guardians are*

powers of evil who institute patterns of belief and rule in defiance of God. They
bring them out of the light into layers of darkness (2:257).

If, however, people are favored with Divine guidance so that belief
enters their hearts and their Pharaoh-like egos are broken, thereby
enabling them to listen to the Book of God, they will resemble me in my
later state. Suddenly the universe will fill with Divine Light, demonstrating the meaning of: *God is the Light of the heavens and the earth* (24:35).
Believers see in this light of belief or right guidance that the past is not a
huge tomb; rather, each past century is the realm of authority of a Prophet
or saints, where the purified souls, having completed the duties of their
lives (worship) with: "God is the All-Great," flew to higher abodes on the
side of the future. Looking to their left and through the light of belief, they
discern, behind the mountain-like revolutions of the Intermediate World
(the world of grave) and the next life, a feasting place set up by the All-
Merciful at palaces of bliss in gardens of Paradise. They understand that
storms, earthquakes, epidemics, and similar events serve a specific function,
just as the spring rain and winds, despite their apparent violence, serve
many agreeable purposes. They even see death as the beginning of eternal
life, and the grave as the gateway to eternal happiness. You can deduce
other realities in the light of the comparison.

THIRD POINT: Belief is both light and power. Those who attain true
belief can challenge the universe and, in proportion to their belief's
strength, be relieved of the pressures of events. Relying on God, they travel safely through the mountainous waves of events in the ship of life.
Having entrusted their burdens to the Absolutely Powerful One's Hand of
Power, they voyage through the world comfortably until their last day. The
grave will be a resting place, after which they will fly to Paradise to attain
eternal bliss. If, however, they do not rely upon God, their worldly life will
force them down to the lowest depths. That means, belief requires affirming
Divine Unity; affirmation of Divine Unity requires submitting to God; submission to God requires relying on God; and reliance on God yields happiness in both worlds. But do not misunderstand reliance on God; it does not
mean ignoring cause and effect and complete negligence of the means to
attain a goal. Rather, it means that one should think of causes or means as a
veil before the Power's hand. One observes them by seeking to comply with
the Divine Will, which is a sort of prayer in action. However, such desire and
seeking is not enough to secure a particular effect. We must understand that,

in accordance with right belief, the result is to be expected only from God, the All-Mighty. As He is the sole producer of effects, we always should be grateful to Him.

The one who relies on God and one who does not are like the two men in the following parable:

Once two people boarded a royal ship with heavy burdens. One put his burden on the deck immediately after boarding and sat on it to keep it safe. The other one, even after being told to lay his burden down, refused to do so and said: "I won't put it down, because it might get lost. Besides, I'm strong enough to carry it." He was told:

> This reliable royal ship, which carries us, is stronger and can hold it better. You will most probably get tired, feel dizzy, and fall into the sea with your burden. Your strength will fail, and then how will you bear this burden that gets heavier every moment? If the captain sees you in this state, he might say you are insane and expel you from the ship. Or maybe he will think you do not trust them and make fun of them, and he will order you to be imprisoned. Also, you will be marked out and become the butt of jokes. Your vanity reveals your weakness, your arrogance reveals your impotence, and your pretension betrays your humiliation. And so you have become a laughing-stock—look how everybody is laughing at you.

These words convinced him to follow his companion's example. He told him: "May God be pleased with you. I have obtained relief and am no longer subject to imprisonment or becoming a laughing-stock." So trust in God and come to your senses, as the man in the parable did. Put your trust in God and be delivered from begging from creation and trembling in fear at each happening. Doing so will deliver you from self-conceit, being ridiculous, the pressures of this life, and the torments of the Hereafter.

FOURTH POINT: Belief enables us to attain true humanity, to acquire a position above all other creatures. Thus, belief and prayer are our most fundamental and important duties. Unbelief, by contrast, reduces us to the state of a brutal but very impotent beast.

A decisive proof for this truth is the difference between how human beings and animals come into existence. Almost from the very moment of birth, an animal seems to have been trained and perfected its faculties somewhere else. Within a few hours or days or months, it can lead its life according to its particular rules and conditions. A sparrow or a bee, for example, acquires or is inspired with the skill and ability to integrate into its environment within a matter of twenty days, while it would take a person twenty years to do so. This means that an animal's basic obligation and essential role does not include seeking perfection through learning, progress through scientific knowledge, or prayer and petitioning for help by displaying their impotence. Rather, their sole purpose is to act within the bounds of their innate faculties, which is the mode of worship specified for them.

People, however, are born knowing nothing of life and their environment and so must learn everything. As we cannot do this even within twenty years, we must continue to learn until we die. We are sent here with so much weakness and inability that we might need as many as two years to learn how to walk. Only after fifteen years can we distinguish good and evil. Only by living in a society can we become smart enough to choose between what is beneficial and what is harmful.

Thus the essential and intrinsic duty of our existence is to seek perfection through learning and to proclaim our worship of and servanthood to God through prayer and supplication. It is to seek answers for such essential questions as: "Through whose compassion is my life so wisely administered? Through whose generosity am I being so affectionately trained? Through whose favors and benevolence am I being so solicitously nourished?" It is to pray and petition the Provider of Needs in humble awareness of our needs, even a thousandth of which we cannot satisfy on our own. In short, it is flying to the highest rank of being worshipful servants of God on the wings of consciousness of our innate impotence and poverty.

And so our purpose here is to seek perfection through knowledge and prayer. Everything is, by its nature, essentially dependent on knowledge. And the basis, source, light, and spirit of all true knowledge is knowledge of God, of which belief is the very foundation. After belief, prayer is our essential duty and the basis of worship, for despite our infinite impotence, we are exposed to endless misfortune and innumerable enemies, and despite our infinite poverty, we suffer limitless need and demands.

Children express their need for something they cannot reach with words or tears. Both are a sort of plea or prayer, in word or deed, with the tongue of weakness. Eventually they get what they want. Similarly, we are quite like a beloved child in the world of living beings, who should either weep at the All-Merciful and Compassionate's Court through our weakness and impotence, or pray through to our poverty and need, so that our need may be satisfied. In return, we should perform our duty of gratitude and thanksgiving for this provision. Otherwise, the ingratitude of those who claim to have so much intelligence and power over everything that they can meet their own needs finally will come to the point where they resemble mischievous, lazy children moaning about irritating flies. Such ingratitude is against our essential nature and makes us worthy of severe punishment.

FIFTH POINT: Belief requires prayer for attainment and perfection, and our essence needs it. God Almighty says: *Say (O Muhammad): "My Lord would not concern Himself with you but for your prayer"* (25:77), and: *Pray to Me and I will answer you* (40:60).

Question: If you say that you pray so many times but that your prayers are unanswered, despite the assurance given in the above verse, the answer would be as follows:

The Answer: An answered prayer does not necessarily mean its acceptance. There is an answer for every prayer. However, accepting the prayer and giving what is requested depends upon the All-Mighty's Wisdom. For example, a sick child asks a doctor for a certain medicine. The doctor will give either what is asked for or something better, or he will not give anything. It all depends upon how the medicine will affect the child. Similarly the All-Mighty, Who is the All-Just and Omnipresent, answers His servants' prayer and changes their loneliness into the pleasure of His company. But His answer does not depend on the individual's fancies; rather, according to His Wisdom, He gives what is requested, what is better, or nothing at all.

Moreover, prayer is a form of worship and worship is rewarded mainly in the Hereafter. Worldly needs and purposes are only causes or occasions for prayer. For example, praying for rain is a kind of worship occasioned by the lack of rain. If rain is the prayer's only aim, the prayer is unacceptable, for it is not sincere or intended to please God and obtain His approval.

Sunset determines the time for the evening Prayer, while solar and lunar eclipses occasion two particular kinds of worship. Since such eclipses—the veiling of two luminous signs of day and night—are two means of manifesting Divine Majesty, the All-Mighty calls His servants to perform a form of worship—the Prayer of Eclipse—particular to these occasions. This Prayer has nothing to do with causing the eclipse to end, for this is known already through astronomical calculations. Similarly, drought and other calamities are occasions certain kinds of prayer. At such times, we best realize our impotence and so feel the need to take refuge in the high Presence of the Absolutely Powerful One through prayer and supplication.

If a calamity is not lifted despite many prayers, we should not say that the prayer has not been accepted. Rather, we should say that the time for prayer has not yet ended. If God removes the calamity because of His endless Grace and Munificence, this is light upon light, profit upon profit, and marks the end of the special occasion for prayer.

Praying is a mystery of servanthood to God through worship. Worship is done solely to please God and for His Sake. We should affirm and display our poverty and weakness, and seek refuge with Him through prayer. We must not interfere in His Lordship, but rather let God do as He wills. We must rely on His Wisdom and not accuse His Mercy.

Every creature offers its unique praise and worship to God. What reaches the Court of God from the universe is prayer.

- One kind of prayer is that which is done through the tongue of potential. Plants pray through the tongue of their potential to achieve a full form and manifest certain Divine Names.

- Another kind of prayer is expressed in the tongue of natural needs. All living beings ask the Absolutely Generous One to meet their vital needs, as they cannot do so on their own.

- Yet another kind of prayer is done in the tongue of complete helplessness. A living creature in straitened circumstances takes refuge in its Unseen Protector with a genuine supplication and turns to its All-Compassionate Lord. These three kinds of prayer are always acceptable, unless somehow impeded.

- The fourth type of prayer is the one done by humanity. This type falls into two categories: active and by disposition, and verbal and with the heart. For example, acting in accordance with causes or fulfilling the prerequisites is an active prayer. We try to gain God's approval by complying with causes or fulfilling the prerequisites, for causes alone or the fulfillment of prerequisites cannot produce the result—only God can do that. For example, plowing the soil is an active prayer, for this means knocking at the door of the treasury of God's Mercy. Such a prayer is usually acceptable, for it is an application to the Divine Name the All-Generous.

The second type of prayer of humanity, done with the tongue and the heart, is the ordinary one. This means that we ask God from the heart for something we cannot reach. Its most important aspect and finest and sweetest fruit is that we know that God hears us, is aware of our heart's contents, that His Power extends everywhere, that He can satisfy every desire, and that He comes to our aid out of mercy for our weakness and inadequacy.

And so, O helpless and poor person. Never abandon prayer, for it is the key to the Treasury of Mercy and the means of gaining access to the Infinite Power. Hold on to it. Ascend to the highest rank of humanity and, as creation's most favored and superior member, include the whole universe's prayer in your prayer. Say, on behalf of all beings: *From You alone do we seek help* (1:5), and become a beautiful pattern for creation.

Second chapter

(Five remarks on human happiness and misery)

[Human beings have been created of the best stature as the perfect pattern of creation, and given a comprehensive potential. They have been sent to the world as miracles of power, the ultimate pinnacle of creation, and wonders of art. For them, this world is arena of trial, where the two ways are open before them, one leading to infinite ascent, the other to infinite descent. So, by following either of these ways, they either will rise to the highest of the high or descend to the lowest of the low. I will expound the mystery of humanity's ascent and descent in five remarks.]

FIRST REMARK: We have some relationship with and are in need of most species. Our needs range into all parts of the universe, and our desires range as far as eternity. We desire a single flower as well as a whole spring, a garden as well as an eternal Paradise. We long to see our friend as well as the All-Beautiful, Gracious One of Majesty. As we have to knock on our beloved friend's door for a visit, so too in order to be able to rejoin the ninety-nine percent of our friends, who have left for the Intermediate World, and be saved from eternal separation, we also need to seek refuge at the Court of the Absolutely Powerful One, Who will close this huge world's door and open the door of the Hereafter, the world of wonders, and will replace this world with the next one.

Given this, our true object of worship can only be an All-Powerful One of Majesty, All-Compassionate One of Beauty and Grace, All-Wise One of Perfection, in Whose hand are the reins of all things, in Whose possession is the provision of every existence, Who sees everything and is omnipresent, unbounded by space, and free of any constraint, flaw, defect, and deficiency.

For only One with infinite power and all-encompassing knowledge can satisfy our unlimited need and therefore it is only He Who is worthy of worship.

So, O humanity! If you worship Him alone, you will attain a rank above all other creatures. If you do not, you will become a disgraced slave to impotent creation. If you rely upon your selfhood and power instead of prayer and trust in God, and claim an arrogant superiority, you will become lower than a bee or an ant and weaker than a fly or a spider with respect to positive acts and constructive invention. But your evil and destruction will weigh heavier than a mountain and be more harmful than a pestilence.

So, O humanity! You have two aspects of being. One is positive and active, and has to do with constructive invention, existence, and goodness. The other is negative and passive, and concerns destruction, nonexistence, and evil. As for the first aspect of your being, you cannot compete with a bee or a sparrow, are weaker than a fly or a spider, and cannot achieve what they can. As for the second aspect of your being, however, you can surpass mountains, the earth, and the heavens, for you can bear a burden that they cannot. Thus your acts have a wider impact than theirs. When you do something good or build something, it reaches only as far as your hand and strength. But your evil and destructive acts are aggressive and expandable.

For example, unbelief is an evil, an act of destruction, an absence of affirmation. It may look like a single sin, but it implies an insult to creation, the debasement of all Divine Names, and the degradation of all humanity. For creation has a sublime rank and important task, for each part of it is a missive of the Lord, a mirror of His Glory, and a dutiful servant of His Divinity. Unbelief denies them this rank bestowed on them by virtue of these functions and reduces them to playthings of chance, and insignificant, useless, and worthless objects doomed to decay and decomposition.

Unbelief is also an insult to the Divine Names, Whose beautiful inscriptions and manifestations are seen in the mirrors of all created forms throughout the universe. Furthermore, it casts humanity down to a level more wretched and weak, helpless and destitute, than the lowliest animal. It reduces us to an ordinary, perishable sign-board without meaning, confused and swiftly decaying. And this when humanity, in reality, is a poetic work of Wisdom that manifests all Divine Names; a great miracle of Power that, like a seed, contains the Tree of Creation; and God-appointed ruler of the earth, who is superior to angels and higher than mountains, the earth, and heavens by virtue of the Supreme Trust we accepted.

In short: As regards evil and destruction, the carnal, evil-commanding soul may commit countless crimes and cause unlimited destruction, while its capacity to do good is very limited. It can destroy a house in a day but cannot rebuild it in a hundred days. But if it abandons self-reliance and vanity and relies upon Divine aid to do good and constructive things, if it abandons evil and destruction and seeks Divine forgiveness and so becomes a perfect servant of God, it becomes the referent of: *God will change their evil deeds into good deeds* (25:70). That is, our infinite capacity for evil is changed into an infinite ability for good. We attain the worth of "the perfect pattern of creation" and rise to the "highest of the high."

Consider then, O heedless one, the All-Mighty's Grace and Munificence. In reality, it is absolute justice to record one sin as a thousand sins, [due to its consequences and effects,] and a good act as only one. But God does the reverse: He records a sinful act as one and an act of goodness as ten, seventy, seven hundred, or, in some cases, seven thousand. From this we can understand that entering Hell is the result of one's deeds and pure justice, while entering Paradise is the result of His absolute Grace.

SECOND REMARK: Human beings have two faces. The first face looks to this worldly life because of our selfhood. Here our capital consists of a free will as feeble as a hair, a power restricted to a most limited talent with respect to positive, constructive acts, a life or lifespan as short as a flash of light, and a material existence bound to decompose swiftly. In this state, we are no more than a feeble member of one species among countless others spread throughout the universe.

The second face looks to the eternal life because of our nature as God's servants charged with and in need of worshipping Him. Our perception of helplessness and insufficiency as God's servants needy of Him make us extremely important and inclusive beings. For the All-Wise Originator has implanted an infinite impotence and poverty in our nature so that each of us may be a comprehensive mirror reflecting the boundless manifestations of an All-Compassionate One of infinite Power, an All-Munificent One of infinite Richness.

We resemble seeds. A seed is endowed with great potential by Divine Power and a subtle program by Divine Destiny, so that it may germinate underground, emerge from that narrow world and enter the spacious world of air. Asking its Creator in the tongue of its capacity to become a tree, it may attain a perfection particular to it. If, due to its malignant disposition, the seed abuses its potential to attract harmful substances, it will soon rot away in its narrow place. If it uses its potential properly, however, and in compliance with the creational commands of *The Splitter of grain and fruit-stone* (6:95), it will emerge from its narrow place and grow into an awe-some, fruitful tree. In addition, its tiny and particular nature will come to represent a great and universal truth.

In just the same way, our essence is equipped by Power with great potential and is inscribed by Destiny with important programs. If we use our potential and faculties in this narrow world under the soil of worldly life to satisfy the fancies of our carnal, evil-commanding soul, we will, like a rot-ten seed, decay and decompose for an insignificant pleasure in a short life amidst hardships and troubles. Thus we will depart from this world with a heavy spiritual burden on our unfortunate souls.

But if we germinate the seed of our potential under the "soil of worship" with the "water of Islam" and the "light of belief" according to the Qur'an's decrees, and use our faculties for their true purposes, we will grow into eter-nal, majestic trees whose branches extend into the Intermediate World and the World of Representations or Immaterial Forms, and which will be favored with countless bounties and yield innumerable fruits of perfection in the next world and Paradise. We will, in fact, become the blessed, luminous fruit of the tree of creation.

True progress is possible only when we turn our faculties (e.g., intel-lect, heart, spirit, and even imagination) to the eternal life and make them occupied with its own kind of worship. What the misguided consider progress—being immersed in the life of this world and subjecting all our faculties to the carnal, evil-commanding selfhood to taste all worldly pleas-ures down to the basest—is nothing but decline and degradation. I once observed this truth in a vision, which is as follows:

I reached a huge city full of large palaces. Outside some of them, I noticed ongoing spectacles and shows to amuse and entertain. As I drew near to one of them, I saw that its owner was playing with a dog at the door. Women were chatting with young strangers, and young girls were organiz-ing children's games. The doorman was behaving as if he were their mas-ter. I realized that the palace was empty, with all important tasks left unat-tended, for its corrupted inhabitants were pursuing useless affairs.

I then came across another palace. A faithful dog was lying at the door, and beside it was a doorman with a stern, serious, and sober expression. The palace seemed so quiet that I entered in wonder and amazement. Inside was a scene of great activity,: one flour above another, the inhabitants were engaged in different, important tasks. The people on the first floor were managing the palace. On the second floor, girls and boys were studying. The women on the third floor were producing beautiful works of art and delicate embroidery. On the top floor, the owner was in constant communication with the king to secure his household's well-being and so that he could perform noble duties for his own progress and perfection. As they did not see me, I walked about unhindered.

Then I came out and looked around. I saw that the city was full of similar palaces. I asked and was told that the palaces like the first one belonged to the foremost unbelievers and misguided, while those of the second type belonged to upright Muslim notables. In one corner, I came across a palace on which my name was written: "Said." As I looked at it closely, I felt as if I saw my image on it. Crying in bewilderment, I came to my senses and awoke.

The city is our social life and the terrain of human civilization. Each palace is a human being, and the inhabitants are human senses and faculties (e.g., eyes, ears, intellect, heart and spirit, and powers of anger and lust). Each sense and faculty has a particular duty of worship, as well as particular pleasures and pains. The carnal soul and fancies, as well as the powers of anger and lust, correspond to the dog and the doorman. Thus, subjugating the sublime senses and faculties to carnal desires and fancies so that they forget their essential duties is decline and corruption. It certainly is not progress. You may interpret the other details for yourself.

THIRD REMARK: With respect to our constructive actions and bodily endeavors, we are like weak animals and helpless creatures. The realm at our disposal is so limited that our fingers can touch its circumference. Our weakness, impotence, and indolence are so great that even domesticated animals are influenced by them. If a domesticated animal is compared with its undomesticated counterpart, great differences can be seen.

But as recipient beings conscious of our need to pray and petition, we are honored, worthy travelers allowed to stay for a while in the guest-house of this world. We are guests of such a Munificent One that He has put His infinite treasures of Mercy at our disposal and subjugated His unique works of creative Power and special servants to us. Also, He has prepared for our use, pleasure and recreation such a vast arena that its radius is as far as sight or even imagination can reach.

If we rely on our physical and innate abilities, taking the worldly life as our goal and focusing on its pleasures in pursuit of our livelihood, we will suffocate within a very narrow circle. Moreover, our bodily parts, senses, and faculties will bring suit and witness against us in the Hereafter. But if we know that we are guests and so spend our lives within the limits established and approved by our All-Munificent Host, we will lead a happy and peaceful life in a broad sphere and gain a long, eternal life. We can rise to the highest of the high, and all of our bodily members and faculties will testify in our favor in the Hereafter.

Our wonderful faculties are not meant for this trivial worldly life; rather, they are for our eternal life of great significance. For when compared with animals, we see that we are far richer than animals in respect of faculties and senses, while in regard to worldly pleasures and animal life we fall a hundred times lower. This is because every worldly pleasure we taste bears many traces of pain. Pains of the past, fears of the future and the pains at the cessation of every pleasure spoil our enjoyment. However, animals experience pleasure without pain, enjoyment without anxiety, and are neither wounded by the pains of the past nor distressed by the fears of the future. They enjoy comfortable lives and praise their Creator.

This means that if humanity, created of the best stature as the perfect pattern of creation, concentrates on this worldly life, we are far lower than a sparrow, although we have far more developed faculties than any animal. In order to explain this reality, I will repeat a parable which I wrote in another treatise.

A man gives his servant ten gold coins and tells him to have a suit made out of a particular cloth. He gives another servant a thousand gold coins and sends him to the market with a shopping list. The former buys an excellent suit of the finest cloth. The latter acts foolishly, for he neither notices how much money he was given nor reads the shopping list. Thinking that he should imitate his friend, he goes to a shop and asks for a suit. The dishonest shopkeeper gives him a suit of the very worst-quality cloth. The unfortunate servant returns to his master and receives a severe reprimand and a terrible punishment. Anyone can see that the thousand gold coins were not given for a suit, but for a very important transaction.

In the same way, our spiritual faculties, feelings, and senses are much more developed than those of animals. For example, we can see all degrees of beauty, distinguish all the varieties of the particular tastes of foods, penetrate the many details of realities, yearn for all ranks of perfection, and so on. But animals, with the exception of a particular faculty that reaches a high state of development according to its particular duty, can realize only slight development, if any.

We are rich in faculties because our senses and feelings have developed a great deal owing to our mind and intellect. Our many needs have caused us to evolve different types of emotions and to become very sensitive to many things. Also, due to our comprehensive nature we have been given desires turned to several aims and objectives. Our senses and faculties have greatly expanded due to the diversity of our essential duties. Furthermore, since we are inclined and able to worship, we have the potential to realize all kinds of perfection.

Such rich faculties and abundant potentialities cannot have been given to us for an insignificant, temporary, worldly life. In reality, they were given to us because our essential duty is to perceive our obligations, which are directed toward endless aims; to affirm our impotence, poverty, and insufficiency in the form of worship; to study creation's glorifications of God with our far-reaching sight and penetrating understanding, and to bear witness to them; to discern and be grateful for the All-Merciful One's aid sent in the form of bounties; and to gaze, reflect upon, and draw warnings from the miracles of His Power as manifested in creation.

O world-adoring one charmed by the worldly life and ignorant of the meaning of your nature as the perfect pattern of creation! Once I saw the true nature of this worldly life in a vision, as follows:

I found myself a traveler going on a long journey. My lord who set me making this journey gradually gave me some of the sixty gold coins He had allotted to me. This went on for some time, and after a while I arrived at an inn that provided some entertainment. In one night I spent ten gold coins on gambling and entertainment, and in pursuit of fame. The next morning, I had no money left. Nor could I do trade and buy provisions I would need at my destination. All I had left was pain, sorrow, and regret left by sins and illicit pleasures. While I was in this wretched state, a man appeared and said to me: "You have lost all you had and deserve to be punished. Moreover, you will go on to your destination with no money. But if you use your mind, the door of repentance is not closed. When you gradually receive the remaining fifteen gold coins, keep half in reserve and use it to buy what you will need at your destination."

My soul did not agree, so the man said: "Save a third of them then." Still my soul balked. The man insisted: "Then a quarter." I saw that my soul could not abandon its addictions, so the man turned away indignantly and disappeared. At once, I found myself on a high-speed train travelling through a tunnel. I was alarmed, but there was no escape. To my surprise, I saw very attractive flowers and tasty-looking fruits alongside the track, hanging out from the sides of the tunnel. I foolishly tried to pick some of them. But all around them were thorns that, due to the train's speed, tore at my hands and made them bleed. They cost me very much. Suddenly an attendant came and said: "Give me five cents and I'll give you as many flowers and fruits as you want. With your hands all cut up, you are losing a hundred instead of five cents. Besides, there is a punishment for picking them without permission."

Depressed by this condition, I looked out the window to see when the tunnel would end. But there was no end in sight. The tunnel's walls had many openings into which passengers were being thrown. Suddenly I caught sight of an opening just opposite me with a gravestone on either side. When I peered out, I made out my name, "Said," written in capital letters on a gravestone. I gave a cry of bewilderment and repentance. Unexpectedly, I heard the voice of the man who had advised me at the inn, asking: "Have you come to your senses?" I replied: "Yes, but I've been left powerless, and there is nothing I can do." He told me to repent and trust in God, to which I replied that I would. Then I woke up and I found myself transformed into the New Said; the Old Said had gone away.

I will now interpret some aspects of this vision: The journey is our life, a journey from the Worlds of Spirits to all eternity, passing through the stages of the mother's womb, youth, old age, the grave, the Intermediate World, Resurrection, and the Bridge. The sixty gold coins are the sixty years of an average lifetime. I was forty-five when I had this vision. Only God knows when I will die. A sincere student of the Qur'an showed me the true path so that I might spend half of the remaining fifteen years for the Hereafter. The inn, I came to understand, was Istanbul for me. The train was time, and each wagon was a year. The tunnel was this worldly life. The thorny flowers and fruits were illicit pleasures and forbidden amusements that make the heart bleed with the idea of separation at the very moment you reach for them. Disappearance of pleasures increases sorrow, and besides, being unlawful, cause one to suffer punishment. The attendant had said: "Give me five cents, and I'll give you as many flowers and fruits as you want." This means that the permissible tastes and pleasures, obtained in lawful ways, are enough to satisfy us and so there is no need to pursue illicit ways.

FOURTH REMARK: Humanity, among the creatures, is much like a tender child. Our strength is in our weakness, and our power in our impotence. This lack of strength and power has caused creation to be subjugated to us. So if we perceive our weakness and become humble servants of God through verbal and active prayer, and if we recognize our impotence and seek God's help, we will have shown our gratitude to Him for this subjugation of nature to us. Moreover, God will enable us to reach our goal and achieve our aims in a way far beyond our own capability. Sometimes we wrongly attribute a wish's attainment to our own power and ability, when in reality it has been obtained for us through the prayer offered by the tongue of our disposition. Consider how great a source of power is a chick's weakness, for it causes the mother hen to attack even a lion. A lion cub's weakness subjugates a great lioness, which will suffer hunger to feed its baby. How remarkable is the powerful appeal inherent in weakness, and what a spectacular manifestation of Compassion for importunate beings.

Tender, beloved children obtain their goals by weeping, wishing, or making sad faces, all of which can cause mighty people to serve them. If children rely on their own strength, in practical terms they can achieve nothing. Their weakness and powerlessness, as well as feelings of affection and protection, are so in their favor that a single gesture may allow them to subjugate powerful persons to themselves. Should such children arrogantly deny the care and affection shown to them and claim to do all of this on their own, they would receive a sour face and resentment. Similarly, if like Korah who said: *I have been given it (my possessions) on account of my knowledge* (28:78), we attribute our achievements to our own power and ability in a way that demonstrates ingratitude and denies our Creator's Mercy and accuses His Wisdom, we will certainly deserve punishment.

This shows that our observed dominion in nature, and our advancement and progress in civilization and technology, are mainly due to our essential weakness and helplessness, which attract Divine aid. Our poverty is the source of Divine provision, our ignorance is compensated for by Divine inspiration, and our need draws Divine favors. Divine Mercy, Affection, and Wisdom, not our own power and knowledge, have empowered us with dominion over creation and have put things at our disposal. It is Divine

Authority and Mercy Which, due to our weakness, enable us, beings so weak that we can be defeated by a blind scorpion and a footless snake, to dress in silk produced by a worm and to eat the honey produced by a stinging insect.

Since this is the reality, O humanity, renounce arrogance and self-trust. Rather, declare and affirm your impotence and weakness in God's Court by asking for His help, and by praying and entreating Him. Show that you are His true servant. Then say: *God is sufficient for us. How excellent a Guardian He is!* (3:173) and ascend to the higher ranks.

Do not say: "I am nothing. Why should the absolutely All-Wise One put creation at my disposal and demand universal gratitude?" In physical terms and with respect to your evil-commanding soul you are almost nothing, but your duty or rank makes you an attentive observer of this magnificent universe, an eloquent tongue of beings declaring Divine Wisdom, a perceptive student of this Book of Creation, an admiring overseer of the creatures glorifying God's praise, a respected master of worshipping beings.

You are, O humanity, an insignificant atom, a poor creature and weak animal in terms of your physical being and soul. And so you are being carried away by creation's huge waves. But if you are perfected through the training of Islam, which is illumined by the light of belief containing the radiance of Divine love, you will find a kingliness in your being a servant, a comprehensiveness in your particularity, a world in your small entity, and a very high rank in your insignificance. The realm of your supervision of the rest of creation will be so broad that you can say: "My Compassionate Lord has made the world a home for me. He has given me the sun and moon as lamps, spring as a bunch of roses, summer as a banquet of favors, and animals as obedient servants. He has put plants and vegetation at my disposal, as ornaments and provisions to my home."

In conclusion, if you obey your evil-commanding soul and Satan, you will fall to the lowest of the low; but if you follow the truth and the Qur'an, you will rise to the highest of the high and become the perfect pattern of creation.

FIFTH REMARK: We have been sent here as guests with a special responsibility. Endowed with important potentials, we have been assigned important duties and strongly urged to carry them out. If we do not, we will be punished. To make "being the perfect pattern of creation" more comprehensible, I will summarize the essentials of worship and duties.

Our worship has two aspects. The first aspect concerns reflection and consciousness without having to address Him directly. The second aspect is worship and prayer, done in His presence by addressing Him directly.

The first aspect is:

- to obediently affirm the Sovereignty of His Lordship over creation and observe Its beauties and perfections in amazement;

- to draw the attention to and herald the unique arts in creation, which consist of the embroideries of sacred Divine Names; to weigh on the scales of perception and discernment the gems of the Lord's Names, each of which is a hidden spiritual treasure, and evaluate them with our hearts' grateful appreciation;

- to study the pages of creation and the sheets of the heavens and the earth, each of which is a missive of Divine Power, and contemplate them in great admiration; and

- to gaze in amazement and admiration upon the subtle ornamentation and refined skills seen in creation, and ardently desire to know their All-Beautiful and Gracious Originator and yearn to enter His Presence, where we hope to be received into His favor.

The second aspect of our worship is done in His presence by addressing Him directly. We pass from the works to their Producer and:

- we see that an All-Majestic Maker wills Himself to be known through His Art's miracles, and in response we believe in Him and know Him;

- we see that an All-Compassionate Lord wills to make Himself loved through His Compassion's beautiful fruits, and in response we love Him and make ourselves loved by Him through devoting our love and adoration to Him;

- we see that an All-Munificent Provider nourishes us with the best and dearest of His material and spiritual favors, and we respond with gratitude and praise, expressed through our works, deeds, lifestyle and, if possible, through all of our senses and faculties;

- we see that an All-Beautiful and Gracious One of Majesty manifests His Grandeur and Perfection, Majesty and Beauty, in the mirrors of beings and draws attention to them, and in response, declaring, "God is the All-Great! All-Glorified is God!" we prostrate before Him in wonder and adoration, and in consciousness of our nothingness before Him;

- we see that One with Absolute Riches displays His limitless wealth and treasuries in an infinitely generous fashion, and, declaring our destitution, we respond with asking for His favors in praise and glorification;

- we see that that Originator of Majesty has arranged the earth like an exhibition to display His matchless works, and in response we appreciate them by saying, "What wonders God has willed and created!"; confirm their beauty by saying, "God bless them!"; show our wonder by saying: "All-Glorified is God!" and express our admiration by saying, "God is the All-Great!";

- we see that One absolutely Unique shows His Oneness throughout creation by His unique signs and specific decrees, and by His inimitable stamps and seals that He has put on each creature; that He inscribes signs of Unity on everything and raises throughout the world the flag of His Unity, proclaiming His Lordship. We respond to this with belief, affirmation, admission, and testimony to His Unity, and with devotion and sincere worship.

We may attain true humanity through such types of worship and reflection. We may show that we are of the best stature as the perfect pattern of creation and, by the grace of belief, become trustworthy rulers of the earth worthy of bearing the Supreme Trust.

Now, O heedless people who move toward the lowest of the low by misusing your will, although you have been created of the best stature as the perfect pattern of creation, listen to me. Like you, I once thought the world was fine and beautiful in heedlessness coming from the intoxication of youth. Then the moment I awoke in the morning of old age, I saw how ugly is the world's face which is not turned toward the Hereafter, which I had previously imagined to be beautiful. To see this and how extraordinarily beautiful is its other face, which is turned toward the Hereafter, you may refer to the two "Tables of Truth" in the Second Station of the Seventeenth Word.

The First Table depicts the reality of the world of the heedless, while the second one describes the reality of the world of the people of right guidance.

> All-Glorified are You! We have no knowledge save what You have taught us. Surely You are the All-Knowing, the All-Wise.

O my Lord, expand for me my breast, and make my task easy for me. Loose any knot from my tongue so they may understand my speech.

O God, bestow peace and blessings on Muhammad, his pure, unique essence, who is the sun of the heavens of mysteries, the manifestation of lights, the point upon which manifestations of God's Majesty are centered, the pivot around which the world of His Grace and Beauty revolves.

O God, for the mystery of him in his relation to You, and for his journeying toward You, secure me from my fears, protect me from falling, diminish my faults, and expel my grief and greed. Be with me, take me away from myself unto You, and favor me with effacement from myself. Do not leave me obsessed with my self, veiled by my feelings. Unveil to me every mystery.

O the All-Living and Self-Subsistent One, O the All-Living and Self-Subsistent One, O the All-Living and Self-Subsistent One! Have mercy upon me and my companions. Have mercy upon all believers and all the people of the Qur'an. Amin, O the Most Merciful of the Merciful, O the Most Munificent of the Munificent!

The conclusion of their call will be: "All praise and gratitude are for God, the Lord of the worlds."

The
Twenty-fourth Word

The Twenty-fourth Word

> ➢ *Manifestations of Divine Names*
> ➢ *Ways of attainment to Truth*
> ➢ *Some criteria to understand certain hadiths*
> ➢ *How beings worship God*
> ➢ *Love, worship, and thanksgiving*

(NOTE: This Word has five branches. Study the fourth one carefully. Hold on to the fifth one; climb it and gather its fruits.)

In the Name of God, the All-Merciful, the All-Compassionate.

God, there is no deity but He; His are the All-Beautiful Names. (20:8)

I will point out five branches of one of the numerous truths contained in the illustrious "tree" of this majestic verse.

Five branches

IRST BRANCH: A KING HAS DIFFERENT TITLES BY WHICH HE IS known and mentioned in his government's various departments, different designations and attributes among his subjects' classes, and different names and signs for his rule's levels. For example, he is the supreme judge in the justice department, chief administrator in the civil service, commander-in-chief in the military, and supreme teacher in the education department. If you know the rest of his names and titles, you will understand that he may have as many names and titles related to his government's departments and levels of his rule.

It is as if, due to his public person and system of communication, he is present in every department. Through his laws, regulations, and representatives, he superintends all officials, watches all subjects, and is seen by them. Behind the veil at every level, he administers, executes his orders, and is watchful through his decree, knowledge, and power.

Similarly, the Lord of the worlds, the Sovereign of eternity, has at the levels of His Lordship's manifestations qualities and designations which are all different but correspond to each other. In the spheres of His Divinity, He has Names and marks which are all different but whose manifestations are concentric with each other. In His majestic execution of His rule, He has representations and appellations which are all different but resemble each other. In the operations of His Power, He has titles which are all different but imply each other. In the manifestations of His Attributes, He has sacred ways of revealing Himself that differ but point to each other. In His modes of acting, He has wise operations which are of numerous sorts but perfect each other. In His colorful artistry and varied works of Art, He has magnificent aspects of Lordship which differ but correspond to each other.

In every world and division of beings, each of His All-Beautiful Names is manifested individually. A particular Name is dominant in a particular sphere, with other Names being subordinate. In every level and division of beings, regardless of size, God has a particular display of Himself, a particular manifestation of Lordship, and a particular manifestation of a Name. Although the Name in question has a universal manifestation, It concentrates on something particular in such a way that you think It is exclusive to that thing.[116]

In addition, although the All-Majestic Creator is nearer to everything than itself, He has seventy thousand veils of light that veil Him from creation. For example, consider how many veils are between the Name of Creator's particular degree of creativity manifested in you and Its universal and greatest manifestation as the Creator of the Universe. This suggests that if you can go beyond the whole universe, you may reach, through the door of being created, to the highest limit of the manifestations of the Name of Creator and draw close to the Sphere of the Attribute of Creativity.

---

[116] For example, God manifests almost all of His Names (e.g., the All-Merciful, the Creator, the All-Fashioning, the All-Wise, the All-Knowing, etc.) on every individual. However, a particular Name's manifestation may be more apparent on one person than the others. If the Name the All-Wise is so manifested, that person may be a wise one. Thus people have different characters and everyone has a capacity and tendency toward a particular profession. (Tr.)

Since the veils have windows opening onto each other, the Names appear to be concentric with each other, the Essential Qualities correspond to each other, the Representations are like each other, the Titles imply each other, ways of Self-Revelation resemble and point to each other, the Operations cooperate with and perfect each other, and Lordship's various dispositions assist each other, then it is surely necessary for one who recognizes Almighty God by one of His Names, Titles, or aspects of His Lordship not to deny His other Titles, acts, and aspects of Lordship. If we do not move from the manifestation of one Name to the other Names, we are in loss.

For example, if we do not see the All-Knowing where we see the works of the All-Powerful and the Creator, we may fall into heedlessness and misguidance by regarding nature as self-originated. Thus we always should recite "He" and "He is God," and listen and hear from everything: "He is God, the One." In unison with all creation, we should proclaim: "There is no deity but He." The Qur'an clear in itself and clearly showing the truth, through the declaration: *God, there is no deity but He. His are the All-Beautiful Names*, points to these truths.

If you want to observe those elevated truths closer, ask a stormy sea or the quaking earth: "What are you saying?" You will hear them repeat: "O the All-Majestic! O the All-Majestic! O the All-Glorious and Mighty! O the All-Compelling!" Ask small creatures and their young who are maintained on the land an the sea with care and compassion: "What are you saying?" They will hymn: "O the All-Gracious! O the All-Gracious! O the All-Compassionate!"[117] Then listen to how the heavens sing: "O the All-Majestic One of Grace!" Listen to the earth, which says: "O the All-Gracious One of Majesty!" Pay attention to animals and hear them invoke: "O the All-Merciful! O the All-Providing!" When you ask the spring, you will hear

---

[117] Once I watched some cats—they only ate, played, and slept. I thought: Why are cats, who have no duties, considered blessed? When I went to bed, a cat approached and, leaning against my pillow, put its mouth to my ear and clearly purred: "O the All-Compassionate! O the All-Compassionate!" It seemed that it was refuting, for its species, my objection about cats' lovability and blessedness. I asked myself if that recitation were unique to that cat or general for all cats, and whether only I could hear it. The next morning I listened to other cats. All repeated this invocation, but not so clearly. At first I heard: "O the All-Compassionate!" among their purring in an indistinct manner. Gradually, their purring and meowing became the same: "O the All-Compassionate!" as a touching, well-articulated recitation. I related this to some visitors. They listened carefully as well, and said that they heard it to a degree. Later, I wondered why they were reciting that Name and why they were reciting it in the way of people and not in an animal tongue. It occurred to me that since they are very delicate, pet-

it reciting such Names as: "O the All-Kind and Caring! O the All- Merciful! O the All-Compassionate! O the All-Munificent! O the All-Subtle and Benevolent! O the All-Affectionate! O the All-Fashioning! O the All-Illuminating! O the All-Favoring! O the All-Adorning!"

Ask those who are truly human. See how they recite and manifest all of God's All-Beautiful Names, and how they are inscribed on their forehead. If you look carefully, you may discern them one by one. It is as if the universe were a huge orchestra singing the Divine Names. With the songs sung in the least notes and tones mixed with the highest, the universe produces a magnificent harmony.

All of the Names are manifested on humanity. However, the variety of the Names and their manifestation in different ways and degrees have caused variety among human beings, as they have in the universe and in the angels' worshipping. It also has caused differences among the laws of Prophets, the ways of saints, and the paths of purified scholars. For example, the All-Powerful was more predominant in Jesus, upon him be peace, than the other Names manifested in him. The All-Loving prevails in those who follow the path of love to God, and the All-Wise in those who follow the path of contemplation and reflection.

Thus, if someone is simultaneously a teacher, officer, lawyer, and civil service inspector, in each office, that person has relations, duties, salaries, responsibilities, promotions, enemies, and rivals. He meets with the king under any or all of these titles, and having recourse to him through many of the king's titles, seeks his help in many ways. Similarly, humanity, upon whom numerous Divine Names are manifested, who has many duties and is the target of many kinds of enmity, seeks refuge in God by invoking many of His Names. In fact, Prophet Muhammad, the pride of humanity and the most perfect human being, upon him be peace and blessings, prayed to God through one thousand and one of His Names in his *al-Jawshanu'l-Kabir* supplication, and sought refuge in Him from Hellfire. This is why God commands us in *Suratu'n-Nas* (114) to seek refuge in Him through three of His

---

ted like children, and live amicably with people, they need great care and compassion. When they receive it, they proclaim the All-Compassionate Creator's Mercy in their own world as thanks for that grace. Cats regard this as a special favor of God, whereas dogs regard this as a favor of people. Cats warn people in the sleep of heedlessness, and through their cry of, "O the All-Compassionate!" remind those who attribute everything to apparent "material" causes who actually sends the help and who is the source of mercy.

Titles, and via *In the Name of God, the All-Merciful, the All-Compassionate,* He teaches us to seek help from Him through three of His Names.

SECOND BRANCH: Here I will address two subtle matters that contain the keys to many subtle truths.

FIRST SUBTLE MATTER: Why do saints differ greatly in their visions and discoveries of hidden truths, although they all agree upon the principles of belief? Why are their discoveries, mainly based on (direct) witnessing or observation, sometimes opposed to reality and contrary to the truth? Why, in their opinions that they consider as true and based on decisive proofs, do thinkers and scholars draw contradictory conclusions while searching for the truth? Why does a truth appear in different colors?

SECOND SUBTLE MATTER: Why did the early Prophets not focus on some pillars of belief and elaborate upon them as much as the Qur'an? Why were they content with a brief exposition, so that some of their later followers denied them?

Why, among saints well-versed in the knowledge of God, have some advanced only in affirming Divine Unity? They attained total certainty coming from direct experience in the truths of belief, yet apparently neglected some pillars of belief. This has caused later followers to pay less attention to those pillars, which, in turn, has caused some to deviate. Although true perfection is attained through full development in all pillars of belief, why have the people of truth advanced greatly in some while remaining backward in others? What is the reason for all these differences while the noblest Messenger, who was endowed with the greatest manifestations of all Divine Names and was the prince of Prophets, as well as the wise Qur'an, the most luminous chief of all sacred Divine Scriptures, described all pillars of belief in detail, clearly, and in a most emphatic way?

The reason is as follows: Humanity is created with a capacity to be able to receive the manifestations of all Divine Names and attain all perfections. However, we search for truth amid thousands of veils and barriers and with a partial will, a slight power, and variable desires and different degrees of abilities. For this reason, insurmountable barriers intervene while we are trying to discover the reality and find out and comprehend the truth. Abilities and levels of understanding differ. Some abilities cannot encompass certain pillars of belief with all their dimensions. Furthermore, the Names' manifestations assume different colors according to the people who receive them. Some can receive them in their universal and original forms, while others can do so only in their partial and shadowy forms. In some people, only one Name predominates and prevails over the others.

To understand this profound, subtle matter and reality with extensive wisdom, heed the following comprehensive and meaningful comparison: Imagine a luxuriant flower, a living drop of water in love with the moon, and a simple dew drop that looks to the sun. Each is conscious and has some goal of perfection to attain. Together with pointing to many other truths, they allude to the journey of the soul, mind, and heart on the way of truth, and correspond to the three types of people searching for truth.[118]

The first group consists of thinkers; those who strive for their particular level of perfection via the physical senses and intellectual faculties only; and those who, keeping their egotism, are preoccupied with and study the physical existence in its elaborate multiplicity and try to reach the truth through deduction and reasoning only. The second group comprises saints or saintly scholars; those who strive through using the mind and refining the soul; and those who search through reason, religious learning, and by acquiring knowledge of God. The third group comprises Prophets; those who pursue the truth through belief, submission, and purifying the heart; and those who travel to the truth swiftly through belief and the Qur'an, and worship and acknowledgment of their poverty and neediness before God.

Under the titles of "Flower," "Drop," and "Dew Drop," I will use a comparison to show how and why these three groups progress [to reach the truth] in their own way. For example, the sun has, by the Creator's leave and command, three kinds of manifestation, reflection, and radiance: its reflection on flowers, its reflection on the moon and the planets, and its reflection and imaging itself in shining objects like glass and water.

The first is in three ways: a universal and general manifestation and reflection that encompasses all flowers simultaneously; a special manifestation that encompasses each species of flowers with a special reflection; and a particular manifestation, whereby it is reflected in a certain flower according to its individual character.[119]

The second manifestation or reflection of the sun is the light that it gives to the moon and planets by the All-Wise Originator's leave. Having

---

[118] Each group has also three subgroups. The three things given in the comparison as representatives of the three groups, in fact, correspond to nine categories.

[119] This accords with the claim that flowers get their colors from the changing reflections of the sun's seven-colored light. So, they are kinds of mirrors to the sun.

received this extensive, universal light and radiance, the moon sends its light, a shadow of the sun's light, onto the seas, air, and earth. In a particular form, it sends it to bubbles on the sea, translucent parts of the earth, and air molecules.

The third is that under God's command the sun has a pure, universal, and direct reflection or self-imaging in the atmosphere and on the seas' surface, which it makes into mirrors. The sun also gives to each bubble, drop of water, air molecule, and snowflake a particular reflection and tiny image of itself.

Thus the sun reflects or images itself on every flower, and in every water and dew drop in two ways in each of the three kinds mentioned above: The first way is direct, without barrier and veil, and represents the way of Prophethood. The second way, that of sainthood, is that in which barriers intervene. The mirrors' capacities, as well as the objects receiving the images or reflections, add their colors to the sun's manifestations.

Thus on the first way, each flower, drop of water, and dew drop can say: "I am a mirror to the sun of the world." But on the second way they can say: "I am the mirror to my own sun only, or the mirror to the sun manifested in my species only," for that is how they know the sun. They cannot see the sun in its direct, universal manifestation, for it appears to each of them or to its species from behind barriers and under restrictions. And so it cannot attribute to that "particular, restricted sun" the works of the unrestricted, unconfined, absolute sun. It cannot ascribe in full conviction to such a sun, which it sees within narrow confines and restrictions, such majestic works as heating and illuminating the earth, stirring plants and animals to life, and making planets revolve around it.

Even if these three (presumably conscious) things attribute those wonderful works to the sun that they see under restrictions, they can do so only through reasoning and dogmatic or unsubstantiated belief or submission to the fact that that restricted thing is the majestic absolute sun. So the judgment of these three things, which we suppose to have a human-like intelligence, depends on or arises from reasoning and not thorough enlightenment coming from direct witnessing and observation. Their conclusion, which depends on unsubstantiated belief, even may conflict with what they see or observe in the outer world. Thus they can be convinced with much difficulty.

To understand this better, let's pretend that we are the flower, drop of water, and dew drop, for we receive enlightenment from our immaterial sun in the way they receive it from their physical sun. So, my friend who cannot renounce the world, is preoccupied with physical subjects, and whose soul is dense, you be the flower. The flower assumes a color as an effect produced by a ray of sunlight having a particular wavelength, and makes it an adorned form in which to be clothed. You have the same capacity.

Let that philosopher who has studied secular science and so explains everything in terms of cause and effect, like the Old Said, be the water drop in love with the moon. The moon sends to it the shadowy light it receives from the sun. The drop shines with that light, through which it can see only the moon. Unable to see the sun, it only believes in its existence.

Let that poor fellow who knows everything to be directly from Almighty God, and who considers cause and effect to be a veil, be the dew drop. A dew drop is poor in itself and has nothing to depend on. It does not rely on itself, as flowers do. It has no color through which to display itself, or anything else toward which it should feel inclined. All it has is a sheer purity and simplicity of heart, by which it holds the sun's image in the "pupil of its eye."

Now that we have taken the place of these three things, we must ask ourselves: What do we have? What must we do? We see that an All-Munificent One, through His favors, is adorning, enlightening, nurturing, and bringing us up. We have an inborn tendency to adore the one who favors us. We want to be close to the one worthy of our adoration and desire to see him. So, in accordance with our capacities, each of us will journey through the attraction of love.

You who are like a flower—you are advancing, so advance as a flower. You have advanced until you reach a universal rank, as if a universal flower to represent all flowers. However, as a flower is a dense mirror in which light is refracted and its seven colors are dissolved, it veils the sun's reflection and image. As you cannot see the face of the sun that you love, for its restricted colors and qualities draw a veil over and obscure it, you cannot be freed from the separation caused by interposing barriers. But you can be freed if you raise your head (now sunk in the love of your selfhood), withdraw your gaze (fixed on the merits you ascribe to your selfhood), and direct it to the face of the sun in the sky. You should also turn your face, looking down to the earth to attract your sustenance, up to the sun, for if you are a mirror of it, you must act as such. Whether you know it or not, your sustenance will come to you from the soil, the door to the treasury of mercy.

Just as a flower is a tiny mirror to the sun, so the huge sun is a drop-like mirror to a gleam from the Name of The Light of The Eternal Sun. So, O human heart, know what Sun you are to serve as a mirror, for only after you are conscious of this will you attain the level of perfection assigned to you. However, you cannot see that Sun in Its essential identity, nor grasp Its truth in Its naked form; rather, your attributes give that truth a color, your cloudy telescope attaches a form to it, and your limited capacity restricts it.

Now, O wise philosopher who represents the drop! Through the telescope of your intellect and by the stairway of science and philosophy, you have advanced as far as the moon and landed on it. On its own, the moon is a dense, dark and lifeless object. Your endeavor has been in vain, and your knowledge has proved useless. You can be saved from the darkness of hopelessness, the desolation of loneliness, the pestering of evil spirits, and the terror of frightening solitude only by abandoning the night of scientism and turning toward the Sun of Truth, believing with certainty that the lights of that night are but shadowy reflections of the lights of the "sun of daytime." If you do this, you will attain to perfection and find the tremendous sun in place of the poor and lightless moon. But like the flower, you will be unable to see the sun clearly, for, you will see it beyond veils with which your reason and philosophy are friendly, behind screens woven by science and learning, and in a color produced by your capacity.

Our third friend, the dew drop, is both poor and colorless. It swiftly evaporates in the sun's heat and, free of egotism, rises into the air. The dense matter in its structure burns in the flames of love and changes into light. It holds on to a ray from the sun's light and draws close to the sun. O friend resembling the dew drop! Since you act as a direct mirror to the sun, whatever your rank, you can find a window through which you can look at it without any barrier. You will experience no difficulty in ascribing the sun's amazing works to it; You will immediately attribute its deserved majestic attributes and the awesome actions of its essential dominion to it. Neither the thickness of barriers, nor the restrictedness of capacities, nor the smallness of mirrors will confuse you or drive you to any falsehood. Since you are turned directly toward it with a pure heart and a sincere intention, you understand that what appears in the objects and mirrors is not the sun itself, but rather its manifestations or colored reflections. Although these reflections describe it, they cannot display all of its majesty's works in their proper splendor.

This comparison, mixed with the reality, contains ways to perfection. They differ in the merits of the perfections to which they lead and in the details of the rank of certainty ultimately reached, but agree in their conclusion and in submitting to truth and affirming reality. Consider people of the night who have never seen the sun, but only its shadow in the mirror of the moon. They cannot understand the sun's uniquely splendid light and awesome gravity, submit only to those who have seen it, and imitate them.

Similarly, those who cannot attain to the most comprehensive degrees of the Names' manifestations such as the All-Powerful and Life-Giver, through succession to the Prophet's mission, accept the Resurrection and Supreme Gathering imitatively and claim that reason cannot understand it. For the Resurrection and Last Judgment will occur due to the most comprehensive manifestation of God's Greatest Name and certain other Names. Those who cannot comprehend it are compelled to believe in it by way of imitation. But those who understand it fully see the world's destruction and the Resurrection, together with the building of a new world, as happening as easily as the alternation of night and day, of winter and spring, and accept it with full conviction of the heart.

The Qur'an speaks of these events most elaborately, at the highest level, and in the most perfect, detailed manner. Our Prophet, who was favored with God's Greatest Name, taught it. The other Prophets, as required by the wisdom in their mission of guiding people to Divine truths, did not instruct their somewhat simple and primitive communities in the Resurrection at the same level and with the same detail as the Qur'an and our Prophet. Due to the restriction of their capacities and the restricted nature of their mission, some saints have not seen or been able to demonstrate some pillars of belief to the greatest degree. There are great differences in the degrees of those who have knowledge of God. In addition to these, this comparison provides clues to understand many other important issues. However, since the comparison contains only some aspects of reality, and reality is quite extensive and profound, I will content myself with the comparison and not try to explain matters beyond my limit and ability.

THIRD BRANCH: Since the *hadiths* (Prophetic Traditions) about the signs of the Last Day, the unusual events at the end of time, and the rewards and merits of certain actions have not been understood fully, some scholars who rely on their intellects have ruled some of them weak or false; others with weak belief, strong egotism, and self-pride deny them. To disperse such doubts, but without going into a detailed discussion, I will explain twelve principles.

FIRST PRINCIPLE: I explained this in greater detail at the end of The Twentieth Word. To summarize: As religion is a means of testing people, of distinguishing exalted spirits from base ones, it speaks of the matters that everyone will see or experience in the future, in such a way that they are neither fully unknown or known so clearly as to make people fell compelled to confirm them. It opens a door to reason but does not deny human free will. If a sign of the Last Day were to be so clear that everyone had to affirm it, exalted and base spirits would be equal, and holding people responsible for their beliefs and actions, as well as the purpose for testing them, would be negated. This explains the apparent ambiguity of the Traditions concerning such issues as the *Mahdi* (the Muslim Messiah) and *Sufyan* (the Anti-Christ expected to appear in the Muslim world), and the great disputes over them.

SECOND PRINCIPLE: Not all Islamic issues have the same degree of importance. One issue demands certain proof, the prevailing opinion is sufficient for another, and yet another requires only acceptance. Secondary issues or historical events are not among the principles of belief. Thus they do not require conviction and decisive proof, but only acceptance or non-rejection.

THIRD PRINCIPLE: While the Companions were alive, many Jewish and Christian scholars accepted Islam. Their former knowledge thus became "Muslim." Some of it, however, was contrary to the truth and, later on, was imagined to belong to Islam.

FOURTH PRINCIPLE: While relating Traditions, some narrators tended to make explanations and included meanings deduced from the Traditions. Later on, such additions came to be considered part of the Tradition's text. Since we are not free of error, some of these erroneous opinions or deductions were considered to be Traditions and declared "weak."

FIFTH PRINCIPLE: There were some among Traditionists (scholars of Hadith) who were mentioned by the Prophet: "Among any community are those who are inspired."[120] Thus, the meanings obtained by some saintly Traditionists through inspiration and communicated to others were considered Traditions in later times. However, due to certain obstructions, some inspirations may be defective and thus contrary to the truth.

---

[120] *al-Bukhari*, "Fada'ilus-Sahaba" 6; *Muslim*, "Fada'ilu's-Sahaba" 23; *at-Tirmidhi*, "Manaqib" 17.

SIXTH PRINCIPLE: Certain widely circulated narrations come to be like proverbs over time. Their literal meanings and the words used are not important, for only the meaning and intent are considered. Thus the Messenger, upon him be peace and blessings, would sometimes mention such narrations in the form of comparisons or metaphors for the purpose of guidance. If there is any error in the original, literal meanings of such sayings, it is due to the people's customs and traditions and to the way the sayings have been circulated.

SEVENTH PRINCIPLE: Over time and misunderstanding, many similes and parables have assumed the form of physical facts. For example, two angels called "The Ox" and "The Fish," represented as an ox and fish in the World of Representations or Immaterial Forms and among those who supervise land and sea animals, were imagined to be a huge ox and a physical fish. As a result, the Tradition related to them was criticized.

Once a rumbling was heard. The Prophet said: "That is the sound of a rock that has been rolling down for seventy years and only now has reached Hell's bottom."[121] Those who do not know the context may reject this. However, about twenty minutes after the Prophet spoke, someone came and related that a well-known hypocrite had died twenty minutes ago. The Prophet had described most eloquently how the hypocrite's life of seventy years had been a continuous descent to the lowest of the low as a stone of Hell. Almighty God let the Prophet and Companions hear that rumbling.

EIGHTH PRINCIPLE: In this arena of testing and experience, the Absolutely Wise One hides certain vital things amidst a multiplicity of things: the Night of Power in the month of Ramadan, the hour when prayers are not rejected in Friday, His favorite friends among the people, the appointed hour of death during a person's lifetime, and the time of Doomsday in the world's life. If we knew when we were going to die, we would spend half of our life in absolute heedlessness and the other half in terror, like that of going step by step to the gallows. To keep the balance between this world and the next, to let people live between hope and fear, living and dying must be possible at any moment. Thus living for twenty years with an unknown end is preferable to living a thousand years with a preknown end.

Doomsday is the world's (a macro-human) appointed hour. If it were known, people of early and middle ages person would have lost themselves in heedlessness, and those of later centuries would be in terror. Just as we

---

[121] *Muslim*, "Janna" 31; Ahmad ibn Hanbal, *al-Musnad*, 3:341.

are concerned with our home's and town's survival in our personal lives, we are also concerned with the world and the earth's continued existence in our social lives and as members of humanity.

The Qur'an announces: *The Hour has approached* (54:1). This was stated fourteen centuries ago, but does not mean that the Hour is not near. Doomsday is the world's death. In proportion to its life, a thousand or two thousand years are like one or two hours in proportion to a year. Doomsday is not only humanity's appointed hour that it should bear any proportion to a human time scale and be seen as remote. Thus the Absolutely Wise One conceals its time in His Knowledge among the "five things of the Unseen (The Qur'an, 31:34)." Such uncertainty has caused people in every age, including the Age of Happiness (the truth-seeing age of the Prophet), to fear its coming. Some have even believed that its signs have appeared already.

Question: Why did the Companions, with their vigilant hearts and keen sight and who were instructed in the Hereafter's details, think that a far-distant future event would be near to their own time?

Answer: Benefiting from the Prophet's enlightening company, they thought of the Hereafter more than anyone else. Well aware of the world's transience and conscious of the Divine Wisdom in the Hour's uncertainty, they remained alert for it and strove seriously for their afterlife. The Prophet's frequent warning: "Expect the Last Hour, wait for it,"[122] was for the same purpose and intended for guidance; it was not a pronouncement of Revelation concerning a fixed time. The cause for something should not be confused with the benefit attached to and expected from it. Such sayings of the Prophet as this arise from the wisdom in leaving certain things vague.

This is also why people of all generations, even that of the Companions' successors, expected such end-time individuals as the *Mahdi* and *Sufyan*, and hoped to live long enough to see them. Some saints even judged that they had passed. As with the Hour, Divine Wisdom requires that the times of these individuals should remain unknown. In every age, people feel in need of the meaning of the *Mahdi*, of one who will come to strengthen their morale and save them from despair. The time of such matters was left vague so that people would not heedlessly follow evil leaders or let the reins of their carnal selves go free out of indifference, and so that they would fear and hold back from terrible individuals who come to lead the

---

[122] *at-Tirmidhi*, "Fitan" 39.

forces of disorder and hypocrisy. If they had been known, the purposes for guiding people would have been unrealized.

Another reason for the differences in the narrations about such end-time individuals as the *Mahdi* is this: The texts of some Traditions have been confused or even mixed with commentaries of interpreters with their own understandings and deductions. For example, the center of power when these Traditions had reached their widest circulation was Madina or Damascus. Thus they thought that events connected with the *Mahdi* and *Sufyan* would take place there or in neighboring places like Basra and Kufa, and interpreted them accordingly. Moreover, in their imaginations, they attributed to those individuals the mighty works and events belonging to the collective identity or community that they would represent, and interpreted relevant Traditions so that people could recognize them when they appeared.

But this world is an arena of trial. A door is opened to reason, but human free will is not denied, nor ignored. For this reason, when those mighty individuals, even the terrible *Dajjal* (Anti-Christ) appear, most people (even himself) may not realize his true identity. These end-time individuals can be known only through the light of belief.

One Tradition about the *Dajjal* says: "His first day is like a year, his second like a month, his third like a week, and his fourth like your normal days. When he appears, the world will hear. He will travel the world in forty days."[123] Some, saying this is impossible, deny the Tradition. However—*the knowledge is with God*—this Tradition must mean that an individual will appear in the north, where unbelief is strongest and at its peak. Leading a mighty current issuing from materialism, he will deny God and religion absolutely.

There is a subtle point here: In latitudes close to the North Pole, the whole year is a day and a night, each comprising six months. The expression, *His first day is like a year*, alludes to his appearance close to those latitudes, in the far north. *His second like a month* means that coming south, there are latitudes where a summer day lasts a month. This means that the *Dajjal* will invade southward toward the civilized world. Coming south, there are places where the sun does not set for one week, and still coming further south, there are barely three hours between the sun's rising and setting—as a prisoner of war in Russia, I was in such a place.

---

[123] *Muslim*, "Fitan" 110; *Abu Dawud*, "Malahim" 14; *at-Tirmidhi*, "Fitan" 59.

The difficulty in understanding *the world will hear when the Dajjal appears* has been solved through radio and telegraph. And, it is now possible to *travel the world in forty days*. What was formerly considered impossible is now commonplace.

As for Gog, Magog, and the Barrier (other end-time signs), consult my *Muhakemat* (Reasonings). Here I will say only this: Some narrations say that various Asian tribes, who forced the Chinese to build the Great Wall and utterly destroyed the civilized world, will reappear, close to Doomsday, to cause chaos in the world and overrun civilization.

Question: Where are the tribes that once performed such extraordinary acts and that will perform them once again?

Answer: Huge numbers of disaster-causing locusts appear in one season. When the season changes, they survive in a few locusts. When it is time, by Divine command, vast numbers grow from those few and again destroy everything in their path. It is as if their national identity's essence becomes fine, but not broken, and resurfaces when its time has come. In just the same way, those same tribes who once destroyed the civilized world will reappear at the appointed time by God's leave and overrun civilization. However, the factors inviting them may be different. *God knows the Unseen.*

NINTH PRINCIPLE: The results of some issues of belief are concerned with this narrow and conditioned world, while others are related to the wide and unconditioned world of the Hereafter. So, though some Traditions about the virtues and rewards of certain religious acts were couched most eloquently to encourage people toward good and away from evil, some consider them exaggerations. However, they are all pure truth and contain no exaggeration.

For example, a most unfairly criticized Tradition relates: "If God valued this world as much as He does a fly's wing, unbelievers could not take even a sip of water from it."[124] This does not allude to the world, but rather to everyone's private world, which is limited to their short lives. It cannot equal an everlasting Divine favor to the extent of a fly's wing from the eternal world. *If God valued* refers to the eternal world. In other words, because it is everlasting, a light from the eternal world to the extent of a fly's wing is greater than the amount of transient light that fills the earth.

---

[124] *Muslim, "Munafiqun" 18; al-Bukhari, "Tafsir Sura 18" 6; Ibn Maja," Zuhd" 3.*

Furthermore, the world has three facets. The first facet contains the mirrors that reflect Almighty God's Names. The second facet is concerned with the Hereafter. That is, this world is the arable field sown with the seeds of the Hereafter, the realm in which we might gain the eternal world. The third facet, looking to transience and non-existence, is the world of the misguided, of which God does not approve. This Tradition refers only to the third facet—the world of the worldly, which is opposed to the Hereafter, the source of all wrong, and the origin of calamities. So, it is not worth one everlasting particle out of what the believers will be rewarded with in the Hereafter. Thus, those who consider this Tradition an exaggeration are ignoring this most exact and serious truth.

Another category of Traditions considered by some to be exaggerations consists of the reward for religious acts and virtues of some Qur'anic *suras*. For example, some Traditions relate that the reward for *Suratu'l-Fatiha* equals that for the Qur'an,[125] *Suratu'l-Ikhlas* equals one-third of the Qur'an,[126] *Suratu'l-Zilzal* equals one-fourth of the Qur'an,[127] *Suratu'l-Kafirun* equals one-fourth of the Qur'an,[128] and *Sura Ya Sin* equals ten times the Qur'an.[129] They base their criticism on the assertion that these more meritorious *suras* are contained within the Qur'an.

The truth of the matter is this. Imagine a field sown with 1,000 maize seeds. If we suppose that some seeds produce 7 shoots and each shoot 100 grains, a single seed equals two-thirds of the original 1,000 seeds. If 1 seed produces 10 shoots, and each shoot yields 200 grains, 1 seed is equal to twice the number of all the seeds originally sown. Many similar analogies can be made. In exactly the same way, if we suppose the wise Qur'an to be a sacred, luminous, heavenly field, each of its 300,620 letters, together with its original reward, is like a seed. Without considering the shoots these seeds may produce, the Qur'an may be compared with the *suras* and verses which bring multiple rewards mentioned by these Traditions.

Out of Divine Grace, the letters of some *suras* may sprout and yield 10, 70, or 700, like the letters of *Ayatu'l-Kursi*. Sometimes they yield 1,500, like the letters of *Suratu'l-Ikhlas*, or 10,000, like verses recited on the Night of

---

[125] *al-Bukhari*, "Tafsir Sura 1" 1; *at-Tirmidhi*, "Thawabu'l-Qur'an" 1; *an-Nasa'i*, "Iftitah" 26.

[126] *at-Tirmidhi*, "Thawabu'l-Qur'an" 10; *Ibn Maja*, "Adab" 52; *Abu Dawud*, "Witr" 18.

[127] *at-Tirmidhi*, "Thawabu'l-Qur'an" 14; Ahmad ibn Hanbal, *al-Musnad*, 3:147.

[128] *at-Tirmidhi*, "Thawabu'l-Qur'an" 9; Ahmad ibn Hanbal, *al-Musnad*, 3:147.

[129] *at-Tirmidhi*, "Thawabu'l-Qur'an" 7; *ad-Darimi*, "Fada'ilu'l-Qur'an" 21.

Forgiveness (*Laylatu'l-Bara'a*) and other blessed occasions. Sometimes they even yield 30,000, like verses recited on the Night of Power (*Laylatu'l-Qadr*). These are like poppy seeds, each of which may produce 10 cones, each of which contains thousands of seeds. As the Qur'an considers the Night of Power equivalent to 1,000 months (97:3), one letter of the Qur'an recited on that night brings 30,000 rewards.

Given this, some *suras* and verses may bring multiple rewards and be compared in certain circumstances with the whole Qur'an, when its letters are considered in their original merits and without producing a new crop of merits. For example, *Suratu'l-Ikhlas* and the *Basmala* (*In the Name of God, the All-Merciful, the All-Compassionate*) both have 69 letters. Since this *sura* equals one-third of the Qur'an and the Qur'an has 300,620 letters, 3 times 69 is 207. Thus each letter of this *sura* has about 1,500 merits or rewards. Similarly, since *Sura Ya Sin* equals 10 times the Qur'an, if all the letters of the Qur'an are multiplied by 10 and the result is divided by the number of the *sura*'s letters, we discover that each letter has about 500 merits or rewards. So, if you apply the others to this, you will understand what a subtle, true and unexaggerated reality related by these Traditions.

TENTH PRINCIPLE: As with most other species, certain people among humankind are extraordinary in their acts and achievements. If they excel in good deeds, they become the pride of humanity; otherwise they are the cause of their shame. They acquire a collective identity and become models for imitators. Since it is not certain who among people has this capacity, theoretically, and sometimes it is even possible, everyone could be like them. Also, as such people can emerge in any place, every place may have some of them.

It follows that any act has the potential to deserve the following reward: The Prophet, upon him be peace and blessings, declared: "The reward for two *rak'ats* of Prayer performed at such and such a time equals the *Hajj* (pilgrimage to the Ka'ba)."[130] This means that all the two-*rak'a* Prayers performed at that time may earn a reward equal to performing the pilgrimage. The reward promised in such narrations is not actual or for everyone at all times. Rather, as certain conditions must be fulfilled, it is possible that the reward will be earned.

Such general promises have to do with possibility or potentiality. For example, one Tradition says: "Backbiting is like murder."[131] This means that there is a sort of backbiting more harmful than deadly poison. Again, for

---

[130] at-Tirmidhi, "Jumu'a" 59; at-Tabarani, *al-Mu'jamu'l-Kabir*, 77:40.

[131] ad-Daylami, *Musnadu'l-Firdaws*, 3:116.

example: "A good word equals in virtue emancipating a slave, which is very meritorious."[132] By indicating the highest reward one may gain from a good deed, the Prophet sought to arouse eagerness for good and aversion to evil. Moreover, the things of the Hereafter cannot be measured on this world's scales, for the greatest thing in this world cannot equal the least thing in the Hereafter. Since rewards for good deeds are related to the Hereafter, we cannot grasp them fully with our worldly, narrow mind.

Another example: God's Messenger, upon him be peace and blessings, declares that people are given the reward of Moses and Aaron if they recite:

> All praise and gratitude are for God, Lord of the heavens, Lord of the earth's layers, Lord of the worlds. His is sublimity in the heavens and the earth. He is the All-Glorious and Mighty, the All-Wise. All praise and gratitude are for God, Lord of the heavens, Lord of the earth's layers, Lord of the worlds. His is grandeur in the heavens and the earth. He is the All-Glorious and Mighty, All-Wise. His is the absolute dominion, Lord of the heavens, and He is the All-Glorious and Mighty, the All-Wise.[133]

This narration has been much criticized. However, we imagine with our narrow minds and limited outlooks what kind of reward Moses and Aaron can receive in the Hereafter. We forget that the Absolutely Compassionate One may give one of His servants in infinite need of everlasting happiness as much reward for one invocation as what we think they received for everything. For example, primitive and uncultured people who have never seen the king are unaware of his kingdom's splendor. So they imagine a village headman and, with their narrow experience, think that the king is a little bit greater than their headman. Some uneducated people in the eastern regions used to say: "Our lord knows what the sultan does, while he cooks his *bulgur* soup in a saucepan over the fire."[134] In other words, they imagined the sultan as someone greater than an ordinary person who still cooked his own bulgur soup. If someone were to tell them: "If you do this for me today, I'll reward you with as much splendor as you think the sultan has," he would be promising those people as much splendor as he could imagine what the sultan has.

Our worldly views and narrow minds cannot know the actual rewards received in the Hereafter. This Tradition compares the actual, unknown

---

[132] at-Tabarani, *al-Mu'jamu'l-Kabir*, 7:230; al-Bayhaqi, *Shu'abu'l-Iman*, 6:124.

[133] Ahmad al-Gumushanevi, *al-Majmu'atu'l-Ahzab*, 263.

[134] A soup made of boiled and pounded wheat. (Tr.)

reward for a believer's invocation not to the actual (and unknown) reward of Prophets Moses and Aaron, upon them be peace, but to the reward we think they received. Moreover, the sea's [smooth] surface and a drop's "pupil" are equal in holding the sun's image. The difference is only in regard to quality, which depends on capacity. The nature of the reward reflected in the mirror of the ocean-like spirits of Moses and Aaron is of the same nature as the reward received by a believer with a drop-like spirit from a Qur'anic verse. They are the same in regard to nature and quantity, while their quality depends on capacity.

Furthermore, sometimes a word or act of glorification opens up a treasury of happiness that one could not open before through a lifetime of Divine service. In certain circumstances, one verse may earn as much reward as the whole Qur'an. Also, the Divine gifts and enlightenment which the noblest Messenger, who was endowed with God's Greatest Name, received through one verse may have been as much as all the gifts and enlightenment received by another Prophet. It may be correct to say that a believer, who through succession to Muhammad's mission is endowed with God's Greatest Name's shadow, may receive reward as much as a Prophet's enlightenment, one that would correspond to his (or her) own capacity in respect of quality.

Also, reward and virtues are from the realm of light, one world of which may be contained in an atom of this world. Just as heaven and its stars may appear in a tiny glass fragment, such reward and virtue, which are of pure light and thus can fill the heavens, may be contained in an invocation or recitation of a Qur'anic verse that acquires transparency through sincerity and pure intention.

In short: O unfair weak in belief but strong in dialectics! Consider these ten principles, and do not use what you consider a "suspect" Tradition as a pretext to slight the reliability and authenticity of the Prophetic Traditions and the Messenger's purity and infallibility. These ten principles make it impossible for you to deny the Traditions and warn you: "If there is a real flaw, it is like what we have explained and cannot be attributed to the Traditions. If there is no real flaw, the problem arises from your misunderstanding." Denying and rejecting these Traditions means you must contradict and refute these ten principles. Therefore, consider them carefully and do not try to deny those Traditions you consider contrary to the truth. Instead of criticizing them, say: "There must be a way to explain or interpret this."

ELEVENTH PRINCIPLE: Just as the Qur'an contains difficult and allegorical verses needing interpretation or requiring total submission, Traditions also have difficulties that sometimes require extremely careful interpretation. The examples above may be sufficient to illustrate this truth.

Those who are awake can interpret a sleeping person's dream, and sometimes those who are sleeping can hear the conversations of those who are awake and interpret their words according to their world of sleep. In the same way, O unfair one stupefied in the sleep of heedlessness and false reasoning! Do not deny in your "dream;" rather, interpret the vision of the one who always and truly was awake and about whom God declared: *His eye never wavered nor swerved* (53:17), and himself said: "My eye sleeps, but my heart sleeps not."[135] If a mosquito bites someone who is sleeping, he may dream that he has been severely wounded. If questioned, he would reply: "I've been wounded. They fired guns and rifles at me." Those sitting by him would laugh at his anguish in sleep. Thus the view of heedlessness and philosophy in its "sleep" cannot be the criterion for the truths of Prophethood.

TWELFTH PRINCIPLE: The way of Prophethood and belief, as well as the doctrine of Divine Unity, deal with everything from the viewpoint of Unity, the Hereafter, and God's Divinity. Thus they see truth and reality from the same perspective. Modern scientific views and philosophy, however, are concerned with nature, causality, and things in their multiplicity. These two points of view are distant from each other. Therefore, the greatest aim of philosophers and scientists is almost imperceptible in comparison with the aims of the scholars of religious methodology and theology.

This is why scientists have advanced greatly in their detailed explanations of beings' structures and natures, but are more backward than a simple believer in the exalted Divine sciences and eschatology. Those who do not understand this consider the meticulous scholars of Islam backward when compared to philosophers. But how can those whose minds see no further than their eyes, who are submerged in the multiplicity of things, reach those who have achieved the sublime sacred aims through succession to the Prophet's mission?

Furthermore, when looked at from two different viewpoints, a thing may display two different truths. For example, science views the earth as a mid-sized planet revolving around the sun among countless stars. When compared to most stars, it is a small body. But as explained in The Fifteenth

---

[135] al-Bukhari, "Tahajjud" 16; at-Tirmidhi, "Adab" 86; Abu Dawud, "Tahara" 79.

Word, the people of the Qur'an see it as something quite different. Despite its small size in comparison with the heavens, the earth is the universe's heart and center with respect to the meaning and art it contains. For the earth is humanity's cradle and dwelling-place, and humanity, despite its impotence, is the fruit of the Tree of Creation, and a most comprehensive, complex, wonderful, and honorable miracle of Divine Power. The earth is also the place where God's miracles of Art are exhibited and the manifestations of Divine Names are concentrated. It reflects God's infinite activity as the Lord of all beings. It is also the center and pivot of the endless Divine creativity displayed in infinite liberality, especially in the numerous small plant and animal species, as well as the place where samples of creatures of the broadest worlds of the Hereafter are shown in small scale. It is the speedily operating workshop for eternal textiles, the fast-changing place of copies of eternal scenes, and the narrow, temporary field and tillage rapidly producing seeds for permanent gardens (in the Hereafter).

It is because of this greatness of the earth with respect to its meaning and its importance in regard to art, that the wise Qur'an puts it on a par with the heavens, although it is like a tiny fruit of a huge tree when compared with the heavens. It places the earth in one pan of a pair of scales and the heavens in the other, and repeatedly mentions them together, saying, the "Lord of the heavens and the earth."

So, compare other issues with this. Understand that the dim, lifeless truths of the modern scientific and philosophical approach cannot compete with the Qur'an's brilliant, living truths. Since the point of view of each is different, they appear differently.

FOURTH BRANCH: Consider the following verse:

> Do you not see that before God prostrate all that is in the heavens and in the earth, and the sun, the moon, the stars, the mountains, the trees, the beasts, and many among humanity? There are still many unto whom the punishment is justly due. Whoever God humiliates has none to give him honor. Surely God does what He wills. (22:18)

From the treasure of this comprehensive verse, I will discuss only one jewel: The Qur'an states that everything in creation prostrates, worships, praises, and glorifies Almighty God according to their capacities and the Divine Names the manifestations of which they are favored. I explain one type of this worship below.

A mighty lord employs four classes of workers to build a large city or a magnificent palace. The first class, consisting of his slaves, receives no wages or salaries and is content with the indescribable enthusiasm and joy coming from every action, all of which are done to please their lord by carrying out his orders. As these slaves praise him and enumerate his virtues, they derive more pleasure and enthusiasm. They have no further demand than their connection with their lord, which they know to be a great honor. They also receive spiritual pleasure from supervising in their lord's name all that is done in his dominion and watching it from his viewpoint. They feel no need for wages, rank, or promotion.

The second class consists of ordinary servants who are unaware of the universal purposes behind their employment and what significant results it will yield. Some imagine that they are working for the small wage that the lord pays them regularly. The third class comprises animals used for certain construction-related tasks and deeds. Since their jobs correspond to their abilities, they get some sort of pleasure. When a potential develops into an actual ability and becomes the origin of certain deeds, it gives exhilaration. This is why there is a certain pleasure in all activities. Members of this class are content with their food and the pleasure they receive as wages. The fourth class consists of those who know what they are doing, why and for whom they are working, why the others are working, and what the lord's overall purpose is. They supervise other workers and are paid according to their rank.

Similarly—*The highest comparison is (and must be put forth) for God*—the Lord of the Worlds, the All-Majestic Lord of the heavens and the earth, the All-Gracious Builder of this world and the next, uses angels, animals, inanimate objects, plants, and humanity in this palace of the universe, in this realm of causality. He does this not out of need, as He is the Creator of everything, but for certain instances of wisdom demanded by His Might and Honor, Grandeur and Lordship. He has charged these four classes with unique duties of worship.

The first class are angels. They are never promoted, for their ranks are fixed and determined. They receive a specific pleasure from the work itself and a radiance from worship each according to their rank. In short, their reward is found in their service. Jus as humanity is nourished by and derives pleasure from air, water, light, and food, so are angels nourished by and receive pleasure from the lights of remembrance, glorification, worship, knowledge, and love of God. They are created from light, and so light is sufficient for their sustenance. Even fragrant scents, which are close to light, are a sort of enjoyable nourishment for them, for pure spirits take pleasure in sweet scents.

Working at the command of the One Whom they worship and for His sake, serving in His name and supervising through His view, gaining honor through connection with Him and being "refreshed" by studying His Kingdom's material and immaterial dimensions, and being satisfied by seeing the manifestations of His Grace and Majesty give them so elevated a bliss that the human mind cannot comprehended or perceive it. Only angels know it.

One class of angels worships and another class works (another form of worship). Working angels appointed for the earth have some sort of human occupation. If one may say so, some are like shepherds or farmers. The earth is like a farm, and an appointed angel supervises its animal species by the All-Majestic Creator's command, leave, power, and strength, and for His sake. Each animal species has a lesser angel appointed as a kind of shepherd.

Also, the earth is an arable field for sowing plants. An angel is appointed to supervise all of them in Almighty God's name and by His power. Angels of lower rank worship and glorify Almighty God by supervising specific plant species. Michael, one of the bearers of God's Throne of Sustenance —an official of the highest rank whom God employs to veil His acts related to providing for all His creatures—superintends these angels.

These angelic shepherds and farmers do not resemble human beings, for they supervise purely for God's sake, in His name, and by His power and command. They only observe the manifestations of God's Lordship in the species entrusted to them, study the manifestations of Divine Power and Mercy in it, communicate to it the Divine commands through some sort of inspiration, and somehow arrange its voluntary actions.

Their supervision of plants in particular consists of representing, in their angelic tongue, the plants' glorification made in the tongue of their being. They proclaim in their angelic tongue the praises and exaltations that plants offer to the All-Majestic Creator through their lives, regulate and use the plants' faculties correctly, and direct them toward certain ends. Such services are actions done through their partial willpower and a kind of worship and adoration. Angels do not originate or create their actions, for everything bears a stamp particular to the Creator of all things, Who has no co-creators. In short, whatever angels do is their worship and so differs from ordinary human acts.

The second class are animals. Since animals also have an appetitive soul and a partial will, their work is not "purely for the sake of God" in the sense that, to some extent, they take a share for their selves. Therefore, since the All-Majestic and Munificent Lord of All Dominion is All-Kind and Generous, He gives them a wage as their share. For example, the All-Wise Originator employs the nightingale,[136] renowned for its love of roses, for five aims:

- It is charged with proclaiming, in the name of animal species, the intense relationship between them and plant species.
- It is an orator of the Lord among animals, which may be considered guests of the All-Merciful One, in need sustenance, and is charged with acclaiming the gifts sent by the All-Munificent Provider and announcing their joy.
- It announces on each plant the welcome offered to them [by animals] in return for the help plants offer animals.
- It announces, in plants' beautiful faces, animals' intense need for plants, a need in the degree of love and passion.
- It offers a most graceful glorification to the Court of Mercy of the All-Majestic and Gracious and Munificent Lord of All Dominion, with a most pleasant yearning, and on a most delicate flower like rose.

God the All-Glorified uses the nightingale for other aims and meanings. The nightingale acts to achieve these aims and meanings for His sake. It speaks in its own tongue, and we understand these meanings from its touching songs. If, unlike angels and spirit beings, it does not know exactly what its songs mean, this does not harm our understanding, for "one who listens may understand better than one who speaks." A clock tells the time although it is unaware of it; a nightingale's lack of detailed knowledge about these aims does not mean that it is not used for these aims. Its wage is the delight it derives from looking on smiling, beautiful roses, as well as the pleasure it receives from talking with them and unburdening itself to them. In other words, its touching songs are not complaints arising from animal grief, but rather are thanks for the All-Merciful One's gifts.

---

[136] Since the nightingale speaks poetically, our discussion also becomes somehow poetic. But it is not fictional; it is the truth.

Compare with the nightingale other small animals or insects like the bee and ant, and you will see that each works for certain purposes. Through a particular pleasure, included in their duties as wages, they serve certain important aims contained in the Lord's creation. Like an ordinary sailor receiving a small wage for working as a steersman on an imperial vessel, each animal employed in its God-assigned duty receives a particular wage.

A COMPLEMENTARY NOTE: Singing God's praise and glorification in this way is not unique to the nightingale. Most species contain one or more members that, like the nightingale, represent its species' finest feelings with the finest glorification in the finest verse. The numerous and various "nightingales" of flies and insects, in particular, sing their glorifications in fine poetry to other members of their species and give them pleasure.

Some are nocturnal. The ode-reciting friends of all small animals sing their praises and glorifications of God when all beings enter night's peaceful silence. Each leads and is followed by their circle of silent reciters which sing God's Names and glorify their Majestic Originator in their hearts. Another group is diurnal. During daytime in spring and summer, they proclaim the All-Merciful and Compassionate One's mercy to all living beings from the "pulpits" of trees with their ringing voices, pleasant tunes, and poetic glorifications. As though each led a circle of loud reciters of God's Names, they arouse their audiences to ecstasy. This causes each species to begin singing the Names of the All-Majestic Originator in its own particular tongue and tone.

Thus every species of beings, even stars, has a leading reciter and light-diffusing nightingale. The most excellent, noble, illustrious, and profound, as well as the greatest and most honorable nightingale, whose voice is the most lyrical and ringing, whose attributes the most brilliant, whose recitation of God's Names the most perfect and comprehensive, and whose thanks the most universal; one with the most perfect identity and the most beautiful form, and who brings all the beings in the garden of the universe to ecstasy through his most rhythmic and most pleasant tunes and most exalted glorification is Prophet Muhammad, who is the glorious nightingale of humanity, the nightingale with the Qur'an. May the best of blessings and peace upon him, his Family, and his peers—the other Prophets.

To conclude: Animals worship and glorify God Almighty by serving in the palace of the universe or by carrying out the duties required by their existence in utmost obedience to God's laws of life, through His power and in

His name. They thus display Divine purposes for their existence in an amazing way. These glorifications and other acts of worship they do are their gifts of praise offered to the Court of the All-Majestic Originator, the Giver of Life.

The third class of workers are plants and inanimate objects. They have no free will and receive no wages. Whatever they do is done purely for God's sake, by His will and power, and in His name. However, as understood from their life cycles, they receive some sort of pleasure from carrying out the duty of pollination and producing fruits. But they suffer no pain, while animals experience both pain and pleasure because they have some degree of choice. The fact that plants and inanimate objects have no will makes their work more perfect than that of animals. Among animal creatures possessing some sort of choice, the work of those like the bee, which are equipped with a kind of inspiration, is more perfect than those that rely on their own will.

Vegetable species pray and ask of the All-Wise Originator, each in the tongue of their beings and potentiality: "O Lord. Give us strength so that, by raising the flag of our species throughout the earth, we may proclaim Your Lordship's sovereignty. Grant us success so that we may worship You in every corner of the mosque of the earth. Enable us to grow in every suitable region, so that we may display the works of Your All-Beautiful Names and Your wonderful, invaluable arts." In response, the All-Wise Originator equips the seeds of certain species (e.g., many thorny plants and some yellow flowers) with tiny "wings of hair" so they can fly away and manifest the Divine Names on behalf of their species. He gives some species beautiful, delicious flesh that is either necessary or pleasure-giving for human beings. He causes us to serve them and plant them everywhere.

Others receive a hard and indigestible "bone"-like flesh so that animals can eat them and then disperse their seeds over a wide area. He equips some with small claws that grip onto whatever touches them. They spread around and raise the flag of their species, exhibiting the most precious artistry of the Majestic Maker. To still other species, such as the bitter melon, He gives the force of a "shotgun" so that when the time is due, small melons fall and shoot their seeds to a distance of several meters so that they may be sown. They work so that, together with recitation of His Names, the All-Majestic Originator may be glorified in numerous tongues.

The All-Wise Originator, Who is the All-Powerful and All-Knowing, has created everything beautiful and with perfect orderliness. He has equipped all beings with whatever they need, directs them toward agreeable aims, and uses them in the most proper duties. He causes them to worship and glorify Him in the best manner. So if you are truly human, do not deform these beautiful things by asserting that they were created by nature, chance, or necessity. Do not foul them thereby with absurdity, purposelessness and misguidance. Do not act in an ugly fashion, and do not be ugly.

The fourth class are human beings. Forming a working class among the servants, they resemble both angels and animals. They resemble angels in their extensive supervision and comprehensive knowledge, and in being the heralds of Divine Lordship. Indeed, we are more comprehensive in nature. Since we have an appetitive soul disposed toward evil (angels do not), we have the potential for almost boundless advance or decline. As we seek pleasure and a share for ourselves in our work, we resemble animals. Given this, we can receive two kinds of wages: one is insignificant, animal, and immediate; the other is angelic, universal, and postponed. Such matters have been discussed elsewhere, particularly in the Eleventh and Twenty-third Words. Therefore, we cut short the discussion here and beseech the All-Merciful to open to us the doors of mercy to enable me to complete this Word and to forgive my faults and shortcomings.

FIFTH BRANCH: This fifth branch has five fruits.

FIRST FRUIT: O my selfish soul! O worldly friend! Love is the cause of the universe's existence, the bond between all things, and the light and life of the universe. Since we are the most comprehensive fruit of existence, a love so overflowing that it can invade the universe has been included in that fruit's heart (its seed or core). One who deserves such an infinite love can only be one with infinite perfection.

Therefore, O soul and friend, our nature contains two faculties: the means of fear and the means of love. Such love and fear is felt for either the created or the Creator. Fear of the created is a painful affliction, and love of the created is a troublesome pain, for you fear such things or persons that they show you no mercy or reject your request. If this is so, fear of the created is a painful affliction. As for love of the created, those you love either do not care for you and, like your youth and possessions, leave you without saying farewell. Or they disdain you because of your love. Ninety-nine percent of lovers complain of their beloved ones, for love of the idol-like worldly beloved from the bottom of one's heart, which is the mirror of the Eternally Besought One, is unbearable in the beloved's view. And so it is rejected, for human nature rejects and repels what is unnatural and unde-served. (Animal love is out of question here.)

In short, those you love either do not care for you, or they despise you, or they do not accompany you. Contrary to your desire, they leave you. So turn your fear and love toward such a One that your fear will be a pleasant humility and your love a happiness free of humiliation. Fearing the All-Majestic Creator means finding a way to His Compassion and taking refuge in Him. In fact, fear is a whip; it drives one into the embrace of His Compassion. A mother frightens her child away from something or someone and attracts him into her arms. That fear is very pleasurable for children, for it draws them into the arms of care and compassion. However, the care and compassion of all mothers is only a ray from His Compassion. This means there is a great pleasure in fear of God. Given this, you can understand what infinite pleasure can be found by loving Him. Furthermore, those who fear God are freed from the worrying, troublesome fear of others, and their love of created beings in God's Name causes no pain or separation.

We, first of all, love our own selves, and then our families and relatives, then our nation, then living beings, then the world or the universe. We have relations with all of these spheres, feel pleasure in their satisfaction and happiness, and pain at their pain. But since everything is impermanent in this tumultuous and ever-changing world, our heart is wounded continuous-ly. What we cling to slips out of our hands, scratching and cutting them on the way. We remain in pain or throw ourselves into the drunkenness of heedlessness.

Since this is so, O soul, if you have sense, give all the love you divide among beings to the One Who truly deserves it and thereby save yourself from all pain and trouble. Only One Who owns infinite perfection and beau-ty deserves infinite love. Only when you can assign that love to its rightful owner can you love, for His sake and in respect of their being mirrors to Him, all things without pain or trouble. Such love must not be assigned directly to existence for the sake of existence itself. Otherwise, while being a most pleas-urable Divine grace, love becomes a most painful ailment.

Another, more important, aspect of the matter, my soul, is that you assign your love to your self. You idolize your self and see it as worthy of ado-ration. You sacrifice everything for your self and revere it as though it were the Lord. However, something is loved either for its perfection (which is loved because of itself), or for the benefit or pleasure it gives, the good it brings, or for another, similar reason. Now, O soul! I have presented convincing arguments in some of the Words that your nature is "kneaded together" out of defect and deficiency, as well as destitution and impotence. As darkness shows light's strength in proportion to its density, by way of contrast, you are a mirror through those essential elements of your nature to the All-Majestic Originator's Perfection, Grace, Beauty, Power, and Mercy.

So, O soul, you should cherish enmity for your self or have pity on it. Or you should treat it with care and mercy after it has full conviction of the truth of the principles of belief and satisfaction in worship.

If you love your (carnal) self, which is addicted to pleasure and always looks after its own interest, you have been captivated by pleasure and self-interest. Do not prefer such insignificant pleasure and self-interest over boundless true pleasure and advantage. Do not be like a firefly, which drowns its friends and everything it loves in the fright and solitude of darkness and contents itself with its own tiny glow. Love the Eternally Beloved One in Whose favor originate, along with your animal pleasures and interests, the interests of all beings with whom you have relations, from whom you receive benefit, and whose happiness makes you happy. This will enable you to take pleasure in their happiness and to receive the same infinite pleasure as you receive from the Absolutely Perfect One.

Your intense self-love is in fact nothing but your innate love for His "Essence," which you unconsciously carry in yourself and wrongly appropriate for your self. Tear apart the "I" in yourself and show the "He." All the love you divide among other beings is nothing but the love implanted in your being for His Names and Attributes. But you misuse it and so suffer pain and trouble, for the return of an illicit love cherished for those who are unworthy of it is pitiless ailment.

An atom of love for the Eternal, Beloved One, Who through His Names the All-Merciful and All-Compassionate has created a Paradise full of *houris* to satisfy all your bodily desires, Who through His other Names has prepared there for you eternal favors to meet all the needs of your immaterial faculties (e.g., your spirit, heart, intellect, and innermost senses), and in each of Whose Names are numerous immaterial treasuries of favor and munificence, may compensate for the universe. However, the universe cannot compensate for even one particular manifestation of His love. Given this, listen and obey the following eternal decree, which the

Eternal, Beloved One made His beloved, His Messenger, declare: *If you really love God, follow me [so] that God may love you* (3:31).

SECOND FRUIT: O soul! Worship of God is not an act through which to demand a Divine reward in the future, but rather the necessary result of a past Divine favor. We have received our wages and, in return, are charged with serving and worshipping Him. For, O soul, the All-Majestic Creator Who clothed you in existence, which is purely good, has given you a hungry stomach and, through His Name the All-Providing, has laid before you all edible things as a table of favors. Also, He has given you a life decked out with senses. It too demands its own particular sustenance like a stomach. All your senses like eyes and ears are like hands before which He has laid a particular table of favors as vast as the earth. In addition, as He has made you human, which demands numerous immaterial favors, He has laid before you a table of favors within reason's grasp and as multidimensional as the material and immaterial worlds. As He has also granted you belief and Islam, which is the greatest humanity and thus demands endless favors and is nourished by the fruits of infinite Mercy, He has opened up for you a table of favors, happiness, and pleasures which encompasses, together with the Sphere of Contingencies, the Sphere of His All-Beautiful Names and sacred Attributes. Moreover, by bestowed on you love, which is a light of belief, He has granted to you still another table of favors, bliss, and pleasures.

In physical terms you are a small, insignificant, impotent, wretched, and restricted particular being. But through His grace and favors you have become a universal, enlightened, and enlightening being. He has endowed you with life and thereby promoted you to the rank of a particular kind of universality. By endowing you with humanity, He has raised you to the rank of true universality, and by granting to you Islam, to the the rank of a sublime and luminous universality; and by bestowing on you love and knowledge of God, He has made you attain an all-encompassing light.

O soul! As you have received these wages already, you are charged with worship, which is an easy, pleasant, and rewarding Divine gift. But you are lazy when it comes to performing it. When you carry it out defectively, as though you consider the advance wages insufficient, you arrogantly demand more. You also put on airs and complain that your prayers are not accepted. Your due is not complaint but offering petitions and supplications to God Almighty. He bestows Paradise and eternal happiness purely out of His Grace and Kindness. Therefore, always seek refugee in His Mercy and Grace, rely on Him, and heed the following Divine declaration: *Say: "Out of His Grace and Mercy," and at that let them rejoice. It is better than what they have been accumulating* (10:58).

If you ask: "How can I respond to those universal, infinite favors through my restricted, particular thankfulness?", the answer will what follows: Through a universal intention and infinitely profound belief and devotion. Suppose a poor man enters the king's presence with a cheap (in materialistic terms) present. There he sees expensive gifts sent by the king's favorites. He thinks: "My present means nothing, but this is what I can afford." Then suddenly he addresses the king, saying: "My lord! I offer all these precious gifts in my name, for you deserve them. If I could, I would offer a double of these."

The king, who needs nothing but accepts his subjects' gifts as tokens of respect and loyalty, accepts the poor man's universal intention, desire, and deep feelings of devotion as though they were the greatest gift. Similarly, a poor servant says in his daily prescribed Prayers: "All worship and veneration is for God," by which he means: "In my name, I offer You all the gifts of worship that all beings present to you through their lives. You deserve all of them, and in reality far more than them." This belief and intention is a most comprehensive and universal thankfulness.

The seeds and stones of plants are their intentions to grow into elaborate plants. For example, with its hundreds of seeds, a melon intends: "O my Creator! I want to exhibit the inscriptions of Your All-Beautiful Names in many places of the earth." Having full knowledge of the future, Almighty God accepts its intentions as worship in deeds. The Prophetic saying: "A believer's intention is better than his action,"[137] expresses this reality. This is also why we glorify and praise Him with phrases expressing infinitude, like: "Glory be to You, and praise be to You to the number of Your creatures, the things pleasing to You, the decorations of Your Supreme Throne, to the amount of the ink of Your words. We glorify You with the sum of all the glorifications of Your Prophets, saints, and angels."

Just as a commander offers the king, in his name, all of his soldiers' services, humanity, the commander of all earthly creatures (including plants and animals) and acting in its own private world as if in the name of everyone, says: *You alone do we worship and from You alone do we seek help* (1:5), and offers the All-Worshipped One of Majesty in humanity's name

---

[137] al-Munawi, *Faydu'l-Qadir*, 6:291.

all of the creation's worship and entreaties for help. Saying: "Glory be to You with the sum of all the glorifications of all Your creatures and with the tongues of all things You have made," humanity makes all creatures speak in its own name.

Also, humanity says: "O God! Bestow blessings on Muhammad to the number of atoms and compounds in the universe." He calls God's blessing on Prophet Muhammad in the name of everything, for everything is connected with the light of Muhammad, upon him be peace and blessings, Understand from all this the wisdom in glorifying God and calling His blessings on Muhammad to the extent of infinity.

THIRD FRUIT: O soul! If you want endless accomplishments with regard to your afterlife during your short life here, if you want to see each minute of your life as fruitful as a whole life, and if you want to transform your ordinary deeds into acts of worship and your heedlessness into constant awareness of being in God's Presence, follow the Prophet's exalted Sunna. For obeying the rules of the Shari'a affords some sort of awareness of God's presence, and becomes a kind of worship that yields many fruits for the Hereafter.

For example, when you follow the principle which the Shari'a requires in a buy-and-sell transaction, this ordinary transaction becomes an act of worship, for remembering the Shari'a reminds you of the Divine Revelation, which causes you to think of the Revealer of the Shari'a and to turn your attention to Him. This produces awareness of His presence. That means, obeying the Sunna can make one's transient life produce eternal fruits to be the means of an eternal life. Therefore, heed the following Divine decree: *So believe in God and His Messenger, the unlettered Prophet who believes in God and His words, and follow him so that you may be guided* (7:158). Try to be a comprehensive object to be enlightened by each Divine Beautiful Name manifested in the rules of the Shari'a and the exalted Sunna.

FOURTH FRUIT: O soul! Do not be deluded by the apparent glitter and illicit pleasure of worldly people, particularly of those leading a dissolute life and, even more particularly, unbelievers. For you will not able to be like them by imitating them. You will fall too low. You cannot be like animals either, for your intellect will be an inauspicious "tool" that will give you endless trouble.

Suppose there is a palace the central room of which has a large electric light. All other rooms have small lights connected to it. If someone turns off that large light, the palace is left in darkness. Another palace has small electric lights in each room that are not connected to its central light. If that palace owner turns off the central light, the other rooms remain illuminated. This allows its inhabitants to do their work and deter thieves.

O soul! The first palace represents Muslims. Our Prophet, upon him be peace and blessings, is the large central light in the Muslims' heart. If they forget him or discard him from their heart, they will be unable to believe in any other Prophet. Moreover, their spirit will have no room for any kind of perfection. They will not recognize their Lord, all their inner senses and faculties will be left in darkness, and their hearts will be ruined and invaded by despair and gloom. What will be able to find to replace the resulting void with and find consolation in?

Christians and Jews are like the other palace. Even if they are not illuminated by the Prophet's light, they can manage with the "light" they think they have. Their form of belief in the Creator and Moses or Jesus, upon them be peace, can still be the means of some sort of moral perfection.

O evil-commanding soul! You can never be like an animal either, for your intellect troubles you continuously with pains of the past and anxieties for the future. It blends one pleasure with a thousand pains. But an animal enjoys itself without pain. So if you want to live like an animal, first discard your intellect and then be an animal. Also, be attentive to the Divine warning: *They are like cattle, rather, more astray (and in need of being led)* (7:179).

FIFTH FRUIT: O soul! Since we are the fruit of the Tree of Creation, we are a most comprehensive being and are related to all creation. We have within ourselves a heart that, like a fruit's pit, is the center in which all parts end and join together. We are mortal and inclined toward the world of multiplicity. But the worship of God is a line of union that turns us from mortality toward permanence, from the created toward the Creator, and from multiplicity toward unity. It is also a point of juncture between the beginning and the end.

If a seed-bearing fruit looks down at those under the tree and, priding itself on its beauty, throws itself into their hands or heedlessly leaps off the tree, it is quickly lost. However, if it is not heedless of its point of support, its seed (in which the tree's whole life is included) will enable the tree to perpetuate its meaning and life. This also enables it to gain a comprehensive reality in a perpetual life.

Similarly, if you are drowned in the multiplicity of things and, deluded with the smiles of mortals in drunkenness with love of the world, leave yourself in their arms, you will certainly suffer utter loss and find yourself in the darkness of eternal execution after a transient life. This will also bring about your spiritual death. But if you listen to the lessons of belief from the Qur'an with the ear of your heart and coming to your senses, turn toward unity, you will be able to reach the summit of perfections through worship and servanthood to God, and gain eternal existence.

O soul! Since this is the reality and since you are from Abraham's nation, say, like he did: "I love not those that set." Turn your face toward the Eternal Beloved One, and weep, saying:

(The verses to be included here have been included in the Second Station of the Seventeenth Word, and have not been repeated here.)

The
Twenty-fifth Word

The Twenty-fifth Word

Treatise on the Qur'an's miraculousness

> While there is a permanent miracle like the Qur'an,
> my mind considers it unnecessary to search for further proof.
> While there is an evidence of truth like the Qur'an,
> would it be heavy for my heart to silence those who deny?

NOTE: Most of the verses discussed in this treatise are those that have either been criticized by heretics or questioned by certain people of sciences or made the subject of doubt by satanic people and jinn. Their truths are herein explained in such a way that the very points that have been made the subject of criticism and doubt are proved to be, in reality, the rays of miraculousness and the sources of the Qur'an's eloquence.

However, since this treatise was composed quickly and amid troubled circumstances, there may be some defects in the expression of ideas. However, it explains several issues that have great scientific importance, and so may be of use even in its present form.

— Said Nursi

In the Name of God, the All-Merciful, the All-Compassionate.

Say: "If humanity and jinn banded together to produce the like of this Qur'an, they would never produce its like, even though they backed one another." (17:88)

(Out of countless aspects of the Qur'an's miraculousness, which is a store of miracles and the greatest miracle of Prophet Muhammad, upon him be peace and blessings, I have so far mentioned about forty in my Arabic treatises, *Isharatu'l-I'jaz* (Signs of Miraculousness, an introductory commentary on the Qur'an) and in the previous 24 Words. I will explain only five here, which briefly mention the others, following an introductory definition of the Qur'an.)

Introduction

THE INTRODUCTION CONSIST OF THREE PARTS.

FIRST PART: Question: What is the Qur'an? How can it be defined?

Answer: As explained in The Nineteenth Word and argued elsewhere, the Qur'an is an eternal translation of the great Book of the Universe and everlasting translator of it multifarious tongues reciting the Divine laws of the universe's creation and operation; the interpreter of the books of the visible, material world and the World of the Unseen; the discloser of the immaterial treasuries of the Divine Names hidden on the earth and in the heavens; the key to the truths lying behind events; the World of the Unseen's tongue in the visible, material one; the treasury of the All-Merciful One's favors and the All-Glorified One's eternal addresses coming from the World of the Unseen beyond the veil of this visible world; the sun of Islam's spiritual and intellectual world, as well as its foundation and plan; the sacred map of the worlds of the Hereafter; the expounder, lucid interpreter, articulate proof, and clear translator of the Divine Essence, Attributes, Names and essential Qualities; the educator and trainer of the world of humanity and the water and light of Islam, which is the true and greatest humanity; and the true guide of humanity leading them to happiness.

For humanity, it is both a book of law, and a book of prayer, and a book of wisdom, and a book of worship and servanthood to God, and a book of command and call to God, and a book of invocation, and a book of thought and reflection. It is a comprehensive, holy book containing books for all spiritual needs of humanity; a heavenly book that, like a sacred library, offers numerous booklets from which all saints, eminently truthful people, all discerning and verifying scholars, and those well-versed in knowledge of God have derived their own specific ways, and which illuminate each way and answer their followers' needs.

SECOND PART: To complete the definition: Having come from God's Supreme Throne, originated in His Greatest Name, and issued from each Name's most comprehensive rank, and as explained in The Twelfth Word, the Qur'an is God's Word on account of God's being the Lord of the Worlds, and His decree on account of His having the title of Deity of all creatures. It is a discourse in the Name of the Creator of the heavens and the earth; a speech and conversation in regard to His absolute Lordship; an eternal sermon on behalf of the All-Glorified One's universal Sovereignty. It is also a register of the All-Merciful One's favors from the viewpoint of His all-embracing Mercy; a collection of messages or communications that sometimes begin with ciphers in respect of His Divinity's sublime majesty; and a wisdom-infusing holy Scripture that, having descended from the Divine Greatest Name's all-comprehensive realm, looks over and surveys the circle surrounded by His Supreme Throne.

This is why the title "the Word of God" has been and will always be given to the Qur'an. After the Qur'an come the Scriptures and Pages or Scrolls sent to other Prophets. Some of the other countless Divine words are conversations in the form of inspirations coming as particular manifestations of a particular aspect of Divine Mercy, Sovereignty, and Lordship under a particular title and with a particular regard. The inspirations coming to angels, human beings, and animals vary greatly with regard to their universality or particularity.

THIRD PART: The Qur'an briefly contains all Scriptures revealed to previous Prophets, and the works of all saints and purified, discerning scholars following different ways of thought and paths to God. Its six sides are bright and absolutely free of doubt and whimsical thought. Its point of support is certainly Divine Revelation and the Divine eternal Speech; its aim is self-evidently eternal happiness; its inside is clearly pure guidance; it is necessarily surrounded and supported from above by the lights of belief, from below undeniably by proof and evidence, from the right evidently by the heart's submission and the conscience, and from the left by the admission of reason and other intellectual faculties. Its fruit is most certainly the All-Merciful's mercy and Paradise. It has been accepted and promoted by angels and innumerable people and jinn throughout the centuries.

All of these qualities mentioned above have either been proven in other places or will be proved in the following pages depending on decisive proofs.

First Light

This Light has three rays.

FIRST RAY: This is the Qur'an's miraculous eloquence, which originates in its words' beauty, order, and composition; its textual beauty and perfection; its stylistic originality and uniqueness; its explanations' superiority, excellence, and clarity; its meanings' power and truth; and its linguistic purity and fluency. Its eloquence is so extraordinary that its eternal challenge to the most brilliant people of letters of humankind, their most celebrated orators, and the most profoundly learned of them, to produce something like it, even if only a chapter, has yet to be answered. Instead, those geniuses who, in their self-pride and self-confidence, consider themselves so great as to touch the heavens have had to humble themselves before it.

I will now point out its miraculous eloquence in two ways:

FIRST WAY: The people of Arabia were mostly unlettered at that time, and therefore preserved their tribal pride, history, and proverbs in oral poetry. They attached great importance to eloquence, and so any meaningful, unique expression was memorized for its poetical form and eloquence and then handed down to posterity. Eloquence and fluency were therefore in such great demand that a tribe treated its eloquent literary figures as national heroes. Those intelligent people, who would govern a considerable portion of the world after Islam's advent, were more eloquent than other nations. Eloquence was so esteemed that two tribes would sometimes go to war over a saying of a literary figure and then be reconciled by the words of another. They even inscribed in gold the odes of seven poets and hung them on the wall of the Ka'ba. They were called the Seven Suspended Poems.

At a time when eloquence was in such demand, the Qur'an of miraculous exposition was revealed. Just as God Almighty had endowed Moses and Jesus with the miracles most suitable to their times—the miracles of Staff and Bright Hand to Moses, and those of raising the dead and healing certain illnesses to Jesus—He made eloquence the most notable aspect of the Qur'an, the chief miracle of Prophet Muhammad, upon him be peace and blessings. When it was revealed, it challenged first the literary figures of the Arabian peninsula: *If you doubt what We have sent down on Our servant, produce a sura like it* (2:23). It defeated their intellectual pretensions and humbled them by continuing: *If you cannot, and you certainly cannot, fear the Fire, whose fuel is people and stones, prepared for unbelievers* (2:24).

Those self-conceited people could not dispute the Qur'an. Although this was an easy and safe course to obstruct and falsify its message, they chose to fight it with swords, the perilous and most difficult course. If those intelligent people, skilled in diplomacy, could have disputed the Qur'an, they would not have chosen the perilous, difficult course and risked losing their property and lives. Since they could not argue with it verbally, they had to fight it with swords.

There were two powerful reasons for trying to produce something like the Qur'an: its enemies strongly wished to dispute it to refute its claim of Revelation, and its friends had the desire to imitate it. The result was, and continues to be, innumerable books written in Arabic. All people, whether scholars or not, who read such books are forced to admit that they do not resemble the Qur'an. So, either the Qur'an is inferior—friend and foe admit that this is inconceivable—or superior to all of them. There are no other options.

Question: How do we know that people have never dared to dispute it, and that their cooperative effort failed?

Answer: If dispute were possible, some disputants would have appeared. For it was a question of honour, and a matter of life and death. Since so many people have opposed the truth, such an attempt would have found many supporters and been well known. When even an insignificant struggle arouses great curiosity, such a historic, unusual contest could not have been kept secret. Although the most insignificant and detestable objections concerning Islam have been circulated widely, nothing other than a few pieces of Musaylima the Liar have been narrated.[138] Whatever his oratorical skills, the historical record of his words show them as utter absurdities when compared with the Qur'an's infinitely beautiful expressions. Thus the Qur'an's miraculous eloquence is indisputable.

SECOND WAY: We will now explain in five points the wisdom in the Qur'an's miraculous eloquence.

First point: There is an extraordinary eloquence and stylistic purity in the Qur'an's word order or composition. This is explained in my *Isharatu'l-I'jaz*. Just as a clock's hands of second, minute, and hour complete and are fitted to each other in precise orderliness, so does every word and sentence—indeed the whole Qur'an—complete and fit each other.

This extraordinary eloquence is visible for all to see. Consider the following examples:

• From *Suratu'l-Anbiya'*:

If but a breath from the punishment of Your Lord touches them. (21:46)

---

[138] Musaylima the Liar claimed that he had been made a partner with the Prophet in authority and composed some "*suras.*" However, he was ridiculed. (Tr.)

To indicate the severity of God's punishment, the above clause points to the least amount or slightest element of it. As the entire clause expresses this slightness, all of its parts should reinforce that meaning.

The words *If but* (*la-in*) signify uncertainty and therefore imply slightness (of punishment). The verb *massa* means to touch slightly, also signifying slightness. *Nafhatun* (a breath) is merely a puff of air. Grammatically, it is a derived form of the word used to express singleness, which again underlies the slightness. The double *n* (*tanwin*) at the end of *nafhatun* indicates indefiniteness and suggests that it is slight and insignificant. The partitive *min* implies a part or a piece, thus indicating paucity. The word *'adhab* (torment or punishment) is light in meaning compared to *nakal* (exemplary chastisement) and *'iqab* (heavy penalty), and denotes a light punishment or torment. The use of *Rabb* (Lord, Provider, Sustainer), suggesting affection, instead of (for example) All-Overwhelming, All-Compelling, or Ever-Able To Requite, also expresses slightness.

Finally, the clause means that if so slight a breath of torment or punishment has such an affect, one should reflect how severe the Divine chastisement might be. We see in this short clause how its parts are related to each other and add to the meaning. This example concerns the words chosen and the purpose in choosing them.

- From *Suratu'l-Baqara*:

Out of what We have provided for them they give as sustenance. (2:3)

The parts of the above sentence point to five conditions that make alms-giving acceptable to God.

First condition: While giving alms, believers must not give so much that they are reduced to begging. *Out of* expresses this.

Second condition: They must give out of what they have, not out of what others have. *We have provided for them* points to this. The meaning is "give (to sustain life) out of what We have provided you with."

Third condition: They must not remind the recipient of their kindness. *We* indicates this, for it means: "I have provided you with the thing out of which you give to the needy as sustenance. As you are giving some of that which belongs to Me, you cannot put the recipient under obligation."

Fourth condition: They must give to those who will spend it only for their livelihood, not in illicit ways. *They give as sustenance* points to this.

Fifth condition: They must give it for God's sake. *We have provided for them* states this. It means: You are giving out of My property, and so must give in My name.

Together with those conditions, the word *what* signifies that whatever God bestows is part of one's sustenance or livelihood. Thus believers must give out of whatever they have. For example, a good word, some help, advice, and teaching are all included in the meaning of *rizq* (sustenance or provision) and *sadaqa* (alms). *What* (*ma*) has a general meaning and is not restricted here. Thus it includes whatever God has bestowed.

This short sentence contains and suggests a broad range of meaning for alms and offers it to our understanding. The word order of the Qur'an's sentences has many similar aspects, and the words have a wide range of relationships with one another. The same is true for the relationships between sentences, as seen in:

- *Suratu'l-Ikhlas*, which is as follows:

  Say: He—(He is) God, (Who is) the Unique One. God is the Eternally Besought One. He begets not, nor was He begotten. And comparable to Him there is none. (112:1-5)

This short *sura* has six sentences, three positive and three negative, which prove and establish six aspects of Divine Unity and reject and negate six types of associating partners with God. Each sentence has two meanings: one *a priori* (functioning as a cause or proof) and the other *a posteriori* (functioning as an effect or result). That means that the *sura* contains thirty-six *suras*, each made up of six sentences. One is either a premise or a proposition, and the others are arguments for it. For example:

  Say: He—(He is) God, because He is the Unique One, because He is the Eternally Besought One, because He does not beget, because He was not begotten, because comparable to Him there is none.

Also:

  Say: Comparable to Him there is none, because He was not begotten, because He does not beget, because He is the Eternally Besought One, because He is Unique One, because He—(He is) is God.

Also:

  He—(He is) God, therefore He is the Unique One, therefore He is the Eternally Besought One, therefore He does not beget, therefore He was not begotten, therefore comparable unto Him there is none.

- From *Suratu'l-Baqara*:

  Alif Lam Mim. That is the Book: there is no doubt about it—a guidance for the God-revering, pious. (2:1-2)

Each of the four sentences has two meanings. One meaning is a proof for the others, and the other, their result. A composite design of miraculousness is woven from the sixteen threads of relationship between them. This design was demonstrated in my *Isharatu'l-I'jaz*. As explained in The Thirteenth Word, it is as if each Qur'anic verse has an eye that sees most of the verses and a face that looks toward them. Given this, it extends to them the immaterial threads of relationship to weave a design of miraculousness. The beauty of composition is elaborated in *Isharatu'l-I'jaz*.

Second point: There is a wonderful eloquence in the Qur'an's meanings. Consider the following examples:

- From several *suras*:

  All that is in the heavens and the earth glorifies God; and He is the All-Glorious and All-Mighty, the All-Wise (57:1, 59:1, 61:1).

To experience the pleasure of eloquence in meanings, imagine that you are living in the desert of pre-Islamic Arabia. At a time when everything is enveloped by the darkness of ignorance and heedlessness and wrapped in the evil of "lifeless" nature, you hear from the Qur'an's heavenly tongue: *All that is in the heavens and the earth glorifies God* or *The seven heavens and the earth and those in them glorify Him* (17:44), or similar verses.

You will see how, in people's mind, those motionless corpse-like entities acquire a purposeful existence at the sound of *glorifying,* and being so raised, recite God's Names. At the cry and light of *glorifying,* the stars, until then lifeless lumps of fire in the dark sky, appear in their understanding as wisdom-displaying words and truth-showing lights in the sky's recitation, the land and sea as tongues of praise, and each plant and animal as a word of glorification.

- From *Suratu'r-Rahman*:

  O company of jinn and humanity! If you are able to penetrate and pass beyond the spheres of the heavens and the earth, then penetrate and pass beyond (them). You will not penetrate and pass beyond them save with an authority. Which then of the blessings of your Lord do you deny? There will be sent on you a flash of fire, and smoke, and no help will you have. Which then of the blessings of your Lord do you deny? (55:33-36)

Indeed, We have adorned the lowest (world's) heaven with lamps, and We have made (out of) them missiles to drive away devils. (67:5)

Listen to these verses, which are discussed in The Fifteenth Word, and pay attention to their meaning. They say:

O humanity and jinn, arrogant and refractory despite your impotence and wretchedness, rebellious and obstinate despite your weakness and destitution! If you do not obey My commands, pass beyond—if you can—the boundaries of My Kingdom. How dare you disobey a King Whose commands are obeyed by stars, moons, and suns as if they were trained soldiers ever ready to carry out their commander's commands. You rebel against a Majestic Ruler Who has such mighty and obedient soldiers that, supposing your satans were to resist, they could stone them to death with mountain-like cannonballs. Your ingratitude causes you to rebel in the Kingdom of such a Majestic Sovereign that among His forces are those that could hurl down upon you mountain-sized or even the earth-sized stars or flaming missiles, if you were unbelievers of that size, and rout you. Moreover, you infringe upon a law to which such beings are bound that were it necessary, they could hurl the earth in your face and rain down upon you stars as though missiles by God's leave.

You can compare the force and eloquence in the meaning of other verses and their elevated style with these.

Third point: The Qur'an has unique, original styles that are both novel and convincing. Its styles, which have always preserved and still preserves their originality, freshness, and "bloom of youth," do not imitate and cannot be imitated. To cite a few examples:

• The *muqatta'at*:

The cipher-like *muqatta'at*, the separated, individual letters (e.g., *Alif-Lam-Mim, Alif-Lam-Ra, Ta-Ha, Ya-Sin, Ha-Mim*, and *'Ayn-Sin-Qaf*, with which some *suras* begin), contain five or six gleams of miraculousness. For example, they comprise half of each category of the well-known categories of letters—emphatic, whispered, stressed, soft, labio-linguals, and *qalqala* (*Ba, Jim, Dal, Ta, Qaf*). Taking more than half from the "light" letters and less than half from the "heavy" letters, neither of which are divisible, the Qur'an has halved every category.

Although it is possible to halve all categories, existing together one within the other, in one out of two hundred probable ways, taking half from each category cannot be the work of a human mind. Chance could not have interfered in it. Together with these individual letters at the beginning of certain *suras* as Divine ciphers displaying five or six further gleams of miraculousness like this, scholars well-versed in the mysteries of letters, as well as exacting, saintly scholars, have drawn many mysterious conclusions and discovered such truths that they consider these letters to form a most brilliant miracle. Since I am unable to discover and demonstrate their secrets clearly, I only refer readers to the five or six gleams of their miraculousness explained in *Isharatu'l-I'jaz*.

Now I will discuss briefly the Qur'anic styles followed in its *suras*, aims, verses, sentences and phrases, and words.

- Consider *Suratu'n-Naba'*:

Suratu'n-Naba' describes the Last Day and the Resurrection, as well as Paradise and Hell, in such an original and unique style that it convinces the heart that each Divine act and the work of Divine Lordship in this world proves the Hereafter's coming and all its aspects. In the interest of space, I mention only a few points.

At the start of the *sura*, it proves the Day of Judgment by meaning:

> I have made the earth a beautiful cradle spread out for you, and the mountains bulwarks of your houses and lives full of treasures. I have created you in pairs, loving and familiar with each other; I have made the night a coverlet for your repose, the daytime the arena in which to gain your livelihood, and the sun an illuminating and heating lamp, and from the clouds I send down water as if they were a spring producing the water of life. I create easily and in a short time from the one, same water all the flowering and fruit-bearing things which bear all your sustenance. Since this is so, the Last Day, which is the Day of Final Judgment, awaits you. It is not difficult for Us to bring about that Day. (78:6-17—not exactly translated but interpreted [Tr.])

Following in the same strain, the *sura* implicitly proves that on the Last Day the mountains will be moved and become as a mirage, the heavens rent asunder, Hell made ready, and the people of Paradise given gardens and orchards. It means: "Since He does all these things before your eyes on the earth and mountains, He will do their likes in the Hereafter." In other words, the mountains mentioned at the *sura*'s beginning have some relationship with the Hereafter's mountains, and the gardens with those in the Hereafter that are mentioned toward the end of the *sura*. Study other points from the same view, and see how elevated its style really is.

- From *Sura Al-i 'Imran:*

Say: O God, Master of all dominion! You give dominion to whom You will and You take away dominion from whom You will, and You exalt whom You will and You abase whom You will. In Your hand is all good. Surely You have full power over all things. You make the night pass into the day and You make the day pass into the night; You bring forth the living out of the dead, and You bring forth the dead out of the living, and You provide whomever You will without measure. (3:26-30)

The Divine acts and operations in this world, the Divine manifestations in the alternation of day and night, the Lordship's control of the seasons, the Lordship's acts in life and death and the world's changes, renewals, transformations, and convulsions are expressed in such a vivid and elevated style that it captivates the minds of the attentive. Since a little attention is enough to see this brilliant, elevated, and comprehensive style, I will go no further.

- From *Suratu'l-Inshiqaq:*

When the heaven is split asunder, obeying its Lord, as is expected indeed, and it always does so. And when the earth is leveled, and casts forth all that is in it and becomes empty, obeying its Lord, as is expected indeed, and it always does so. (84:1-5)

These verses express in a most elevated style to what extent the heavens and the earth submit to and obey Almighty God's command. To accomplish and conclude a war—strategy, fighting, enrolling, and mobilizing soldiers, and so on—a commander-in-chief establishes two offices. After the fighting is over, he turns to change these offices and use them for other business. The offices request him in the tongue of their staffs or suddenly starting speaking, they say through their own tongue: "O commander, let us first clean up and remove the bits and pieces of the former business, and then honor us with your presence." They do so, and then say to the commander: "Now we are at your command. Do what you wish, for whatever you do is right, good, and beneficial."

Similarly, the heavens and the earth were built as two arenas of testing and trial. Following the end of this period of trial for conscious beings, the heavens and the earth will expel the things connected with that trial at God's command. Then will they call: "O Lord, we are at Your command, so use us for whatever You will. Our due is to obey You; whatever You do is right and true." Based on this understanding, reflect upon the verses' elevated style and meaning.

- From *Sura Hud:*

O earth, swallow up your water! O sky, cease (your rain)! And the water was made to subside, and the affair was accomplished. Then (the Ark) came to rest upon al-Judi, and it was said: "Away with the wrongdoing folk!" (11:44)

To point to a drop from the ocean of this verse's eloquence, I will show an aspect of its style through the mirror of an analogy. After the victory won in a world war, a commander orders one firing army "Cease fire!" and another, attacking, army "Halt!" The fire ceases and the attack is halted. The commander announces: "The job is well done. The enemy is defeated, and our flag is raised on the highest tower in the enemy's headquarters. Those aggressive wrongdoers have received their deserts and have gone to the lowest of the low."

Similarly, the peerless Sovereign ordered the heaven and the earth to annihilate Noah's people. After they did so, He decreed: "O the earth, swallow up your water! O the sky, stop! You have completed your duty. The water subsided. The Ark, which is like the royal tent, came to rest upon the mountain. The wrongdoers received their due."

Consider how sublime this style is. The verse says that like two soldiers, the sky and the earth heed God's commands and obey Him. The style suggests that the universe is indignant and that the heavens and the earth are furious with humanity's rebellion. Moreover, it warns humanity that its rebellion against the One Whose commands the heavens and the earth obey is unreasonable and that people must not rebel. The verse expresses a very powerful restraint. In a few sentences, it describes a global event like the Flood, with all its truths and results, in a concise, miraculous, and beautiful manner. Compare other drops of this ocean to this one.

Now consider the style apparent through the window of the Qur'an's words:

- From *Sura Ya Sin:*

And for the moon We have determined mansions till it returns like an old shriveled date-stalk. (36:38)

Look at *like an old shriveled date-stalk.* What a fine style it displays: One of the moon's mansions is the Pleiades. The verse compares the moon in its last quarter—the crescent—to an old shriveled date-stalk. The comparison gives the impression that behind the sky's dark veil is a tree, one pointed shining stalk of which tears the veil and shows itself with the Pleiades like a cluster hanging from that stalk, and other stars like the glittering fruits of that hidden tree. If you have taste, you will appreciate what a proper, beautiful, fine, and noble style this is, especially for desert-dwellers whose most important means of livelihood is the date palm.

• Another example from *Sura Ya Sin*, which was discussed at the end of The Nineteenth Word:

And the sun runs its course to a resting place destined. (36:37)

The expression *runs its course* opens a window on an exalted style: By reminding us of Divine Power's systematic, magnificent, free acts and operations in alternating day and night as well as summer and winter, it makes the Maker's Might and Grandeur understandable, turns one's attention toward the Eternally Besought One's messages inscribed on the season's pages by the Pen of Power, and makes known the Creator's Wisdom.

By using *lamp* in *He has made the sun a lamp* (71:16), the Qur'an opens a window on a particular style, as follows: This world is a palace, and its contents are humanity's and other living beings' adornments, food and other necessities of life. The sun is a lamp illuminating this palace. By making the Maker's Magnificence and the Creator's favors comprehensible in this way, the sentence provides a proof for God's Unity and declares the sun (which the polytheists of that time viewed as the most significant and brightest deity) to be a lifeless object, a lamp subdued for the benefit of living beings.

In *lamp*, the verse signifies the Creator's mercy in His Lordship's might and greatness, reminds us of His favor in His Mercy's vastness, suggests His munificence in His Sovereignty's magnificence, and thereby proclaims His Oneness. It also teaches that a lifeless, subjected lamp is unworthy of worship. By indicating Almighty God's systematic, amazing acts in alternating night and day as well as winter and summer, it suggests the vast Power of the Maker, Who executes His Lordship independently.

Thus the verse deals with the sun and moon in a way to turn our attention to the pages of day and night, summer and winter, and the lines of events inscribed on them. The Qur'an mentions the sun not in its own name but in the name of the One Who has made it shining. It ignores the sun's physical nature, which does not benefit us, and draws our attention to its essential duties: to function as a wheel or spring for the delicate order of Divine creation and making, and as a shuttle for the harmony of Divine design in what the Eternal Designer weaves with the threads of night and day. When you compare other Qur'anic words with these, you see that each word, even if common, is a key to the treasury of fine meanings.

In sum, the vividness and extraordinariness of the Qur'an's styles would sometimes entrance a Bedouin with one phrase, who would then prostrate before its eloquence. Once *Proclaim what you are commanded openly and in an emphatic manner* (15:94) engendered this very reaction. When asked if he had become a Muslim, he answered: "No. I prostrate before the phrase's eloquence."

Fourth point: The Qur'an's wording is extraordinarily fluent and pure. As it is extraordinarily eloquent when expressing meaning, so also it is wonderfully fluent and pure in wording and word arrangement. One proof of this is that it does not bore the senses but rather gives them pleasure, even if it is recited thousands of times. Brilliant scholars of the sciences of rhetoric and grammar also confirm its matchless eloquence with the wisdom it has.

Even a child can memorize the Qur'an easily. Seriously ill people, even if troubled by a few words of ordinary speech nearby, feel relief and comfort upon hearing it. For dying people, it gives their ears and minds the same taste and pleasure as that left by *Zamzam* water in their mouths and on their palates.

The Qur'an does not bore the senses; rather, it feeds the heart, gives power and wealth to the mind, functions as water and light for the spirit, and cures the soul's illnesses. We never tire of eating bread, but might tire of eating the same fruit every day. Similarly, reciting or listening to the Qur'an's pure truth and guidance does not bore us. As it always maintains its youth, it also preserves its freshness and sweetness.

Once the Quraysh[139] sent one of its eloquent leaders to listen to the Qur'an. When he returned, he remarked: "The Qur'an is so sweet and pleasing that no human tongue can resemble it. I know poets and soothsayers very well. The Qur'an is not like any of their work. We could only describe it as magic in order to deceive our people about it." Even its most hardened enemies admired its fluency and eloquence.

It would take too long to explain the sources of the fluency and purity of language in the. One who looks at the arrangement of the letters in:

> Then, after grief, He sent down peace and security for you: a slumber overtook a party of you; and another party being concerned about themselves, were entertaining false notions about God—notions of (the pre-Islamic) Ignorance—and saying: "Do we have any part in the affair?" Say: "The affair wholly belongs to God." Indeed, they concealed within

---

[139] The Quraysh was the Prophet's tribe. (Tr.)

themselves what they would not reveal to you, and were saying: "If only we had had a part in the affair, we would not have been killed here." Say: "Even if you had been in your houses, those for whom killing had been ordained would indeed have gone forth to the places where they were to lie (in death)." (All of this happened as it did) so that He may test what is in your bosoms, and purify and prove what is in your hearts. God has full knowledge of what lies hidden in the bosoms. (3:154)

will see the miraculousness brought about by the letters' extraordinary arrangement. Such an arrangement, subtle relationship, delicate harmony and composition show that the verse is not the work of a person or chance. Such an order may be for other unknown purposes. Since the letters are arranged according to a certain system, there must be a mysterious order and illustrious coherence in the choice and arrangement of words, sentences, and meanings. Those who notice and understand it will remark: "What wonders God wills. How wonderfully God has made them."

Fifth point: The Qur'an's expressions contain a superiority, power, sublimity, and magnificence. Its fluent, eloquent, and pure composition and word order, as well as eloquent meanings, and original and unique styles, lead to an evident excellence in its explanations. Truly, in all categories of expression and address such as encouragement, dissuasion, praise, censure, demonstration, proving, guidance, explanation and overcoming in argument, its expositions are of the highest degree. For example: The expressions in *Suratu'l-Insan* (76), one of many examples of exhorting and encouraging good deeds, are most pleasing, like the water of a river of Paradise, and as sweet as the fruits of Paradise.

Aimed at dissuasion and threat, its explanations at the beginning of *Suratu'l-Ghashiya* (88) produce an effect like lead boiling in misguided people's ears, fire burning in their brains, *Zaqqum* scalding their palates, Hellfire assaulting their faces, and a bitter, thorny tree in their stomachs. That Hell, an "official" charged with torturing, tormenting, and demonstrating the Divine Being's threats, roars to the extent that the Divine Being says about it, *It nearly bursts with rage and fury* (67:8), shows how great and powerful that Being's dissuasion is.

In the category of praise, the Qur'anic explanations in the five *suras* beginning with *All praise and gratitude are for God*[140] are brilliant like the sun, adorned like stars, majestic like the heavens and the earth, lovely like

---

[140] Namely, *al-Fatiha*, *al-An'am*, *al-Kahf*, *as-Saba'*, and *al-Fatir*. (Tr.)

angels, full of the tenderness and compassion shown to the young in this world, and beautiful like Paradise.

As for censure and restraint, consider what follows:

- Would any of you like to eat the flesh of his dead brother? (49: 12).

It censures backbiting in six degrees of censure, and restrains the backbiter with six degrees of severity.

The initial *hamza* (in the original Arabic) is interrogative. This sense penetrates all the phrases of the verse. So through the initial *hamza* it asks: "Do you have no reason or intelligence, the faculty of asking and answering, that you do not perceive how abominable this thing is?" *Like* asks: "Is your heart, with which you love and hate, so corrupted that you love such a repugnant thing?" *Any of you* asks: "What has happened to your sense of social relationship and civilization, which derive their liveliness from collectivity, that you accept something so poisonous to social life?"

To eat the flesh asks: "What has happened to your sense of humanity, that you tear your friend to pieces with your teeth like a wild animal?" *Of his brother* asks: "Do you have no human tenderness, no sense of kinship? How can you sink your teeth into an innocent person tied to you by numerous links of brotherhood? Or do you have no intelligence, and so senselessly bite into your own limbs?" *Dead* asks: "Where is your conscience? Is your nature so corrupt that you can do the most repulsive thing like eating his flesh to your brother who is now in the position where he must be shown the greatest respect?"

Thus slander and backbiting are repugnant to one's intelligence, heart, humanity, conscience, human nature, and religious and national brotherhood. See how this verse condemns backbiting in six degrees very concisely, and restrains people from it in six miraculous ways.

As for proving and demonstration, consider the following from among numerous examples:

- Look upon the imprints of God's Mercy, how He revives the earth after its death. He it is Who will revive the dead [in a similar way]. He has full power over everything. (30:50)

This verse is such a wonderful proof of the Resurrection that no better proof is conceivable. As discussed in The Tenth Truth of The Tenth Word and in The Fifth Gleam of The Twenty-second Word, the annual spring resurrection of countless plants and animals that died during the previous autumn and winter contains uncountable examples of the Resurrection.

Referring to the utmost order and differentiation in the revival of innumerable species that exist all mixed up together in total confusion, the verse states that the One Who does these things can raise the dead with ease after destroying the world. As it is the stamp of the One of Unity to inscribe on the page of the earth countless species with the Pen of His Power, one within the other without confusion, together with proving Divine Oneness like the sun, the verse shows the Resurrection as evidently as sunrise and sunset. As the Qur'an refers to this truth with the adverb *how* in this verse, it describes it in detail in many other *suras*.

Also, in *Sura Qaf* (50), the Qur'an proves the Resurrection in so brilliant, beautiful, lovely, and elevated a manner of expression that it gives as great certainty as the coming of spring. Replying to the unbelievers' denial that decomposed bones can come to life once again, it declares:

- Do they, then, never observe the sky above them, how We have constructed it and adorned it, and that there are no rifts in it? And the earth—We have spread it out, and set therein firm mountains, and caused to grow thereon every lovely pair of vegetation. (All this is a means of) insight and reminder for every servant (of God) willing to turn to Him in contrition. And We send down from the sky blessed water with which We cause to grow gardens and grain to harvest, and tall and stately date-palms with ranged clusters, as a provision for the servants. And We revive with it a dead land: even so will the dead be raised and come forth (from their graves). (50:6-11)

Truly, the manner of its exposition flows like water, glitters like stars and, just as dates give to the body, gives pleasure and nourishment to the heart.

Among the most delightful examples of proof and demonstration is:

- *Ya Sin.* By the wise Qur'an. Certainly you are among those sent (as Messengers of God). (36:1-3)

This oath points out that the proof of Muhammad's Messengership is so certain and true and the truth of his Messengership is so worthy of respect that an oath can be sworn upon it. In other words: "You are the Messenger, for you hold the Qur'an in your hand, and the Qur'an is the truth and Word of God. For it contains true wisdom and bears the seal of miraculousness."

Another concise and miraculous example of this type is:

- ... he says: "Who will revive these bones when they have rotted away?" Say: "He Who produced them in the first instance will revive them. He has full knowledge of every (form, mode and possibility of) creation." (36:78)

As explained in the third comparison in The Ninth Truth of The Tenth Word, if one assembles a huge, dispersed army in a day and someone says, "That person can certainly gather, through a trumpet call, a battalion dispersed for rest and line the soldiers up in their previous positions," and you reject him, this would certainly be a foolish denial.

Similarly, an All-Powerful, All-Knowing One assembles all living beings' atoms, regardless of their location, by the command of *"Be!" and it is* (2:117) with perfect orderliness and the balance of wisdom, and make from them bodies having the most delicate senses and keenest faculties. Each spring He creates innumerable army-like animate species on the earth. Can it be questioned then how He can reassemble at a blow of Israfil's Trumpet the fundamental parts and atoms of a formerly battalion-like living body, which are already familiar with one another?

As for guidance, the Qur'an is so affective, penetrating, tender, and touching that its verses uplift the spirit with ardor, the heart with delight, the intellect with curiosity, and the eyes with tears. Just one example shows this:

- Yet after all this your hearts were hardened and became like rocks, or even harder: For there are rocks from which rivers gush, and some from which, when they are cleft, water issues; and some which fall down for awe of God. God is not unaware of what you do. (2:74)

As mentioned in The First Station of The Twentieth Word, this verse, addressed to the Children of Israel, means: "While even a hard rock cried tears like a spring from its twelve "eyes" before Moses' miracle of the Staff, what has happened to you that you remain indifferent in the face of all his miracles, with your eyes dry and your hearts hard and unfeeling?" Since the verse's meaning was elaborated elsewhere, I will not go further here.

As for silencing and overcoming in argument, consider what follows from among uncountable examples:

- If you are in doubt about (the Divine authorship of) what We have been sending down on Our servant (Muhammad), then pro- duce just a *sura* like it and call for help from all your supporters, all those (to whom you apply for help apart from God), if you are truthful (in your doubt and claim). (2:23)

The verse, directed to humanity and jinn, briefly means: If you have doubt about the Divine authorship of the Qur'an and think a human being is writing it, let one of your unlettered people, as Muhammad the Trustworthy is unlettered, produce something similar. If he cannot, send the

THE TWENTY-FIFTH WORD 405

most famous of your writers or scholars. If he cannot either, let all of them come and work together and call upon all their history, "deities," scientists, philosophers, sociologists, theologians, and writers to produce something similar. If they cannot, let them try—leaving aside its inimitable truths and the miraculous aspects of its meaning—to produce a work of equal eloquence in word order and composition.

By: *Then produce ten suras like it, contrived* (11:13), the Qur'an means: What you write does not have to be true; let it be fabrications or false tales. Neither need it match the Qur'an's length, just produce the like of its ten chapters. If you cannot do that either, produce only the like of one chapter. If you cannot do that, produce only the like of a short chapter. If you cannot do that—which you cannot although you direly need to do it because such inability will put your honor, religion, nationality, lives, and property at risk, and you will die humiliated—*then fear the Fire, whose fuel is people and stones* (2:14). You and your idols will spend eternity in Hell. Having understood your eight degrees of inability, what else can you do but admit eight times that the Qur'an is a miracle? Either believe or be silent!

See how the Qur'an silences the opponents as well while making truths understandable by all and say: "There cannot be and is no need for any other exposition after that of the Qur'an."

- Another example:

  So preach and remind; by God's grace, you are not a soothsayer, nor a madman. Or do they say (of him): "A poet (jinn-possessed). We await for him some calamity ahead"? Say: "Wait on; I am also waiting with you (though I hope for a different outcome)." Or do their minds urge them to such (falsehoods), or are they a rebellious people? Or do they say, "He forges it?" No, indeed. Rather, they have no will to believe. If not, let them produce a Discourse like it, if they are truthful (in their claims). Or were they created in vain and without anyone being before them? Or are they creators? Or did they create the heavens and the earth? Rather, they have no certain knowledge. Or are the treasures of your Lord with them? Or have they been given absolute authority? Or do they have a ladder by which they overhear? Then let their eavesdropper produce some clear authority. Or are there for Him daughters, while for you there are sons? Or do you ask them for a wage so that they are crushed under debt? Or do they have the knowledge of the Unseen, so that they copy from it? Or do they intend a plot (to entrap you)? Yet it is those who disbelieve who are entrapped. Or do they have a deity other than God? All-Glorified is He, above what they associate as partners with Him. (52: 29-43)

I will discuss only one of the countless truths found in these verses to show how the Qur'an makes truths understandable by all and silences the opponents: Through fifteen questions introduced by *or*, which express a rejection and impossibility, it silences all opponents, ends all doubt, and closes all ways to misguidance. It rends all veils under which the misguided may hide and discloses their fallacies. It crushes whatever lie they may fabricate. Each sentence either exposes and demolishes the fallacy of a group of unbelief, or remains silent where a fallacy is evident, or makes a short reference to an assertion of unbelief, which it refutes elsewhere in detail. For example, it refers their assertion that the Prophet is a poet to: *We have not taught him poetry; it is not seemly for him* (36:69), and their claim in the last section finds its answer in: *Were there deities in them (the earth and the heavens) other than God, they would surely go to ruin* (21:22).

In the beginning, it says: "Relay the Divine Commandments. You are not a soothsayer, for their words are confused and consist of conjecture. You speak the truth with absolute certainty and are not possessed. Even your enemies testify to your perfect intellect."

Or do they say: "*A poet (jinn-possessed). We await for him some calamity ahead*"? Say to them: "Wait on; I am waiting, too." The great and brilliant truths you bring are free of poetic fancy and artificial embellishment.

Or do their minds urge them to such (falsehoods)? Or, like senseless philosophers, do they consider their own intellects sufficient and so refuse to follow you? Any sound intellect requires following you, for whatever you say is reasonable. However, human intellect is unable to produce a like of it.

Or are they a rebellious people? Or, like rebellious wrongdoers, is their denial due to their non-submission to truth? Everybody knows the end of such leaders of mutinous wrongdoers as Pharaoh and Nimrod.

Or do they say, "He forges it?" No, indeed. Rather, they have no will to believe. Or, like lying and unscrupulous hypocrites, do they accuse you of inventing the Qur'an? Until this time, however, they knew you as the most trustworthy among them and even called you Muhammad the Trustworthy. In fact, they have no intention to believe. Otherwise they must find a human work similar to the Qur'an [if they are sincere in their claims].

Or were they created in vain and without anyone being before them? Or, like those philosophers who see existence as absurd and purposeless, do they regard themselves as purposeless, without a Creator, and left to themselves? Are they blind? Do they not see that the universe is embellished throughout with instances of wisdom and fruitfulness, that everything has duties and obeys Divine commandments?

Or are they creators? Or, like materialists who are each like a Pharaoh, do they imagine themselves self-existent and self-subsistent, able to create whatever they need? Is this why they refuse belief and worship? It seems that they consider themselves creators. But one who creates one thing must be able to create everything. Self-conceit and vanity have made them so foolish that they suppose such an impotent one defeated by even a fly or a microbe to be absolutely powerful. They are so devoid of humanity and reason that they have fallen lower than animals and even inanimate objects. So do not be grieved by their denial.

Or did they create the heavens and the earth? Rather, they have no certain knowledge. Or, like those who deny the Creator, do they deny God and so ignore the Qur'an? If so, let them deny the existence of the heavens and the earth or claim to be their creators, so that all can see their complete lack of reason. The proofs of Divine Existence and Unity are as numerous as stars and as many as flowers. Such people have no intention of acquiring sure belief and accepting the truth. Otherwise, how can they say that this Book of the Universe, in each letter of which is inscribed a book, has no author when they know that a letter must have an author?

Or are the treasures of your Lord with them? Or, like some misguided philosophers and Brahmans who deny Almighty God's free will, do they deny Prophethood and therefore belief in you? If so, let them deny all prints of wisdom, purpose, order, purposeful results, favors, and works of mercy seen throughout the universe, as well as all the Prophets' miracles. Or let them claim to possess the treasuries of favors bestowed on all creatures, and so show that they are not worthy of address. If this is so, do not feel sorrow for their denial.

Or have they been given absolute authority? Or, like the Mu'tazilis who made reason the absolute authority in judging matters, do they consider themselves overseers and inspectors of the Creator's work and desire to hold Him responsible? Never be disheartened and do not mind their denial, for it is vain.

Or do they have a ladder by which they overhear? Then let their eavesdropper produce some clear authority. Or, like the soothsayers and spiritualists who follow jinn and Satan, do they imagine that they have discovered another route to the Unseen? Do they therefore think they have a ladder by which to ascend to the heavens, which are closed to their satans? Is this why they deny your heavenly tidings? The denial of such people means nothing.

Or are there for Him daughters, while for you there are sons? Or, like philosophers who associate partners with God (e.g., the Ten Intellects and the Masters of Species), the Sabaeans (who ascribe a sort of divinity to heavenly objects and angels), or those who attribute sons to God Almighty, do they assert that angels are His daughters, despite the fact that such is contrary to the necessary Existence of the Unique, Eternally Besought One, to His Unity and absolute Independence, to His being the Eternally Besought One, and to the innocence and servanthood of the genderless angels? Do they consider angels their intercessors with God and therefore not follow you? Reproduction is the means of multiplication, cooperation, and continuance of all contingent and mortal entities. A great example is humanity, who has biological existence and whose members are impotent, mortal, enamored with the world, needy of help and want to be succeeded by children. Therefore, it is sheer foolishness to ascribe fatherhood to God, Who necessarily and eternally exists and with respect to His Essence is absolute free from all physical qualities, and in regard to His Nature is absolutely exempt from multiplication and division, and has Power absolutely free from impotence. Even more amazing is their saying that God has daughters, when they regard their own daughters as sources of shame. Given this, do not mind the denial of such people.

Or do you ask them for a wage so that they are crushed under debt? Or, like the rebellious and insolent, miserly and ambitious, do they find the commandments you convey unbearable and so avoid you? Do they not know that you expect your wage only from God? Is it unbearable to give to the poor among them one-tenth or one-fortieth of the wealth God has given them and as a consequence, both to receive plenty and be saved from the envy and curses of the poor? Do they consider to pay the *Zakah* burdensome and therefore hold back from Islam? Their denial is not worth answering, and their due is only punishment.

Or do they have the knowledge of the Unseen, so that they copy from it? Or, like those who claim to have knowledge of the Unseen and those pseudo-intellectuals who imagine their guesses of future events to be certain, do they not like your tidings of the Unseen? Do they have books of the Unseen that they refute your Book of the Unseen? If so, they fancy that the Unseen, which is only open to Messengers receiving Divine Revelation and cannot be entered by anyone on his or her own, is open to them and that they are just writing down the information they obtain from it. Do not be disheartened by the denial of such conceited people, for the truths you bring will destroy their fancies in a very short time.

Or do they intend a plot (to entrap you)? Yet it is those who disbelieve who are entrapped. Or, like hypocrites and intriguing heretics, do they encourage others to join them in their unbelief or do they want to deceive the people and turn them away from the guidance which they cannot obtain, ad so call you a soothsayer, a magician, or one possessed? They are not truly human, and so do not be disheartened by their denial and tricks. Rather, be more vigorous and strive harder, for their trickery only deceives themselves. Their apparent success in evil-doing is temporary, a gradual perdition prepared for them by God.

Or do they have a deity other than God? All-Glorified is He, above what they associate as partners with Him. Or, like the Magians (Zoroastrians) who believe in two deities (a creator of goodness and a creator of evil), and those who attribute divinity to every physical cause and make causality a point of support for them, do they rely on false deities and argue with you? Do they consider themselves independent of you? If they do, they are blind to the universe's perfect order and delicate coherence: *Were there deities in them (the heavens and the earth) other than God, they would surely go to ruin* (21:22). Two headmen or elders in a village, two governors in a town, or two sovereigns in a country would make order impossible. From a fly's wing to the lamps in the heavens, there is such a fine order that there is left no room for any partners to be associated with God. Since such people act completely contrary to reason, wisdom, common sense, and evident realities, do not let their denial cause you to abandon communicating the Divine Message.

Out of hundreds of jewels in such truth-laden verses, I have sought to summarize only one which concerns clarification and silencing opponents. If I could show a few more of their jewels, you would conclude: "Each verse is a miracle."

The Qur'anic expositions in teaching and explaining are so wonderful, beautiful, and fluent that anyone can understand easily the most profound truths. The Qur'an of miraculous exposition teaches and explains many profound and subtle truths so clearly and directly that it neither offends human sensibility nor opposes generally held opinions. Rather, such exposition conforms with what is familiar to us. Just as one uses appropriate words when addressing a child, the Qur'an, described as "the Divine address to the human mind," uses a style appropriate to its audience's level. By speaking in allegories, parables, and comparisons, it makes the most difficult Divine truths and mysteries easily understood by even the most common, unlettered person. For example: *The All-Merciful has established Himself on the Supreme Throne* (20:5) shows Divine Lordship as though it were a Kingdom, and the aspect of His Lordship administering the universe as though He were a King seated on His Sovereignty's throne and exercising His rule.

The Qur'an, the Word of the All-Majestic Creator of the universe issuing from His Lordship's highest degree of manifestation, surpasses all other degrees. It guides those who rise to those degrees, and passes through seventy thousand veils to illuminate each. Although it has been radiating enlightenment to all levels of understanding and intelligence for so many centuries and still continues to pour out its meaning, regardless of people's ability and scientific level, it maintains its infinite freshness and delicacy. It continues to teach all people in an easy yet most skillful and comprehensible way, and convinces them of its truth. Wherever you look in it, you will find a gleam of its miraculousness.

In short, when a Qur'anic phrase like *All praise and gratitude are for God* is recited, it fills up the ear of a tiny fly as well as that of a mountain (a cave). Likewise, just as its meanings fully saturate the greatest intellects, the same words also satisfy the most simple intellects. The Qur'an calls all levels of humanity and jinn to belief and instructs them in the sciences of belief. Given this, the most unlettered person as well as the most distinguished member of the educated elite will follow its lessons together and benefit from them.

The Qur'an is such a heavenly table spread with intellectual and spiritual foods that beings of all levels of intellect, reason, heart, and spirit can find their sustenance and satisfy their appetites therein. Moreover, the Qur'an has many more treasures of meaning and truths that will be opened by future generations. The whole Qur'an is an example of this truth. All students of the Qur'an—the greatest scholars of Islamic law, those distinguished with truthfulness, Muslim sages and philosophers, saints distinguished with knowledge of God and the spiritual poles distinguished with love of God, and the mass of Muslims—declare: "The Qur'an teaches us in the best way."

SECOND RAY: This ray, the extraordinary comprehensiveness of the Qur'an, consists of five gleams.

FIRST GLEAM: This concerns the Qur'an's comprehensive wording, which is apparent in the verses whose meanings are quoted in previous Words, as well as in this one. As pointed out in a *hadith*, each verse has outer and inner meanings, limits and a point of comprehension, as well as boughs, branches, and twigs.[141] Each phrase, word, letter, and even an omission has many aspects. Each person who hears it receives his or her share through a different door.

- From *Suratu'n-Naba'*:

And the mountains as masts. (78:7)

---

[141] Abdu'r-Razzaq, *al-Musannaf*, 3:358; Abu Ya'la, *al-Musnad*, 9:278.

God Almighty means: "I have made mountains like masts and stakes for your earth." Ordinary people see mountains as if driven into the ground and, thinking of the benefits and bounties thereof, thank the Creator. Poets imagine the earth as a ground on which the heavens' dome is pitched, in a sweeping arc, as a mighty blue tent adorned with electric lamps. Seeing mountains skirting the heavens' base as tent pegs, they worship the All-Majestic Creator in amazement.

Desert-dwelling literary people imagine the earth as a vast desert, and its mountain chains as multifarious tents of nomads. They see them as if the soil were stretched over high posts and as if the posts' pointed tips had raised the "cloth" of the soil, which they see as the home for countless creatures. They prostrate in amazement before the All-Majestic Creator, Who placed and set up such imposing and mighty things so easily. Geographers with a literary bent view the earth as a ship sailing in the ocean of air or ether, and mountains as masts giving balance and stability to the ship. Before the All-Powerful One of Perfection, Who has made the earth like a well-built orderly ship on which He makes us travel through the universe, they declare: "All-Glorified are You. How sublime is Your Glory!"

Sociologists or anthropologists see the earth as a house, the pillar of whose life is animal life that, in turn, is supported by air, water, and soil (the conditions of life). Mountains are essential for these conditions, for they store water, purify the atmosphere by precipitating noxious gases, and preserve the ground from becoming a swamp and being overrun by the sea. Mountains also are treasuries for other necessities of human life. In perfect reverence, they praise the Maker of Majesty and Munificence, Who has made these great mountains as pillars for the earth, the house of our life, and appointed them as keepers of our livelihood's treasuries.

Naturalist scientists say: "The earth's quakes and tremors, which are due to certain underground formations and fusions, were stabilized with the emergence of mountains. This event also stabilized the earth's axis and orbit. Thus its annual rotation is not affected by earthquakes. Its wrath and anger is quietened by its coursing through mountain vents." They would come to believe and declare: "There is a wisdom in everything God does."

- From *Suratu'l-Anbiya'*:

   The heavens and the earth were of one piece; then We parted them. (21:30)

To learned people who have not studied materialist philosophy, *of one piece* means that when the heavens were clear and without clouds, and the earth was dry, lifeless, and unable to give birth, God opened the heavens with rain and the soil with vegetation, and created all living beings from fluid through a sort of marriage and impregnation. Such people understand that everything is the work of such an All-Powerful One of Majesty that the earth's face is His small garden, and all clouds veiling the sky's face are sponges for watering it. They prostrate before His Power's tremendousness.

To exacting sages, it means: "In the beginning, the heavens and the earth were a formless mass, each consisting of matter like wet dough without produce or creatures. The All-Wise Originator separated them and rolled them out and, giving each a comely shape and beneficial form, made them the origins of multiform, adorned creatures." These sages are filled with admiration at His Wisdom's comprehensiveness. Modern philosophers or scientists understand that the solar system was fused like a mass of dough. Then the All-Powerful and Self-Subsistent One rolled it out and placed the planets in their respective positions. He left the sun where it was and brought the earth here. Spreading soil over its face, watering it with rain, and illuminating it with sunlight, He made the world habitable and placed us on it. These people are saved from the swamp of naturalism, and declare: "I believe in God, the One, the Unique."

- From *Sura Ya Sin*:

    The sun runs its course to a resting place destined. (36:38)

The particle *li* (written as the single letter *lam*), translated here as "to," expresses the meanings of "toward," "in," and "for." Ordinary people read it as "toward" and understand that the sun, which is a moving lamp providing light and heat, one day will reach its place of rest and, ending its journey, assume a form that will no longer benefit them. Thinking of the great bounties that the Majestic Creator bestows through the sun, they declare: "All-Glorified is God. All praise and gratitude are for God."

Learned people also read *li* as "toward," but see the sun as both a lamp and a shuttle for the Lord's textiles woven in the loom of spring and summer, as an ink-pot whose ink is light for the letters of the Eternally Besought One inscribed on the pages of night and day. Reflecting on the world's order, of which the sun's apparent movement is a sign and to which it points, they declare before the All-Wise Maker's Art: "What wonders God has willed," before His Wisdom: "May God bless it," and prostrate.

For geographer–philosophers, *li* means "in" and suggests that the sun orders and propels its system through Divine command and with a spring-like movement on its own axis. Before the All-Majestic Creator, Who created and set in order a mighty clock like the solar system, they exclaim in perfect amazement and admiration: "All greatness and power is God's," abandon materialistic philosophy, and embrace the wisdom of the Qur'an.

Precise and wise scholars consider *li* to be causal and adverbial. They understand that since the All-Wise Maker operates behind the veil of apparent causality, He has tied the planets to the sun by His law of gravity and causes them to revolve with distinct but regular motions according to His universal wisdom. To produce gravity, He has made the sun's movement on its axis an apparent cause. Thus *a resting place* means that "the sun moves in the place determined for it for the order and stability of its own (solar) system." For it must be a Divine law that motion produces heat, heat produces force, and force produces gravity. On understanding such an instance of wisdom from a single letter of the Qur'an, wise scholars declare: "All praise and gratitude be to God! True wisdom is found in the Qur'an. Human philosophy is worth almost nothing."

The following idea occurs to poets from this *li* and the stability mentioned: "The sun is a light-diffusing tree, and the planets are its moving fruits. But unlike trees, the sun is shaken so that the fruits do not fall. If it were not shaken, they would fall and be scattered." They also may imagine the sun to be a leader of a circle reciting God's Names, ecstatically reciting in the circle's center and leading the others to recite. Elsewhere, I expressed this meaning as follows:

> The sun is a fruit-bearing body;
> It is shaken so that its traveling fruits do not fall.
> If it stopped moving and gravity ceased,
> Its ecstatic followers would scatter through space and weep.

- From *Suratu'l-Baqara*:

  They are those who will certainly prosper. (2:5)

This general verse does not specify how they will prosper. Thus each person may find what they pursue in it. The sense is compact so that it may be comprehensive. People seek to be saved from the Fire, enter Paradise, or acquire eternal happiness. Others seek God's good pleasure or the vision of God. In many places, the Qur'an neither narrows nor specifies the sense, and so expresses many meanings by leaving certain things unsaid. By not specifying in what way they will prosper, it means: "O Muslims, good tidings! O God-reverent, pious one, you will be saved from Hell. O righteous one, you will enter Paradise. O one with knowledge of God, you will gain God's good pleasure. O lover of God, you will be rewarded with the vision of God."

- From *Sura Muhammad:*

  Know that there is no deity but God, and ask forgiveness for your error. (47:19)

This verse has so many aspects and degrees that all saints consider themselves in need of it during their whole journey and derive from it a fresh meaning and spiritual nourishment appropriate to their ranks. This is because "God" is the Divine Being's all-comprehensive Name, and thus it contains as many affirmations of Divine Unity as the number of the Divine Names: There is no provider but He, no creator but He, no merciful one but He, and so on.

- The story of Moses, upon him be peace:

The story of Moses has, like Moses' Staff, thousands of benefits and pursues many purposes, such as calming and consoling the Prophet, threatening unbelievers, condemning hypocrites, and reproaching Jews. Thus it is repeated in several *suras* to stress different aspects. Although all purposes are relevant in each place, only one is the main purpose.

Question: How do you know the Qur'an contains and intends all those meanings?

Answer: As the Qur'an is an eternal discourse speaking to and teaching humanity at all levels and times, it contains, intends, and alludes to all of those meanings. In my *Isharatu'l-I'jaz*, I use Arabic grammatical rules, as well as the principles of rhetoric, semantics, and eloquence, to prove that the Qur'an's words include and intend various meanings. As Muslim jurists, Qur'anic interpreters, and scholars of religious methodology agree and the differences in their understanding of verses and conclusions they derive demonstrate, all aspects and meanings understood from the Qur'an can be considered among its meanings if they accord with Arabic's grammatical rules, Islam's basic principles, and the sciences of rhetoric, semantics, and eloquence. The Qur'an has placed a sign, either literal or allusive, for each meaning according to its degree. If allusive, there is another sign from either the context—the preceding or the following verses—or another verse to point to the meaning. Thousands of Qur'anic commentaries prove its wording's extraordinary comprehensiveness. Interested readers can refer to my *Isharatu'l-I'jaz* for a more extensive (yet still partial) discussion.

SECOND GLEAM: This relates to the Qur'an's extraordinarily comprehensive meaning. In addition to bestowing the sources for exacting jurists, the illuminations of those seeking knowledge of God, the ways of those trying to reach God, the paths of perfected human beings, and the schools of truth-seeking scholars from the treasuries of its meaning, the Qur'an always has guided them and illuminated their ways. All agree on this.

THIRD GLEAM: This relates to the extraordinary comprehensiveness of the knowledge contained in the Qur'an. Not only is its vast knowledge the source of countless sciences related to the Shari'a, truth (*haqiqa*), and religious orders (*tariqa*), but the Qur'an also contains true wisdom and scientific knowledge of the Sphere of Contingencies (the material world), true knowledge of the Realm of Necessity (the Divine Realm), and profound knowledge of the Hereafter. For examples, consider the previous Words, which are only twenty-five drops from the oceans of the Qur'an's knowledge. Any errors in those Words come from my defective understanding.

FOURTH GLEAM: This relates to the Qur'an's extraordinarily comprehensive subject matter. It deals with humanity and its duties, the universe and its Creator, the heavens and the earth, this world and the next, and the past, future, and eternity. It explains all essential matters related to our creation and life, from correct ways of eating and sleeping to issues of Divine Decree and Will, from the universe's creation in six days to the functions of winds alluded to in such oaths as: *By those that (like winds) sent forth* (77:1) and *By those that (like winds) that scatter far and wide* (51:1).

It discusses so many other topics: from God's intervention in our heart and free will: *(God) intervenes between a person and his heart* (8:24), and *But you cannot will not unless God wills* (76:30), to His grasp of the heavens: *The heavens will be rolled up in His "right hand"* (39:67); from the earth's flowers, grapes, and dates: *We made therein gardens of palms and vines* (36:34) to the astounding event described in *When the earth quakes with a violent quaking destined for it* (99:1); from the heaven's state during creation: *Then He turned to the heaven when it was smoke* (41:11), to its splitting open and the stars being scattered in endless space; from building this world for testing and trial to its destruction; from the grave, the other world's first station, to the Resurrection, the Bridge, and eternal happiness in Paradise.

It also discusses the past, including the event which took place in the eternity in the past and pointed to in *"... Am I not your Lord? ...* (7:172), the creation of Adam's body and the struggle between his two sons, the

Flood, the drowning of Pharaoh's people, and the Prophets' life-stories, to what will happen on the Day of Judgment: *Some faces on that day will be radiant, looking up toward their Lord* (75:22-23).

The Qur'an explains all such essential and important matters in a way befitting an All-Powerful One of Majesty, Who administers the universe like a palace, opens and closes the world and the Hereafter like two rooms, controls the earth like a garden and the heavens like a lamp-adorned dome, and in Whose sight the past and future are like day and night or two pages, and all eternity (in the past and future) like a point of present time.

Like a builder describing two houses he has built and listing what he will do, the Qur'an is—if one may express it—a list or program written in a suitable style by the One Who has built and administers the universe. It contains no trace of artifice, pretence, or unnecessary trouble, and no strain of imitation, trickery, or deception. It does not pretend to speak in another's name. Like daylight announcing to be from the sun, with its absolutely genuine, pure, clear, solemn, original, and brilliant style, it declares: "I am the Word of the Creator of the universe."

Can the Qur'an belong to someone other than the Maker, the Bestower of Bounties, Who has decorated this world with the most original and invaluable works of art and filled it with the most pleasant bounties? It resonates throughout the world with cries of acclamation and commendation, litanies of praise and thanks, and has made the earth into a house where God's Names are recited, where God is worshipped and His works of art are studied in amazement. Where can the light illuminating the world be coming from, if not from the sun? Whose light can the Qur'an be, other than the Eternal Sun's, which has unveiled the universe's meaning and illuminated it? Who could dare to produce a like of it?

It is inconceivable that the Artist Who decorated this world with the works of His Art should not address humanity, who appreciates and commends that Art. Since He knows and makes, He will speak. Since He speaks, He will speak through the Qur'an. How could God, the Lord of all dominion Who is not indifferent to a flower's formation, be indifferent to a Word resonating throughout His dominion? Could He allow others to appropriate it, thereby reducing it to futility and to nothing?

FIFTH GLEAM: This relates to the Qur'an's extraordinarily comprehensive style and conciseness. It has five beams.

First beam: The Qur'an is so wonderfully comprehensive in style that a single *sura* may contain the whole ocean of the Qur'an, in which the universe is contained. One verse may comprehend that *sura*'s treasury. It is as if most verses are really small *suras* and most *suras* are little Qur'ans. This miraculous conciseness is a great gift of Divine Grace with respect to guidance and easiness, for although everyone always needs the Qur'an, not all people read the whole of it. So that they are not deprived of its blessings, each *sura* may substitute for a small Qur'an and each long verse for a short *sura*. Moreover, all people of spiritual discovery and scholars agree that the Qur'an is contained in *Suratu'l-Fatiha*, which is itself contained in the *basmala* (*In the Name of God, the All-Merciful, the All-Compassionate*).

Second beam: The Qur'an contains references to all knowledge, categories of explanation and human needs, such as command and prohibition, promise and threat, encouragement and deterring, restraint and guidance, narratives and parables, Divine knowledge and teachings, "natural" sciences, the laws and conditions of personal life, social life, spiritual life, and the life of the Hereafter. It gives people whatever they need, so that: *Take from the Qur'an whatever you wish, for whatever need you have* has been widely circulated among verifying scholars. Its verses are so comprehensive that the cure for any ailment and the answer for any need can be found therein. This must be so, for the Book that is the absolute guide of all perfected people who each day move forward on the way of God must be of that quality.

Third beam: The Qur'an's expressions are concise but all-inclusive. Sometimes it mentions the first and last terms of a long series in a way that shows all of it; other times it includes in a word many explicit, implicit, allusive, or suggestive proofs of a cause.

- From *Suratu'r-Rum*:

  And among His signs is the creation of the heavens and the earth and the diversity of your tongues and colors. (30:22)

By mentioning the universe's two-part creation—the creation of the heavens and the earth and the varieties of human languages and races—it suggests the creation and variety of all animate and inanimate beings as signs of Divine Unity. This also testifies to the All-Wise Maker's Existence and Unity, Who first created the heavens and the earth and then followed this with other links—from adorning the heavens with stars to populating the earth with animate creatures; from giving the sun, the earth, and moon regular orbits, as well as alternating day and night, to differentiating and individualizing speech and complexion in cases of extreme multiplication.

Since there is an amazing purposeful system in the differentiations of complexions and countenances, which one may suppose to depend on chance more probably than other aspects of creation, for sure the other links of creation , which clearly manifest a deliberate order, will point to the All-Designing. Also, since creating the vast heavens and the earth displays certain artistry and purposes, the artistry and purpose of a Maker Who founded universe on the heavens and the earth will be much more explicit in other parts of His creation. Thus, by manifesting what is concealed and concealing what is manifest, the verse displays an extremely beautiful conciseness.

The chain of proofs beginning six times with *And among His signs* from *so glorify God when you enter the evening and when you enter the morning* (30:17), to *The highest comparison in the heavens and the earth is for God; He is the All-Glorious and All-Mighty, the All-Wise* (30:27), is a series of jewels, lights, miracles, and miraculous conciseness. However much I desire to show the diamonds in those treasures, I must, in the present context, postpone doing so.

- From *Sura Yusuf:*

  Then said he: "So send me forth." "Joseph, O man of truth!.." (12:45-46)

The narrative omits several events between *so send me forth* and *"Joseph, O man of truth:"* [So send me forth] to Joseph so that I may ask him about the dream's interpretation. They sent him. He came to the prison and said: [Joseph ...]. In such a way does the Qur'an narrate briefly and to the point without any loss of clarity.

- From *Sura Ya Sin:*

  He Who has made for you fire from the green tree. (36: 80)

In the face of rebellious humanity's denial of the Resurrection, *Who will revive these bones when they have rotted away?* (36:78), the Qur'an says: "The One Who originated them will give them life anew. The One Who creates knows all aspects of all things. Moreover, the One Who made fire for you from the green tree can revive decayed bones." The part of the verse quoted deals with and proves the Resurrection from different viewpoints.

First, it reminds us of Divine favors. Since the Qur'an details them elsewhere, here it only alludes to them and refers the detail to the intelligence. It actually means: "You cannot escape or hide from the One Who made fire for you from trees, causes them to give you fruits, provides you with grains and plants from earth, has made the earth a lovely cradle containing all your provisions, and the world a beautiful palace containing whatever you require. You have not been created in vain and without purpose, and so you are not free or able to sleep in the grave eternally without being woken up."

Second, in pointing to a proof of the Resurrection, it uses *the green tree* to suggest: "O you who deny the Resurrection, look at trees. How can you challenge the Power of the One Who revives in spring innumerable trees that died and hardened in winter? By causing them to blossom, come into leaf and produce fruits, He exhibits three examples of the Resurrection on each tree." It points to another proof and means: "How can you deem it unlikely for One Who makes a refined and light-giving substance like fire out of hard, dark, and heavy trees? How can you say that He cannot give a fire-like life and a light-like consciousness to wood-like bones?"

Another proof: "Everything in the universe is subject to and depends on the decrees of the One Who creates fire when nomads rub two green tree branches together, and reconciles opposing natures to produce new things. How can you oppose Him and deem it unlikely for Him to bring forth humanity from earth after He created them from it and restored into it?" Moreover, it alludes to the well-known tree near which Prophet Moses received the first Revelation and suggests that the causes of Prophet Muhammad and Moses, upon them be peace, are the same. Thus it refers indirectly to all Prophets' agreement on the same essential points and adds yet another meaning to the compact treasures of that word's—green tree—meaning.

Fourth beam: The Qur'an's conciseness is like offering the ocean in a pitcher. Out of mercy and courtesy for ordinary human minds, it shows the most comprehensive and universal principles and general laws through a particular event on a particular occasion. The following examples are only a few of many such concise examples:

• From *Suratu'l-Baqara*:

This concerns the three verses (31-34), which were explained in the First Station of The Twentieth Word. They suggest several things. Teaching Adam the names of all things means that humanity were given the potential to obtain all knowledge and science; the angels' prostration before Adam and Satan's refusal to do so signify that most creatures have been placed at humanity's disposal, while harmful beings (e.g., Satan and snakes) will not be so docile. Mentioning the Israelites' slaughtering of a cow (2:67-71) means that cow-worship (borrowed from Egypt and shown in the Israelites' adora-

tion of the calf made for them by the Samiri: 20: 85-88) was destroyed by
Moses' knife. Mentioning that rivers gush forth from some rocks, that others
split so that water issues from them, and that still others crash down in fear of
God (2:74) states implicitly that subsurface rock strata allow subterranean
veins of water to pass through them and that they had a role in the earth's origin.

- Second example (from *Suratu'l-Mu'min*):

Each phrase and sentence of Moses' repeated story points to and
expresses a universal principle. For example, in: Haman, *build for me a tower* (40:36), the Qur'an means: "Pharaoh ordered his minister Haman: 'Build
a high tower for me. I will observe the heavens and try to find out through
heavenly events whether there is a god such as Moses claims.'" Through
this particular event and by *tower*, the Qur'an alludes to a curious custom
of the Pharaohs: Worshippers of nature who lived in a vast desert without
mountains, believers in sorcery and reincarnation because of unbelief in
God, they cherished a deep desire for mountains and claimed absolute sovereignty like that of Divine Lordship over people. To eternalize their names
and fame, they built mountain-like pyramids for their mummified bodies.

- From *Sura Yunus*:

So today We will deliver you with your body. (10:92)

By mentioning Pharaoh's drowning, the Qur'an suggests: "Since all
Pharaohs believed in reincarnation, they mummified their bodies to eternalize themselves. Thus their bodies have survived until now. Although
not mummified, the body of the Pharaoh who drowned while pursuing
Moses with his army was found prostrate beside the Nile in the closing
years of the nineteenth century. This is an explicit Qur'anic miracle, which
foretold it centuries ago in the verse in question.

- From *Suratu'l-Baqara*:

(The Pharaoh's clan), who were afflicting you with the most evil suffering, slaughtering your sons and sparing your women [to use them]. (2:49)

This verse mentions the Pharaohs' evils and cruelties to the Israelites.
It also implicitly refers to the mass murder of Jews in many places and times,
and the notorious part played by some Jewish women in history:

You will find them the greediest of all people for life. (2:96)

You see many among them vying in sin and enmity, and consuming
unlawful earnings; evil indeed is what they have been doing. (5:62)

They hasten about the earth causing disorder and corruption; God does not love those who cause disorder and corruption. (5:64)

We decreed for the Children of Israel in the Book: You will most certainly cause disorder and corruption on the earth twice. (17:4)

Do not go about acting wickedly on earth, causing disorder and corruption. (2: 60)

These verses express the two general disastrous Jewish intrigues against humanity's social life. The Jews have pitted labor against capital, driven the poor to struggle against the rich, used compound usury, have caused the building of banks and accumulated wealth through unlawful ways. Thus they have shaken human social life. Also, it has usually been the same nation who, to revenge themselves upon states or governments who have wronged or defeated them, have entered seditionist committees or participated in revolutions.

- From *Suratu'l-Jumu'a*:

    If you assert that you are the friends of God, apart from other peoples, then long for death if you speak truly. But they will never long for it.... (62:6-7)

Revealed to refute an assertion of Madina's Jewish community, these verses state that Jews, renowned for their love of life and fear of death, will not give up these traits until the Last Day.

- From *Suratu'l-Baqara*:

    Humiliation and misery were stamped on them (2:61)

The verse states the general fate of the Jews. Due to such general and awful aspects of their nature and fate, the Qur'an deals with them severely and criticizes them harshly. Compare with these other aspects of the Qur'anic account of Moses and the Children of Israel. Notice the many gleams of miraculousness behind the Qur'an's simple words and particular topics, like the gleam of miraculous conciseness described in this beam.

Fifth beam: This relates to the Qur'an's extraordinarily comprehensive aim, subject matter, meaning, style, beauty, and subtlety. When its *suras* and verses, particularly the former's opening sections and the latter's beginnings and ends, are studied attentively, it is clearly seen that the Qur'an contains all types of eloquence, all varieties of fine speech, all categories of elevated style, all examples of good morals and virtues, all principles of natural sciences, all indexes of knowledge of God, all beneficial rules of individual and social life, and all enlightening laws of creation's exalted reasons and purposes, and yet not a single trace of confusion is apparent in it.

Indeed, such a perfect and comprehensive work can be the work of an overwhelming miraculous order. It only can be the extraordinary work of a source of miracles like the Qur'an, which sees and shows the truth, is familiar with the Unseen, and bestows guidance—it only can be the Qur'an's work to, together with having such degree of comprehensiveness and order, rend with its penetrating expressions the veil of the commonplace over things and events, which causes the compound ignorance leading to unbelief (e.g., atheism and materialism), and show the extraordinariness behind that veil. Only its diamond-like sword of proof can destroy naturalism (the source of misguidance), remove thick layers of heedlessness with its thunder-like cries, and uncover existence's hidden meanings and creation's mysteries, which are beyond the abilities of all philosophers and scientists.

If the Qur'an's verses are considered carefully and fairly, it will be seen that unlike other books, they do not resemble a series of arguments gradually unfolded on one or two subjects. Rather, they give the impression that each verse or each group of verses was sent separately at one time as the codes of a very solemn and important communication. Who, other than the universe's Creator, can carry on a communication so concerned with the universe and its Creator as the Qur'an? Who can make the All-Majestic Creator speak according to their wish and cause the universe to "speak" so truly? In fact, it is the universe's Owner Who speaks and makes the universe speak most seriously and truthfully, and in the most elevated style, in the Qur'an.

No one can find any signs of imitation in it, for it is He Who speaks and makes to speak. If, supposing the impossible, someone like Musaylima the Liar appeared and managed to make the All-Glorious, All-Compelling, and All-Majestic Creator speak as he wishes and make the universe speak to Him, there would certainly be countless signs of imitation and pretence. Every manner of those who put on great airs, even in their basest states, shows their pretence. Consider the following verses, which declare this with an oath: *By the star when it goes down, your companion is not astray, neither errs, nor speaks on his own, out of caprice. That is but a Revelation revealed* (53:1-4).

THIRD RAY: This relates to the Qur'an's miraculous prediction, as well as its freshness and ability to address all levels of understanding regardless of time and place. This ray consists of three radiances.

FIRST RADIANCE: This relates to the Qur'an's predictions and has three light-giving aspects.

First aspect: The Qur'an gives news of the past. Although communicated by an unlettered one, the wise Qur'an mentions in a solemn and powerful manner the important experiences of Prophets from the time of Adam to the Age of Happiness as well as the main aspects of their mission. The information it provides usually coincides with the commonly agreed descriptions of the previous Scriptures. It also corrects the points on which their corrupted forms disagree. Thus the Qur'an has an all-seeing vision that knows the past better than the previous Scriptures.

Its account of the past is not based on intellectual study, but it is transmitted knowledge. Transmitted knowledge is particular to lettered persons, whereas Prophet Muhammad was completely unlettered and known as Muhammad the Trustworthy. The Qur'an speaks of past events as if seeing them. It extracts the kernel of a long series of events and presents its argument through that kernel. The extracts, summaries, and indications found therein therefore demonstrate that the One Who presents them sees all dimensions of the past. Just as a substantial summary, a fine extract, or a telling example shows a specialist's skill or expert knowledge, the Qur'an's chief points and main themes, chosen from certain events, show that the One Who chooses them has an all-encompassing knowledge of the whole and is describing them with an extraordinary skill.

Second aspect: This relates to the Qur'an's many categories of predictions. One category is particular to saints and spiritual unveiling. For instance, Muhyi'd-Din ibnu'l-'Arabi found many predictions in *Suratu'r-Rum.* Imam ar-Rabbani discovered signs of many future events in the *muqatta'at* (the individual, separated letters at the beginning of certain *suras*). For scholars of the inner aspects and innermost meanings of the Qur'an and creation, the Qur'an is full of predictions. I will concentrate on only one and be content with mentioning some examples, without going into detail.

The Qur'an says to the Messenger, upon him be peace and blessings:

> So be patient: Surely God's promise is true. (30:60)

> You will enter the Sacred Mosque, if God wills, in full security, with your heads shaved, your hair cut short, and without fearing. (48:27)

> It is He who has sent His Messenger with the guidance and the Religion of truth, that He may uplift it above every religion. (48: 28)

The Byzantine Romans have been defeated in the nearer part of the land; and, after their defeat, they will be the victors in a few years. To God belongs the Command. (30:3-4)

Soon you will see, and they will see, which of you is demented. (68:5-6)

Or do they say: "He is a poet. We await for him some calamity ahead." Say: "Wait on; I am also waiting with you." (52:30-31)

God will protect you from people. (5:67)

If you are in doubt about (the Divine authorship of) what We have been sending down on Our servant (Muhammad), then produce just a *sura* like it... If you fail to do that—and you will most certainly fail... (2:23-24)

... They will never long for it. (2:95)

We will show them Our signs in the outer world and in themselves, until it is clear to them that it is the truth. (41:53)

Say: "If humanity and jinn banded together to produce the like of this Qur'an, they would never produce its like, even though they backed one another." (17:88)

God will bring a people He loves and who love Him, humble toward believers, mighty and dignified against unbelievers, (people) who strive in God's cause, and fearing not the reproach of any reproacher. (5:54)

Say: "All praise and gratitude are for God. He will show you His signs and you will recognize them." (27:93)

Say: "He is the All-Merciful. We believe in Him and in Him we put all our trust. Assuredly, you will soon know who is in manifest error." (67:29)

God has promised those of you who believe and do righteous deeds that He will make them successors in the land, even as He made those (of the same qualities) who were before them successors, and that He will establish their religion for them, that He has approved of for them, and He will replace their present state of fear with security. (24:55)

All of the predictions made in these verses came true. So if a person who is subject to the severest criticisms and objections, in whom even one fault is certain to lead to his cause's failure, makes predictions so unhesitatingly and confidently, and in such a serious manner, it shows without doubt that he speaks not of himself but of what he receives from his Eternal Teacher.

Third aspect: This relates to what the Qur'an says about the Unseen, Divine truths and the Hereafter's realities. Certain truths of creation also may be considered in this category.

The Qur'an's explanations concerning Divine truths and its statements about the realities of creation which solve the mystery of creation and unveil the talisman of the universe are among the most important pieces of information about the Unseen. For humanity cannot advance in a straight direction amid paths of misguidance and reach the Unseen's truths or realities. The deep, endless disagreements between schools of philosophy and scientists show that even their greatest geniuses cannot discover even the least of these truths by unaided reasoning. Only after purifying their souls, refining their hearts, evolving their spirits, and perfecting their intellects, humanity can perceive and accept those truths and realities, and then say: "May God bless the Qur'an."

This point has partly been explained in The Eleventh Word. As for the Hereafter's events, states, conditions, and stages, including the life of the grave, no one can discover and perceive them by himself or herself. However, one can penetrate and comprehend them through the Qur'an's light, as if seeing and observing them clearly. You may refer to The Tenth Word, which discusses how right and true are the Qur'an's explanations of that Unseen world of the Hereafter.

SECOND RADIANCE: This relates to the Qur'an's freshness, which is maintained as if it were revealed anew in every epoch. As an eternal discourse addressing all human beings regardless of time or place and level of understanding, it should—and does—have a never-fading freshness.

The Qur'an so impresses each new generation that each one regards it as being revealed to itself and receives its instructions therefrom. Human words and laws become old and so need to be revised or changed. But the Qur'an's laws and principles are so established and constant, so compatible with essential human nature and creation's unchanging laws, that the passage of time has no effect upon them. Instead, it shows the Qur'an's truth, validity, and force even more clearly! Especially the people of this twentieth century, including particularly its People of the Book,[142] who rely on themselves more than any preceding people's self-reliance and close their ears to the Qur'an's calls, are most in need of the Qur'anic calls of guidance beginning with: O *People of the Book*. As this phrase also means "O people of schooling and education," it is as if those messages were directed toward

---

[142] Jews and Christians. (Tr.)

this century exclusively. With all its strength and freshness, the Qur'an makes the whole world resound with its call: *Say: "O People of the Book! Come to a word common between us and you, that we worship none but God, and that we associate none as partner with Him, and that none of us take others for Lords, apart from God."* (3:64)

Modern civilization, the product of human ideas and perhaps of the jinn, has chosen to contend with the Qur'an, which no one has ever been able to do. It tries to contradict its miraculousness through its charm and "spells." To prove the Qur'an's miraculousness or inimitability against this new, terrible opponent, and affirm its challenge of: *Say: "If humanity and jinn banded together to produce the like of this Qur'an, they would never produce its like, even though they backed one another"* (17:88), I will compare modern civilization's basic principles and foundations with those of the Qur'an.

First, all of the comparisons and criteria put forward from The First Word to this Twenty-fifth One, and the truths and verses contained therein and upon which they are based, prove the Qur'an's miraculousness and indisputable superiority over modern civilization.

Second, as convincingly argued in The Twelfth Word: By reason of its philosophy, modern civilization considers force or might to be the point of support in social life, and the realization of self-interest is its goal. It holds that the principle of life is conflict. The unifying bonds between the members of a community and communities are race and aggressive nationalism; and its ultimate aim is the gratification of carnal desires and the continuous increase of human needs. However, force calls for aggression, seeking self-interest causes fighting over material resources, which do not suffice for the satisfaction of all desires; and conflict brings strife. Racism feeds by swallowing others, thereby paving the way for aggression. It is because of these principles of modern civilization that despite all its positive aspects, it has been able to provide some sort of superficial happiness for only twenty per cent of humanity and cast eighty per cent into distress and poverty.

As for the Qur'anic wisdom, it accepts right, not might, as the point of support in social life. Its goal is virtue and God's approval, not the realization of self-interests. Its principle of life is mutual assistance, not conflict. The only community bonds it accepts are those of religion, profession, and country. Its final aims are controlling carnal desires and urging the soul to sublime matters, satisfying our exalted feelings so that we will strive for human perfection and true humanity. Right calls for unity, virtues bring solidarity, and mutual assistance means hastening to help one another. Religion secures brotherhood, sisterhood, and cohesion. Restraining our carnal soul and desires and urging the soul to perfection brings happiness in this world and the next.

Thus despite its borrowings from previous Divine religions and especially the Qur'an, which accounts for its agreeable aspects, modern civilization cannot offer a viable alternative to the Qur'an.

Third, I will give a few examples of the Qur'an's many subjects and commandments. As its laws and principles transcend time and space, they do not become obsolete; they are always fresh and strong. For example, despite all its charitable foundations, institutions of intellectual and moral training, and severe disciplines and laws and regulations, modern civilization has been unable to contest the wise Qur'an even on the following two matters and has been defeated by it:

First comparison: Perform the Prescribed Prayer, and pay the Zakah (2:43); and: *God has made trading lawful and interest and usury unlawful* (2:275). As explained in my *Isharatu'l- I'jaz*, as the origin of all revolutions and corruption is one phrase, so is the cause and source of all vices and moral failings also one phrase: The first is: "I am full, so what is it to me if others die of hunger?" And the second: "You work so that I may eat."

A peaceful social life depends on the balance between the elite (rich) and common (poor) people. This balance is based on the former's care and compassion and the latter's respect and compliance. Ignoring the first attitude drives the rich to wrongdoing, usurpation, immorality, and mercilessness; ignoring the second attitude drives the poor to hatred, grudges, envy, and conflict with the rich. As this conflict has destroyed social peace for the last two or three centuries, it has also caused social upheavals in Europe due to the struggle between labor and capital.

Despite all its charitable societies, institutions of moral training, and severe laws and regulations, modern civilization has neither reconciled these two social classes nor healed those two severe wounds of human life. The Qur'an, however, eradicates the first attitude and heals its wounds through the *Zakah*, and eradicates the second by outlawing interest and usury. The abovementioned Qur'anic verse stands at the door of the world and says to interest and usury: "You are forbidden to enter!" It decrees to humanity, "If you want to close the door of strife, close the door of interest and usury," and orders its students not to enter through it.

Second comparison: Modern civilization rejects polygamy as unwise and disadvantageous to social life. Indeed, even though if the purpose of marriage were sexual gratification, polygamy would be a lawful way to realize it.

But as observed even in animals and plants, the basic purpose for and wisdom in sexual relations is reproduction. The resulting pleasure is a small payment determined by Divine Mercy to realize this duty. Thus, as marriage is for reproduction and perpetuation of the species, being able to give birth at most once a year, to be impregnated only during half of a month, and entering menopause around fifty, one woman is usually insufficient for a man, who can sometimes impregnate even until the age of a hundred. That is why, in most cases, modern civilization has been compelled to tolerate numerous houses of prostitution.

Third comparison: Modern civilization criticizes the Qur'an for giving a woman one-third of the inheritance (half of her brother's share) while giving a man two-thirds. However, general circumstances are considered when establishing general rules and laws. In this case, a woman usually finds a man to maintain her, whereas a man usually has to live with one of whom he must take care. Given this, a woman's husband is to make up the difference between her share of the inheritance and that of her brother. Her brother, on the other hand, will spend half of his inheritance on his wife [and children], equaling his sister's share. This is true justice.

Fourth comparison: The Qur'an severely prohibits idolatry and condemns the adoration of images, which can be an imitation of idolatry. However, modern civilization sees sculpture and the portrayal of living beings, which the Qur'an condemns, as one of its virtues. Forms with or without shadows (sculptures and pictures of living beings) are either a petrified tyranny (tyranny represented in stone), embodied ostentation or solidified passion, all of which excite lust and urge people to tyranny, ostentation, and capriciousness.

Out of compassion, the Qur'an orders women to wear the veil of modesty to maintain respect for them and to prevent their transformation into objects of low desire or being used to excite lust. Modern civilization, however, has drawn women out of their homes, torn aside their veils, and led humanity into corruption. Family life is based on mutual love and respect between men and women, but immodest dress has destroyed sincere love and respect, and poisoned family life. Sculptures and pictures, especially obscene ones, have a great share in this moral corruption and spiritual degeneration. Just as looking at the corpse of a beautiful woman who deserves compassion with lust and desire destroys morality, looking lustfully at pictures of living women, which are like little corpses, troubles and diverts, shakes and destroys elevated human feelings.

In conclusion, then, besides securing happiness for all people in this world, the Qur'anic commandments serve their eternal happiness. You can compare other matters with those mentioned.

Just as modern civilization stands defeated before the Qur'an's rules and principles for social life and humanity, and bankrupt before the Qur'an's miraculous content, so also the Words written so far, primarily the Eleventh and Twelfth, demonstrate that European philosophy and scientism, the spirit of that civilization, are helpless when confronted with the Qur'an's wisdom. In addition, when compared to the Qur'an's literary merits—which may be likened to an elevated lover's uplifting songs arising from temporary separation or heroic epics encouraging its audience to victory and lofty sacrifices—modern civilization's literature and rhetoric appear as an orphan's desperate, grief-stricken wailing or a drunkard's noise.

Styles of literature and rhetoric give rise to sorrow or joy. Sorrow is of two kinds: it comes from either the feeling of loneliness and lack of any protection and support, or separation from the beloved. The first is despairing and produced by modern misguided naturalist, and heedless civilization. The second is lofty and exhilarating, and arouses a hope and eagerness for reunion. This is the kind given by the guiding, light-diffusing Qur'an.

Joy also is of two kinds. The first incites the soul to animal desires (so-called "fine" arts, drama, and cinema, etc.). The second restrains the carnal soul and urges (in a mannerly, innocent way) the human heart, spirit, intellect, and all inner senses and faculties to lofty things and reunion with the original, eternal abode and with friends who have passed on already. The Qur'an of miraculous exposition encourages this joy by arousing an eagerness to reach Paradise, eternal happiness, and the vision of God.

Thus the profound meaning and great truth contained in: *Say: "If humanity and jinn banded together to produce the like of this Qur'an, they would never produce its like, even if they backed one another"* (17:88), is not, as some assert, an exaggeration. It is pure truth and reality, which the long history of Islam has proved. The challenge contained here has two principal aspects. One is that no human or jinn work can resemble or equal the Qur'an's style, eloquence, rhetoric, wording, comprehensiveness, conciseness, and profundity. Nor can their most beautiful and eloquent words, all arranged in a volume by their most competent representatives, equal the Qur'an. The second aspect is that all human and jinn civilizations, philosophies, literatures, and laws, which are the products of the thought and efforts of humanity and the jinn and even satans, are dim and helpless when faced with the Qur'an's commandments, wisdom, and eloquence.

THIRD RADIANCE: The wise Qur'an addresses all people, regardless of time, place, or level of understanding, and calls them and teaches them about belief, the highest and most profound science, and about knowledge of God, the broadest and most enlightening branch of knowledge, and about the laws of Islam, the most important and elaborate of sciences. Therefore it has to teach each group and level in an appropriate manner. As people are very diverse, the Qur'an must contain enough levels for all of them. You may refer to the examples given earlier. Here I will point out only a few particular points briefly and refer to a few classes' share of understanding in it.

- From *Suratu'l-Ikhlas:*

  He begets not, nor was He begotten. And comparable to Him there is none.. (112:3-4)

Ordinary people, the majority of humanity, understand that Almighty God has no parents, children, wives, and equals. Those having relatively higher levels of understanding will infer that the verses reject Jesus' supposed (by Christians) Divine sonship and divinity, and the divinity of angels and all beings who beget and are begotten. Now, since rejecting a negation or an impossibility is useless, according to the science of eloquence, it must have another important, useful import. As God does not beget and was not begotten, this rejection must serve another purpose: Whoever has parents, children, and equals cannot be God and so does not deserve worship. This is one reason why *Suratu'l-Ikhlas*, from which the above verses are quoted, is of such great use for all persons at all times.

Those with a higher degree of understanding derive the meaning that Almighty God is free of all relationships with the creation that suggest begetting and being begotten, and that He has no partners, helpers, or fellow deities. He is the Creator, and everything and everyone else is the created. God creates whatever He wills and however and with the command *"Be! and it is."* He is absolutely free of every quality and relationship which suggests compulsion or obligation, and unwilled action, and is therefore contrary to perfection.

Another group with an even higher level of understanding infers the meaning that Almighty God is eternal, without beginning or end, and is the First and the Last. He has no equals, peers, likes, or anything similar or analogous to Him in His Being, Attributes, or acts. However, to make His acts understandable, the Qur'an allows us to have recourse to proper comparisons. You may compare to these understandings the shares of those distinguished with knowledge of God, ecstatic lovers of God, and most truthful, pains-taking scholars.

- From *Suratu'l-Ahzab:*

Muhammad is not the father of any of your men. (33:40)

Ordinary people understand that Zayd, the servant of God's Messenger and whom he had adopted as his son, divorced his wife Zaynab because he found her superior to him in virtue. By God's command, God's Messenger then married her. Therefore the verse says: "If the Prophet calls you 'son,' this is because of his mission as Messenger. Biologically, he is not the father of any of your men, which would prevent him from marrying one of your widows."

A second group derives this meaning: "A superior treats his subjects with fatherly care and compassion. If that superior is both a worldly ruler and a spiritual guide, his compassion will be far greater than a father's, and his subjects consider him a real father." Since this may cause people to have difficulty in seeing the Prophet, whom they consider more fatherly than a father, as the husband of their women, the Qur'an corrects this view: "The Prophet considers you with the view of Divine compassion and treats you in a fatherly manner. You are like his children from the viewpoint of his mission. But he is not your biological father so that it would be improper for him to marry one of your women."

A third group understands that merely because of their connection with the Prophet, as well as their reliance on his perfections and fatherly compassion, believers cannot believe that their salvation is assured even though they commit sins and errors. (For example, some Alawis do not perform the prescribed Prayers and say that their Prayers have been performed already.[143])

A fourth group deduces a prediction: The Prophet, upon him be peace and blessings, will not have a son to continue his line. His sons will die young. As expressed by *men*, that is, as he will not be the father of *men*, he will be the father of daughters. Thus his line will continue through his daughter. All praise be to God, the blessed children of his daughter Fatima, his two grandsons Hasan and Husayn, the "light-giving full moons" of the two illus-

---

[143] Similarly, Christians delude themselves that Jesus sacrificed himself for their salvation, and so rely on their leader's or guide's perfections and are lazy when it comes to observing religious commandments. (Tr.)

trious lines, continue the line of the Sun of Prophethood both biologically and spiritually. O God, bestow blessings on him and his Family.

Second light

This second light has three rays.

FIRST RAY: The Qur'an is a book of perfect fluency, superb clarity and soundness, firm coherence, and well-established harmony and proportion. There is a strong, mutual support and interrelation among its sentences and their parts, and an elevated correspondence among its verses and their purposes. Such leading figures in Arabic philology, literature, and semantics as az-Zamakhshari, as-Sakkaki, and 'Abdu'l-Qahir al-Jurjani[144] testify to this.

In addition, although seven or eight factors counter fluency, soundness, coherence, harmony, proportion, interrelation, and correspondence, these factors rather enrich the Qur'an's fluency, soundness, and coherence. Like branches and twigs stemming from a fruit-bearing tree's trunk and completing the tree's beauty and growth, these factors do not cause discord in the fluent harmony of the Qur'an's composition, but rather express new, richer, and complementary meanings. Consider the following facts:

- Although the Qur'an was revealed in parts over twenty-three years for different needs and purposes, it has such a perfect harmony that it is as if it were revealed all at once.

- Although the Qur'an was revealed over twenty-three years on different occasions, its parts are so mutually supportive that it is as if it were revealed all at once on one occasion.

- Although the Qur'an came in answer to different and repeated questions, its parts are so united and harmonious with each other that it is as if it were the answer to a single question.

- Although the Qur'an came to judge diverse cases and events, it displays such a perfect order that it is as if it were the judgment delivered on a single case or event.

---

[144] Abu'l-Qasim Jarullah Mahmud ibn 'Umar az-Zamakhshari (1075–1144) was one among the most well-known interpreters of the Qur'an. He lived in Kwarazm. His interpretation of the Qur'an called *al-Kashshaf* was famous for its deep linguistic analysis of the verses. *Abu Ya'qub Yusuf ibn Abu Bakr as-Sakkaki (?–1229): Miftahu'l-'Ulum ("Key to Sciences") and al-Miftah fi'n-Nahw wa't-Tasrif wa'l-Bayan ("A Key to Grammar, Inflection, and Syntax and Style") are among his most well-known works. * 'Abdu'l-Qahir al-Jurjani (d., 1079) was known as the master of eloquence. Asraru'l-Balagha ("Mysteries of Eloquence") and Dalailu'l-I'jaz ("Evidences of Miraculousnes") are his most famous books. (Tr.)

- Although the Qur'an was revealed by Divine courtesy in styles varied to suit innumerable people of different levels of understanding, moods, and temperament, its parts exhibit so beautiful a similarity, correspondence, and fluency that it is as if it were addressing one degree of understanding and temperament.

- Although the Qur'an speaks to countless varieties of people remote from each one in time, space, and character, it has such an easy way of explanation, pure style, and clear way of description that it is as if it were addressing one homogenous group, with each different group thinking that it is being addressed uniquely and specifically.

- Although the Qur'an was revealed for the gradual guidance of different peoples with various purposes, it has such a perfect straightforwardness, sensitive balance, and beautiful order that it is as if it were pursuing only one purpose.

Despite being the reasons of confusion, these factors add to the miraculousness of the Qur'an's explanations and to its fluency of style and harmony. Anyone with an undiseased heart, a sound conscience, and good taste sees graceful fluency, exquisite proportion, pleasant harmony, and matchless eloquence in its explanations. Anyone with a sound power of sight and insight sees that the Qur'an has an eye with which to see the whole universe, with all its inner and outer dimensions, like a single page and to read all the meanings contained in it. Since I would need many volumes to explain this truth with examples, please refer to my *Isharatu'l-I'jaz* and the Words written so far.

SECOND RAY: This relates to the Qur'an's miraculous qualities displayed by means of the conclusive parts of its verses and its unique style of using God's Beautiful Names to conclude many of its verses.

> NOTE: This ray contains many verses that serve as examples for this ray as well as for other previously discussed matters. Since it would therefore be too lengthy to explain them, I will discuss them briefly.

The verses of the Qur'an generally conclude either with certain Divine Beautiful Names or phrases which summarize them or comprehensive, general principles concerning the Qur'an's main aims. These conclusive parts sometimes corroborate the verses, or incite the mind to reflection. Given this, these parts contain traces from the Qur'an's elevated wisdom, drops from the water of life of Divine guidance, or sparks from the lightning of the Qur'an's miraculousness.

I will discuss briefly only ten of the numerous traces, and mention only one of the many examples of each trace's several aspects. I will append a brief statement of the meaning of one of the many truths contained in each example. Most traces are found together in most of the verses and form a real design of miraculousness. Most of the verses to be given as examples are also examples for most of the traces. With respect to verses mentioned in previous Words, I will make a short reference to the meanings of those cited here.

FIRST QUALITY OF ELOQUENCE: With its miraculous expression, the Qur'an spreads out the All-Majestic Maker's acts and works before eyes. It then concludes either with the Divine Name or Names originating those acts and works or with proof of an essential aim of the Qur'an (e.g., Divine Unity or Resurrection). Examples:

- He has created for you all that is in the earth. Then He turned to the heaven, and formed it into seven heavens. He is the All-Knowing of everything (2:29)

The verse relates, in a manner leading to a particular result or important goal, the most comprehensive works, all of which testify to Divine Knowledge and Power together with their purposes and organizations, and concludes with the Name "the All-Knowing."

- Have We not made the earth a cradle, and the mountains masts? And We have created you in pairs ... Surely the Day of Judgment and Distinction is a time appointed (76:6-8, 17).

The verse mentions Almighty God's mighty acts and tremendous works and concludes with the Day of Resurrection (the Day of Judgment).

SECOND POINT OF ELOQUENCE: The Qur'an lays out the works of Divine Art before eyes without specifying the Divine Name originating each work, and concludes by either mentioning the Names together or referring them and their meanings to the intellect. For example:

- Say: "Who provides for you from the heaven and the earth; or who owns all hearing and sight; and who brings forth the living from the dead and the dead from the living; who rules and directs all affairs?" They will say: "God." Then say: "Will you not then keep your duty to Him in reverence for Him? That is God, your Lord, the Ultimate Truth." (10:31-32)

At the beginning, it asks: "Who, having prepared the heaven and the earth as two sources of your provision, sends rain from there and brings forth grains from here? Who but He subjugates the heaven and the earth as two stores of your provision? That being so, praise and thanksgiving are due to Him exclusively."

In the second part it means: "Who owns your eyes and ears, which are your most precious bodily parts? From which shop or factory did you buy them? Only your Lord can give you these subtle faculties of hearing and sight. It is He Who creates and nurtures you, and gave you them. Therefore, there is no Lord but He, and only He deserves worship."

In the third part it signifies: "Who is it that revives the dead earth and innumerable dead species? Who but the Truth, the Creator of the whole universe, can do that? As He gives life to the earth, He will also resurrect you and send you to a Supreme Tribunal."

In the fourth part it explains: "Who but God can administer and maintain this vast universe with perfect order like a city or a palace? Since only He can do that, the Power easily governing the universe and its various spheres is so perfect and infinite that It needs no partners and helpers. The One Who governs the universe does not leave smaller creatures to other hands. Therefore you must admit God willingly or unwillingly."

The first and fourth parts suggest God, while the second suggests the Lord and the third suggests the Truth. Understand from this the miraculousness of *That is God, your Lord, the Ultimate Truth*. After presenting the mighty acts of Almighty God, and the important works of His Power, the Qur'an mentions the Names God, the Lord and the Truth, and thereby points out the origin of those acts and works: God, the Lord, the Ultimate Truth.

- An example of how the Qur'an urges the human intellect to reflect on His works and recognize Him is presented below:

> Surely in the creation of the heavens and the earth, the alternation of night and day, the ships sailing on the sea for humanity's benefit, the water which God sends down from the heaven and thereby reviving the earth after its death, and dispersing all kinds of living creatures therein, (in His) directing and disposal of the winds, and the clouds subjugated between the heaven and the earth, are signs for people who reason and understand. (2:164)

The verse enumerates the works of Divine Art or acting which indicate the perfection of Almighty God's Power and the grandeur of His Lordship and testify to His Oneness. They do so by drawing the attention to the manifestation of the Sovereignty of Divinity in the creation of the heavens and the earth; and the manifestation of Lordship in alternation of night and day;

and the manifestation of Mercy in subduing the sea and the ship, which are of great use for human social life; and the manifestation of Power's grandeur in sending rain and thereby reviving the earth and its innumerable creatures, making it like an exquisite place of resurrection and gathering; and the manifestation of Power and Compassion in creating innumerable animals from simple soil; and the manifestation of Mercy and Wisdom in charging and using the winds to pollinate plants and to allow animate beings to breathe; and the manifestation of Lordship in accumulating and dispersing the clouds (means of mercy), and suspending them between the heavens and the earth.

After enumerating such works and manifestations of Divine acting without mentioning the Names originating them, the verse concludes ...*are signs for people who reason and understand* and urges the intellect to reflect fully on the truths they contain.

THIRD QUALITY OF ELOQUENCE: Sometimes the Qur'an describes Almighty God's acts in detail and concludes with a summary. It uses detailed description to give conviction, and then impresses them on the mind by summarizing them.

• From *Sura Yusuf*:

So will your Lord choose you, and teach you about the inner meaning of all happenings (including the interpretation of dreams), and complete His favor upon you and upon the family of Jacob, as He completed it formerly on your forefathers Abraham and Isaac. Surely our Lord is All-Knowing, All-Wise. (12:6)

This verse points to the Divine blessings on Prophet Joseph, his father and forefathers, and says: "He has distinguished you (Joseph) with Prophethood and, by connecting the chain of Prophets to yours, made your lineage the most honored and prominent. He has made your house a place of education and guidance in which knowledge of God and Divine wisdom are taught, and combined in you, through that knowledge and wisdom, felicitous spiritual sovereignty of the world with eternal happiness in the Hereafter. He will also equip you with that knowledge and wisdom and make you a dignified ruler, a noble Prophet, and a wise guide."

By concluding with *Surely your Lord is All-Knowing, All-Wise*, the verse summarizes all those blessings and means: "His Lordship and Wisdom require that He will manifest His Names the All-Knowing and the All-Wise through you and make you a knowledgeable and wise one, as He did your father and forefathers."

- From *Sura Al-i 'Imran*:

  Say: "O God, Master of all dominion! You give dominion to whom You will, and take away the dominion from whom You will. You exalt whom You will and You abase whom You will. In Your hand is all good. Surely You have full power over everything. You make the night pass into the day and you make the day pass into the night. You bring forth the living out of the dead and the dead, and You bring the dead out of the living; and You provide whomever You will without measure." (3:26-27)

These verses point out God's execution of His Laws in humanity's social life and the universe. They emphasize that honor and degradation, as well as wealth and poverty, depend directly on Almighty God's Will and Choice. Nothing, not even the most insignificant happenings in the realm of multiplicity, is beyond the domain of Divine Will, and so there is no place for chance.

After pointing out this essential principle, the verse affirms that our provision, which is most essential in this worldly life, originates directly from the Real Provider's treasury of Mercy, and means: "Your provision depends on the earth's vitality, the revival of which is possible through the coming of spring. Only the One Who has subdued the sun and the moon, and alternates night and day, can bring spring. If this is so, then only the One Who fills the earth's surface with fruits can provide someone with an apple and become one's real provider."

By concluding with *and You provide whomever You will without measure*, the verses summarize all acts previously described in detail and affirm that the One Who provides you without measure does all those things.

FOURTH POINT OF ELOQUENCE: Sometimes the Qur'an mentions God's creation and creatures in a certain series. By showing that their existence and life have a purposeful order and balance, it seems to give them a certain radiance and brightness. Then it points to the Divine Name or Names originating that order, which, like mirrors, reflect Him. It is as if each mentioned creature were a word and the Names were those words' meanings, or each creature were a fruit and the Names were their seeds or substantial parts. For example:

- From *Suratu'l-Mu'minun*:

  We created humanity from an extraction of clay. Then We made it into a fertilized ovum in a safe lodging; then We created of the fertilized ovum a clot clinging (to the womb wall), and (afterwards in sequence) We created of the clinging clot a chew of lump, and We created of a

chew of lump bones, and We clothed the bones in flesh. Then We
caused it to grow into another creation. So Blessed and Supreme is God,
Who is of the highest and most blessed degree of creating. (23:12-14)

The Qur'an mentions the extraordinary and wonderful, well-ordered,
well-proportioned stages of humanity's creation in such a manner that, as
if in a mirror, *So Blessed and Supreme is God, Who is of the highest and most
blessed degree of creating* is seen in it, with the result that whoever reads or
listens to it cannot help but utter that same phrase of blessing. A scribe
employed by God's Messenger to record the Revelations uttered this phrase
before the Messenger recited it, so that he wondered whether he too was
receiving Revelation. But in reality, it was the verses' perfect order, coherence, and clarity that led to that phrase even before its recitation.

- From *Suratu'l-A'raf:*

  Your Lord is God, Who has created the heavens and the earth in six
  days—then set Himself upon the Supreme Throne, covering the day
  with the night, each pursuing the other urgently, with the sun, the
  moon, and the stars subservient, by His command. Truly, His are the
  creation and the command. Blessed and Supreme is God, the Lord of
  the worlds. (7:54)

Here the Qur'an shows the grandeur of God's Power and His Lordship's
sovereignty in such a way that He is an All-Powerful One of Majesty, Who,
"seated" on the Throne of Lordship, makes the sun, moon, and stars
absolutely obey His commands and by causing night and day continuously
to follow each other like white and black ribbons or lines, inscribes His
Lordship's sign on the pages of the universe. Therefore, whoever reads or
hears this verse feels eagerness to utter *Blessed and Supreme is God, the Lord
of the worlds.* Thus this phrase summarizes the preceding lines in the context, and is the substance or seed or fruit of the truths contained in them.

FIFTH QUALITY OF ELOQUENCE: The Qur'an sometimes mentions certain physical or material things or substances of various qualities and subject to change and disintegration. Then, in order to transform them into
stable and unchanging realities, it connects and concludes them with certain universal and permanent Divine Names, or concludes with a summary urging reflection and taking a lesson.

- From *Suratu'l-Baqara:*

  And He taught Adam the names, all of them; then He presented
  them unto the angels and said: "Now tell me the names of these, if

you speak truly." They said: "All-Glorified are You, we have no knowledge save what You have taught us. Surely You are the All-Knowing, the All-Wise." (2:31-32)

The verses first mention that Adam's superiority over angels is due to the knowledge he received as a Divine gift, and then relates the angels' defeat before Adam with regard to knowledge. The Qur'an concludes its description of these two events with two universal Names: *the All-Knowing, All-Wise.* Thus the angels acknowledge: "Since You are the All-Knowing and All-Wise, You instructed Adam in the Names and made him superior to us through that knowledge. You are the All-Wise, and therefore give us according to our capacities and give him superiority because of his capacity."

- From *Suratu'n-Nahl:*

There is a lesson for you in cattle. We give you to drink of what is in their bellies, between filth and blood, pure milk, sweet to drinkers. You take from the fruits of the date-palms and vines a strong drink and a fair provision. Surely in that is a sign for a people who reason and understand. Your Lord inspired the bee, saying: "Take for yourself dwelling-place in the mountains, houses, and trees, and of what they are building. Then eat of every kind of fruit and follow the ways of your Lord, easy to go upon." Then comes out of their bellies a fluid of diverse hues wherein is healing for people. Surely in that is a sign for a people who reflect. (16:66-69)

After demonstrating that for humanity, Almighty God has made some animals (sheep, goats, cows, and camels) sources of pure and delicious milk; some of His vegetable creatures such as date palms and vines tables of sweet, pleasant, and delicious bounties; and some of His Power's miracles like the bee a producer of honey that contains healing, to urge humanity to compare similar gifts with these and so reflect and take lessons, the verses conclude with *In that is a sign for a people who reflect.*

SIXTH POINT OF ELOQUENCE: Sometimes a verse lays out many results and decrees of Divine Lordship and unites them with a bond of unity or inserts a universal principle.

- From *Suratu'l-Baqara:*

God, there is no deity but He, the All-Living, the Self-Subsistent. Slumber overtakes Him not, nor sleep. To Him belongs all that is in the heavens and all that is in the earth. Who is there that will intercede with Him save with His permission? He knows what is before them (in time and space) and what is behind them (in time and space), and they comprehend nothing of His Knowledge save such as He wills. His Seat embraces the heavens and the earth, and the preserving of them does not weary Him. He is the All-Exalted, the Supreme. (2:255)

Together with proving Divine Unity in ten ways, this verse, called the Verse of the (Supreme) Seat, rejects and refutes associating partners with God with the question: *Who is there that will intercede with Him save with His permission?* Further, since God's Greatest Name is manifested in this verse, the meanings it contains concerning Divine truths are of the highest degree. It also shows an all-encompassing control and act of Lordship in Its highest degree. Moreover, after mentioning God's all-encompassing preserving or upholding in the greatest degree—His simultaneous control of the heavens and the earth, as a bond of unity or an aspect of oneness, it summarizes the origins of all these acts and manifestations in *He is the All-Exalted, the Supreme*.

- From *Sura Ibrahim:*

God is He Who has created the heavens and the earth and sends down from heaven water wherewith He brings forth fruits for your provision. He has subjected to you the ships to run upon the sea at His command, and He has subjected to you the rivers; and He has subjected to you the sun and moon constant in their courses, and He subjected to you the night and day; and He has granted you from all that you ask Him. Were you to attempt to count the bounties of God, you can never number them... (14:32-34)

These verses show how Almighty God has created this universe like a palace and how, sending the water of life from heaven to the earth, He has made the heavens and the earth like two servants for us. They also state that He has subjected ships to us so that all may benefit from fruits and grains grown elsewhere and may make their livelihood through bartering their produce. In other words, He created the sea, the winds, and trees in such a way and with such qualities that the wind serves as a whip, the ship as a horse, and the sea as a desert.

In addition to enabling us to have global relations through ships, He has made mighty rivers a natural means of transportation. To bring about seasons and present His bounties produced therein to us, the True Giver of Bounties has made the sun and moon run in their courses and created them like two obedient servants or wheels to steer that vast revolving machine. He has appointed the night as a cloak, a cover for our rest and sleep, and the day as a means for making our livelihood.

After enumerating these favors to show how broad is their circle and how uncountable are the favors in themselves, the verses end in this summary: *He has granted you from all that you ask Him. Were you to attempt to count the bounties of God, you can never number them.* In other words, God gives to us whatever we ask for in the tongue of capacity and natural neediness. His favors are beyond counting. If the table of bounties presented to us is the heavens and the earth, with the sun, the moon, the night and the day being some of the bounties on it, then of course it is impossible to count them.

SEVENTH MANIFESTATION OF ELOQUENCE: To show that apparent causes have no creative part in bringing about the associated effect or result, the Qur'an sometimes presents the purposes for something's existence and the results it yields. This shows that unconscious and lifeless causes are only apparent veils, and that very wise purposes and significant results can be willed and pursued only by an All-Knowing and All-Wise One.

By mentioning the purposes and results, the Qur'an shows the great distance between the cause and result, regardless of what our eyes tell us. No cause, no matter how great, can produce the smallest result. Thus the Divine Names appear as stars in the distance between causes and effects or results [and connect them together]. Like a line of mountain peaks seeming to meet the sky on the horizon, despite the vast space between them in which the stars rise and set, the distance between causes and results is so great that it can only be seen through belief and the Qur'an's light.

- From *Sura 'Abasa*:

> Let human consider his food: We pour down rain abundantly, then We split the earth in clefts and therein make the grains grow, as well as grapes and fresh herbage, and olives and date-palms, and gardens dense with foliage, and (diverse other) fruits and herbage, as provision for you and your livestock. (80:24-32)

The verses first mention Divine Power's miracles in a purposeful order and, connecting the apparent causes with their results, draw the attention to the purpose behind them through *as provision for you and your livestock*. This purpose proves that there is a free Agent pursuing it along with the series of all those causes and results, and that causes are only a veil before Him. Indeed, with the phrase *as provision for you and your livestock* the verses declare that material or natural causes have no creative part in bringing about the results and mean: "The water necessary for you and your cattle comes from heaven. Since it cannot have mercy on you and your cattle and thereby provide for you, it does not come by itself; rather, it is sent down. Then the earth splits in clefts for vegetation to grow in and provide you with food. As the unfeeling, unconscious earth cannot consider your provision or have mercy on you, it does not split by itself; rather, someone opens that "door" to you and hands you your provision. Since pastures and trees do not think about your provision or producing fruits and grains for you out of mercy, they are only threads, ropes, or cables that an All-Wise, All-Merciful One stretches out from behind a veil to extend His bounties to living beings." Thus several Divine Names like the All-Merciful, the All-Compassionate, the All-Providing, the All-Giver of Bounties, and the All-Munificent manifest themselves in these verses, even though they are not mentioned.

- From *Suratu'n-Nur*:

> Do you not see that God gently drives the clouds, then gathers them together in piles (completing the formation of a circuit between them). Then you see rain issuing out of their midst. He sends down hail out of snow-laden mountains (of clouds) from heaven, and smites with it whom He wills, and averts it from whom He wills. The flash of its lightning almost takes away the sight. God turns about the night and the day. Surely in that is a lesson for people of insight. God has created every living creature from water. Among them are such as move on their bellies, and such as move on two legs, and such as move on four. God creates whatever He wills. Surely God has full power over everything. (24:43-45)

These verses explain the curious Divine disposals in sending rain from accumulated clouds, which are among the Divine Lordship's most important miracles and the most curious veils over the Divine treasuries of Mercy. While the cloud's atoms are scattered in the atmosphere, they come together to form a cloud at God's command, just like a dispersed army assembling at the call of a trumpet. Then, like small troops coming from different directions to form an army, God joins the clouds together to enable the completion of an electric circuit between them. He causes those piled-up clouds, which resemble the moving mountains at the Resurrection and are charged with rain or snow or hail, to pour down the water of life to all living beings on the earth.

Rain does not fall by itself, but is sent to meet certain purposes and according to need. While the atmosphere is clear and no clouds can be seen, the mountain-like forms of clouds, gathered like a striking assembly, assemble because the One Who knows all living beings and their needs gathers them together to send rain therefrom. These events suggest several Divine Names:

the All-Powerful, the All-Knowing, the All-Disposer of Things, the All-Arranging, the All-Upbringing, the All-Helping, and the All-Giver of Life.

EIGHTH QUALITY OF ELOQUENCE: To convince our hearts of God Almighty's wonderful acts in the Hereafter, and to prepare our intellects to confirm them, the Qur'an sometimes mentions His amazing actions in the world. In other places, it describes His miraculous acts pertaining to the future and the Hereafter in such a manner that we are convinced of them due to something with which we are familiar in our own lives.

- From *Sura Ya Sin:*

> Does human not consider that We created him of a drop of (seminal) fluid? Yet he turns into a manifest, fierce adversary. And he has coined for Us a comparison, having forgotten his own origin and creation, saying, "Who will give life to these bones when they have rotted away?" Say: "He Who produced them in the first instance will revive them. He has full knowledge of all creation. He Who has made for you fire from the green tree and see, you kindle fire with it." Is not He Who has created the heavens and the earth able to create the like of them (whose bones have rotted away under the ground)? Surely He is; He is the Supreme Creator, the All-Knowing. When He wills a thing to be, He but says to it "Be!" and it is. So All-Glorified is He in Whose hand is absolute dominion of all things, and to Him you are being brought back. (36:77-83)

In the verses above, the Qur'an proves the Resurrection in seven or eight ways. First, it presents humanity's first creation and means: "You see you are created through the stages of a sperm-drop, something suspended on the wall of your mother's womb, something like a lump of chewed flesh, the bones and the clothing of bones in muscular tissue. As you can see this, how can you deny the other creation (the Resurrection), which is even easier than the first one?"

By reminding people of His great favors to them through *He has made for you fire from the green tree*, Almighty God means: "The One Who bestows such favors does not leave you to yourselves, so that you enter the grave and lie there, not to be raised again." Also, He suggests: "You see how dead or dried trees are revived and turn green, so how can you deem it unlikely that wood-like bones will be revived? Further, is *He Who has created the heavens and the earth* unable to create humanity, the fruit of the heavens and the earth? Does One Who governs a huge tree attach no importance to its fruit and leave it to others? Do you think He will leave humanity, the result of the Tree of Creation, to it own devices or to others, and thereby allow that Tree of Creation, all parts of which have been kneaded with wisdom, to go to waste?"

Again He means: "The One Who will revive you on the Day of Judgment is such that the whole universe is like an obedient soldier before Him. It submits with perfect obedience to His command of *"Be!" and it is.* For Him, creating spring and a flower are equal. It is as easy for His Power to create all animals as a fly. It is absolutely improper and irrational to see Him as impotent and challenge His Power by asking: 'Who will revive the bones?'"

Through *So All-Glorified is He, in Whose hand is the absolute dominion of all things,* the Qur'an signifies: "He controls everything and has the keys to everything. He alternates night and day, and winter and summer, as easily as turning the pages of a book. He is such an All-Powerful One of Majesty that, like closing one house and opening another, He closes this world and opens the next. Given this fact and its proofs, you will be returned to Him. He will resurrect everyone and gather them in the Place of Mustering, where He will call you to account for what you did while in the world." Such verses prepare one's mind and heart to accept the Resurrection, because they show how it resembles many events in our lives.

The Qur'an sometimes mentions God's acts in the other world in such a manner that it suggests their like in the world and leaves no room to deny the Resurrection.

- From *suras at-Takwir, al-Infitar,* and al-*Inshiqaq,* beginning with the following respective verses:

  When the sun is folded up. (81:1) When the heaven is cleft open. (82:1) When the heaven is split asunder. (84:1)

In these *suras,* the Qur'an describes the tremendous events of the world's destruction and the Resurrection in such a way that since we see their like especially during spring and autumn, we easily affirm those revolutions, which cause dread to the heart and cannot be comprehended by the mind. As it would be too lengthy even to summarize the meaning of those *suras,* I will point out only one verse as an example:

When the scrolls (of deeds) are laid open (81:10) states that on the Day of Judgment, everyone will be confronted with a role of pages containing the record of their deeds. This is hard for us to comprehend. However, every year we witness similar events during the general revival in spring, as well as many other events that are similar to those the *sura* mentions concerning the world's destruction and the Resurrection.

Every fruit-bearing tree or flowering plant has deeds, actions, and duties. Its type of worship shows the Divine Names manifested in it. All of its deeds (its life-cycle from germination to blossoming and yielding fruits) are recorded in its seeds to be exhibited in a subsequent spring on the earth. As it clearly displays the deeds of its source or origin in the tongue of its form and shape, its branches, twigs, leaves, blossoms, and fruits lay open the pages of those deeds. Thus the One Who does this work before our eyes as manifestations of His Names the All-Wise, the All-Preserving, the All-Arranging, the All-Upbringing, and the All-Subtle, is He Who says: *When the scrolls (of deeds) are laid open.* Compare other points with this and understand.

However, for further help, also consider the explanation of: *When the sun is folded up* (81:1). Besides the brilliant metaphor in *folded up* (meaning "rolled" or "wrapped up"), the verse alludes to several related events: First, by drawing back the veils of non-existence, ether, and the heaven respectively, Almighty God brought a brilliant lamp (the sun) out of His Mercy's treasury to illuminate and be displayed to the world. After the world is destroyed, He will rewrap it in its veils and remove it.

Second, the sun is an official of God charged with spreading its goods of light and folding light and darkness alternately round the world's head. Each evening it gathers up and conceals its goods. Sometimes it does little business because a cloud veils it; sometimes it withdraws from doing business because the moon draws a veil over its face and closes its account book for a short, fixed time. At some future time, this official will resign from its post. Even if there is no cause for its dismissal, due to the two black spots growing on its face, as they have begun to do, the sun will obey the Divine command to draw back the light it sends to the earth and wrap it around its own head. God will order it: "You no longer have any duty toward the earth. Now, go to Hell and burn those who, by worshipping you, insulted an obedient official with disloyalty as if you had claimed divinity." Through its black-spotted face, the sun exhibits the meaning of: *When the sun is folded up.*

NINTH POINT OF ELOQUENCE: Sometimes the wise Qur'an mentions a particular purpose and, to urge our minds to think in universal terms, confirms and establishes that purpose through Divine Names, which are the origin of certain universal rules.

- From *Suratu'l-Mujadila*:

God has indeed heard the words of the woman who pleads with you concerning her husband and refers her complaint to God. God hears your conversation. Surely God is All-Hearing, All-Seeing. (58:1)

The Qur'an says: "Almighty God is All-Hearing. He hears through His Name the Ultimate Truth a wife arguing with you and complaining about her husband, a most particular matter. A woman is most compassionate among human beings, and a mine of care and tenderness leading to self-sacrifice. So, as a requirement of His being the All-Compassionate, Almighty God hears her complaint and considers it a matter of great importance through His Name the Ultimate Truth." By concluding a universal principle from a particular event, the verse suggests that One Who hears and sees a particular, minor incident must hear and see all things. One Who claims Lordship over the universe must be aware of the troubles of any creature who has been wronged and hear its cries. One Who cannot do so cannot be Lord. Thus *God is All-Hearing, All-Seeing* establishes these two mighty truths.

- From *Suratu'l-Isra'*:

All-Glorified is He Who took His servant for a journey by night from the Sacred Mosque (*al-Masjidu'l-Haram*) to the Farthest Mosque (*al-Masjidu'l-Aqsa'*), whose neighborhood We have blessed, that We might show him of Our signs. Surely He is the Hearing, the Seeing. (17:1)

This verse relates the first stage of the noblest Messenger's Ascension, upon him be peace and blessings. "He" in *Surely He is* refers to either the Prophet or Almighty God. If it refers to the Prophet, it means: "This journey is a comprehensive one, a universal ascension. During it, as far as the *Lote-tree of the utmost boundary* (where the Realm of the Created ends) and at a *distance between two bow strings, or less*, he heard and saw God's signs and amazing works of art that were displayed before his eyes and ears in the Divine Names' universal degrees of manifestations." Thus the verse presents the journey from *al-Masjidu'l-Haram* in Makka to *al-Masjidu'l-Aqsa'* in Jerusalem as the key to a universal journey.

If *He* refers to Almighty God, its means: "To admit His servant to His Presence at the end of a journey and to entrust him with a duty, He took him from *al-Masjidu'l-Haram* to *al-Masjidu'l-Aqsa'*. He caused him to meet the Prophets, who were gathered there. After showing that he is the heir to the principles of all Prophets' religions, He caused him to travel through the realms of His dominion in all their inner and outer dimensions, to *the distance between two bow strings, or less.*"

The Prophet is a servant and made a particular journey. But together with him was a trust pertaining to the universe and a light that would change the universe's color. There was also a key with him to open the door to eternal happiness. Therefore, Almighty God describes Himself with the attributes of hearing and seeing all things to demonstrate the global purposes for the trust, the light, and the key.

- From *Suratu'l-Fatir:*

> All praise and thanks are for God, the Originator of the heavens and the earth, Who appoints angels as messengers having wings, two, three, or four (or more). He increases in creation what He wills. Surely God has full power over everything. (35:1)

This verse means: "By adorning the heavens and the earth and demonstrating His Perfection's works, their All-Majestic Originator causes their innumerable spectators to extol and praise Him infinitely. He decorated them with uncountable bounties so that the heavens and the earth praise and exalt endlessly their All-Merciful Originator in the tongue of all bounties and those who receive them."

The verse also shows that the All-Originating One of Majesty, Who has equipped humans, animals and birds (the inhabitants of the earth's regions) with the necessary limbs, faculties, and wings to travel throughout the world, and Who has equipped angels (the heavens' inhabitants) with wings to fly and travel throughout the heavenly palaces of stars and lofty lands of constellations, must be powerful over all things. The One Who has given wings to fly from one fruit to another, and to a sparrow to fly from one tree to another, is He Who gives the wings with which to fly from Venus to Jupiter and from Jupiter to Saturn.

Furthermore, unlike the earth's inhabitants, angels are not restricted to particularity or confined by a specific limited space. Through *two, three, or four. He increases in creation what He wills,* the verse suggests that angels may be present on four or more stars at the same time. Thus by stating that God has equipped angels with wings (a particular event), the Qur'an points to the origin of a universal, tremendous power and establishes it with the summary: *God has full power over everything.*

TENTH POINT OF ELOQUENCE: Sometimes the Qur'an mentions humanity's rebellious acts and restrains its members with severe threats.

But so as not to cast people into despair, it concludes with certain Divine Names pointing to His Mercy and consoles them.

- From *Suratu'sh-Shura:*

> Say: "If there were, as they assert, deities besides Him, they would certainly seek a way against the Master of the Supreme Throne." All-Glorified is He, and absolutely exalted, immeasurably high above what they say. The seven heavens and the earth and all that is therein glorify Him. There is nothing but it glorifies Him with praise, but you do not comprehend their glorification. Surely He is All-Clement, All-Forgiving. (42:4)

The verses mean: "Say: 'If there were deities with Him in His Sovereignty, they would have sought a share in His absolute rule over creation. This would have caused disorder in the universe. However, every creature, universal or particular, big or small, from the seven levels of the heavens to microscopic organisms, glorifies the All-Majestic One signified by the All-Beautiful Names in the tongue of the inscriptions of the Divine Names manifested on them. They declare Him free of any partners. Just as the heavens declare Him to be All-Holy and testify to His Unity through their light-diffusing words of suns and stars, as well as through the wisdom and order they display, the atmosphere glorifies and sanctifies Him and testify to His Unity through the words of clouds, thunder, lighting, and rain."

Similarly, just as the earth glorifies its All-Majestic Creator and declares Him to be One through its living words of plants and animate creatures, each tree glorifies Him and testifies to His Oneness through its words of leaves, blossoms, and fruits. Likewise, even the smallest and most particular creature glorifies the All-Majestic One, many of Whose Names it displays through their inscriptions that it bears, and testifies to His Unity.

The verses state that humanity is the issue and result of the universe, its delicate fruit that has been honored with ruling the earth in God's name. However, while the universe glorifies its All-Majestic Creator with one voice, testifies to His Oneness, and worships in perfect obedience, unbelievers and those who associate partners with God commit an ugly act that deserves punishment. So that such people will not give in to utter despair and in order to show the wisdom in why, despite such an infinitely ugly rebellion and crime, the All-Overwhelming One of Majesty gives them respite without destroying the world on them, the verses conclude with *He is All-Clement, All-Forgiving,* and thus leave a door open for repentance and the hope of being forgiven.

Understand from these foregoing signs of miraculousness that the conclusive parts of the verses contain many aspects of guidance and gleams of miraculousness. Even the greatest geniuses of eloquence have admired and been astonished by the Qur'an's eloquent styles and, concluding that it cannot have a human origin, have believed with absolute certainty that *it is a Revelation revealed* (53:4). Together with the points and qualities already mentioned, verses contain many further qualities such that even the "blind" can see the impress of miraculousness in their totality.

THIRD RAY: The Qur'an cannot be compared with other words and speeches. This is because speech is of different categories, and in regard to superiority, power, beauty, and fineness, has four sources: the speaker, the person addressed, the purpose, and the occasion on which it is spoken. Its source is not only the occasion, as some literary people have wrongly supposed. So do not consider only the speech itself. Since speech derives its strength and beauty from these four sources, from the answers given to the questions "Who spoke it? To whom did he speak it? Why did he speak it? On what occasion did he speak it?", if the Qur'an's sources are studied carefully, the degree of its eloquence, superiority, and beauty will be understood. Since speech is first considered according to the speaker, if it is in the form of command and prohibition it contains a will and power proportional to the speaker's rank. Then it may be irresistible and have an effect like electricity, increasing in superiority and power.

- From *suras Hud* and *Fussilat*, respectively:

  "O earth, swallow up your water, o sky, cease (your rain)!" (11:44)

  He said to them (the heaven and the earth): "Come both of you, willingly or unwillingly." They said: "We have come in willing obedience." (41:11)

That means: "O heaven and earth, come willingly or unwillingly, and submit yourselves to My Wisdom and Power. Come out of non-existence and appear as places where My works of Art will be exhibited." They answered: "We come in perfect obedience. We will carry out, by Your leave and Power, all duties You have assigned us."

Consider the sublimity and force of those compelling commands bearing an irresistible power and will, and imagine how absurd and wishful our commands toward inanimate objects would be: "O earth, stop! O heaven, rend asunder! O world, destroy yourself!" Can such commands be compared with His? How can our wishes and insensible commands be compared with the compelling commands of a supreme ruler having all of rulership's essential qualities?

The difference between a supreme commander's compelling command to march to a mighty, obedient army, and that of an ordinary private is as great as the difference between the commander and the private. Consider the force and superiority of the commands in: *When He wills a thing to be, He but says to it "Be!" and it is* (36:82), and *When We said to the angels: "Prostrate before Adam!"* (2:34) with human orders, and see whether the difference between them is not like that between a firefly and the sun.

Consider how masters describe their work while doing it, how artists explain their artistry while working, and how benefactors discuss their goodness while doing it. We see how effective their combined actions and words and the affect of their words when they say that they have done that in a certain way and for a certain purpose, and in the way it must be done. For example:

- From *Sura Qaf*:

   Do they not observe the sky above them, how We have built and adorned it, and that there are no rifts in it?. And the earth—We have spread out, and set therein firm mountains, and caused to grow thereon every lovely pair of vegetation. (All this is ea means of) insight and reminder for every servant willing to turn to Him in contrition. And We send down from the sky blessed water whereby We cause to grow gardens and grain to harvest, and tall and stately date-palms with ranged clusters as a provision for the servants. And We revive with it a dead land: even so will the dead be raised and come forth (from their graves). (50:6-11)

The descriptions which shine in the constellation of this *sura* like starry fruits of Paradise introduce, with perfect eloquence, many proofs of the Resurrection derived from the observable part of the universe, which is in action. By concluding with *even so will the dead be raised and come forth (from their graves)*, they silence those whom the *sura* says deny the Resurrection at its beginning. How different this is from the people's discussion of happenings with which they have little concern. The difference is greater than that between real and plastic flowers. I will interpret these verses very briefly.

The *sura* begins with the unbelievers' denial of the Resurrection. To convince them of its truth, the *sura* asks: "Don't you see in how magnificent and orderly a fashion We have built the sky and how We have adorned it with the sun, the moon, and stars, with no rifts therein? Do you not see how

We have spread the earth out for you, and how wisely We have furnished it? Having fixed mountains thereon, We protect it against the oceans' invasion. Do you not see how We have created on it all kinds of multicolored and beautiful pairs of vegetation and pasturage and then embellished the earth with them? Do you not see how We send blessed water abundantly from the sky and cause to grow with it gardens, orchards, grains and lofty trees like date-palms bearing delicious fruits, with which We provide Our servants? Do you not see that I also revive the dead soil with that water and bring about thousands of instances of resurrection? In the same way that I cause vegetation to grow on the dead earth through My Power, you will be resurrected on the Day of Judgment, when the earth will die and you will rise out of it alive!" How exalted is the eloquence displayed in these verses that prove the Resurrection, how superior to the words humans use to prove a claim!

From the beginning of this treatise up to here, I have left secret many of the Qur'an's rights for the sake of objective reasoning and verification to convince unbelievers of the Qur'an's miraculousness. I have brought that "sun" in among candles and drawn comparisons. Now, I will briefly point out its incomparable rank in the name of truth.

When compared with the Qur'an, all other words are like tiny reflections of stars in a glass in comparison with the stars themselves. In fact, how far are the meanings that human minds picture in the mirrors of their thoughts and feelings, from the Qur'an's words, each of which describes an unchanging truth! How great is the distance between the Qur'an's angel-like, life-giving words, the Word of the All-Majestic Creator of the sun and moon, which also diffuses the lights of guidance, and the stinging words originated by bewitching souls and affected manners that incite desire! When compared with the Qur'an, our words are like stinging insects in comparison with angels and other luminous spirit beings. This is not a mere assertion; rather, as is apparent in our discussions in The Words written so far, it is a conclusion based on evidence.

How far are our words, full of fancies and fantasies, from the Qur'an's words and phrases. This eternal Divine address, which originated from the All-Merciful's Supreme Throne, came in consideration of humanity as an independent being superior to all other creatures, and is founded upon God's Knowledge, Power, and Will. Each word and statement is the source of a pearl of guidance and of the truths of belief, as well as the mine of an Islamic principle. How great is the distance between our vain, fanciful, futile words and those of the Qur'an.

Like a blessed tree under which the universe lies, the Qur'an has produced the leaves of all Islamic spiritual values and moral perfections, public symbols and rules, principles and commandments. It has burst into blossoms of saints and purified scholars, and yielded fruits of all perfections, Divine truths and the truths concerning the Divine laws of creation and the operation of the universe. The pits or stones in those fruits have grown into "fruit-bearing trees" as principles of conduct and programs of practical life.

Every person and land has benefited from the gems of truth exhibited by the wise Qur'an for almost fourteen centuries in the market of the universe. During that time, neither too much familiarity nor the abundance of its truths, neither time's passage nor the great changes and upheavals in human life, have made people indifferent to its invaluable truths and fine, authentic styles. Nor have these things damaged or devalued them, or extinguished its beauty and freshness. This is miraculous by itself.

If someone were to arrange some Qur'anic truths into a book of his own and claim to have brought about a book similar to the Qur'an, it would be like the following: Suppose a master-builder built a magnificent palace of various jewels, all laid in a symmetrical manner, and embellished it proportionally to each jewel's position and the palace's general design. Then imagine that an ordinary builder, knowing nothing of the palace's jewels, design, and embellishments, were to enter it and destroy the master-builder's work to make it look like an ordinary building. Suppose this person hangs some beads on it to satisfy certain childish fancies, and then says: "Look! I am more skillful than the original builder and have more wealth and more valuable adornments." Could anyone take such an absurd claim seriously?

Third light

This consists of three rays.

FIRST RAY: A significant aspect of the Qur'an's miraculousness is explained in The Thirteenth Word. I mention it here as well, as the context makes it appropriate to do so.

If you want to see and appreciate how each star-like Qur'anic verse removes the darkness of unbelief by spreading the light of miraculousness and guidance, imagine yourself in pre-Islamic Arabia. Everything in that time of ignorance and desert of savagery was enveloped in the veil of lifeless nature amidst the darkness of ignorance and heedlessness. Suddenly, you hear from the Qur'an's sublime tongue such verses as: *All that is in the heavens and the*

earth glorifies God. He is the All-Glorious and All-Mighty, the All-Wise (57:1);
*All that is in the heavens and all that is on the earth glorifies God, the Absolute
Sovereign, the All-Holy and All-Pure, the All-Glorious and Mighty, the All-Wise*
(62:1). See how those creatures, considered lifeless and unfeeling, spring to
life in the audience's minds at the sound of *glorifies*, how they awaken, spring
up, and begin to extol God by praising His Names! At the sound of, *The seven
.heavens and the earth glorify Him* (17:44), the dark heaven appears to those
who hear it as a mouth, with each star being a wisdom-displaying word and
a truth-radiating light; and the earth as a head, with the land and sea each a
tongue, and all animals and plants words of glorification.

If you consider these verses from a modern viewpoint, if you look at it
through a superficial veil of familiarity, after the darkness of the ignorance
of the pre-Islamic age has long been changed into the "already known" by
the Qur'an's "sun" and Islam's light, you cannot see what sort of darkness
each verse removes in a sweet melody of miraculousness, and so cannot
appreciate this aspect of its miraculousness.

If you want to see one of the Qur'an's highest degrees of miraculousness,
consider the following parable: Imagine an extremely vast and spreading tree
hidden behind a veil of the Unseen. You know that just as between the members of a human body, there has to be and is a harmony and balance between
various parts of a tree—between its branches, leaves, flowers, and fruits— and
each part has its proper form and shape according to the tree's nature. If someone draws an exact replica of that hidden tree, correctly displaying all its parts,
relationships, and proportions without seeing it, no one can doubt that the
artist sees and depicts the hidden tree with an eye penetrating the Unseen.

In the same way, the Qur'an's explanations on the reality of things,
namely, the reality of the Tree of Creation stretching from the beginning
of creation to eternity, from the earth to the Divine Throne, from particles
to the sun, maintain the proportion between all parts to such a degree, and
give each part and fruit such a suitable form that all exacting and truth-
seeking scholars have concluded: "What wonders God has willed. May God
bless it. Only you, O wise Qur'an, solve the mystery of creation."

The highest comparison is (and must be put forth) for God—let us represent
His Names and Attributes, as well as His Lordship's acts and qualities, as a tree
of light so vast and great that it stretches through eternity. It encompasses the
whole universe and includes Divine acts in an infinitely vast sphere stretching from: *He intervenes between a person and his heart* (8:24), *Surely God is the
Splitter of the seed-grain and the date-stone* (6:95), and: *It is He Who fashions you*

in the wombs as He wills (3:6), to: *And the heavens rolled up in His Right Hand* (39:67), *He has created the heavens and the earth in six days* (7:54), and: *He made the sun and the moon subservient to His command* (13:2). The wise Qur'an describes this radiant reality, the truths of those Names, Attributes, Qualities, and acts in all of their ramifications and results in so harmonious, fitting, and appropriate a way that all who have penetrated the reality of things and discovered the hidden truths, as well as all sages journeying in the Realm of the Inner Dimension of Existence, have declared: "All-Glorified is God! How right, how conformable with reality, how beautiful, and how fitting!"

Take the six pillars of belief, which relate to both the Sphere of Contingency (the Realm of Creation) and the Sphere of Necessity (the Realm of Divine Existence), and may be regarded as a branch of these two mighty "trees." The Qur'an describes these six pillars of belief with all their elements and furthest fruits and flowers such proportionately, observes their harmony to such a degree, and presents them in such a balanced and well-measured way that we are amazed and scarcely able to grasp its beauty. It also observes the perfect relationship, complete balance, and amazing harmony among the five pillars of Islam, which form a twig of the branch of belief, down to the finest details, most insignificant points of conduct, furthest aims, most profound wisdom, and most particular fruits. With its perfect order and balance, as well as its due proportion and soundness, the supreme Shari'a, which originated from the comprehensive Qur'an's decisive statements, different aspects or dimensions of wording and meaning, indications, and allusions, is an irrefutable and decisive proof, and just and undeniable witness for this.

Given this, the Qur'an's explanations could not have issued from any human being's knowledge, especially from that of an unlettered person. Rather, its explanations rest on an all-comprehensive knowledge and is the Word of One Who sees all things together like a single thing, Who simultaneously observes all truths between two eternities. In this we believe.

SECOND RAY: We discussed in the Twelfth and other Words to what extent human philosophy is inferior to the Qur'an's wisdom. Here we will compare them from another perspective.

Philosophy and science view existence as permanent and discuss creatures' nature and qualities in detail. If they mention their duties toward their Creator at all, they do so only very briefly; they discuss only the designs and letters of the Book of the Universe and ignore its meaning. Whereas the Qur'an views the worldly existence as transient, moving, illusory, unstable, and changing. It speaks of creatures' nature and outward, physical qualities rather briefly, but mentions in detail the duties of worship with which their Creator has charged them, the ways they manifest His Names, and their submission to the Divine laws of creation and operation of the universe. Thus, in order to distinguish truth from falsehood, we should see the differences between human philosophy and Qur'anic wisdom related to summarizing and elaborating.

However unmoving, constant, and static a clock outwardly appears, it is in a state of continuous movement in essence and inwardly. Likewise the world, which is a huge clock of the Divine Power, rolls or revolves unceasingly in continuous change and upheaval. Its two "hands" of night and day show the passage of its seconds, and its "hands" of years and centuries show the passage of its minutes and hours respectively. Time plunges the world into waves of decay and, leaving the past and future to non-existence, allows existence for the present only.

The world also is changing and unstable with respect to space. Its atmosphere changes rapidly, filling with and being cleared of clouds several times a day and displaying weather-related changes. Such activity corresponds to the passage of seconds. The earth, the world's floor, undergoes continuous change through cycles of life and death and in vegetation and animals. Such cycles correspond to the passage of minutes and demonstrate the world's transience.

Such cycles can also be found in the earth's interior, where convulsions and upheavals such as earthquakes that result in the emergence of mountains and sinking of lands occur. These are like an hour hand and also show the world's mortality. The movements of heavenly bodies in the sky (the world's roof), the appearance of comets and new stars while some others are extinguished, as well as solar and lunar eclipses, demonstrate that it is not stable and therefore is making its way toward a final ruin. However slow its changes are, like the hand counting the days in a weekly clock, they also show that the world is mortal and moves to its inevitable end.

Thus, the world, with respect to its worldly existence, was founded upon these seven unstable "pillars." They shake it continually. However, when considered with respect to its Maker, its movements and changes are the results of the movements of the Divine Power's Pen writing the Eternally Besought One's missives, and the transformations it undergoes function as ever-renewed or ever-polished mirrors reflecting the Divine Names' manifestations in all different aspects.

Thus, when considered with respect to itself and being a material, created entity, the world continually convulses and moves toward decay and death. Although it moves like flowing water, heedlessness has frozen it and (philosophical) naturalism has solidified it so that it has become a veil before the Hereafter. Philosophy, nourished by modern scientific thought and supported by corrupt modern civilization's alluring amusements, as well as the intoxicating desires it arouses in people, makes the world more turbid and increase its solidity, which causes people to forget the Creator and the afterlife. Whereas through such verses as: *The sudden, mighty strike! What is the sudden, mighty strike?* (101:1-2); *When the event to happen happens* (56:1); and: *By the Mount, and by a Book inscribed* (52:1-2), the Qur'an shatters this world and cards it like wool. Through such verses as: *Do they not consider the inner dimension of the heavens and the earth, and God's absolute dominion over them?* (7:185); *Do they not observe the sky above them, how We have built it?* (50:6); and: *Do those who disbelieve consider that the heavens and the earth were of one piece, then We parted them?* (21:30), it gives that world a transparency and removes its turbidity. Through its bright, light-diffusing "stars" like: *God is the Light of the heavens and the earth* (24:35), and: *The present, worldly life is but a play and pastime* (6:32), it melts that solid world.

Through its threatening verses that recall death, such as: *When the sun is folded up* (81:1); *When the heaven is cleft open* (82:1); *When the heaven is split asunder* (84: 1); and: *The Trumpet is blown, and so all who are in the heavens and all who are on the earth fall dead, save those whom God wills* (39:68), it destroys the delusion that the world is eternal. Through its thunder-like blasts, such as: *He knows whatever goes into the earth and whatever comes forth out of it, and whatever descends from the heaven and whatever ascends into it. He is with you wherever you may be. God sees all that you do* (57:4); and: *Say: "All praise and gratitude are for God, Soon He will show you His signs, and you will come to know them. Your Lord is never heedless and unmindful of what you do"* (27: 93), it removes heedlessness, which gives rise to naturalism.

Thus all the Qur'anic verses concerned with the universe follow the principle outlined above. They unveil the world's reality and display it as it is. By showing the world's ugly face, they turn us away from it; by pointing out its beautiful face, which is turned toward the Maker, they turn our face toward it. The Qur'an instructs us in true wisdom and teaches us the meanings of the Book of the Universe, with little attention to its letters and decorations. Unlike human philosophy, it does not give itself over to what is ugly and, causing people to forget the meaning, lead them to waste their time on such meaningless things as the letters' decorations.

THIRD RAY: In the Second Ray, we pointed out the inferiority of human philosophy to the Qur'an's wisdom as well as the latter's miraculousness. In this Ray, which compares the Qur'an's wisdom with the philosophy of its students (e.g., purified scholars, saints, and the Illuminists (*Ishraqiyyun*), who were the more enlightened class of philosophers), we will discuss briefly the Qur'an's miraculousness in this respect.

We now present a most true evidence for the wise Qur'an's sublimity, the clearest proof of its truth, and a most powerful sign of its miraculousness. Consider this: The Qur'an contains and explains all degrees, varieties, and requirements of Divine Unity's manifestation and belief in it in a perfectly balanced manner. Moreover, it maintains the equilibrium among all elevated Divine truths, contains all commandments and principles required by the Divine Names, and maintains exact and sensitive relationships among them. Also, it holds together all the acts and essential characteristics of God's Divinity and Lordship with perfect balance.

All of these show its matchless virtue and characteristics, which cannot be found in the greatest human works, in those of saints who penetrate the inner realities or dimension of things, or of those Illuminists who discern the inner aspects of things and events, or of those wholly purified ones who penetrate the World of the Unseen. It is as if, according to a certain division of labor, each group devoted itself to one branch of the mighty tree of truth and busied itself only with its leaves and fruits, all the while being unaware of the others.

Absolute, unlimited truth cannot be comprehended by restricted minds and vision, but only by the Qur'an's universal and all-encompassing vision. All that is not the Qur'an cannot comprehend the universal truth in its entirety, even if they benefit from it, for their minds are limited, restricted, and wholly absorbed in only a couple of its parts. They frequently go to extremes, dwelling on one or two points more than the others, and thereby destroy the balance and accurate relations among the truths. This point was discussed with a significant parable in the Second Branch of The Twenty-fourth Word. We will approach it here with another parable.

Imagine a treasure under the sea full of jewels. Many divers look for it but, since their eyes are closed, they search for it with their hands. One seizes a large diamond and concludes that he has found the whole of the treasure.

When he hears that his friends have found other jewels, such as a round ruby or a square amber, he thinks that they are facets or embellishments of what he has found. Each diver has the same idea.

Such a thought and attitude destroys the balance and accurate relations among truths. It even changes the color of many of them, for one is compelled to make forced interpretations and detailed explanations to see the true color of truths or show them to others. Some even deny or falsify them. Those who make a careful study of the Illuminists' books, or of the works of Sufi masters who rely on their visions and illuminations without weighing them on the scales of the Qur'an and the Sunna, will confirm this judgment. Although they have benefited from the Qur'an and generally have been taught by it, their teachings have certain shortcomings and defects because they are not the Qur'an itself. The Qur'an, that ocean of truths, encompasses and sees in its verses the entire treasure and describes its jewels in such a harmonious and balanced way that they show their beauty perfectly.

For example, just as the Qur'an sees and shows the Divine Lordship's grandeur in: *The whole earth is in His Grasp on the Day of Resurrection, and the heavens are rolled up in His Right Hand* (39:67); and: *On the Day when We will roll up the heaven as written scrolls are rolled for books* (21:104), it sees and shows the all-encompassing Mercy expressed by God, *Nothing whatever on the earth or in the heaven is hidden from Him. It is He Who shapes you in the wombs as He wills* (3:5-6); *No living creature is there but He holds it by its forelock* (11:56), and: *How many a living creature there is that bears not its own provision, but God provides for it, and indeed for you* (29:60).

Just as it sees and points out the vast creativity expressed by: *(He) has created the heavens and the earth and made the veils of darkness and the light* (6:1); it sees and shows the comprehensive Divine control of things and His encompassing Lordship in: *He creates you and what you do* (37:96). It also sees and shows the mighty truth expressed in: *He revives the earth after its death* (30:50) and the truth concerning His munificence expressed in: *Your Lord has inspired the bee* (16:68), and the great truth concerning His Sovereignty and command expressed in: *The sun and the moon and the stars (are) subservient by His command* (7:54).

The Qur'an sees and shows the truth of compassion and administration expressed in: *Do they not consider the birds above them (flying) in lines, spreading and closing their wings? None holds them up save the All-Merciful; indeed He sees all things* (67:19); the vast truth expressed in: *His Seat embraces the heavens and*

the earth, and the preserving of them does not weary Him (2:255); the truth concerning His overseeing, expressed by: *He is with you wherever you may be*
(57:4); the all-embracing truth expressed by: *He is the First and the Last, the*
All-Outward and the Al-Inward, and He has full knowledge of everything (57:3);
His being nearer to beings than themselves, expressed by: *Assuredly, We have*
created human and know what his soul whispers to him; We are nearer to him than
his jugular vein (50:16); the elevated truth expressed by: *The angels and the*
Spirit ascend to Him in a day the measure of which is fifty thousand years (70:4);
and the all-encompassing truth expressed by: *God enjoins justice and devotion*
to doing good, and generosity towards kinsfolk, and He forbids all shameful deeds,
things abominable to sound conscience, injustice and rebellion (16:90).

In short, the Qur'an sees and shows in detail all truths pertaining to
knowledge and practice concerning this world and the next, and each of the
six pillars of belief. It points out purposefully and earnestly each of the five
pillars of Islam and all other principles of securing happiness in both worlds.
It preserves the exact balance and maintains the accurate relationship and
proportion among them. The subtlety and beauty originating from the harmony of the entirety of those truths give rise to a form of the Qur'an's miraculousness.

Scholars of theology study the Qur'an and have written numerous volumes on the pillars of belief. But some of them, like the *Mu'tazilis*, have preferred reason over transmitted knowledge originating from Divine
Revelations and so have not been able to explain these truths as effectively
as even ten Qur'anic verses. It is as though they have dug tunnels under
mountains as far as the end of the world to obtain and convey water. They
have gone along with the chains of cause and effect as far as the beginning of
time and then, cutting the chains, jumped over to eternity to obtain the
knowledge of God (the water of life for people) and prove the Necessarily
Existent One's Existence.

On the other hand, each Qur'anic verse can extract "water" from every
place like the Staff of Moses, opening up a window from everything and making the All-Majestic Maker known. In addition, because they could not preserve the exact balance between the truths, leaders of all heretical groups, those
who have delved into the inner nature of things by relying on their visions
instead of the Prophet's Sunna, have returned half-way and formed different
sects. This caused them to fall into heresy and misguidance, and to cause others to deviate. Their failure also demonstrates the Qur'an's miraculousness.

Conclusion

Among the gleams of the Qur'an's miraculousness, its reiterations and brief mentions of scientific facts and developments, which are wrongly thought to be a cause of defects, were discussed in the Fourteenth Droplet of The Nineteenth Word. Another gleam of the Qur'an's miraculousness, radiating in its mention of the Prophets' miracles, was shown in the Second Station of The Twentieth Word. You will find many other gleams discussed in other Words and my Arabic treatises. However, I will add here another aspect.

Just as the Prophets' miracles exhibit an aspect of the Qur'an's miraculousness, the Qur'an with all its miracles is a miracle of Muhammad, upon him be peace and blessings, and all of his miracles constitute a miracle of the Qur'an. They demonstrate its Divine authorship, through which each word becomes a miracle, for just like a seed, each word may contain a tree of truths; just like a heart's center, it may have relations with all parts of a mighty truth. Also, since it depends on an All-Encompassing Knowledge and Infinite Will, it may be interrelated by means of its letters, position, meaning, connotations, and in its entirety, with countless other things. This is why specialists in the science of letters assert that each letter of the Qur'an contains as many mysteries as may cover a page, and prove it to those who have expert knowledge in that science.

Consider all the Lights, Rays, Gleams, Radiances, and Beams discussed so far, and see how the claim at the beginning becomes a decisive, undeniable conclusion. In other words, this entire treatise decisively proclaims the truth of: Say: *"If humanity and jinn banded together to produce the like of this Qur'an, they would never produce its like, even though they backed one another"* (17:88).

All-Glorified are You. We have no knowledge save what You have taught us. Surely You are the All-Knowing, All-Wise.

Our Lord, take us not to task if we forget or make mistakes.

My Lord, expand for me my breast. Make my task easy for me. Loose any knot from my tongue so that they can understand my speech clearly.

O God, bestow blessings and peace; the best, finest, most pleasant and most manifest, purest, most gracious and most abundant, mightiest, greatest, most honored and most elevated, most flourishing and most prosperous, and the most subtle of your blessings; the most sufficient and most abundant, most ample and most exalted, most sublime and most constant of Your peace; and as blessing, peace, mercy, good pleasure, forgiving, and pardoning, in increase and continuity along with the rains from the clouds as favors of Your Generosity and Munificence, and in continuous multiplication along with the fine and exquisite bounties of Your Generosity and Benevolence; eternally, without beginning or end, along with Your eternity—on Your servant, Your beloved, and Your Messenger, Muhammad, the best of Your creatures, the brightest light, the clearest and most decisive proof, the most profound ocean, the most comprehensive light, having shone grace and overwhelming majesty and superior perfection; bestow blessings on him through the grandeur of Your Being, and blessings on his Family and Companions through which You may forgive our sins, expand our breasts, purify our hearts, uplift our spirits, bless us, refine our memories and thoughts, remove the filth from our souls, cure us of our diseases, and open the locks on our hearts.

Our Lord! Do not let our hearts swerve after You have guided us and bestow upon us mercy from Your Presence. Surely You are the All-Bestowing.

The conclusion of their call will be: "All praise and gratitude are for God, the Lord of the worlds."

First addendum[145]

The tireless and insatiable traveler, who knew the aim and essence of life in this world to be belief, addressed his own heart and said: "Let us have recourse to the book known as the Qur'an of miraculous exposition, which is said to be the Word of the Being Whom we are seeking: let us examine the most famous, most brilliant and wisest book in the world, one which issues a challenge in every age to whoever refuses to submit to it. Let us see what it says. But first, we must establish that this book is from our Creator." Saying this, he began to search.

Since the traveler lives in the present age, he looked first at the *Risale-i Nur*, which comprises gleams from the miraculousness of the Qur'an, and he saw that its one hundred and thirty parts consist of the subtle meanings, lights and well-founded explanations of certain verses from that Criterion between truth and falsehood—the Qur'an. He understood from its content and forceful diffusing and defending of the Qur'anic truths in this age of unbelief that the Qur'an, its master, source, authority and sun, is a revealed book. Among the hundreds of proofs for the Divine authorship of the Qur'an in the different parts of the *Risale-i Nur*, The Twenty-Fifth Word, which is a single proof of the Qur'an, and the end of The Nineteenth Letter establish forty aspects of the

---

[145] This part consists of the Seventeenth Rank of the First Station of The Supreme Sign, which is the Seventh Ray in *The Rays*.

Qur'an's miraculousness in such a way that whoever sees them will, far from raising any criticism or objection, admire their arguments and praise them in appreciation. Therefore, leaving to the *Risale-i Nur* the establishment of the Qur'an as God's Word and the explanation of its various aspects of miraculousness, the traveler noticed a few points that demonstrate its greatness briefly.

FIRST POINT: Just as the Qur'an, with all its aspects of miraculousness and truths that show its veracity, is a miracle of Muhammad, upon him be peace and blessings, he himself, with all his miracles, proofs of Prophethood and perfections of knowledge, is a miracle of the Qur'an and a decisive proof of the its being the Word of God.

SECOND POINT: As well as bringing about a about a substantial, happy, and enlightening transformation in human social life, the Qur'an has brought about a revolution in the souls, hearts, spirits and intellects of people, and in their individual, social and political lives. Furthermore, it has perpetuated this revolution in such a way that at every moment in the past fourteen centuries, its more than six thousand and two hundred verses have been read with the utmost respect by more than a hundred million people, training and refining their souls and purifying their hearts. For spirits it has been a means of development and advancement; for intellects, a guidance and light; and for life, it has been life itself and felicity. Such a book is without doubt unparalleled in every respect: it is a wonder, a marvel and a miracle.

THIRD POINT: From the age of its advent down to the present day, the Qur'an has demonstrated such eloquence that it caused the value attached to "Seven Hanging Poems"—poems which were chosen as the best, written in gold and hung on the walls of the Ka'ba during the age of ignorance— to fall to such a low level that the daughter of (the famous poet) Labid, when taking down her father's ode from the Ka'ba, said, "Compared with the verses of the Qur'an, this no longer has any worth."

A Bedouin poet once heard this verse being recited: *Proclaim what you are commanded openly and in an emphatic manner* (15:94), and immediately prostrated. When they asked him, "Have you become a Muslim?" he replied, "No! I was merely prostrating before the eloquence of this verse!"

Also, thousands of scholars, litterateurs and geniuses of the science of eloquence and rhetoric such as 'Abdu'l-Qahir al-Jurjani, Sakkaki and Zamakhshari have concluded unanimously that the eloquence of the Qur'an is beyond human capacity and cannot be replicated by man.

Moreover, from the outset, the Qur'an has also invited all arrogant and egoistic litterateurs and rhetoricians, and, in a manner to break their arrogance, challenged them by saying: "Either produce a single *sura* like mine or accept perdition and humiliation in this world and the Hereafter." Despite this challenge, the obstinate rhetoricians of that age abandoned the shorter route of attempting to produce a single sura like the Qur'an and instead chose the longer route of casting their persons and property into danger. This proves that the shorter route cannot be taken.

Millions of Arabic books are in circulation, written since that time either by friends of the Qur'an in order to imitate it or by its enemies in order to confront and criticize it; and such books have been improved over time along with the developments in science and thought. However, to this day not one of them has been able to attain the level of the Qur'an. Should even a common man listen to them, he would be sure to say: "The Qur'an does not resemble these other books and is in a different class entirely. It must be either below them or above them." And since no-one in the world—not even an unbeliever or a fool—can say that it is below them, one must therefore conclude that in eloquence it is higher than all of them.

A man once read the verse, *Whatever is in the heavens and on the earth glorifies God* (57:1). He said: "I cannot see any miraculous eloquence in this verse." He was told: "Go back to that age in your mind and listen to the verse as it was recited there." Imagining himself to be there, he saw that all the beings in the world were lifeless and without either consciousness or purpose, living in an unstable, transient world, surrounded by empty, infinite and unbounded space, and floundering in confusion and darkness. Suddenly he heard the above verse proclaimed by the tongue of the Qur'an. At once the verse removed the veil from the face the universe and illumined it. This pre-eternal Speech, this eternal Decree, gave instruction to all conscious beings, drawn up in the ranks of succeeding centuries, in such fashion that the universe became like a vast mosque. The whole of creation, and in particular the heavens and the earth, was engaged in vital remembrance of God and proclamation of His Glory, fulfilling its function with joy and contentment. All of this the traveler observed. Thus tasting one degree of eloquence of the Qur'an and comparing the other verses to it, he understood one of the many thousands of wise reasons why the eloquence of the Qur'an has conquered half of the earth and a fifth of humanity; he saw how it has increased without let or hindrance its majestic dominion with utmost respect throughout the fourteen centuries since its advent.

FOURTH POINT: While repetition of even the most pleasant thing eventually leads to disgust, the sweetness of the Qur'an is such that however many times it is recited, it causes neither tiredness nor repulsion. Indeed, it has become axiomatic that for those whose hearts are not corrupted and taste spoilt, repeated recitation of the Qur'an leads not to weariness but, rather, to an increase in its sweetness and appeal. Also, the Qur'an demonstrates such freshness, youth and originality that even though it has lived for fourteen centuries and been available to everyone, its vitality is such that one would think it has only just been revealed. Every century sees the Qur'an enjoying a new youth, as though it were addressing itself in particular. Similarly, even though they keep the Qur'an at their side constantly in order to benefit from it and follow its method of exposition, scholars of every branch of learning see that the Qur'an continues to maintain the originality of its style and manner of explanation.

FIFTH POINT: One wing of the Qur'an is in the past and one is in the future. Its root and one wing are the unanimously confirmed truths of the former Prophets, who affirm it with the tongue of unanimity, and whom it in turn affirms and corroborates. Similarly, all saints and purified scholars, those fruits of the Qur'an who have received life from it, have shown through their vital spiritual progress that their blessed "Tree" is living and most radiant means to truth, and beneficial in every respect. All the true spiritual paths or ways of sainthood and Islamic sciences, which have all grown under the protection of the Qur'an's second wing, which looks to the future, unanimously testify that the Qur'an is truth itself and a collection of truths and unequaled in comprehensiveness.

SIXTH POINT: The Qur'an is luminous in each of its six aspects or sides, all of which point to its truthfulness and veracity. Beneath it lie the pillars of argument and proof; above it shine the gleams of the stamp of miraculousness or inimitability; before it are the gifts of happiness in both worlds as its goal; behind it are the truths of the heavenly Revelation as its point of support; to its right is the well-documented and substantiated confirmation of innumerable sound and upright minds; to its left one sees the true satisfaction, sincere attraction and submission of sound hearts and pure consciences. These six, taken together, prove that the Qur'an is an extraordinary, firm and unassailable heavenly citadel standing on earth.

From these six aspects it is clear that the Qur'an is pure truth, that it is not a human word, and that it contains no errors at all. The Controller and Director of the universe, Who has made it His practice to always exhibit beauty in the universe, to protect goodness and truth, and to eliminate imposters and liars, has confirmed and set His seal on the Qur'an by giving it the most acceptable, highest and most dominant place of respect and success in the world.

Also, the person who represented and communicated Islam and interpreted and explained the Qur'an throughout his life, upon him be peace and blessings, held it in greater respect than anybody else; he assumed a different state when it was revealed; other words uttered by him outside the context of his revelatory experience did not resemble the Qur'an and could never be on the same level; despite being illiterate he was, with the Qur'an as his basis, he described with complete confidence many past and future events and numerous cosmic phenomena from behind the veil of the Unseen; as the supreme translator of the Qur'an, in whose behavior no trickery or shortcoming had ever been witnessed even by the sharpest eyes, believed in and affirmed every pronouncement of the Qur'an with all his might, allowing nothing to shake him in his conviction—all of these facts serve to confirm beyond doubt that the Qur'an is the Divinely-revealed Word of his All-Compassionate Creator.

Furthermore, more than a fifth of humankind have been attached to the Qur'an with piety and rapture, paying heed to it eagerly in their desire to know the truth. According to the testimony provided by many indications, events and spiritual unveilings, the jinn, the angels and the spirit beings gather around it in truth-adoring fashion like moths whenever it is recited. This too serves to confirm that the Qur'an enjoys universal acceptance and occupies the highest position.

In addition, each of the different classes of humankind, from the most simple and lowly to the most clever and learned, is able to take its full share of the Qur'an's instruction and understand its most profound truths (each according to their capacity). Moreover, all of the celebrated scholars in all branches of the religious sciences, the great interpreters of the Supreme Shari'a in particular, together with the brilliant and exacting scholars of theology and the basic principles of the Religion are able to exact from the Qur'an all the answers needed for their various disciplines. All of these facts confirm that the Qur'an is a source of truth and a mine of reality.

Also, although the disbelieving ones among the Arab litterateurs who are most advanced in literature and eloquence felt the greatest need to dispute the Qur'an, they have never been able to match it in eloquence by producing the like of even a single sura, despite the fact that eloquence is only one of the seven most prominent aspects of the Qur'an's miraculousness. Up until this day, not even those renowned rhetoricians and linguistic experts who have contested the Qur'an in order to make a name for themselves have been able to oppose even a single aspect of its miraculousness, and as a result have been forced to remain in impotent silence. This is further confirmation that the Qur'an is a miracle and completely beyond human capacity.

The value, superiority, and eloquence of a speech are based on the answers given to these questions posed with regard to it: "From whom has it come, for whom is it intended, and to what purpose?" In respect of these points, the Qur'an can have no like, and none can reach it. For the Qur'an is a speech and address by the Lord and Creator of all the worlds, and a conversation of His that is in no way derivative or artificial. It is addressed to the one who was sent in the name of all humanity, indeed of all beings, who is the most famous and renowned of humankind, the strength and breadth of whose belief gave rise to mighty Islam and raised its owner to the station of *The distance between two bow strings, or less,* and returned him as the addressee of the Eternally Besought One. It describes and explains matters concerning happiness in this world and the next, the results of the creation of the universe, and the purposes of the Lord within it. It expounds also the belief of its first and primary addressee—the Prophet Muhammad—which was the highest and most extensive belief, encompassing all of the truths of Islam. It shows every facet of the huge universe like a map, a clock or a house, describing it in a manner which befits the Craftsman Who made it. To produce the like of this Qur'an of miraculous exposition is therefore not possible, nor can the degree of its miraculousness be attained.

Also, thousands of meticulous, learned scholars of high intelligence have written commentaries expounding the Qur'an, some of which consist of as many as seventy volumes, proving with clear evidence and argument its innumerable qualities, characteristics, mysteries, subtleties and elevated meanings, and showing its numerous indications concerning every sort of hidden and unseen matter. And the one hundred and thirty parts of the *Risale-i Nur* in particular, each of which proves with decisive arguments one quality or subtle point of the Qur'an. Each part of it—such as The Twenty-Fifth Word on the miraculousness of the Qur'an; The Second Station of The Twentieth Word, which deduces many things from the Qur'an concerning the wonders of civilization such as the railway and the airplane; The First Ray, called Signs of the Qur'an, which makes known the indications of verses alluding to electricity; the eight short treatises known as The Eight Signs, which show how well-ordered, full of meaning and mysterious the words of the Qur'an actually are; the small treatise ("The Seventh Gleam" in The Gleams) proving in five aspects the miraculousness of the verses at the end of *Suratu'l-Fath* (*sura* 48) from the perspective of their giving news of the Unseen—each part of the

Risale-i Nur shows one truth or one light of the Qur'an. All of this serves to confirm the fact that the Qur'an has no like: it is a miracle and a wonder; it is the tongue of the World of the Unseen in this visible earthly realm, and it is the Word of One Who is the All-Knowing of the Unseen.

It is on account of these qualities and characteristics of the Qur'an that we have indicated above in six points, that its sublime, luminous sovereignty and its sacred, mighty rule have continued with perfect splendor, illuminating the faces of the centuries and the visage of the earth for (more than) thirteen centuries. It is also on account of these qualities of the Qur'an that each of its letters has the sacred distinction of yielding at least ten rewards, ten merits and ten eternal fruits; indeed, the letters of certain verses and suras yield a hundred or a thousand fruits, or even more, while at certain blessed times the light, reward and value of each letter multiplies a hundredfold. Our traveler journeying through the world understood this and said to his heart: "The Qur'an, which is thus miraculous in every respect, through the consensus of its suras, the agreement of its verses, the accord of its lights and mysteries, and the concurrence of its fruits and works, testifies with its proofs to the Existence, Unity, Attributes and Names of a Single Necessarily Existent One, and its testimony has caused to issue forth the permanent testimony of all the believers."

Thus in a brief reference to the instruction in belief and Divine Unity that the traveler received from the Qur'an, it was said in the Seventeenth Step of the First Station:

> There is no deity but God, the Necessarily Existent, the One and Unique, Whose necessary Existence in His Unity is demonstrated clearly by the Qur'an of miraculous exposition, the Book accepted and desired by all species of angels, humanity and jinn; the verses of which are read each minute of the year, with the utmost reverence, by hundreds of millions of people; and whose sacred sovereignty is permanent over all regions of the earth and the universe and the face of time: its spiritual and luminous authority has run over half the earth and a fifth of humanity, for fourteen centuries, with the utmost splendor. This is also testified to and evidenced by the unanimity of its sacred and heavenly suras, the agreement of its luminous, Divine verses, the congruence of its mysteries and lights, and the correspondence of its fruits and effects, by witnessing and clear vision.

The flower of Emirdağ[146]

The following is a persuasive response to the objections raised about the apparent repetitions in the Qur'an.

My dear, faithful brothers (and sisters)!

Confused and ill-expressed though it may be on account of my distressing situation, the following is a reflection on one aspect of the Qur'an's miraculousness. While I find it difficult to articulate, since it concerns the Qur'an, it will be instructive and lead to reflection. It may be likened to the wrapper on a bright, invaluable gem. So consider the gem being offered rather than its shabby covering. I wrote it with some speed and concision during a few days in Ramadan while I was malnourished and ill, so please forgive any shortcomings it may have.

My dear, faithful brothers (and sisters)!

The Qur'an issues, first of all, from the greatest and most comprehensive rank of the Eternal Speaker's universal Lordship. It is addressed, first of all, to the comprehensive rank of the one who received it in the name of the universe. Its purpose is to guide humanity from the time of its revelation until the end of time. It therefore contains entirely meaningful and comprehensive explanations concerning the Lordship of the Creator of the universe, Who is the Lord of this world and the Hereafter, the earth and the heavens and eternity, and clarifications of the Divine laws which pertain to the administration of all creatures. It is because of these and similar other attributes of the Qur'an that this Divine discourse is so comprehensive and elevated, and therefore so inclusive and miraculous – so much so that even its most apparent, literal meanings which target the simple minds of ordinary people, who make up the most numerous group of the Qur'an's addressees, is enough to satisfy those among the people who have attained the highest and most sophisticated levels of understanding. Even its narratives are not a collection of historical stories that were revealed to teach only the people of a certain age, but it addresses and is revealed to every age and all levels of understanding and learning as a collection of universal principles. For example, while describing the punishments meted out to the people of Pharaoh or of 'Ad and Thamud for their sins, and with its severe threats against wrongdoers, it warns all tyrants and criminals, including those of our own time, of the consequences of their tyranny and wrongdo-

---

[146] A district of Afyon province (western Turkey) where Said Nursi lived for some time. (Tr.)

ing. By mentioning the final triumphs of Prophets such as Abraham and Moses, upon them be peace, it consoles wronged believers of all eras.

The Qur'an of miraculous expression revives the past, which, for those mired in heedlessness and misguidance, is a lonely and frightful realm, a dark and ruined cemetery. It transforms the past centuries and epochs into living pages of instruction, into a wondrous, animated realm under the direct control of the Lord—a realm that has significant connections with us. By transporting us back to those times or displaying them to us like the scenes on a cinema screen, the Qur'an teaches us in its own inimitable and most elevated and miraculous style. In the same manner, it shows the true nature of the universe. The misguided see it as an unending, lifeless, lonely and frightful place, replete with decay and separation, while the Qur'an shows it to be a book of the Eternally Besought One, a city of the All-Merciful and a place where the Lord's works of art are exhibited. In it, lifeless objects become animate beings performing their particular duties and helping one another within a perfect system of communication.

This most glorious Qur'an, which enlightens and instructs angels, jinn and humanity in Divine Wisdom in the most pleasing manner, has sacred distinctions which are such that, at times, a single letter sometimes brings ten merits, sometimes a hundred and sometimes a thousand or, indeed, thousands. If all jinn and human beings pooled their talents, they would not be able to produce anything to rival or equal the Qur'an in any way. It speaks to all people and the whole universe in the most appropriate way; it is inscribed continuously and with great facility on the minds of millions of people; however frequently it is recited, it never bores or tires its listeners; despite its similar sentences and phrases which may confuse some, children are able to commit it to memory with ease; and it gives pleasure and tranquility to the sick and the dying, for whom listening to even a few human words causes great discomfort. The Qur'an causes its students to attain felicity in both this world and the next.

Observing the unlettered nature of the one who conveyed it, and without any hint of pretentiousness or ostentation, the Qur'an preserves its stylistic fluency and purity while never ignoring the level of understanding of the common masses. At the same time it instructs people in the extraordinary miracles of Divine Power and meaningful instances of Divine Wisdom which underpin all events which occur in the heavens and the earth, thereby displaying a fine aspect of miraculousness within the grace of its status as a book of guidance.

The Qur'an shows that it is a book of prayer and invocation, a call to eternal salvation, and a declaration of God's Unity, all of which require reit-

eration. Consequently it repeats this or that sentence or story, gives numerous meanings to many different groups or categories of addressees, and
informs its readers that its Author treats with compassion even the slightest
and apparently most insignificant things and events, including them in the
sphere of His Will and Control. By paying attention to even the most particular or apparently trivial events involving the Companions of the Prophet in
the establishment of Islam and legislation of its laws, it presents universal
principles and suggests that those events function as though they were seeds,
destined to produce numerous important fruits in the establishment of Islam
with its Law. In this way it demonstrates another aspect of its miraculousness.

When needs are expressed repeatedly, answers must be repeated accordingly. Therefore the Qur'an answers many questions which were asked
repeatedly during the twenty-three years of its revelation and seeks to satisfy
all levels of understanding and learning. To prove that all things, from
minute particles to vast stars, are controlled by a Single One, and that He will
destroy the universe in order to bestow on it a new form on Doomsday,
replacing it with the extraordinary realm of the Hereafter; to establish a
mighty and all-comprehensive revolution in minds that will, for the sake of
the purposes and results of the creation of the universe, show Divine rage and
wrath in the face of the human injustice and wrongdoing which fill the universe, the earth and the heavens with rage, the Qur'an repeats certain verses
and phrases that are the conclusions of innumerable proofs and which have
a weight as great as that of thousands of conclusions. In such cases, repetition
is an extremely powerful aspect of Qur'anic miraculousness, an extremely elevated example of its eloquence and the beauty of its language in conformity
with the requirements of the subject matter.

For example, as is explained in the Fourteenth Gleam and the First
Word of the *Risale-i Nur*, the phrase *In the Name of God, the All-Merciful,
the All-Compassionate*, which appears a total of 114 times in the Qur'an—
at the beginning of every *sura* apart from *at-Tawba* and once in the middle
of the *Suratu'n-Naml*—is a truth which links the earth to God's Supreme
Throne and all spheres of the universe, thus illuminating the cosmos. As
everybody is in constant need of this, it is worth repeating millions of times.
We need it not only every day in the same way that we need bread, but at
every moment, in the same way that we need oxygen and light.

Another example is *Your Lord is He Who is the All-Glorious and All-Mighty,
the All-Compassionate*, which has the strength of thousands of truths and is
repeated eight times in *Suratu'sh-Shu'ara*. It tells of the Prophets' final triumph

and salvation and the ruin of their rebellious peoples. If, for the sake of the purposes or results of the universe's creation, in the name of God's universal Lordship, and to teach people that the Lord's Glory and Dignity require the wrongdoers' ruin and His Compassion demands the Prophets' triumph and salvation, this sentence were repeated thousands of times, there would still be a need for it. Thus it is a concise and miraculous aspect of the Qur'an's eloquence.

Also, the verses *Which of the favors of your Lord will you two deny?* (55:13) and *Woe on that day to the deniers* (77:15), which are repeated several times in their respective suras are threats repeated in front of jinn and humanity down the ages, and across the heavens and the earth, concerning the ingratitude, unbelief and wrongdoing of all those whose unrighteousness provokes the fury of the heavens and the earth, ruin the results of the universe's creation, and show contempt and denial in the face of the Divine Sovereign's Majesty. They also denounce their violation of the rights of all creatures. Since they constitute a universal teaching which has the strength of a thousand truths, even if these two verses were repeated thousands of times, it would still not be enough. Therefore it represents a majestic example of conciseness and the miraculousness of eloquence in grace and beauty.

Also, the invocation of the Prophet known as *al-Jawshanu'l-Kabir* (The Great Shield), inspired by the Qur'an, consists of a hundred sections, each of which ends with the words: *All-Glorified are You! There is no deity but You. Mercy! Mercy! Deliver us from the Fire!* These sentences contain affirmation of God's Unity, which is the greatest truth in the universe. This affirmation is the greatest of the mighty duties of all created beings toward the Lord, namely glorification, praise, and declaring Him to be All-Holy and free from all defect, exalted above what polytheists attribute to Him. It is also a supplication for humanity to be saved from eternal punishment, which should be our most vital concern and is the expected result of our servanthood to God and our helplessness before Him. And so even if we were to repeat those phrases thousands of times over, it would still not be enough.

Thus the Qur'an includes reiterations on account of such substantial principles. As required by the occasion and the demands of literary eloquence, and to facilitate understanding, it sometimes expresses the truth of Divine Unity twenty times in one page, be it explicitly or implicitly. Yet it never bores its listener; rather, it enforces the meaning and gives its reader encouragement.

The *suras* revealed in Makka and Madina differ from each other in eloquence and miraculousness, and in degrees of elaboration and conciseness. The

Makkans were mainly Qurayshi polytheists and unlettered tribesmen. Given this, the Qur'an uses forceful, eloquent and concise language with an elevated style, repeating certain points to better establish its truths. In the Makkan *suras*, the pillars of belief and the categories and degrees of Divine Unity's manifestations are expressed repeatedly in a forceful, emphatic, concise and most miraculous language. They prove the beginning and end of the world, the existence of God and the coming of the Hereafter with such powerful proofs and are expressed not only on a single page, verse, sentence or word, but sometimes even in a single letter, through such subtle changes in word order, through the use or non-use of definite articles or the inclusion or omission of certain words, phrases and sentences that masters of the art of literary eloquence have been amazed. The sublime eloquence and conciseness of the Makkan chapters have been discussed in *Isharatu'l-I'jaz* and The Twenty-fifth Word, which explain forty aspects of the Qur'an's miraculous inimitability.

The *suras* revealed in Madina, during the second phase of the mission of the Prophet, upon him be peace and blessings, are in the main addressed to believers, Jews, and Christians. As required by the rules of eloquence and the practical need for guidance, rather than the pillars and principles of belief, they focus more on explaining the laws and commands of the Shari'a in a simple, clear and detailed language. In the unique, matchless style particular to the Qur'an, they usually end their explanations with an elevated, powerful sentence or phrase related to belief, Divine Unity or the Hereafter, thus securing obedience to them by relating them to belief in God and the Last Day. By doing so, it also uses certain particular events as a basis upon which the universality of the Shari'a's laws is established.

For an understanding of the elevated aspect of eloquence and the subtleties to be in the phrases which come at the end of certain verses, such as *God has full power over everything; God has full knowledge of all things; He is the All-Glorious and All-Mighty, the All-Wise;* He is the All-Glorious and All-Mighty, the All-Compassionate, the reader may refer to the Second Ray of the Second Light in The Twenty-fifth Word.

While explaining Islam's secondary principles and social laws, the Qur'an draws its audience's attention suddenly to elevated, universal truths, leading them from the lesson of the Shari'a to the lesson of Divine Unity, and changes from a plain style to an elevated one. In so doing it demonstrates its aim of guidance on every occasion and shows itself to be a book of law and wisdom, a book of creeds, belief, reflection, invocation, prayer and the call to the Divine Message. Thus, the Qur'an's Madinan chapters display a most miraculous eloquence and purity of language which is different from the styles evident in the Makkan chapters.

For example, by modifying "Lord" with "your" (*your Lord*) or "the worlds" (*the Lord of the worlds*), the Qur'an declares, respectively, God's Oneness in His particular relationship with a person as his or her Lord or His Unity in His universal relationship with the whole creation. In introducing God as *the Lord of the worlds*, it introduces Him with all His Majesty, while in using *my Lord* or *your Lord*, it introduces Him from the perspective of His special attentiveness and compassion, expressing the former within the latter. Sometimes when it sees and fixes an atom in the pupil of the eye, it uses the same "hammer" to fix the sun in the sky and make it an eye of the heavens.

For example, in the expressions, *He has created the heavens and the earth* (57:4), and: *He makes the night pass into the day and He makes the day pass into the night* (57:6), it considers the understanding of common people, including those who are unlettered among them. However, in concludes the verses with *He has full knowledge of whatever lies in the bosoms* (57:6), and means: "Together with the magnificent creation and administration of the earth and the heavens, He has also full knowledge of whatever occurs to people's hearts." Thus the simple style of speech aimed at ordinary people is manifested here as an elevated and appealing address for the guidance of all.

QUESTION: Sometimes an important truth may remain hidden for superficial views. Also, the reason for ending the narration of an ordinary event with a universal principle or an aspect of Divine Unity cannot always be readily discerned. Some may consider this Qur'anic style defective. For example, after narrating how Prophet Joseph, upon him be peace, managed to detain his brother (12:69–76), the Qur'an mentions an exalted principle: *Above every owner of knowledge, there is (always) one more knowledgeable.* From the perspective of the rules of eloquence, this seems unrelated to the actual context. What is the reason for this?

ANSWER: The Qur'an is a book of belief, reflection and invocation, as well as a book of law, wisdom, and guidance; it therefore contains numerous "books." For this reason, in many pages and passages of long and medium-length suras, each of which is a small Qur'an, many teachings and aims are pursued. For example, in order to express the all-comprehensive and magnificent manifestations of Divine Lordship, since it is a kind of copy or reflection of the great Book of the Universe, the Qur'an gives instructions on every occasion concerning knowledge of God, aspects of Divine Unity and the truths of belief. Whenever a suitable occasion arises, no matter how insignificant it seems, the Qur'an expounds different teachings, thus using that occasion to present new instructions or to reveal certain universal rules or principles. This corresponds perfectly to the discussion and adds to the Qur'an's eloquence.

QUESTION: Be it implicitly or explicitly, the Qur'an dwells too much on Divine Unity, the Hereafter and God's Judgment of humanity. Why is this so?

ANSWER: The Qur'an was revealed to teach man about the Existence of God, Divine Unity and the absolute control that He exercises over the universe and the changes, upheavals and revolutions which take place in it; it was revealed to dispel all doubts concerning these truths and to break the obstinacy of those who continue to desist from confirming them. It was also revealed to instruct humanity, who has accepted to bear the Supreme Trust as vicegerent of the earth, which they are to rule and develop in accordance with Divine laws, in the mightiest and most important aspects of its duties concerning eternal happiness or perdition. In order to have humanity confirm the instructions of the Qur'an and assent to the most essential matters concerning them, even if the Qur'an were to focus attention on these matters a million times, it would still not be a waste of time or words, and they would be read and studied over and over again without causing the least boredom.

For example, we read in *Suratu'l-Buruj*:

> Those who believe and do good, righteous deeds, for them there are Gardens through which rivers flow. That is the great triumph. (85:11)

This verse teaches us that death, which stands ever present before us, is something that saves us, our world and our loved ones from eternal annihilation, for it leads us to a magnificent, everlasting life. Even if this verse were repeated billions of times, and if as much importance were attached to it as is attached to the whole of existence, it would still not be excessive enough to devalue or detract from its meaning. In teaching countless, invaluable matters of this sort and in trying to prove and make people aware of the awesome revolutions that continuously change and renew the universe, the Qur'an draws attention to those matters repeatedly, either in an explicit manner or through allusions. Since they are bounties like light, air, food and medicine – things which we always need and which require constant renewal and refreshment—the fact that they are repeated so often in the Qur'an is an instance of Divine grace.

Also, consider the following:

The Qur'an reiterates severely, angrily and emphatically such threatening verses as: *For the wrongdoers there is a painful punishment* (14:22); and:

As for those who disbelieve, for them is the fire of Hell (35:36). As discussed in detail in the *Risale-i Nur*, humanity's unbelief is such a heinous violation of the rights of the universe and most of its creatures that it angers the earth and infuriates the elements. It is for this reason that they smite unbelievers with floods and similar disasters.

As is stated explicitly in: *When they are cast into it, they will hear its raucous breath (by which they are sucked in) as it boils up, almost bursting with fury...* (67:7–8) Hell is so furious with the unbelievers that it is described as almost bursting with rage. If, in the face of such a heinous crime and such boundless aggression, and not from the perspective of the physical insignificance of humanity but of the enormity of the unbeliever's wrongdoing and the awesomeness of unbelief, and in order to show the importance of His subjects' rights as well as the ugliness and iniquity of unbelief, the Sovereign of the universe were to describe and denounce such crimes a billion times, it would still not count as a defect. Countless people have read these words every day for fourteen centuries with the utmost eagerness and without the slightest feeling of boredom or weariness.

Every day, for each person a world disappears and the door of a new world is opened. Thus by repeating *There is no deity but God* a thousand times out of need and with the desire to illuminate each of our transient worlds, we make each repetition a lamp for each changing scene. In the same way, one of the reasons the Qur'an repeats the Eternal Sovereign's threats and punishments so often is to seek to break humanity's obduracy and free them from their rebellious carnal soul. It thus seeks to prevent them from darkening the changing scenes and the freshly-recruited worlds, from disfiguring the images of them which are reflected in the mirror of their lives, and from turning against them those fleeting scenes that will testify for them in the Hereafter. For this reason, even Satan does not consider the Qur'an's severe and forceful repetition of its threats as being out of place. These threats demonstrate that the torments of Hell are pure justice for those who do not heed them.

Another example is the repetition of the stories of the Prophets, particularly that of Moses, upon him be peace.

Such stories contain many instances of wisdom and benefit. The Qur'an shows the Prophethood of all previous Prophets as an evidence of Muhammad's Messengership, upon him be peace and blessings. This means that from the point of view of truth, no-one can deny Muhammad's Messengership unless one denies all the other Prophets. Also, since not everyone can recite the whole of Qur'an every time they open it, it includes those stories, together with the essentials of belief, in almost all the long and medium-length suras, thus making each one like a miniature Qur'an. This is done because it is demanded by the principles of literary eloquence and also because the Qur'an wishes to show that Muhammad, upon him be peace and blessings, is the most important of people and the noblest phenomenon in the cosmos.

The ritual declaration of belief in Islam—the *Kalimatu't-Tawhid*—is *There is no deity but God and Muhammad is God's Messenger.* The Qur'an accords the highest status to the person of Muhammad and since part of this declaration—*Muhammad is God's Messenger*—points to four of the six pillars of belief, it has been considered equal to the first part, namely *There is no deity but God.* Muhammad's Messengership is the universe's greatest truth, as an individual he is the most noble of God's creatures, and his collective personality and sacred rank, known as the *Muhammadan Truth* is the brightest sun of both this world and the next. Among many of the proofs in the *Risale-i Nur* which show how worthy he is of occupying such an extraordinary position, the following are but a few:

According to the rule "The cause is like the doer," an amount of reward equal to the number of the good deeds that his community has ever done or will do in the future is added to the Prophet's account. Since he illuminated the universe with the light he brought, not only jinn, humanity and angels but also the heavens and the earth are indebted to him. We see clearly that the supplications of the plants and animals that they offer through the tongue of potentiality and need are accepted. This shows that the prayers of millions of righteous ones among Muhammad's community must be acceptable. They have been praying to God many times a day for centuries to bestow peace and blessings on him and give him the same reward as they have earned. Furthermore, his record of good deeds also contains countless lights from his followers' recitation of the Qur'an, each letter of which brings as many as ten, a hundred or a thousand rewards.

Knowing beforehand that his collective persona—the *Muhammadan Truth* —would be like a blessed, elaborate tree of Paradise in the future, and considering him as a person to be the seed of that majestic tree, the All-Knower of the Unseen attached the greatest importance to him in His Qur'an. In His Decree He emphasized the need for others to obey him and to gain the honor of his intercession by following his *Sunna* or path and confirmed it as the most important and serious matter of humanity.

Thus since the truths repeated in the Qur'an have such a great value, anyone with a sound, uncorrupted nature will testify that in its repetitions is a powerful and extensive miracle, unless one is afflicted with some sickness of the heart and malady of the conscience due to the plague of materialism, and is therefore included under the rule below:

A person denies the light of the sun because of his diseased eye,
A mouth denies the taste of sweet water on account of sickness.

ۈ ۈ

Two concluding notes

FIRST NOTE: Twelve years ago, I heard that a dangerous and obstinate unbeliever ordered the Qur'an to be translated so that people could see its reiterations and understand just what it really is. He also intended to substitute the translation for the original in the prescribed prayers. However, as the *Risale-i Nur* shows decisively, an exact translation is impossible, for no other language can preserve Arabic's virtues and fine points, as Arabic is very strict in syntax and grammar. No translation can replace the Qur'an's miraculous phrases and words, which are comprehensive in meaning, and each letter of which brings from 10 to 1,000 merits.

The *Risale-i Nur* also stopped the plan to have only translations of the Qur'an recited in mosques. But since hypocrites taught by that heretic continue to seek a way to extinguish the sun of the Qur'an in the name of Satan, I felt compelled to write the Flower of Emirdağ. As they do not allow me to meet with people, I have no knowledge of the latest developments.

SECOND NOTE: After our release from Denizli prison, I was sitting on the top floor of the well-known Hotel Şehir. The graceful dancing of the leaves, branches, and trunks of the poplar trees in the fine gardens opposite me, each with a rapturous motion like a circle of dervishes touched by a breeze, pained my heart, which was grievous and melancholy at being parted from the brothers and remaining alone. Suddenly I recollected autumn and winter, and a heedlessness overcame me. I so pitied those graceful poplars and living creatures swaying with perfect joy that my eyes filled with tears. Since they reminded me of the separations and deaths beneath the universe's ornamented veil, the grief at a world full of death and separation pressed down on me. Suddenly, the light of the Muhammadan Truth came and changed that grief and melancholy into joy. Indeed, I am eternally grateful to the person of Muhammad for the help and consolation that came to me at that time, for only a single instance of the boundless grace of that light for me, as for all believers and everyone. It was as follows:

Picturing those blessed and delicate creatures as trembling at death and separation, and going into non-existence in a fruitless season (the view of the heedless), weighed heavily on my feelings of passion for permanence, love of beauty, and compassion for fellow creatures and living things. It changed the world into a kind of hell, and the mind into an instrument of torture. Just at that point, the light that Muhammad brought as a gift for humanity lifted the veil and showed not extinction, non-existence, nothingness, futility, and separation, but meanings and purposes as numerous as the poplars' leaves, and, as demonstrated in the *Risale-i Nur*, results and duties that may be divided into certain types, as follows:

One type relates to the Majestic Maker's Names. For example, everyone applauds an engineer who makes an extraordinary machine: "What wonders God has willed. May God bless him (or her)." By carrying out its functions properly, the machine congratulates and applauds its engineer. Everything, every living creature, is such a machine and congratulates and applauds its Maker.

Another type of purpose for the lives of things like poplar trees is that they each resemble a text that, when studied, reveals knowledge of God to conscious living beings. Having left their meanings in such beings' minds, their forms in these beings' memories and on the tablets of the World of Symbols or Immaterial Forms, and on the records of the World of the Unseen and in the sphere of existence, they leave the material world for the World of the Unseen. In other words, they are stripped of apparent existence and gain many existences pertaining to meanings, the Unseen, and knowledge.

Since God's Existence and Knowledge encompass all things, there is no room in a believer's world for non-existence, eternal extinction, annihilation, and nothingness. But an unbeliever's world is full of non-existence, separation, and extinction. A famous proverb says: "Everything exists for the one for whom God exists; nothing exists for the one for whom God does not exist."

In short, then, just as belief saves us from eternal punishment when we die, it saves everyone's particular world from the darkness of extinction and nothingness. Unbelief, especially denying God, changes life's pleasure into painful poison, terminates the individual and his or her particular world with death, and casts such people into dark Hell-like pits. Those who prefer this world over the Hereafter should heed this. Let them find a solution for this or accept belief, and save themselves from a fearful, eternal loss.

> All-Glorified are You. We have no knowledge save what You have taught us. Surely You are the All-Knowing, the All-Wise.

Your brother who is in much need of your prayers and misses you greatly.

— Said Nursi

The
Twenty-sixth Word

The Twenty-sixth Word

Divine Destiny and Decree and human free will

There is not a thing but its treasuries are with Us, and We send it down but in a due and certain measure. (15:21)

Everything We have written down and kept in a Manifest Record. (36:12)

DESTINY AND HUMAN FREE WILL ARE A PAIR OF IMPORTANT RELATED matters. We will try to explain them in some respects in four topics.

First topic

Destiny and human free will, which mark the final limits of belief and being a Muslim, are related to believers' inner experiences and spiritual states; they are not of the kind of theoretical matters to be discussed scientifically. That is, believers attribute everything (and every act in the universe) to God, even their actions and selves. However, in order that they should not consider themselves to be free of responsibility and sins, human free will confronts them and says: "You are responsible and under obligation, therefore you are accountable for your actions." Then, so that they should not feel proud of their good deeds, attainments and personal perfections, Divine Destiny stands before them and warns: "Know your limits, it is not you who does these." Thus, marking the final limits of belief and being a Muslim, Divine Destiny and human free will have been included among the articles of belief to save the human carnal soul from conceit and unaccountability, respectively. They are not scientific matters which will provide grounds for obdurate evil-commanding carnal souls to attribute their evils to Destiny and clean themselves of their responsibility, and to become proud of the achievements bestowed on them.

Common people who have not progressed spiritually may have an excuse to make reference to Destiny; they may relate any past events and calamities to Destiny so as not to fall into despair and grief. However, no one can be absolved of their sins and exempted from their obligations by attributing everything to Destiny. Belief in Destiny has been included among the pillars of faith to preserve us from self-conceit, not to absolve us from responsibility and obligations; and human free will has been recognized among the articles of creed to be the source of evils and sins, not to be the source of virtues and attainments so that people exult in and become proud of them.

As declared in the Qur'an, we are completely responsible for our sins, for only we will and commit them. Evils and sins mean and cause much disorder and destruction, and so may merit a terrible punishment. They are like, for example, destroying a house by striking a match. On the other hand, we have no right to boast about our good acts since we have only a minute share in them—Divine Compassion demands them, and the Lord's Power creates them. God guides us to good acts and makes us will and do them. We own our acts only by belief and praying to deserve them, consciously believing in the necessity to perform them and be pleased with what God has ordained. However, just as some substances liable to decomposition go bad and putrefy in the pure, bright light of the sun—and this is because of their nature or disposition—, so our carnal soul wishes sins and evils either through its nature and disposition or through choice, and we commit them. But it is God Almighty Who creates these evils due to a law He established for our life and for the universe, and for many good purposes. Thus, since it is we ourselves who wish, cause and commit evils, we are responsible for them. As for their creation, it is good on account of many of its results which are good. Based on this subtle reality, *willing and committing evil deeds is evil, whereas creating them is not*. Although we derive great benefit from rain, those who have been harmed by it due to their faults cannot deny that rain contains God's grace for all people. Although there may be some evil in creating our evil deeds, creation is by its very nature absolutely good and contains many instances of good (for the universe's general operation, life, and for the person who wills and commits that evil). To abandon greater good for a minor evil becomes a greater evil. Ugliness in our human acts lies in our will and potential, not in God's creating it.

As Divine Destiny is absolutely free of evil and ugliness in relation to results, it also is exempt from injustice on account of causes. Divine Destiny always considers the primary cause, not the apparent secondary cause, and always does justice. On the other hand, we judge according to apparent causes and draw wrong conclusions. For example, a court may imprison an innocent person for theft. However, Divine Destiny actually passes this judgment because of that person's real crime, such as murder, that has remained unknown. So while the court unjustly jailed this person for a crime that he or she did not commit, Divine Destiny justly punished that person for his or her secret crime.

From this example, we see that Divine Destiny and creation is just, while we are liable to do injustice. Divine Destiny and Creation is absolutely free of evil and ugliness at the beginning and end of all events, and on account of cause and results.

QUESTION: If our partial free will has no creative ability and gives us only a nominal share in our acts, why does the Qur'an of miraculous exposition show humans to be rebellious and hostile to the Creator of the heavens and the earth? Why does the Creator of the heavens and the earth take our rebellion so seriously and come to the aid of His believing servants together with His angels?

ANSWER: Unbelief, rebellion, and sinfulness mean destruction. Vast destruction can result from a tiny act of disobedience, just as a vessel may sink due to the helmsman's negligence, despite the crew's efforts to save it. Human free will, no matter how limited and when guided by unbelief and sinfulness, can cause terrible results. Unbelief is only one evil, but it is such a great sin that it renders the entire universe worthless and futile, contradicts creation's witnessing to God's Existence and/or Oneness, and denies and disparages the Divine Names' manifestations.

Given this, it is entirely just for God to take unbelief seriously, to threaten unbelievers severely in the name of creation and the Divine Names, and to condemn them to Hell's eternal torment. Since unbelievers and sinful people cause vast corruption, believers need God's succor against them. A mischievous child can set a house on fire although it is guarded by ten strong people, and those guards may need to ask the child's parents, even the government, to prevent the child from committing such a crime. So too do believers need the help of God Almighty against rebellious and sinful people.

In short, believers can speak of Divine Destiny and human free will when their belief is perfect and they are mature enough to perceive that all creation, including themselves, is at God's disposal. Believers assume their responsibilities because they have free will, and glorify God by proclaiming Him free of any involvement with their sins. Always aware that they are

God's servants, they try to follow all Divine commandments. They remain thankful to God by ascribing all of their good deeds to Divine Destiny and never boasting about them. In addition, they find the strength to bear all misfortunes by discerning Destiny's role in them.

It is not proper for those who neglect Divine commandments to argue about Divine Destiny and human free will, since their defective thinking will lead them to ascribe creation to causes and ignore God. They appropriate all their skills and good deeds, regarding them as having originated with themselves, and attribute their defects and failures to Destiny. They also impute to Destiny the responsibility for their evils. This makes the discussion of Divine Destiny and human free will meaningless and reduces their discussion to a trick employed by the own evil-commanding soul (*nafs ammara*) to save it from responsibility; this is entirely contrary to the wisdom in them.

Second topic

What follows is a profound, scholarly discussion addressing scholars in particular. Divine Destiny and human free will can be reconciled in seven ways:

FIRST WAY: Creation's order and harmony witness that God is All-Wise and All-Just. Wisdom and Justice demand that, even though we do not know its exact nature, we possess free will so that we may be rewarded or punished for our acts. Just as we do not know many of the numerous aspects of the All-Just and Wise One's wisdom, our ignorance of how human free will can be reconciled with Divine Destiny does not mean that it does not exist and is not reconcilable with Destiny.

SECOND WAY: Every person feels that he or she has free will and perceives its existence. Knowing something's nature is different from knowing that it exists. The existence of many things is obvious to us, even though we do not understand their nature. Our free will may be one of them. Also, existence is not restricted to the number of things known to us, so our ignorance of something does not indicate its non-existence.

THIRD WAY: Human free will does not contradict Divine Destiny; rather, Destiny confirms its existence. For Divine Destiny is in some respects identical with Divine Knowledge, Which parallels our free will, in determining our actions. Thus It confirms free will.[147]

---

[147] That is, God has pre-knowledge of everything, including our acts. However, we do not do something or act in some way because God has pre-knowledge of it. So God's pre-knowledge of our acts and our acting in the way He knows confirms our free will and shows its reconcilability with Destiny. (Tr.)

FOURTH WAY: Divine Destiny is a kind of knowledge, and knowledge is dependent on the thing known. In other words, conceptual knowledge is not fundamental to determining the external existence of what is known. In its external existence, the known depends upon the Divine Power acting through the Divine Will.

Past eternity (*azal*) is not, as people imagine, just the starting-point of time and therefore essential for a thing's existence. In fact, past eternity is like a mirror that reflects the past, present, and future all at once. Excluding themselves from time's passage, people tend to imagine a limit for past time that extends through a certain chain of things. They call this past eternity. Such a method of reasoning is neither right nor acceptable. The following subtle point may clarify this matter. Imagine that you are holding a mirror. Everything reflected on the right represents the past, while everything reflected on the left represents the future. The mirror can reflect only one direction, since it cannot show both sides simultaneously while you are holding it. For it to do so, you would have to rise so high above your original position that left and right become one and there is no longer any difference between first and last, beginning or end.

In some respects, Divine Destiny is identical with Divine Knowledge. It is described in a Prophetic Tradition as containing all times and events in a single point, where first and last, beginning and end, what has happened and what will happen are united into one. Neither we nor our viewpoint and reasoning are excluded from It, so that we could imagine a final point for It in the past and think of It like a mirror containing and reflecting only the space of the past.

FIFTH WAY: In the view of Destiny, cause and effect cannot be separated. This means that a certain cause is destined to produce a certain effect. For this reason, it cannot be argued that killing someone with a gun is acceptable because the victim was destined to die at that time and would have died even if he or she had not been shot. Such an argument is baseless, for the victim actually is destined to die as a result of being shot. The argument that he or she would have died even without being shot means that the victim died without a cause. If this were so, we could not explain how he or she died.

There are not two kinds of Destiny—one for the cause and one for the effect. Destiny is one. Deceived by such a paradox, the Mu'tazili school concluded that the victim would not have died if he or she had not been shot (forgetting that it was the victim's destiny to be shot to death), while the Mujabbira (Fatalists) argued that he or she would have died even without being shot (ignoring the cause). The *Ahlu's-Sunna wal-Jama'a* (the broad majority of Muslims) follow the correct view: "We do not know whether or not the victim would have died if he or she had not been shot."

SIXTH WAY: According to the followers of Imam al-Maturidi, a subschool of the *Ahlu's-Sunna wal-Jama'a*, human free will is based on inclinations. (An inclination is not something so forceful as to compel one to do something.) It has only a nominal and relative value and existence and therefore can be attributed to servants. The *Ash'aris*, however, do not regard human free will as consisting of inclinations, for they consider inclinations to have a real or substantial existence. According to them, we have only a nominal or theoretical control of inclinations in the name of free will.

Something with nominal and relative existence does not require a perfect, efficient cause that would annul human free will in our actions. Rather, when its cause acquires the weight of preference, it might have an actual existence. In that case, the Qur'an commands us to do or avoid something. If we created our own actions, we would be their ultimate cause and our will would be cancelled. According to the science of established principles or methodology and logic, something will not exist if it is not necessary. In other words, there has to be a real complete, creative cause before something can exist. But as a complete cause makes the existence of something compulsory, there can be no room for choice.

Question: Our actions are the result of our preference between two alternatives, which is of nominal significance. If a necessary cause that would force a preference does not exist, the act of preference takes place without a necessary cause. Is this not a logical impossibility that contradicts one of the most important principles of theology?

Answer: We can make a preference without a necessary cause, for it is an attribute of our free will to do such things. However, something cannot be preferable by itself, nor can it make a choice out of alternatives by itself without an external agent.

Question: Since God creates the act of murder, why is one who kills called a murderer?

Answer: According to Arabic grammar, the active participle functioning as the subject is derived from the infinitive, which denotes a relative affair or deed, not from the word which denotes the result of the action done by the active participle and which expresses an established fact. Thus as the person denoted by the infinitive commits the murder, he or she is called the murderer. Since we want to do something and so do it, we are the doers or agents of our acts and so responsible for them. As we are the ones who kill, we should be called the murderer. God creates our acts by giving them external existence; He does not perform them. That is, He is the One Who creates death as the result of our act of murdering. If this were not the case, our free will would be meaningless.

SEVENTH WAY: Although our free will cannot cause something to happen, Almighty God, the absolutely Wise One, uses it to bring His will into effect and guides us in whatever direction we wish. He in effect says: "My servant! Whichever way you wish to take with your will, I will take you there. Therefore, the responsibility is yours!" For example, if a child riding on your shoulder asks you to take him up a high mountain, and you do so, he might catch a cold. How could he blame you for that cold, as he was the one who asked to go there? In fact, you might even punish him because of his choice. In a like manner, Almighty God, the Most Just of Judges, never coerces His servants into doing something, and so His Will considers our free will in our actions.

In sum, as human beings, we have a degree of free will. Although it is so limited that it makes almost no contribution to our good acts, it can cause deadly sins and destruction. So use your free will for your benefit by praying to God continuously. If you do so, you may enjoy the blessings of Paradise, a fruit of the chain of good deeds, and attain to eternal happiness, which a flower of them. In addition to praying, always seek God's forgiveness so that you may refrain from evil and be saved from Hell's torments, a fruit of the accursed chain of evil deeds. Prayer and trusting God greatly strengthen our inclination to do good, and repentance and seeking God's forgiveness defeat our inclination to evil and break its transgressions.

Third topic

Believing in Divine Destiny is a pillar of belief. That is, everything is determined by God, the All-Mighty. While there are countless proofs of Destiny, we will make only some introductory remarks to show just how important this pillar is for creation.

The Qur'an specifically explains that everything is predetermined and recorded after it comes into existence, as in: *Not a thing, fresh or withered, wet or dry, but it is in a Manifest Book* (6:59), and many other verses. This is confirmed by the universe, this macro-Qur'an of the Divine Power, through its creational and operational signs like order, harmony, balance, forming and shaping, adornment and distinguishing. All seeds, fruit pits, measured proportions, and forms show that everything is predetermined before its earthly existence. Each seed or fruit pit has a protective case formed in *the factory of Kaf Nun*,[148] into which Divine Destiny has inserted a tree's or plant's life-history. Divine Power uses the atoms, according to the measure established by Divine Destiny, to cause the particular seed to grow miraculously into the particular tree. This means that the tree's future life-history is as though written in its seed.

Individuals and species differ, but they are formed from the identical basic materials. Plants and animals grow from the same constituent basic elements, yet display such harmony and proportion amid abundant diversity that we can only conclude that each one has been given its unique form and measure by Divine Power according to the measure established for it by Divine Destiny. For example, consider how vast and innumerable are the inanimate atoms that shift, cohere, and separate so that this seed grows into this tree or that drop of semen grows into that animal.

Since Divine Destiny is manifested to this extent in visible material things, the forms with which things are clothed over time and the states they acquire through their motions also depend on Divine Destiny's ordering. A seed displays Destiny in two ways. The first is by showing the Manifest Book (*Kitabun Mubin*), another title for Divine Will and God's creational and operational laws of the universe. The second is by showing the Manifest Record (*Imamun Mubin*), another title for Divine Knowledge and Command.[149] If we regard these two as different manifestations of Divine Destiny, the former can be understood and referred to as "Actual Destiny" and the latter as "Formal (Theoretical) Destiny." The future physical form a tree will assume with all its roots, trunk, branches, leaves, blossoms, and fruits can be understood as its Actual Destiny. Its general (theoretical) form, represented by its seed and comprised of all the life stages it will pass through, is its Formal Destiny. Such manifestations of Divine Destiny, so easily observed in a tree's life, illustrate how everything has been predetermined in a Record before its worldly existence.

On the other hand, all fruits (signs of the Manifest Book and Manifest Record), and all human memories indicating the Supreme Preserved Tablet

---

[148] The Qur'an says that His Command, when He wills a thing to be, is to say *"Be,"* *and it is* (36:82). The original Arabic words are *kun fa yakun*. In the Islamic tradition, creation is considered to result from the Divine Command *kun*. The letters *k* (*kaf*) and *n* (*nun*) make up the word *kun* (be). (Tr.)

[149] See also p. 565, the footnote 170.

(*Lawhun Mahfuz*), prove that just as everything has been prerecorded, everything's life-history has been recorded. Each tree's life-history is recorded in each fruit, the outcome of its life. Humanity's life-history, including events occurring in the external world, is recorded in human memory. Thus Divine Power registers our deeds with the Pen of Destiny by lodging it in our memory so that we will remember them on the Day of Reckoning. We should also realize that this world of transience and upheaval contains numerous "mirrors" pertaining to eternity, in which the All-Powerful and Wise One depicts and makes permanent the identities of mortals. There also are many tablets upon which the All-Knowing Preserver records the eternal meanings of transient beings.

In short, while plants (the simplest and lowest level of life) are completely dependent upon Divine Destiny, human life (the highest level) also has been determined by Destiny. Just as raindrops indicate a cloud, water trickles disclose a spring and receipts and vouchers suggest a ledger's existence, so fruits, sperms, seeds, and forms indicate the Manifest Book and the Manifest Record or the (Supreme) Preserved Tablet. The former is a title for or a notebook of Divine Will and God's creational and operational laws of the universe, while the latter represents Divine Knowledge.

While a living creature is being formed, atoms move continuously, travel to their destinations by complicated routes, and remain there. Their movement results in many benefits, uses, and instances of wisdom. Evidently, Divine Destiny appoints an apparent measure and form for each thing. If this is so, even the immaterial states of living beings result in certain fruits. Thus Divine Power is the agent, and Divine Destiny is the pattern upon which Divine Power writes the book of meanings. We see that each movement and stage experienced by a living creature are predetermined by Divine Destiny. Moreover, its whole life forms a harmonious unity.

Since Divine Destiny has appointed a destination and a certain purposeful result for everything, and since all of its life-stages also have been predetermined by the same Destiny, the life-history of humanity, the most perfect fruit of the Tree of Creation and ruler of the earth and bearer of the Supreme Trust, is more subject than anything else to the law of Divine Destiny.

QUESTION: If we are so bound by Divine Destiny, is belief in Destiny not a burden for the heart and spirit, which are so desirous of activity and self-perfection?

ANSWER: Absolutely not! Rather, it provides the spirit with relief, security, and comfort. If we do not believe in Destiny, the spirit has to endure a burden as heavy as the earth for the sake of an illusory, temporary, and very limited freedom. For we are connected with the whole universe, and cherish limitless desires and ambitions, none of which we can satisfy on our own. Eventually, we will be left alone with insupportable trouble and torment. Belief in Destiny places this burden on the vessel of Destiny, and allows the heart and spirit to work for their perfection with perfect ease and freedom. It only takes away the carnal soul's illusory freedom and breaks its tyrannical hold over us. Belief in Destiny gives us a pleasure and happiness beyond description.

Consider this comparison: Two people enter a splendid palace. One does not recognize the king and tries to live there on theft and usurpation. However, he finds it hard to control the palace and its inhabitants, take care of the garden, carry out the king's affairs with the necessary calculation and management, operate the machines, and feed the animals. As a result, this "paradise" turns into "hell" for him. Finally, he is imprisoned because of his defective management and corruption. The other person recognizes the king and is aware of being his guest. He perceives and believes that the affairs of the palace and the garden are carried out under the king's rule and authority. Understanding that the king assumes full responsibility for governing the palace, he enjoys the pleasures of living there and does not interfere. He overlooks certain things that appear disagreeable, trusting in the king's compassion and his administration's justice and wisdom. As a result, he lives a contented and pleasant life. Reflect on this comparison and understand the adage: Whoever believes in Destiny is free from anxiety.

Fourth topic

QUESTION: The First Topic proves that whatever is determined by Destiny is good, that even apparently evil deeds are actually good, and that ugly things are essentially beautiful. But do the calamities and tribulations suffered in this world not contradict this?

ANSWER: O my carnal soul and my friend, you feel agony because of your strong connections with existence and affection toward beings. Existence is entirely good, for it generates every beauty and perfection; non-existence [which absorbs every good like black holes] is purely evil, for all sin and misfortune originate in it. Given this, whatever contains a hint of non-existence contains an element of evil. So, life, the most brilliant light of existence, becomes stronger as it is confronted with different circumstances. It is purified and perfected through contradictory events and happenings, and produces the desired results by assuming different qualities. Thus it testifies to the impresses of Names of the Giver of life. It is because of this subtle reality that living creatures pass through many states and experience pains, tribulations and hardship, through which the lights of existence are continuously renewed in their lives, and the darkness of non-existence draws distant and their lives are purified. In quality and as conditions, idleness, inertia, and monotony are aspects of non-existence. Monotony reduces even the greatest pleasure to nothing.

In short, since life displays the impresses of God's All-Beautiful Names, everything occurring in it is beautiful. Consider this: A very rich and infinitely skilled clothes designer uses an ordinary model to display his works of art in return for wages. He requires the model to dress in a jeweled and artistically fashioned garment that illustrates his work's art and his invaluable wealth. He continues to modify the garment while the model wears it. Does the model have any right to say: "Your orders to bow and stand up are causing me trouble. Your cutting and shortening of this garment, which makes me more beautiful, spoils my beauty." Can the model accuse the designer of treating him unkindly and unfairly?

Similarly, in order to display the impresses of His All-Beautiful Names, the Maker of Majesty, the peerless All-Originating, alters within numerous circumstances the garment of existence He clothes on living creatures, bejeweled with senses, reason, intellect, and heart. Circumstances that appear to be calamitous and painful are actually rays of Divine Mercy within gleams of Wisdom and contain subtle beauties. They show the acts and impresses of the Divine All-Beautiful Names.

Conclusion

This consists of Five Paragraphs which silenced the Old Said's obstinate, proud, and conceited soul, and compelled it to submit.

FIRST PARAGRAPH: Since things exist and have been made with skill, a Supreme Maker must exist. If everything's existence is not ascribed to One Being, the existence of a single thing would become as difficult as the existence of all things. But if everything is ascribed to One Being, the creation of all things becomes as easy as the creation of one thing. Since One Being has created the earth and the heavens, for sure that All-Wise and Skillful Creator would not allow disorder to arise by allowing others to create and administer living beings, who are the fruits and aims of the heavens and the earth, and so He would not mock His Divine purpose for creation. He would certainly not give others their worship and thanks.

SECOND PARAGRAPH: O my haughty carnal soul! You are like a grapevine. The vine itself has not attached the bunches of grapes; someone else has attached them, so do not boast.

THIRD PARAGRAPH: O my ostentatious carnal soul! Do not be proud of your services to God's religion. As stated in a Prophetic Tradition, God may strengthen this religion by means of a dissolute person. You are not pure, so regard yourself as that dissolute person. Purge yourself of self-admiration and pride by considering your service and worship as thanksgiving for God's past favors to you, a duty required by your humanity and a consequence of your being God's work of art.

FOURTH PARAGRAPH: If you want to acquire knowledge of the truth and true wisdom, try to attain knowledge of God. For all truths and realities of creation consist in the rays of the Divine Name of the Ultimate Truth and Ever-Constant and the manifestations of His Names and Attributes. The reality of each human being and every existence, whether material or spiritual, substantial or accidental, originates in the light of one of His Names. Otherwise they would be mere forms without any substantial reality and truth.

O my carnal soul! If you are attached to this temporary worldly life and try to flee from death, know that life is the present moment. The past and what existed therein have passed away, and the future and what will exist therein is still non-existent. Thus the material life upon which you rely is of momentary duration. Some truth-knowing scholars even say that life consists of an instant. For this reason, some saints believe that the world is non-existent on account of itself. As this is the reality, abandon the corporeal, carnal life and rise to the level of life of the heart, spirit, and innermost faculties. See what a broad sphere of life they have. The past and future, which are dead for you, are living for them; they are existent and full of life. Given this, O my carnal soul, shed tears like my heart, and cry out and say:

I am mortal, so I do not want the mortal.
I am impotent, so I do not desire the impotent.
I surrendered my spirit to the All-Merciful, so I desire none else.
I want only one who will remain my friend forever.
I am but an insignificant particle, but I desire an everlasting sun.
I am nothing in essence, but I wish for the whole of creation.

FIFTH PARAGRAPH: This paragraph occurred to me in Arabic and so was written in Arabic. It expresses one of the 33 stations of reflection upon "God is the All-Great" (*Allahu Akbar*).

God is the All-Great: He is the All-Powerful, the All-Knowing, the All-Wise, the All-Munificent, the All-Compassionate, the All-Beautiful, the Eternal Inscriber. The truth and reality of these worlds, in whole and in parts, and in "sheets," and layers, as well as the truths and realities of these beings as a whole and individually, and in their existence and continuation, are but:

- the lines drawn by the Pen of God's Decree and Destiny, and His ordering and determining with knowledge and wisdom;

- and the skillful inscriptions made with the compasses of His Knowledge and Wisdom, and forming and arranging, with art and favor;

- and the embellishments of the shining "hand" of His Art, Favor, decorating, and illuminating, with grace and munificence;

- and the flowers of the subtleties of His Favor and Munificence, and making Himself known and loved, with mercy and bountifulness;

- and the fruits of the effusions of His Mercy and Bountifulness, Pitying and Affection, with grace and perfection.

- and the radiations of the manifestations of His Grace, Beauty and Perfection, as attested to by the disappearance of mirrors (of beings) and the flux of objects despite the permanent manifestation and constant reflection of the transcendent, eternal Grace and Beauty throughout all seasons, centuries, and ages, and by the perpetual bestowal of bounties throughout the passage of creatures, days, and people.

Indeed, a perfect work points, for an intellectual one, to a perfect act; a perfect act points, for an intelligent one, to a perfect title; a perfect title self-evidently points to a perfect attribute; a perfect attribute necessarily points to a perfect capacity; and a perfect capacity certainly points to the perfection of the Essence, the Agent, in a way proper for that Essence, Who is the Most Evident Truth.

The mortality of mirrors (wherein manifestations are reflected) and the decay of crea-tures, despite the perpetual manifestation (of the Titles, Attributes, and acts) in utmost abun-dance, is a clear sign and convincing argument that the manifest beauty does not belong to those on whom they are manifested. This is a most eloquent explanation and evident proof of the abstract Beauty and ever-renewed Benevolence, of the Necessarily Existent and the All-Loving, Permanent One.

> O God. Bestow blessings on our master Muhammad from past eternity to future eternity to the number of things encompassed by Divine Knowledge, and on his Family and Companions, and bestow peace on peace.

Addendum

In the Name of God, the All-Merciful, the All-Compassionate.

(This addendum is very important and benefits everyone.)

There are many ways to Almighty God. All true ways have been derived from the Qur'an, but some are safer, more comprehensive, and direct than others. The way I have derived from the Qur'an depends upon our perception and admission of our innate impotence or helplessness and poverty before God's Might and Riches, and upon affection and reflection.

This way is as sure as the way of love, or even safer, for it elevates you so as to be loved by God on account of your sincere devotion to Him. Your perception and admission of your impotence leads you to the Divine Name the All-Merciful. Affection is more effective than love and leads to the Name the All-Compassionate. Reflection is brighter and more comprehensive than love, and leads to the Name the All-Wise. This way does not resemble the way of those Sufi orders that have developed a ten-step method to purify and sharpen their members' ten outer and inner senses or faculties, and that prefer silent recitation and invocation. Neither does it resemble those orders that practice public recitation and seek to purify their members from all defects contained in the soul's seven stations. Let it not be misunderstood. Our way means and demands the sincere admission of one's innate impotence and poverty and one's sinfulness before God; it does not mean making show of one's impotence, poverty and sinfulness before people.

Our way consists of four steps and is the truth (*haqiqa*), rather than a Sufi way (*tariqa*). It is the Shari'a. Its fundamental principles consist in following the Sunna, performing the religious obligations, avoiding the major sins, performing the Prescribed Prayers properly and carefully, and saying words of praise, glorification, and exaltation of God after every Prayer. The steps are as follows:

- The first step is expressed by: *Do not justify and hold yourselves pure* (53:32)
- The second step is indicated by: *Be not like those who are oblivious of God—and so He has made them oblivious of their own selves* (59:19)
- The third step is pointed to by: *Whatever good happens to you is from God; whatever evil befalls you is from yourself* (4:79)
- The fourth step is shown by: *Everything is perishable (and so perishing) except His Face (and His good pleasure)* (28:88).

The following is a brief explanation of these four steps.

FIRST STEP: We should never regard ourselves as infallible and sinless. As humans, we love ourselves first on account of our nature and innate disposition. We love our own selves before all else, so much so that we sacrifice anything for ourselves. We praise ourselves as if praising an object of worship, and hold ourselves free of faults and defects. We do our utmost in order not to ascribe any faults to us, and defend ourselves so passionately that it is as if we deify our selves. We exploit the faculties given to us for praising and thanking God by using them to glorify ourselves and resemble him who is mentioned in: *who has taken his lusts and fancies for his deity* (25:43). We praise, rely on, and admire ourselves. To be purified of such attitudes, we should never hold ourselves pure; instead, we should regard ourselves as fallible and susceptible to error.

SECOND STEP: As the verse: *Be not like those who are oblivious of God— and so He has made them oblivious of their own selves* teaches, we are oblivious and unaware of ourselves. We do not want to remember death, while we always consider others mortal. We hold back when confronting hardship and rendering service, but believe that you should be the first one rewarded when it is time to collect the wages. Purifying ourselves at this step involves carrying out our responsibilities, being prepared for death, and forgetting ourselves when it comes to pleasures, ambitions and collecting wages.

THIRD STEP: As the verse: *Whatever good happens to you is from God; whatever evil befalls you is from yourself* teaches, our evil-commanding soul always ascribes good to itself and feels conceited. In reality, we should perceive our defects, insufficiency, impotence and poverty and then thank and praise God for whatever good we can do and whatever virtue we have. According to the meaning of: *He is indeed prosperous who has grown it in purity* (91:9), our purification at this step consists of knowing that our perfection lies in confessing our imperfection, our power in perceiving our helplessness, and our wealth in accepting our essential poverty and inadequacy.

FOURTH STEP: As the verse: *Everything is perishable except His Face (and His good pleasure)* teaches, the carnal, evil-commanding soul considers itself completely free and existent in its own right. It even claims Lordship for itself and harbors hostile rebelliousness against its Creator, the All-Worshipped. We can save ourselves from this perilous situation only by perceiving the truth that everything, with respect to its own self, is essentially non-existent, contingent, ephemeral, and mortal. But in respect of being like a letter in a word to signify something other than itself, and in respect of being a mirror reflecting the All-Majestic Maker's Names and entrusted with various duties, it is existent, experiencing and experienced.

Here, we can purify ourselves by perceiving that our existence lies in acknowledging our essential non-existence. Considering ourselves self-existent, we fall into the darkest pit of non-existence. In other words, relying on our personal existence and thus ignoring the Real Creator causes our ephemeral, firefly-like personal existence to be drowned in the infinite darkness of non-existence. But if we abandon pride and egoism and recognize that we are only a mirror in which the Real Creator manifests Himself, we attain to infinite existence. One who discovers the Necessarily Existent Being, the manifestations of Whose Names cause all things to come into existence, is counted as having found everything.

Conclusion

This way is the method of recognizing our innate impotence and poverty, as well as that of affection and reflective thought. This four-stage way leads to its objective rapidly, since it is the easiest and most direct way. Recognizing our incompetence or impotence leads us to be freed from our evil-commanding soul's influence and rely on the All-Powerful One of Majesty alone. Love, regarded as the quickest route, can lead to the true Beloved only after we have directed our love to Him and love others on account of Him. This method is safer than other ways, for it enables us to recognize our limits, and find within us nothing other than impotence, poverty and defects, and it saves us from high-flown claims.

This way is a main highway, very broad and more universal, for it allows us to attain a constant awareness of God's presence without denying or ignoring the universe's actual existence, as demanded by the followers of the Way of the Unity of Being (*Wahdatu'l-Wujud*) or the Unity of the Witnessed (*Wahdatu'sh-Shuhud*), respectively. Instead, it admits the universe's actual existence, as proclaimed in the Qur'an, but it ascribes it directly to the All-Majestic Creator. It admits that all things consist in the manifestations of Divine Names, devoted to His service, and are charged with being mirrors reflecting them. It saves from heedlessness by allowing us to travel to Him through everything, by making us always aware of His presence.

In short, this way considers beings as neither existent nor working on their own behalf; rather, it states that beings function as signs and officials of God, the All-Mighty.

The
Twenty-seventh Word

The Twenty-seventh Word

> Ijtihad in Islamic jurisprudence
> The Prophet's Companions

NOTE: To put in their place those who overstep the limits in this matter, the following treatise on *ijtihad*[150] is included here at the request of two of my brothers.

In the Name of God, the All-Merciful, the All-Compassionate.

If they would but refer it to the Messenger and those with authority among them, certainly those who are capable of deductions among them would know it and bring it to light. (4:83)

The door to *ijtihad* is open, but six obstacles block the way to it.

Six obstacles

 IRST OBSTACLE: DURING A WINTER STORM OR A FLOOD, WHEN EVEN smaller holes are closed, to open new and larger ones is unreasonable. Likewise, under the onslaught of a mighty flood, making openings in a wall to repair it leads to being drowned. So, at this time of the un-Islamic and even anti-Islamic practices, the onslaught of customs from Europe, the legion of religious innovations and the destruction of misguidance, to open new holes and invasion routes in the citadel of Islam in the name of *ijtihad* is a crime against Islam.

---

[150] *Ijtihad* means, after acquiring the required knowledge and competence, deducing rules of law through juristic reasoning from original sources—the Qur'an and Sunna—if they present no decisive ruling on a particular matter. (Tr.)

SECOND OBSTACLE: The essentials of Islam are not subject to *ijtihad*. They are specified and definite, and are like basic food and sustenance without which life is impossible. At present, they are abandoned and neglected. We must strive to restore and revitalize them with all our strength. The principles which early generations of Islam established for deduction of new rules from the main legal sources and the rules they deduced with perfect authority and pure intention are adequate for almost all times and places. Therefore, abandoning them and seeking new ones in an indulgent and fanciful fashion is a harmful innovation and a betrayal of Islam.

THIRD OBSTACLE: Various products are sought in the marketplace according to season and demand. This is also true of humanity's social life and civilization as well. For example, in our age people seek to secure their worldly life and pursue philosophy and politics, and so the demand for those "products" increases. Attention is given to them and minds are preoccupied with them. However, during the early generations of Islam, the most sought-after "product" was learning from the Word of the Creator of the heavens and the earth what He approves of and wants from us, and how to obtain eternal happiness in the world of the Hereafter, the doors of which had been opened so widely by the light of Prophethood and the Qur'an that they could not be closed.

At that time, all minds, hearts, and souls were focused on understanding the things approved of by the Lord of the heavens and the earth. All conversations, discussions, correspondences, and events were devoted to that point. Therefore, whoever had the capacity was naturally and automatically taught by the ethos of the time. It was as if everything were a teacher that prepared one's mind and soul, and developed one's capacity for *ijtihad*. Such a natural and automatic kind of teaching was so enlightening that one could engage in *ijtihad* almost without requiring the necessary formal education. With a match-like capacity ready to ignite, such a person displayed the meaning of "light upon light" and quickly became a *mujtahid* (a practitioner of *ijtihad*).

But now European civilization is dominant. We face naturalistic philosophy's heavy pressure, and the conditions of modern life scatter our minds and hearts and divide our efforts and cares. Our minds are estranged from spiritual issues. Thus even if one was as intelligent as Sufyan ibn Uyayna, a great *mujtahid* who memorized the Qur'an at the age of 4 and later held discussions with scholars, in contrast with the time of Sufyan, one would now need ten times longer to become a *mujtahid*. If Sufyan became qualified to perform *ijtihad* in ten years, we would need a hundred years. This is because Sufyan's natural study began at the age of reason. His capacity developed gradually, was sharpened, and reached the degree where he could learn from everything. In the end, he became like a match (ready to ignite and give light).

As for his counterparts in our own time, our capacity has grown too dull to qualify for being a *mujtahid*. Our thoughts are absorbed in philosophy, our minds preoccupied with politics, and our hearts giddy with worldly life. We have removed our faculties from *ijtihad* to the degree of our preoccupation with modern sciences, and have remained backward in regard to it to the extent that we have concentrated on physical and worldly matters. Therefore we cannot say: "I am as intelligent as him. Why can't I be on a level with him?" We have no right to say this, and we cannot be on the same level as Sufyan.

FOURTH OBSTACLE: A living body has an inherent tendency to expand and grow. Since this tendency is inherent in or comes from within the body, it serves for the body's development and perfection. If this tendency is an external intervention, it will tear up the body's skin and destroy it; it is not a growth and development. Similarly, if, like the pious, righteous early generations, those who have entered the sphere of Islam through the door of perfect piety, righteousness and God's consciousness, and conform to Islam's essentials strictly have the inclination to expand and the desire to engage in *ijtihad*, it is a virtue and serves for perfection. But this inclination and desire in those who neglect Islam's essentials, prefer the world over the afterlife, and occupy themselves with materialistic philosophy destroys Islam's body and leads to breaking away from the Shari'a.

FIFTH OBSTACLE: The Law of Islam is heavenly and revealed. Since *ijtihad* uncovers its hidden rules and commandments, it also is heavenly. However, three factors now make *ijtihad* worldly:

First factor: The cause for establishing a rule differs from the wisdom and benefit expected of it. Wisdom or benefit is the reason for its preference, while the cause requires its existence. For example, traveling Muslims can shorten their Prayers. The cause for this Divine dispensation is traveling, and the underlying wisdom is the hardship of traveling. Prayers are shortened even if no hardship is encountered, for the cause exists. Muslims who are not traveling and yet encounter hardship cannot shorten the Prayers, for the wisdom or benefit cannot be the cause for this dispensation.

In our day, however, people substitute wisdom or benefit for the cause and act accordingly. Such *ijtihad* is worldly, not heavenly.

Second factor: People now give priority to worldly happiness; the Shari'a gives absolute priority to otherworldly eternal happiness, and only a secondary priority to worldly happiness and in the context of its being a means of eternal happiness. Since the present viewpoint is alien to the Shari'a's spirit, it cannot exercise *ijtihad* in the Shari'a's name.

Third factor: The principle that *absolute necessity makes permissible what the Shari'a forbids* is not always valid, regardless of time and place. If the necessity does not arise from a forbidden act, it may be the cause for permission. But if it arises from a misuse of willpower and unlawful acts, it cannot be the means for any dispensation. For example, if someone becomes drunk and commits some crimes, he cannot be excused for his actions. If he divorces his wife, the divorce is in force. If he murders someone, he is punished. But if his drunkenness is due to force or threat, and not from his own willpower, the divorce and the punishment are considered non-binding. Thus a chronic drunkard cannot claim innocence by saying: "I am forced to drink it, and so it is lawful for me."

These days, many things that are not necessary for people's life have become necessary and an addiction because of people's voluntary misuse of their will-power, unlawful inclinations, and forbidden acts. Thus they cannot be the means for a dispensation or making the unlawful lawful. Those who favor exercising *ijtihad* in the present circumstances build their reasoning on such "necessities," and so their *ijtihad* is worldly, the product of their fancies, and under the influence of modern trends of thought. In short, it does not accord with the Shari'a and therefore is worldly. If any exercise of authority in the Divine ordinances of the Creator of the heavens and the earth, and interference in the worship of His servants does not depend on that Creator's permission, that exercise of authority and interference are rejected.

SIXTH OBSTACLE: Respected *mujtahids* who lived close to the time of the Prophet and the Companions (the Age of Light and Truth) were purified by that light and exercised *ijtihad* with pure intentions. Their modern counterparts look at the Qur'an from such a great distance and from behind so many veils that it is very hard for them to see even its clearest letter.

Question: The Companions were human beings who could make mistakes and contradictions. However, the Shari'a commandments established by the Sunna and the early *mujtahids'* conclusions reached through *ijtihad* are founded upon the Muslim community's general belief and unanimous agreement that all Companions are just, truthful, and do not lie.

Answer: The absolute majority of Companions were lovers of truth, devoted to truthfulness, and desired justice. In that age, the ugliness of lying and deception was demonstrated in all its ugliness, and the beauty of truth and truthfulness in all its beauty. The distance between them was as great as that between the ground and God's Supreme Throne, or between the degree of the truthfulness of Prophet Muhammad (the highest rank) and the deceptiveness of Musaylima the Liar (the lowest rank). Inded, just it was lying that brought Musaylima to the lowest of the low, so it was truthfulness and right which elevated Muhammad the Trustworthy to the highest of the high.

The Companions, illumined by the light of companionship with the Sun of Prophethood, had lofty emotions and sentiments and adored good morals. They never lied voluntarily, as this is infinitely ugly and degrading. They avoided lying just as they avoided unbelief, for the two usually go together. While narrating and communicating the Shari'a's commandments, they took great care to seek the truth, be truthful, and conform to the truth. They understood that the truth is infinitely beautiful, a means of pride and glory, and a stairway to spiritual perfection. It is in greater demand than the other "gems" in the Pride of Messengership's elevated treasury, and illuminates humanity's social life with its splendid beauty.

In our time, the distance between truth and lying has become so narrow that they stand side by side. It is extremely easy to pass from truth to lying. In fact, political propaganda has made lying preferable to truth. Thus if the ugliest and most beautiful things are sold together and for the same price, the brilliance of truth, which is infinitely sublime and priceless, is not to be bought in blind reliance on the merchant's skills and word.

Conclusion

Laws change over time. Prior to Prophet Muhammad, the Seal of Prophets, different Prophets were sent to different people with different laws in even one age. As the Prophet's most comprehensive Shari'a suffices for all people in every age, there has been left no need for different Laws. However, various secondary matters showed that different legal schools were needed. Just as clothes are changed seasonally and cures may differ according to temperaments, rules governing secondary matters may differ, as they are based on time's passage and people's characters and capacities. This allows them to answer newly arising questions and situations.

At the time of the early Prophets, people were physically and intellectually distant from each other. Their characters were somewhat coarse and violent, and their minds were primitive. Thus the laws for that time were different and appropriate to their conditions. There were even different Prophets and laws in the same continent during the same age.

The Last Prophet came with an all-comprehensive religion to lead us forward in all areas of science, education, and civilization, and to bring us to the point where all of us could receive one lesson, listen to one teacher, and act in accord with one law. Therefore there was no longer any need for different laws or teachers. But because all people cannot be on the same level or lead the same sort of social life, different schools of legal thought are needed. If this were not the case, all the schools could be united.

QUESTION: Given that the truth is one, how can the rulings of these various legal schools be true?

ANSWER: The same water functions in five different ways when given to five sick people. It will cure the first person's illness, and so, according to the science of medicine, it is necessary. It will be like poison for the second person, making him even sicker, and therefore is medically forbidden. It will be slightly harmful for the third person, and therefore should be avoided. It will be beneficial for the fourth person, and thus medicine advises it. It will be neither harmful nor beneficial for the fifth person, and because he can drink it with good health it is medically permissible. Thus all five approaches are valid. Can you argue that water is only a cure, and that it must be consumed regardless of its effect?

Similarly, Divine Wisdom requires that Divine ordinances of secondary importance should differ according to those who follow them. This results in different schools, all of which are right. For example, most members of the Shafi'i school are closer to village life and less familiar with the social life that makes the community like a single body. This is why, in a congregational Prayer, each one recites Suratu'l-Fatiha behind the imam to unburden themselves at the Court of the Dispenser of needs and relate their private wishes. This is right and pure wisdom.

However, since over time the majority of Islamic governments have adopted the Hanafi school of law as their official code, those who follow this school have been closer to civilization and city life and more inclined to social life. As social, civilized life makes a community like a single individual, one person can speak for the community. Therefore, since all people affirm and support the leader with their hearts and his word becomes the word of all, Hanafi congregations do not recite *Suratu'l-Fatiha* behind the imam. This is also right and pure wisdom.

As most adherents of the Shafi'i school are villagers and manual laborers, they are prone to filth and closer intermingling of the sexes. However, the Shari'a aims at physical cleanness, spiritual purity, and moral chastity, and trains and educates the soul. Thus this school states that one's ablution is invalidated by touching the skin of a woman whom he can legally marry and by a small amount of filth on his body or clothes. The Hanafi school, most of whose adherents are more socialized and civilized, says that neither of these invalidate one's ablution.

Consider a manual laborer and a gentleman. Pursuing his livelihood, the former comes into contact with dirty things and mixes with unknown women. As he might be unable to resist the associated temptations, the Shari'a warns him with a heavenly tune: "You'll lose your ritual purity if you touch the women. Your Prayers will be invalid if you become tainted." The gentleman, in line with social custom and common morality, and provided he remains chaste and modest, does not have to mix with unknown women and seldom becomes dirty. In the Hanafi school, therefore, the Shari'a shows its permissive side and saves the gentleman from scruples: "Simply touching her with your hand does not invalidate your ablution. If you can't remove the dirt from your body or clothes, any amount less than three grams is permitted. So, you don't have to renew your ablution."

These examples are like two drops from an ocean. Try to judge in this way the Shari'a ordinances according to Imam Sha'rani's criteria.

> All-Glorified are You! We have no knowledge save what You have taught us. Surely You are the All-Knowing, the All-Wise.
>
> O God, bestow blessings and peace on him who, by being a comprehensive mirror to Your All-Beautiful Names' manifestations, embodied the lights of Your love for the beauty of Your Attributes and Names; being Your most perfect and wonderful creature, and the sample of Your Art's perfections and the index of Your inscriptions' beauties, in whose being were focused the rays of Your love for Your inscriptions; being the most elevated herald of the Your Art's beauties, the one who proclaimed in the loudest voice his admiration for Your inscriptions' beauty, and is the most unique in praising Your Art's perfections, dis-

played in his being the subtleties of Your love and desire for the appreciation of Your Art; having all good morality through Your favor and all beautiful attributes through Your grace, gathered together in his being the varieties of Your love and appreciation of You for the good morals of Your creatures and the beauties of Your creatures' attributes; and who is the most exact criterion and superior standard for all whom You mention in the Qur'an—Your Criterion of Truth and Falsehood— You love from among those who always do good, are patient, believers, God-conscious, those who turn to You in penitence and submission, and all classes of those whom You love and have honored with love of You in Your Criterion of Truth and Falsehood, so he became the leader of those who love You and the master of those whom You love. Bestow blessings and peace on his Family, Companions, and followers. Amin, through Your Mercy, O Most Merciful of the Merciful.

Addendum on the Prophet's Companions

Like Mawlana Jami', I say:

O Messenger of God.
If only like the dog of the Companions of the Cave,
I could be in Paradise in the company of your Companions.
Is it right that their dog is in Paradise while I am in Hell?
It was the dog of the Companions of the Cave,
I am the dog of Your Companions.

In His Name, All-Glorified is He.
There is nothing but it glorifies Him with praise.

In the Name of God, the All-Merciful, the All-Compassionate.

Muhammad is the Messenger of God, and those who are in his company are firm and unyielding against the unbelievers and compassionate among themselves... (48:29)

QUESTION: Some narrations say: "At a time when religious innovation is widespread and heresy is on the attack, some righteous God-conscious believers who try to conform to God's laws of religion and life may attain to the Companions' rank or even be more virtuous." Are these authentic? If so, what do they mean?

ANSWER: The Ahlu's-Sunna wa'l-Jama'a are unanimous that, after the Prophets, the Companions are the most virtuous people.[151] Therefore the authentic ones among such narrations refer to particular virtues [not virtuousness in general]. A less virtuous person may excel a more virtuous one in particular virtues. As regards general superiority, however, no one can equal or better the Companions, whom God describes (in 48:29) as having praiseworthy qualities, and whom the Torah and Gospel predicted and praise highly. Three of the innumerable reasons for this are as follows:

FIRST REASON: Companionship with the Prophet and being taught by him is such an elixir that one honored with it for even a minute may receive as much enlightenment as that which another person receives only after years of spiritual journeying. Companionship and the Prophet's education cause one to be colored with the Prophet's color and receive his reflections. Following the Prophet and being illumined by the greatest light of Prophethood enables a person to rise to the highest spiritual level. This is like a great king's servant who, through servanthood and absolute allegiance to the king, reaches the rank that an ordinary king cannot.

Even the greatest saint cannot rise to the same degree as the Companions. Great saints like Jalalu'd-Din as-Suyuti, who, having come centuries later, talked with God's Messenger many times while awake, cannot equal the Companions, for the latter were illumined by the light of Muhammad's Prophethood. He lived among them and communed with them as a Prophet. Saints who see him after his death are honored only with his sainthood's light, for now there is no Prophethood. Given this, these two types of communication with God's Messenger, upon him be peace and blessings, are as different as Prophethood and sainthood.

His conversation and companionship was such an enlightening elixir that when a wild and hard-hearted Bedouin who had murdered his daughter by burying her alive was honored with an hour of his companionship, he would become so compassionate and tender-hearted that he no longer even trod on an ant. Savage and ignorant persons honored in this way for only a day went as far as India and China to teach truths and guide civilized people to human perfection.

SECOND REASON: As explained in The Twenty-seventh Word's discussion of ijtihad, most of the Companions attained the highest degrees of human perfection, for Islam revealed good and truth in their full beauty and evil and falsehood in their full ugliness. These were actually experienced. The difference between good and evil, as well as truth and lying, was a great as that between belief and unbelief, and Paradise and Hell.

---

[151] Ibn Hibban, as-Sahih, 10:477; al-Haysami, Majma'u-z-Zawaid, 1:153.

The Companions had lofty emotions, were enamored of moral virtues and inclined to dignity and glory. Therefore, they never approached evil and falsehood voluntarily and fell to the level of Musaylima the Liar, the sample and herald of lying, evil, and falsehood who eventually became an object of ridicule. Witnessing the Beloved of God as the highest example, sample and herald of human perfections, truth, right, and good, their pure characters impelled them to exert all their strength and effort to follow him.

Sometimes, due to their dreadful results and detestable effects, people flee from certain things in the market of human civilization and the shop of human social life. At the same time, like beneficial cures or brilliant diamonds, certain things are in much demand and draw everybody's attention because of their good effects and valuable results. Everybody tries to buy them. During the Age of Happiness, such articles as unbelief, lying, and evil yielded results like eternal doom and torment and produced laughing-stocks like Musaylima the Liar. The Companions, enamored of high moral qualities and praiseworthy virtues, fled from them in disgust. With their pure and elevated characteristics, as if they were most beneficial cures and most precious diamonds, they strove to be the best and most ardent customers of truth, right, and belief, which result in eternal happiness and produced illustrious fruits like God's Messenger, upon him be peace and blessings.

However, after that time, the distance between truth and lying gradually lessened so that now they now stand side by side in the same shop and are sold together. Social morality has been corrupted, and political propaganda encourages lying and causes it to be in demand. When lying's awesome ugliness remains concealed and truth's brilliant beauty is invisible, who could claim to have the same degree of strength, firmness, and meticulousness as the Companions in matters of justice, truthfulness, and moral sublimity? I will clarify this by relating one of my experiences.

Once it occurred to me why saints with extraordinary qualities (like Muhyi'd-Din ibnu'l-'Arabi) cannot equal the Companions. While reciting "All-Glorified be my Lord, the All-High" during the prostration, a portion of this phrase's full meaning was unveiled and its truth was revealed to me. I thought: "If only I could perform one prescribed Prayer as perfectly as I discovered that phrase's meaning. It would excel one year's usual worship in virtue." I came to see that this experience was to guide me to perceive why one cannot reach the Companions' degrees.

In the mighty social revolutions brought about by the Qur'an's lights, opposites were completely separated from each other. Evil (with all its darkness, details, and consequences) and good and perfection (with all their lights and results) stood face to face. Thus in that exciting, stimulating time, all levels of the meaning of words and phrases of recitation, praise, and glorification were revealed in their full freshness and originality. This stirred up and awakened the feelings and spiritual faculties of those fully experiencing all stages of this mighty revolution, and even caused such senses as fancy and imagining to wake up fully, receive, and absorb these meanings based on their own perception.

Thus the Companions, all of whose senses were awakened and faculties alert, pronounced the blessed words and phrases containing all the lights of belief and glorification in all their meanings, and derived their shares with all their faculties. Over time, people gradually lost the taste and pleasure they received from these phrases, for familiarity and insensitivity caused their faculties to sleep and their senses to become heedless. All that has remained of those fruits is some moisture (superficiality). Only a reflective and contemplative operation can restore our faculties and senses to their former state. This is why people cannot attain in forty days or even forty years what a Companion reached in forty minutes.

THIRD REASON: As explained in the Twelfth, Twenty-fourth, and Twenty-fifth Words, compared to sainthood, Prophethood is like the sun in relation to its images in mirrors. Thus, however much superior Prophethood is to sainthood, the Companions, the servants of Prophethood and the planets around that sun, are must be superior to saints to the same degree. Even if a saint reaches the rank of absolute truthfulness, loyalty, and succession to the Prophet (the highest rank of sainthood belonging to the Companions), they cannot reach the Companions' degree. I will explain three of the many aspects of this third reason:

First aspect: No one can equal the Companions in *ijtihad* (deducing God's ordinances and what He approves of from the Qur'an and Sunna). For the mighty Divine revolution at that time sought to learn and understand God's commandments and the things of which He approves. All minds were concentrated upon deducing Divine ordinances, and all hearts wondered what their Lord wanted from them. All events and circumstances impelled people toward that goal. Conversations, discussions, and stories taught

Divine ordinances and what He approves of in His servants. These all perfected the Companions' capacities and enlightened their minds.

Moreover, since their potentials to make deductions and exercise *ijtihad* were as ready to ignite as matches, even if we had their level of intelligence and capacity we could not attain in ten or even a hundred years the level of deduction and *ijtihad* they attained in a day or a month. For at present, people consider worldly happiness rather than eternal happiness and so concentrate on other aims. Since the struggle to make a living and not relying on God have bewildered and stupefied spirits, and naturalistic and materialistic philosophy have blinded intellects, the social environment only scatters and confuses people's minds and capacities in exercising *ijtihad*. While discussing *ijtihad* in The Twenty-seventh Word, I explained why no modern person, even if having the same intelligence as Sufyan ibn Uyayna, could obtain in a hundred years what Sufyan obtained in ten years.

Second aspect: No saint can reach the rank of the Companions in nearness to God Almighty, Who is nearer to us than everything while we are infinitely far from Him. One can acquire nearness to Him in two ways. The first way is through God's favor to make one near to Him and to make one realize His nearness. Through companionship with and succession to the Prophet, the Companions were endowed with this sort of nearness. The second way is through continuous promotion to higher ranks until honored with nearness to God. Most saints follow this way and make a long spiritual journey in their inner world and through the outer world.

The first way is a gift of God and thus does not depend upon one's efforts. Such nearness is realized through the Merciful One's attraction and being beloved by Him. This way is short but extremely elevated and sound, perfectly pure and free of obscurity. The other is long, depends on one's endeavors, and has obscurities. Even if the one following it is endowed with miracle-like wonders, this way is inferior to the former in acquiring nearness to God Almighty. Consider this example: One can experience yesterday once more in two ways. Without following the course of time, one rises by a sacred spiritual power to a position from which all time is seen as a single point. Or, following the course of time, one lives a whole year and reaches the same day next year. Despite this, one cannot preserve yesterday or prevent it from passing.

Similarly, one can pass from the external observation of religious commandments to the realization of their truth in two ways. Without entering the intermediate world of religious orders, one submits to the truth's attraction and finds it directly in its external aspect. [In other words, one sees the external and the internal combined into a single unity.] Or, one is initiated into a spiritual way and continually promoted to higher ranks. But however successful they are in self-annihilation and killing their carnal, evil-commanding souls, saints cannot reach the Companions, who were purified, had refined souls, and were honored with all varieties of worship and sorts of praise and thanksgiving with the selfhood's multiple inborn faculties. The worship of the saints who completely annihilate their selfhood becomes simple and one dimensional.

Third aspect: No one can reach the Companions in merits of deeds, rewards for actions, and virtues pertaining to the Hereafter. A soldier guarding a dangerous point under perilous conditions for an hour can gain the merits of a year of worship, and a soldier who achieves martyrdom in one minute can attain the rank of a type of sainthood that others can reach only after at least forty days. The Companions' services in establishing Islam, spreading the Qur'an's commandments, and challenging the world for Islam's sake were so meritorious and rewarding that others cannot gain in one year the merits they acquired in a minute. It can even be said that every minute of theirs equals the minute of that soldier martyred while in that sacred service. Every hour of theirs is like the hour of watch of a self-sacrificing soldier under perilous conditions. Even though it seems a small act, it is extremely valuable and meritorious.

Since the Companions were the first line in establishing Islam and disseminating the Qur'an's lights, according to the rule of "The cause is like the doer," they share in all Muslims' rewards, regardless of time or place. Muslims invoke God's peace and blessings on them, saying: "O God, bestow blessings and peace on our master Muhammad, his Family, and Companions," thereby showing that the Companions share in all Muslims' rewards [without causing any reduction in the Muslims' rewards].

Just as an insignificant characteristic in a tree's roots assumes a great form in its branches and is larger than the largest branch, just as a small amount at the beginning becomes a large mass, and just as a little point in the center forms a wide angle in the circumference, the Companions' few actions were multiplied and their small service acquired a huge consequence. They formed the roots of the blessed, illustrious tree of Islam, were among the Muslim community's leaders and first in establishing its traditions, and were the nearest to the center of the Sun of Prophethood and the Lamp of Truth, upon him be peace and blessings. Only another Companion can reach them.

> O God, bestow blessings and peace our Master Muhammad, who said: "My Companions are like stars; whichever of them you follow, you will be rightly guided."[152] The best of the ages is my age."[153]—and on his Family and Companions.

> All-Glorified are You! We have no knowledge save what You have taught us. Surely You are the All-Knowing, the All-Wise.

QUESTION: Some people argue: "The Companions saw God's Messenger, upon him be peace and blessings, and believed. But we believed without seeing him, and so our belief must be stronger. In addition, there are narrations indicating the strength of our belief."

ANSWER: At a time when the world's public view opposed the truths of Islam, the Companions saw God's Messenger only in his apparent human form. Many of them believed even without seeing a single miracle. Yet their belief was so firm that opposing views had no effect. And you compare your belief with theirs?

Although the public view of the Muslim world and Islam's magnificent history form a formidable proof and support for your belief, and although you have seen God's Messenger with his collective personality formed of all of Islam's lights and the Qur'an's truths and enveloped by as many as a thousand miracles, not with his apparent human form and character, which was the seed of the blessed universal tree of his Prophethood, one word from an European philosopher can cause you to doubt and waver in belief. How can your belief equal that of the Companions, who never wavered in the face of total opposition from the forces of unbelief and polytheism, among them philosophers, Christians, and Jews?

Also, how can your weak and dim belief which cannot even make you perform the religious obligatory duties regularly and accurately can be compared with the Companions' strong piety and perfect righteousness which originated in their belief and showed its strength? As for the Prophetic tradition: "The belief of one who believes at the end of time without seeing me is greater in value,"[154] this deals with particular virtues and pertains to certain individuals. Here we are discussing general superiority and the majority.

---

[152] al-Munawi, *Faydu'l-Qadir*, 6:297., 10:477.
[153] *al-Bukhari*, "Fadailu Ashabi'n-Nabiyy" 1; *at-Tirmidhi*, "Fitan" 45.
[154] Ahmad ibn Hanbal, *al-Musnad*,5:248, 257, 264.

QUESTION: Saints and people of perfection usually renounce the world. A tradition says that love of the world is the beginning of all sins and faults.[155] However, the Companions, may God be pleased with them, indulged in the world to such an extent that some enjoyed it more than the worldly people of that time. How can you say that the greatest saint cannot reach a Companion of the lowest degree?

ANSWER: As convincingly argued in the *Risale-i Nur*,[156] loving the facets of the world that look to the Hereafter and manifest God's Names is a means of perfection. The more profound one is in appreciating and loving these two facets of the world, the deeper one is in worship and knowledge of God. The Companions concerned themselves with these two facets. Considering the world an arable field of the Hereafter, they sowed it with seeds to grow in the Hereafter. They saw all creatures as mirrors reflecting the Divine Names and observed them lovingly. The world is evil in its mortal facet which looks to our animal appetites.

QUESTION: Religious spiritual orders are ways to truth. Some assert that the *Naqshbandi* order is the most famous, most elevated, and broadest way. Some inspired *Naqshbandi* leaders describe its foundations as follows: "In the *Naqshbandi* way, four things should be renounced: the world, the Hereafter (it should not be taken as the main aim in the name of the carnal soul), being or becoming, and the idea of renunciation (in order not to get into self-pride and vanity)." Does this mean that true knowledge of God and human perfection can be attained by renouncing all that is other than God?

ANSWER: If we were no more than a heart, we would have to renounce everything other than God. We would even have to give up our concern for God's Names and Attributes and completely give ourselves to His Essence. In reality, however, we have many senses and faculties (e.g., the intellect, spirit, soul, and the innermost ones), each of which has particular duties and functions. Perfect people are those who, using each sense and faculty in its particular type of worship, strive to reach the truth. With their hearts serving as the commander and the other faculties as soldiers, they advance heroically like the Companions in a broad sphere and in a manifold way toward their goal. For the heart to leave its soldiers in order to save itself and proceed on its own is a cause of distress, not of pride.

---

[155] al-Bukhari, *Tarikhu'l-Kabir*, 3:472; al-Bayhaqi, *Shu'abu'l-Iman*, 7:323, 338.

[156] In the second and third Stations of the 32nd Word.

QUESTION: Why do some claim superiority to the Companions? Who puts it forward? Should such a claim be discussed? From where does the claim of equality with the great *mujtahids* arise?

ANSWER: Two groups of people put forward these claims. One group comprises some pure-hearted religious scholars and pious people who, seeing certain Traditions, start such discussions to encourage and hearten righteous and devoted Muslims. We have nothing to say to them. Anyway, they are few and quickly are made aware of the matter's truth. The other group consists of very conceited and dangerous people seeking to spread their denial of the legal schools by claiming such equality, and to promote their heresy by claiming equality with the Companions.

First, such misguided people are addicted to dissipation. To excuse their neglect of religious duties (which forbid dissipation), they argue: "Those matters are secondary and depend on *ijtihad*. The legal schools disagree about them. Since the *mujtahids* were people like us, and therefore fallible, we can exercise *ijtihad* and worship in whatever way we wish. Why should we follow the early *mujtahids*?" This is how Satan leads people out of the legal schools' bounds. To see how groundless their claim is, refer to The Twenty-seventh Word.

Second, those misguided people do not only claim equality with *mujtahids*, who concerned themselves only with religion's theoretical matters, but pursue their ultimate goal: abandoning and changing Islam's basic obligations. *Mujtahids* can rule only in theoretical matters and secondary, noncategorical issues. But these misguided people, who refuse to follow a legal school, want to mix their ideas in the basic obligations of the Religion, change unalterable matters, and oppose Islam's definite pillars. Therefore, they feel compelled to criticize the Companions, the bearers and supports of Islam's basic obligations. No one, not only these apparently human ones, but even the greatest saints, who are the most perfect of true human beings, can equal even the least virtuous Companion.

> O God. Bestow blessings and peace on Your Messenger, who said: "Do not reprove my Companions. If one of you spent gold equivalent to Mount Uhud (in the cause of God), you could not attain (the virtue) of a handful of one of my Companions."[157] God's Messenger told the truth.
>
> All-Glorified are You! We have no knowledge save what You have taught us. Surely You are the All-Knowing, the AllWise.

---

[157] al-B:ukhari, "Fadailu Ashabi'n-Nabiyy" 5; *Muslim*, "Fadailu's-Sahaba" 221, 222.

The
Twenty-eighth Word

The Twenty-eighth Word

Answers to questions about Paradise

In the Name of God, the All-Merciful, the All-Compassionate.

Give glad tidings to those who believe and do good, righteous deeds: for them are Gardens through which rivers flow. Every time they are provided with fruit therefrom, they say: "This is what we were provided with before," for they are given to them in resemblance. Furthermore, for them are spouses eternally purified, and therein they will abide. (2:25)

BELOW ARE BRIEF ANSWERS TO QUESTIONS ABOUT PARADISE, WHICH is everlasting. The Qur'anic descriptions, which are more beautiful than Paradise, more delightful than its *houris*, and sweeter than its springs' pleasant water, leave nothing to be added. We will only point out some steps so that such brilliant, eternal, elevated, and beautiful verses can be understood easily, and explain some fine points, resembling flowers from that Qur'anic paradise, through five significant questions and answers.

QUESTION: What does the defective, changing, unstable, and pain-stricken body have to do with eternity and Paradise? The spirit's elevated pleasures must be enough. Why should a bodily resurrection take place for bodily pleasures?

ANSWER: Soil, despite its darkness and density when compared to water, air, and light, is the means and source of all works of Divine Art.

Therefore it is somehow superior in meaning over other elements. Likewise, human selfhood or soul, despite its density but due to its being comprehensive and provided it is purified, gains some kind of superiority over all other senses and faculties. Similarly, the physical body is a most comprehensive and rich mirror for the Divine Names' manifestations, and has been equipped with instruments to weigh and measure the contents of all Divine treasuries. For example, if the tongue's sense of taste were not the origin of as many measures as the varieties of food and drink, it could not experience, recognize, or measure them. Furthermore, the body also contains the instruments needed to experience and recognize most of the Divine Names' manifestations, as well as the faculties for experiencing the most various and infinitely different pleasures.

The universe's conduct and humanity's comprehensive nature show that the Maker of the universe wants, by means of the universe, to make known all His Mercy's treasures and all His Names' manifestations, and to make us experience all His bounties. Given this, as the World of Eternal Happiness is a mighty pool into which the flood of the universe flows, a vast exhibition of what the loom of the universe produces, and the everlasting store of crops produced in the field of this (material) world, it will resemble the universe to some degree. It will preserve all its bodily and spiritual foundations. So, the All-Wise Maker, the All-Compassionate, All-Just One, will give pleasures particular to each bodily organ as wages for their duty, service, and worship. To act otherwise would be utterly contrary to His Wisdom, Justice, and Compassion.

QUESTION: A living body is in a state of continuous formation and deformation, and so is subject to disintegration and is non-eternal. Eating and drinking perpetuate the individual; sexual relations perpetuate the species. These are fundamental to life in this world, but are irrelevant and unnecessary in the World of Eternity. Given this, why have they been included among Paradise's greatest pleasures?

ANSWER: A living body declines and dies because the balance between what it needs to maintain and takes in is disturbed. From childhood until the age of physical maturity, it takes in more than it lets out and grows healthier. Afterwards, it usually cannot meet its needs in a balanced way, and eventually dies. In the World of Eternity, however, the body's particles remain constant and are immune to disintegration and re-formation, or the balance between the body's income and consumption remains constant.[158] Like moving in perpetual cycles, a living body gains eternity together with the constant operation of the factory of bodily life for pleasure. In this world, eating, drinking, and marital sexual relations arise from a need and serve a purpose. Thus a great variety of excellent (and superior) pleasures are ingrained in them as immediate wages for the purpose served. Since in this world of ailments, eating and marriage lead to many wonderful and various pleasures, for sure, Paradise, the Realm of Happiness and Pleasure, will contain these pleasures in their most elevated form. Adding to them otherworldly wages as pleasures for the duties performed in the world by them and the need felt for them here in the form of a pleasant and otherworldly appetite, they will be transformed into an all-encompassing, living source of pleasure that is appropriate to Paradise and eternity.

According to: *The life of this world is but a pastime and a game, but the Abode of the Hereafter—it is all living indeed* (29:64), all lifeless and unconscious substances and objects in this world are living and conscious in the other world. Like people and animals here, trees and stones there will, respectively, understand and obey commands. If you tell a tree to bring you such-and-such a fruit, it will do so. If you tell a stone to come, it will come. Since stones and trees will assume such an elevated form, it will be necessary for eating, drinking, and marital relations to assume a form that is superior to their worldly forms to the same degree as Paradise is superior to this world. This includes preserving their bodily realities.

QUESTION: A Tradition states that "a person is with the one he or she loves,"[159] and so friends will be together in Paradise. Thus a simple Bedouin who feels a deep love for God's Messenger in one minute of companionship with him should be together with him in Paradise. But how can a simple nomad's illumination and reward cause him to share the same place with God's Messenger, whose illumination and reward are limitless?

ANSWER: I will point to this elevated truth by a comparison. A magnificent person prepared a vast banquet and a richly adorned event in an extremely beautiful and splendid garden. It included all delicious foods that

---

[158] In this world, human and animal bodies are like guesthouses, barracks, or schools for particles. Lifeless particles enter them, become worthy of being particles for the eternal world, and then leave them. In the Hereafter, however, according to: *The Abode of the Hereafter—it is all living indeed* (29:64), the light of life encompasses everything. There is no need for its particles to make the same journey and undergo the same training as particles or atoms in this world must do.

[159] al-Bukhari, "Adab" 96; Muslim, "Birr" 165.

taste can experience, all beautiful things that please sight, all wonders that amuse the imagination, and so on. Everything that would gratify and please the external and inner senses was present. Two friends went to the banquet and sat at a table in the same pavilion. One had only limited taste and so received little pleasure. His weak sight and inability to smell prevented him from understanding the wonderful arts or comprehending the marvels. He could benefit only to the degree of his capacity, which was miniscule. But the other person had developed his external and internal senses, intellect, heart, and all faculties and feelings to the utmost degree. Therefore he could perceive, experience, and derive pleasure from all subtleties, beauties, marvels, and fine things in that exquisite garden.

This is how it is in our confused, painful, and narrow world. There is an infinite distance between the greatest and the least who exist side by side. So, in Paradise, the Abode of Happiness and Eternity, where friends will be together, it is more fitting that each receives his or her share from the table of the All-Merciful, All-Compassionate according to the degree of his or her ability. Even though they are in different Gardens or on different "floors" of Paradise, they will be able to meet, for Paradise's eight levels are one above the other and share the same roof—the Supreme Throne of God.[160]

Suppose there are walled circles around a conical mountain, one within the other and one above the other, each one facing another, from its foot to the summit. This does not prevent each one from seeing the sun. Indeed, various narrations or Traditions indicate that the levels or floors of Paradise are somewhat like this.

QUESTION: Prophetic Traditions say: "*Houris* are clothed in seventy garments (one over the other), yet the marrow of their leg-bones may be seen."[161] What does this mean? What sort of beauty is this?

ANSWER: This Tradition has a very fine meaning and a lovely beauty. In this world, which is ugly, lifeless, and for the most part just a covering, it is sufficient as long as beauty and loveliness appear to the eye as beautiful and until too much familiarity conceals it. In Paradise, which is beautiful, living, brilliant, and entirely essence or kernel without covering, like the eye, all our senses and faculties will want to receive their different

---

[160] al-Bukhari, "Tawhid" 22; at-Tirmidhi, "Sifatu'l-Janna" 4.

[161] al-Bukhari, "Adab" 96; Muslim, "Birr" 165.

pleasures from *houris* and from the women coming from this world, who will be even more beautiful than *houris*. This Tradition indicates that from the beauty of the top garment to the marrow in the bone, each will be the means of pleasure for a sense and faculty.

It also points out that the *houris'* adornment, physical and spiritual beauty and charm, will please, satisfy, and gratify all the yearnings of our senses, feelings, powers, and faculties for beauty, and their great fondness for pleasure and adornment. Clothed in seventy sorts of adornment of Paradise in such a way that one does not conceal another, *houris* display more than seventy sorts of bodily and spiritual beauty and elegance, and thereby demonstrate the truth contained in: *In it (Paradise) is whatever the souls desire and the eyes delight in* (43:71).

This Tradition also points out that since Paradise contains no unnecessary, peeled, or shelled waste matter with sediment,[162] its inhabitants will not excrete waste after eating and drinking. In this world, trees, the most ordinary of living beings, do not excrete despite taking in much nourishment. So why should Paradise's inhabitants, the highest category of life, excrete waste?

QUESTION: Some Prophetic Traditions say that some inhabitants of Paradise will be given a place as large as the world, and that hundreds of thousands of palaces and *houris* will be granted to them. What is the reason for this, and why and how does one person need all these things?

ANSWER: If we were only a solid object, a vegetable creature consisting of a stomach, or only had a limited, heavy, simple, and transient corporal or animal body, we would not own or deserve so many palaces or *houris*. But we are so comprehensive a miracle of Divine Power that if we ruled this world and used all of its wealth and pleasure to satisfy our undeveloped senses' and faculties' needs, we still could not satisfy our greed during our brief life. However, if we have an infinite capacity in an eternal abode of happiness, and if we knock on the door of infinite Mercy in the tongue of infinite need and with the hand of infinite desires, we will receive the Divine bounties described in such Traditions. We will present a comparison to illustrate this elevated truth.

---

[162] *al-Bukhari*, "Bad'ul-Khalq" 8; *Muslim*, "Janna" 17-19.

[163] The garden of Süleyman, who served this poor one with perfect loyalty for eight years, where this Word was written in one or two hours.

Like this valley garden[163], each vineyard and garden in Barla has a different owner. Each bird, sparrow, or honey-bee, which has only a handful of grain, may say: "All of Barla's vineyards and gardens are my places of recreation." Each may possess Barla and include it in its property. The fact that others share it does not negate its rule. A truly human person may say: "My Creator made the world a home for me, with the sun as its chief lamp, the stars as its electric lights, and the earth as my cradle spread with flowered carpets," and thanks God. This conclusion is not negated because other creatures live in this "house." On the contrary, the creatures adorn this home and are like its decorations. If, on account of being human, we or even a bird were to claim the right of control over such a vast area in this narrow, brief world and to receive such a vast bounty, why should we consider it unlikely that we will own property stretching for five hundred years in a broad, eternal abode of happiness?

Also, just as the sun is present here in many mirrors simultaneously, so a spiritually enlightened being may also be present in many places at the same time, as discussed in The Sixteenth Word. For example, Gabriel, upon him be peace, can be on a thousand stars while being present at God's Supreme Throne, in the Prophet's presence, and in the Divine Presence. Prophet Muhammad, upon him be peace and blessings, can meet with most of the devoted, God-conscious members of his community in the Place of Gathering after the Resurrection, just as he can appear in many places and to numerous saintly people in this world simultaneously. A group of saints (abdal: substitutes) can appear in many places at the same moment. Ordinary people sometimes can do as much as a year's work or observe its being done in a minute while dreaming, and everyone can be in contact with and concerned with many places at the same time in heart, in spirit, and in imagination. Such things are well-known and witnessed.

Given this, the inhabitants of Paradise, which is luminous, unrestricted, broad, and eternal, will have bodies with the spirit's strength and lightness and the imagination's swiftness. They will be able to be in countless places simultaneously, talk with innumerable houris, and receive pleasure in an infinite number of ways. This is fitting for that eternal Paradise and infinite Mercy, and the Truthful Reporter, upon him be peace and blessings, says that this is the reality and the truth. But such truths cannot be weighed on the scales of our tiny minds.

All-Glorified are You. We have no knowledge save what You have taught us. Surely You are the All-Knowing, the All-Wise.

Our Lord, take us not to task if we forget or make mistakes.

O God, bestow blessings on Your beloved, who opened the doors of Paradise through being beloved by You, and through his prayers, and whose community which helped him opening those doors through calling Your blessings on him. On him be blessings and peace. O God, let us enter Paradise among the pure, righteous ones through the intercession of Your chosen beloved. Amin.

Addendum: About Hell

As argued in the Second and Eighth Words, belief bears the seed of a sort of Paradise experienced by the spirit, while unbelief contains the seed of a sort of Hell experienced by the spirit. Just as unbelief is the seed of Hell, Hell is a fruit of unbelief. Unbelief is the cause of entering Hell as well as of its existence and creation. If an insignificant ruler with a small dignity, pride, and majesty were confronted by someone who challenged him: "You cannot punish me," he would have to cast that person into prison or build a prison if one did not exist already. Denying Hell means that the unbeliever contradicts the infinitely Powerful One, Who has infinite dignity, glory, majesty, and greatness. Such a person accuses Him of impotence and lying, both of which are great affronts to His honor and dignity, and offends His pride, glory, and majesty. If it did not exist already, Hell would have to be created to punish such unbelief and its possessor.

O Lord. You did not create this in vain. All-Glorified are You. Save us from the torment of the Fire.

The
Twenty-ninth Word

The Twenty-ninth Word

> ➤ *The permanence of the spirit and angels,*
> ➤ *The Resurrection and the afterlife*

I seek refuge in God from Satan, the accursed.

In the Name of God, the All-Merciful, the All-Compassionate.

The Angels and the Spirit descend in (the Night of Power) by the leave of their Lord. (97:4)

Say: "The Spirit is of my Lord's Command." (17:85)

[NOTE: This treatise consists of an Introduction and two chapters of Aims.]

Introduction

THE EXISTENCE OF HEAVENLY BEINGS, WHICH THE SHARI'A CALLS angels and other spiritual beings is as evident as that of humanity and animals. As explained in the First Step of the 15th Word, reality and universal wisdom require that like the earth, the heavens should have conscious or intelligent inhabitants particular to themselves. For the earth, despite its small size and apparent insignificance when compared with the heavens, is continually filled with and emptied of conscious beings. This indicates that the heavens, which resemble decorated castles with awe-inspiring towers, are filled with living beings, the light of the existence's light, and conscious, intelligent beings who are the light of living creatures. These beings, just like jinn and humanity, are observers of this palace of the world, students and readers of this book of the universe, and heralds of the Lord's Sovereignty. Through their comprehensive and universal worship, they represent the glorifications of the creatures of universal nature or identity.

The nature of the universe requires the existence of these beings, for its finely adorned art works, meaningful decorations, and purposeful, delicate embroideries demand sentient beings to reflect upon, as well as praise and commend, them in full appreciation. Just as a beauty needs a lover and food is given to the hungry, so the food provided for souls and hearts through this infinite beauty of art is first of all related to the existence of angels and other spirit beings. The universe's infinite beauty and majesty calls for a response that must be of an infinite duty of reflection and worship. Since jinn and humanity can fulfill only a miniscule part of this duty, there must be countless varieties of angels and spirit beings to fill this universal mosque of existence with rows arranged in worship of the Creator.

Indeed, there is a band or species of spirit beings and angels in every corner of the universe, each performing its own specific duty of servanthood. Based on certain Prophetic Traditions and the wisdom in the universe's order, it can be said that some mobile lifeless bodies from planets to raindrops provide vehicles for some species of angels. They mount them by God's leave and travel through the material world, representing their glorifications.

Furthermore, certain types of living bodies provide vehicles for some species of souls or spirit beings. For example, a Tradition says that the souls of the people of Paradise enter the "green birds" of Paradise in the Intermediate World of the grave and travel around Paradise in them.[1] Such birds, even some flies, belong to these groups of living bodies. Souls enter them by God's command, observe creation's wonders through their senses, and glorify the Creator on their behalf. Like reality, Divine Wisdom also require this. For just as the All-Wise Originator breathes life into gross clay and muddy water, which have little to do with the spirit, and thereby produces numerous conscious beings, so does He create certain types of intelligent beings from light and darkness, and other subtle substances (e.g., air and electricity), as they are more appropriate for the creation of the spirit and life.

Two aims

First aim

Confirming the existence of angels is a pillar of belief. This First Aim contains four fundamentals:

FIRST FUNDAMENTAL: The perfection of existence is through life. In fact, life is the real basis and light of existence. Consciousness, in turn, is the light of life. Life constitutes the foundation of everything and appropriates everything for each living thing. Only through life can a living creature claim that everything belongs to it, that the world is its home and the universe its property conferred by the Owner. Just as light causes (concrete) things to be seen and, according to one theory, is the real cause of color, so too, life unveils creation. Life causes qualities and natures to be manifested and realized. It makes the particular universal and the universal concentrated in a particular.

Life also causes existence to attain all its perfections; it causes countless things to come together to achieve unity and thereby the rank of having a soul. Furthermore, life is the manifestation of unity in the levels of multiplicity; it reflects the essential oneness of existence in plurality. See how lonely even a mountain-sized object is without life. Its interactions are restricted to its location, and all that exists in the universe means nothing to it, for it is unconscious of other existents. But as such a minute living being as a honeybee can have close interactions with the universe, particularly with plants and flowers, it can say: "The earth is my garden; my marketplace where I do business." Through the "instinctive" senses of impetus or motivation and enthusiasm in addition to the well-known outer and inner senses that living beings have, a bee has close relations, interaction and familiarity with most species.

If life's effect upon this small creature is so great, how much greater will it be upon humanity, as it expands into our consciousness, reason, and intellect! Through reason and consciousness, which is the light of life, we travel through the higher worlds of corporeal and spiritual existence as easily as passing from one room to another. Just as conscious and living beings may visit those worlds in spirit, those worlds come as guests to our mirror-like spirit by being reflected there. Life is a clear evidence of God's Unity, the greatest source of His bounty, a most subtle manifestation of His Compassion, and a most hidden and delicate embroidery of His Art. Life is so mysterious and subtle that even the life of plants (the simplest level of life) and the awakening of the life-force in seeds (the beginning of its life) are still not understood fully. Although it is something common to us, it has remained a mystery since the time of Adam, for no person has ever grasped its nature.

In its outer (material) and inner (immaterial) aspects, life is pure. Divine Power creates life without the participation of causes, while It uses "natural" causes as a veil before the creation of everything else so that those unable to discern Divine wisdom and essential beauty in things and events may attribute to them certain base qualities that they cannot reconcile with the dignity of Divine Power.

In short, without life, any existent thing cannot be regarded as existent or as substantially different from non-existence. Life is the spirit's light, and consciousness is life's light. Since life and consciousness are so important, and a perfect harmony prevails over all creation and the universe displays a firm cohesion, and since our small rotating planet is full of countless living and intelligent beings, those heavenly castles and lofty constellations must surely have conscious living inhabitants unique to themselves. Just as fish live in water, those spirit beings may exist in the sun's heat. Fire does not consume light; rather, fire makes light brighter. Seeing that the Eternal Power creates countless living beings from inert, solid substances and transforms the densest matter into subtle living compounds by life, thus radiating the light of life everywhere in great abundance and furnishing most things with the light of consciousness, the All-Powerful, All-Wise One would certainly not make such subtle forms of matter as light and ether, which are close to and fitting for the spirit, without life and consciousness. He creates countless animate and conscious beings from light and darkness, ether and air, and even from meanings (conceived) and words (uttered). As He creates numerous animal species, He also creates different spirit creatures from subtle forms of matter. Some of these are angels, various spirit beings, and jinn. Consider the following parable if you are not convinced.

An uncivilized nomad and a civilized person went to a magnificent city like Istanbul. In a remote corner of that well-ordered, splendid city, they saw an old building containing a factory full of miserable workers. The local people around it lived on either vegetables or fish. While watching them, they had, in the distance, a vision of lofty, adorned castles and palaces, among which were huge workshops and broad squares. They could see no inhabitants in that area, for they either had defective sight or the inhabitants were hiding. As there was also no comparison between the two living conditions, the uncivilized person concluded that no one lived there. The other man said:

> You can see that this poor, dilapidated factory is inhabited by workers—somebody very powerful and wise is employing and then replacing them with new ones. Also, there is no empty space around the factory, for every spot is being used. How could those adorned, lofty palaces and castles be unoccupied? They must be inhabited by beings who have different conditions of life. You can't see them because of the distance or your defective sight or because they are hiding. Just because you can't see something doesn't mean it doesn't exist.

The earth, although much smaller than other heavenly bodies, is so densely inhabited by living creatures that even its grossest and most rotten parts are full of living things, such as micro-organisms. This shows that those infinite firmaments, with their numerous stars and constellations, are inhabited by conscious, living beings created from fire, light, air, ether, electricity, voices, scents, words, and other subtle forms of matter. The Qur'an or the Shari'a calls such beings angels, jinn, and spirit entities. They have their own kinds or species, just like earthly creatures. For example, the angel in charge of a raindrop is certainly different from the angel in charge of the sun.

In conclusion, and as may be established empirically, matter is not essential. Therefore existence is not subject to or dependent on it. Rather, matter subsists by means of a meaning, and that meaning is life, is spirit. As may be established through observation, existence does not serve matter and thus everything does not have to be ascribed to it. Rather, matter exists so that it may serve and perfect a reality: life. Spirit is the foundation of life.

As matter does not rule existence, perfections do not have to be sought from it. Rather, it is dominated, subject to the decree of a fundamental, and fashioned according to that decree's dictates. That fundamental is life, spirit, consciousness. Matter is not the unchanged essence of existence and the source of perfections; rather, it is a form and outer covering subject to disintegration. A micro-organism has acute senses: It hears its mate's voice and sees its food. This shows that as matter becomes more refined, life's effects become more manifest and the spirit's light grows brighter. It is as though the more closely matter resembles the realm of spirit and consciousness, the more ethereal it becomes. This causes life's light to be manifested more brightly.

Given this, how could the inner world of existence not be occupied with conscious living beings while the reflections of life and consciousness continue to be manifested upon the veil of matter? Besides, is it possible that the countless manifestations and reflections of meaning, spirit, life, and consciousness in the corporeal world could be ascribed solely to matter and its motion? On the contrary, they indicate that the corporeal world is only a lace veil over the World of the Spirit and the inner worlds.

SECOND FUNDAMENTAL: Most philosophers and religious scholars agree that angels and spirit beings exist, although there have been differences in naming them. Among philosophers, the Peripatetics (*Mashshaiyyun*), who were inclined to explain existence in materialistic terms, had to admit the existence of angels on the ground that each species has a spiritual, incorporeal essence. The Illuminists (*Ishraqiyyun*) did not deny the existence of angels, but wrongly called them the "Ten Intellects" and "Masters of Species." Followers of Divine religions, guided by Divine Revelation, believed that an angel is in charge of each kind of existence. They named them according to that kind of existence: the Angel of the

Mountains, the Angel of the Seas, the Angel of Rain, and so on. Even naturalists and materialists, who restrict themselves to what they see, admit the meaning of angels by calling them (incorrectly) "pervasive forces."

If you do not admit the existence of such beings, on what proof do you base your denial? Can these vast spaces and beautiful firmaments be devoid of inhabitants while, as explained in the First Fundamental, life unveils the reality of creation and is its result and essence, and the earth is animated by numerous living beings? How can so-called natural laws have any influence upon creation? Being no more than nominal and imaginary principles, they cannot be the origin, nor even the cause, of any kind of existence, nature, identity and external reality if there are no angels to represent, manifest, and administer them. Since life is an external observed reality, such nominal principles as natural laws cannot be the origin of this reality.

Scientists, philosophers and religious scholars agree that creation is not limited to this visible world. Although this world is material and thus unsuitable for being a home for spirit beings, it has been decorated by countless living creatures. Therefore, there must be many degrees of existence over which this material world is but a lace curtain. Furthermore, as the sea houses fish, the unseen world of the spirit houses spirit beings. In short, all arguments presented so far and all others that can be deduced from the universe's operation indicate the existence of angels.

The Qur'an explains the meaning of angelic existence so reasonably that anyone can understand it: The human community is responsible for carrying out Divine Commandments issuing from the Divine Attribute of Speech, whereas angels are a huge community whose "working" stratum carry out Divine laws of nature issuing from the Attribute of Will. They are God's honored servants who have subtle, luminous bodies, are divided into classes, and do whatever He tells them to do. They obey the commandments issuing from the Eternal Will and the Creative Power, Which rules the universe. Each heavenly body is a place of worship for them.

THIRD FUNDAMENTAL: The existence of angels and other spirit beings can be established by proving the existence of one angel, and denying (or accepting) the existence of one amounts to denying (or accepting) the species. From the beginning of time, all people of religion have believed in their existence. There is a consensus that some people have seen, conversed with, and related news from angels. If angels did not exist, if one had not been seen, if the existence of one or more had not been established through observation, how could such a general belief continue? If this belief were not based on strong evidence, how could it come down to us despite changing ideas and beliefs and the passage of time? Besides, might not such a religious belief and a consensus of religious scholars be based on an experienced reality originating in countless signs and experiences? So, we can conclude that belief in angels and other spirit beings is based on the experiences that Prophets and godly people have had with them, and that these accounts were narrated by reliable sources.

How can you doubt their existence after it has been reported by all Prophets and saints, who are like suns, moons, and stars in our social life? Such people are specialists in this matter, and obviously two specialists in a matter are preferable to thousands of non-specialists. It also is an established principle that once a matter is confirmed by two persons, its denial by thousands carries no weight. Moreover, how can you doubt the Qur'an, shining like the sun in the realm of truths, and the testimony and experiences of Prophet Muhammad, the sun of Prophethood?

Although establishing the existence of one individual proves the existence of the species of spirit beings, the best, as well as the most rational and acceptable way of establishing their existence, is expounded by the Shari'a, described by the Qur'an, and witnessed by the one who performed the Ascension, upon him be peace and blessings.

FOURTH FUNDAMENTAL: When we carefully examine creation, we discern that like particulars, each universal thing has a collective identity and performs a unique, universal function. For example, a flower displays a superlative design and symmetry and recites the Creator's Names in the tongue of its being. Likewise, the earth performs a universal duty of glorification as though it were a flower. A fruit and a tree glorify God within an order and regularity, although the latter does so on a larger scale through the "words" of its leaves, blossoms, and fruits. Similarly, the vast "ocean" of heavens praises and glorifies the All-Majestic Maker through its suns, moons, and stars, all of which are like its words. In short, each of the inert and outwardly inanimate and unconscious material bodies performs a vital function in praising and glorifying God. Angels represent such bodies in the World of the Inner Dimensions of Things and express praise and glorification on their behalf. In turn, these bodies are the angels' representatives, dwellings, and mosques in the material world.

As explained in the Fourth Branch of the 24th Word, angels and spirit beings constitute the first class of the laborers that the All-Majestic Maker of this palace of creation employs. Among others, inanimate things and the vegetable creation are quite important servants who work without wages; animals serve unconsciously in return for their food and pleasures; and humanity, taking a share in everything for themselves, supervises the other servants (on the earth) and works consciously according to the Majestic Creator's purposes in return for wages: a reward here and in the Hereafter.

As the foremost category of servants, angels resemble humanity because they know and conform to the Creator's purposes. But they differ from us, because they work solely for God's good pleasure and ask only for the spiritual pleasure and happiness of nearness to their Creator. Their worship varies according to their nature and function as representatives of most species. Their services and praises differ in the different departments of Divine Lordship, as do the duties performed by a government's departments. For example, Archangel Michael superintends the growth of corn and provision upon the earth by God's permission and Power. If one may say so, he is the head of all farmer-like angels. Another great angel leads the "incorporeal shepherds" of all animals, by the All-Majestic Originator's permission, Command, and Power.

Since an angel represents each kind of creature and presents its service and worship to the Divine Court, the Prophet's descriptions of them are entirely reasonable and credible: "There are angels with forty thousand heads, each with forty thousand mouths, and forty thousand praises sung by forty thousand tongues in each mouth." This Prophetic Tradition means that angels serve universal purposes and that some creatures worship God with forty thousand heads in forty thousand ways. For example, the firmament praises the Majestic Creator through its suns and stars, while the earth worships with countless heads, each with countless mouths, and each mouth containing countless tongues. Thus this Tradition is said to refer to the angel representing the earth in the World of the Inner Dimensions of Things.

Once I saw a medium-sized almond tree with forty branches (the equivalent of forty heads), each of which had forty twigs (the equivalent of forty tongues). Each twig had forty blossoms, each of which had forty differently colored stamens. These "forty"s are each a manifestation of a Divine Name. Is it possible that the All-Wise One of Grace, the All-Majestic Maker of that almond tree, Who charged it with so many duties, would not appoint a specific angel to know it, introduce it to the universe, and present it to the Divine Court?

The above explanations seek to encourage the heart to believe, the intellect to accept, and the carnal soul to admit the truth. If you have acquired some understanding and wish to encounter angels more closely, purify yourself of doubt and enter the garden of the Qur'an—its gates are open. You can see angels in the Paradise of Qur'an, and its verses are like an observatory from which you can look at them:

> By the companies (of angels) sent one after another, and then moving fast and forcefully like tempests; and by those enfolding the Scrolls of Revelation, and serving (for right and wrong) to be separated, and so bringing down the Revelation, so that some may have the means to ask for forgiveness and that some may be warned. (77:1–6)

> By those who immediately fly out and plunge (with God's command); by those who move gently and eagerly; by those who swiftly float and so hasten along as if in a race, and thus fulfilling the commands. (79:1–5)

> ... in (the Night of Power) angels and the Spirit descend, by the leave of their Lord, with His decrees for every affair. (97:4)

> ... a Fire whose fuel is human beings and stones, and over which are angels stern and strict, who disobey not God in what He commands them and do what they are commanded. (66:6)

> All-Glorified is He. Nay, but they are honored servants: they speak only what He has spoken to them, and they act by His command. (21:26–27)

If you desire to meet jinn, enter into the Qur'anic chapter that discusses them (72) and listen to what they are saying:

> "We have heard a Qur'an wonderful, guiding to rectitude. We believe in it and we will not associate with our Lord anyone." (72:1–2)

Second aim

[This is about Doomsday, the world's destruction, and the afterlife. This Aim consists of an Introduction and four Fundamentals.]

INTRODUCTION: If one were to claim that a city or a palace will be destroyed and then reconstructed firmly, one would be asked the following six questions:

- Why will it be destroyed, and is its destruction necessary?
- Can its destroyer and its rebuilder really do these things?
- Is such destruction possible?
- If possible, will it really be destroyed?
- Is such rebuilding possible?
- If possible, will it actually be rebuilt?

There is a necessary cause for the destruction and re-building of this palace of the world and the city of the universe. Both can and will be destroyed and re-built. Their destroyer and rebuilder can do both.

FIRST FUNDAMENTAL: The spirit is undoubtedly eternal. All the proofs for the existence of angels and other spirit beings prove its eternity as well. We are too close to the souls of the dead, who are waiting in the Intermediate Realm to go to the Hereafter, to require proof of their existence. It is commonly known that people of spiritual unveiling get in contact with them, and the saints who have insight into the reality of the life of grave can see them; some people can communicate with them, and almost everyone encounter them in true dreams. As modern materialism causes doubt in such obvious matters, we provide an Introduction and four Sources from which persuasive knowledge can be obtained.

Introduction: An eternal, matchless beauty requires an eternal lover through whom it will be reflected permanently. A faultless, eternal, and perfect art demands a permanent contemplative herald. An infinite mercy and benevolence require the continued sustenance and happiness of needy ones who thank it. The human soul is the foremost of those lovers, contemplative heralds, and needy thankful ones. Given this, it will accompany that beauty, perfection, and mercy on the way to eternity.

Not only human spirits, all creatures, even the most primitive, are created for some kind of eternity. Even the spiritless flower has a sort of postdeath immortality in countless ways: its form is preserved in memories, and the law of its formation and life gains permanence via new flowers growing from its seeds. Since this law, which has the same significance for it as our spirit has for us, and the model of its form are preserved amidst turbulent events through its seeds by the All-Preserving, All-Wise One, the human spirit, which has a sublime comprehensive nature and consciousness and has been clothed with external existence, is far more deserving of being eternal. How could an All-Wise One of Majesty, an All-Preserving One of Eternity, Who maintains a huge tree's life-cycle and the law of its formation through a tiny seed, not preserve the spirits or souls of dead people?

First source: This concerns us as individuals and relates to our inner world. Look carefully into your life and inner aspect, and you will discern the existence of an eternal spirit. Every person changes his or her body at least annually through a complete renewal, but the spirit remains unchanged.

Since this is so and the body is ephemeral, the spirit inhabiting it is permanent. The formation or deformation of your body's molecules, or its composition and decomposition, does not affect the spirit, which annually changes or renews its bodily garment. When it strips off this garment at death, neither its permanence nor its essential nature is affected because, as established through experiences and observation, the spirit does not depend upon the body for its life. The body is only its dwelling place, not its cover. The spirit has a subtle cover, its "energetic or ethereal envelope," and leaves its dwelling place at death and is dressed in this ethereal cover.

Second source: This relates to the outer world. Repeated observations, and countless incidents and experiences indicate the spirit's eternity. If a single spirit's permanence is established in the afterlife, this confirms the spirit's perpetuation after death. For the science of logic says that an essential or intrinsic quality an individual has is common to the whole species, for qualities originating in the essence are shared by all individuals. There are so many observations, incidents, signs and experiences indicating the permanence of the spirit that it is as certain as the existence of a continent that we have never visited. So there are numberless spirits which have left their corporeal bodies and continue to exist in the Intermediate Realm. They have a relationship with us; our prayers for them and acts of charity on their behalf reach them and we receive their blessing in return.

It is also commonly perceived that an essential aspect of each person exists after physical death: his or her spirit. As the spirit is a simple unitary entity, it is not subject to disintegration or decomposition like composite material things. Life ensures a form of unity within multiplicity and causes a sort of permanence. In other words, unity and permanence are essential to the spirit, through which multiplicity gains some sort of unity and permanence.

The spirit's mortality would be due either to its decomposition and disintegration or its annihilation. The first option is impossible, for the spirit has a simple unitary essence. The second option also is impossible, for it is contrary to the Absolutely All-Generous One's infinite Mercy. His boundless Munificence and Mercy would not allow the human spirit to be deprived of the blessing of existence that He has bestowed on it, for it ardently desires and is worthy of this blessing.

Third source: The spirit is a living, conscious, luminous entity; a comprehensive, substantial law or command of God furnished with external existence and has the potential to achieve universality. Even "natural" laws, which are insubstantial when compared to the spirit, have stability and permanence. For all kinds of existence, although subject to change, possess a permanent dimension that remains unaltered through all stages of life. Thus each person is an individual and, on account of his or her comprehensive nature, universal consciousness and far-reaching powers of conception, like a species. A law that operates upon humanity also applies to the individual. Since the All-Majestic Creator endowed us with a sublime nature, caused us to be comprehensive mirrors through which His Names and Attributes are reflected, and charged us with a universal duty of worship, then each individual's spiritual reality remains alive forever by Divine permission, even though its form undergoes countless changes. Thus the human spirit, which constitutes our conscious, living element, is eternal and has been made so by God's command and permission.

Fourth source: The Divine laws of "nature" resemble the spirit, for they also belong to the world of the Divine Will and Command. However, they operate upon categories that do not have a perceptive existence. When we analyze these laws, we see that they would have been the spirits of the categories themselves if they had been given external existence. As they are permanent and unchanging, their unity and simplicity (uncompositeness) is not affected by any alteration or transformation. For example, the seeds of a dead fig tree still contain the permanent, spirit-like law relating to its formation.

Since insubstantial and ordinary laws have such sort of permanence and continuance, the human spirit must not only have permanence in the world but also be immortal and eternal. According to: *The spirit is of My Lord's Command* (17:85), the spirit is a conscious and living law from the world of Divine Command and has been endowed with external existence by Eternal Power. Since unconscious laws issuing from the Divine Attribute of Will and the World of Divine Command are permanent, the spirit is even worthier of such permanence, for it comes from the same source and, additionally, has an external reality. Furthermore, it is more sublime and powerful because it has consciousness, and more permanent and valuable because it is living.

SECOND FUNDAMENTAL: Eternal happiness is necessary, and the All-Majestic One is absolutely able to create it. Both the destruction of our universe and the resurrection of everything are possible and will occur. Addressing the reason or intellect, we will explain these realities briefly.

There is a necessary cause for the eternal happiness. Consider the following ten points:

First point: Creation displays a perfect harmony and a purposeful order, and every aspect of the universe shows signs of a will and indications of a purpose. As testified by their fruits or results, everything and every event displays a light of purpose, intention, and will; every movement, a gleam of choice and preference; and every compound and composition, a ray of wisdom. If creation were not meant to produce eternal happiness, its harmony and order would be a deceit. All meanings, relations, and connections, which are the spirit of order, would come to nothing. It is eternal happiness which underlies this order. In which case, the order of the universe points to eternal happiness.

Second point: The universe's creation displays perfect wisdom. Divine Wisdom, the representation of eternal Divine Favoring, proclaims the coming of eternal happiness through the tongue of the benefits and purposes that It observes throughout the universe. If there were no eternal happiness, all benefits and purposes observed in the universe would have to be denied.

Third point: Human intellect, wisdom, experience, and deductive reasoning point out that nothing superfluous or vain occurs in creation. For the universe's All-Majestic Maker chooses the best and easiest way in creation, and apportions many duties, purposes and results to each creature, no matter how insignificant it may appear. This indicates the existence of eternal happiness. Since there is no waste and nothing in vain, there must be eternal happiness, for eternal non-existence would make everything futile and wasteful. The absence of waste in creation, particularly in human body, as testified to by several sciences, demonstrates that our countless spiritual potentialities, limitless aspirations and ideas, and inclinations will never go to waste. Our basic inclination toward perfection indicates perfection's existence, and our desire for happiness proclaims that an eternal happiness awaits us. If this were not so, all the basic features of our existence and nature and all our sublime aspirations would be wasteful and lose their essential meaning.

Fourth point: The alternation of day and night, as well as spring and winter, atmospheric changes, our body's annual renewal, and our awakening and rising every morning after sleep all indicate a complete rising and renewal. Seconds forecast a minute, minutes predicts an hour, and hours anticipate a day. The dials of God's great clock—the earth—point, in succession, to the day, the year, our lifetime, and the ages through which the world passes. As they show morning after night and spring after winter, they intimate that the morning of the Resurrection will follow the death of creation.

A person's life contains many cycles that can be regarded as a kind of death and resurrection (e.g., daily, seasonal, and annual changes; sleeping and waking; and various revivals and renewals). Nature's revival every spring is a promise of the final Resurrection; during that season countless kinds of resurrection take place among animals and plants. Thus the All-Wise Creator reminds us of the Resurrection to come.

The human individual is like a species in animal kingdom. For the light of intellect has given such breath to the aspirations and ideas of humanity that they encompass both the past and the future. Even if they consumed the entire world, they would not be satisfied. In all other species, an individual's nature is particular, its value is personal, its view is restricted, its qualities are limited, and its pleasure and pain are instantaneous. Human beings, however, have a sublime nature and the greatest value, limitless perfection, and a more permanent spiritual pleasure and pain. Given this, the kinds of resurrection experienced by other species suggest that every human being will be resurrected completely on the Day of Judgment.

Fifth point: Humanity is endowed with unlimited potentialities that develop into unrestricted abilities. These, in turn, give rise to countless inclinations that generate limitless desires, which are the source of infinite ideas and conceptions. All of these, as confirmed by thinkers and scholars, indicate the existence of a world of eternal happiness beyond this material world. Our very nature, which is the origin of our innate inclination toward eternal happiness, makes one sure that such a world will be established.

Sixth point: The all-encompassing Mercy of the universe's All-Merciful, All-Compassionate Maker requires eternal happiness, which gives Divine bounty and grace their true nature. Were it not for this happiness, God's chief grace for humanity, all people would raise lamentations over eternal separation, acts of favor would turn into requital, and Divine compassion would be negated. However, Divine mercy is a substantial reality and more evident than the sun in the universe. Observe the three manifestations of Divine Mercy: love, affection, and intellect. If human life resulted in eternal separation with unending pangs of parting, that gracious love would turn into the greatest affliction, affection into a most painful ailment, and the light-giving intellect into an unmitigated evil. Divine Compassion, however, (for it is Compassion) never inflicts the agony of eternal separation upon true love.

Seventh point: All known and observable pleasure-giving experiences, beauties, perfections, attractions, ardent yearnings, and feelings of compassion are spiritual articulations and manifestations of the All-Majestic Creator's Favor, Mercy, and Munificence made known to the intellect. Since there is a substantial reality underlying the universe, there is true Mercy; since there is true Mercy, there will be eternal happiness.

Eighth point: Our conscience (conscious nature) indicates eternal happiness. Whoever listens to their alert conscience hears it saying eternity over and over again. Even if we were given the entire universe, we would not be compensated for the lack of eternity, for we have an innate longing and were created for it. Thus our natural inclination toward eternal happiness comes from an objective reality—eternity's existence and our desire for eternity.

Ninth point: Prophet Muhammad, upon him be peace and blessings, who spoke the truth and whose words have been confirmed throughout the centuries, preached and promised the coming of everlasting life and eternal happiness. His message concentrated almost as much on the Resurrection as on Divine Unity, referring to the consensus of all Prophets and saints.

Tenth point: The Qur'an, a matchless miracle with forty aspects, announces the Resurrection and the coming of eternal happiness. It unveils creation's mystery and offers uncountable rational arguments for the Resurrection. Such verses as: *He has created you by stages* (71:14), and, *Say: "He Who has originated them the first time will bring them to life again"* (36:79), which contains a comparison and an analogy, and, *Your Lord does not wrong His servants* (41:46), which indicates God's justice, provide us with telescopes to see the Resurrection and everlasting happiness. I have discussed the proofs within the first two verses in my treatise *Nuqta* (The Point: included in *al-Mathnawi an-Nuri*) as follows:

Each human being undergoes ordered and systematic changes during the process of development, which goes through the stages of a fertilized ovum, blood-clot, a chew of lump, bones, the flesh, and another creation or (distinct) human-shaped being. Each of these stages follows precise principles particular to it. This development and the principles it follows indicate the exercise of a definite purpose, will, and wisdom. The All-Wise Creator, Who creates human beings by these stages, also causes the body to renew itself each year. This renewal demands the replacement of decomposed cells by new ones produced by the All-Providing One's provision of food according to the needs of each bodily part.

If we observe the atoms of the food used to renew or repair the body, we see them come together from the atmosphere, soil, and water. Their motions are so precise that it seems they have received marching orders to go to a certain place. In addition, their manner of going indicates the operation of the Real Agent. Starting from the inanimate world of elements and chemical substances, they pass into the animated world of vegetables and animals. Having developed into *sustenance* in agreement with definite principles, they enter the body as food. After being "cooked" in different "kitchens" and transformed and passed through some "filters," they are distributed to the body's parts according to need following the principles established by the All-Munificent Providing.

All of these processes take place in accordance with the All-Providing One's laws and without the intervention of blind chance, lawless coincidence, deaf nature, and unconscious causes. They display perfect knowledge, wisdom, and insight. At whatever stage an atom enters the body's cell from the surrounding element, it does so in an orderly fashion and conforms to that stage's specified laws. To whichever level it travels, it steps with such order that it appears self-evidently to be proceeding at an All-Wise Mover's command. Never deviating from its aim and object, it gradually advances from stage to stage and from level to level until, at the command of its Sustainer, it reaches its appropriate position. Once there, it establishes itself and begins to work.

The provision of food and its reaching the cells for which it is destined show Divine Will and Divine Determination. So perfect is this process' order and arrangement that each particle seems to have its final destination written on its "forehead." Is it conceivable that the All-Majestic Creator, Who exercises Lordship over creation with boundless power and all-encompassing wisdom, from particles of matter to planets, and spins them with order and balance, could fail to revive creation? Qur'anic verses open our eyes to this revival by comparing it with our first creation:

> Say: "He Who has originated them the first time (with definite purpose) will bring them to life again (in the Hereafter)." (36:79)

> He originates creation, then brings it back again, and it is easier for Him. (30:27)

Soldiers of a battalion dispersed to rest come together again at a bugle call more readily and easily than when they had been collected to form the battalion. Similarly, the mind will conclude that it is easier than their original creation that a body's essential particles, which had established mutual close relations and familiarity during their worldly life, are assembled when the angel Israfil blows the Trumpet. Not all of the component parts even have to be present; rather, the fundamental parts and essential particles, which are like nuclei and seeds and which a Prophetic Tradition calls "the root of the tail" (the *os coccyx*), may suffice for the second creation's basis and foundation. The All-Wise Creator will rebuild the human body upon this foundation.

The following section summarizes the truth expressed by the analogy of justice in such verses as: *Your Lord does not wrong His servants.*

We observe that cruel, sinful, and tyrannical persons usually lead a comfortable and luxurious life while godly, oppressed people live in poverty and difficulty. Death makes them equal, for both would have departed forever with their deeds unquestioned if there were no supreme tribunal. However, Divine Wisdom and Justice never allow any wrongdoing to go unnoticed and forbid injustice, and therefore require the establishment of a supreme tribunal to punish evil and reward good.

As this world is not exactly propitious for a complete development of human potentialities, we are destined to find realization in another world. Our essence is comprehensive and is bound for eternity. As we have an extremely comprehensive nature, we can commit tremendous crime and wrongdoing. Therefore, we cannot be left to our own devices without an order and discipline, nor can we left to deteriorate into non-existence. Hell is waiting for us with a wide-open mouth, and Paradise is expecting us with open arms.

Study the verses like those mentioned above, which contain rational arguments for the Resurrection. Also, the Ten Points you have been following give you a clear insight and strong evidence for the absolute necessity of the Resurrection. Moreover, most of the All-Majestic Maker's Beautiful Names such as the All-Wise, All-Compassionate, All-Preserver, and All-Just actually require that the Resurrection should occur, that eternal life should come, and that eternal happiness should be realized. Consequently, the Resurrection's necessity and requirement is so strong that there is no room for doubt or uncertainty.

THIRD FUNDAMENTAL: Just as the Resurrection's necessity and requirement is certain, so the One Who will bring it about can do so. His Power is absolute and has no deficiency. Everything is the same in relation to His Power. He creates the spring as easily as a flower. All suns, stars, worlds, and atoms bear witness to His Power and Majesty. Given this, how can one doubt that He can raise the dead for the Last Judgment? It is observed that an All-Powerful One of Majesty causes a new environment to come into existence each century, renews the universe every year, and creates a new world every day. He hangs many transient worlds upon the string of time as centuries, years, or even days pass for a perfect, definite purpose. He displays His Wisdom's perfection and His Art's beauty by clothing the earth in the garment of spring as if it were a single flower, and then decorating and embellishing it with countless examples of Resurrection.

The verse: *Your creation and resurrection are as but a single soul* (31:28) announces that creating and resurrecting the greatest thing or countless things is easy for God's Power as the least, single thing. This is so because

Divine Power is intrinsic in the Divine Essence and inseparable from Him, so there can be no incapacity connected with It. Divine Power operates (in) the inner, immaterial dimension of existence, so no obstacle can interfere with Its operation. Divine Power operates like a law that has the same relationship with everything, so particulars are equal to universals in relation to It. Now we will explain these three arguments:

First argument: Divine Power is intrinsic in the Divine Essence and inseparable from Him, so there can be no incapacity connected with It. Otherwise, the simultaneous existence of two opposites would have to be supposed. Since impotence cannot be involved with Divine Power, It can have no degrees, for degrees in a thing's existence come about only through the intervention of opposites. Degrees of temperature occur because of cold's intervention, and degrees of beauty exist because of ugliness' intervention. This is true of all qualities in the universe. Since contingent things and beings do not exist essentially of themselves and have no absolute qualities intrinsic in and inseparable from and originating in themselves, they contain opposites and degrees. Because of this, the contingent world is subject to change and transformation.

Since Eternal Divine Power contains no degrees, it is equally easy for It to create and operate particles and galaxies. Resurrecting humanity is as easy for It as reviving one person, and creating spring is as easy as creating a flower. If creation or resurrection were ascribed to causes, creating a flower would be as difficult as creating spring. But when attributed to the One of Unity, creating everything is as easy as creating one thing.

Second argument: Divine Power operates in the inner, incorporeal dimension of things (the metaphysical kingdom). Like a mirror, the universe has two sides: corporeal (resembling a mirror's colored face) and incorporeal (resembling the mirror's shining face and looking to the Creator). Opposites exist in the corporeal side, which manifests beauty and ugliness, good and bad, big and small, difficulty and ease. The All-Majestic Creator of the universe veils His Power's acts behind the veil of observed causes in this side so that those who lack understanding do not regard His Power's relation to simple things as unbecoming to Him. His Dignity and Majesty require this. Causes have no real effect upon creation, for that would violate His Oneness and Unity. The incorporeal world, absolutely clear and transparent, contains none of the physical world's grossness. As Divine Power operates directly there, cause and effect have no effect, obstacles cannot interfere, and creating a particle is as easy as creating a sun.

To conclude, Divine Power is simple, infinite, and an indispensable Attribute of Divine "Essence." This Power operates directly in a realm that is clear, refined, and transparent, one in which there is nothing to oppose or intervene in it. Thus there is no difference between a community and an individual, particular and universal or big and small in relation to Power.

Third argument: Divine Power operates like a law that has the same relationship with everything. We will make this subtle matter comprehensible through several features of creation. Transparency, correspondence and reciprocity, balance, orderliness, abstraction, and obedience are the phenomena in the universe that render many equal to few, and great equal to small.

First feature: Transparency. The reflection of the same sun on both the ocean's surface and in a drop of water has the same identity. If the earth consisted of pieces of glass, each one would reflect the sun without hindrance and without one interfering with the other. If the sun were a conscious independent being with willpower that could reflect its own light knowingly or consciously, its giving of light to or being reflected in one particle or on the whole of the earth would be equally easy.

Second feature: Correspondence and *reciprocity.* If we stand with a lit candle in the center of a large circle of people, each of whom is holding a mirror, each mirror will hold the same reflection without any one hindering any other.

Third feature: Balance. If we weigh a pair of things—two stars or two eggs or two atoms—with a balance that measures each item with perfect precision, any extra force exerted upon either scale would disturb the balance.

Fourth feature: Orderliness. We can steer a huge ship as easily as a small toy, for all the parts of its orderly system are interrelated.

Fifth feature: Abstraction or Incorporeality. A living creature's size has no bearing on its real essence or nature, for these abstract and incorporeal features are the same for every creature. Differences in individualized forms do not cause confusion. For example, a minnow has the same essence or nature as a basking-shark (both are fish), and a micro-organism has the same essence as a rhinoceros (both are living animals).

Sixth feature: Obedience. A commander moves an army as easily as a single soldier by ordering it to march. The reality of obedience in the universe is as follows: Everything inclines toward its own perfection. An inclination grows into a need, an increased need becomes a yearning, and an increased yearning becomes an attraction. Inclination, need, yearning, and attraction work as Divine laws and operate in ways designed to lead things to realize their perfection. Creation's final, absolute perfection occurs when it grows into absolute existence. A thing's relative perfection is the relative existence that gives effect to all its potentialities. This is why the universe's obedience to the Divine Command of *"Be!" and it is* (36: 82) does not differ from that of a particle.

Creation obeys this Divine Command, coming from the Creator's Eternal Will, via the same forces of inclination, need, yearning, and attraction. All of these are urged to operate on all creatures by the same Divine Will. Delicate water, which cracks or even shatters iron when ordered to freeze, shows the power of this obedience.

If defective, limited, weak, and non-creative contingencies display such effects in the face of these six features or phenomena, for sure, everything is equally susceptible to the Divine Power's order. This Power, Which brought the universe into existence from non-existences and shows Itself through Its amazing works, is infinite, eternal, and absolutely perfect. Nothing is difficult for It. Note that Divine Power cannot be measured in the scales of these features; they are mentioned only to have some grasp of the matter.

In conclusion: The eternal Divine Power is infinite; It is intrinsic in and inseparable from the All-Sacred Being; It operates in the pure, incorporeal dimension of existence. This dimension is directly turned to It. In the face of or in relation to Divine Power, this dimension's material existence or non-existence is equally possible. Also, it is free from any impediments before the operation of Divine Power and having different, confusing characteristics. Besides, it obeys all Divine laws of creation. Thus Divine Power can create everything with equal ease. It can revive all the dead people on Resurrection Day as easily as It revives an insect in spring. Given this, the Divine announcement of: *Your creation and resurrection are as but a single soul* is true and unexaggerated. This proves that the Agent Who will destroy and re-create the universe on the Last Day can do this.

FOURTH FUNDAMENTAL: As there is a necessary cause for the Resurrection and the One Who will bring it about can do this, so also the world is exposed to the Resurrection. There are four related matters here: The world can perish, it will perish, the destroyed world can be rebuilt as the Hereafter, and it will be resurrected and rebuilt.

First matter: The death of the universe is possible. For if something is subject to the law of development, it must evolve to a final end. That which develops to a final end must have a limited lifetime and, therefore, a fixed natural end. That which has a fixed end inevitably dies. Just as humanity is a microcosm subject to death, so the universe, a macro-human being, is also subject to death. Accordingly, it will perish and be resurrected on the morning of the Resurrection. Just as a living tree (a miniature universe) cannot save itself from annihilation, the universe (the branch of creation growing from the tree of creation) can neither be saved from destruction and disintegration to be repaired and renewed.

If the universe is not destroyed by an external destructive event, with the Eternal Will's permission, it eventually will begin to die. Even scientists say this. Begin to suffer death agonies, it will give a sharp cry and what the following verses pronounce will happen: *When the sun is folded up, and when the stars fall, and when the mountains are set moving* (81:1-3); and *When heaven is cleft open, and when the stars fall in disorder and are scattered, and when the seas burst forth* (82:1-3).

A significant subtle point: Water freezes to its detriment (loses its essential liquid form); ice melts to its detriment (loses its essential solid state); an item's essence becomes stronger at the expense of its material form; a language becomes coarse to the detriment of the meaning; the spirit weakens as the flesh becomes more substantial, and the flesh weakens as the spirit becomes more illuminated. Similarly, the solid world is refined through life in favor of the afterlife. The Creative Power breathes life into dense, solid, and inanimate substances through an astonishing activity. This suggests that It melts, refines and illuminates that solid world to the advantage of the Hereafter through the light of life.

Unlike forms, no truth, even though weak, ever perishes. Rather, it assumes various forms in the corporeal world. A truth flourishes and expands, while forms grow weaker and gains greater refinement to be able to become suitable for the stable, developed truth. The truth that constitutes an item's essence is inversely proportional to its form's strength: the form grows denser as the truth weakens, and the truth becomes stronger as the form weakens. This law is common to whatever develops and evolves. Given this, the corporeal world, which is a form containing the great truth of the universe, will shatter, with the All-Majestic Creator's permission, and be rebuilt more beautifully. One day, *On the day the earth is changed into another earth* (14:48) will be realized. In short, the death of the world is possible and it will certainly die.

Second matter: The world's eventual death is confirmed by all God-revealed religions, supported by all pure and saintly persons, and indicated by the universe's changes, transformations, and alterations. The constant replacement of this guest-house's living inhabitants, all of whom are welcomed and then leave at their appointed time (through death) so that they can be replaced by newcomers, also indicates this world's death.

If you want to imagine the death of the world as the Qur'an describes it, consider how and in what minute and precise interrelationship the constituent parts of the universe have been organized into a sublime and delicate system. If any heavenly body were told to leave its axis, the universe would be thrown into the throes of death. Stars would collide, planets would be scattered, and the sound of exploding spheres would fill space. Mountains would fly, oceans would burst forth in masses of fire and the earth would be flattened. The Eternal Power will shake andrefine the universe, with the result that the elements of Paradise and Hell will be separated from each other.

Third matter: The universe can be resurrected, for as proved in the Second Fundamental, Divine Power is not defective. Moreover, there is a strong necessity for it and it is possible. If there is a strong necessity that something possible should occur, it comes to be regarded as something that will certainly occur.

Another significant point: A close examination of what occurs in the universe shows that two opposite elements in it have spread everywhere and become rooted. Their clash accounts for good and evil, benefit and harm, perfection and defect, light and darkness, guidance and misguidance, belief and unbelief, obedience and rebellion, and fear and love, and so on. Such ongoing conflict causes the universe to manifest a continuous alteration and transformation in order to produce the elements of a new world.

These opposed elements eventually will lead to eternity in two different directions and materialize as Paradise and Hell. The eternal world will be made up of this transitory world's essential elements, which will be given permanence. Paradise and Hell are the two opposite fruits growing on the tree of creation's two branches, the two results of the chain of creation, the two cisterns being filled by the two streams of things and events, the two poles to which beings flow in waves, and the places where Divine Grace and Divine Wrath manifest themselves. They will be filled with their particular inhabitants when Divine Power shakes up the universe.

This is so because God, the Eternal All-Wise and as the requirement of His Eternal Grace and Wisdom, has created this world as a testing arena, a mirror to reflect His All-Beautiful Names, a vast page upon which to write with the Pen of His Destiny and Power. People are tested here to develop their potentialities, and the development of potentialities causes the manifestation of their abilities. The manifestation of abilities gives rise to the emergence of relative truths, which, in turn, causes the All-Majestic Maker's All-Beautiful Names to manifest their inscriptions and make the universe a missive of the Eternally Besought One. It is through this testing that the diamond-like essences of sublime souls to be separated from the coal-like matter of base ones.

For many other subtle, sublime instances of wisdom like these, God willed that creation, as well as its change and alteration, should take place. He made opposites confront one another—mingling benefit with harm, good with evil, and beauty with ugliness. Kneading them together like dough, He subjected the universe to the law of alteration and the principle of perfection. The day when the abode of testing has been closed, the time of testing and trial has ended, the All-Beautiful Names have fulfilled their mission, the Pen of Divine Destiny has finished its writing, Divine Power has completed the inscriptions of Its art, creatures have fulfilled their duties and services, seeds have been sown in the field of the afterlife, the earth has displayed all the miracles of Divine Power's miracles, this transitory world has hung all eternal scenes upon the picture-rail of time, and the All-Majestic Maker's eternal Wisdom and Favor has required that the test's results be announced, the truths of the Divine All-Beautiful Names' manifestations and the Pen of Divine Destiny's missives be unveiled, the originals of the sample-like inscriptions of the Power's art be exhibited, the benefits and purposes of the duties performed by creatures be displayed and their services be paid, the truths of the meanings expressed by the Book of the Universe's words be seen, the seeds of potentialities be developed fully, a supreme court be established, the scenes bearing the meanings of whatever belongs to and has occurred in the world be displayed, and the veil of "natural" apparent causes be removed so that everything is submitted directly to the All-Majestic Creator—on that day the Eternal All-Wise will destroy the universe in order to save it from change and transience and eternalize it and to separate its opposites. This separation will cause Hell to appear with all its awfulness, and Paradise to appear with all its beauty and splendor. The people of Hell will be threatened with: *Now keep yourselves apart, you sinners, upon this day* (36:59), while the people of Paradise will be welcomed with: *Peace be upon you. Well you have fared; enter in, to dwell forever* (39:73). By means of His perfect Power, the Eternal All-Wise will give an everlasting, unchanging existence to the inhabitants of both dwelling places. They will not age or suffer bodily disintegration or decomposition, for there will be nothing to cause any change.

Fourth matter: After destroying this world, the One Who created it will re-form it more beautifully and convert it into a mansion of the

Hereafter. The Qur'an, which contains thousands of rational evidences, and other Divine Scriptures agree on this, as do the All-Majestic One's Attributes of Majesty and Grace as well as His Beautiful Names. Moreover, He promised that He would bring about the Resurrection and the Supreme Gathering through all of His heavenly decrees sent to His Prophets, all of whom agree that He carries out His promises. Prophet Muhammad is the foremost to confirm this, along with the strength of his one thousand miracles. All saints and righteous scholars confirm this as well. Lastly, the universe predicts it with all the evidence it contains.

In short, it is as certain as the sun's rising the next morning after setting this evening that the "sun of truth" will appear in the form of the Hereafter's life after this world's life sets.

Inspired by the Divine Name the All-Wise and the Qur'an's grace, I have elaborated the proofs of this truth to convince the intellect and ready the heart to accept it. But the words of the Creator of the universe have the greatest right to speak in this matter. So, listen to the Eternal Discourse of the All-Wise Maker, in which He addresses everyone regardless of time and place. In response, we must believe and affirm what He says:

> When the earth quakes with a violent quaking destined for it and throws up its burdens, and human cries out: "What is the matter with it?" That day it will proclaim its tidings because Your Lord has inspired it. That day humans will come forth in scattered groups to be shown their deeds. Whoever does an atom's weight of good will see it, whoever does an atom's weight of evil will see it. (99:1–8)

> Give glad tidings to those who believe and do good, righteous deeds: for them are Gardens through which rivers flow. Every time they are provided with fruits therefrom, they say, "This is what we were provided with before." For they are given to them in resemblance (to what was given to them both in the world, and just before in the Gardens). Furthermore, for them are spouses eternally purified. They will abide there (forever). (2:25)

> All-Glorified are You. We have no knowledge save what You have taught us. Surely You are the All-Knowing, the All-Wise.

> Our Lord, take us not to task if we forget or make mistakes. O God, bestow blessings on our master Muhammad and on his Family, as You bestowed blessings on our master Abraham and his family. You are the All-Praiseworthy, the All-Sublime.

The
Thirtieth Word

The Thirtieth Word

- *An exposition of ego or human selfhood*
- *The movement of atoms*

HIS WORD EXPLAINS AN IMPORTANT TALISMAN OF THE WISE Qur'an, which reveals the mystery of creation: *ana* (I, human selfhood) and *dharra* (atom) to the measure of an *alif* and a *nuqta*, respectively.[164] This Word consists of two Aims: The First Aim discusses the Selfhood's essential nature and final state, and the Second Aim discusses the motion and function of atoms.

Two aims

In the name of God, the All-Merciful, the All-Compassionate.

We offered the Trust to the heavens, and the earth, and the mountains, but they shrank from bearing it, and were afraid of it (fearful of being unable to fulfill its responsibility), but humanity has undertaken it; it is indeed prone to doing great wrong and misjudging, and acting out of sheer ignorance. (33:72)

First aim

We point out a single gem from the vast treasure-house of this verse: Human selfhood is one aspect of the Trust which the heavens, the earth and the mountains shrank from bearing. From the time of Adam up to the present, it has been the seed of the terrible tree of *Zaqqum* and of the illustrious tree of *Touba*, which have shot out branches around the world of humankind. Before shedding some light on this great truth, we offer the following introductory explanation.

---

[164] The *alif* is a short, vertical line representing the first letter of the Arabic alphabet and the word *ana*. The *nuqta* is the dot in the Arabic script from which all letters are made by either a horizontal or vertical extension. This same dot is used in Arabic to represent zero. (Tr.)

Selfhood is the key to the Divine Names, which are hidden treasures. Being a mystery and a wonderful talisman, it also is the key to creation's mystery. When its essence is known, its mystery is resolved, and that, in turn, discloses creation's mystery and the Necessary Existence's treasures. I discussed this in my Arabic treatise, A *Whiff from the Breezes of the Qur'an's Guidance* (included in *al-Mathnawi an-Nuri*), as follows:

The key to creation is in our hand and attached to our selfhood. The doors to creation seem to be open, but in fact are closed. The All-Mighty has entrusted us with a key (Ego or Selfhood) that will open creation's doors and reveal the hidden treasures of the Creator of the universe. However, Selfhood itself is a difficult mystery and an enigma, but if its true nature and purpose are known, both itself and creation's mystery will be solved.

The All-Wise Maker has entrusted each human being with selfhood having clues and samples to urge and enable him or her to recognize the truths about His Lordship's attributes and essential characteristics. Selfhood is the measure or means of comparison that makes Lordship's attributes and Divinity's characteristics known. A measure or means of comparison does not have to have actual existence, for its posited or supposed existence can serve as a measure, just like hypothetical lines in geometry.

QUESTION: Why did God make our selfhood a means to know His Attributes and Names?

ANSWER: An absolute and all-encompassing entity has no limits or terms, and therefore cannot be shaped or formed; neither can it be determined in such a way that its essential nature can be comprehended. For example, an endless light undetermined by darkness cannot be known or perceived. But whenever a real or hypothetical bounding line of darkness is drawn, it becomes determined and known. In the same way, the Divine Attributes and Names (e.g., Knowledge, Power, Wisdom, and Compassion) cannot be determined, for they are all-encompassing and have no limits or like. Thus what they essentially are cannot be known or perceived. A hypothetical boundary is needed for them to become known.

In our case, this hypothetical boundary is our selfhood. It imagines within itself a fictitious lordship, power, and knowledge, and so posits a bounding line, hypothesizes a limit to the all-encompassing Divine Attributes, and says: "This is mine, and the rest is His." Selfhood thus makes a division. By means of the miniature measures it contains, Selfhood slowly comes to understand the true nature of the Divine Attributes and Names.

For example, through this imagined lordship in its own sphere, Selfhood can understand the Lordship of the Creator in the universe. By means of its own apparent ownership, it can understand the real Ownership of its Creator, saying: "As I am the owner of this house, the Creator is the Owner of this universe." Through its partial knowledge, Selfhood comes to understand His Absolute Knowledge. Through its defective, acquired art, it can intuit the All-Majestic Maker's matchless, originative Art. It says: "I built and arranged this house, so there must be One Who made and arranged this universe."

Human ego or selfhood contains thousands of states, attributes, and perceptions that, to some extent, disclose and make knowable the Divine Attributes and essential Characteristics. Like a mirror, a measure, an instrument for discovering, or a letter which has no meaning in itself but serves the word's meaning, Selfhood is a strand of consciousness from the thick rope of human existence, a fine thread from the celestial weave of humanity's essential nature, an *alif* from the book of human identity and character.

That *alif* (I) has two aspects or faces. One aspect relates to good and existence and only receives passively what is given; it cannot create. The other aspect or face relates to evil and derives from non-existence. Here Selfhood is active. Its real nature is indicative—like a letter that has no meaning by or in itself—and points to the meaning of things other than itself. Its lordship is fictitious and hypothetical, and its own existence is so weak and insubstantial that it cannot bear or support anything on its own. Rather, Selfhood is a kind of scale or measure, like a thermometer or barometer, that indicates the degrees and quantities of things. The Necessary Being's absolute, all-encompassing and limitless Attributes can become known through it.

Those who know and realize that this is the reality of their essential nature and act accordingly are included in: *He is indeed prosperous who has grown it in purity (away from self-aggrandizing rebellion against God)* (91:9). Such people truly carry out the Trust and, through the telescope of selfhood, see what the universe is and what duties it performs. When any information about the universe comes to their soul, they see that their selfhood confirms it, and this information remains as light and wisdom, without changing into darkness and futility. When Selfhood has performed its duty in this way, it renounces its claim to lordship and hypothetical ownership (mere devices of measurement) and proclaims: "His is the sovereignty and ownership of all beings, and to Him is due all praise and gratitude. His is the judgment and

rule, and to Him you are returning." Thus it achieves true worship and servanthood and attains the rank of the best pattern of creation.

But if Selfhood forgets the Divine purpose of its creation, abandons its
duty of creation, and views itself as a self-existing being independent of the
Creator, it betrays the Trust and falls into the class of those referred to in: *And
he is indeed lost who corrupts it* (91:10). This attitude or this aspect of Selfhood
is responsible for all the kinds of polytheism, evil, and deviation that have
caused the heavens, the earth, and the mountains to be terrified of assuming
the Trust—lest they might be led to associate hypothetical partners with God.

If Selfhood, which is only an insubstantial *alif,* a thread, a hypothetical
line, is not perceived in its true essence, it grows and swells under the soil of
ignorance until it gradually permeates all parts of a human being. Like some
huge monster, it completely swallows such people so that they and their faculties may consist of nothing more than Selfhood. Eventually, the tribal or
national zealotry and human racism give strength to the individual selfhood.
This causes it to contest, like Satan, the All-Majestic Maker's commands.
Finally taking itself as a yardstick, it compares everyone and everything with
itself, divides God's sovereignty between them and other causes, and begins
to associate partners with God in the most grievous manner. Such people are
referred to in: *Surely associating partners with God is indeed a tremendous wrong*
(31: 13). Just as a man who has stolen money from the public treasury
attempts to justify his action by saying that he took a certain sum for each of
his friends, so too, one who claims self-ownership ends up believing and
claiming that everything owns itself.

While in this treacherous position, Selfhood is in absolute ignorance.
Even if it has absorbed thousands of branches of science, its ignorance is
only compounded by its knowledge. For whatever glimmers of knowledge
of God its senses and reflective powers may have brought to it from the universe, they are extinguished because it can no longer find within its soul
anything with which to confirm, polish, and maintain them. Whatever
comes to Selfhood is stained with the colors within it. Even if pure wisdom
comes, it becomes absolutely futile within a selfhood stained with by atheism, polytheism, or other forms of denying the All-Mighty. If the whole
universe were full of shining signs of God, a dark point in that selfhood
would hide them from view, as though they were invisible.

In truth, however, the essential quality proper to human nature and to
Selfhood within that nature is to point out what is other than itself. As discussed in the Eleventh Word, true to that nature, Selfhood is a most sensi-

tive scale and accurate measure, a comprehensive index and perfect map, a comprehensive mirror, and a fitting calendar and diary for the universe.

We now shed some light on the truth of this subject. Consider the following: From Adam's time until the present, two great currents or lines of thought have spread their branches in all directions and in every class of humanity, just like two tall trees. One is the line of Prophethood and religion; the other is that of philosophy and human wisdom. Whenever they agree and unite, whenever philosophy joins religion in obedience and service to it, humanity has experienced brilliant happiness and collective life. But whenever they have followed separate paths, truth and goodness have accumulated on the side of Prophethood and religion, whereas error, evil, and deviation have been drawn to the side of philosophy. We will elaborate on the origin and foundations of those two lines.

Philosophy, whenever it has split from religion, has taken the form of a tree of *Zaqqum* spreading its dark veils of ascribing partners to God and of misguidance. On the branch of the faculty of intellect or reason, it has yielded the fruits of atheism, materialism, and naturalism for the intellect's consumption. On the branch of the faculty of anger and passion, it has produced such tyrants as Nimrod, Pharaoh, and Shaddad to tyrannize people.[165] On the branch of the faculty of lusts and appetites, it has produced the fruits of goddesses, idols and those who have claimed divine status for themselves.[166]

In contrast, the blessed line of Prophethood, which takes the form of the *Touba* tree of worship, has borne the fruits of Prophets, Messengers, saints, and the righteous in the garden of the earth and on the branch of intellect. On the branch of anger and passion, the branch of defense against and repelling of evil, it has yielded the fruits of virtuous and just rulers. On the branch of attractiveness, it has borne the fruits of generous, benevolent persons of good character and modest bearing throughout history. As a result, this line has demonstrated how humanity is the perfect fruit of creation.

We will now shed light on selfhood's two aspects or faces as the origin and principal seed of these two lines of thought. One face is represented by Prophets and the other by philosophers.

---

[165] Shaddad was a tyrannical king of Antiquity who ruled in Yemen. (Tr.)

[166] The philosophies of ancient Egypt and Babylon, which either practiced magic or were thought to do so because they were represented by a small elite, produced and nurtured Nimrods and Pharaohs. The mire of naturalist philosophy gave birth to idolatry and planted deities in the ancient Greek mind. When humanity draws the veil of nature between Divine light and itself, people attribute divinity to everything and cause themselves nothing but trouble.

The face represented by Prophethood is the origin of pure worship and servitude to God, for our selfhood knows that it is His servant. Selfhood realizes that it serves One other than itself and that its essential nature has only an indicative function. It understands that it bears the meaning of one other than itself and that it can be meaningful only when it points to that One upon Whom its existence depends. Selfhood believes that its existence and life depend upon that One's Creativity and Existence. Its feeling of ownership is illusory, for selfhood knows that it enjoys only an apparent, temporary ownership by the real Owner's permission and that it has only a shadow-like reality. It is a contingent entity, an insignificant shadow manifesting the true and necessary Reality. Its duty is consciously serving as a measure and balance for its Creator's Attributes and essential Characteristics.

This is how Prophets, pure and righteous ones, and saints who follow the Prophets' line perceive selfhood's nature. As a result, they resign sovereignty to the All-Majestic Sovereign and Master of creation and believe that He has no partner or like in His Sovereignty, Lordship, and Divinity. He does not need an assistant or a deputy. In addition, He possesses the key to and has absolute power over all things. "Natural" causes are but a veil of appearances, and that nature is the sum of His creation's rules, an assemblage of His laws, of how He displays His Power.

This radiant, luminous, beautiful face of Selfhood always has been like a living seed full of meaning. From it, the All-Majestic Creator has created the *Touba* tree of worship, the blessed branches of which have adorned all parts of our world with its illustrious fruits. Through this face, the darkness over the past is removed and we understand that the past is not a domain of eternal extinction or a vast graveyard, as conceived by philosophy, but rather a source of light and a bright, shining ladder with many rungs from which all souls traversing it may leap into the future and eternal happiness. It is also a radiant abode and a garden for souls that have left this world, cast off their heavy loads, and been set free.

The second face, represented by philosophy, regards Selfhood as having an essential meaning of its own. It says that Selfhood has an independent existence, is an index only to itself, and labors wholly on its own behalf. It considers Selfhood's existence as necessary and essential, and falsely assumes that selfhood owns its being and is the real lord and master of its own domain. Philosophy supposes Selfhood to be a permanent reality that has, as its duty, the quest for self-perfection for the sake of self-esteem.

As a result of such mistaken views, philosophers have built their schools of thought on corrupt foundations. Even such eminent philosophers as Plato and Aristotle, Ibn Sina (Avicenna) and al-Farabi (Alfarabius), maintained that people's ultimate aim is to make themselves like the Necessary Being; in other words, to actually resemble Him. Such views provoked Selfhood and set it free to run in the valleys of polytheism. This opened the way to associating partners with God via such practices as the worship of causes, idols, natural forces, and stars. They closed the doors to people's perception and confession of their innate impotence and weakness, insufficiency and need, deficiency and imperfection, and thus blocked the road to worship and servitude to God. Immersed in naturalism and unable to escape from ascribing partners to God, they could not locate the wide open doors of gratitude.

In contrast, Prophethood considered that humanity's aim and duty is to be molded by Divine values and achieve good character. Prophets believed that people should perceive their impotence and seek refuge with Divine Power, perceive their weakness and rely on Divine Strength, realize their insufficiency and essential poverty and trust in Divine Mercy, know their need and seek help from Divine Riches, see their faults and plead for pardon through Divine Forgiveness, and perceive their inadequacy and glorify Divine Perfection.

Philosophy's deviation from the Straight Path, in disobedience to religion, caused Selfhood to take up the reins and gallop into error. Consequently, a tree of *Zaqqum* has grown out of such selfhood and swallowed up more than half of humanity. The fruits it has presented on the branch of lusts and appetites are idols and female deities, for according to the principles of philosophy, power is approved. "Might is right" is the norm. Its maxims are: "All power to the strongest"; "Winner takes all," and "In power there is right."[167] It has given moral support to tyranny, encouraged dictators, and urged oppressors to claim divinity. By ascribing the beauty in "works of Art" and the threads of which they are made to the works and threads themselves, and not to the Maker and Fashioner's pure, sacred Beauty, it says: "How beautiful it is," not: "How beautifully made it is," and thus considers each as an idol worthy of adoration.

In addition, philosophy adulates a cheap, self-conceited, ostentatious, superficial, transient, physical beauty that may be sold to anyone. This has

---

[167] The principle of Prophethood says: "Power is inherent in right; right is not inherent in power." It thus halts tyranny and secures justice.

led people into pretension and caused these new "idols" to display hypocritical reverence before their admirers.[168] On the branch of anger and passion, it has nurtured the fruits of greater and lesser Nimrods, Pharaohs, and Shaddads to tyrannize unfortunate people. On the branch of intellect or reason, it has yielded such fruits as atheism, materialism, and naturalism, all of which it has embedded into the human mind and thereby thrown people into confusion. To clarify this truth, we will give a few examples and compare the results originating from Prophethood's sound foundations with those arising from philosophy's rotten foundations.

FIRST EXAMPLE: According to one of Prophethood's principles concerning individual life, namely, the rule: "Be molded by Divine values," there is the instruction: "Seek distinction through Divine values and turn toward the All-Mighty with humility, recognizing your impotence and insufficiency, and be a servant in His Court." But philosophy, due to its self-oriented principle of seeking human perfection in being like the Necessarily Existent Being, instructs: "Try to be like the Necessarily Existent Being." This is impossible, for while the Necessarily Existent Being is infinitely powerful, omnipotent, self-sufficient, and without need, our essence has been mixed with infinite impotence, weakness, poverty, and need.

SECOND EXAMPLE: Among Prophethood's principles of social life's fundamental conditions are mutual assistance, magnanimity, and generosity. These function in the reciprocal cooperation of all things—from the sun and the moon down to particles. For example, plants help animals, animals help people, and particles of food help the body's cells. Philosophy, however, considers conflict to be social life's fundamental condition. In fact, conflict springs from tyrants, brutes, and savage people and wild animals misusing their innate dispositions. Conflict is so fundamental and general to the philosophers' line of reasoning that they absurdly claim that "life is conflict."

THIRD EXAMPLE: One sublime result and exalted principle of Prophethood about Divine Unity is: "That which has unity can proceed only from one (of unity)." That is, the unity and universal accord or harmony in existence is because of the Creator's Oneness. Whereas philosophy states that "Only one proceeds from one." Thus, as only one thing can proceed from one person, everything comes from that one by means of intermediaries. This misleading principle opened the way to a most grievous polytheism. By present-

---

[168] In order to appear desirable to their admirers and gain their attention, such people display a kind of "worshipful" attitude through a hypocritical show.

ing the absolutely All-Powerful and Self-Sufficient as needing impotent intermediaries, it gave all causes and intermediaries a kind of partnership in His Lordship and allotted only the creation of the "First Intellect" to the All-Majestic Creator. If the Illuminists (*Ishraqiyyun*), considered among the foremost of philosophers, exerted themselves for such nonsense, just imagine how absurd are the theories of such inferior philosophers as materialists and naturalists.

FOURTH EXAMPLE: According to one of Prophethood's wise principles that *There is nothing but it glorifies Him with His praise* (17:44), the purpose and wisdom in creation, particularly of living creatures, may have one aspect relating to the creature itself but many aspects relating to the Creator. For example, a fruit has as much wisdom and as many purposes involved in its creation as all fruits of a tree. However, according to philosophy's principles, which lack true wisdom, every living creature's purpose relates to itself or is connected with benefits for humanity. This means that creation is so senseless that the purpose of a mountain-like tree is only to yield a tiny fruit. It is one of the disastrous results of philosophy that such great Muslim philosophers as Ibn Sina and al-Farabi, infatuated by philosophy's apparent glamour and deceived into following it, were considered only ordinary believers. Hujjatu'l-Islam al-Ghazzali did not accord them even that rank.

The leaders of the *Mu'tazili* school, who were among the most learned scholars of Islamic theology, were attracted by philosophy's glitter and became closely involved with it. Considering reason to be a self-sufficient and sound measure for determining the truth, they could not rise above the rank of heretical or novitiate belief. Furthermore, since they took pleasure in philosophy's flattery of their evil-commanding souls, such famous literary figures in Islamic history as Abu'l-A'la al-Ma'arri, notorious for his pessimism, and Omar Khayyam, known for his pitiful weeping, basked in philosophy's applause. However, they earned contempt, condemnation, and restraining reproofs from people of truth and perfection, who told them: "You are being impertinent. You are approaching heresy and leading others to heresy."

Another consequence of philosophy's rotten basis is that Selfhood, instead of being viewed as insubstantial, is seen as self-regarding and self-dependent. This view has caused it to change from a "light vapor" into a "viscous liquid." Due to our indifference to creation's miraculous truths (as we now are "too familiar" with them) and our preoccupation with this world and natural sciences, that liquid hardens. After this, due to our neglect and denial, Selfhood "freezes." It loses its refinement and becomes opaque, due to its rebelliousness, gradually becoming denser and enveloping the person. It then expands with all sorts of human fancies.

Finally supposing all people and even causes to be like itself—though they deny it—it considers each one a Pharaoh. At this point, it contests the All-Majestic Creator's commands: *Who will revive these bones when they have rotted away?* (36:78) and, in defiance, accuses the absolutely All-Powerful of impotence. Selfhood even goes so far as to debase the All-Majestic Creator's Attributes by rejecting or deforming the Attributes it deems unsuited to its interest or disagreeable to its Pharaoh-like evil-commanding soul.

For example, some philosophers considered the All-Mighty "self-bound" (i.e., constrained by His own decree) and thus denied Him choice. They rejected creation's endless testimony which proves that He has choice. Although all creatures show that the Creator has choice, each with its own individuality and order, wisdom and measure, this blind philosophy refuses to see it. Other philosophers claimed that Divine Knowledge does not contain the particulars, thereby denying the Attribute of all-encompassing Knowledge and refusing to accept creation's true witnessing.

Philosophy also has attributed a creative effect to causes and thereby attributing creative power to nature. Since it does not see the clear stamp upon everything signifying the Creator of all things, philosophy assumes nature to be the originator. It ignores the facts that nature, whose supposed power is ascribed to blind chance and necessity, is impotent, inanimate, unconscious, and blind. It attributes a part of creation to nature, although every element is but a missive from God, the Eternally Besought, relaying thousands of instances of exalted wisdom.

Moreover, philosophers did not find the door to the Resurrection and the Hereafter, which the All-Mighty (with all of His Names), the universe (with all of its truths), the line of Prophethood (with all of its verifications), and the revealed Books (with all of their verses) demonstrate. As a result, they denied bodily resurrection and ascribed pre-eternity to souls. Such superstitions give an idea of what their views on other matters would be. Indeed, the powers of evil have raised up (flattered) the intellects or reason of disbelieving philosophers as though with the beaks and talons of their ego or selfhood and thrown them into the abyss of deviation. In the microcosm (human), they have made Ego or Selfhood into an idol or a false deity; in the macrocosm, they have made nature an object of worship. *Hence, he who rejects the false deities (and powers of evil which institute patterns of faith and rule in defiance of God) and believes in God has indeed taken hold of the firm, unbreakable handle; and God is All-Hearing, All-Knowing (2:256).*

It is useful to mention here, to elucidate the aforementioned truth, the meaning of an imaginary event I described as a visionary journey in *Gleams of Truth*. In İstanbul, eight years before I wrote this treatise, during Ramadan, at a time when the Old Said (concerned with philosophy) was about to become the New Said, while pondering over the three ways indicated at the end of *Suratu'l-Fatiha—The Path of those whom You have favored, not of those who have incurred (Your) wrath, nor of those who are astray* (1: 7)—I saw the following:

I was in a vast desert. The earth's face was covered by a layer of murky, depressing, and suffocating clouds. There was no breeze, light, or water. I imagined that dangerous and dreadful monsters were everywhere. It occurred to me that there should be a light, a breeze, and some water at the other side of this land, and I should get there. I noticed that I was driven on involuntarily. Worming my way into an underground tunnel-like cave and gradually traveling through the earth, I saw that many people had passed this way before me. They were submerged on all sides. Sometimes I saw their footprints and heard their voices, which later ceased.

> O friend who is with me on this imaginary journey. That land is nature and the philosophy of nature-worship. The tunnel is the way opened by philosophical thought to reach the truth. The footprints belonged to famous philosophers like Plato and Aristotle, and the voices I heard were those of such geniuses as Ibn Sina and al-Farabi.[169] I occasionally encountered some of Ibn Sina's ideas and principles but, after a time, they would disappear completely. Being unable to proceed, he was submerged before reaching the truth. Anyhow, I showed you a small part of the truth to save you from anxiety. Now I return to my journey.

As I went on, I found that I had been given two things: a torch to dispel the darkness and a device that was opening a way for me through mighty boulders and rocks, which fell apart one after the other. I was told: "This torch and device have been given to you from the treasury of the Qur'an."

---

[169] If asked: "Who are you to challenge these famous philosophers? While you are like a fly, how dare you challenge the flight of eagles?" I would reply: "I have an eternal teacher like the Qur'an, and so, in matters of the truth and knowledge of God, do not need to attach as much value as a gnat's wing to such eagles, who were students of misguided philosophy and deluded reason. However inferior I am to them, their teacher is far more inferior than mine. With the help of my "teacher"—the Qur'an—nature and materialistic tendencies that led them to drown cannot even wet my toes. An insignificant private who serves a great ruler's laws and commands can achieve more than an insignificant ruler's chief general."

After continuing on for a long time, I suddenly realized that I had come out on the other side. I saw a world where everything was rejoicing, and which had bright sunshine in the most beautiful springtime and an enlivening breeze and delicious life-giving water. I thanked and praised God.

Then I realized that instead of being in command of myself, I was being tested by someone. I again found myself under the suffocating cloud in that vast desert. Though now on another path, I still felt urged on by an unseen motive. This time I was traveling on the earth's surface to reach the other side. I saw things so strange and curious that they cannot be described: raging seas, threatening storms—everything caused difficulties for me. As before, I felt my way through them with the help of the equipment that had been given to me from the Qur'an, and so overcame all of them. On the way, I frequently encountered the corpses of other travelers. Barely one in a thousand had completed this journey. However, I was saved from that suffocating cloud and came out the other side, happily, in full view of the shining sun. I breathed in the enlivening breeze and said: "All praise be to God."

Then I started looking around that Paradise-like world. But someone would not let me stay there, for instantly I was returned to that dreadful desert as if I had to see another path. There I saw different sorts of apparatuses—some like airplanes, others like cars and hoists—all of which had descended like lifts. Those who jumped onto them were taken up as far as their power and capacity allowed. I jumped onto one of them, and, in a moment, was raised high above the cloud. I came out among the most beautiful, green, and spectacular mountain tops. The cloud layer only reached halfway up the mountains, and mild breezes, delicious water, and gentle light were everywhere, as were those lift-like luminous vehicles. Although I had seen them in the first two parts of my journey and on the earth's other face, I had not understood what they were. Now I came to realize that they were manifestations of the All-Wise Qur'an's verses.

The first way, indicated by *nor of those who are astray*, is that of people submerged in nature and followers of naturalism. You have seen how many difficulties this way contains. The second way, indicated by *not of those who have incurred Your wrath*, is followed by those who attribute creative power and creative effect to causes and intermediaries, and those (like the Peripatetic philosophers) who seek to open the way to the ultimate truth and knowledge of the Necessarily Existent Being through reasoning and thinking alone. The third way, indicated by *those whom You have favored*, it is the radiant highway of those who follow the Qur'an, the people of the Straight Path. This radiant highway is a brilliant path revealed and bestowed by God, the All-Merciful. It is the shortest, easiest, and safest way, and is open to everyone.

Second aim

This Aim is about the motion and transformation of atoms as well as their duty.

In the Name of God, the All-Merciful, the All-Compassionate.

The unbelievers say: "The Hour will not come upon us." Say: "No indeed, by my Lord—and He is the Knower of the Unseen—it most certainly will come upon you." Not an atom's weight of whatever there is in the heavens or in the earth escapes Him, nor is there anything smaller than that, or greater, but it is in a Manifest Book." (34:3)

In this Aim, I point to a gem of only an atom's weight from this verse's great treasure. It consists of an introduction and three points.

INTRODUCTION: The transformations of atoms are their vibrations and circulations while the Pen of the Eternal Inscriber's Power writes creation's signs in the book of creation. They are not games of chance or random and meaningless motions, as materialists and naturalists assume. For each atom, like all of creation and with the tongue appropriate to its disposition, says: "In the Name of God" when it starts to move. It does so because it bears loads that infinitely exceed its strength. For example, a grain-sized seed shoulders a load the size of a huge pine tree. After completing its duty, it says: "All praise and gratitude are for God." For by exhibiting a wise beauty of art, as well as meaningful and subtle ornament, that amaze all minds, it has displayed a work of art like an ode in praise of the All-Majestic Maker. Look carefully at pomegranates and ears of corn, for example.

Indeed, the transformations of atoms are their motions and meaningful circulations caused by Divine Power's transcribing "words of Power" from the Manifest Book onto the Tablet of Effacement and Confirmation, which is the reality and, metaphorically, a page of the stream of time. The Manifest Book is a title for Divine Power and Will, Which operate in the present time and the corporeal world to create things. Divine Power's transcription of Its words—all things and events—from the Manifest Book onto the Tablet of Effacement and Confirmation or on the page of time takes place according to the dictates and principles of the Manifest Record,[170]

---

[170] The Qur'an mentions the Manifest Record and the Manifest Book in several places. Some interpreters (of the Qur'an) consider these to be identical in meaning, while others say they have different meanings and connotations. The explanations of their true nature differ, but all

which is a title for Divine Knowledge and Command and secures the harmonious arrangement of things coming from the realm of the Unseen with their seeds and roots and their future progeny.

---

are in agreement that both describe Divine Knowledge. However, through the enlightenment of the Qur'an, I have arrived at the following conviction:

The Manifest Record, which relates more to the World of the Unseen than to the visible, material world, expresses one aspect of Divine Knowledge and Command. That is, it relates more to the past and future than to the present. It is a book of Divine Destiny that contains the origins, roots, and seeds of things, rather than their flourishing forms in their visible existence.

By growing into their full bodies with perfect order and art, the origins, sources, and roots of things show that they are arranged according to a book of the principles contained in the Divine Knowledge. Likewise, the seeds, results, and fruits of things, which contain the indexes and programs of beings that will come into existence, demonstrate that each is a miniature register of the Divine Commands. For example, it can be said that a seed is the miniature embodiment of the program and index according to which a tree may be formed and of the Divine principles or commands which determine this program and index. In short, the Manifest Record is an index and program of the tree of creation as a whole, which spreads its branches through the past and future and the World of the Unseen. In this sense, it is a book of Divine Destiny or a register of its principles. By means of the dictates and demands of these principles, atoms are used and managed for things to come into existence and to continue their existence.

As for the Manifest Book, it relates more to the visible, material world than to the World of the Unseen, and more to the present than to the past and future. It expresses Divine Power and Will rather than Divine Knowledge and Command. If the Manifest Record is the book of Divine Destiny, the Manifest Book is the book of Divine Power. In other words, the perfect art and orderliness in everything's essence and existence, as well as its attributes and functions, show that everything is made to exist in accordance with the laws of an effective, all-penetrating Will and the principles of a perfect, absolute Power. Everything is specifically formed and given an appointed measure and particular shape. This shows that Divine Power and Will have a universal, comprehensive register of laws, a great book, according to which a particular existence and form are determined for each entity.

Curiously, although the people of neglect, misguidance, and corrupt philosophy are aware of the existence of the Supreme Preserved Tablet (*Lawhun Mahfuz*) of the Creative Power and the manifestations and reflections of the Manifest Book of Divine Wisdom and Will on things, they name it "nature," thus making it completely meaningless. In sum, through the dictates of the Manifest Record, that is, through the decrees and instructions of the Divine Destiny, Divine Power uses atoms to create or manifest the chain of beings, each link of which is His sign, on the metaphorical or "ideal" page of time, which is called the Tablet of Effacement and Confirmation. Thus, atoms are set to move so that beings may be transferred from the World of the Unseen to the material, visible world, from (the Realm of) Knowledge to the (Realm of) Power.

The Tablet of Effacement and Confirmation is the tablet on which beings are inscribed and then removed or effaced according to their origins in, or the dictates of, the Supreme Preserved Tablet. Therefore, it displays continuous change. The Tablet of Effacement and Confirmation constitutes the essence of time. Time, a mighty river that flows through existence, has its essence in the Divine Power's inscription of beings and in the ink It uses. Only God knows the Unseen.

FIRST POINT: This Point consists of two matters.

First matter: In each atom, through its motion and rest, two lights of Divine Unity shine like two suns. For if each atom were not acting under God's authority and with His permission, if it were not undergoing change within His Knowledge and Power, it would have to possess infinite knowledge and limitless power, as well as eyes to see and an authority to command everything, for each atom acts in an orderly fashion within the body of all living beings.

The order within things and the rules of their formation differ from one to the other. If each thing's specific order is unknown, acting within it is impossible. If we suppose that acting is possible, acting without error would be impossible. Since we observe a perfect order and harmony in each animate being's body, either those atoms of which it is made up or which act in it have an all-encompassing knowledge and power, or someone with infinite knowledge and power is using them under his irresistible will and command.

Each air atom can enter every living being's body, every flower's fruit, and every leaves' structure, and can act within them. However, each of these things has a different formation and a unique order. If a fig may be likened to a textile mill or a pomegranate to a sugar factory, the programs of these fruits (or those factories' structures) differ from each other. Despite such structural differences, an air atom can enter all of them, assume the appropriate position, and act in a wise and lordly fashion without error. Thus a mobile air atom must know the forms, shapes, measures, and formations of whatever it enters, or must be acting under the command and will of one who has that all-encompassing knowledge.

This also is true of an apparently motionless soil atom. Each soil atom has the capacity to be the means and place of cultivation for each plant and tree seed, for any seed can find therein whatever it needs to germinate and grow. Therefore, either that soil must contain functioning mechanisms that can adapt to any number of such species, or its atoms must have a marvelously comprehensive knowledge and miracle-working power that creates everything from nothing. Alternatively, those duties must be performed at the command, with the permission, and through the power and might of an all-knowing and all-powerful one.

If an untrained and inexperienced blind person entered an industrial city and performed so excellently in each trade and craft that everyone was speechless, who could doubt that that person was being taught and employed by a master of all trades and crafts? Or say that another crippled and blind person, rendered helpless by his or her disability, lived in a small house. People see small fragments of stone and bits and pieces of material like bone and cotton go in, and sacks of sugar, rolls of cloth, boxes of jewelry, finely-made bejeweled clothes, delicious foods, and so on come out of it. The only logical conclusions would be that that person was just the doorkeeper of some extraordinary miracle-working being, and that he or she had as little share in those products as the factory's lock.

In the same way, the motion and functions or service of air atoms in these living objects, each of which is a letter from the Eternally Besought, a precious work of the Lord's art, a miracle of His Power, and a marvel of His Wisdom, tells us that those atoms are acting according to the Command and Will of an All-Majestic, All-Wise Maker, an All-Gracious, All-Munificent Originator. Likewise, soil atoms are the place and means of cultivation for seeds to grow into young plants and tall trees. Each tree is a unique factory and workshop, a unique printing press and treasury, a unique precious object and declaration proclaiming the All-Majestic Maker's Names. It is also like a unique ode singing a hymn to His perfections. These soil atoms tell us that they are acting under the Command and through the Power of an All-Majestic Maker Who owns the command, "*Be! and it is,*" and to Whose Command everything is subject.

Second matter: This is a brief indication of the functions and instances of wisdom in the motion of atoms. Materialists, whose reason is limited to what they receive through their five senses, consider the transformations of atoms random and coincidental, and yet they base their approaches and ideas on and attempt to explain all existence with these random and coincidental movements. But how can that which has no consciousness (let alone meaning and purpose) create existence, which overflows with instances of wisdom and purpose?

According to: *There is nothing but it glorifies Him with His praise* (36: 82), and many other similar verses, the transformations of atoms are based on various purposes and duties and demonstrate many instances of wisdom. We will mention some of these purposes by way of illustration.

First: Through His Power, the All-Majestic Originator moves and uses atoms. He takes each spirit as a model and, renewing and refreshing the manifestations of His acts of creating, annually clothes it with a fresh body. Also, He miraculously copies out countless books from each book of creation through His Wisdom, shows one truth in ever-differing forms, and prepares the ground and makes ways for beings, worlds, and universes to follow each other.

Second: The All-Majestic Master of all dominion created this world, especially its surface, in a way that allows cultivation to flourish and produce ever-fresh crops so that He might sow and reap His Power's countless miracles. Thus, by causing atoms with wisdom to move and employing them in order in His field of the earth, He continuously displays a new form of the universe through miracles of His Power and makes His field produce ever-differing crops. Through the atoms' movement, He demonstrates gifts from His Mercy's infinite treasury and samples of His infinite Power's miracles.

Third: The Eternal Inscriber causes atoms to move with perfect wisdom and employs them with perfect order so that, in order to set forth the manifestations of His Names by displaying their limitless embroideries, He may exhibit infinite inscriptions in a finite arena and write endless signs, which will express limitless meanings, on a small page. Although this year's crops are like those of last year in respect of their nature, their meanings are different. As their relative determinations and identifications have changed, they display many different meanings. They are almost the same in form, structure, and appearance, but in truth they are renewed annually. Though they are ephemeral in respect of their material existence, their beautiful meanings are preserved, constant, and permanent.

Since a tree's leaves, blossoms, and fruits have no spirit, they are the same every spring both in meaning and in appearance. But as they are formed anew each spring, a tree repeatedly comes to leaf, blossoms through the years, and yields fruit to show the meanings of the acts of the Divine Names, Whose manifestations are renewed constantly.

Fourth: In order to produce things like crops or items for decoration or provision appropriate for the most broad World of the Inner Dimensions of Things and the World of Ideal Forms or Representations, and endless worlds of the Hereafter, the All-Wise One of Majesty sets atoms moving in the narrow tillage of this world, in the workshop and field of the face of the earth, and keeps the cosmos continuously moving and its beings circulating. From His Power's infinite treasury, He causes an endless flow into the World of the Unseen, and some of it enters the worlds of the Hereafter.

Fifth: The All-Mighty causes atoms to move through His Power and with perfect wisdom, and uses them with perfect order, to display infinite

Divine perfection, endless manifestations of His Grace and Majesty, and countless glorifications of His Lordship in this limited material field and in a short, limited time. He creates numerous realities concerning the Unseen, and many fruits for the Hereafter, and invents from the lasting identities of the mortal numerous embroideries pertaining to the World of Ideal Forms and meaningful weavings to be recorded and eternalized on preserved Tablets. Therefore, the One Who causes atoms to move is the same Being Who manifests these great purposes and instances of wisdom. If it were otherwise, each atom would need a brain as large as the sun.

Materialist philosophers assume that the motion of atoms is aimless. Blind to the infinite instances of wisdom in their motion, which are far more than the five points above, they consider them stunned and aimless. In reality, however, these atoms revolve like Mevlevi dervishes glorifying God and reciting His Names in two ecstatic movements, one spinning upon its axis and the other reeling in circles.

SECOND POINT: Every atom contains two truthful testimonies to the Necessarily Existent Being's Existence and Unity. Despite being powerless and insentient, it bears decisive witness to the Necessarily Existent Being's Existence by carrying out important duties and functions as though it were conscious. It also testifies to the Unity of the same Being, Who owns all material and immaterial dominions, by conforming to the universal order in general, and to the rules of each place it enters in particular. It settles in every place as if it were its homeland. All of this shows that the One Who owns the atom owns all the places it enters.

By carrying out very heavy duties incompatible with its size and weakness, the atom shows that it acts at the command and in the name of One with absolute power. By conforming to the cosmos's universal order and entering everywhere without obstacle, as though knowingly, it shows that it acts through the power and wisdom of a single Being with absolute knowledge. A private is connected with all the divisions of the army, from his squadron to the corps, and has duties with respect to each connection. By performing those duties and receiving training and instruction under the general military order, in essence he is obeying a single supreme commander who is in charge of the whole army. Similarly, an atom positioned in any of the parts of a compound within many other compounds has a different purposeful connection with every other part and compound and a well-regulated function to yield beneficial results. This shows that the Being Who holds the universe in His grasp of power can position each atom in such a way that it preserves these connections and functions without damaging any of those beneficial results. For example, an atom positioned in the eye's pupil has a well-arranged connection with the eye's vessels, and motor and sensory nerves, and then with the face, and further with the head, the trunk, and the whole body. It also has functions and duties in relation with each. This shows that only the One Who creates all bodily members can position the right atom in the right place.

Atoms entering the body as sustenance make their journey in the food caravan with an astonishing order and wisdom. They pass through modes and stages in an orderly manner and, progressing as if deliberately and without confusion, carry on until they are strained through the "filters" (digestive organs) in a living being's body. They are then loaded onto the red blood corpuscles to assist those members and cells needing sustenance according to a law of munificence. This shows that the One Who drives these atoms and makes them pass through thousands of different stages of necessity must be an All-Munificent Provider, an All-Compassionate Creator, in relation to Whose Power particles and stars are equal.

Furthermore, atoms cooperate to produce or weave miraculous works of art in such a wonderful way that each atom is in a position of both dominance and subjection to every other atom individually, and to all others collectively. Given this, each atom either knows and creates that wonderful demonstration of wisdom and art (infinitely impossible), or is assigned to its place and motion and proceeds by the decree of Divine Destiny, by the Pen of the Power of an All-Wise Maker.

For example, the stones set in the Hagia Sophia's dome are both dominant and subject to each other. If we deny that they were put in place by a skillful architect, we must admit that each stone is just as great an architect as Sinan, for each stone would have to convince the others to take their proper places. Similarly, if all atoms making up creatures, which are infinitely more skillfully fashioned, wonderful, and full of wisdom than the Hagia Sophia's dome, were not dependent upon the Master Builder of the universe's command, we would have to ascribe to each one as many attributes of perfection as those belonging to the Maker of the universe. Since unbelievers deny a Necessarily Existent Being, they are compelled to accept as many false deities as there are atoms. Thus all of them are in a state of profound and absolute ignorance.

THIRD POINT: One Divine purpose in making atoms move on in animate bodies and causing them to pass through several transformations is to enliven and illuminate them with meaning. This makes them suitable material from which to build the Hereafter. It is as if human, animal, and even plant bodies were guesthouses, barracks, or schools to train and instruct inanimate atoms so that they may be illumined and refined. By performing various duties, they become worthy of being atoms in the World of Permanence, the abode the Hereafter, all of whose elements are living.

Question: How can we become aware that there is that Divine purpose (mentioned above) in each atom's motions?

Answer: *First:* We can become aware through the Maker's Wisdom, Which is established and proved by the purposiveness or instances of wisdom and orderliness observed in all creatures. The Wisdom, Which attaches universal instances of wisdom to a most particular thing would not leave the motion of atoms, which exhibit the greatest activity in the universe's flow and are the means for embroideries full of wisdom, without purpose. Also, the Divine Wisdom and Sovereignty, Which give even the smallest creature a suitable wage and recompense for its duty and its proper perfection, would not leave their most numerous and important servants without light, without a wage.

Second: By setting the elements moving and employing them, the All-Wise Maker elevates certain atoms to the degree of minerals as if that were their wage of perfection, and instructs them on how to glorify Him in the way of minerals. He causes inanimate minerals to move and employs them to reward them with the degree of vegetable life. He sets vegetables in motion and uses them as food for animals, thus favoring them with the rank of animal life. He employs the atoms in animal bodies as food for human beings and promotes them to the rank of human life. Lastly, by refining many of the atoms in a human body through repeated filtering, He raises them to the most delicate and subtle organs of the body: the brain and the heart. Given this, we can understand that each atom's movement is neither random nor aimless; rather, they are made to race to a sort of perfection worthy of themselves.

Third: Among the atoms in animate beings, some—like those in small fruit seeds and other seeds—are favored with such a light, refinement, and quality that they become like a spirit or a king to the rest of the atoms and, say, to a mighty tree. So among a mighty tree's atoms, some are promoted to higher ranks (e.g., to being the atoms of fruit) by performing many delicate duties and passing through many stages in a tree's life-cycle. This shows that through the All-Wise Maker's command, these atoms acquire a refinement, light, and rank in honor of the Divine Names manifested in them and according to the sorts of motion determined by the Divine law of creation.

In conclusion, the All-Wise Maker has appointed for each thing an attainable rank of perfection and an appropriate level of existence. Accordingly, He has endowed it with a potential to work for and attain that rank. He urges everything toward its rank of perfection and level of existence. This is a law He established as the Lord of all creation, one that is operative in the realms of both plants and animals as well as in that of inanimate things. Thus plain soil can become the source of all jewelry like priceless diamonds. This indicates a universal law of God as being the Lord, One Who sustains, evolves, and trains all creatures.

The All-Munificent Creator gives animals a particular pleasure, which He uses in the comprehensive law of reproduction, as a reward. He rewards animals such as bees and nightingales, which He employs in certain other duties pertaining to His Lordship, with a wage of particular perfection. He grants to each a level of excellence that is a source of eager industry and pleasure. This reality reveals the tip of a comprehensive law of Munificence.

The reality of everything originates in the manifestation of a Divine Name, for Which the thing is a mirror. Whatever beauty appears in it is owed to the Name that requires it to be thus. Whether the individual thing is aware of it or not, the beauty apparent in it is there because it is desired to be so. This demonstrates the tip of a comprehensive law of Grace and Beautifying.

As required by His law of Munificence, the All-Munificent Originator does not take back the rank and perfection He has bestowed upon something when it dies. Rather, He makes permanent the fruits, the real meaning and identity and (if it has one) the spirit of that bearer of perfection. For example, He makes permanent the meanings and fruits of the perfections He has bestowed on humanity in this world. He will even return the thanks and praise of thankful believers to them—embodied as fruits of Paradise. In this, the tip of a mighty law of Mercy is apparent.

The Peerless Creator wastes nothing and does nothing without purpose. For example, He uses the material remains of creatures which died in autumn in the creation and formation of springtime creatures. According to the meaning of: *On the day the earth is changed into another earth* (14: 48), and the indication of: *The Abode of the Hereafter—it is all living indeed* (29:64), His Wisdom requires that soil atoms, which are inanimate and unconscious yet perform important duties in this world, be used and included in some constructions of the Hereafter, all elements of which, including its stones and trees, will be animate and conscious. For to abandon the destroyed world's atoms or throw them into non-existence would be wasteful. In this, the tip of a mighty law of Wisdom is apparent.

This world's many fruits, consequences, and meanings, as well as the books containing or composed of the actions of those (jinn and human beings) charged with performing Divine commands while here, and their bodies and spirits , are sent to the market of the Hereafter. Justice and wisdom require that, after receiving their individual perfection in accordance with performing their duties, the atoms accompanying and serving those meanings be included in the Hereafter's construction. They will be included along with this world's debris, having received and served many times the light of life, and after being the means for sentient beings' glorifications. In this, the tip of a mighty law of Justice is apparent.

Just as the spirit dominates the body, the commands of creation, existence and life determined and decreed by Divine Destiny dominate inanimate matter. Inanimate substances assume a disposition and order due to Divine Destiny's rule and determination. Thus, in innumerable varieties of eggs and sperms, as well as of seeds and grains, they achieve different levels of existence and refinement according to the Divine commands and laws of creation, all of which Destiny determines differently.

All substances, being compositions of hydrogen, nitrogen, oxygen, and carbon, issue into innumerable entities due to Destiny's different commands and determination. In this way, they achieve different ranks of existence and refinement in different kinds and species. So if an atom has repeatedly served life and the glorifying of the Lord that is inherent in life, then the Lord must record the wisdom of the meanings it realizes, so to speak, on its immaterial forehead with the Pen of Destiny, which overlooks nothing. This is required by His Knowledge being all-encompassing. In it, the tip of a mighty law of All-Encompassing Knowledge is apparent.

In sum, and given all of the above, atoms cannot be considered random entities. Beyond the visible tip of each of the seven laws just mentioned (namely, Lordship, Munificence, Grace, Mercy, Wisdom, Justice, and All-

Encompassing Knowledge) as well as many others, a Greatest or most universal Name of God and Its greatest manifestation is intimated. From that intimation, we may understand that all atoms, like all entities in this world, move in a delicate balance calculated with Knowledge. They follow Power's commands of creation, existence and life, and within the bounds determined by Destiny. As atoms are being prepared for another, higher existence,[171] we should see animate bodies as a sort of school, barracks, or temporary lodging-house for their training. This proposition can be put forward with certainty.

To conclude: As stated and demonstrated in The First Word, all things say: *In the Name of God.* Thus all atoms and groups and assemblages of atoms say: *In the Name of God* with the tongue of their individual dispositions. It is with that formula that they are in motion.

According to the argument of the three points above, all atoms say: *In the Name of God, the All-Merciful, the All-Compassionate* with the tongue of their individual dispositions as they begin their motion. That is: "I am moving in God's name, for His sake, with His permission, and through His Power." As they conclude their motion, they say: "All praise and gratitude are for God, the Lord of the worlds." Each thus shows itself as a miniature tip of the Pen of Power tracing the embroideries of intricately worked creatures, each of which is like an ode of praise (for the Creator). Each can be seen as the point of a record player needle turning on creatures, each of which is like a record on a mighty, non-material Divine record player with an infinite number of arms.

Thus atoms cause creatures to recite odes glorifying their Lord and to hymn their praises of God.

> Therein, their invocation will be: "All-Glorified You are, O God!
> And their greeting will be: "Peace!" And their invocation will close
> with "All praise and gratitude are for God, the Lord of the worlds!"

---

[171] It is observed that in this dense, lowly world life's light is kindled and diffused most freely and in great abundance with an extraordinary dynamism; that a spark of life is kindled over a broad expanse in the most unpromising material and in the most decayed substances. In this way, heavy and unpromising matter is made subtle and given a sheen by the light of life. That tells us that this agitated, dense and lowly world is being melted, refined and made more beautiful through the activity of atoms and the light of life for the sake of another subtler, more exalted, pure, and ever-living world. It is as if it were being adorned for passage to a finer world. If those so narrow-minded as to be unable to understand and believe in bodily resurrection look with the light of the Qur'an, they will see that a Divine law (issuing from God's being Self-Subsistent) as infinitely comprehensive and mighty as to resurrect and rearrange all atoms like a well-ordered army, is clearly in force in the maintenance of creation.

All-Glorified are You. We have no knowledge save what You have taught us. Surely You are the All-Knowing, the All-Wise.

Our Lord, do not let our hearts swerve after You have guided us, and bestow upon us mercy from Your Presence. Surely You are the All-Bestowing.

O God, bestow such blessings on our master Muhammad as will be pleasing to You and a fulfillment of his due, and also on his Family, Companions, and followers in religion, and grant them peace. Protect us and our religion. Amin, O Lord of the worlds.

The
Thirty-first Word

The Thirty-first Word

The Ascension of Prophet Muhammad

(NOTE: Belief in the Prophet's Ascension is the result of, and draws its light and strength from, belief in the pillars of belief.[172] The Ascension may not be proved independently to those who do not accept these pillars, without first proving them. Therefore we address believers who doubt it. From time to time, however, we will address unbelievers. Some aspects of the Ascension's truth have been mentioned elsewhere in the *Risale-i Nur*. At the insistence of my brothers, we seek God's grace and help to unite them with the essence of that truth and make them into a mirror to reflect the total beauty of the perfections of Muhammad, upon him be peace and blessings.)

In the Name of God, the All-Merciful, the All-Compassionate.

All-Glorified is He Who took His servant for a journey by night from *al-Masjidu'l-Haram* to *al-Masjidu'l-Aqsa'*, the environs of which We had blessed, so that We might show him of Our signs. Surely He is the Hearing, the Seeing. (17:1)

It is but a Revelation revealed. One with mighty power has taught it, one firm, with the ability to penetrate and perfect in spirit, rose with all splendor, when he was in the highest horizon. Then he drew near and came close, so he was at a distance between the strings of two bows or even nearer. And He revealed to His servant what He revealed. The heart did not contradict what he saw. Will you then dispute with him concerning what he saw? Surely he saw him during a second descent, by the Lote-tree of the farthest limit, near it is the Garden of Refuge and Dwelling. It was when what enveloped the

---

[172] These are belief in God's Existence and Unity, angels, Scriptures, Prophethood and Divine Messengership (including belief in all of God's Prophets and Messengers), and the Resurrection, and Divine Decree and Destiny, without excluding human free will. (Tr.)

Lote-tree enveloped it. The sight did not swerve, nor did it stray. Truly did he see one among the greatest signs of his Lord. (53:4-18)

UT OF THE FIRST VERSE'S VAST TREASURY, WE WILL DESCRIBE ONLY TWO points which the pronoun *He* in *Surely He is* refers to as a principle of eloquence, as they are included in our present concern.

After mentioning the Prophet's journey from the *Masjidu'l-Haram* in Makka to the *Masjidu'l-Aqsa'* in Jerusalem (the beginning of his Ascension), the Qur'an concludes: *Surely He is the Hearing, the Seeing.* The pronoun *He* in *Surely He is*, which alludes to the furthest point of the Ascension which is indicated in 53:4-18 above, refers either to Almighty God or the Prophet.

If it refers to the Prophet, according to the rules of the language and the preceding part of the verse, it means: This apparently particular journey is, in reality, comprehensive. It signifies such a universal ascent that, during it, the Prophet heard and saw all of the Lord's signs and the Divine art's wonders that caught his sight and encountered his ears due to the Divine Names' manifestations in universal degrees as far as the *Lote-tree of the farthest limit* and *the nearness of the distance between the strings of two bows.* Thus, through its conclusive phrase, the verse describes that particular journey as the key to a journey that is universal and full of extraordinary events.

If this pronoun refers to God Almighty, it means: In order to invite one of His servants on a journey to His Presence and and entrust him with a duty, God Almighty took him from the *Masjidu'l-Haram* to the *Masjidu'l-Aqsa'*, where the Prophets came together. There, He caused him to meet with them and showed that he is the absolute, indisputable heir of all the Prophets' principles of religion. Then He took him through both the external and inner dimensions of His dominion as far as the *Lote-tree of the farthest limit* and the nearness of the *distance between the strings of two bows.*

We know that he was a servant and that his Ascension was a particular event. However, since he was given a trust connected to the whole universe, was accorded a light that would change the universe's color, and also had a key that opens the door to eternal happiness, Almighty God describes Himself as the One Who hears and sees all things so that His world-embracing, comprehensive and all-encompassing wisdom in the trust, the light, and the key might be observed and understood.

This mighty truth contained in the Ascension may be dealt with under four principles: Why was the Ascension necessary, what is its reality, what is its wisdom, and what are its fruits and benefits?

First principle: Why was the Ascension necessary?

QUESTION: Almighty God is nearer to one than one's jugular vein, closer to everything than itself, and absolutely free of corporeality and space. Therefore, while all saints can converse with Him in their hearts, why did the sainthood of Muhammad have to make a long journey (the Ascension) to talk to God?

ANSWER: We will discuss this profound matter via two comparisons from The Twelfth Word, which concern the mystery of the Qur'an's miraculousness and of the Ascension.

First comparison: A king has two forms of speech and address. He either speaks on his private phone to a common subject regarding a minor matter or private need, or, in his capacity or position as the supreme sovereign, supreme head of the religious office, and supreme ruler, conveys his orders in the form of an exalted decree manifesting his majesty by means of an envoy or high official.

As in the comparison, the Creator of this universe, the Master of existence in its external and inner dimensions, and the Lord of eternity has two kinds of conversing and speaking and two manners of favoring. One is particular and private; the other is universal and general. The Ascension is the manifestation of Muhammad's sainthood in a universal and most exalted form and much superior to all other sainthoods. It is the Prophet's being honored with the conversation and direct address of Almighty God through His Name the Lord of the entire universe and His title the Creator of all existence.

Second comparison: A person holds a mirror up to the sun. According to its capacity, the mirror receives what it can from the sun's seven-colored light. That person has a relation with the sun through the mirror and according to its ability to reflect the sun. If he or she directs the mirror's shining side toward his or her dark house or small, private, and roof-covered garden, he or she can benefit only according to the mirror's capacity, not in proportion to the sun's value.

Another person puts down the mirror and, facing the sun directly, sees its splendor and comprehends its grandeur. He or she then climbs a very high mountain and faces the sun without veil, witnessing the majesty of its broad dominion. Coming back, this person tries to have a direct connection with the sun's constant light by making large windows in his or her house or garden's roof, and obtains other means of benefiting from the sun directly. Facing it, that person may say in indebtedness: "O amiable sun, beauty of the world and darling of the skies, who gilds the earth's face with light and makes it and all flowers smile in joy and happiness! You have illuminated and heated my house and garden, as you illuminate the world and heat the earth's face." The first person cannot say this, for the sun's reflection in his or her mirror is restricted to the mirror's capacity.

Likewise, the Single, Eternally Besought One, Who is the Sun without beginning and the Lord of eternity, manifests Himself in the nature of humanity in two forms that comprise innumerable degrees. The first manifestation occurs in the heart's mirror through one's relationship with the Lord. Everyone may receive a manifestation of the Eternal Sun's light and conversation in certain degrees in accordance with their capacity, the character of their spiritual journey toward sainthood, and their ability to receive manifestations of Divine Names and Attributes. As a result, the kind of sainthood which is attained through journeying within the shade of some particular Name(s) or Attribute(s) contains innumerable degrees.

The second is that since we have a comprehensive nature and are the most enlightened fruit of the tree of creation, we can reflect all Divine Names in the mirror of our spirits. Thus Almighty God manifests Himself and all His Beautiful Names most comprehensively in humanity's best and greatest representative. This form of manifestation occurred during the Ascension of Prophet Muhammad, upon him be peace and blessings, in which his sainthood found its meaning and became the first stage of his Messengership.

Sainthood contains veils between one's heart and the Divine Names' manifestations, as in the case of the first person in the second comparison above. Messengership contains no veils, as in the case of the second person in the second comparison, for it is connected directly with the the All-Majestic Being's manifestation with all His Names, in a single being. Since the Prophet's Ascension was the greatest wonder of his sainthood and marked its final and greatest station, it was transformed into Messengership.

In its inner aspect, the Ascension signifies sainthood and is a journey from the created to the Creator. In its outer aspect, it is Messengership and signifies a return from the Creator to the created (to guide them). Sainthood is the journey through the degrees of nearness to God. As such, it requires the attainment of many ranks and so takes a long time. Messengership, whose light is greatest, proceeds from the realization of Divine nearness—God's choosing one and making him near to Himself personally—in all its comprehensiveness. This may occur in an instant, which accounts for the Tradition: "The Ascension took place in an instant. The Prophet went and returned in the same instant."

Here we must say to the unbeliever: Since this universe resembles a most orderly country, magnificent city, or adorned palace, it must have a ruler, owner, and builder. There is such a magnificent, All-Majestic Owner, All-Perfect Ruler, All-Gracious Maker. There is also a man with a universal view, who has a relationship with that entire country, city, or palace and is connected to each by means of his senses, feelings, and faculties. Given this, the All-Magnificent Maker will have a sublime relationship to the fullest degree with that man, who has a universal view and comprehensive consciousness, and will favor him with a sacred address.

Among those honored with this relationship, Prophet Muhammad displayed this relationship to its fullest degree. His achievements speak for themselves: One-half of the world and one-fifth of humanity are under his control and influence, and he enlightened the universe by giving it a new spiritual form and furnishing it with a sublime meaning. The Ascension, the fullest degree of that relationship, is most deserved by and suitable for him.

Second principle: What is the Ascension's reality?

ANSWER: It is Prophet Muhammad's journey through the degrees of perfection. Almighty God has various Names and Titles manifested in the arrangement and disposition of creatures, and displays diverse works of His Lordship—His upbringing, training, sustaining, and providing—as the results of executing His absolute authority in inventing and administering creatures in the levels of the "heavens" where He executes His Lordship in different ways and according to each level's conditions.

Thus, to show His Lordship's works to His special servant and thereby enable him to encompass all human perfections, receive all Divine manifestations, view all levels of the universe, announce His Lordship's sovereignty, proclaim what He approves of, and unveil creation's enigmatic meaning, God Almighty mounted him on *Buraq* (heavenly mount). God raised him through the heavens like lightning, promoted him to higher and higher ranks, and displayed Divine Lordship to him from mansion to mansion and from sphere to sphere. He also showed him the Prophets, his brothers, whose abodes are in the heavens of those spheres, one after the other. Finally He raised him to the station of *the nearness of the distance between the strings of two bows* and honored him with the special manifestation of all His Names to the fullest degree, with His Speech, and with the vision of Himself.

We may examine this sublime truth through two comparisons.

First comparison: As explained in The Twenty-fourth Word, a king has different titles by which he is known and mentioned in his government's various departments, different designations and attributes among his subjects' classes, and different names and signs for his rule's levels. For example, he is the supreme judge in the justice department, chief administrator in the civil service, commander-in-chief in the military, and supreme teacher in the education department. He has a seat or a chair in each sphere and department, which has the meaning of a throne. That one king may have a thousand names and titles in his sovereignty's spheres and his government's departments, as well as a thousand thrones of sovereignty one within the other. It is as if, due to his public person and system of communication, he is present in every department. Through his laws, regulations, and representatives, he superintends all officials, watches all subjects, and is seen by them. Behind the veil at every level, he administers, executes his orders, and is watchful through his decree, knowledge, and power. He has a different center and headquarters in each sphere. Each sphere and department has different rules. The king designates one of his subjects, shows him to all those spheres and departments, and makes him witness his imperial dominion and commands unique to each. He then brings him to his presence, entrusts him with certain general and universal commands concerning all spheres and departments, and sends him back.

Similarly, the Lord of the worlds, the King of eternity, has at the levels of His Lordship's manifestations Qualities and Designations which are all different but correspond to each other. In the spheres of His Divinity, He has Names and marks which are all different but whose manifestations are concentric with each other. In His majestic execution of His rule, He has representations and appellations which are all different but resemble each other. In the operations of His Power, He has titles which are all different but imply each other. In the manifestations of His Attributes, He has sacred ways of revealing Himself that differ but point to each other. In His modes of acting, He has wise operations which are of numerous sorts but perfect each other. In His colorful artistry and varied works of Art, He has magnificent aspects of Lordship which differ but correspond to each other.

He organized the universe in an amazing and wonderful fashion because of this mysterious reality. The universe has different formations one over the other, from particles to the heavens, from the heavens' first level to God's Supreme Throne. Each heaven is the roof of a different world, a chair for exercising Divine Lordship, a center for Divine operations. Due to His absolute Oneness demonstrating Itself through the concentrated manifestation of all His Names on single entities, all Divine Names may be found in all spheres and levels, and He may show Himself with all of His Titles in them.

However, just as the title of just ruler belonging to the king in the comparison dominates in the department of justice and the others are subordinate, in each level of creatures and in each heaven, a Divine Title dominates and the others are subordinate to It. For example, in whichever heaven Prophet Muhammad met Prophet Jesus, who was distinguished with the manifestation of the Divine Name the All-Powerful, Almighty God is in constant manifestation in that heaven, primarily with that very Name. Again, in the sphere of the heaven which is the abode of Prophet Moses, God's title as the All-Speaking, with Which He distinguished Moses, is predominant.

Finally, since Prophet Muhammad was honored with the manifestation of God's Greatest Name and of all His other Names as well as being given a universal Prophethood, he must be connected with all of His Lordship's spheres. Therefore, the Ascension's reality required Prophet Muhammad to meet with the Prophets whose seats are in those spheres and pass through all of those levels.

Second comparison: The title of commander-in-chief, a title of a king, is seen throughout an army's ranks. A private sees his corporal as a sample of that imposing title, and so listens to and obeys him. A corporal sees his sergeant in the same way, and so obeys him. A sergeant sees his lieutenant in the same way, and so on. He will see the title in each sphere (e.g., captain, major, colonel, general, and field-marshal) in proportion to the sphere's size.

If the commander-in-chief entrusts a soldier with a duty connected to all military ranks, or gives him a rank that allows him to appear in every office and control it like an inspector, the soldier must be given the necessary knowledge and be recognized by the personnel. Thus the commander-in-chief arranges for him to make a study and inspection tour of all the ranks. After that, the soldier will be admitted into the commander-in-chief's presence to have a private conversation, receive a decoration and decree, and be sent back from whence he came.

The following point must be noted: If, in addition to his political power, the king has spiritual, saintly power, he will not deputize others to act in his name in different offices. Rather, he will be present everywhere in person and give orders directly, appearing in the form of persons of certain rank. In fact, there are narrations of sultans who reached sainthood's highest level and so executed their rule in many spheres in the form of certain individuals. Since the commander-in-chief in our parable is such a saintly, powerful king, the decrees and commands come directly from him in every office and are executed through his command, will, and power.

Similarly, the Ruler of the heavens and the earth, the Absolute Sovereign and Lord of eternity having the command of *"Be!" and it is*, has a sphere of Lordship, a level of rulership in the levels of creatures and classes of beings, ranging from particles to planets, from flies to the heavens, all of which differ but are related to each other. In each sphere, His regulations, statutes, and commands are carried out in perfect order and obedience. Thus in order to comprehend this universe's elevated aims and tremendous results, witness the duties of worship particular to each level and class, observe the sovereignty of the One of Grandeur's Lordship and His rule's majesty, understand what is pleasing to Him, and be a herald of His sovereignty, one must travel through all levels and spheres of His rulership until reaching the Supreme Throne (the title of the greatest, all-encompassing sphere) and attaining to the ultimate rank that a servant can reach (called *the nearness of the distance between the strings of two bows*), and meet with the One of Majesty and Grace. This journey is the reality of the Ascension.

Like ordinary people travelling in their minds with the speed of imagination, saints journeying in their hearts with the speed of lightning, angels, whose bodies are of light, circulating between God's Supreme Throne and the earth with the speed of spirit, the people of Paradise rising from the Place of Supreme Gathering to Paradise covering a distance of five hundred years with the speed of *Buraq*, Prophet Muhammad's body will certainly accompany his elevated spirit in his journey as far as God's Supreme Throne. For the body of Muhammad, upon him be peace and blessings, is the storehouse of all of his faculties and serves his spirit, which is pure light and has the capacity and characteristics of light, and is more refined than saints' hearts, lighter than the deceased's spirits and the angels' forms, and finer than the beings' ethereal bodies, in performing its duties.

Now we say to the unbeliever who does not recognize God or know of the Prophet, and so does not believe in the Ascension: The universe and all of those creatures exist, and diverse acts and a continual creation are observed in the universe. An orderly act must have an author; a meaningful book must have a writer; and a skillful design must have a designer. Therefore, the wise and purposeful acts filling the universe must have an author, and the meaningful letters and amazing inscriptions or designs covering the earth and renewed seasonally must have a writer and a designer.

In addition, the result of two rulers interfering in the same affair is disorder. But we can see that there is perfect order in everything, from a fly's wings to the sky's lamp (the sun). So the ruler is One, for if this were not true, and given that the art and wisdom seen in everything are so wonderful and amazing that they require an All-Powerful and All-Knowing Maker, there would have to be as many deities as there are creatures. Since such deities would be both opposite and similar to each other simultaneously [because the acts and creatures in the universe have infinite diversity and yet resemble each other in many ways], it is inconceivable that this amazing order would not be upset.

Also, since those creatures clearly move by a command and in a far more organized form than an army, and since each group of creatures, from heavenly objects to almond flowers, displays in a perfect and organized manner and in far more orderly fashion than an army, the uniforms, decorations, and other beautiful garments given to it by the Eternal All-Powerful One and carries out the duties and drills He has assigned to them, this universe has an Absolute Ruler behind the veil of the Unseen, Whose commands are heeded and carried out by all creatures.

As His wise acts and majestic works testify, that Ruler is a Majestic Sovereign. As shown by His favors, He is an extremely Compassionate Lord. As His most beautiful works of art bear witness, He is a Maker Who is a Lover of art and Who loves His own art. As is apparent from the decorations and curiosity-exciting arts He exhibits, He is a Wise Creator Who wills to attract the appreciative gaze of conscious beings to His works of art. As is understood from His Lordship's wisdom, He wills to inform conscious beings of what the amazing and wonderful decorations displayed in the universe's creation mean, and where creatures come from and where they go. Therefore this All-Wise Ruler and All-Knowing Maker wills to demonstrate His Lordship.

He also wills to make Himself known to and loved by conscious beings through all these traces of grace and mercy, as well as the wonders of the art He displays. Given this, He will use an envoy to inform conscious beings of what He wants them to do and what pleases Him. He will choose a conscious being and declare His Lordship through him. To show His favorite arts, He will honor a herald with the nearness of His presence, and use him to exhibit them. To display His perfections by informing conscious beings of His lofty purposes for creating the universe, He will appoint one of them as a teacher and a guide so that the mystery of creation and the enigma of existence do not remain meaningless.

So that the beauties of the art He displays will not remain useless, He will choose a guide to teach the purposes contained in them. To inform them of the things that please Him, He will select a conscious being, raise him above all others, and use that person to inform others of those things. Reality and wisdom require this. As the one most worthy to perform these duties was Prophet Muhammad, who performed them perfectly, a fact attested to by the truthful and just witnesses of the world of Islam that he founded and the light of Islam that he showed, he would have to rise above all creatures and attain the rank of holding a universal and elevated conversation with the Creator of the universe. In this lies the Ascension's reality.

In short, Since Almighty God formed, organized, and decorated this universe for mighty purposes and great aims, such as those mentioned above; and since among beings there is humankind to see the universal Divine Lordship with all Its subtleties, and this mighty Divine sovereignty with all its truths, most certainly that Absolute Ruler will speak to and inform us of His purposes. But not everyone can rise to the highest, universal position to receive the Ruler's universal address directly. Given this, certain special people will be entrusted with that duty. Being human beings themselves, they can teach other human beings. They also should be extremely exalted spiritually, for only such people can receive God's direct address.

The one who taught the purposes of the universe's Maker most perfectly, unveiled the universe's and creation's mysterious meaning, and best heralded the beauties of His Lordship's dominion was Prophet Muhammad, upon him be peace and blessings. He would therefore make a spiritual journey and rise above all others and to the most exalted and comprehensive rank; he would make an Ascension by journeying through the corporeal world and then reaching beyond the "seventy thousand veils" of the manifestations of Divine Names, Attributes and acts, and all levels of creation. This is the Ascension.

QUESTION: How can I believe this? What does it mean to journey thousands of years to a Lord Who is nearer to all things than themselves and to meet with Him after passing through seventy thousand veils?

ANSWER: Almighty God is nearer to everything than itself, but everything is infinitely far from Him. If the sun were conscious and could speak, it would talk to you via a mirror in your hand. It could do with you as it wished. Although it is nearer to you than your eye's pupil, which is like a mirror, you are millions of miles away from it and cannot draw closer to it. If you rose to a position corresponding to the moon and came face to face with it, you would only be a kind of mirror to it.

Likewise, the All-Majestic One, the Sun of Eternity, is nearer to everything than itself, yet everything is infinitely far from Him. To be honored with a sort of nearness to Him, one should pass through all levels of existence. Freed from the restrictions of being a single particular, one should rise above the thousands of veils in the degrees of universality, draw near to a Divine Name encompassing all creation, and then traverse many other degrees beyond it.

A private is far below the commander-in-chief. He views him through an insignificant sample of command that he sees in a corporal, at a great distance and beyond many veils. To be nearer to his position, the private should be promoted to the higher and comprehensive ranks of lieutenant, captain, major, and so on. The commander-in-chief, however, is always present with the private through his rules, decrees, knowledge, and commands. If he is a saint having certain spiritual rank, he can be present with him personally, without the private seeing him. This truth has been argued convincingly in The Sixteenth Word.

QUESTION: I believe neither in the levels of heavens nor in angels. How can I believe that one can travel through the heavens and meet with angels?

ANSWER: It is really hard to convince those whose minds depend on their eyes. But since the truth is so brilliant that even the blind can see, we say the following: (Scientists generally agree that) space is full of "ether." Such subtle and refined matters as light, electricity, and heat point to the existence of a more subtle and refined matter that fills space.

Just as fruits demonstrate the existence of the trees that bear them, flowers their flower-bed, shoots their field, and fish the sea, so too stars present the existence of their origin to the mind's eye. Since there are different formations in the celestial realm and different rules are in force under different conditions, the heavens requiring the existence of those rules must be different. Just a person has, in addition to their bodily existence, immaterial forms of existence such as mind, heart, spirit, imagination, and memory, certainly the universe, the macro-human and the tree of which humanity is the fruit, contains other worlds beside the physical one. Also each world, from the earth to Paradise, has a heaven.

As for angels, we say: the earth is a medium-sized one among planets and highly small and dense among stars. And yet life and consciousness, which are luminous and of the greatest value among creation, are found on it in great abundance. So the stars, adorned castles and perfectly built palaces compared to the dark house of the earth, and the heavens, which are like the stars' seas, are inhabited by conscious, animate, numerous, and different kinds of angels and spirit beings. The Twenty-ninth Word discusses angels in more detail.

In conclusion, the heavens are formed of "ether" and are the source of such subtle and refined matters, energies, or forces as light, heat, electricity, and gravity. As pointed to in the Tradition "Heaven is a wave stretched and restrained," they were created in such a way that certain stars and planets can move easily within them. Wisdom and reason require that from the Milky Way to the nearest planet, there should be heavenly levels of different formations and a heaven as the roof of a world from the world of the earth to the Intermediate World (of the grave) and the World of Ideal Forms or Representations, and to the World of the Hereafter.

QUESTION: We can ascend only to a certain height by aircraft. How can someone bodily travel within a few minutes a distance that would normally take thousands of years to cover?

ANSWER: According to science, whose findings you accept without question, a heavy body like the earth travels about four hundred miles in a minute, and about two hundred million miles in a year. Should an All-Powerful One of Majesty, Who causes the earth to make that regular motion and revolves it like a stone in a sling, be unable to convey a human being to His Supreme Throne? Should a Wisdom that causes the heavy earth to revolve around the sun like a dervish through a law of Divine Lordship (gravity) be unable to raise a person, like lightning, to the All-Merciful One's Throne through the "gravity" of the All-Merciful One's Mercy and the attraction of the Eternal Sun's love?

QUESTION: Even if he could ascend, why did and why should he? Would it not have been enough for him to ascend in heart and spirit like saints?

ANSWER: The All-Majestic Maker wanted to show His amazing signs in His domain's inner and outer dimensions, make this world's workshops and sources observed, and display the results of our actions pertaining to the Hereafter. Given this, and as required by reason and wisdom, He would take Muhammad to His Supreme Throne not only with his eyes (the key to the world of visible objects) and ears, (which perceived His signs in the world of sound and voices,) but also with his entire blessed body, which, as his spirit's machine composed of different members and faculties, is the means for the fulfillment of his uncountable duties. Just as Divine Wisdom makes the body accompany the spirit in Paradise, because the body enables numerous duties of worship to be performed and innumerable pleasures and pains to be experienced, it also is pure wisdom that He would make Muhammad's blessed body accompany his spirit in ascending to the *Lote-tree of the furthest limit*, the "trunk" of the Garden of Refuge and Dwelling.

QUESTION: How, in the name of reason, can the distance that normally takes thousands of years to cover be covered in a few minutes?

ANSWER: In the All-Majestic Maker's art, motions have infinitely different degrees. For example, the speeds of electricity, spirit, imagination, and sound are quite different from each other. Also, science has established that the speeds of planetary movements are astonishingly different. So why should it be unreasonable that Muhammad's body acquired a sort of refinement, accompanied his spirit in the Ascension, and moved at its speed? Sometimes you sleep for ten minutes but have a year's worth of experiences. If the words spoken and heard in a dream lasting for only a minute were collected, it would take a day and even longer to speak or hear them while awake. Thus a single period of time means a day for one and a year for another.

Consider this analogy: A clock measures the speed of a person, a cannonball, sound, light, electricity, spirit, and imagination. It has ten hands to show the hours, minutes, and seconds down to fractions of an hour to the tenth power. It also has ten circles, one round the other and sixty times larger than it, respectively. If the circle with the hour hand is the size of a normal clock, the circle with the fraction-of-an-hour hand to the tenth power would have to be the size of the earth's annual orbit or much greater.

Suppose there are two people. One is mounted on the hour-hand and observes according to its motion, while the other is on the hand showing fractions of an hour to the tenth power. There would be a huge difference, as great as the proportion between a normal clock and the earth's annual orbit, with respect to what they could see during the same time period.

Since time is like an aspect or a "ribbon" of motion, a rule that is in force in motion is also in force in time. While we would see the same amount of things during an hour as the one mounted on the hour-hand, which moves in the smallest circle at the slowest speed, God's Messenger, like the one mounted on the hand showing fractions of the hour to the tenth power, gets on the mount of Divine assistance and, in the same space of time, traverses the entire sphere of contingency like lightning. Seeing the wonders in the inner and outer dimensions of contingent existence and rising as far as the boundary of the immaterial realm of the necessary existence (Divine realm's limits), he is honored with Divine conversation and vision of His Beauty, receives the decree, and returns to his duty of Messengership on the earth. It was possible for him to do that, and he did it.

QUESTION: Even if this were possible, not everything possible occurs. Is there something similar that we can accept? How can we accept the occurrence of something unique, only because it is possible?

ANSWER: There are countless similar cases. For example, people with sound sight can ascend with their eyes to Neptune in a second. Astronomers can mount the laws of astronomy in their minds and travel beyond the stars in a minute. Believers can mount in thought on the acts and pillars of the prescribed Prayers and, leaving the universe behind through a sort of Ascension, go as far as the Divine Presence. Perfected saints can make a spiritual journey and travel the spiritual ranks beyond the realms of God's Supreme Throne and His Names and Attributes in forty days. Such people as 'Abdu'l-Qadir al-Jilani and Imam ar-Rabbani truthfully reported that they used to ascend spiritually as far as the Divine Throne in a minute.

Angels, whose bodies are of light, come and go between the ground and the Divine Throne in a very short time. The people of Paradise will ascend to the gardens of Paradise from the Supreme Plain of Gathering in a short period of time. Many such examples demonstrate that it is pure wisdom, completely rational, and that it undoubtedly occurred that Prophet Muhammad, the lord of all saints, leader of all believers, head of all people of Paradise, and accepted by all angels, realized an Ascension, which marks his journey through and beyond all ranks of sainthood, in a form appropriate to his position.

Third principle: What is the Ascension's wisdom?

ANSWER: The wisdom here is so elevated that human minds cannot reach it, so profound that human minds cannot comprehend it, and so subtle and fine that the intellect cannot grasp it. However, even if we cannot know its wisdom or the exact Divine purposes for it, some indications allow us to show the existence of several purposes. They are as follows.

To show the light of His Unity and the manifestation of His absolute Oneness in the levels of publicity, the Creator of this universe distinguished an eminent individual with an Ascension in the form of a link between the realm of multiplicity and corporeality's furthest limit and the Dominion of Pure Unity and spirituality's starting point. Addressing him on behalf of all creatures, He explained all Divine purposes to him in the name of conscious beings, and made them known through him. He also willed to observe through his sight His Art's beauty and His Lordship's perfection in the mirrors of His creatures and to cause them to be observed by others.

Furthermore, His works testify that the Maker of the world has infinite beauty and perfection, both of which are loved because of themselves. Thus the One with infinite beauty and perfection has a boundless love for His Beauty and Perfection, a love that manifests itself in the works of His Art, which He loves because He sees His Beauty and Perfection in them. The most lovable and elevated of His works of Art are animate beings. The most lovable and elevated animate beings are conscious beings. By virtue of their comprehensiveness, the most lovable conscious beings are found among humanity. The most loveable person is the one who has developed his or her potentiality most fully and manifested the samples of the perfections observed in all creatures.

To see at one point and in one mirror all manifestations of His Love pervading all creatures, and to display all varieties of His Beauty focused on one individual, the Maker of beings chose one person, an illustrious, enlightened fruit of the tree of creation, one whose heart is like a seed containing all the essential truths contained in that trees. To demonstrate how He loves that individual in the name of the universe, He drew him to His Presence through an Ascension, which is like a thread linking the seed (the origin) with the fruit (the end), and honored him with the vision of His Essential Beauty. So that others could imitate his holiness and excellence, He favored him with His speech and entrusted Him with His decree.

To understand this exalted wisdom, consider the comparisons below.

First comparison: As explained in The Eleventh Word, imagine a glorious king with vast treasuries containing many varieties of jewels. He is well-versed in all industries, and had a vast knowledge of all artistic and scientific disciplines, and countless fine arts. As anyone with perfect beauty and perfection tend to see and show themselves, that glorious king wants to open up an exhibition and display his kingdom's magnificence, his wealth's splendor and extent, and the wonderful products of his artistry and skill. He so desires in order to behold his beauty and perfection with his own discerning eye and through the eyes of others.

And so he begins to build a very large, magnificent palace. Dividing it into many apartments and rooms, he decorates it with his finest and most beautiful works of art, and embellishes it with his precious stones. Designing it according to his artistic and scientific principles and disciplines, he furnishes it with the miraculous products of his knowledge. Finally, he sets up therein tables containing most delicious specific foods and drinks, and specifies an appropriate table for each tribe of his subjects. He prepares a general banquet.

Then, to show his perfection, the king invites his subjects to eat and see the palace. He appoints a representative or supreme commander and gives him the highest rank with himself. He invites him to rise above the bottom floor in order to tour all mansions and floors one after or above the other. Showing him the successive machinery, all workshops of his wonderful art and storehouses for the produce coming from below, he brings him to his private apartment. There he honors him with his presence and the vision of his blessed person, who is the origin of all those perfections, and informs him of the palace's true nature and of his own perfections.

Appointing him to guide the rest of his subjects, he sends him back to describe the palace's maker through its contents, inscriptions, and wonders. The guide also will explain the inscriptions' meanings, what the works of art and well-proportioned and well-arranged furniture and decorations signify, and how they point to the perfections and skills of the palace's owner. He will teach them the correct behavior and formalities when visiting the palace and beholding the exhibition, and describe the protocol and ceremonies that meet with the pleasure and desires of the learned and skillful king, who does not appear to them.

Similarly, the All-Majestic Maker, the Lord of Eternity, willed to see and display His infinite Beauty and Perfections. So He made the palace of this world in such a fashion that each creature voices His Perfections in numerous tongues and points to His Beauty with many signs. Through all its inhabitants, this universe shows how numerous immaterial treasuries are hidden in each of His All-Beautiful Names and how many subtleties are concealed in each sacred Title. It shows this in such a way that although scientists, together with all of science's laws and principles, have studied this book of the universe since the time of Adam, they still have not discovered one-hundredth of that book's meanings and signs concerning the Divine Names and Perfections.

Thus the Wisdom of the All-Majestic One of Beauty, the Beautiful One of Majesty, the Maker having infinite Perfection, Who has made that palace of the universe like an exhibition to see and display His Perfections and transcendent Beauty, requires that He inform someone of the meanings of His signs contained therein so that they do not remain useless and without benefit for conscious beings on the earth; that He have someone travel through the exalted worlds, which are the sources of the palace's wonders and the store-houses where the results of their lives accumulate; that He raise him above all others, honor him with nearness to Him in His Presence, have him tour the Hereafter's worlds, and entrust him with such duties as teaching His servants, heralding His Lordship's sovereignty, informing His servants of things pleasing to Himself, and expanding His signs in the universe's creation and operation; that He should show his pre-eminence through the decorations of miracles; and that He should proclaim through a decree like the Qur'an that that person is a truthful personal interpreter of the All-Majestic One.

So far, we have demonstrated through this comparison a few instances of wisdom in the Ascension. You may infer others by analogy.

Second comparison: Suppose a knowledgeable, skillful person writes a miraculous book, each page of which contains as many truths as would fill a hundred books, each line of which contains as many subtle meanings as would fill a hundred pages, and each word of which would contain as many truths as would fill a hundred lines. If all the meanings and truths of such a book point to its miracle-displaying writer's transcendent perfections, he surely would not leave it closed and therefore worthless. Rather, he would teach it to others so that others could benefit, so that his hidden perfections would be unveiled and his beauty (intellectual and spiritual excellence) would be seen, and so that he would be pleased and make himself loved. To this end, he would have someone go through that entire wonderful book, all the while instructing him in its meanings and truths so that the person would then instruct others in them.

Similarly, in order to show His Perfections, Beauty, and the truths of His Names, the Eternal Inscriber has "written" the universe in such way that all creatures proclaim and express His infinite Perfections, Names, and Attributes in innumerable ways. If a book's meaning is not known, it has no value. But a book (such as the universe), each letter of which contains thousands of meanings, cannot be reduced to nothing. Given this, the One Who wrote it will make it known and cause it to be explained in parts according to the capacity of each group of creatures.

He will teach the whole of it to one with the most comprehensive view, most universal consciousness, and greatest capacity. But to teach such a book in its entirety and with all its universal truths requires that, starting from the furthest limits of the levels of multiplicity (the corporeal world, the book's first page) as far as the Realm of Unity (its final page), the individual should make a most elevated and universal journey. Through this comparison, one can gain some understanding of the exalted instances of wisdom in the Ascension.

QUESTION: Those deniers who are beginning to believe still might face some confusion over such things as:

- Why is this Ascension special to Prophet Muhammad?
- What do you mean by saying that Muhammad is the seed of the universe, that the universe was created from his light, and that he is its farthest and most enlightened fruit?
- You say that he made his Ascension to rise to the elevated realm, to see the machinery and workshops whose produce or works are exhibited on the earth, as well as the storehouses where the results of those works are kept. What does this mean?

ANSWER: The first question was answered in previous Words, and so we give only a brief list of signs showing Muhammad's Prophethood and perfections, and why he is the most worthy to make the Ascension.

Firstly: Despite the great corruption in the Torah, the Gospels, and the Psalms, Husain al-Jisri found in them one hundred and ten signs indicating Muhammad's Prophethood. These are presented in his *Risala al-Hamidiya*.

Secondly: History also records the words of many pre-Islamic soothsayers, such Shiq and Satih, who accurately foretold the Prophethood of Muhammad, upon him be peace and blessings, and that he was the Last Prophet.

Thirdly: Many extraordinary events before his Prophethood (*irhasat*) foretold his imminent advent. For example, on the night he was born, the Ka'ba's idols toppled over and the pinnacles of the famous palace of the Persian ruler Chosroes broke.

Fourthly: Prophet Muhammad was distinguished with approximately a thousand miracles, which have been related by historians and biographers. To cite only a few examples, he satisfied an army's thirst with the water flowing from his fingers and split the moon (54:1). The dry wooden pole against which he leaned while preaching in the Mosque moaned like a camel in front of many people when it was separated from him.

Fifthly: Friend and foe who are fair agree that all good qualities were found in him to the highest degree, and that, as demonstrated by his conduct, all attributes and character of the highest excellence were apparent in the way he performed his mission. As testified to by Islam's moral principles, praiseworthy virtues of the highest order are found in the Law he brought.

Sixthly: Wisdom requires that Divinity manifest Itself and be responded with worship. Prophet Muhammad, upon him be peace and blessings, manifested God's Divinity at the highest level and in the most brilliant fashion through the most perfect and comprehensive way of worship contained in the religion that he brought. Due to the wisdom in the universe's creation, the Creator of the world wants to display His most perfect Beauty and Grace through the most appropriate means. Clearly, Prophet Muhammad showed and described His Beauty and Grace in the most perfect fashion.

The Maker of the world wills to exhibit and draw attentive gazes toward His perfect Art of infinite beauty; Prophet Muhammad proclaimed that Art with the clearest voice. Muhammad, in response to the desire of the Lord of the worlds to proclaim His Oneness in the realms of multiplicity, most perfectly announced Unity with all Its aspects.

As a consequence of His Wisdom, the Owner of the world wills to see and show His infinite essential Beauty and Grace, with all their manifestations, in the mirrors of all beings; Prophet Muhammad, upon him be peace and blessings, reflected them in the most brilliant fashion and made others love them. Also, Muhammad, in response to the will of the Builder of the palace of the world to describe His Perfections by exhibiting His unseen treasuries of invaluable gems, most perfectly displayed and described them.

The Maker of the universe has decorated the universe with the most beautiful and exquisite embellishments, and has included therein His conscious creatures so that they may travel to receive enjoyment and reflect. As required by wisdom, He also wills to communicate the meaning and value expressed by the works of His Art to people who observe and reflect. Prophet Muhammad, upon him be peace and blessings, guided humanity, jinn, and angels in the most comprehensive way, in this respect, through the Qur'an.

The All-Wise Ruler of the universe wills to use an envoy to provide for all conscious beings the answers to three perplexing questions: Where do we come from? Where are we going? What are we?, and therefore to reveal the purpose of the changes and transformations in existence. By means of the Qur'an's truths, Muhammad, upon him be peace and blessings, revealed this purpose and provided the answers in the clearest and most perfect way.

The Maker of this world wills to make Himself known to conscious beings through His exquisite works and to be loved by them through the precious bounties He bestows on them. Thus He wants to communicate to them, by means of an envoy, what He wants them to do and how they may obtain His approval and good pleasure in return for those bounties. By means of the Qur'an, Prophet Muhammad communicated the things that please God in the most exalted and perfect way.

The Lord of the worlds has endowed humanity, the fruit of the tree of creation, with a comprehensive disposition that can encompass the universe, and with a corresponding ability—and even need—to perform a universal worship. But humanity inclines to the world and its attractions. So God wills, by means of a guide, to turn humanity's attention from worldly multiplicity to Divine Unity, from transience to eternity. In response to this will and by means of the Qur'an, Prophet Muhammad, upon him be peace and blessings, guided humanity to this goal in the most desirable fashion and performed the duty of Messengership in the most perfect way.

Thus the most superior members of creation are living beings, the most superior living beings are conscious beings, the most superior conscious beings are true human beings, and the true human being who carried out all of the duties mentioned in the most perfect and comprehensive way naturally would rise through an all-embracing Ascension to *the nearness of the distance between the strings of two bows*, the station nearest to God, to knock at the door of eternal happiness, open Mercy's treasury, and witness directly belief's unseen truths.

Seventhly: Everything displays the most pleasing instances of beauty and utmost degree of adornment, thereby demonstrating that their Maker wills to make things beautiful and adorn them. In turn, this shows that the Maker has a strong inclination and sacred love toward His Art. Therefore the person with the most comprehensive disposition to display this Art's wonders in himself; one who knows them, makes them known, and thus makes himself lovable; and who deeply appreciates the beauties manifested in other beings in full appreciation of their coming from the Maker, will be the most beloved in the sight of the Maker, Who nurtures art and loves His Art greatly.

This same being, in full awareness of the exquisite beauties and qualities adorning all beings and of the perfections illuminating them, makes the heavens echo: "All-Glorified is God! What wonders God has willed!" and "All these are from God! God is the All-Great!" This same being causes the universe to reverberate with the sounds of the Qur'an, and enraptures land and sea with his appreciative reflections and glorification as well as with his proclamation and demonstration of Divine Unity.

Such a being, according to the principle of "The cause is like the doer," receives a reward equivalent to his community's good deeds. His spiritual perfections draw strength from the blessings invoked upon him by his community, and the duties he performed during his Messengership cause him to receive an immaterial recompense and infinite emanations of Divine Mercy and Love. Given this, the result of pure truth and absolute wisdom is that this being should advance by means of Ascension as far as Paradise, *Sidratu'l-Muntaha*—the Lote-tree, contingency's farthest limit—the Divine Throne, and to the *nearness of the distance between the strings of two bows.*

Answer to the second question: The truth behind the second question is so elevated and profound that the human mind cannot comprehend it. It can be discerned only through the light of belief. However, we will try to indicate it through comparisons.

This universe, when considered with regard to the wisdom in its purposes, appears to have the meaning of a mighty tree. Just like a tree, this world, which is a branch of the tree of creation, has branches (elements), leaves (plants), flowers (animals), and fruits (humanity). His Name the All-Wise requires that any law of the All-Majestic Maker that is prevalent in trees be prevalent in this supreme tree. Therefore, like any other tree, this tree of creation must also have been formed from a seed. It must have been such a seed that, besides those of this material world, it would encapsulate the models and foundations of all other worlds. For the origin and essential seed of the universe, which comprises thousands of different worlds, cannot be a dried, inanimate piece of matter.

Since there was not another tree prior to this tree of creation, the Divine Name the All-Wise requires that the meaning or light constituting its seed or origin be clothed within a fruit. A seed cannot remain naked for ever. As it was not clothed within a fruit at the beginning of creation, it would certainly be clothed in it in the end. Since this seed is humanity, and since Prophet Muhammad, as pointed out earlier, is the best-known and illustrious among humanity—one who has attracted humanity's attention to himself and has fixed the attention of half of the globe and one-fifth of humanity on himself, and one who, through his exceptional virtues and excellencies, has made the world consider him with love and amazement—for sure, the light constituting the universe's seed would be clothed in Muhammad's person and appear in the form of the final fruit.

Why should it be considered unlikely that this amazing, mighty universe was created out of a man's nature? Why should the All-Powerful One of Majesty, Who creates a huge, world-resembling pine tree from a grain-sized seed, not create—or be unable to create—the universe from the light of

Muhammad, upon him be peace and blessings? The tree of the universe being (like the *Touba* tree of Paradise) upside down, with its roots and trunk spreading upward and branches downward, contains a link of light and a link in meaning between the position of the fruit below and that of the essential seed above. The Ascension is that link's form: Prophet Ahmad (Muhammad) opened the way of traveling along it; he ascended through sainthood, returned with Messengership, and left the door open to a sort of ascension. Saints travel in heart and spirit on that highway of light under the Prophetic Ascension's shadow, and rise to the elevated stations according to their capacity.

While answering the first question, we saw that the Maker of the universe made it in the form of a palace for the purposes mentioned. Since the Prophet is the means for accomplishing those purposes, he would have to be under the eyes of the favor of the universe's Maker and receive His Manifestation before the universe was created, for something's result or fruit is considered first. Thus the latest in existence is the first in meaning and consideration. Since Prophet Muhammad is the most perfect fruit, the means for valuing all other fruits and the cause for realizing all purposes (for the universe's creation), his light must receive the first manifestation of Divine creation.

As for the third question, it is so extensive that people like us cannot comprehend it. We can only glimpse it from afar. The "immaterial factories" producing the material world are in the celestial worlds and its governing laws are determined or issue from there. The results of the acts performed by the earth's innumerable inhabitants, and the consequences of what is done by humanity and jinn, also assume form in those worlds. Together with the testimony of many indications and Prophetic Traditions, the Qur'an suggests, and the wisdom in the universe and the Divine Name the All-Wise require, that the good deeds done by humanity and jinn assume the forms of Paradise's fruits, while their evil deeds assume the forms of the bitter, poisonous fruits of the tree (*Zaqqum*) of Hell.

Creatures exist on the earth in such abundance, and creation has been divided into so many branches, that the groups and species of beings and divisions of creatures are found here in far greater numbers than anywhere else in the universe. These beings and creatures are replaced constantly by newer ones, for the world is filled and emptied of them continuously. All of these multiple beings and creatures have their sources and origins in the universal laws and manifestations of Divine Names, which are first reflected in and received by the heavens.

To some degree simple and pure, each heaven is like a different world's roof, and represents a center for the administration of that world and regulation of its affairs. One of those worlds is the Garden of Refuge and Dwelling, an apartment of Paradise beside the *Lote-tree of the farthest limit*. The Truthful Reporter (the holy Prophet) says the praises and glorifications of God performed on the earth assume the forms of that Garden's fruits. In other words, the storehouses containing the results or fruits of the works done here are located in those heavenly worlds; the harvest obtained here is sent there (to "reap" on a predetermined day.)

So do not say how an utterance, such as "All praise and gratitude are for God," which is lost in the air, become embodied in a fruit of Paradise? Sometimes you say an agreeable word while awake and eat it in the form of a delicious apple in your dream at night. A disagreeable word said during the day returns at night as a bitter thing to swallow. If you backbite someone, they will make you eat it as decaying flesh. So whatever good or bad words you utter in this worldly sleep, you will eat them in the forms of fruits in the Hereafter, the world of being awake.

Fourth principle: What are the Ascension's fruits and benefits?

ANSWER: Out of the numerous fruits of the Ascension, which is like an elaborate tree of Paradise in meaning, we will mention only five as examples.

First fruit: The vision of the original forms of the pillars of belief or the truths from which they originate, as well as seeing angels, Paradise, and the Hereafter, and even the vision of the All-Majestic Being (beyond all features of quality and quantity), resulted in a vast treasury, an eternal light, and a gift for the universe and humanity. Through it, the universe could no longer be seen as a disordered heap of things doomed to destruction, for its reality was revealed: It is the harmonious collection of the Eternally Besought's sacred writings and the lovely mirrors where the Single One's Grace and Beauty are reflected. It has pleased and caused the universe and all conscious beings to rejoice.

It also freed us from our confused state of misguidance, in which we considered ourselves wretched, helpless, and destitute beings entangled in infinite need and hostility and doomed to eternal annihilation. It showed us our reality as beings of the fairest composition and creation's best pattern, miracles of the Eternally Besought's Power, a comprehensive copy of His writing, and beings addressed by the Sovereign of Eternity. It also revealed that we are His private servants appreciating His Perfections, His friends beholding His Beauty in amazement, and His beloved and honorable guests designated for Paradise. It implanted infinite joy and enthusiasm in those who are truly human.

Second fruit: The Ascension brought to jinn and humankind as a gift the essentials of Islam, including primarily the prescribed five daily Prayers, which comprise whatever is approved by and pleasing to the Ruler of Eternity, the Maker of creatures, the Owner of the universe, and the Lord of the worlds. To perceive the things that are pleasing to Him are so curiosity-exciting and brings such happiness that it cannot be described. For everyone wants to know the wishes of a renowned benefactor or a benevolent king, and so wishes that they could talk with him directly to know what he asks of them and what pleases him.

All creatures are in the grasp of His Power, and their grace, beauty, and perfections are but dim shadows when compared to His Beauty, Grace, and Perfection. See to what degree humanity, who needs Him in infinite respects and receives His boundless bounties every moment, should be curious about and want to know His will and what pleases Him. One of the Ascension's fruits was that after passing through "seventy thousand" veils, Prophet Muhammad heard what pleases the King of Eternity directly from Him with absolute certainty, and then relayed this information to us as a gift.

Humanity is very curious about the moon and other planets. We hope that someone will go there and tell us what they see, and are ready to make great sacrifices for this end. But the moon travels in the domain of the Master Who makes it fly around the earth like a fly. The earth flies around the sun like a moth, and the sun is only one of thousands of lamps and functions as a candle in a guest-house of the All-Majestic Master's Kingdom. During the Ascension, Prophet Muhammad, upon him be peace and blessings, observed the essential Characteristics of such an All-Majestic Being, as well as the originals of His Acts, His Art's wonders, and His Mercy's treasuries in the eternal world. He observed these and returned to tell us about them. How contrary to reason and wisdom it would be if humanity did not listen to him with utmost curiosity and in perfect amazement and love.

Third fruit: The Prophet saw the hidden treasury of eternal happiness during the Ascension and brought its keys to humanity and jinn as a gift. He saw Paradise, observed the everlasting manifestations of the Majestic All-Merciful One's Mercy, and perceived eternal happiness with absolute certainty. He then gave humanity and jinn the glad tiding that the eternal happiness exists (in an everlasting world).

The great happiness that surged in the mortal, wretched human beings and jinn, all of whom before this event had considered themselves condemned to eternal annihilation, cannot be described. They learned of this at a time when all creatures were pouring out heart-rending cries at the thought of being in a flux amid the convulsions of death and decay in an unstable world, entering the ocean of non-existence and eternal separation through time's flow and atoms' motion. Consider how happy such people become when they learn, just before they are to be hanged, that the king has given each of them a palace near his own palace. Add together the joy and happiness of all human beings and jinn, and then you will understand the value of this good tiding.

Fourth fruit: Prophet Muhammad received the fruit of the vision of God's Beautiful "Countenance," and brought it to humanity and jinn as a gift so that every believer may be honored with the same vision. You can understand how delicious, fine, and beautiful that fruit is by the following comparison: Anyone with a heart loves a beautiful, perfect, and benevolent one. This love increases in proportion to the extent of beauty, perfection, and benevolence; expands to adoration and self-sacrifice; and increases to the point that one may sacrifice possessions and life for a single vision of the beloved one.

When compared to His, all beauty, perfection, and benevolence in creation do not even resemble a few flashes of the sun in comparison to the sun itself. Understand from this what a pleasant, beautiful, rejoicing, and blissful fruit it is to receive in eternal happiness the vision of an All-Majestic One of Perfection, Who is worthy of infinite love, the sight of Whom deserves to inspire an infinite eagerness.

Fifth fruit: Another fruit is that this event made it understood that humanity is a valuable fruit of the universe and a darling beloved of the Maker of the universe. Though outwardly an insignificant creature, a weak animal, and an impotent conscious being, humanity has risen through this fruit to a position so far above all other creatures that it is the cause of pride for us. The joy and happiness it gives is indescribable. If you tell an ordinary private that he has been promoted to the rank of field-marshal, he will feel infinite joy. While being a mortal, helpless, reasoning, and articulating animal knowing only the blows of decay and separation, we were told unexpectedly through the Ascension: As you may realize all your heart's desires in an everlasting Paradise, enveloped by the Mercy of an All-Merciful, All-Compassionate, and All-Magnificent One, and in recreation, in traveling with the speed of imagination and in the broad sphere of the spirit and the mind, you also may see His All-Beautiful "Countenance" in eternal happiness.

Imagine the great joy and happiness one who is truly human will feel in his or her heart upon hearing this. O unbelievers, tear the shirt of denial and irreligion and put on the ears of a believer and the eyes of a Muslim. Consider the following two comparisons.

First comparison: Suppose we are in an unfriendly land in which everything and everyone is hostile and strange to us and to each other. Dreadful corpses are everywhere. All we hear are cries of orphans and laments of the oppressed. While there in that situation, if one goes and brings the good news from the king, which somehow changes hostility into friendship; enemies into friends; dreadful corpses into worshippers occupied with praising and glorification, in veneration and humility; cries and wailings into shouts of approval or acclamation; and death, killing, and robbery into discharges from life's duties— and if we somehow share the joy and happiness of others, while experiencing our own joy and happiness, you can understand how joyful that tiding is.

Prior to the light of belief, a fruit of Prophet Muhammad's Ascension, all creatures seemed to be strange, harmful, troublesome, and frightening objects. Mountain-like bodies seemed like dreadful corpses, death cut off everyone's head and threw it into the well of eternal non-existence, and all voices were cries of lament coming from death and separation. At a time when misguidance presented everything in such a way, the truths contained in the pillars of belief, a fruit of the Ascension, showed every creature as a friend or sibling, something that mentions and glorifies its All-Majestic Maker, death as a discharge from life's duties, and voices as praises and glorifications of God. If you want to comprehend this truth perfectly, refer to the Second and Eighth Words.

Second comparison: Suppose we are trapped at night in a desert sandstorm. We cannot see even our hands and are hungry, thirsty, hopeless, and exposed. Just then, someone appears unexpectedly with a car and takes us to a Paradise-like place, where an extremely merciful lord welcomes us and extends his protection to us. Our future has been secured, and a banquet has been prepared for us. You can well imagine our great happiness.

The desert is the world, and the sandstorm is the violent disturbances of time and events. All of us are anxious about our future. Since we look at it through the view of misguidance, we see it in a thick darkness. No one we know can hear our cries. Moreover, we are very hungry and thirsty. But thanks to the pillars of belief, ways of worship and principles of good conduct that Prophet Muhammad brought as a fruit of the Ascension, the world is the guest-house of an extremely Munificent One and we are His guests and officers. In such a guest-house, the future appears as beautiful as Paradise, as lovely as mercy, and as brilliant as eternal happiness. Given this, understand how lovely, pleasant, and beautiful that fruit is.

The unbeliever remarks: "Boundless praise and gratitude be to Almighty God! I am convinced and reject my unbelief. I am a believer." We congratulate you, and may God Almighty include us in His Messenger's intercession.

O God, bestow blessings from the beginning of the world until the end of the Day of Judgment, on him by whose sign the moon split, and from whose fingers water gushed forth like the spring of Paradise; who made the Ascension and whose eyes did not swerve— our master Muhammad, and on his Family and Companions.

All-Glorified are You! We have no knowledge save what You have taught us. Surely You are the All-Knowing, the All-Wise.

O Lord, accept from us (all our good deeds); surely You are the All-Hearing, the All-Knowing. Our Lord, take us not to task if we forget or make mistakes. O Lord, do not let our hearts swerve after You have guided us. O Lord, complete our light for us and forgive us. Surely You have full power over all things. The conclusion of their call will be: "All praise and gratitude are for God, the Lord of the Worlds."

❧ ❧

Addendum

The miracle of splitting the moon

In the Name of God, the All-Merciful, the All-Compassionate.

The Hour has drawn near, and the moon split. But whenever they see a sign (miracle), they turn away in aversion, saying: "This is sorcery like many others, one after the other." (54:1-2)

QUESTION: Materialist philosophers and their imitators, who want to eclipse this bright miracle of Prophet Muhammad with their vicious delusions, say: "If the event had really happened, it would have been known all over the world and related in all historical documents."

ANSWER: This miracle was demonstrated before a group of people as an evidence of Prophethood of Muhammad, upon him be peace and blessings. It happened momentarily at a time of night when people were sleeping; such obstacles as mist, clouds, and time differences prevented others from seeing it; and, moreover, at that time science and civilization were not yet advanced or widespread. Thus the practice of observing the sky was quite limited. Last but not least, there is no reason why it should have been seen worldwide.

In order to remove such clouds of delusion, consider the following five points:

FIRST POINT: The stubbornness of Muhammad's unbelieving contemporaries is well-known and recorded. When the Qur'an announced this incident in *The moon split*, not one unbeliever dared contradict it. If they had not seen this event, they would have used this verse as a pretext to attack the Prophet more formidably. However, neither the biographies of the Prophet nor history books report anything that even suggests their denial of this event. Their reaction was recorded as: *This is sorcery like many others, one after the other*. They declared the event to be magic, and added further that if Makkan caravans in other places had seen it, it had truly happened; otherwise, the Prophet had bewitched them. When caravans arriving the following morning from Yemen and other places announced that they had seen this miracle, the unbelievers replied: "The magic of Abu Talib's orphan has affected even the heavens!"

SECOND POINT: The majority of the foremost scholars of meticulous research, such as Sa'dud-Din at-Taftazani, concluded that, like the miracles of water flowing from the Prophet's fingers and satiating a whole army, and the audible grieving of the wooden pole against which the Prophet used to lean while delivering sermons, when it was separated from him following the construction of a pulpit, the splitting of the moon is *mutawatir*. This means that it has been transmitted down the generations by numerous truthful groups after another, and that the transmitters form such a vast community that they are unable to agree on a lie. It is as certain as Halley's comet, which appeared a thousand years ago, or the existence of an island we have not seen. Therefore it is unreasonable to foster baseless doubts about such certain, witnessed matters. In fact, it is enough for their acceptability that they are not impossible. Splitting the moon is just as possible as splitting a mountain by a volcanic eruption.

THIRD POINT: Prophets work miracles to prove their claim of Prophethood and to convince deniers, not to compel belief. Therefore, every miracle is shown to convince those who heard the claim of Prophethood. If miracles somehow compelled everyone to see or believe in them, the All-Wise's Wisdom in or the Divine purpose for creating us with free will and sending religion, which entails that the ground be prepared for the mind's willing acceptance but the free choice not be negated or canceled, would be violated.

Thus if the All-Wise Originator had left the moon split for several hours so that everyone could see and record it in their historical records, it would have been only another astronomical event instead of an event unique to Muhammad's Messengership or an evidence of his Prophethood. Or it would have been so evident a miracle that everyone had been forced to believe, free will would be annulled and people of coal-like spirit like Abu Jahl would be equal to those of diamond-like spirit like Abu Bakr. Thus the purpose of creating humanity with a special function and responsibility, as well as the purpose for sending Revelation, would be negated. That is why this miracle was not shown worldwide so that it could be recorded.

FOURTH POINT: Since this event occurred instantaneously at night while everyone was sleeping, it would certainly not be seen all over the world. Even if some people had seen it, they would not have believed their eyes. And even if it had made them believe, such a significant, miraculous event would not have been recorded by histories based on individual reports.

Some additional reports that after the moon split into two halves, it fell to earth have been rejected by veracious scholars as a false addition made by hypocrites to reduce to nothing the value of this evident miracle.

This miracle would certainly not be mentioned in Chinese, Japanese, and Native American historical accounts because, in addition to other obstacles, it was barely sunset in such European countries as Spain, France, and England (all enveloped in mists of ignorance), daytime in America, and morning in China and Japan when it happened.

FIFTH POINT: This miracle is not an ordinary incident that happened due to particular causes or randomly so that it should be criticized based on ordinary "laws of nature." Rather, the All-Wise Creator of the sun and the moon made it an extraordinary event to confirm His Messenger's Prophethood and support his claim. Therefore it was shown as a convincing proof to certain people specified by Divine Wisdom, for the nature of Divine guidance and human responsibility as well as the reason for raising a Messenger required this. If it had been seen by those who were not intended to see it and who had not yet heard of Muhammad's Prophethood, and if it had occurred according to ordinary "laws of nature," it would have been an ordinary astronomical event instead of a miracle specific to and connected with his Messengership.

In conclusion, these arguments are enough for any mind to be convinced of the possibility that this miracle occurred. Out of many evidences of its occurrence, we will mention only six, as these six have the strength of a six-fold consensus:

- The Companions, all people of justice and truthfulness, agree that it took place.
- All exacting Qur'anic interpreters agree that *The moon split* indicates that a gesture of Muhammad's fingers caused this event.
- All truthful *Muhaddithun* (Traditionists) narrated this incident through various authentic channels of transmission.
- All people of truth and sainthood, as well as of inspiration and spiritual discovery, testify that this event took place.
- All foremost theologians and learned scholars confirm this event, despite their other differences of opinions.
- Muhammad's community, which an authentic Prophetic Tradition states can never agree on an error, accepts its occurrence.

These six evidences clearly prove the splitting of the moon.

In conclusion, then, we have established the reality of this miracle by refuting objections to its possibility. In a few concluding sentences, we will speak in the name of the truth and for the sake of belief.

By making the Seal of the Prophets, an earthly body, yet the light-diffusing moon of the heaven of Messengership, travel through the heavens (Ascension), which is the greatest wonder or miracle of his sainthood achieved through the quality of his worship which elevated him to the status of God's beloved, God showed the inhabitants of the heavens and those of the highest realms that Muhammad is their superior and His beloved.

So too, by allowing a man's gesture to split the moon, which is set in the sky and bound to the earth, people saw another great evidence of his Messengership. Thus Prophet Muhammad flew to the summit of perfections on the two brilliant wings of Messengership and sainthood—like the moon's two bright halves. He ascended to the point *of two bows' length* (to the highest rank and nearest station to God) and became the cause of pride for all inhabitants of the heavens and the earth.

> Upon him and his Family be blessings and peace such as to fill the earth and the heavens.

> Glory be unto You. We have no knowledge save what You have taught us. You are the All-Knowing, All-Wise.

> O God, for the sake of him by a gesture of whom the moon split, make my heart and the hearts of the *Risale-i Nur*'s students as devoted and loyal to the "sun" of the Qur'an as the moon is to the sun. Amin.

The
Thirty-second Word

The Thirty-second Word

> Creation rejects associating partners with God
> Arguments for God's Unity
> The way of destruction and the way of happiness

(NOTE: This Word consists of three Stations. The First Station is an appendix explaining the Eighth Gleam of The Twenty-second Word and interpreting the first of the fifty-five languages by which universal entities bear witness to God's Oneness. It also discusses one truth, in the form of a parable, of the many truths expressed in: *Had there been in them (the heavens and the earth) any deities other than God, both would certainly have fallen into ruin* [21:22].).

Three stations

In the Name of God, the All-Merciful, the All-Compassionate.

First station

Had there been in them (the heavens and the earth) any deities other than God, both would certainly have fallen into ruin.

There is no deity but God, He alone; having no partner; His is the Dominion and to Him belongs all praise; He alone gives life and causes to die; He is All-living and dies not; in His hand is all good. He has full power over everything, and to Him is the homecoming.

ONE NIGHT DURING RAMADAN I MENTIONED THAT EACH OF THOSE eleven statements of affirmation of Divine Unity contained an aspect of Unity and a particular good tiding (for believers). I explained only the meaning of *having no partner* in the form of an allegorical conversation or parable. Now, at the request of brothers at the mosque and friends attending me, I am committing this conversation to writing.

Imagine someone who, on behalf of all kinds of associating partners with God and varieties of unbelief and other ways of misguidance—such as attributing everything to nature or material causes or idol-worship—presumes to be Lord or exercise Lordship over some part of creation. That is, this being alleges that he or she owns or rules, controls or disposes, of that part. Coming upon an atom first, he or she informs it in the language or according to the presumptions of materialistic science or natural philosophy that he or she is its true master and owner. The atom answers in the language of truth and revealed wisdom:

> I perform innumerable tasks; I work within, alongside, or upon an infinite variety of created entities. Do you have the knowledge and power to direct me in these tasks? I work and move in a measured relationship with innumerable other atoms of a like constitution.[173] Can you command and employ all of these? If you own, arrange, or manage the infinite complexity of entities of, for example, red blood corpuscles, of whose atoms I am but one, and do so with perfect knowledge and discipline, then presume to be my Lord, and only then presume me to be attributable to any other than God.
>
> But you cannot do so, so be silent! You do not own me and cannot interfere in my operation, for all of my movements and activities are so purposeful and arranged that only one with infinite wisdom and all-encompassing knowledge can run them. If any other had a hand in it, there would be confusion. How can anyone who, like you, cannot even give himself life, whose seeing and feeling are blind to truth, who sees himself as subject to chance and accidents of nature, even presume to interfere in my functioning?

The pretender responds as all materialists do: "Be your own master then! Why do you claim to be in the service of some other power?" The atom replies:

---

[173] Each object that moves, from minute particles to planets, displays the Eternally Besought's stamp and Unity. Also, by virtue of its motion, each takes possession of the places in which it enters in Unity's name, thus adding them to the property of its true Owner. Each immobile entity, from plants to fixed stars, is like a seal of Unity that shows its location as missives of their Maker. Each plant and fruit is a stamp and seal of Unity that demonstrates, in Unity's name, that its habitat and native place is the missive of its Maker. In short, by moving in Unity's name, each entity takes possession of all entities, which means that one who cannot master all stars cannot master a single particle.

> If I had a mind with knowledge as all-encompassing as the sun's light and with power as intense as its heat; if I had powers of feeling as all-embracing as the seven colors in its light; if I had faces and eyes turned to every being and every place with which my being and my place are connected; and if I had authority in and over all these connections—then perhaps, perhaps, I might have claimed to be my own master. Yet even then, had I done so, I only would have been as foolish as yourself. Now get away from me, for I can have no business with you!

The pretender, despairing of the atom, hopes to pursue the matter with a red blood corpuscle. Coming upon one, he or she speaks to it in the name of material causality and the language of natural philosophy: "I am your Lord and Master." The red blood corpuscle answers in the language of truth and Divine Wisdom:

> I am not alone. If you also possess all my fellows in the blood army with whom I share the same formation pointing to our Maker, as well as the same duties and functions, and if you have the full and detailed knowledge, the awesome and subtle power, as well as the perfect wisdom to direct all the body cells through which we move and in which we operate, there might be some sense to your pretensions. But as you depend on blind and deaf nature or natural forces, you can have no influence over us, let alone mastery over me. Our order is so perfect and intricate that only one who sees, hears, and knows all things could be our true sovereign and master. So, be silent! I have so important duties and we work in such discipline that I have no time to answer your nonsensical pretensions!

Unable to deceive the red blood corpuscle, the pretender moves on and comes across a larger entity they call "cell." Addressing it in the familiar language of natural philosophy, he or she says: "True, the atom and the red blood corpuscle did not listen to me. I hope you can understand me. As I can see, you are composed of several smaller elements, like things arranged in a room. I can have a hand in this arrangement, and arrange and rearrange it. You can be my creature, and I can have power over you." The body cell answers with wisdom and in the language of truth:

> Although I am small, I perform vital tasks. I have the subtlest and yet strongest connections with all my neighboring cells, and with the whole organism of which I am a part. I perform vital functions with, for example, arteries and veins, sensory and motor nerves, electrical forces of attraction and repulsion, and the principles or elements determining my size, shape, and reproduction. If you have the knowledge and power to form an entire organism, to order and regulate the

arteries and veins and nerves, and to put to work all the diverse forces and principles managing our form and function; if you can direct, with irresistible power and all-comprehending wisdom, the innumerable body cells similar to me in artistry and quality, then show your ability. Then perhaps, perhaps, you might claim to master or make me.

But as you cannot, leave me—there are even now red blood cells carrying nourishment for me, white blood cells confronting diseases that might threaten me—I am busy, so do not waste my time any further with your vanity. No one as empty as you are of true understanding, of true hearing and seeing, could ever meddle in our being. Our order is so precise, delicate, and perfect that only one with absolute wisdom, knowledge, and power could control us.[174] If it were otherwise, our cohesion and order would not exist or would quickly fall into chaos.

Disappointed, the pretender comes across a human body, reiterates the argument in the language of unenlightened nature and erring philosophy: "I can say that you are mine, that I have a share in owning and managing you." The human body answers in the language of wisdom and truth and in the tongue of its order:

---

[174] The All-Wise Maker has created the human body like a well-ordered city. Some nerves function as telephones and telegraphs, while some of the blood vessels function as pipes carrying blood (the water of life). Blood contains two types of corpuscles: red ones convey nutrients to the body's cells, their sustenance, according to a Divine law (analogous to merchants and officers distributing food); white ones, fewer in number, defend (analogous to soldiers) against such invaders as disease. When actively engaged in defense, they perform two revolutions like Mevlevi dervishes and display a striking and rapid fluidity.

Blood repairs damage to the cells and cleans the body by collecting waste matter from the cells. As for arteries and veins, one forms channels to transport purified blood while the other forms channels for the unclean blood that gathers waste.

The All-Wise Maker created two elements in the air: nitrogen and oxygen. When oxygen encounters blood during respiration, it draws the impure carbon element polluting the blood to itself, just like amber. Combining with carbon, it transforms both substances into carbonic acid gas. Oxygen also helps to maintain body temperature and purifies the blood. The All-Wise Creator has given oxygen and carbon a mutual ardor, a sort of chemical affection, so that, according to Divine law, they approach each other and then combine. Science has explained how this combining, being a form of combustion, generates heat as follows.

Oxygen and carbon atoms have distinct motions that, when combined, become one motion, each pair of atoms now having the motion of one atom. Thus one of the original two motions is "lost." This "lost" motion is transformed into heat by a law of the All-Wise Creator. "Motion produces heat" is an established principle. This chemical combination removes carbon from the blood and maintain bodily temperature while, at the same time, purifying the blood. While inhaling, oxygen cleanses the body's water of life and kindles its fire for life. While exhaling, oxygen enables words (miracles of Divine Power) to form in the mouth.

All-Glorified is He at Whose works minds are amazed.

Do you have the knowledge and power to control and direct all human bodies similar to me that manifest the same signs of supreme power and creation? Do you have dominion over the treasuries of light, air, and water, as well as of all plants and animals, which are the ground and store of my provision and sustenance? Do you have the boundless wisdom and infinite power by which such invaluable, immaterial entities as the mind, intellect, and soul are so securely disposed in a narrow, bodily envelope, such as me, and made to "worship" by performing extremely important tasks? If you have such power, knowledge, and wisdom, demonstrate it—only then claim to own and manage me.

But as you cannot, be silent! My Maker is All-Powerful, All-Knowing, All-Seeing, and All-Hearing—this is testified to by the perfection with which I am organized and by the sign of Oneness in my face. A being as ignorant and incompetent as you could never have the least hand in His Art.

The pretender, nonplussed that all points in the human body reject his or her claim to have a say, moves on and surveys humanity as a species, thinking: They live in diverse and complex societies. I see that Satan finds ways to interfere in their affairs of will and their social life. Therefore I can find a way to enter into the creation, constitution, and operation of their bodies? If I can find a point of control in their bodies, I will be able to control the body and its cells that turned me down.

With this intention, he or she addresses the species in the familiar language of blind nature and erring philosophy: "You appear very diverse and at great odds. I am your master and owner or, at the very least, I have a share in your making and life." To this, humanity responds in the language of truth and reality, and in the tongue of wisdom and order:

Do you have the power, knowledge, and wisdom to create the rich texture covering the earth's face, woven with perfect wisdom from varied fabrics, thousands of mineral and plant and animal species? Can you, with a like wisdom, renew this texture and do so continuously? Do you possess the all-extensive power and all-comprehending science that manages the earth, of which we are a fruit, and the universe, of which we are the seed? Can you send us, from across the universe and in measured amounts, the provisions we need for our sustenance? Can you generate all individuals of my kind, past and future, whose faces bear the same sign of supreme majesty and power as mine? If so, you might then, perhaps, claim Lordship over me.

But as you cannot, be silent! Do not dare to say that you have a hand in me just from remarking the diversity in my kind, for that

diversity is part of our ordering's perfection. Diversity and multiplicity are copies made with a perfect order from the Book of Destiny
[containing the origins of beings in a perfect order] by Power. Our
diversity of appearance is a sort of reproducing of our forms [dictat-
ed by Destiny]—as the perfect diversity and order of plants and animals (which are inferior to us, under our vigilance, and which we
study) also testifies.

Is it at all plausible that the One Who weaves the diverse fabrics
spread over and through this world's texture with great skill is other
than its Maker, that the Creator of a fruit is other than the Creator
of the tree from which it grows, and that the Creator of a seed is
other than the Creator of the plant or tree into which it grows? You
are blind, for you do not see the miracles of Power in my face and the
wonders of His Creation in my constitution. If you had seen, you
would have understood that nothing escapes my Maker's observation or tasks Him capriciously. He makes the stars as easily as He
makes an atom. He creates springtime as smoothly as He creates a
flower. He has placed the vast universe's index in my constitution
with perfect correspondence. Could anyone who is, as you are, corporeal, incompetent, blind, and deaf have had a hand in such a
Being's artistry? So be silent, and be gone!

The pretender then turns to the widespread texture overlaying the earth's
face like an embellished cloak and speaks to it in the name of causality and in
the language of natural philosophy: "I can manage you. I own you, or at least
have a share in you." The texture[175] answers in the name of truth and in the
language of wisdom:

If you have the skill and power to create and weave all the textures in
which the earth is closed anew every year and every century, and
which have been hung on the line of past time, laid, unlaid, and relaid
seamlessly throughout all time, and that will be hung on the line of
future time, according to programs and patterns predesigned with the
greatest precision and in accordance with Destiny's framework, each
elegant, purposeful, and uniquely adorned; if you possess immaterial
hands that can reach out from the earth's creation to its destruction,
or rather, from the eternity of no-beginning to the eternity of no end;
if you have the power and science to create all individuals within this
texture, restoring and renewing them in exact order and wisdom; if
you can create and possess the earth itself which is, as it were, a model

---

[175] In fact, the texture is animated, continuously giving the signs of life in a regular fashion. Its
embroideries are renewed continuously with perfect wisdom and order to display the various,
ever-differing manifestations of its Weaver's Names.

for me and puts me on like a veil—only if you can, only then claim
Lordship over me—if not, leave! You have no business here!

In my rich and harmonious diversity are demonstrated clear signs
of Oneness, and the clear stamp of His Uniqueness. Only He Who
controls the whole cosmos, Who can do innumerable tasks simultaneously, Who can see all beings and their actions, whether inner or
outer, at the same instant, Who is present and vigilant everywhere
while being unbounded by time, space, or dimension, and Who has
infinite wisdom, science, and power—only such a Being could ever
own or have dominion over me.

The pretender turns to the earth, hoping to deceive it,[176] and repeats
the same argument in the name of causality and in the language of mere
naturalism: "I see that you roam about idly in the universe. Certainly you
can have no master, and so I claim you." Upon hearing this, the earth roars
like thunder in the name of truth and in the language of reality:

> Do not be foolish! How can I roam about without a master? Have
> you ever seen any disorder, lack of wisdom or skill, in the making of
> my dress or in any little point or fabric of it, that you dare to say that
> I roam about idly? Do you presume to own my orbit, which would
> take some twenty-five thousand years to traverse at a human being's
> pace but which I complete in my annual round with perfect disci-
> pline and precision?[177] Do you claim to own my ten fellow planets,
> which carry on their appointed tasks along their individual orbits as
> I do? Do you claim to have the unlimited science and power to cre-
> ate and control the sun, which gathers and focuses our orbits, orbits
> to which we are bound through the gravitation of mercy, and to
> make me and other planets revolve around it?
>
> Since you cannot plausibly make such a claim, leave me, for I
> have work to do. Our awesome circling, purposeful submission, and
> magnificent discipline show that our Maker is a Being to Whom all
> entities submit, and submit perfectly—as a dutiful soldier submits to
> his superior's orders. He is the Wise and Absolute Ruler of Majesty,

---

[176] Briefly, beginning with the atom, each thing visited referred the pretender to the next level:
from the atom to the red blood corpuscle, the cell, the body, humanity, the earth's outer garment, the earth as a globe, the sun, and the stars, respectively. Each said: "Be off! If you can
subjugate the next one up from me, do so, and then return and seek to master me. If you cannot subjugate that level, you also cannot subjugate me!" Thus one whose authority does not
embrace stars can have no acceptable claim to mastery over a single atom.

[177] If half the diameter of a circle is roughly 180 million kilometers, the circle covers a distance of
roughly 25,000 years [to cover on foot, provided one covers five kilometers (less than 3 miles)
an hour and walks for 6 hours a day.]

Who holds the sun and planets in their proper order as easily as He adorns each tree with its proper fruit.

Having failed to find a place in governing the earth, the pretender turns to the sun in the expectation that he or she can open a path there. Since the sun is so great an entity, he or she hopes to use it to gain control of the earth. Addressing the sun in the name of the way of associating partners with God Almighty and in the language of satanic philosophy, as sun-worshippers do, the pretender says: "You are a monarch. You are your own master. You do whatever you will."

The sun answers in the name of truth and reality and in the language of Divine Wisdom:

> No, indeed! How can you utter such an untruth! I am but an obedient officer, no more than a candle in my Master's guest-house. I could not own and master so much as a fly, even its wing, for even such a small thing has such immaterial faculties and fine, exquisite works of art as its eye and ear that I do not have their like in any of my workshops. I cannot make even the smallest of them.

Though rebuked by the sun, the pretender argues in the manner of Pharaohs, arrogant creatures who promote themselves as deities: "I claim you as mine in the name of causality, since you are not your own master but merely a servant." The sun replies in the name of truth and in the language of obedience to its Creator: "I can belong only to that Being Who has created me and all resplendent stars like me, Who, having fixed them in their stations with perfect wisdom, rotates them in glory and adorns the wide heavens thereby."

The pretender then comes among the stars and thinks: "Perhaps I can find some clients here." Talking to them in the name of causality and its partners and in the language of corrupt philosophy as star-worshippers do, he says: "You must be under the control of many different rulers, seeing that you are situated at such vast distances from each other." Upon this, one star, speaking for all others, answers him:

> How senseless and mindless you must be, not to see or understand the signs of the Creator's Oneness and the stamp of His Uniqueness in our nature. Do you not know how absolute is our organization, how secure the laws we obey? You think we have no order. In fact, we are the handiwork and servants of a Unique One of Unity that He holds the sky (our sea), the universe (our tree), and the vastness of space (our wide, maneuvering field) in His control. Like the

many-colored lamps indicating human festivities, we are luminous witnesses of His perfect Dominion, brilliant evidence blazing across boundless space, of His Kingdom and Lordship.

Each group of us are shining servants displaying His Majesty, near and far, in this world and the next, and in the many worlds beyond, within the infinitude of His Creation. Each of us is a miracle of the Power of the Unique One of Unity, a perfectly ordered fruit on the tree of creation, a bright evidence of God's Unity, a home and mount and mosque for His angels, a sun or a lamp of higher worlds, a witness of Divine Lordship, an ornament, a flower, a palace of the celestial sphere, a luminescent fish in the heavenly ocean, and each a beautiful eye set in the face of the heavens.[178] Throughout our vast community, there exists profound silence amidst tranquility, movement in wisdom, shining ornament with majestic grandeur, the most varied beauty in perfect harmony, and the highest art in absolute balance.

While we therefore proclaim in innumerable tongues the Unity of our All-Majestic Maker and His being the Eternally-Besought, together with His Attributes of perfection, grace, and beauty, you accuse us of disorder and of having no duty and no master. Since you accuse us, who are infinitely pure and obedient servants, you merit a slap in the face in payment for your absurd effrontery!

A star strikes the pretender's face in a gesture like the stoning of the devil, and hurls him from the stars' domain to the bottom of Hell. It also hurls natural philosophy[179] into the valleys of delusion, and chance into the well of non-existence. It hurls all who arrogate to themselves some portion in the One God's Dominion into the utter darkness of improbability and impossibility, and every argument against true religion into the lowest of the low. Then the stars together recite the holy decree: *Had there been in them (the heavens and the earth) any deities other than God, both would certain-*

---

[178] That is, we are pointers beholding the wonders of the Almighty's creation and pointing others to behold them also. The heavens observe the wonders of the earth's Divine artistry with innumerable eyes. As angels do in the skies, stars observe the earth, a display hall of wonders, and their doing so urges conscious beings to observe it attentively.

[179] After its lapse, nature repented. Understanding that its proper purpose and duty is not to be active and cause effects, but rather to receive and to be acted upon, it realized that it is a sort of notebook of Divine Destiny, susceptible to mutation and change; a sort of program of the Lord's Power, analogous to the corpus of rules of creation instituted by the All-Powerful of Majesty, an assemblage of His laws. It assumed its duty of worship in perfect submission, admitting its absolute powerlessness and therein achieved the title of God's creation and the Lord's handiwork.

ly have fallen into ruin (21:22), and affirm: "There is no place for any partner with God, from a fly's wing to the heavens' lamps."

> All-Glorified are You! We have no knowledge save what You have
> taught us. Surely You are the All-Knowing, the All-Wise.

> O God, bestow peace and blessings on our master Muhammad,
> the lamp of Your Unity amidst the multiplicity of Your creatures,
> and the herald of Your Oneness in the display hall of Your universe,
> and on his Family and Companions altogether.

ৰ্জ ৰ্জ

> In the Name of God, the All-Merciful, the All-Compassionate.

> Look upon the imprints of God's Mercy, how He revives the earth
> after its death! (30:50)

The following points to a flower from the eternal garden of this verse:

> Every tree in blossom is an ode
> rhythmic and well-composed,
> singing the high and manifest praises of the Originator.
> Or it is something with multiple eyes opened to watch,
> and cause the attentive to watch the wonders
> of the Maker's art displayed.
> Or it has clothed its members in green for their festival
> so that its Master may observe
> His illustrious works and gifts upon it,
> while itself displays in the display hall—the earth—
> His Mercy's embellishments before humanity's eyes,
> thereby proclaiming the wisdom in its creation,
> in that significant treasuries are stored in it
> by the Generosity of the Lord of its fruits:
> All-Glorified is He, how generous His favoring,
> how clear the arguments for Him,
> how manifest are His proofs!

The imagination sees angels clothed in bodies from the (branches of)
these trees resembling thousands of flutes, and from these flutes are heard
songs of praises of the All-Living. The leaves are each a tongue reciting: "O
the All-Living!" and chanting all together: "There is no deity but He."
They incessantly utter: "O the Truth!" announce: "O the All-Living!" and
together proclaim: "God."

> We send down from heaven blessed water. (50:9)

A short addendum

Listen to the following verse:

> Do they not observe the sky above them how We have constructed
> it and adorned it. (50:6)

> Look at the sky's face, where you see a silence in restful serenity; a
> wise, purposive motion; radiance in majesty; a smile in adornment; all
> combined in creation's orderliness and art's symmetry. Its candle's
> brilliance, its lamp's dazzle, and its stars' glitter manifest infinite
> Sovereignty for those with insight and sound reasoning.

The following expounds the lines above in interpreting the verse (50:6):

The verse draws attention to the sky's adorned and beautiful face.
People who observe it with care must notice the silence in the extraordinary calmness and apparent rest observed there, and conclude that the sky
has assumed that form through an Absolutely Powerful One's order and
subjugation. If the heavenly bodies roamed at random, with their enormous
size and speed of motion, the resulting noise would deafen everybody. They
also would cause such tumult and confusion that the universe would collapse. If twenty buffaloes move together in the same area, you can guess
what great uproar and confusion they would cause. However, according to
astronomy, some moving stars are a thousand times larger than the earth
and move at a speed seventy times faster than a cannonball. Given this,
from the silence of the heavenly bodies in calmness and rest, you may
understand the extent of the Power of the All-Majestic Maker, the All-
Powerful One of Perfection, as well as the degree of His subjugation and the
degree of the stars' submission and obedience to Him.

A *wise, purposive motion*: The verse orders us to see the purposive
motion in the sky. That extremely strange and mighty motion takes place
in absolute dependence on an extraordinarily subtle and comprehensive
purpose. The immensity and order of a factory whose wheels and machinery turn and toil in wisdom, in perfect order and for wise purposes, show to
what extent its engineer is learned and skillful. In the same way, with the
sun in the center and mighty planets revolving around it in a perfect, subtle order for many wise purposes, the solar system shows the extent of the
All-Powerful One's Power and Wisdom.

Radiance in majesty and a smile in adornment: The sky manifests a radiance of such majesty and a smile of such adornment that it shows how magnificent Sovereignty and how beautiful Art the All-Majestic Maker has. In

the same way as innumerable illuminations used on special occasions to show the king's majesty and his country's advanced civilization, the vast heavens, with their majestic glittering stars, show to attentive eyes the perfection of the All-Majestic Maker's Sovereignty and the beauty of His Art.

All combined in the orderliness of creation and the symmetry of art: The verse says: See the order and subtle balance of the objects in the sky and know how powerful and wise their Maker is. When you see someone turning numerous different objects one round the other or directing numerous animals in a perfect order and with a special, delicate balance for many wise purposes, you may guess how wise, powerful, and skillful that one is. Likewise, together with their numberless stars of awesome size and speed, the vast heavens in their tremendous immensity have performed their duties for billions of years according to an established measure and with a certain, sensitive balance. They have never transgressed their limits, and have never caused even the slightest disorder. This shows to attentive eyes just how sensitive and exact is the measure according to which their All-Majestic Maker exercises His Lordship. Like similar verses in *Suratu'n-Naba'*, among others, the verse indicates that the All-Majestic Creator has subjugated the sun, moon, and other heavenly bodies.

Its candle's brilliance, its lamp's dazzle, and its stars' glitter manifest the infinite Sovereignty for those with insight and sound reasoning: Almighty God has hung on the world's adorned roof a lamp—the sun—that gives heat and light. He uses this as a "pot" of light to write the Eternally Besought's "letters" on the lines of day and night on the pages of the seasons.

Like the phosphorescent hour-hands of a clock in a tall tower, He has made the moon in heaven's dome the hour-hand of the largest clock of time. He causes it to move through its mansions according to a perfect measure and fine calculations, as if He leaves a different crescent to each night and then folds all of them in itself (making it invisible). Furthermore, He has gilded the sky's beautiful face with stars that glitter and smile in that dome. All this points to His Lordship's infinite Sovereignty and His Divinity's magnificence and invites thinking people to believe in His Existence and Unity.

> Look at the colorful page of the book of the universe,
> and see how the golden Pen of the Power has inscribed it!
> No point has been left dark for those
> who can see with the eyes of their hearts.
> It is as if God has written His signs with light.
> See what an astounding miracle of wisdom the universe is!

See how tremendous a spectacle the space of the universe is!
Listen to the stars and heed their beautiful sermons.
See what Wisdom has written in these luminous missives of It.
They are all delivering this discourse with the tongue of truth:
"Each of us is a radiant proof for the majestic Sovereignty
of an All-Powerful One of Glory.
We are light-diffusing witnesses to the Existence of the Maker,
and also to His Unity and Power.
We are His subtle miracles gilding the face of the skies,
for the angels to make excursions on.
We are the innumerable discerning eyes of the heavens
directed to Paradise, and overseeing the earth.
We are the exquisite fruits attached to the heavenly branch
of the Tree of Creation; and to the twigs of the Milky Way,
attached by the hand of wisdom of
the All-Gracious One of Majesty.
For the inhabitants of the heavens, we are traveling mosques,
revolving houses and exalted homes,
light-diffusing lamps, mighty ships, and planes.
We are miracles of the Power of the All-Powerful One of Perfection,
the All-Wise One of Majesty.
Each of us is a wonder of His creative Art, a rarity of His Wisdom,
a marvel of His creation, a world of light.
To the people who are truly human, we present
countless proofs in countless tongues;
The eyes of the materialists, may they be blind,
never see our faces, nor do their ears hear our speech;
we are signs that speak the truth.
On us is the same stamp and seal. We obey and glorify our Lord,
and mention Him in worship.
We are ecstatic lovers in the widest circle of the Milky Way,
the circle reciting our Lord's Names.

Second station

In the Name of God, the All-Merciful, the All-Compassionate.

Say: "He—(He is) God, the Unique One of Absolute Oneness. God
—(is He Who is) the Eternally Besought (Himself in no need of anything).

This Station consists of three Aims.

FIRST AIM: Having been cast down by a star, the representative of those attributing partners to God gave up the attempt to find a part of creation that would accept him or her as God's partner. However, to incite doubt about God's Unity, he or she sought to arouse suspicions in the minds of its adherents by asking three questions.

Question: In the language of the irreligious, he or she asks: "I have found no evidence to prove my cause. But how can you prove the existence of a single One of infinite power? How do you reject everything but His Power in the universe's creation and operation?

Answer: As argued convincingly in The Twenty-second Word, from atoms to stars, each creature is a clear proof for the Necessarily Existent Being, the Absolutely Powerful One's necessary existence. Each link in the chain of creation proves His Unity. Among the many Qur'anic arguments, particularly like: *If you ask them who has created the heavens and the earth, they will certainly say: God* (39:38); and *Among His signs are the creation of the heavens and the earth, and the variety of your tongues and colors* (30:22), the creation of the heavens and the earth is presented as a proof of God's Existence and Unity. Conscious people who consider the creation of the heavens and the earth must confirm the Majestic Creator's existence. When asked who their creator is, they will answer: "God."

In The First Station, we started from an atom and showed the stamp of Divine Unity on every object as far as the heavens and the stars. The Qur'an rejects any form of partnership with God. This means that the Absolutely Powerful One, Who has created the heavens and the earth in perfect order, must hold the amazing solar system in His Power's grasp. Since that absolutely All-Powerful One holds the sun and its planets in His Power's grasp, managing it and regulating its movements, the earth must be in His Power's grasp and management. Given this, all of its creatures, which are its fruits and may be regarded as the goal of its existence, are in His Lordship's grasp (raising, administering, and sustaining). Since all creatures, spread over the earth singly or in groups and replaced after adorning it for a while, fill and empty the earth in a continuous cycle, are in the grasp of His Power and Knowledge and are managed and arranged according to the measure of His Justice and Wisdom, for sure, each member of each species, each of which is a well-designed and perfectly formed miniature of the universe, a pattern or specimen of its species, and a tiny index of the book of the universe, are in His grasp of Lordship, invention, raising, and management.

Given this, each living being's cells, corpuscles, limbs, and nerves are under His command, at His disposal, and move according to His laws. Since this is so, all particles or atoms, the essential building blocks constituting all creatures and their parts as well as being the means for their design and formation, are in His Power's grasp and His Knowledge's sphere. They move most regularly and perform perfect duties by His command, permission, and strength.

Since every atom moves and functions by His law, permission, and command, then most certainly, it is His Knowledge and Wisdom that distinguish each face by making it unique, their sounds and tongues differ. Consider this verse that, in mentioning only the first and most universal link and the last and most individualized one, points to this chain of creation and the series of His signs in creation: *Among His signs is the creation of the heavens and the earth, and the variety of your languages and colors. Indeed, in this are signs for those who know* (30:22).

Now we say: "O representative of those associating partners with God! These evidences are as strong as the chains of creation, which point to an Absolutely Powerful One and prove His Unity."

Since the creation of the heavens and the earth shows an All-Powerful Maker and His boundless and infinitely perfect Power, certainly, He is absolutely independent of partners. While He has no need for them, why do you follow the dark way of associating partners with Him? As He has no partners in His Divinity, any partnership in His Lordship and creativity is impossible. The Power of the Maker of the universe and the earth is boundless and infinitely perfect, and everything is equal before It. If there were a partner, this would require that a limited power defeat a boundless and infinitely perfect power, or somehow limit it and infect it with incapacity. Such assertions are completely untenable.

There is no need for partners, and their supposed existence is inconceivable. Therefore, claiming partnership is no more than forced and arbitrary judgments that cannot be substantiated by reason or logic. It is a principle of theology and methodology that any probability or possibility not arising from evidence cannot be considered, and that it does not injure conviction or certainty based on knowledge. For example, it is theoretically conceivable that Lake Eğridir might change into oil or grape juice or a heavy syrup. But since this is a mere possibility raised on the basis of no circumstantial evidence, it does not harm our certainty that the lake is water.

Similarly, we have asked each part of the universe: from atoms to stars in the First Station, and from the creation of the heavens and the earth to the variety of tongues and uniquely identification of each face in the Second Station. Each part testified to God's Oneness and shows the stamp of His Unity. Therefore there is no circumstantial sign upon which any partnership with God could be found. Given that this claim is forced, meaningless, and insubstantial, all such claims are clear nonsense and pure ignorance.

Question: Those who reject Divine Unity raise another objection: Everything depends on a cause and takes place according to the cycle of cause and effect. Since causality is apparent throughout the universe, causes must have a part in the creation and operation of things. If they have a part, they may be partners.

Answer: As required by Divine Will and Wisdom, and as the Divine Names tend to manifest themselves, results are made dependent on causes. However, as is convincingly argued in the *Risale-i Nur*, causes have no creative effect. Here we add the following:

Conscious beings are the most effective causes in bringing about effects. Humanity, which has a free and most comprehensive willpower and a vast field in which to exercise it, is the most elevated conscious being. Speaking, thinking, and eating are the most apparent acts arising from our free will. They include numerous well-ordered chains of events, but only one is directly connected to our free will. For example, out of all the processes related to eating from the formation of food to its becoming nourishment in cells, only chewing them depends on free will. In the case of speaking, free will is limited to inhaling and exhaling the air needed by the vocal organs to produce sounds. A word is like a seed in the mouth, becomes like a tree when uttered, produces millions of fruits that resemble that single word, and enters millions of ears. We can only imagine this multiplication, free will has nothing more to do with it after it has been said.

If humanity, the most honored cause and agent, the freest in using will, has no part in creation, how can nature (e.g., inanimate objects, elements, plants, animals) have any real effect or part in creation? How can natural laws, which have no consciousness, will, or knowledge and only a nominal existence, originate such a miraculous system as the universe, the creation and operation of which require infinite knowledge, will, and power? How can they create a miraculous living, conscious, speaking, reasoning, thinking, and learning organism like a man or a woman?

Together with causes, nature is only an envelope for the Lord's creatures, a tray for the All-Merciful One's gifts. The tray bearing the gift, the cloth in which it is wrapped, even the one who brings it, cannot be a partner in the king's sovereignty. One who does not understand this is blinded by delusion. In the same way, apparent causes and means have no part in Divine Lordship; their only duty is to worship.

SECOND AIM: In despair of proving the existence of any partners with God, this being tries to demolish belief in Divine Unity through doubt, and asks another question:

Question: You argue that the universe's Creator is absolutely One and the Eternally Besought, Who needs nothing while everything else is absolute need of Him. He is Single yet has absolute and free control of everything. He exercises His absolute authority over all things simultaneously and can do innumerable things at the same time, without doing one thing hindering Him from doing another thing simultaneously. How can we believe such a bewildering assertion? How can one being do countless things in countless places at the same instant and without difficulty?

Answer: Our answer requires that we analyze an extremely profound and subtle, as well as very elevated and comprehensive, mystery of God's being One and the Eternally Besought. The mind can discern that mystery only by comparison. Although His Essence and Attributes have no like or equal and are not comparable, His acts may be considered through comparison.

First comparison: As argued convincingly in The Sixteenth Word, a single thing can acquire universality through various mirrors. While being particular in essence, it can be universal by having numerous aspects at the same time. Just as a single corporeal thing acquires universality through reflection in things like glass and water, which mirror corporeal things, more refined and transparent matters (e.g., air, ether, certain objects from the World of Representations and Ideal Forms) become like mirrors to bodies of light and spirit beings. Such matters transport them, allowing them to travel in such clear realms as air or ethereal arena with the speed of lightning and imagination.

Seated on them, these bodies of light and spirit beings can be present in thousands of places at once. Since they are of light and their reflections are identical with themselves and have exactly the same qualities, they act in every place as if they were personally present. The reflections of solid, corporeal bodies are not identical with themselves and, not having the same qualities as themselves, are lifeless.

For example, the sun is a concrete particular object that acquires universality by shining on transparent objects. It lends its reflections and images to all shining things on the earth according to each one's capacity. Even a drop of water and a piece of glass reflect the sun's image. The sun is present, through its light, heat, image, or the seven colors in its light, in every transparent or shining object on the earth. If it had knowledge and consciousness, each object, especially shining and transparent ones, would be like a seat or chair through which it could contact everything. It also would be able to communicate with all conscious beings, through mirrors or each one's eye, while communicating with all others. While present and acting everywhere on the earth through its knowledge, power, and other attributes, it would be nowhere in person.

If the sun, which is like a solid, particular, and lifeless mirror to only the Name the Light out of the All-Majestic Being's one thousand and one Names, can therefore display such universal activity, should the All-Majestic Being, with the Oneness of His Essence, be unable to do countless things at the same time?

Second comparison: Since the universe is like a tree, each tree may be an example of the universe's realities. Taking the huge tree in front of my room as a tiny specimen of the universe, we will demonstrate Divine Oneness' manifestation in the universe. This tree has at least a thousand fruits, and each fruit has at least a hundred seeds. All fruits and seeds were created at the same time. However, that tree has the same single node of its nucleus of life in its single original seed. This node contains the laws of the entire tree's formation issuing from Divine Will and Divine Command, and permeates all parts of the tree by being present in its roots and trunk, as well as in each branch, blossom, leaf, fruit and seed, without being divided or fragmented.

Unlike light, heat, and air, this nucleus of life, which is a single display of Divine Will and a law of Divine Command, does not dissipate but it is present in every part. Its manifold actions are not contrary to its singleness. In fact, the manifestation of Divine Will, that law of Divine Command and nucleus of life, may be present in each part and nowhere at the same time. It is as if that law of Divine Command had as many eyes and ears as that magnificent tree's fruits and seeds. Or it is as if each part of the tree had a control center for the "senses and feelings" of that law of Divine Command. The tree's veins and parts, such as branches, are like telephone wires in facilitating that law's operation or functioning, rather than forming obstacles, and the farthest become like the nearest through them.

Given that a single particular manifestation of God's Attribute of Will is observably the means of millions of acts in millions of places at the same time, we are convinced, as if seeing it with our own eyes, that the All-Majestic Being controls the tree of creation and all of its parts and atoms through the manifestation of His Power and Will.

As convincingly argued in The Sixteenth Word, such single, fixed, and helpless luminaries as the sun, restricted by matter, and His laws of Command and manifestations of His Will, such as those comprising the nucleus of that tree's life and that are like its spirit, can be present, through luminosity, in many places and perform numerous tasks simultaneously. Although each such object is a particular thing restricted by matter, it resembles a universal thing and can accomplish many things at once. You see this with your own eyes, and so cannot deny it.

The All-Sacred Being is absolutely free of matter, exempt from restrictions and the darkness of density. All lights and luminaries, as well as all creatures of pure light, are a single shadow of His Sacred Names' lights. The whole existence and life, as well as the worlds of spirits and ideal forms or representations and the Intermediary World of the grave are semi-transparent mirrors of His All-Pure "Face." His Attributes and essential Qualities are all-encompassing, and all His manifestations or operations upon things individually and collectively are underlain or underpinned by His universal Will, absolute Power, and all-encompassing Knowledge. How can therefore something hide from or escape the manifestation or operation of His Oneness—the concentrated manifestation or operation of His Names? What can be hard for or concealed from Him? Who can be far from Him or draw near to Him without acquiring universality? What can prevent Him from doing something else?

As Ibn 'Abbas, may God be pleased with Him, pointed out, why should He not have immaterial "eyes" and "ears" to see and hear every individual creature? Why should chains of things not be like veins or wires that quickly convey His laws and commands? Why should things that are considered obstacles and impediments not be the means of His free disposition of creation? Why should causes and means not be only apparent veils (to His direct control of the universe and free operation)? Why should He not be present everywhere while being nowhere? Why should He need to reside in a certain place? Why should distance, size, or veils of the levels of existence be obstacles to His nearness to things, or to seeing and controlling them as He wills?

Why should change, alteration, containment by space, and division (all intrinsic qualities of physical, restricted, contingent, solid, and multiplying beings) be accidental or necessary to the Sacred Being, the Light of Lights, the Single One of Unity, the Necessarily Existent One, Who is free of matter and restriction, exempt from defect and fault? Does impotence ever befit Him? Does defect ever appear in His Honor and Dignity?

Conclusion of the Second Aim: Reflecting on God's Oneness displayed by each individual thing while looking at the fruit tree in front of my room, a series of reflections occurred to me. I relate them below.

All-Glorified is Him Who has made His garden of earth a display hall of His Art, an exhibition of His Wisdom, a manifestation of His Power, a flower garden of His Mercy, the arable field of His Paradise, a place where His creatures come and depart in floods and each with its particular life and features. Adorned animals, ornamented birds, fruit-bearing trees, and flowering plants are all miracles of His Knowledge, wonders of His Art, gifts of His Munificence, and offerings of His Favoring. Flowers smiling because of beautiful fruits, birds singing at the dawn breeze, raindrops glittering on flowers' cheeks, and mothers' compassion for their infants—all this is because the All-Loving One wills to make Himself known, the All-Merciful One wills to make Himself loved, the All-Compassionate One wills to make His Compassion known, and the All-Favoring One wills to make His Affection recognized by humanity, jinn, angels, and other spirit beings.

Each fruit and seed is a miracle of Divine Wisdom, a wonder of Divine Art, a gift of Divine Mercy, a proof of Divine Oneness, and a sign of God's bounties in the Hereafter. They are true witnesses that their Creator has full power over everything and full knowledge of everything. All fruits and seeds are mirrors to His Oneness in this world of multiplicity, for in the tongue of its being, each one says: "This elaborate tree is included in me. Don't be absorbed in its elaboration. All its parts and features are encapsulated in me." A seed is like the fruit's heart, a mirror to Divine Oneness. In the tongue of its being, it "recites" in its heart the Divine Names recited by the entire tree loudly.

Seeds are also signs of Divine Destiny and embodied symbols of Divine Power. Through them, Destiny indicates and Power alludes to the fact that each elaborate tree has grown from one seed and so points to its Maker's Oneness, Who has no partner in His creation and fashioning. After it has grown and elaborated itself fully, it encapsulates all its laws, realities, and life-history in a fruit. As all of its meaning contained in a seed, it shows the All-Majestic Creator's wisdom in His creation and government. As in the case of that tree,

Oneness also is the source of the tree of creation's existence and growth. Similarly, being the fruit of the universe, humanity points to Unity in the multiplicity of beings, and the human heart sees the meaning of Unity in multiplicity with the eye of belief.

These fruits and seeds are also tablets of Divine Wisdom through which Wisdom speaks to conscious beings like this: This tree's life and the efforts spent for its growth are aimed at its fruits, which represent it and is the aim of its growth. Its life is aimed at the seeds, because each seed is an index bearing the tree's entire meaning. Thus, the One Who creates the tree and the necessary conditions for its growth aims all manifestations of His Names concerned with the tree's life at the fruit, the reason for its existence. Furthermore, that huge tree is sometimes pruned to control its growth and make it yield better fruits for many years; they cut off some parts of it so that it may rejuvenate.

Similarly, as humankind is the tree of creation's fruit, we are the reason for the universe's creation and existence, and the human heart is the most illumined and comprehensive mirror of the Maker of the universe. Because of this, humanity undergoes frequent pruning in the form of convulsions, revolutions, upheavals, and physical and social change, and it will cause the destruction and re-construction of the universe. The door of this world will be closed and the door of a new one be opened for its judgment.

Here it is appropriate to explain a point showing the eloquence and force of Qur'anic expressions dealing with the Resurrection. As argued above, the universe must be destroyed and a new one built for the judgment and eternal happiness of humanity. There is a Power that will do this. However, the Resurrection will be done in stages. We must believe in and acquire knowledge of some of those stages. In order to perceive and acquire knowledge of other stages, we must evolve spiritually and intellectually. To prove the simplest stage, the Qur'an draws our attention to a Power that will open up the Resurrection's broadest sphere.

This is the simplest stage that all people must know and believe in: When people die, their spirits go to other abodes. Their bodies rot underground, but a tiny part (a seed) remains intact. During the Resurrection, God re-creates us from it and returns the spirit to it.

This stage is so easy that countless examples of it are seen every spring. Many Qur'anic verses call our attention to the operations of the Power Which will gather and then disperse all atoms. Sometimes they show the works of a Power and Wisdom that will send creation into non-existence and then re-create it, or rend the heavens asunder and scatter the stars.

They also show the operations and manifestations of a Power and Wisdom that will cause to die and then revive all living creatures at once through a single call, or the works of a Power and Wisdom that will toss mountains into the air, completely level and then re-shape the world in a new and more beautiful form. This means that, together with the phase in which all people will be re-created and which all people must believe in and have knowledge of, Almighty God will perform all tasks connected with the Resurrection with the same Power and Wisdom.

Question: You often use analogies in the form of comparisons or parables in *The Words*. According to logic, such analogies do not offer certainty, and issues requiring conviction for belief must be based on logical proofs. Analogy is used in jurisprudence for potential solutions and for cases in which a fairly certain presumption is enough. Furthermore, you set forth analogies and comparisons as parables, which by definition are not real.

Answer: According to logic, analogies in the form of comparisons do not offer certainty. But one type of analogy is stronger than logical proof and gives greater certainty than induction: You point to the tip of a universal truth through a particular analogy based on concrete facts and base your conclusion on that truth. To teach that mighty truth and deal with particular incidents and realities in accordance with it, you show the general or universal law on which the truth is based in a certain, particular thing or event. For example, through the analogy that the sun is a single body that can be present in all shining objects at once because it emits light, we show the law of a truth: Light and things of light are not restricted. Distance, size, and quantity make no difference to such items, and they cannot be contained in space.

Another example: A tree's leaves and fruits are formed easily and perfectly at the same time and in the same center through a law of Divine Command. This shows the tip of a mighty truth and a universal law, and proves that truth and law. Like a tree, this vast universe is the result of that law and the manifestation of oneness. All analogies and comparisons in *The Words* are of this kind. They offer greater conviction and certainty than logical proofs.

As for the second part of the question, according to the science of eloquence, a metaphor is a word or phrase used to suggest or express a meaning other than its original one. In such statements, the metaphorical (and not the original) meaning is considered. If the metaphorical meaning conforms to reality, you are saying the truth. For example, height can be conveyed by the phrase: "The sheath of so-and-so's sword is long." If that man is tall, this statement is true whether or not he has such a sword. If he is not tall, this statement is false even if he has such a sword, for the phrase is only figurative in meaning.

Such parables as those in the Tenth and Twenty-second Words contain realities that are to be sought in metaphors. Their original meanings are like telescopes through which to see the truth being discussed. We speak in parables so that readers may understand subtle realities through such comparisons. However, to make them understandable to everyone, states and dispositions are presented in the forms of speeches, and the community's character is presented as a particular individual.

THIRD AIM: Receiving a convincing answer to the second question (discussed at the beginning of the Second Aim), the misguided one asks:

Question: Qur'anic expressions like *the Best of Creators* and *the Most Merciful of the Merciful* suggest the existence of other creators and merciful ones comparable to God. Also, you assert that the Creator of the universe has infinite perfections by encompassing the highest degree of all perfections. But perfections are judged by way of contrast. Pleasure's perfection cannot be perceived without pain, light cannot be recognized without darkness, and union gives no pleasure if there is no separation.

Answer: We answer the first part through five indications.

First indication: Being a book that emphasizes Divine Unity, the wise Qur'an could not have used those phrases as you understand them. Rather, *the Best of Creators* means that the Creator has the highest rank of creativity. This does not suggest the existence of other creators for, like other Attributes, Creativity has ranks of manifestation. Thus this phrase means that He is the All-Majestic Creator having the ultimate rank of creativity.

Second indication: Such phrases as *the Best of Creators* do not suggest a plurality of creators. Rather, they relate to species of beings or the variety of being created and mean that He is the Creator Who creates everything in the best and most appropriate fashion. This is the same meaning as that which is expressed by verses like *He Who makes excellent everything that He creates* (32:7).

Third indication: Such phrases as *the Best of Creators, God is the Greatest, the Best of Judges,* and *the Best of the Benevolent* do not compare those acts and Attributes of God that are manifested in the universe with those of creatures. [Whatever beings have is a gift from God. We see because God is All-Seeing, and hear because He is All-Hearing.] All perfections shared by humanity, angels, and jinn are only indistinct shadows in relation to His, which are beyond compare.

People, especially the misguided, cannot measure God properly and are usually forgetful of Him. For example, a private pays his corporal perfect respect and attributes to him whatever good he enjoys. He is oblivious of the king; even if he remembers him, it is still to the corporal that he shows gratitude in return for any good he receives. Such a private should be warned: "The king is greater and more benevolent than your corporal, so you must thank the king." This does not mean to compare the king's actual, magnificent commandership with the corporal's—such a comparison would be meaningless. What is meant is to warn the private who prefers the corporal in gratitude and forgets the king.

Similarly, means, nature, and causes blind heedless people to the True Bestower of bounties. They attribute the bounties which they receive to means and nature and creativity to causes, as if they were the actual sources, and praise and thank them. Therefore, the Qur'an warns: Almighty God is much greater and a far better Creator and Benefactor (actually meaning that He is the sole Creator and Benefactor). Regard Him and thank Him.

Fourth indication: Just as actually existent things may be compared with each other and preferred over each other, so possible, and even hypothetical things may also be compared with and preferred over each other. Since there are numerous grades or degrees in qualities and natures, people may imagine infinite grades in the essences and manifestations of Divine Names and Attributes. Almighty God is, however, of the highest, most perfect, and most beautiful of all grades that His Names and Attributes are imagined to have. The universe bears witness to this. His description of all His Names as the best or most beautiful, as in: *His are the Most Beautiful Names* (20:8), points to this fact.

Fifth indication: Such phrases also should be considered from the following viewpoint. Almighty God has two kinds of Attributes and ways of manifestations. In the first one (*Wahidiya*), in the form of an all-encompassing law, He manifests His Names and exercises His authority throughout the universe from behind apparent means and causes. In the second one (*Ahadiya*), He focuses His manifestations on one being without any means or veils. When shown in this second way, His kindness, creation, and grandeur are brighter, more beautiful and splendid than their manifestations in the first way.

Suppose a saintly king executes his authority directly, with all his officials and commanders being only veils or screens. His execution of his authority is in two ways: by some general laws he has established and using officials and governors in every office, or through direct governance by being present everywhere at the same time in different forms and without officials. This second way is better and more excellent in the sight of his subjects. Similarly, the Creator of the universe, the Eternal Sovereign, uses means and causes to veil or screen His rule and to demonstrate His Lordship's majesty in this life. However, He also has installed a "private telephone" in His servants' hearts so that, leaving all means and causes behind, they can contact Him and declare: *You alone do we worship and from You alone do we seek help* (1:5). Phrases like *the Best of Creators, the Most Merciful of the Merciful,* and *God is the Greatest* also underline this fact.

As for how we can judge something as perfect if it has no opposites, consider the following five points:

FIRST POINT: One who asks such a question is unaware of true perfection and imagines relative perfections to be true. Any virtue, perfection, or superiority that manifests itself in comparison to or in contrast with others is not true; rather, it is of relative value and significance. Thus losing its opposite causes it to lose its value.

For example, heat is desired over severe cold and food is delicious in proportion to one's hunger. Without cold and hunger, heat and food have no or little value. True pleasure, love, perfection or virtue do not show themselves in comparison with others or in proportion to their opposites' degree—they are by and of themselves, and so are substantial and constant realities.

Existence, life, love, knowledge (especially knowledge of God), belief, permanence, mercy, compassion or affection, as well as light, sound sight and hearing, eloquence, munificence, good conduct or moral virtues, appropriate form, and the perfections any people have either in their persons or characters and attributes or acts—these are all virtues by their very nature. With or without opposites, they are virtues and perfections in themselves. Neither they themselves nor their pleasure and beauty do not need comparisons or opposites to perceive and appreciate. Thus, all perfections of the All-Majestic Maker, the All-Gracious and Beautiful Originator and the Creator of Perfection are true in and of themselves. Whatever other than Him can have no effect on Him. The perfections in creation are only their reflections according to the capacity of each being.

SECOND POINT: In *Sharhu'l-Mawaqif*, Sayyid Sharif al-Jurjani writes: "The cause of love is either pleasure or benefit or sexual or natural inclination or perfection. Perfection is loved because of itself." In other words, you love something or someone either because of the pleasure you find in them or their benefit or your sexual or natural (e.g., fatherly, motherly, filial, etc.) inclination, or its perfection. If love arises from perfection, there is no need to search for another cause. For example, people tend to love people of perfection and of perfect virtue although they have no relation to them whatsoever.

Thus, as they are true, indisputable, and infinite, all of Almighty God's Perfections and His All-Beautiful Names are loved because of themselves. The All-Majestic Being, Who is absolutely worthy of love and is the True Beloved One, loves His Perfections and the beauties of His Names and Attributes in a manner appropriate to Himself. He also loves the works of His Art and the beauties in His creatures, which mirror His Perfections. He loves His Prophets and saints, particularly His noble beloved, the lord of Messengers and master of saints—Prophet Muhammad, upon him be peace and blessings.

Due to His love for His Own Beauty, He loves His beloved, who mirrors that Beauty. Due to His love for His Own Names, He loves His beloved, who manifests those Names in a most comprehensive way, as well as all other Prophets. Due to His love for His Art, He loves His beloved, who displays that Art, and those who are like him (the other Prophets). Due to His love for His creatures, He loves His beloved, who welcomes those creatures with due appreciation and applause, saying: "What wonders God has willed! God bless them! How beautifully they have been created!" and those who follow him. Due to His love for the beauties of His creatures, He loves His beloved, who is the most comprehensive embodiment of all those beauties and all moral virtues shared by them, and his followers.

THIRD POINT: All perfections in the universe are signs of an All-Majestic One's Perfections and indications of His Beauty. In relation to His Perfection, all beauty and perfection in the universe is an indistinct shadow. I now present brief pointers to five evidences of this reality.

First evidence: A splendid, perfectly built and decorated palace points to perfect engineering, architecture, and joinery. This perfect engineering, architecture, and joinery point to one worthy of called by such titles as builder, engineer, architect, decorator, and joiner. These titles show the perfection of the builder's artistry, which points to his competence. This perfect competence shows that the builder is a perfect one of a most sublime nature.

Similarly, this world, a perfectly built and decorated palace, points to the perfection of Acts, for a perfect work results from perfect acts. Perfect acts point to such perfect Names as the All-Organizing, the All-Fashioning, the All-Wise and the All-Decorating, Which are involved in building the palace. Perfect Names and Titles show perfect Qualities or Attributes, for if the latter are imperfect, the Names originating from them also are imperfect. Perfect Attributes demonstrate the inherent, perfect Competence, Which, in turn, shows that the One Who built that palace is perfect. Although His Perfection is manifested through the veils of Essential Competence, Attributes, Names, Acts, and works, it still reveals the faultless perfection and beauty seen everywhere.

After you see that infinite Perfections originating in the Essence of the One Who has them, you may understand how imperfect and dim are the relative perfections manifested in comparison to others or by way of contrast.

Second evidence: When viewed with attentive eyes and considered reflectively, the universe reveals to the heart and sound conscience that the One Who has made it so beautiful and decked it out with such varieties of adornment has such infinite beauty and perfection that He has made it so.

Third evidence: Perfect and well-proportioned works of art depend on perfect planning that, in turn, is based on comprehensive knowledge, a productive mind, intellectual refinement, and spiritual purity. It is the spirit's purity that shows itself in the work through knowledge. So, with all its material beauties, this universe consists of the drops issuing from an infinite knowledge belonging to One Who has infinite and eternal beauty and perfection.

Fourth evidence: As you know, something which gives light must have light, and that which illuminates must be luminous. Similarly, benevolence comes from wealth and generosity and grace originates from a gracious one. Since this is so, like light pointing to the sun, all the beauty and perfection observed in the universe point to a perpetual beauty. Like a mighty river glittering with reflections of the sun's light, creatures flow over the earth's face glittering with reflections of beauty and perfection. Just as reflections of light in bubbles on a river's surface do not originate from the bubbles themselves, so the beauties and perfections glittering temporarily on the flood of creatures do not belong to the creatures themselves; rather, they are reflections of the lights of an Eternal Sun's Names.

> The disappearance of mirrors and the death of creatures, in contrast
> to the perpetual reflections in them of inseparable grace and beauty,
> are among the most manifest proofs that the apparent beauty does

not belong to those reflecting it, and that there is One with pure beauty and ever-manifested kindness and grace, One Whose existence is absolutely necessary, Who is Eternal and All-Loving.

Fifth evidence: If several people coming from the same place through different ways report the same event, it means that the event occurred. In the same way, all people who can uncover hidden truths and are as sure of them as if they had seen them with their own eyes, whether truth-seeking purified scholars or saints belonging to different spiritual orders or sages belonging to different schools of thought, regardless of time, place, or capacity, have agreed that the beauties and perfections seen in the mirrors of the universe's creatures are reflections of the Perfection of a Single Necessarily Existent One and manifestations of the beauty of His Names. This consensus is an unshakable and decisive testimony.

FOURTH POINT: A person's or a thing's pleasure, good, and beauty are judged according to those who receive and manifest them, not according to their opposites. For example, generosity is a beautiful and praiseworthy virtue. Generous people receive far greater pleasure from the happiness of those whom they have favored than from their superiority to others in generosity. Caring and compassionate people feel greater pleasure in proportion to the comfort of those for whom they feel compassion. For example, a mother's compassion for her children causes her to have such a great and strong pleasure in her children's happiness and well-being that she nearly sacrifices her life for them. The pleasure of such compassion even causes a hen to attack a dog to protect her young.

Thus, since the true pleasure, beauty, and perfection of laudable virtues and praiseworthy qualities are judged according to that with which they are related, not to their likes or opposites, for sure, the beauty of the Mercy of One of Beauty, Grace and Perfection, the All-Living and Self-Subsistent, the All-Kind and Caring, the All-Bounteous and Favoring, the All-Merciful and the All-Compassionate, should be considered in view of those toward whom He has mercy. According to the degree of happiness and well-being of those whom He favors with His mercy, particularly their enjoyment of His bounties in Paradise, the All-Merciful and All-Compassionate One feels what we call sacred love, sacred pleasure, sacred exhilaration, and sacred joy. All of these accord with His Holy, Transcendent Being, and are infinitely greater, as well as more sacred, elevated, and refined, than their counterparts in creation.

You may see one manifestation of this mighty truth's comprehensive meaning via the following comparison: Suppose a kind, compassionate, and generous man wills to feed some very poor, hungry, and destitute people. So, he prepares a banquet on his fine ship and watches them from above while they eat. You may understand how much their enjoyment of the food in gratitude and their happiness in praise and thankfulness please and exhilarate that noble and generous person.

Similarly, the All-Merciful and All-Compassionate One has spread out a vast food-laden table on the face of the earth, which He causes to travel in the space with all of its inhabitants. He feeds all living beings, primarily including humanity, jinn and animals, from the food on this table and invites His hungry and needy servants to Paradise's everlasting gardens. He prepares each garden as if it were a magnificent table laid out with all kinds of food and drink, which are of pure pleasure and delight. Consider the pleasure and happiness that the above-mentioned person feels at his guests' enjoyment, although he is not the true owner of what he offers, and then compare it with the indescribable sacred love and pleasure felt by the All-Merciful One.

Also consider this: A skillful technician invents something like a gramophone which plays without records. If it works and gives the desired results perfectly, how proud its inventor will feel and how pleased he will be. He will but utter, "How beautiful! May God bless this!" The All-Majestic Maker has invented the vast universe (in general) and the earth with each creature in it (in particular), especially our head, as such a Divine gramophone or orchestra that science should be lost in admiration. Each creature displays the expected results to the utmost degree and in a very beautiful way. Their obedience to God's laws of creation and life, which comprise their worship, glorification, and specific praise and exaltation of Him, as well as the attainment of Divine purposes for their lives, please Him to a degree beyond our comprehension.

Or, say a just judge receives great pleasure from doing and establishing justice, and becomes extremely happy when able to restore the rights of the oppressed. Compare with this the sacred meanings arising from the reality that the Absolutely Just Ruler, the All-Majestic Overwhelming One, gives all creatures the right of existence and protects and maintains their existence and lives against aggression, restores rights in the universe, and acts with justice. Compare with this especially the sacred meanings to arise from the fact that He will judge humanity and jinn in the Hereafter and establish absolute justice.

As in the examples above, each Divine Name contains many sorts or degrees of beauty, grace, and perfection, as well as many levels of love, pride, honor, and grandeur. This is why exacting saintly scholars honored with the manifestation of the Divine Name the All-Loving, have concluded: "The essence of the universe is love. All creatures move with the motive of love. All laws of attraction, rapture, and gravity originate in love." One of them even said:

> The spheres are intoxicated, and so are angels and stars;
> The heavens, the sun, the moon, and the earth are all intoxicated.
> Intoxicated are the elements and plants, and trees and human beings.
> All animate beings are intoxicated, and so are all atoms of creation.

Every creature is intoxicated, according to its capacity, with the "wine" of Divine love. People love those who are kind to them as well as true perfection and transcendent beauty. They also love those who are kind to those whom they love and for whom they have mercy.

Given this, we can understand that the All-Gracious and Beautiful One of Majesty, the All-Loved of Perfection, in each of Whose Names are innumerable treasuries of kindness, Who makes all those whom we love happy with His favors and is the source of countless perfections and levels of beauty and grace, is worthy of infinite love and the creation's intoxication with His love. This is why some saints who have been honored with the manifestation of the Divine Name the All-Loving have said: "We do not even want Paradise. A gleam of the Divine love is eternally sufficient for us," and why, as Prophet Muhammad said: "A single minute spent in beholding the Divine Beauty in Paradise excels all the bounties of Paradise."

So, perfect love and perfections attained through love are possible within the spheres of the Divine Unity and Oneness, displayed, respectively, through the universal manifestations of Divine Names on beings as a whole and their particular manifestations on individuals. Any perfections imagined outside those spheres are false.

FIFTH POINT: The representative of the misguided says: "Your Traditions condemn the world, describing it as flesh. Also, all people of truth and sainthood deplore it, considering it evil and foul. But you say it is the means for the manifestation of all Divine perfections, and speak of it like a lover."

Answer: The world has three facets or aspects. The first facet is concerned with Almighty God's Names and shows their inscriptions and activity; it mirrors them. This facet is the Eternally Besought's collection of innumerable "letters." Therefore it is extremely beautiful and worthy of love. The second facet relates to the Hereafter. It is the field to sow for the Hereafter, the tillage of Paradise, the flowerbed of Divine Mercy. Like the first one, it is beautiful and worthy of love.

The third facet is a veil of heedlessness, a plaything for human fancy and desire. This facet is ugly because it is mortal, painful, and deceptive, and thus condemned by the Traditions and disliked by the people of truth. The Qur'an praises creation and attaches importance to it due to the first two facets of the world. The Companions and other saints sought these two facets.

Four groups of people condemn and deplore the world. The first group, those with knowledge of God, condemn the world because it builds a barrier in front of the knowledge, love, and worship of Almighty God. The second group consists of those who aim solely at the Hereafter. They abhor the world because its affairs and occupations prevent them from striving for the Hereafter seriously, or because their firm belief and conviction show it to be very ugly when compared with Paradise's beauties and perfections. Just as all men are ugly when compared with Prophet Joseph, upon him be peace, all the world's beauties and charms mean nothing when compared with those of Paradise. The third group, those who cannot conquer the world, condemn it out of their love for—not their dislike of—the world. The fourth group condemn the world because whatever its members grasp slips out of their grasp. They become angry and console themselves by declaring the world ugly. Such condemnation also arises from love of the world. Agreeable condemnation comes from those who love the Hereafter and knowledge of God.

For the sake of the master of Messengers, may Almighty God include us among the first two groups. Amin.

Third station

In the Name of God, the All-Merciful, the All-Compassionate.

There is nothing but it glorifies Him with His praise.

This Third Station consists of two Topics.

FIRST TOPIC: According to the meaning of *There is nothing but it glorifies Him with His praise*, everything has many aspects, like windows, opened on Almighty God. All truths contained in creation are based on the Divine Names. Each thing owes its existence and essential nature to one or several of God's Names. The variety of art in things and the sciences also are based on a Divine Name. For example, philosophy, in its true sense, depends on the Name the All-Wise, medicine on the Name the All-Healing, and geometry and engineering are based on the Names the All-Determining, the All-Proportioning, and the All-Giving of exact measure.

In the same way that all sciences are based on Divine Names, all human arts, levels of human perfections, and the attainments of those who are the most advanced in knowledge and skills have their sources in Divine Names. Some exacting saintly scholars have concluded: "The realities of things consist in Divine Names, and their nature is the inscription of those realities. The manifestations of around twenty Divine Names can be seen in one living creature." We will discuss this subtle and comprehensive truth through a comparison and an analysis.

When an extremely skillful artist well-versed in painting and sculpture wants to paint pictures of a beautiful flower and a member of the fair sex and to sculpt them, he first determines the general shape of each with a few lines. This determination is based on certain geometrical measurement and planning. This means the measurement and planning depend on knowledge and wisdom or purposiveness. With the compasses of knowledge and purpose (or wisdom), the artist draws the outer lines of the eyes, ears, and the nose, and the leaves and seed-producing parts in a proportionate manner, thereby displaying artistry and accordance with the parts' functions or vital duties. This shows that it is the artistic skill and the functionalism which use the compasses of knowledge and purpose.

The artist's skill and following a certain purpose determined by the vital duties and functions of bodily parts show that he pursues excellence and beauty in his art. Therefore, his works—the statute and flower—give the impression of life and happiness. This suggests that the artist is gracious and munificent. These attributes dominate him to the extent that it is as if the flower were an embodied grace and the statute, an embodied munificence. What causes these attributes to display themselves is that the artist wants everyone to recognize and love him so that they may have recourse to him without hesitation whenever they are in need, a desire arising from the artist's compassion and desire to benefit others. So, he fills the statute's arms and pockets with all varieties of bounty and attaches jewels to the flower. While himself in need of nothing, it is the artist's personal perfections and virtues that cause him to do all these. Compassion, love and tenderness, which are the most delightful and the sweetest among human virtues and perfections, manifest themselves in striving for the happiness of others and find the greatest happiness in seeing others happy. In short, human perfection and virtue are both beauty and love. The union of beauty and love stems from this reality. They both love and are loved and they want to be known by others. Thus the lovable bounties which were set on the statute and the extra gifts attached in the form of the flower reflect the artist's virtues and laudable qualities.

Similarly, the All-Wise Maker creates, determines, specifies, and shapes Paradise and the world, the heavens and the earth, animals, jinn and humanity, angels and spirit beings, and all things whether of universal or particular nature by manifesting His Names. He determines each according to certain measures and gives each a certain form. This displays His Names the All-Determining, the All-Designing, and the All-Fashioning. Determining or giving certain measures, designing and fashioning are based on Knowledge and Wisdom, and therefore point to the Divine Names the All-Knowing and the All-Wise. He begins fashioning everything with the rulers of Knowledge and Wisdom according to the form He has determined for each. He does this in such a manner that He displays the meanings of perfect artistry or making excellent. With the shining hand of art and the brush of munificence, He equips His creatures with all necessary well-proportioned parts and gives each part many complex functions. He furnishes and adorns human beings with beautiful, well-proportioned eyes, ears and so on, the flower with petals and stamens, the earth with minerals, plants, and animals, and Paradise with gardens, palaces, and *houris*, each of which has a particular beauty and functions.

The All-Wise Creator equips His creatures in such a fashion and He is so gracious and munificent that it is as if each well-proportioned and richly adorned creature were an embodied grace and munificence and causes the Names the All-Gracious and the All-Munificent recited. What leads His Munificence and Graciousness to such a display is His love of creatures and His will to be known by animate beings and loved by conscious ones. Thus the Names the All-Gracious and the All-Munificent exhibit the Names the All-Loving and the All-Recognized or Known One.

Then, He decorates all beautiful creatures with delicious fruits and agreeable benefits and results in such a way that He makes each decoration or adornment into an item of bounty and each act of grace into mercy. This points to the Names the Giver of bounties and the All-Compassionate, and shows their manifestations from behind apparent veils. The All-Independent One's will to manifest His Compassion and Munificence is because He has infinite care, kindness and mercy for His creatures, which causes creatures to recite the Names the All-Merciful and the All-Kind and Caring. It is His Essential Beauty and Perfection Which stimulate the meanings of His Mercifulness and Kindness to demonstrate themselves, and cause the Name the All-Beautiful together with the All-Loving and the All-Compassionate, Which are contained in It, to be recited. Absolute beauty is loved for itself, and the One with absolute beauty loves Himself. Therefore it is both beauty and love. This is also true with perfection, which is loved for itself and not because of anything else. Therefore it is both lover and beloved.

Since a beauty of infinite perfection and a perfection of infinite beauty are loved to an infinite degree, they wish to manifest themselves in mirrors according to the mirror's capacity. As the Essential Beauty and Perfection of the All-Majestic Maker, the All-Wise One of Beauty, the All-Powerful One of Perfection, will to show mercy, kindness and care, the Names the All-Merciful and the All-Kind and Caring must manifest themselves. Since the will to show mercy, kindness and care is associated with compassion and bountifulness, it urges the Names the All-Compassionate and the Giver of bounties to be manifested. Compassion and Bountifulness lead to showing compassion and being known and therefore require and cause the Names the All-Loving and the All-Recognized or Known to manifest themselves.

The will to be loved and recognized incite manifestations of grace and munificence and cause creatures to demonstrate the Names the All-Gracious and the All-Munificent. Grace and munificence provokes the acts of decorating and illuminating and therefore cause the Names the All-Decorating and the All-Illuminating to be manifested and recited via the beauty and illumination seen in creatures. Decoration and illumination have the meanings of making artistically and benevolence and therefore cause the Names the Maker and the All-Benevolent to be recited via all creatures' beautiful countenances. Making and benevolence are based on knowledge and wisdom and show the Names the All-Knowing and the All-Wise via the well-ordered and purposeful bodily members all creatures and their harmonious and purposeful organization. Demanding acts of organizing or arranging, fashioning and forming, knowledge and wisdom demonstrate the Names the All-Fashioning and the All-Determining or Giver of measure via all creatures' general forms.

In short, the All-Majestic Maker has made all creatures in such a fashion that most of them, particularly living ones, display most of the Divine Names. It is as if He clothed each creature in twenty different garments, one over the other, and inscribed several of His Names on each one. For example, as pointed out in the above comparison, there are many layers of loveliness in the apparent creation of a beautiful flower and a member of the fair sex. Compare vast and universal bodies with these two particular examples.

FIRST LAYER: Their general forms and appearances, which recite: "O the All-Fashioning, O the All-Determining, O the All-Arranging."

SECOND LAYER: Their forms and appearances including all bodily members and parts, that show many Names like the All-Knowing and the All-Wise.

THIRD LAYER: The forms of beauty and adornment particular to each bodily member and part, on which are inscribed many Names like the Maker and the All-Holy Creator (the One Who creates subtly and perfectly).

FOURTH LAYER: The detail of ornament, beauty, and elegance given to creatures as if in the embodied form of grace and munificence. They recite: "O the All-Gracious One, O the All-Munificent One," and many other Names.

FIFTH LAYER: The delicious fruits attached to that flower and lovely children, as well as the laudable virtues given to that woman as gifts, show Names like the All-Loving, the All-Compassionate, and Giver of bounties.

SIXTH LAYER: This layer of bountifulness and benevolence recites: "O the All-Merciful, O the All-Kind and Caring," and several other Names.

SEVENTH LAYER: The bounties given to them and the results attached to their existence demonstrate such gleams of beauty and grace that they deserve pure gratitude and love kneaded with true eagerness and tenderness. This layer manifests such Names as the All-Beautiful One of Perfection and the All-Perfect One of Beauty.

If a flower and a beautiful woman display so many Names through their outward forms, you may compare how many Names of universal manifestation all flowers, animate beings, and vast and universal bodies demonstrate. You may understand how many sacred, enlightening Names of God (e.g., the All-Living, the Self-Subsistent, and the Giver of life) a person manifests through his or her spirit, heart, reason, life, and all other senses and faculties.

Paradise, the community of *houris*, the earth's face, and springtime are all flowers. Heaven is a flower; the stars are its gilded embroideries. The sun is a flower; the seven colors in its light are its dyes. The cosmos is a beautiful, macro-human being; humanity is a normo-universe or micro-universe. *Houris*, spirit beings, angels, jinn, and humanity have been fashioned, organized, and created as if they were beautiful individuals. As they collectively and individually manifest the All-Majestic Being's Names, each one is a different mirror to His Beauty, Perfection, Mercy, and Love. Each is also a different and true witness, as well as a different sign, of His Infinite Beauty, Perfection, Mercy, and Love. As all such boundless perfections are possible only in the sphere of Divine Unity and Oneness or Uniqueness, any perfections imagined outside of this sphere are false.

Thus, understand that the realities of things are based on the Divine Names, or rather they are manifestations of those Names, and all things mention their Maker in numerous tongues. Also, know one of the meanings of *There is nothing but it glorifies Him with His praise*. Say: "All-Glorified is He Who is veiled through His manifestation's intensity." Understand the reason why He is the All-Glorious, the All-Wise; He is the All-Forgiving, the All-Compassionate; He is the All-Knowing, the All-Powerful," and similar phrases repeated at the end of Qur'anic verses.

If you cannot see clearly the Names displayed on a flower, ponder on Paradise, look at spring attentively, or examine the earth's face. You can read clearly the Names inscribed in those huge flowers of Mercy and see the Names' distinct manifestations.

SECOND TOPIC: Left without any support, the representative of the misguided reveals his or her real intention: "Since I find worldly pleasure, happiness, and advancement in civilization in denying God and the Hereafter, in loving this world, and in human freedom and self-confidence, I bring others to this path, with Satan's help, and will continue to do so."

Answer: I say in the Qur'an's name: O helpless fellow, come to your senses and do not listen to the representative of the misguided. If you do, you will suffer such loss that the spirit, mind and heart shudder even to imagine it. There are two paths before you: the path of wretchedness offered by the representative of the misguided and the path of happiness described in the Qur'an. You have already seen many comparisons between these two paths in *The Words*, primarily in the first nine short ones. Now heed only one among a thousand, which befits the occasion:

The path of associating partners with God and other kinds of misguidance, and of transgression and dissipation causes us to fall to bottomless depths of degradation. It places an unbearable load on our weak backs and burdens our hearts with boundless sorrow. For if we do not recognize and place our trust in Almighty God, we become like very weak, impotent, infinitely poor, and destitute animals, or mortal beings afflicted with pain and grief, subject to countless calamities. We suffer incessantly, for we remain separated from all things and people that we have loved and to which we have been connected. Leaving all things and people amidst the pain of separation, we enter the grave's dark depths alone.

We struggle in vain, with a limited will, little power, a short life-span, and a dull mind against infinite pain and ambition. We strive to realize our countless desires and goals, but without any considerable result. While we cannot bear even the burden of our own being, we load our minds and backs with the burden of the world. We suffer Hell's torments even before going to it.

In order to avoid feeling such a painful spiritual torment, people of misguidance seek out heedlessness as a kind of anesthesia. But they begin to feel this pain most acutely as they approach the grave. Not being true servants of Almighty God, they believe that they own themselves. In reality, however, with their limited free will and insignificant power, they cannot govern their being in this tumultuous world. They encounter many enemies from harmful microbes to earthquakes ready to attack them. They look at the grave in fear and terror.

As human beings, they are related to humanity and the world. But since they deny that the world and humanity belong to and under the authority of the One Who is the All-Wise, the All-Knowing, the All-Powerful, the All-Compassionate, and the All-Munificent, they attribute their existence and lives to chance and nature. And so the world's fearful events (e.g., convulsions, earthquakes, plagues, calamity, death, and famine) and humanity's conditions and experiences always trouble them. Moreover, they must contend with their own pain and the troubles that other creatures cause them to suffer.

As their own unbelief brought them to this deplorable state, how can they deserve mercy and affection? This reminds us of The Eighth Word's parable of two brothers who fell into two wells. If one, without being content with a fine banquet's agreeable and lawful enjoyment and entertainment among honest friends in a beautiful garden, drinks wine to obtain an unlawful pleasure and, imagining themselves surrounded by wild beasts in a dirty place on a winter day, trembles and cries in fear, they will not deserve pity. For they see their honest friends as wild beasts and insult them. They see delicious food as foul; clean, fine plates and bowls as worthless, dirty stones; and attempt to break them. Moreover, they judge the invaluable, meaningful books that they are to read and study as ordinary, meaningless collections of sheets, and tear them up and scatter them. Such people are not merely unworthy of pity, rather, they deserve to be punished.

Similarly, unbelief and misguidance arise from abusing one's willpower. Such people assert that the All-Wise Maker's guest-house of the world is a plaything of chance and nature and that the transference of beings to the World of the Unseen, after completing their duty of refreshing the Divine Names' manifestations, is going into absolute non-existence. Also, they judge beings' glorifications and recitations of the Divine Names as outcries of death and eternal separation; sheets of creatures, each being a missive of the Eternally Besought, to be confused, meaningless collections; the grave's door, which opens onto the World of Mercy, as opening onto a dark world of non-existence; and death as separation from—not re-union with—all friends and beloved ones. Thus, they deliver themselves to an extremely painful punishment. Since they also deny, reject, and insult all creatures, the Divine Names, and His inscriptions and missives, they deserve punishment. They are in no way worthy of pity.

So, unfortunate people of misguidance and dissipation, can any of your progress, evolution, science, technology, and civilization compensate for such a terrible loss, collapse, and crushing hopelessness? Where can you find the true consolation that the human spirit urgently needs above all else? What nature or causality, what thing upon which you rely and to which you attribute His works, bounties, and favors, which of your discoveries, inventions, idols, and fetishes can save you from the darkness of death, which you suppose to be eternal extinction? Which one can take you through the Intermediate World of the grave, the Place of Resurrection and Supreme Gathering, and over the Bridge to the Abode of eternal happiness? Since you cannot close the grave's door, you are bound to travel and tread this way (passing through the stations mentioned.) To travel it safely, you must depend on the One Who commands and controls all those worlds and abodes.

O unfortunate, misguided, and heedless people. Any love directed to other than that which deserves it brings suffering. In view of this, misusing the potential of loving and knowing given to you to know and love God and His Attributes and Names, you love your selves and the world. This, as well as your similar misuse of your body and faculties that were given so that you could worship and thank Him, causes you to suffer deserved punishment. Assigning to your selves the love that must be felt for Almighty God, you suffer the resulting troubles. You are suffering the endless troubles that your own selves cause you. You do not provide true peace and happiness for what you adore: your soul or self. Since you do not submit and entrust it to the Absolutely Powerful One, the True Beloved One, you always suffer pain.

Since you assign the love belonging to Almighty God's Names and Attributes to the world and attribute the works of His Art to causality and nature, you are suffering the resulting pains. That which you love either leaves you without saying good-bye or does not recognize you. Even if it recognizes you, it does not love you. Even if it loves you, it gives you no benefit. You always suffer from incessant separation and death without hope of re-union.

This is the reality of what the people of misguidance call the happiness of life and human perfection, beauty of civilization, and pleasure of freedom. Dissipation and drunkenness temporarily veil the suffering and pain that eventually will come upon them.

As for *the Qur'an's light-diffusing way*, it heals the wounds afflicting the misguided with the truths of belief, disperses the darkness enveloping them, and closes the doors of misguidance and perdition.

This way removes our weakness, impotence, poverty, and need, for it enables us to trust in an All-Powerful One of Compassion. Submitting the burden of being and life to His Power and Mercy, we are saved from their mount; instead, we transform the self and life into a mount for us. We learn that we are true human beings and the All-Merciful One's welcomed guests, not "speaking animals." Showing the world as the All-Merciful One's guesthouse, and its creatures as mirrors of Divine Names and ever-recruited missives of the Eternally Besought, it heals perfectly all our wounds caused by the transience of the world, the decay of things, and love for mortals. It also saves us from the darkness of whims and fancies. Also, showing life as the prelude to re-union with deceased friends and beloved ones, it heals the wounds of death, which the misguided regard as eternal separation, and shows that separation is actually re-union.

By proving that the grave is a door opened onto the World of Mercy, the Abode of Happiness, the gardens of Paradise, and the luminous Realm of the All-Merciful One, the way of the Qur'an removes our greatest fear and shows that our journey in the Intermediate World, which seems to be most depressing and troublesome, is really most pleasant and exhilarating. It demonstrates that the grave is not like a dragon's mouth, but rather a door opened onto the gardens of Divine Mercy. It informs believers:

> If your willpower is very limited, entrust your affairs to your Owner's universal Will. If your power is slight and insignificant, rely on the Absolutely Powerful One's Power. If your life is short, consider eternal life. If your mind is dull, come into the Qur'an's sun, and look with the light of belief, so that in place of your mind, which gives light like a

firefly, each Qur'anic verse gives you light like a most shining star. If you have endless ambition and pain, boundless reward and infinite mercy await you. If you have limitless desire and aims, do not be anxious, for you cannot realize all of them here. This is only possible in another realm, and the One Who gives them to you is not your self.

And:

You do not own yourself, but are owned by One infinitely Powerful and an infinitely Compassionate One of Majesty. So, do not trouble yourself by placing your being and life on your shoulders, for the One Who has given and governs your life is He. Also, the world is not without an owner. So do not be anxious thinking of the state of it and load that burden onto your mind, for the world's Owner is All-Wise and All-Knowing. You are His guest in His world, so do not interfere with what is beyond your power and responsibility. Such living beings like humanity and animals are not left to themselves. Rather, they are officials charged with certain duties and are controlled and favored by an All-Wise, All-Compassionate One. He has far more compassion for them than for you. Furthermore, from microbes to catastrophes like plagues, floods, droughts, and earthquakes, which, in appearance, are hostile to you, all things and events are controlled and governed by that All-Compassionate, All-Wise One. He is the All-Wise and so does nothing useless, and the All-Compassionate Whose every act contains a kind of grace.

It adds:

This transient world provides the necessities of the afterlife. It decays, but yields everlasting fruits and displays an All-Permanent One's Eternal Names. In return for its few pleasures, it causes one to suffer many pains and afflictions. However, the favors of the All-Merciful, All-Compassionate One are true and lasting pleasures, and its pains cause one to obtain many spiritual rewards. What is lawful is sufficient for the spirit's enjoyment and pleasures, as well as for the heart and carnal soul, so do not enter upon what is unlawful. Any illicit pleasure results in numerous pains and causes one to lose the All-Merciful One's favors, which are pure, lasting pleasures.

Misguidance so debases humanity that no philosophic trend, scientific development, or human civilization and progress can lift people out of that deep pit of darkness. It is only the wise Qur'an that it takes us out of the lowest pit and raises us to the highest rank through belief and righteous deeds. It fills that deep pit with the steps of spiritual progress and the means of spiritual perfection.

The Qur'an also facilitates our long, troubling, and stormy journey toward eternity. It shows us how to traverse in a day the distance that normally takes fifty thousand years to cover. By enabling us to know the the All-Majestic Being, the King of all eternity, it honors us with being His dutiful servants and guests and secures for us an easy and comfortable journey through the world and through the mansions of the Intermediate World of the grave and the Hereafter.

Just as a king's righteous, dutiful official travels in his domain in security, via the fastest modes of transportation, and easily cross provincial boundaries, so those connected with the Eternal King through belief, as well as those who show obedience to Him through righteous deeds, travel through the stations and across the boundaries of the world and the realms of the grave and the Hereafter with the speed of lightning or *Buraq*, the mount of Paradise. Such people find eternal happiness. The Qur'an proves the truth of this, and purified religious scholars and saints see it clearly.

The Qur'an also says:

O believers, do not waste your God-given infinite capacity of loving on your ugly, defective, evil, and harmful carnal soul. Do not adore it or follow its desires and fancies as if it were an object of worship, but direct it toward the One worthy of infinite love, Who does you infinite good and will make you infinitely happy; Who through His favors makes happy those with whom you have connections and whose happiness pleases you; One with infinite perfection and infinitely sacred, transcendent, pure, perfect, and undecaying beauty; Whose every Name radiates numerous lights of beauty and grace; the beauty of Whose Mercy and the mercy of Whose Beauty are displayed in Paradise; and Whose Beauty and Perfection all the beauty, grace, and perfection in the universe, which are lovable, point to and signal. Love Him, and make Him the sole object of your worship.

Furthermore it says:

O humanity, do not use your infinite capacity of loving, which has been given to you to love His Names and Attributes, to love impermanent beings. All that exists, except for Him, is transitory, whereas the Divine All-Beautiful Names displayed on mortals are permanent and constant. Each Name and Attribute has thousands of degrees of favoring and thousands of levels of perfection and love. Consider, for example, the Name the All-Merciful: Paradise is one of Its manifestations, eternal happiness is one of Its radiances, and all provisions and bounties bestowed on worldly creatures are just one of Its drops.

To see how the Qur'an expresses the difference between these two ways, consider: *Surely We have created humanity of the best stature as the perfect pattern of creation; then We reduced it to the lowest of the low, save those who believe and do good, rihgteous deeds* (95:4-6); and *Neither the heavens nor the earth wept over their destruction* (44:29). See in what elevated and miraculous style they express the difference! A detailed explanation of the first verse can be found in The Eleventh Word. Here we present a few remarks on the exalted truth contained in the other verse, which explicitly states that the heavens and the earth do not weep when unbelievers die. This implies that the heavens and the earth weep when believers die.

Unbelievers do not know the meaning of the heavens and the earth, do not recognize their Maker, deny their duties, and so reduce their value. Such insults and hostility cause the heavens and the earth to be pleased when such people die. But they weep when believers die, for believers know the duties of the heavens and the earth and affirm the reality they bear. As their belief enlightens them about these meanings, they say: "How beautifully they have been created. How well they perform their duties." Believers acknowledge their value and respect them accordingly. They also love them and the Names to which they are mirrors in Almighty God's name. And so the heavens and the earth grieve for them.

An important question: Loving is not voluntary. I have a natural need to love delicious foods and fruits, my parents and children, my spouse and friends, virtuous people, life, youth, this world, spring, and beautiful things. Why should I not? How can I appropriate all such instances of love only to the Divine Being and His Names and Attributes?

Answer: Listen to the following four points.

FIRST POINT: However involuntary loving is, you can direct it to a certain object. For example, by convincing yourself that something beloved is ugly, or an obstacle to or only a mirror for an object worthy of true love, this feeling of love can be diverted to the true object of love.

SECOND POINT: You can love such things, but do so in Almighty God's name and for His love's sake. Loving delicious foods and fruits because they are favors and bounties of Almighty God, the All-Merciful and the All-Compassionate, means loving the Names the All-Merciful and Giver of bounties and is a sort of thanksgiving. Love, when done in the All-Merciful One's name and not the carnal soul's name, is reflected by lawful earning, contentment with what is lawful, and consuming in gratitude and reflection.

Loving and respecting one's parents on behalf of the Mercy and Wisdom that equipped them with affection and tenderness, and that raised you through their compassionate hands, are included in God's love. If done for Almighty God's sake, you must show your parents much more love, respect, and care when they only can cause you difficulty. The verse: *If either or both of them reach old age with you, do not say to them "Uff!"* (17:23), which tells children to love and respect their parents in five ways and degrees, shows how important parents' rights are in the eyes of the Qur'an and how degrading and detestable filial ingratitude is.

Since a father typically prefers his children to be superior to him, children cannot claim rights against him. There can be no justifiable cause of dispute between parents and children, for a dispute arises either from envy or a violation of rights. A father never envies his children, and children cannot claim rights against him. Even if they consider his treatment of them wrong, they cannot rebel. Those who do so, or who annoy him, are cruel and ungrateful.

Loving one's children with utmost care and compassion, as they are the All-Compassionate, All-Munificent One's gifts, is included in one's love of Almighty God. The sign that such love is for God's sake is to show "becoming patience" at their death and not to wail in despair and rebelliousness against Destiny. One should submit to God, believing that judgment belongs only to Him, and think: "My child was a loveable creature of God whom He placed in my custody. His Wisdom required Him to take the child from me and to a far better place. Even if I have one apparent share in that servant of His, thousands of true shares belong to Him."

Your love for friends, on account of their being believing friends of Almighty God who do good deeds according to the principle of loving for the sake of God, also is included in love of God. In addition, this is true of the love you feel for your spouse, your companion in life, because he or she is a sweet gracious gift of the Divine Mercy. Do not set your heart on his or her transient good looks.

A woman's greatest charm and beauty lie in her lovable good conduct accompanied with the kindness and grace particular to womanhood, and in her elevated, serious, and sincere compassion. That beauty of compassion and good conduct increase until she dies. It is through the love and respect for her compassion and good conduct that one can observe her rights to the end. If she is loved because of her physical beauty, she is deprived of her rights and the love and respect due to her at a time when she needs them most.

Loving virtuous people like Prophets and saints because they are approved servants of Almighty God, and in His name and for His sake, are included in His love. If you love your life because it is a most valuable capital given by Almighty God to gain eternal life, a treasury containing the faculties with which to acquire all kinds of virtues and perfections, and if you spend it in His service, then this love is included in love of Almighty God, the All-Worshipped One. Loving the prime of youth because it is a sweet, fine gift of Almighty God, and thus spending it in His cause is a sort of lawful love wedded to gratitude.

Loving nature reflectively, especially in spring, because it is a realm displaying the most beautiful inscriptions of the All-Wise Maker's light-diffusing Names and the most splendid and embellished works of His Art, means to love Almighty God's Names. If you love the world only because it is the field to sow for the Hereafter, the mirror of the Divine Names, the collection of Almighty God's missives, and a temporary guest-house of His, then this love is also in Almighty God's name—provided you are not under your carnal soul's influence.

In short, love the world and its creatures not for themselves but in the name of their Creator and the meaning they contain. Do not say: "How beautiful they are!" Rather, say: "How beautifully they have been made!" In your heart, do not love that which is not Him. Do not set your heart on that which is not Him, for the heart is the Eternally Besought's mirror and belongs to Him. So pray to Him: "O God, provide me with love of You and the love of what will make me near to You."

And so if all the types of love mentioned so far are in God's name, then they give a painless, pure pleasure and are the means of a union that does not allow separation. In addition, they cause your love of God to grow and can be considered gratitude that gives pure pleasure and a reflection that is itself pure love.

For example, if a noble king grants you an apple in his presence, you will receive two sorts of pleasure and feel two kinds of love. The first type is your love for the apple because it is an apple. Thus you receive as much pleasure as an apple can give. Such a love is not in the king's name, but arises from your love of yourself, for you love the apple because of the pleasure it gives you. This kind of pleasure is transient and ends when you finish eating the apple, leaving behind regret for the cessation of the pleasure. Moreover, the king may not be pleased with such an attitude.

The second sort of pleasure and love are directly related to the king. If you love and respect the apple because it embodies the royal compliment to you, then this love is in the king's name and for his sake. The pleasure arising from such a compliment is far greater than the pleasure coming from eating the apple. Such an attitude is pure gratitude to the king for his gift, and the love shown for the apple is a respectful love for the king himself.

Likewise, loving bounties—all foods and fruits—granted to us because of themselves and the pleasure they give is a carnal love, for it is for the carnal soul's sake. The pleasure coming from eating and drinking is transient and mixed with pain. If you love the bounties you receive on account of their being favors of Divine Mercy and fruits of Divine Bountifulness and Benevolence, and if you receive pleasure from them and have an appetite for them in appreciation of the Divine grace in them, this love is pure gratitude and pure pleasure without any pain.

THIRD POINT: Love of the Divine Names has degrees and levels. As pointed out above, sometimes you love the Divine Names because you love their works in the universe, and sometimes because they are titles of Divine perfections. It sometimes occurs that you are in limitless need due to your comprehensive nature and love the Divine Names in need of them.

For example, while you are seeking help in utter despair for your relatives or for poor, weak, and needy creatures, someone appears unexpectedly and does for them what you wish to do for them. How much would you love such a person for his munificence and benevolence, and always be thankful to him for those qualities? Similarly, consider only the Names the All-Merciful and the All-Compassionate. As the manifestations of these Names, Almighty God favors your believing parents and ancestors, as well as your friends and beloved ones, in this world with all His bounties. He will also make both you and them happy in Paradise, in the World of eternal happiness, with all varieties of pleasure and bringing you together. Thus, you may understand how much these two Names are worthy of your love, to what extent your spirit needs them, and how proper and necessary it is to say: "All praise and gratitude are for God for His being All-Merciful and All-Compassionate."

Also, with its creatures being its amiable residents and lovable adornments, with which you feel a profound connection and for whose wretchedness you grieve, the world is like a home for you. Through reflection, you may perceive how much your spirit loves and to what degree you need the Names the All-Wise and the All-Sustaining of the One Who has organized the world and it creatures and thus governs, grows, and sustains them with perfect wisdom. You also may understand to what extent your spirit needs the Names the Heir, the All-Quickening, the All-Permanent, the All-Munificent, the All-Reviving, and the All-Benevolent, of the One Who brings all of the people to whom you feel connected and at whose death you are grieved, out of the darkness of eternal extinction and settles them in a place far more beautiful than this world.

Since we, as human beings, are noble, elevated beings with comprehensive natures, our endless needs and aspirations make us needy of one thousand and one Divine Names in their numerous degrees of manifestation. Compound or intense need is eagerness, compound or intense eagerness is love, and compound or intense love is adoration. In proportion to the degree of the spirit's perfection, love increases and flourishes in degrees according to the levels of the Divine Names' manifestations. Since the Names are titles with which the Majestic Being manifests Himself, love of all Names turns into love of the Divine Being. Out of thousands of levels of manifestations of the Names the All-Just, the All-Wise, the (Ultimate) Truth, and the All-Compassionate, we present one as an example as follows:

If you want to see the Names the All-Merciful, the All-Compassionate, and the (Ultimate) Truth in full manifestation in wisdom and justice, consider the following comparison: Suppose an army formed of four hundred companies. Each company has unique uniforms, rations, weaponry, and medicines. If these companies are situated together mixed with one another without the uniqueness of each considered, and yet, out of his perfect compassion and through his extraordinary power and miraculously encompassing knowledge, and with utmost justice and wisdom, a peerless king equips each with unique uniforms and weapons and provides them with appropriate foods and medicines without mistake or help, you may understand what a powerful, compassionate, just, and munificent king he is.

Similarly, if you want to see the manifestations of the Divine Names the (Ultimate) Truth, the All-Merciful and the All-Compassionate in wisdom and justice, you can look at magnificent armies of plants and animals, which consist of countless different families, genera, and species. All of these set up their tents on the earth's face in spring, are infinitely mixed with each other, and yet have unique uniforms, provisions, weaponry, instructions, lifestyles, and demobilizations. Although they have no tongues with which to voice their needs and no power to meet them, see how the One with the Names of the (Ultimate) Truth, the All-Merciful, the All-Providing, the All-Compassionate, and the All-Munificent provides, maintains, and raises them in perfect justice and wisdom and without confusing and forgetting any of them.

Is it possible that another hand could share in this amazing order and all-comprehensive organization based on an absolute measure and balance?

Who other than the Unique One of Unity, the Absolutely All-Wise and All-Powerful One, could share in this art, this regulation and government, and this raising and sustaining?

FOURTH POINT: You ask: "What are the uses and results of my love for foods, and my selfhood, spouse, parents, children, and friends, and for virtuous people, beautiful things like spring and the world if that love must be in line with the Qur'an's commands?"

Answer: It would take a comprehensive book to explain all of the uses and results of such a love. Therefore I will restrict myself to pointing out briefly only a few of its immediate consequences here and its permanent results in the Hereafter.

As explained above, any love in the carnal soul's name, like that of worldly, heedless people, causes much pain, trouble, and affliction in this world, and the ease, pleasure and enjoyment it gives is little. For example, compassion turns into a painful affliction because you cannot do something. Love becomes a consuming feeling because of separation. Pleasure becomes like a poisonous drink because it is subject to transience. Since such love is not love in Almighty God's name, it will be useless in the Hereafter. Also, it will bring torment if it has driven the lover into illicit dealings.

Question: How does one's love for Prophets and saints become fruitless?

Answer: Love for Prophets and saints, such as that found among Christians who believe in the Trinity, and the *Rafidis* (a Shi'a sect) who cherish enmity toward almost all Companions due to their love of 'Ali, is fruitless.[180] Any love in God's name and in the Qur'anic manner yields good results in both this world and the Hereafter. I briefly mention its worldly results below:

- Loving delicious foods and fruits in God's name makes them a favor and grace unmixed with pain, an ease that yields pure thankfulness.
- Loving your carnal soul leads you to pity so that you will educate it and prevent it from harmful desires and fancies. When you do this successfully, your carnal soul cannot take you wherever it wishes and enslave you to its desires. On the contrary, you will mount it and guide it to truth, not drive it to passions.

---

[180] Such love is rooted in love for the person loved. As it is not in God's name, it leads to unforgivable excesses in belief. Due to such excesses, Christians deified Jesus and the *Rafidis* broke from the majority Muslim community (Tr.).

- If you love and has mercy for your spouse sincerely based on her good conduct and her being a mine of compassion and a gift of Divine Mercy, she (or he) will love and respect you. As you both age, this mutual love and respect will grow and increase your happiness. Carnal love based on physical beauty is fleeting. When it disappears, so do your mutual good relations.

- Loving your parents for Almighty God's sake is an act of worship and increases as they age. With a most elevated feeling and endeavor, you pray for them to live long so that you may get more rewards because of them and receive a pure spiritual pleasure by respecting and serving them. If you find their existence unbearable when they need you and thus desire their deaths, you have descended to barbarism and will suffer a painful spiritual ailment.

- Loving your children because they are Almighty God's lovable gifts that He has entrusted to you to raise and educate in an agreeable way is a love that brings happiness and blessing. You will not suffer much because of the calamities striking them or wail in despair if they die. Since their Creator is All-Wise and All-Compassionate, you will conclude: "Since it was better for them to die than to live, Almighty God took them away from me." Thinking that your patience will draw God's Mercy and that He will bring [both of] you together in an Abode of eternal happiness, you will be saved from the pains of separation.

- Loving your friends for God's sake means that separation or death will not break the relationship you currently enjoy. You will benefit from this mutual love and spiritual connection. The pleasure of re-union for His sake is lasting. While a second of union for His sake gives the pleasure of a year of union, a year of being together for worldly purposes means a second of union and ends in painful separation.

- Loving virtuous people like the Prophets and saints shows you the Intermediate World of the grave, which appears to the heedless as a dark, frightening solitude, as a mansion illuminated by the existence of those blessed ones. You will not be afraid to go to that world. Rather, you will feel an inclination and eagerness to go there, and the pleasure you receive from your life will not be spoiled. But if you love them as the "civilized" people love famous individuals, you will be grieved at their death, and the thought of their decay and oblivion in the past's "vast grave" will increase your pain. Thinking that you will enter the grave, which causes even the best people to rot away, you will utter sighs of grief and fear death. But if you love in Almighty God's name, you will see the grave as a place of perfect rest after discarding the body, and you will look forward to it in warm anticipation.

- Loving beautiful things in their Maker's name and in a way reminding you of their Creator is a pleasant reflection and will turn your view, which adores beauty, toward the sources of a far more elevated, sacred, and subtler beauty. You will turn from those beautiful works toward the beauty of Divine acts, then to the beauty of Divine Names, and then to the beauty of Divine Attributes and the All-Majestic One's matchless Beauty. This love is pure pleasure, an act of worship, and a reflection.

- Loving youth because it is a fine blessing of Almighty God, you will spend it in worship and not waste it in dissipation. When you do that, the worship done while you are young yields permanent fruits. Youth disappears, but those fruits remain and you will be protected from the evil consequences of a youth spent in rebellion and dissipation. When you grow old, you will concentrate even more on worshipping God and deserve more from Divine Mercy. Unlike the heedless, you will not weep or regret your five or ten years of youthful pleasures as you enter the twilight of your life. You will not be like the heedless, who say: "If only my youth would return, I would tell it what old age has made happen to me."

- Loving such exhibits as spring because they are works of Divine Art means that the pleasure of observing them does not disappear when they are removed, for you can recall the meanings they have left in your mind like gilded letters. Like movie scenes, your imagination and time enable you to take pleasure in seeing them, and your mind refreshes the beauties and meanings of the past spring. In such a case, your love continues to give pleasure and enjoyment and does not become painful and temporary.

- Loving this world in Almighty God's name makes all of its creatures like amiable friends. Seeing it as a tillage for the Hereafter, you find in everything a capital that can be used for the good of your afterlife. Calamity does not scare you, and the transience of your life does not trouble you. You will stay in that guest-house peacefully until your appointed hour. But if you love the world as the heedless do, you will suffocate in a troublesome, calamitous, transient, and fruitless love.

If, after indicating the pleasures and benefits that the kind of love taught in the Qur'an will give here, you want to hear and know such love's other-worldly results, read the introduction and nine indications that follow:

Introduction: Through His majestic Divinity, gracious Mercy, supreme Lordship, munificent Caring, vast Power, and subtle Wisdom, Almighty God has equipped the insignificant-sized human body with so many senses and feelings, such a variety of organs and members and systems, and numerous faculties so that He may make each one of us sense and know the innumerable varieties of His bounties, kinds of His favors, and instances of His Mercy. Also, He has done this so that we can measure and love His Names' countless manifestations. Each bodily member, system, and faculty has different types of service and worship as well as different sorts of pleasures, pains, duties, and rewards.

For example, eyes see the beauties of forms and various miracles of Divine Power in the sphere of sight. Their duty is thoughtful and contemplative observation and gratitude to the Maker. Everyone knows the pleasures and pains particular to sight. Ears perceive different sounds, creation's sweet melodies, and the subtleties of Divine Mercy in the sphere of hearing. They have their own unique type of worship, pleasure, and reward. The sense of smell is aware of Mercy's subtleties in the sphere of smelling, and also has its own unique pleasure, duty of gratitude, and reward. Like the others, the sense of taste performs many duties of thanksgiving by being aware of the tastes of everything consumed.

In short, all of our senses, organs, and faculties (e.g., the heart, intellect, and spirit) have unique duties, pleasures, and pains. Almighty God, the Absolutely All-Wise One, will undoubtedly reward all of them accordingly. Everyone is aware of their immediate rewards in the world. As for their rewards in the Hereafter, as they are briefly proved in the Twelfth Truth of The Tenth Word, the six Fundamentals of The Twenty-Ninth Word, and The Twenty-Eighth Word, they are also either stated explicitly or alluded to in the Qur'an, the truest word, the most perfect system, the Word of God, the Sovereign, the All-Glorious, the All-Knowing.

First indication: Lawful love in gratitude for delicious foods and fruits yields paradisiacal foods and fruits in the Hereafter and arouses in us an appetite for them. Even saying: "All praise and gratitude are for God" after you eat something will be returned to you as a fruit of Paradise. As suggested by the Qur'an and required by Divine Wisdom and Mercy, any pleasurable thanks given to Almighty God for His bounties and favors will be returned to you in Paradise as the most delicious food.

Second indication: In return for loving your selfhood or soul in a lawful manner (pitying it and working to perfect it and guiding it to good), you will be given that which you love in Paradise. Since you gratified your soul's desires and ambitions and used its organs and faculties in the way Almighty God approves of while here, the Absolutely Munificent One will reward your (lawful) love of it by clothing you in seventy different celestial garments as samples of seventy different kinds of beauty and adornment of Paradise. These will please all of your senses. He also will adorn your body with seventy varieties of beauty and present the *houris* to you, each of whom is like an animate miniature Paradise. Your love for youth in the world, which manifests itself in your using it to worship God, will result in eternal youth in the Abode of eternal happiness.

Third indication: In reward for the sincere love you feel for your spouse due to her (or his) delightful compassion, laudable virtues and good conduct, and protecting her (or him) against disobedience to God and other sins, the Absolutely Compassionate One will make her (or him) an immortal friend for you in the Abode of eternal happiness. She will be more beautiful, better dressed and ornamented, and more charming than the *houris*. Spouses will be seated on thrones face to face and will take great pleasure in relating to each other their worldly lives they spent together.

Fourth indication: As the result of lawful love for parents and children, Almighty God, the All-Merciful and All-Compassionate, will allow them to come together in Paradise and reward them with eternal happy communion, even though the rank and place of each may be different. He will re-create children who died before puberty as the lovable and most beautiful immortal children of Paradise (56:17), in a form worthy of Paradise, and return them to their parents' arms so that they may enjoy eternally the pleasure of parenthood. Since Paradise is not the place of reproduction, some thought that the pleasure of having children would be absent there. But as Paradise contains every pleasurable thing in its highest degree, the pleasure of having children, at its best, will be there by means of the children who died before reaching puberty. This is a good tiding for those parents whose prepubescent children have died.

Fifth indication: The Qur'an explicitly states that, as the result of loving righteous friends for God's sake, they will be seated on couches face to face in Paradise (15:47) and will enjoy eternally the pure pleasure of talking to each other about their worldly lives in a most delightful manner.

Sixth indication: Your Qur'anic love for the Prophets and saints will cause you to benefit from their intercession in the Intermediate World of the grave and in the Place of Supreme Gathering. You also will receive enlightenment from their elevated positions. According to the rule that "One will be with whom he or she loves," each believer can have a part in the highest rank or position through closeness to the one with that position.

Seventh indication: Your love for beautiful things and spring, expressed in seeing them as the Creator's beautiful works, as well as in appreciating the beauty and harmony of the Acts behind those works, the manifestations of the Names behind those Acts, and the manifestations of the Attributes behind those beautiful Names, will cause you to behold, in the World of Permanence, the manifestations of those Names, which are far more beautiful than their counterparts in this world, and witness His Beauty and Attributes in those Names. Imam Rabbani says: "Paradise's beauties and subtleties are the embodiment of the Divine Names' manifestations." Reflect upon these words.

Eighth indication: Your reflective love for this world, on account of its being the Hereafter's tillage and the Divine Names' mirror, will be rewarded with an everlasting garden of Paradise as large as the world. Only the shadowy manifestations of the Names from behind numerous veils result in the world's amazing beauties. In Paradise, the Names will manifest themselves in a most splendid form. God will give Paradise, in relationship to which this world is like a small seedbed, to those who loved this world as the afterlife's tillage. Also, as required by Mercy and Wisdom and pointed to in the Prophetic Traditions and some Qur'anic verses, our senses and feelings, which are like small shoots here, will be perfected there; our potentials, which are like seeds here, will develop into varieties of perfection and pure pleasure there.

Since we loved the world only in its two aspects concerned with the Hereafter and the Divine Names and not in its contemptible aspect (the cause of all errors), and caused it to prosper through our worship as if we had spent all our lives and body, senses, and faculties in worship, Mercy and Wisdom require that we receive a reward as great as the world. Since we loved the world as the Hereafter's tillage for the sake of loving the Hereafter and loved it as the mirror of Almighty God's Names for His sake, we will be rewarded with a world-like object of love—a garden of Paradise as vast as the world.

Question: What is the use of such a vast and empty garden?

Answer: If you could travel throughout the world and most of the stars with the speed of imagination, you could assert that the world belonged to you. The fact that angels, other people, and animals share this space with you would not negate your assertion. Likewise, if Paradise is thus full, you would be able to say, "Paradise is mine." The meaning of the Tradition, "Some people of Paradise will be given a Paradise that would take five hundred years (to traverse on foot)," has been explained in The Twenty-eighth Word and "The Treatise on Sincerity" in *The Gleams.*

Ninth indication: The result of your belief and love of God is the eternal life of Paradise and vision of Him. People of spiritual unveiling and verification all agree that a thousand years of a happy life in this world is not worth an hour of life in Paradise, and that a thousand years of life in Paradise is not worth an hour's vision of the All-Majestic One in His absolute sacred Beauty and defect-free Perfection. Seeing Him is established by the Qur'an and authentic Prophetic Traditions, one of which says: "That vision far excels all the other pleasures of Paradise, so much so that it causes them to be forgotten. After the vision of God, the people of Paradise will have increased in beauty and loveliness to such a degree that the couples will be able to recognize each other only with great difficulty."

All people feel in the depths of their being a great longing to see such great people of the past as Prophet Solomon, famous for his magnificent perfection, and Prophet Joseph, distinguished for his beauty. So compare how deeply desired and yearned for, and with what degree of passion, is our desire to see Him. And remember that one manifestation of His Beauty and Perfection contains all the beauty and perfection of Paradise, which are far more elevated than all the beauty and perfection seen in this world.

> O God, provide us in this world with love of You and of what will draw us near to You, with the uprightness You command, and in the Hereafter with Your Mercy and the vision of You.

> All-Glorified are You! We have no knowledge save what You have taught us. You are the All-Knowing, the All-Wise.

> O God, bestow blessings and peace upon him whom You sent as a mercy for all worlds, and upon his Family and Companions. Amin.

~ ~

NOTE: Do not regard as too lengthy the detailed explanation in this Word's last section. It is short in proportion to its importance and, in fact, requires further elaboration. Truth speaks in *The Words* in the name of indications from the Qur'an. Truth speaks the truth. If you see anything incorrect, know that it originated from my mind.

Supplication

O Lord! A person knocks on the door of a palace which is not opened to him or her, with the call of him or her who is esteemed in that palace and whose call is familiar with its inhabitants. So, since I am too wretched to knock on the door of the Court of Your Mercy, I knock on it with the call and supplication of Uwaysu'l-Qarani, one of Your servants whom You love. Open that Court of Yours to me, as you opened it to him. I call as he did:

O God, You are my Lord; I am a servant.
You are the Creator; I am the one created.
You are the All-Providing; I am the one provided.
You are the Master, the Owner; I am a slave, the one owned.
You are the All-Glorious; I am the one abased and wretched.
You are the All-Wealthy; I am the one absolutely poor.
You are the All-Living; I am the one dead,
You are the All-Permanent; I am the one mortal.
You are the All-Munificent; I am the one miserly.
You are the All-Benevolent; I am the one doing ill.
You are the All-Forgiving; I am the one sinful.
You are the All-Supreme; I am the one despicable.
You are the All-Strong; I am the one weak.
You are the All-Granting; I am the one begging.
You are the All-Trustworthy, One giving security; I am the one in fear.
You are the All-Generous; I am the one in utmost need.
You are the One Answering pleas; I am the one pleading.
You are the All-Healing; I am the one sick.

So forgive my sins, spare me, and heal my ills, O God! O the All-Sufficing One! O Lord! O the All-Faithful! O the All-Compassionate! O the All-Healing! O the All-Munificent! O Restorer to health! Pardon all my sins, restore me to health from all illnesses, and be pleased with me for all eternity! Through Your Mercy, O the Most Compassionate of the Compassionate!

The conclusion of their call will be: All praise and gratitude are for God, the Lord of the worlds.

The
Thirty-third Word

The Thirty-third Word

Thirty-three windows opening on God's Existence and Unity from the universe and humanity

In the Name of God, the All-Merciful, the All-Compassionate.

We will show them Our manifest signs in the horizons of the universe and within their own selves, until it becomes clear to them that it (the Qur'an) is indeed the truth. Is it not enough that your Lord is a witness over all things? (41:53)

UESTION: WE WOULD LIKE A BRIEF, CONCISE EXPLANATION OF how humanity (the microcosm) and the universe (the macrocosm) point to God's necessary Existence and Unity, as well as His Lordship's characteristics, attributes, and acts, which the two parts of the comprehensive verse above denote.

ANSWER: The thirty-two Words written so far are thirty-two drops from the ocean of the truths poured out by that verse. Your question is answered therein. The following only points to the droplets of a drop from that ocean.

If a miracle-displaying person wants to build a large palace, first he lays the foundation firmly according to his purpose for building it. Next, he divides it into apartments and rooms skillfully and then furnishes and decorates them. After that, he illuminates the palace with electric lights. Then, in order to show his other skills and ever-renewed bountifulness, he makes additions, changes, and transformations in every floor, wing and apartment. Furthermore, he establishes a communication system linking every apartment and room, and opens windows in every room so that his rank and true identity may be displayed and the inhabitants of the palace may contact him.

Similarly—*The highest comparison is (and must be put forth) for God*—the Maker of Majesty, the Originator, Who is beyond compare and called by one thousand and one holy Names, such as the All-Wise Ruler and the All-Just Judge, willed to make that palace of the universe, that tree of creation, which is the macrocosm. He laid the palace's (and tree's) foundations in six "days" and built the main body with the principles of His Wisdom and rules of His eternal Knowledge. Dividing it into higher and lower levels and branches, He ramified and elaborated it with the principles of His Decree and Destiny. Then He formed and organized creatures in groups, families, and species and ordered the life of each with the principles of His Art and Favoring. After that, He adorned each thing and world in a unique way. For example, He adorned the sky with stars and the earth with flowers. He manifested His Names in those vast arenas where His universal laws and all-inclusive principles are in force and illuminated them. Following that, by manifesting His Names the All-Merciful and the All-Compassionate, He came to the aid of each individual creature, which cried at the pressure of those universal laws. That means that He has, within His universal and all-inclusive rules or laws, special favors and help, as well as particular manifestations, that encourage every being to turn to Him at any time and ask Him to meet any of its needs. Also, in order to make His Existence and Unity evident, He opened windows on Himself from all apartments, all levels of creation and worlds, all groups of existence and individuals, and all things. Furthermore, He left a phone in every heart.

Now referring those innumerable windows to the all-comprehensive Divine Knowledge, the discussion of which is beyond our capacity, in a happy correspondence with the thirty repetitions of the phrases of glorifying and praising God, and of affirming His Greatness after each prescribed Prayer, and under the title of The Twenty-third Word, we will be content with a brief allusion to thirty-three of them originating from the Qur'an's verses.

Thirty-three windows

FIRST WINDOW: We clearly observe that all things, particularly living ones, have many different needs and demands. They are properly met on time from somewhere unknown and unexpected. Unable to reach their objects by themselves, they cannot meet even the least of their needs. For example, consider yourself: consider how many needs you have to satisfy your outer and external senses and organs, which you are unable to procure. Extend this comparison to all other living beings. These needs and demands, as well as their gratification, point singly and as a whole to an Absolutely Necessary Being's Existence and His Oneness. Like the sun's light pointing to the sun, they show Him to the mind behind the veil of the Unseen with His Names the All-Munificent, the All-Compassionate, the All-Training and Upbringing, the All-Organizing the All-Providing. How can you explain this universal reality displaying wisdom, awareness, and compassion? Can you explain it by attributing it to deaf nature, blind force, random coincidence, or lifeless and powerless causes?

SECOND WINDOW: While on the way to existence and individualization things and beings have an infinite variety of potential forms, each is given, all at once and wisely and with perfect wisdom, a particular, distinct and extremely well-ordered individuality and countenance equipped with outer and inner senses with perfect wisdom. This countenance bears a unique mark that distinguishes the individual from all other members of its species. Thus one's countenance is a very brilliant stamp of Divine Oneness and Uniqueness displayed especially by His purposeful choice and preference. Just as each face bears witness in countless ways to an All-Wise Maker's Existence and points to His Oneness, that stamp of Oneness displayed by all faces as a whole shows to the mind's eye that it is a seal belonging to the Creator of all things.

To what workshop can you attribute those stamps that cannot be imitated, and the brilliant seal of God's being the Eternally Besought that they form as a whole?

THIRD WINDOW: The huge army of countless plant and animal species on the earth are each given with perfect measure and order, and without any confusion and forgetfulness, a particular form and garment, and a particular provision and weaponry; and each species is trained and demobilized in a unique way.[181] This is a stamp of Him Who is the One and the Unique, a stamp as brilliant as the sun and thus beyond doubt. Who but the One with limitless Power, all-encompassing Knowledge, and infinite Wisdom can dare to share in that infinitely wonderful administration? If one who could not administer and train all these species and races together, which exist intermixed, were to interfere with one of them, confusion would certainly arise. However, we read: *Look yet again, can you see any rifts?* (67:3). As there is no sign of any void or confusion, no one could have a part in creation.

---

[181] Among those species are some whose numbers in a year exceed all people who have ever lived, and who ever will live, from the time of Adam to the end of the world.

FOURTH WINDOW: Seeds pray in the tongue of their disposition and potentiality, animals pray in the tongue of their natural needs, and all who are in straitened circumstances in the tongue of compulsion or utter need and constraint. Each prayer is answered. As each answered prayer bears witness to and points to God's necessary Existence and Unity, all of them self-evidently point to an All-Compassionate, All-Munificent, and All-Answering Creator as a whole and on a larger scale.

FIFTH WINDOW: We see that things, especially living ones, apparently come into existence as if all at once. Given this, we would expect them to be simple, coarse, and without any art. Instead, they are so finely created that many skills are required, embellished so carefully and delicately that a long time is demanded, ornamented so artistically that many tools are needed, and made so elaborately that a great amount of material is necessary. So, just as the beautiful form given to each and all things simultaneously, as well as the wonderful artistry manifested on them, testify to an All-Wise Maker's necessary Existence and point to His Lordship's Unity, so too, as a whole they point in a most brilliant fashion to a Necessarily Existent Being Who is infinitely Powerful and Wise.

How do you explain this? Can it be attributed to ignorant nature? Can you call that All-Holy Maker "nature" and ascribe the miracles of His Power to it? Will it not be a greatest mistake, and mean regarding something utterly impossible as possible?

SIXTH WINDOW

> Surely in the creation of the heavens and the earth, and the alternation of night and day (with their periods shortening and lengthening), and the vessels sailing in the sea with profit to people, and the water that God sends down from the sky, therewith reviving the earth after its death and dispersing therein all kinds of living creatures, and His disposal of the winds, and the clouds subservient between sky and earth—surely there are signs for a people who reason and understand. (2:164)

This verse, which demonstrates God's necessary Existence and Unity, is an extremely large window through which one of God's Greatest Names is seen. Briefly, all worlds situated at the universe's higher and lower levels point to the same result in different tongues: the Lordship of a single All-Wise Maker. It is as follows:

- Well-organized and systematic movements in the heavens for extensive results show an All-Powerful One of Majesty's Existence and Unity and His Lordship's perfection.

- Likewise, the tremendous seasonal and other changes on the earth resulting in utterly comprehensive benefits show the necessity of that All-Powerful One of Majesty's Unity and His Lordship's perfection.

- All land and water animals are fed through perfect mercy, given forms with perfect wisdom, and equipped with senses and faculties through perfect Lordship. As each of them testifies to that same All-Powerful One of Majesty's Existence and points to His Unity, as a whole, they demonstrate His Divinity's grandeur and His Lordship's perfection on a large scale.

- Similarly, all well-formed plants in gardens and orchards and their ornate flowers, the well-proportioned fruits that replace the flowers, and the rich embellishments displayed by the fruits bear witness to that All-Wise Maker's Existence and point to His Unity individually. Collectively, they show His Mercy's grace and His Lordship's perfection in a splendid way.

- All drops sent from the atmosphere and charged with important purposes, necessary consequences, and benefits show to their number that All-Wise Maker's necessary Existence and Unity and His Lordship's perfection.

- In the same way, all mountains and minerals of great variety deposited in them for various purposes show, as firmly as mountains, that All-Wise Maker's Existence and Unity and His Lordship's perfection.

- All beautiful flowers decorating hills and plains attest, individually, to an All-Wise Maker's necessary Existence and point to His Unity. Collectively, they show His Sovereignty's majesty and His Lordship's perfection.

- Likewise, all well-proportioned shapes and positions of herb and tree leaves, as well as their rapturous and systematic movements, show to the number of the leaves that All-Wise Maker's necessary Existence and Unity and His Lordship's perfection.

- All growing bodies are equipped with various members and systems during their growth, and begin to move in an ordered manner and are directed toward yielding fruits. Each one testifies to that All-Wise Maker's necessary Existence and points to His Unity. As a whole, they demonstrate His Power's comprehensiveness, His

Wisdom's inclusiveness, His Art's beauty, and His Lordship's perfection on a very large scale.

- Establishing souls and spirits in all animal bodies with perfect wisdom, equipping them with appropriate systems with perfect order, and mobilizing them for unique services and purposes with perfect wisdom—all of this bears witness, to the number of animals, indeed to the number of their faculties, and points to that All-Wise Maker's necessary Existence and Unity. Collectively, these acts show His Mercy and His Lordship's perfection in a most brilliant fashion.

- All Divine inspirations that instruct humanity in all sorts of knowledge and truth, as well as teach animals how to procure their needs, suggest the Existence of an All- Compassionate Lord and point to His Lordship.

- Also, like the rays of light coming from the eye and collecting together all the "flowers" in the garden of the universe before eyes, all outer and inner senses function each as a key to a different world. This demonstrates, as brightly as the sun, the necessary Existence of that All-Wise Maker, All-Knowing Originator, All- Compassionate Creator, All-Munificent Provider, and His Unity and Lordship's perfection.

Thus a huge window is opened through the twelve windows mentioned above. It shows through a twelve-colored light of truth the Oneness or Uniqueness of God Almighty and His Lordship's perfection. How can you close that window, which is as wide as the earth or even its orbit around the sun? How can you extinguish that source of light, which is as bright as the sun? Behind what veil of heedlessness can you hide it?

SEVENTH WINDOW

- Countless kinds and species of creatures come into existence easily and resemble each other in many ways. They are spread on the earth with perfect order and show a perfect proportionateness and equipment. This demonstrates an All-Wise Maker's necessary Existence and Unity and His Power's perfection on a broad scale.

- Likewise, the creation of innumerable and unique well-composed compound beings out of simple lifeless elements also testifies to that All-Wise Maker's necessary Existence and points to His Unity. As a whole, these beings show His Power's perfection and His Unity in a most brilliant way.

- Also, there is an infinite degree of differentiation and compounding within infinite profusion in the composition, dissolution and reformation of beings. For example, while seeds and roots exist underground in very confused positions, they are amazingly distinguished in growth. Like food particles entering the body in confusion and then separated and shared among organs and tissues with perfect measure and wisdom, the substances entering trees in confusion are distinguished and distributed among leaves, blossoms, and fruits. This shows the necessary Existence of that absolutely Wise, Knowing, and Powerful One, as well as His Unity and His Power's perfection.

- It also demonstrates the necessary Existence of that same All-Powerful One Majesty and the Maker of Perfection, His Power's perfection, and His Lordship's grandeur and perfection that He makes the world of atoms into a boundless, vast field and then sows and harvests it every moment with perfect wisdom. He obtains fresh crops of different worlds from it and causes those unconscious, powerless, and ignorant atoms to perform innumerable systematic functions, just as if they were extremely learned, conscious, and capable.

Thus a large window is opened onto knowledge of God through these four ways, and they display an All-Wise Maker to the mind on a large scale. If you do not want to see Him through this window and recognize Him, rid yourself of reason so as to become like an animal and be saved!

EIGHTH WINDOW: The testimony of all Prophets, upon them be peace, (those people with luminous spirits), based on their manifest and evident miracles; the testimony of all saints (those distinguished with illumined hearts), relying on their wonder-working and spiritual discoveries; and the testimony of all purified scholars (those with enlightened minds), relying on their research and quest for truth, all testify to the necessary Existence and Unity of One, the Creator of all things, and His Power's perfection. They form a vast and enlightening window through which His Lordship   sustaining, training, raising, etc.—shows Itself continually.

Who do you rely on so that you do not heed those people? Or, by closing your eyes in the daytime, do you imagine the world to be in darkness?

NINTH WINDOW

- The worship of all beings shows an Absolutely Worshipped One. As testified by those who penetrate the world of spirits and the inner dimension of things, where they meet with angels and spirit beings, all angels and spirit beings worship an Eternally Worshipped One in perfect obedience. We all observe that all living beings perform duties in perfect order in a manner resembling worship, and that all inanimate things render services with perfect submission in a like manner. All of this shows the necessary Existence and Unity of an All-Worshipped One, Who is absolutely worthy of worship.

- This is also the case with the true knowledge of all saints knowing Him (which bears the weight of consensus), all thankful people's fruitful thanks, the blessed recitations of those who regularly recite God with His Names and Attributes, the praises (which increase Divine bounties) of those who praise God, the pronouncements and descriptions of Divine Unity (based on decisive proofs) of those who believe in it, the true love of all lovers of God, the true will and desires of those who seek Him, and the earnest searching and inclinations of those who turn to Him. All of this shows the necessary Existence and Unity of that Eternally Worshipped One, the One Who is the All-Recognized, the All-Mentioned, the All-Praised, the All-Beloved, the All-Desired, and the All-Sought, as well as His Lordship's perfection.

- Also, the acceptable worship and supplications of perfected people, as well as their spiritual radiance, visions, and illuminations resulting from their worship, demonstrate that Everlasting and Eternally Worshipped One's necessary Existence and Unity and His Lordship's perfection.

These three aspects open up a broad, light-giving window onto Divine Unity.

TENTH WINDOW

God is He Who has created the heavens and the earth, and sends down water from the sky with which He brings forth fruits for your provision; and He has made the ships serviceable for you, so that they run upon the sea by His command; and He has made the rivers serviceable for you. And He has made the sun and the moon constant in their courses, (and so) serviceable for you; and He has made the night and the day of service to you. He has granted you from all that you ask Him; were you to attempt to count God's blessings, you could not compute them. (14:32-34)

The mutual helping and solidarity of beings and their responding to each other's call for assistance shows that all creatures are trained by one

Instructor, administered by one Director, controlled by one Disposer, and serve one Master. Through a universal law of mutual helping, the sun cooks, by the Lord's command, that which is needed by the earth's living creatures to continue living. The moon acts as a calendar; light, air, water, and sustenance hasten to help animate beings; plants hasten to help animals; animals and plants hasten to help human beings; bodily members hasten to help each other; and food particles hasten to help cells.

This most wise and generous cooperation among unconscious beings, their responding to each other's needs and supporting each other under a law of munificence and grace, a law of compassion and care and a principle of mercy, show that they are the servants, officers, and creatures of a Unique One of Unity, a peerless, Eternally Besought One, an Absolutely Powerful, Absolutely Knowledgeable, Absolutely Compassionate, Absolutely Munificent, and Necessarily Existent One. How do you, O follower of materialistic philosophy and scientism, respond to this mighty window? Can chance have a hand in this?

Eleventh window

> Be aware that it is only in the remembrance of and whole-hearted devotion to God that hearts find rest and contentment. (13:28)

Only through recognizing their One Creator can all spirits and hearts be delivered from the distress and confusion of misguidance, and from the spiritual pains arising from that distress. Attributing all beings to a Maker of Unity allows them to find salvation, and they find rest and contentment in the remembrance of One God. For, as proved in The Twenty-second Word, if all those innumerable beings are not attributed to a Single Being, one thing must be ascribed to numberless causes. In which case, the existence of a single thing becomes as difficult as the whole creation; a fruit becomes as difficult as the universe, indeed, more difficult. Consider this: If one soldier is commanded by a hundred officers, a hundred difficulties will arise. But if a hundred soldiers are commanded by one officer, they will be as easy to command as one soldier. This also is true in the case of creation, for creating one thing by multiple causes would face as many problems as there are causes. Given this, belief in the Creator's Unity and knowledge or recognition of God will deliver us from the endless distress arising from the curiosity and desire to find the truth, which is inherent in our nature.

Unbelief and associating partners with God engenders so many difficulties and pains that they clearly cannot contain any truth. In contrast, we see how easily things and beings come into existence in great variety and multiplicity and yet with utmost beauty and artistry. This ease of creation can be explained only by ascribing all of creation to One God. As there is infinite ease in the way of believing in One God, it is certainly necessary and the truth itself. See how dark and distressing is the way of misguidance. Why do you take it, when you can see how easy and pleasant is the way of belief and affirming Divine Unity? Take that way and be delivered.

TWELFTH WINDOW: As declared in:

> Glorify the Name of your Lord, the Most High, Who creates and fashions in due proportions; and Who determines (a particular life, nature, and goal for each creature), and guides (it toward its own way and the fulfillment of that goal). (87:1-3)

all things, especially living ones, have a form and well-measured proportions according to their functions, as if they have emerged from a mold of wisdom. Each has been given a unique shape, with curves and twists according to its appointed benefits and uses. Their resulting outer and inner changes and renewals proceed according to certain measures and purposes determined for their lives. All of this shows that the shapes and proportions of these innumerable creatures are planned within the frame of an all-inclusive Determining or Destiny of an All-Powerful One of Majesty, an All-Wise One of Perfection, and they are given forms and bodies in the workshop of the Divine Power. All this points to His necessary Existence and bears witness in endless tongues to His Unity and His Power's perfection.

Look at your own body and its parts. Reflect on the uses and benefits of each one's curves and twists, and see the perfection of the Power embedded in perfect Wisdom!

THIRTEENTH WINDOW: As stated in: *There is nothing but it glorifies Him with His praise* (17:44), each thing mentions and glorifies its Creator in its own tongue. These glorifications, whether vocal or in the tongue of their lives and dispositions, show a single All-Holy One's Existence.

The testimony of disposition or nature is not rejected. The proof produced by practical life, especially when it issues from many aspects of that life, cannot provoke doubt. See how well-ordered forms of these creatures, which exhibit countless testimonies of creation and disposition, and bear witness in the language of their lives and manners, and which all turn to a single center like concentric circles, are each an expressive tongue. Their well-proportioned structures and organizations are tongues of testimony, and their well-organized lives are tongues of glorification. As convincingly argued in The Twenty-fourth Word, these glorifications and exaltations testify to a single All-Holy Being, demonstrate His necessary Existence as certainly as light shows the sun, and point to His Divinity's perfection.

FOURTEENTH WINDOW

Say: "In whose hand is the absolute dominion of all things?" (23:88)

There is nothing but the stores (for its life) are with us. (15:21)

No living creature is there but He holds it by its forelock. (11:56)

Surely my Lord keeps watch and record of all things. (11:57)

These verses state that everything, in all circumstances and aspects of its life and existence, needs a single Creator of Majesty. Looking at creatures, we see the manifestation of an absolute force within absolute weakness and the impressions and inscriptions of an absolute power in absolute impotence. For example, the awakening of the life-force in plant seeds and roots is extraordinary.

There also are manifestations of absolute wealth within absolute poverty and sterility, like the poverty of soil and trees in winter and their glittering profusion in spring. Sparks of absolute life are observed in absolutely lifeless matter (e.g., the transformation of mineral elements into living entities). Manifestations of all-encompassing consciousness are seen in absolute ignorance, as when everything from stars to atoms acts as if consciously conforming to the universe's order, life's principles, and wisdom's demands. All these manifestations—power within impotence, force or strength within weakness, richness within poverty, and life and consciousness within lifelessness and ignorance—open windows onto the necessary Existence and Unity of One Absolutely Powerful, Strong, Wealth, and Knowing, as well as Living and Self-Subsistent. In their totality, they point to a luminous highway (the way of believing in God and His Oneness) on a large scale.

If you ascribe creativity to nature and accept it as self-originated instead of recognizing Divine Power, you must acknowledge that everything contains an infinite force and power, wisdom and skill, and the capacity to see, know, and direct most other things.

FIFTEENTH WINDOW: As declared in: *He Who makes excellent everything that He creates* (32:7), everything is clothed in existence and a form tailored to its nature's receptivity with perfect measure and order, assembled with the finest art, and by the most direct method, in the best shape and the easiest manner, and with the most practicable features. Look at the "dress" of birds and see how easily they can ruffle up and continually use their feathers. Giving things bodies and dressing them in forms in so wise a manner as mentioned and without waste and futility bears witness, to the number of those things, to an All-Wise Maker's necessary Existence and points to an Absolutely Powerful and Knowing One.

SIXTEENTH WINDOW: The order and organization in the creation and management of creatures, recruited every season on the earth, show a universal purposiveness and wisdom. Since an attribute cannot be without the one it qualifies, that universal wisdom shows a Wise One. The wonderful adornment within that veil of wisdom shows an all-embracing grace, which shows an All-Gracious Creator of Munificence. The all-encompassing favoring and benevolence within that veil of grace show an all-encompassing mercy, which shows an All-Merciful, All-Compassionate One. The sustenance and provision of all living creatures on that veil of mercy, all perfect and appropriate for their needs, show an upbringing and training providence and a compassionate lordship. That training and administering show an All-Munificent Provider.

Each creature raised with perfect wisdom, equipped and adorned with perfect graciousness, favored with perfect mercy, and nurtured with perfect caring and compassion, bears witness to the necessary Existence of an All-Wise, Munificent, Compassionate, Providing Maker and points to His Unity. Consider the all-encompassing wisdom manifested on whole of the earth and which clearly shows a purpose and will; the perfect grace encompassing all creatures in accordance with wisdom; the extensive mercy comprising both grace and wisdom and embracing all creatures; and the most generous providing and nurturing comprising the mercy, wisdom, and grace, and embracing all living creatures. Just as the seven colors form the light and the light illuminating the earth shows the sun, so too that grace within wisdom, mercy within grace, and providing and nurturing within mercy show brilliantly, and on a vast scale and at a high degree, the Unity and Lordship of an All-Wise, All-Munificent, All-Compassionate, All-Providing, and Necessarily-Existent One.

How can you explain this wise as well as compassionate, generous, providential sustaining and raising; this extraordinary, wonderful, miraculous state of affairs before your eyes? By random chance and coincidence, blind force, deaf and mute nature, or by powerless, lifeless, and ignorant causes? By giving the name of "nature," which is infinitely impotent, ignorant, deaf, blind, contingent, and helpless, to the All-Majestic One, Who is infinitely Powerful, Knowing, Hearing, and Seeing? Do you want to commit such a serious mistake? How can you extinguish a truth as brilliant as the sun? Under what veil of heedlessness can you hide it?

SEVENTEENTH WINDOW

Surely in the heavens and the earth are signs for believers. (45:3)

Consider the following points:

- During spring and summer we see in the creation of things an infinite generosity and absolute liberality, which could be expected to cause disorder and confusion, within an infinite order and harmony. See all the plants adorning the earth's face.

- The absolute speed in creating things, which normally would result in imbalance and loss of decorum, is observed within a perfect equilibrium and proportion. See all the fruits decorating the earth's face.

- The absolute multiplicity and variety, which normally would bring about triviality and even ugliness, is apparent within art's perfect beauty. See all the flowers gilding the earth's face.

- The absolute ease in creating things, which normally would cause simplicity and lack of art, is seen within an art, skill, and attention of infinite degree. See all the seeds, which are like tiny containers and programs of all plants and trees, and also like small cases containing their life-histories.

- The great distances, which normally would necessitate difference and diversity, appear within an absolute correspondence and conformity. See all the varieties of cereal grains sown throughout the world.

- The utter intermingling, which normally would cause confusion and mess, is seen within perfect differentiation and separation. Consider how seeds, cast into the ground all mixed together and resembling each other with regard to their substance, are perfectly differentiated when they are about to sprout. See how the various substances entering trees are separated perfectly for leaves, blossoms, and fruits, and how the foods entering the stomach all mixed together are separated perfectly for the body's members and cells. Consider all this and see the perfect power within perfect wisdom.

- The infinite abundance and profusion, which normally would cause triviality and worthlessness, are seen to be most valuable and most worthwhile in regard to the earth's creatures and art. Among all those innumerable wonders of art, consider only the varieties of mulberry, those sweets of Divine Power, on the table of the All-Merciful One on the earth, and observe the perfect mercy combined with the perfect art.

Just as daytime shows light and light shows the sun, the great value despite infinite profusion; within infinite profusion, the infinite differentiation and separation despite boundless intermingling; within infinite differentiation and separation, the infinite conformity and resemblance despite the great distances; within infinite resemblance, the infinite care and attention in the making despite infinite ease and facility; within the most beautiful making, the infinite equilibrium, balance, and lack of waste despite absolute speed and rapidity; within the utmost lack of waste, the highest degree of beauty of art despite the utmost abundance and multiplicity; within the highest degree of art, the absolute order and harmony despite the utmost liberality—all of these bear witness to the necessary Existence, Unity, and Oneness of an All-Powerful One of Majesty, an All-Wise One of Perfection, an All-Compassionate One of Grace and Beauty, and His Power's perfection and His Lordship's grace and beauty. They demonstrate the meaning of: *His are the All-Beautiful Names* (20:8).

So, unfortunate, obstinate, and heedless one! How can you interpret this mighty truth or explain this infinitely miraculous and wonderful state of affairs? To what can you attribute these truly extraordinary arts? What veil of heedlessness can you draw across this window as broad as the earth and then close it? Where is your chance and coincidence? Where is your unconscious companion on which you rely and call "nature," your friend and support in misguidance? Is it not utterly impossible for chance and coincidence to have a hand in these affairs? Is it not inconceivable to attribute to nature even a minute fraction of ordering these things? Or does lifeless, ignorant, unconscious nature have machines and printing presses within each thing, made from each, and equal in quantity to the number of individual things?

EIGHTEENTH WINDOW

Do they never consider the inner dimension of the heavens and the earth and God's absolute dominion over them? (7:185)

Consider the following comparison explained in The Twenty-second Word:

A perfect, well-designed and artistic construction like a palace points to a perfect act, that is, an act of construction. A perfect, well-performed act points to a perfect actor, to a skillful master-builder. The title of a skillful master-builder points to a perfect attribute, to an artistic ability. A perfect attribute, a perfect competence in an art points to the existence of a perfect capacity. A prefect capacity or potentiality points to the existence of a noble spirit, an exalted being.

Likewise, the ever-renewed, refreshed, and replaced works filling the earth's face and the universe show acts of perfect degree. Those acts, occurring in an infinitely wise and well-ordered system, show an agent or an actor with perfect titles and names. For it is clear that well-arranged and wise acts must have someone doing them. Infinitely perfect titles point, in turn, to that agent's infinitely perfect attributes. This is also a rule of grammar—according to the (Arabic) grammar, the origins of nouns are adjectives. Perfect attributes point to perfect personal potentialities, and perfect potentialities point to the one with a limitless degree of perfection.

Thus, since each work of art and all creatures in the universe are perfect, and since each bears witness to an act, the act to a name, the name to an attribute, the attribute to a potentiality, and the potentiality to a being, then—as well as all of them testifying to a single Maker of Majesty's necessary Existence and Unity to their number—as a whole they constitute a stairway of knowledge of God, which leads to Him in a form as strong as the chain of creatures, and a proof of truth in series that cannot be doubted.

So, O poor, heedless unbeliever, can you break this proof as strong as the chain of beings? Can you shut up this window that has as many openings as the numbers of creatures to show the rays of truth? What veil of heedlessness can you draw across it?

NINETEENTH WINDOW

> The seven heavens and the earth and all in them glorify Him. There is nothing but it glorifies Him with His praise. (17:44)

According to the meaning of this verse, the All-Majestic Maker has attached so many instances of wisdom and meanings to heavenly bodies that, as if to express His Majesty and Grace, He has adorned the heavens with suns, moons, and stars. He has also attached such instances of wisdom and meanings to the creatures in the atmosphere as if to make the atmosphere speak in words like lightning, thunder, and raindrops. He also teaches the perfection of His Wisdom and the beauty of His Mercy.

Just as He makes the earth speak in meaningful words like plants and animals, and thereby shows His Art's perfection to the universe, He also shows His Art's perfection and His Mercy's beauty by making plants and trees speak in their words of leaves, flowers, and fruits. By making flowers and fruits speak in words of seeds and pollen, He teaches the subtleties of His Art and His Lordship's perfection to conscious beings. Among these countless words of glorification, we will consider the manner in which a flower or an ear of wheat expresses its glorification and discover how it bears witness:

Each plant and tree shows its Maker in numerous tongues in a way that amazes observers and causes them to say: "All-Glorified is God, how excellently it bears witness." Each plant's glorifications when it blossoms and grows ears or spikes—the time when it speaks in smiles—are beautiful like itself and evident. For the order or system displaying the wisdom or purposiveness expressed in all flowers' speaking, in the tongues of well-formed spikes or ears, and in the words of well-proportioned seeds and well-made grains, is perfectly measured and balanced, which visibly points to knowledge. The balance or measure is in a design of art, which indicates skill in art, and the design of art is in an adornment showing grace and munificence. The adornment is in pleasant fragrances showing mercy and benevolence. These meaningful states of things, one within the other, form such a tongue of testimony that they define their All-Majestic Maker with His Names, describe Him with His Attributes, exemplify His Names' manifestations, and express His being loved and recognized.

Hearing such a testimony from a flower, if you can hear the voices of all flowers in all of the Lord's gardens on the earth's face and how powerfully they announce the All-Majestic Maker's necessary Existence and Unity, how can you have any remaining questions, doubts, and hesitations?

Look at a tree and see its fine expressiveness—how in spring its leaves appear all regularly, its blossoms open all proportionately, its fruits grow and ripen in wisdom and mercy, and itself dances at the blowing of breezes. Then consider the exact balance in the wise order expressed through the leaves becoming green by a hand of munificence, and the tongue of the blossoms smiling with a joy of grace, and the words of the fruits smiling with a display of mercy. Also, consider the delicate arts and designs within the balance demonstrating the exact measure; and the different tastes and pleasant fragrances within skillfully made designs and ornaments showing mercy and benevolence, and the seeds and stones, each of which is a miracle of Power, in pleasant fragrances and sweet tastes. See how such facts show most clearly the necessary Existence and Unity of an All-Wise, All-Munificent, All-Compassionate, All-Benevolent Maker, the Bestower of bounties, All-Beautifying, One Making Excellent, and His Mercy's beauty and His Lordship's perfection. If you could hear all the tongues of all trees, you would see what beautiful gems there are in the treasury of: *Whatever is in the heavens and the earth glorifies God* (61:1).

So, O unfortunate heedless one who supposes yourself to be left to your own devices in ingratitude! If you do not want to recognize an All-Munificent One of Majesty, Who makes Himself known to you and wills to be loved by you in such innumerable tongues, then these tongues should be silenced. But since they cannot be silenced, you should listen to them. Just closing your ears will not make you able to escape from them, for the universe does not stop speaking and creatures are not silenced. As testifiers to Divine Unity, they cannot be silenced; for sure, they will condemn you.

TWENTIETH WINDOW[182]

All-Glorified is He in Whose hand is the absolute dominion of all things. (36:83)

There is nothing but the stores (for its life) are with Us, and We send it not down but with a due, determined measure. We send the winds

---

[182] The truth in this Twentieth Window occurred to me at one time in Arabic as follows:

The radiance of light is through Your illuminating
and making things known through it;
The movements of winds in waves is through Your dispatching and
employing them so that they serve His commands to be carried out swiftly.
All-Glorified are You, how mighty is Your Rule!
The gushing out and flowing forth of rivers is through
Your storing them up and subjugating them.
The formation and decoration of all kinds of stones and minerals is through
Your arranging and fashioning them.
All-Glorified are You, how unique and splendid is Your Wisdom!
The smiling of flowers is through Your adorning and beautifying them.
The emergence of fruits in splendor is through Your bestowal and favoring.
All-Glorified are You, how beautiful is Your Art!
The singing of birds is through Your making them
speak and communicate with each other.
The hymning of rain is through Your sending it down, Your bestowal.
All-Glorified are You, how vast is Your Mercy!
The motion of moons is through Your determining, arranging, directing, and illuminating.
All-Glorified are You, how brilliant are Your proofs, how clear Your Sovereignty!

>to fertilize, and so We send down water from the sky and give it to you
>to drink; it is not you who are the keepers of its stores. (15:21-22)

Just as a perfect wisdom and the beauty and grace of art are apparent in particulars, results, and details in creation, so also universal elements, which seem to be in confusion as well as random and coincidental, assume positions dictated by wisdom and art. Thus, as indicated by its other wise duties, light shines to show and expose God's creatures on the earth by the leave of its Lord. That is to say, light is employed by an All-Wise Maker; He uses it to make His unique arts visible in the market of this world.

Consider the winds: as seen by its other great and wise benefits and functions, they run to carry out numerous, vital duties. Thus, their wave-like movements show that they are employed, sent, and used by an All-Wise Maker. They move in order to speedily carry out the Lords' orders.

Now consider springs, streams, and rivers! Their gushing forth from the ground and mountains is not by chance. Rather, their benefits and uses, all of which are works of Divine Mercy, their storage in mountains according to need, and their being sent according to wisdom show that an All-Wise Lord has subjugated and stored them and causes them to gush forth in obedience to His commands.

Now consider stones, jewels, and minerals of great variety! They have wise specific purposes and benefits and are arranged to meet human and animal needs. This shows that an All-Wise Maker has decorated, arranged, organized, and fashioned them, and given them their particular, beneficial properties.

Now consider the flowers and fruits! The smiles, colors, tastes, beauties, embroideries, and scents that each species are given specific for them and different from those of others are in effect an invitation to and menu on the table of an All-Munificent Maker, an All-Compassionate Bestower of bounties.

Now consider the birds! A decisive proof that their twittering and chirping is due to an All-Wise Maker's making them speak is the amazing way in which they relay their feelings and express their intentions to each other with these sounds.

Clouds are also amazing. The sound of falling raindrops, as well as the noise of thunder and lightning, are not meaningless; rather, creating these strange atmospheric events in space, milking from clouds raindrops like the water of life and making living creatures on the earth needy of and longing for them suckle them—all this shows that that pattering and crashing are most meaningful and full of purposive wisdom. At an All-Munificent Lord's command, the rain calls out to those longing for it: "Good tidings! I am coming!"

Look at the sky, particularly the moon among the innumerable bodies in it! The important instances of wisdom attached to it in connection with the earth—which are discussed elsewhere in the *Risale-i Nur*—demonstrate that it moves at the command of an All-Powerful and All-Wise One.

These universal elements from light to the moon open a vast window. They proclaim and show a Necessarily Existent One's Unity, His Power's perfection, and His Sovereignty's grandeur. So, O heedless one, if you can silence this voice resounding like the crashing of thunder, as well as extinguish this light as brilliant as the sun, forget God. Otherwise, come to your senses and say: *All-Glorified is He, Whom the seven heavens and the earth and all within them glorify.*

Twenty-first window

The sun runs the course appointed for it for a term to its resting-place for the stability of it(s system). This is the measured determining of the All-Glorious with irresistible might, the All-Knowing. (36:38)

The sun, the universe's lamp, is a window onto the Maker of the universe's Existence and Unity, which are as brilliant and radiant as itself. Despite their great differences in size, position, and speed, the twelve planets[183] move and revolve with perfect order, wisdom, balance, and without confusion, and are bound to the sun through a Divine law known as gravity, that is, they follow their leader. This shows on a large scale the Divine Power's grandeur and the Lord's Unity. Just imagine and compare how tremendous must be the Power and Wisdom Which rotate those lifeless bodies, those vast, unconscious masses, in infinitely perfect orderliness and with infinitely wise balance and in various forms and over varying distances. If any degree of chance were to interfere in this vast and complex event, it would cause such a great explosion that the universe would be ripped apart. If it were to stop a planet's motion for even a minute, that planet would leave its orbit and collide with another planet. Imagine the awesome collision of bodies thousands of times larger than the earth.

Referring the wonders of the other planets to God's All-Encompassing Knowledge, we consider only our own earth. As discussed in The Third Letter (in *The Letters*), it is caused to make a long journey around the sun at the Lord's command to carry out a most important duty and in a way showing the grandeur of the Lord's imperial Power and Majesty, the loftiness of

---

[183] In 12:4, the Qur'an alludes that there are twelve planets. (Tr.)

Divine Sovereignty, and the perfection of His Mercy and Wisdom. Being a ship belonging to the Lord, it has been filled with God's wonderful creatures and made like a moving place of recreation for His conscious servants. The moon has been attached to it with precise reckoning for mighty instances of wisdom like being an hour-hand telling the time, and it has been given various mansions through which to journey. These aspects of this blessed planet prove an All-Powerful One's necessary Existence and Unity with a testimony as strong as the earth itself. You can make an analogy with the rest of the solar system from this.

Moreover, the sun is made to turn on its own axis like a spinning-wheel in order to wind the immaterial threads called gravity into a ball and tie the planets to it with them and set them in order. One theory says the sun is driven together with its planets at a speed of 20 km/s toward the constellation Hercules. This self-evidently occurs by the All-Majestic One's Power and Command, the Sovereign of Eternity. It is as if He makes the solar system move like an army of soldiers under orders, thereby showing His Lordship's majesty.

So, O astronomer, can chance have a hand in these affairs? Tell me what causes can reach them, what force can draw close to this! Would such an All-Majestic Sovereign display impotence and give others a share in His Sovereignty? Would He give this, especially living beings, which are the universe's fruit, result, aim, and cream, to other hands? Would He permit others to interfere? Would He leave us to our own devices, while we are the most comprehensive fruit, the most perfect result, His guest and vicegerent on the earth (one who must rule according to His laws), and serve as a mirror (reflecting His Names)? Would He leave us to nature and chance, thereby reducing His Sovereignty's majesty and His perfect Wisdom to nothing?

TWENTY-SECOND WINDOW

Have We not made the earth a cradle, and the mountains masts? And We have created you in pairs. (78:6-8)

Look at the imprints of God's Mercy, how He revives the earth after its death! (30:50)

The earth is a head containing innumerable mouths with innumerable tongues, each of which has innumerable proofs testifying in innumerable ways to an All-Majestic One's necessary Existence and Unity, to One Who is All-Powerful over all things and knows everything, and to His sacred Attributes and All-Beautiful Names.

We consider the first creation of the earth: a rock stratum was created from matter in a fluid state and the layer of soil was created from rock. If it had retained its fluid form, it would have been uninhabitable. If it had remained as rock, hard like iron, it would not have been suitable for us. And so we know that an All-Wise Maker's Wisdom, One Who is aware of the needs of the earth's inhabitants, gave it its present form.

Afterwards, mountains were driven into the earth like masts in order to stabilize it or made to burst out from the interior of the earth so that they might provide an outlet for its internal quakes and so it could continue its duty and movements without diversion. Mountains also protect the earth's surface from the oceans' invasion. Furthermore, they are treasuries for the vital necessities of living creatures, air filters that purify the air of harmful gasses, store water, and are sources of necessary minerals. All these facts testify to an Absolutely Powerful, All-Wise, All-Compassionate One's necessary Existence and Unity.

So, O geologist, how do you explain this? Could chance have made this Divine ship a display of wonders, full of wonderful creatures? Can chance cause this ship to travel at an incredible speed without losing anything arranged on its surface? Look at the wonderful kinds of art on the earth's face. See how wisely elements [chemical substances and the universal elements of air, water, soil, and fire] have been charged with duties, how beautifully they look after the All-Merciful One's guests here at the command of the All-Powerful, All-Wise One, and hasten to serve them!

Among unique and wonderful works of art, consider those lines of embroidery on the earth's multicolored face that display striking instances of wisdom. See how He makes brooks and streams, seas and rivers, mountains and hills serve as dwellings and means of transport for His creatures and servants. In addition to these, populating the earth with countless plant and animal species with perfect wisdom and order, and causing it to prosper with life; and discharging those inhabitants in regular cycles from their duties through death, and regularly refilling it and reviving it after its death in a way analogous to the Resurrection are innumerable tongues that testify to an All-Powerful One of Majesty's necessary Existence and Unity, to an All-Wise One of Perfection.

In short, the earth's face exhibits the wonders of His Art, is an assembly arena of exquisite creatures, a thoroughfare for the troops of creatures, and a place of worship and dwelling for His servants. Being like the universe's heart, the earth shows a light of Divine Unity as broad as the universe.

So, O geographer! If you do not recognize God while the earth makes Him known via innumerable mouths containing infinite tongues, and if you submerge your head in the swamp of naturalism, consider the extent of your error. Becoming aware of the severe punishment you will thereby deserve, come to your senses. Raise your head from the swamp and say: "I believe in God, in Whose hand is the absolute dominion of all things!"

TWENTY-THIRD WINDOW

He has created death and life. (67:2)

Life is the Divine Power's most luminous and beautiful miracle, the Divine Unity's most brilliant and strongest proof, the most comprehensive and polished mirror reflecting the Eternally Besought One. Life makes known the All-Living and Self-Subsistent One with all His Names and essential Characteristics, for it is a compounded light formed by the manifestations of many Divine Attributes together, just as the seven colors are compounded in light and various medicinal substances in natural confections. Similarly, life is a reality compounded of many Divine Attributes' manifestations causing it to have many attributes. Some of these attributes develop through senses and become distinct. Most of them, however, make themselves felt through sentiments, feelings and emotions and are manifested as a result of life's "boiling."

Life also comprises providence, mercy, grace, and wisdom, which are the most substantial elements in maintaining and administering the universe. It is as if life brings them along wherever it goes. For example, when life enters a body, the Divine Name the All-Wise also shows Itself therein and builds and arranges that "nest" of life with perfect wisdom. The Names the All-Munificent and the All-Compassionate become manifest at the same instant, furnishing and decorating that nest in accordance with its needs, and, respectively, bestowing on it all kinds of favors to continue and perfect that life. And, the Name the All-Providing manifests Itself by supplying life with the material and spiritual nourishment necessary for its maintenance and flourishing, as well as by storing a certain amount of that nourishment in its body.

This means that life is like a focal point at which various Names or Attributes meet or, rather, are united into each other to form one entity. It is as if life is entirely knowledge while simultaneously being power, wisdom, mercy, and so on. Due to its comprehensive nature, life is a mirror to God's being the Eternally Besought that reflects the essential Characteristics of the Divine Being's Essence. For this reason, the Necessarily Existent One, the All-Living and Self-Subsistent, creates and shows life in the greatest profusion. He also concentrates all things around life to make them serve it, for life is entrusted with a very important duty.

It is not easy to be a mirror to God as the Eternally Besought One. The innumerable new lives and the spirits, which the essences or identities of lives, that we constantly witness being brought into existence instantly and from nothing show the necessary Existence, sacred Attributes, and All-Beautiful Names of the Necessarily Existent, All-Living and Self-Subsistent One, just as gleams of light show the sun. If you do not recognize the sun and admit its existence, you have to deny the light pervading daytime. In the same way, if you deny the Sun of Oneness, the All-Living and Self-Subsistent, the Giver of life and the One causing to die, you have to deny the existence of all living beings on this planet from their appearance to the earth's final destruction. You would have to admit to yourself that you are like the unconscious, most ignorant beings.

TWENTY-FOURTH WINDOW

There is no deity but He. All things are perishable except His "Face;" His is the sovereignty and to Him you are being brought back. (28:88)

Death is a proof of Divine Lordship to the degree of life, a very strong evidence of His Oneness. According to the meaning of: *He has created death and life* (67:2), death is neither total non-existence or extinction, nor absolute annihilation or decay without one who authors it. Rather, as discussed in The First Letter, it is a discharge from worldly service by an All-Wise Author, a change of place and bodily renewal, a freeing from duties, a release from the body's prison, a well-ordered work of wisdom. Just as the earth's lively face, as well as its creatures and animate beings, testify to an All-Wise Maker's necessary Existence and Unity, so do those living creatures bear witness through their death to an All-Living, All-Permanent One's Unity and Eternity. As such matters were explained in The Twenty-second Word, we will explain here only the following subtle point.

Through their lives, living beings testify to a Necessarily Existent One's Existence; through their death, they bear witness to an All-Living Permanent One's Eternity and Unity. For example, the face of the earth, which is an alive entity, shows the Maker through all of its features and orderliness. When it dies during winter and is covered with a white shroud, our view of its face is distracted or this wintry corpse of spring diverts our attention to the past and brings a broader spectacle to our eyes. In other words, all past springs, each a miracle of Divine Power covering the earth's face, urge the conviction that a new spring will come and that earth's face will be revived and refilled with living creatures. Thus, all past springs, as well as the earth's face [which has experienced cycles of life and death for millions of years] bear witness to the necessary Existence, Unity, Permanence, and Eternity of an All-Majestic Maker, an All-Powerful One of Perfection, a Self-Subsistent, All-Permanent One, so brilliantly and strongly and on such a vast scale, and present such clear proofs, that one cannot help but proclaim: "I believe in God, the One of Unity, the Unique."

According to the meaning of: *He revives the earth after its death*, just as this lively earth testifies to the Maker through spring, it also attracts attention to the Divine Power's miracles arranged on the two wings of time— the past and the future—through its death. In place of one spring it shows thousands. It also points to thousands of Power's miracles in place of just one. The testimony of one of those past springs is more decisive than that of the present spring, for all past springs have disappeared, together with their apparent causes, and been replaced by new ones like themselves.

This shows that apparent causes mean nothing, for an All-Powerful One of Majesty creates and dispatches them. However, He makes them dependent on certain causes due to His Wisdom. As for the earth's lively faces arranged in sequence in time to come, their witness is also more forceful, for they will be made while there is yet no sign of them. Each one will be original and, after being sent for definite duties, will be removed.

So, O heedless one about to drown in the swamp of naturalism, how can something without a wise and powerful hand reaching all past and future interfere with the earth's living face? Can chance and nature, which mean nothing like you [with respect to creating, sustaining, and causing to die) have a hand in this? If you want to be freed from this swamp, say: "Nature is no more than a notebook of Divine Power, and chance is the veil of a hidden Divine Wisdom that hides our ignorance," and draw close to the truth.

TWENTY-FIFTH WINDOW: A work of art shows an artist. Something born requires the existence of something giving birth. Being below implies being above. And so on. Like all relative things or qualities in pairs existing in relation to each other and requiring the existence of each other, the contingency of all that exists, whether the particular or the whole, shows necessity, for it is equally possible for something to exist or not exist. The being or becoming or being acted upon observed throughout the universe show activity. Their being created shows the activity of creating. Their observed multiplicity and composition necessitate unity. Necessity, acting, doing, creating, and unity demand the attributes of being necessary, active, creative, and one, all of which are not contingent, passive, multiple, composed, and created. Given this, all contingencies, actions, formations, creations, multiplicities, and compositions in the universe testify to a Necessarily Existent One, One doing whatever He wills, the Creator of all things, One and Unique.

In short, contingency shows necessity, being or becoming points to the act of doing or making, and multiplicity points to unity. In the same way, being created and provided, as observed in existence, point to the existence of the acts of making, creating, and providing. These, in turn, point to the existence of an All-Compassionate Maker, Who is the Creator and the All-Providing. This means that each creature, through the tongues of its hundreds of attributes, bears witness to hundreds of the Necessarily Existent Being's All-Beautiful Names. If this is not admitted, then all such qualities also must be denied.

TWENTY-SIXTH WINDOW[184]: The beauties and comeliness observed in creatures in the universe appear for a fixed period and then are renewed and refreshed after they disappear. This shows that they are some sort of shadows of an Eternal Beauty's manifestations. Just as sparkling troops of bubbles on a river's surface show that the bubbles are mirrors of a perpetual sun's rays, the rays of beauty glittering on creatures traveling in the flowing river of time point to and are the signs of an All-Permanent Beauty.

The earnest love inherent in the universe's heart also shows a Never-Ending Beloved One. As something that does not exist in a tree's nature has no place in its fruits, the solemn, transcendent love existing in humanity, the tree of creation's most sensitive and delicate fruit, shows that the universe contains true love, though in different forms and of different kinds. Such a true love in the universe's heart shows an Eternal, All-Beloved One.

The attractiveness, attractions, and attachments manifesting themselves in the universe's bosom show all alert and aware hearts that they issue from the attractiveness of an attractive, eternal truth. In addition, saintly people and those who can unveil hidden truths in creation, who form the most sensitive and enlightened group of beings, unanimously

---

[184] This Window concerns people of heart and love.

report that they receive an All-Beautiful One of Majesty's manifestations and are aware, through their illuminations and visions, that the All-Beautiful One of Majesty makes Himself known and loved. This testifies to the existence of a Necessarily Existent One, an All-Beautiful One of Majesty, and to His making Himself known by human beings. Also, the Pen of beautification and decoration working on the face of the universe and creatures shows the beauty of the Names of that Pen's Owner.

Thus the universe, through the beauty on its face, the love in its heart, the attraction in its bosom, the illumination and vision in its eyes, and the beauty and decoration it has as a whole, opens a pleasant, clear window. To the intellects and hearts that are alert and awake, it displays an All-Beautiful One of Majesty, a Never-Ending Beloved One, an Eternal All-Worshipped One—all of Whose Names are Beautiful.

So, O heedless one struggling in the darkness of materialism and illusions, in suffocating doubts and conjectures, come to your senses! Ascend in a way befitting humanity and look through these openings. See the grace and beauty of Oneness, obtain perfect belief, and be a true human being.

TWENTY-SEVENTH WINDOW

> God is the Creator of all things, and He is the Guardian (with power of disposition) over all things. (39:62)

Looking at visible things as causes and effects in the universe, we see that the greatest cause—by itself—cannot cause even the most insignificant thing to exist. Thus causes are only a veil, for there must be one who brings effects (things) into existence. Out of innumerable creatures, consider the human faculty of memory, located in a mustard-seed-sized place in a person's head. Despite its tiny size, it is so comprehensive that it contains a book, or rather a library, in which his or her entire life-history is recorded.

What cause can you present as the origin of that miracle of Divine Power? The brain's entangled nerves? The cell's simple, unconscious atoms or particles? The winds of chance? In reality, that miracle of art can only be the work of such a One, an All-Wise Maker that, in order to remind us in the Hereafter's Supreme Place of Gathering of what we did in this world, He copies our deeds' register and gives it to our intellect as memory.

Compare all eggs, seeds, and fruit pits to our memory, and then compare all other effects to these tiny miracles of Power. Whatever effect or thing you look at, you will see that it contains such a wonderful artistry that if not only its own cause but all causes were gathered together, they would display their impotence in front of it. For example, supposing the sun, thought by some to be a huge cause or agent, were conscious and had willpower, if you asked it to make a fly's body, it obviously would answer: "Thanks to my Creator's grace, my shop contains a great deal of light and heat and several colors. However, a fly's body contains eyes, ears, life, and other things that are not in my shop or within my capacity."

A thing's amazing art and decoration refute causes (as accounting for its existence) and point to the Necessarily Existent Being, the Producer of all causes—according to the meaning of: *To Him alone is the whole of the affair referred* (11:123)—and acknowledge Him as the true Originator of all things and events. Similarly, the results, purposes, and benefits connected to things show that they are products (of the Acts) of an All-Munificent Lord, an All-Compassionate, All-Wise One acting behind the veil of causes.

Since unconscious causes cannot pursue a purpose, how can we explain the fact that every creature comes into existence for many definite purposes and benefits, and according to many instances of wisdom? The only answer is that an All-Wise and All-Munificent Lord brings them into existence, and makes those benefits the reason for their existence.

Consider the coming of rain. Rain's apparent causes have no consideration or concern for animate beings. Therefore it is sent to help animate beings through the Wisdom of an All-Compassionate Creator Who creates and then provides for them. Rain is called "mercy," for it bears many results of mercy and brings many benefits. It is as if mercy is embodied in raindrops and falls in drops.

The show and embellishment in all adorned plants and animals, which smile at all creatures, also point to an All-Majestic Being's necessary Existence and Unity and to the One Who, behind the veil of the Unseen, wills to make Himself known and loved through that adornment and embellishment. All of this points to the qualities of making known and loved, which, in turn, testify to the necessary Existence and Unity of One All-Known, All-Loving, and All-Powerful Maker.

In short, causes are infinitely ordinary and impotent when compared to effects (things), which are full of art and valuable. So how can they have any real part in creation? Also, the benefits of things and the purposes pursued through and for them deny causes any real role in creation, for they attribute their existence to an All-Wise Maker. Moreover, their decorations and the skills apparent in their coming into existence point to an All-Wise Maker Who wills to make His Power known to conscious beings, Who wills to be loved.

O helpless one who deifies causes! How do you explain these important realities? Why do you deceive yourself? If you are a rational being, tear the veil of causes apart and, proclaiming: "He is One, without partner," be saved from innumerable illusions.

TWENTY-EIGHTH WINDOW

> Among His signs are the creation of the heavens and the earth and the variety of your tongues and colors. Surely in this are signs for those who know. (30:22)

We see an all-inclusive wisdom and ordering in the universe, from a body's cells to the entire creation. When looking at a body's cells, we see a significant organization and arrangement by the command and law of the One Who sees and governs all bodily functions and needs. Just as some nourishment is stored up in the body in the form of fat to use in case of need, so there is the same kind of storage facility in the cells. We also see a wise organization, cultivation, and nursery in plants; a generous subsistence and breeding in animals; and a majestic management and illumination in the universe's pillar-like parts, each of which serves important purposes. We see the entire universe to have been perfectly planned and ordered as a country or a city or a palace for certain sublime instances of wisdom and exalted purposes.

As explained and argued in the First Station of The Twenty-second Word, these facts make it impossible to associate any partners with God. From the tiniest particles to the largest stars, everything is intertwined and interrelated in such a way that one who does not subjugate and manage stars cannot dominate a particle. In order to dominate a single particle, one must be able to subdue and manage all of the stars. Also, as explained and argued in the Second Station of The Twenty-second Word, one who cannot create the heavens and put them in an exact order cannot give anyone a unique face. One unable to be a lord over all the heavens cannot inscribe the heavenly mark on the face of an individual which distinguishes him or her from others.

All of this forms a window as large as the universe so that, if we look through it, both the person's and the mind's eye see clearly that the meanings of: *God is the Creator of all things and He is a Guardian (with power of disposition) over all things. His are the keys of the heavens and the earth...* (39:62-63) are inscribed on the pages of the universe in capital letters. Those who do not see them have no eyes or heart, or only appear to be human.

TWENTY-NINTH WINDOW

> There is nothing but it glorifies Him with His praise. (17:44)

Once during spring, I was traveling amid thoughts and feelings of loneliness. At a hill's base, I saw a yellow wild flower that reminded me of similar flowers I had seen in the past in my hometown and other places. It then struck me whose stamp that flower was, whose seal and inscription it was, all similar flowers on the earth's face were His stamps and seals. This thought led to the idea that just as a letter's seal announces the one who wrote and sent it, so is that flower a seal of the All-Merciful One, and that hill, which has been worked with such inscriptions and "lines" of meaningful plants [and sealed with that flower], a letter of that flower's Maker.

The hill in itself is also a seal, and the plain ahead of it is a letter of the All-Merciful One [sealed with it]. These thoughts led to the following truth: Each thing, being like a seal of the Lord, attributes all things to its Creator and proves that it is a letter of its Author. Thus each thing forms such a window on Divine Unity that it submits all things to a Unique One of Unity's ownership. This is especially true of living things, each of which contains such a wonderful design and miraculous art that the One Who makes it so and designs it so meaningfully is also the One Who makes all things. This means, one who cannot make everything cannot create one thing.

O you who are unaware of the reality of things, look at the universe's face! Who can deny the testimony of the pages of creatures, all of which are like innumerable letters of the Eternally Besought, one within the other? Who can deny the testimony of the seals put on them to Divine Unity? What power can silence them? If you listen to any of them with your heart, you will hear it say: "I bear witness that there is no deity but God."

THIRTIETH WINDOW

> Had there been deities in them (the heavens and the earth) other than God, both would certainly have fallen into ruin. (21:22)

> All things are perishable except His "Face;" His is the sovereignty and to Him you are being brought back. (28:88)

This window is the window of all theologians who base their arguments on the facts that all things are contingent (not absolutely necessary) and have come into existence over time. They follow this way in proving the Necessarily Existent One's Existence. Referring their detailed explanations to such voluminous scholarly books as *Sharhu'l-Mawaqif* and *Sharhu'l-Maqasid*, we will try to reflect a few rays coming to the soul from the light of the Qur'an through that window, as follows:

Authority and sovereignty do not allow rivalry, partnership, or interference. If a village had two headmen, its order and peace would be destroyed. A district or town with two governors would experience great confusion, and a country with two kings (or governments) would be in constant turmoil. Since these pale shadows of absolute authority and sovereignty enjoyed by powerless people who are not self-sufficient reject rivalry and the intervention of their opposite, consider how strongly true Sovereignty, in the form of supreme, absolute Kingdom and Authority at the degree of Divine Lordship enjoyed by an Absolutely Powerful One, rejects interference and partnership. This means, Oneness and absolute Independence without partners is the most indispensable and constant requirement of Divinity and Lordship.

The universe's perfect order and most beautiful harmony testify to this. There is such a perfect order in the universe from a fly's wing to the heavens' lamps that our minds prostrate before it in amazement and admiration, declaring: "All-Glorified is God! What wonders God has willed! God bless it!"

If there were any room for associating partners with God to interfere with Him, according to the meaning of: *Had there been deities in them (the heavens and the earth) other than God, both would certainly have fallen into ruin* (21:22), order would be destroyed and the universe's form and shape would change. But, as stated in: *Look yet again: can you see any rifts? Then look again and yet again, your sight will fall back to you dimmed and dazzled, and awed and weakened* (67:3-4), however hard we look for a flaw in creation, our gaze will return exhausted and inform our fault-finding reason: "I have exhausted myself in vain, for there is no flaw." This shows that the order is perfect, which means that this perfect order testifies to God's Oneness.

Given that the universe came into existence contained in time and so is not eternal, theologians argue:

> The world is subject to change. Anything subject to change has a beginning and came into existence within time and is time-bound. Anything that came into existence within time has someone who brought it into existence. That being the reality, this universe has an Eternal Creator.

We say:

> The universe certainly has a beginning, for it came into existence within time. For we see one world replaced by a new one every century, every year, even every season. Thus there is an All-Powerful One of Majesty Who invents and creates a new world every year, every season, or even every day.

After showing it to conscious beings, He replaces it with a newer one. He makes these worlds succeed each other, attaching them to the string of time in a series. It is surely the Power of an All-Powerful One Which creates this series of renewed worlds in this way. The One Who does this obviously created the universe. He has made this universe and the earth a guest-house for those mighty guests.

As for contingency, theologians argue:

Contingency means equality between two possibilities. That is, if it is equally possible for something to come into existence or not, there must be one to prefer either possibility, one to create according to this preference, for contingent beings cannot create each other one after the other. Nor can they go back to eternity in cycles with the former having created the latter. Given this, there is a Necessarily Existent Being Who creates all.

Theologians have disproved the chain of creative cause and effect, as well as the notion of successive creators, with twelve decisive arguments, some of which they call "argument in ascension" and "argument in steps." Breaking the chain of cause and effect, they have proved the Necessarily Existent Being's Existence.

We say: Rather than showing the impossibility of the chain of cause and effect in creation or the cycle of successive creators to prove the necessary Existence of a Creator Who has no beginning and has created all things, it is better and easier to show the stamp on everything belonging to the Creator of all things. Through the Qur'an's enlightenment, all the Words and the Windows in this Word follow this principle. Even though the subject of contingency embraces a broad range of arguments to display the Necessarily Existent Being's Existence in innumerable ways, the subject does not need to be restricted to the way theologians treat it. Rather, it opens up innumerable ways to knowledge of the Necessarily Existent Being. For example, when each thing hesitates amidst innumerable possibilities concerning its existence, being, features, qualities, and lifespan, we see that it follows a well-ordered, well-established way so that it acquires the most appropriate body, and that it is equipped with the qualities necessary for its existence, as well as for all the state, conditions, and features it will experience during its life. This is through the will of One Who assigns to everything its specialties, through the choice of One Who chooses, and through the creation of a wise Creator Who directs it for wise purposes along its unique way.

He then clothes it with befitting features and qualities and makes it a part of a composite entity, which increases the possibilities before it, for it is equally possible for it to have a place in that entity in thousands of ways. However, it is positioned in the most appropriate way so that it can perform the fruitful and purposeful duties expected of it. The entity then becomes part of a larger entity, which multiplies possibilities still further. Just like before, it is positioned so that it can carry out its important duties. This accurately and decisively demonstrates an All-Wise Director's necessary Existence and shows that things are directed through an All-Knowing Authority's command.

A private has certain duties and specially determined services to perform in relation to his squad, company, battalion, regiment, corps and army, and wisely arranged relations specific to each. Likewise, a cell in your eye's pupil has a certain relation to your eye and then to your head, veins, nervous system, and body as a whole. It also has duties apportioned to it wisely in relation to each. If it did not perform its least duty, you would become ill and the body would suffer.

Thus, just as each creature proclaims a Necessarily Existent One via its being, features, body, form, and attributes, each one also proclaims its Maker in other tongues when positioned in different larger and larger composite entities. With respect to its services and duties in each entity, it bears witness to the All-Wise Maker's necessary Existence, Will, and Choice. For only the Creator of all composite entities, Who positions a thing in such a way that the wise relations between them are maintained, can do such things. This means that one thing testifies to Him in thousands of tongues. As a result, such testimonies of the Necessarily Existent Being's Existence far surpass the number of the creatures in the universe. In fact, they reach the number of possible qualities, features, forms, positions, and duties assigned to each, as well as the relations they maintain in the composite entities in which they are located.

So, you who are unaware, just how deaf do you have to be not to hear this testimony filling the universe? What do you say?

THIRTY-FIRST WINDOW

Surely We have created humanity of the best stature as the perfect pattern of creation. (95:4)

On the earth there are signs for those who seek certainty, and also in your own selves. Will you not then see (the truth)? (51:20-21)

This window is the window of humanity and opened from the inner aspect of its being. As detailed explanations are available in the books of numerous saintly scholars, we will mention only a few fundamentals we have obtained from the Qur'an's enlightenment. As explained in The Eleventh Word and others, each human being is such a comprehensive copy (of existence) that God Almighty makes all of His Names perceived by the individual through his or her self. Referring the details to other Words, here we will discuss only the following three points:

FIRST POINT: Human beings are mirrors to the Divine Names in three aspects:

First aspect: Just as the night's darkness suggests light, humanity points, through its weakness and impotence, destitution and neediness, imperfection and defects, to an All-Powerful One of Majesty's Power, Force, Wealth, Mercy, and so on. Thus each person becomes a mirror to many of God's Attributes. Moreover, searching for a point of support against countless obstacles and hostilities in our infinite weakness and impotence, our conscience is always turned toward the Necessarily Existent Being. Besides, our infinite destitution and neediness compel us to look for a point of seeking assistance in order to realize our innumerable aims, and so our conscience has recourse to the Court of an All-Compassionate, All-Wealthy One, and we petition Him for our needs. Thus, with respect to our need for a point of support and a point of seeking assistance, two small windows open from each person's conscience onto the All-Compassionate All-Powerful One's Court of Mercy, through which we can look to Him.

Second aspect: Each of us has a specific God-given knowledge, power, sight, hearing, ownership, and sovereignty. As a result, we function as a mirror to the (Attributes of) Absolute Knowledge, Power, Sight, Hearing, and Ownership of the universe's Owner and His Lordship's sovereignty. Each person understands them and makes them known. For example: "I built this house and know how to build it. I own, see, and manage it. So this huge palace of the universe must have a builder who knows, sees, and administers it."

Third aspect: Each person functions as a mirror to the Divine Names inscribed upon him or her. As stated at the beginning of the Third Station of The Thirty-second Word, the inscriptions of more than seventy Divine Names are apparent in our comprehensive nature. For example, our creation manifests the Names the Maker, the Creator, and the Giver of form. By being of the best stature as the perfect pattern of creation, we demonstrate the Names the All-Merciful and the All-Compassionate. Our good sustenance and upbringing display the Names the All-Munificent and the All-Gracious. All our bodily systems and parts, members and organs, faculties and features, and senses and feelings display different inscriptions of different Divine Names. Just as there is the Greatest Name among the Divine Names, the greatest among the inscriptions of the Names is humanity.

If you know yourself to be human, read yourself. Otherwise, you may remain human only in appearance.

SECOND POINT: This relates to a significant mystery of God's Oneness—His being One as displayed by the concentrated manifestations of His certain Names on individual beings. It is as follows:

Each person's spirit has a unifying function in regard to his or her body, that it causes all bodily members and parts to help each other. In other words, the spirit, a conscious law of Divine Command issuing from Divine Will and a faculty breathed into each of us by God and clothed in a perceptible existence, is not confused by the signals coming from all bodily elements and meeting their needs simultaneously. Distance or nearness are irrelevant, and bodily organs do not prevent each other from communicating with it. When necessary, the spirit can send most bodily elements to help a single one or move all bodily parts at once. It also can know, perceive, and govern through any of them. If it has refined and purified itself, thereby acquiring sufficient luminosity, it can see and hear through any bodily part.

Seeing that the spirit, a law of Divine Command, displays such abilities in our bodies—*The highest comparison is (and must be set forth) for God*— the Necessarily Existent Being cannot be confused by countless actions, sounds and voices, invocations and deeds in the universe, which is the macrocosm. His universal Will and absolute Power deal with all of them all at once and without confusion, for the All-Majestic Creator sees all things and hears all sounds and voices. As distance has no meaning for Him, He can send, if He wills, all things to help one thing.

THIRD POINT: Life has a very significant nature and important duty. Since this has been detailed in the Twenty-third Window as well as The Twentieth Letter's Eighth Phrase, we recall here only the following point: The interwoven embroideries that life has profusely in the form of complex senses, feelings and sentiments point to many of God's Names and function as clear mirrors to the All-Living, Self-Subsistent One's essential Characteristics and Acts. Since it is not appropriate to discuss this matter before those who deny God and belief in Him, we stop here.

THIRTY-SECOND WINDOW

He it is Who has sent His Messenger with the Divine guidance and the Religion of truth that He may make it prevail over all religions. God suffices for a witness. (48:28)

Say: "O humankind! Surely I am the Messenger of God to you all, for Whom is the sovereignty of the heavens and the earth; there is no deity but He. He gives life and causes to die." (7:158)

This window is formed of the Prophet Muhammad, the sun of the heaven of Messengership, indeed, the sun of suns, upon him be peace and blessings. Having explained this most brilliant, large and light-diffusing window in great detail in the Nineteenth and Thirty-first Words, as well as in The Nineteenth Letter, we discuss only the following point:

On the wings of Messengership and sainthood, that is, equipped with a power formed of the absolute consensus of all Prophets preceding him and the unanimous agreement of all saints and pure scholars to come after him, Prophet Muhammad, himself an articulate proof of Divine Unity, proclaimed and demonstrated Divine Unity throughout his life with all his strength. He opened up onto knowledge of God a broad and radiant window, namely the world of Islam. Hundreds of thousands of pure, truth-seeking and truthful scholars like Imam al-Ghazzali, Imam ar-Rabbani, Muhyid-Din ibnu'l-'Arabi, and 'Abdu'l-Qadir al-Jilani look through this window and point others to knowledge of God through it. Is there a veil to draw across such a window? Can one who criticizes this window and does not look through it be considered sensible? You give the answer.

THIRTY-THIRD WINDOW

All praise and gratitude are for God, Who has sent down on His servant the Book and has allowed therein no crookedness. (18:1)

Alif Lam Ra. A Book which We have sent to you so that you may lead humankind forth from all kinds of darkness to light. (14:1)

Consider that all the previous Windows are a few drops from the ocean of the Qur'an and try to understand how many lights of Divine Unity, like water of life, there are in the Qur'an. Even if you have a simple, superficial look at the Qur'an, which is the source and mine of all those previous Windows, still it is a most shining, luminous, comprehensive Window. To understand how brilliant and luminous that Window is, you may refer to the Treatise of the Qur'an's Miraculousness, which is the Twenty-fifth Word, and the Eighteenth Sign of the Nineteenth Letter. Supplicating the Throne of Mercy of the All-Majestic Being, Who sent us the Qur'an, we say:

Our Lord, take us not to task if we forget or make mistakes! Our Lord, do not let our hearts to swerve after You have guided us! Our Lord! Accept from us, surely You are the All-Hearing, the All-Knowing. Accept our repentance, surely You are the One Who accepts repentance and returns it with liberal forgiveness, the All-Compassionate.

A note

I hope this Thirty-third Word with thirty-three windows may help an unbeliever to accept belief, and that it may strengthen the belief of one whose belief is weak, and lead one with strong belief based on imitation to have substantial belief, and then to expand that substantial belief. I hope that it may lead one with expanded belief to progress in knowledge of God, which is the source of all kinds of true progress and evolution, and open up before him more luminous, more brilliant scenes. For this reason, you should not regard one window to be sufficient for you, because even if your mind has received its share and obtained conviction, your heart will also demand its share, as will your spirit. Even the imaginative faculty will demand its share from that light. It is because of this that each window has benefits of its own.

The Treatise on the Ascension of the Prophet Muhammad, upon him be peace and blessings, primarily addressed the believer, while the materialist was in the position of listener. But this treatise addresses the denier, and the believer is in the position of listener. This should be considered when studying it.

Unfortunately, because an important reason, this letter was written very speedily and has remained in the state of the first draft. Therefore, there will certainly be some flaws of expression, which are due to me. I request my brothers to look at it with tolerance, and correct it if they are able, and pray for my forgiveness.

Peace be upon those who follow the true guidance. May those who follow their whims and illusions receive what they deserve.

All-Glorified are You. We have no knowledge save what You have taught us. Surely You are the All-Knowing, the All-Wise.

O God, bestow blessings and peace upon him whom You sent as a mercy for the worlds, and upon his Family and Companions. Amin.

Gleams of Truth

Gleams of Truth

Flowers from the Seeds of Truth from between the Crescents of Ramadan and the 'Iyd Day

This is a short "*Mathnawi*" on Islamic belief, thought, and action for students of the *Risale-i Nur*.

NOTE: In both its composition and subject-matter, this collection is unlike other mathnawis or compilations of poetry. It bears the title *Lemeat* (Gleams of Truth) and was written in order to explicate, to some degree, the writer's previous work, *Hakikat Çekirdekleri* (Seeds of Truth); moreover, it is in prose form and does not contain entertaining images or unbalanced emotions. It was written as scholarly instruction for some of the students of Bediüzzaman, including his nephew, who was with him at the time of writing; in it are included the truths of the Qur'an and belief, entirely in accordance with logic. This is a lesson about the Qur'an and belief. As our master himself said, and as we can understand, Bediüzzaman had no predisposition to verse or poetry, and did not occupy himself with them.

Working for two or two and a half hours every day, Bediüzzaman wrote this work in versified form (though it was not poetry); the work was completed in twenty days during Ramadan. At that time, he was a member of the *Darü'l-Hikmeti'l-İslamiyye* ("The House of Islamic Wisdom"), and had numerous preoccupations. Although it was dictated "extempore" and completed very quickly, the work was not edited and was published as it was. In our opinion, it is a wonder, on account of its relation to the *Risale-i Nur*. No other compilation of poetry seems to be as remarkable as this one is, as easy to read as prose. God willing, this work will become a sort of Mathnawi for students of *Risale-i Nur*. It acts as a form of index for the *Risale-i Nur*, or a forerunner for it, as the *Risale-i Nur* appeared ten years later and was completed over twenty-three years.

The *Risale-i Nur* students,
Sungur, Mehmed Feyzi, Hüsrev

REMINDER: AS THE SAYING GOES: "A PERSON IS HOSTILE TO WHAT THEY do not know." I have thought a great deal about poetry and rhyming simply because I do not know much about them. I have never wanted to change the reality of what I mean to fit into the demands of poetry. So, in this book, I have dressed sublime truths in an inelegant garment that is bereft of rhyme or meter.

In the first place, I do not know any better way and am only thinking of conveying the meaning. Secondly, I wanted to give form to my criticism of those poets who chisel the body to suit the clothes. Thirdly, a childish style such as this is preferable and more suited to occupy the carnal soul and heart during Ramadan. But, my reader, I must confess I have made a mistake and want to alert you to avoid making the same – do not be misled by the poor style into being carelessly disrespectful of its exalted truths!

AN EXCUSE: O Reader! I confess at the beginning that I have worried about my abilities in the art of writing and versification. As for verse and rhyme, I had never been able to produce even one poem. But suddenly I felt a desire to put things in verse, a desire which has persisted. There is an epic in Kurdish about the expeditions of the Companions called *Qawl-i Nawala Sisaban*. My spirit enjoyed its natural cadence, which is similar to a hymn. So I chose to use its verse form, but in a way particular to myself. I made a composition which somehow resembled verse, although I took no pains with the meter. Anyone who wishes may read it as easily as prose, without thinking of its verse-like form. Indeed, it would be better to consider it as prose so that the meaning can be better understood. The verses of each section are interrelated in respect of meaning. Readers should not ask about rhyming. A fez can be without a tassel, and meter can be without rhyme, verse without rules. I think that if a composition draws attention to itself through its artistry, the mind is preoccupied then with the art. Therefore, a composition is better when artless, thus not distracting attention away from the meaning.

My teacher in this work was the Qur'an, my book was life, and the one I addressed was myself. And you, my reader, are an eavesdropper. Eavesdroppers have no right to criticize; they must take what pleases them and ignore what they do not like. It is my hope that the readers' tongues will utter a prayer of forgiveness for me, or recite a *Fatiha*, God willing.

The Supplicant

I am a ruined grave, in which are piled up
Seventy-nine dead Saids with his sins and sorrows.
The eightieth is a gravestone for this grave;
All together they weep at the decline of Islam.
Together with my gravestone and the moaning grave of dead Saids
I advance toward my abode of tomorrow.
I am fully certain that the heavens and earth of the future
Will together surrender to Islam's clear, shining hand.
For its strength lies in its belief and blessings,
It affords peace and security to all beings.

In the Name of God, the All-Merciful, the All-Compassionate.

All praise and gratitude are for God; and may God's blessings be upon the master of the Messengers and upon him Family and Companions, altogether.

Two supreme proofs of Divine Unity

With whatever is in it, the universe is a supreme proof; with its tongues of the unseen and manifest worlds, it declares God's Unity and glorifies Him. Announcing the Unity of the All-Merciful, it continuously proclaims:

There is no deity but He!

All the atoms of its cells, all its parts and members, are tongues mentioning God. Together they pronounce in that resounding voice:

There is no deity but He!

The tongues are infinitely various, the voices are of differing pitch, but they are united on one point—the mention of Him, saying:

There is no deity but He!

The universe is the macro-human; it mentions God in a loud voice, while all its elements and atoms add to that loud voice their tiny voices, declaring in unison:

There is no deity but He!

The universe is a circle of God's remembrance, reciting the Qur'an section by section. Its light comes from the Qur'an, and all beings with spirits reflect on the truth:

There is no deity but He!

The Qur'an, this Mighty, Glorious Criterion of Truth and Falsehood, is the most articulate proof of Divine Unity. All of its verses are truthful tongues, and rays from the lightning of belief. All together they declare:

There is no deity but He!

If you attach your ear to the bosom of that Criterion, in its profoundest depths you will hear clearly a heavenly voice which recites:

There is no deity but He!

Its voice is utterly exalted, utterly solemn, truly sincere, most friendly, utterly convincing, and equipped with proofs. Repeatedly it declares:

There is no deity but He!

All the six aspects of this proof of light are transparent: upon it is the flower and stamp of miraculousness and in it shines the light of guidance, which says:

There is no deity but He!

Beneath it lies subtly interwoven logic and proof; on its right the intelligence or reason is made speak and the mind completely affirms it, saying:

There is no deity but He!

On its left, identical to the right, the conscience is produced as a witness; before it lies pure good and its aim is happiness and prosperity, the key of which at every instant is:

There is no deity but He!

Its support beyond it, identical to "before it," is heavenly, pure Divine Revelation. All these six aspects are luminous and manifested in the sign of each is:

There is no deity but He!

Can any lurking suspicion, any conceivable, piercing doubt, any treacherous deviance sneak into that resplendent, shining castle with its lofty walls of suras, every word of which is an angel uttering:

There is no deity but He!

The Qur'an of mighty stature is an ocean of Divine Unity. To take a single drop as an example from that ocean, look at only a single, slight allusion out of the short sura, *Suratu'l-Ikhlas*; there are innumerable allusions: its six phrases, three positive, three negative, refute all kinds of attribution of partners to God and prove Divine Unity in its seven aspects:

THE FIRST PHRASE: *Say, He*: it is a clear indication of Him, requiring no evidence. That is, it defines Him without considering Him with

His Names, Attributes, and acts. This definition indicates Him directly. That is:

There is no "he" but He!

This is an allusion to the experiential affirmation of Divine Unity. When a truth-seeing view becomes immersed in Divine Unity, it says:

There is nothing observed but He!

THE SECOND PHRASE: *God, the absolutely One, the Unique* is an explicit affirmation of God's Unity as the Divine Being or of His Divinity. Reality declares in the tongue of truth:

There is nothing to be worshipped but He!

THE THIRD PHRASE: *God, the Eternally Besought One.* This is the shell of two pearls of Divine Unity. The first is God's Unity as the Lord (of all creation). The order of the universe declares:

There is no creator but He!

The second pearl is God's Unity as the Self-Subsistent, by Whom all subsist. The universe in its entirety declares through the language of absolute need for an Author, an Ultimate, Creative Cause, both for its coming into being and its continued existence:

There is no self-subsistent, by whom all subsist, but He!

THE FOURTH PHRASE: *He begets not.* This indicates God's Unity as the All-Majestic One. It rejects all kinds of attribution of partners to God, and decisively refutes unbelief. That is, one who is subject to change or production or division can be neither Creator, nor Self-Subsistent, nor Deity.

The negating *not* (*lam* in the Arabic) decisively refutes the idea of begetting for the Divine Being. This kind of attribution of partners to God (that is, accepting paternity for the Divine Being) has made the majority of humankind sinful. It has given rise to creeds such as Jesus, Ezra, angels, or "the ten intellects" are offspring of the Divine Being.

THE FIFTH PHRASE: *Nor is He begotten* indicates God's Unity as the All-Eternal. That is, one whose existence is not necessary, pre-eternal, or uncontained by time cannot be God. That is, one who came into existence within time, or was born of matter, or descended from a progenitor, cannot be the universe's Refuge and Protector.

The attribution of existence to causes (causality), the worship of stars, idolatry, and naturalism are all varieties of associating partners with God, all pitfalls of misguidance.

THE SIXTH PHRASE: *And comparable to Him there is none* is a comprehensive phrase that expresses all aspects of Divine Unity. That is, the negating *is none* refers to God having no like, partner, or peer either in His Essence, or in His Attributes, or in His acts.

In meaning, each of these six phrases is both the result and proof of the others; proofs in sequence and the results arising from them in order are included in this sura to construct it as a fortress.

That is to say, included in *Suratu'l-Ikhlas*, appropriately to its stature, are thirty-six suras the parts of which are set in order to form both proofs and results of one another; this single sura is the horizon at which the thirty-six suras rise.

None knows the Unseen save God

Causes are purely apparent

Divine Grandeur and Dignity require that natural causes are, in the view of reason, a veil before the Hand of Power;

At the same time Divine Unity and Majesty require that natural causes have no hand in the coming into existence of the works of Power.

Existence is not restricted to the physical world

The unbounded forms of existence cannot be confined to this visible world; it cannot contain them;

The physical world is but a lace veil over the radiating worlds of the Unseen.

The universality of the Pen of Power demonstrates Divine Unity

The faultless works of art explicitly refute the creativity of causes at every point of origination;

The inscriptions of the Pen of Power necessarily reject the existence of intermediaries at every point of creation.

Nothing can exist without the existence of everything

Throughout the universe there is harmony and solidarity that is both concealed and observable—both in the inner and outer aspects of existence.

Both this solidarity and the cooperation—mutual assistance or reciprocal answering of needs—demonstrate that only an all-encompassing Power could do this: thus an atom is created and situated in a way appropriate for all its relations.

Every line and word of the book of the universe is animated; need urges them toward each other and acquaints them with each other.

Wherever it comes from, every call for help receives response: in the name of Divine Unity, all the surroundings are moved to help it in its need.

Every living word has a face that is turned and an eye that looks to all the sentences.

The sun's motion is for gravity and gravity provides the stability of the solar system

The sun is a fruit bearing body; it shakes itself so that its fruit—which are mobile—do not fall.

If it were to stop moving and come to rest, then gravity would cease and its ecstatic followers would scatter through space and weep.

Small things are interconnected to larger things

Certainly, the one who has created the eye of a mosquito has created both the sun and the Milky Way.

And the one who has ordered the flea's stomach doubtlessly has set in order the solar system.

Also, the one who has given sight to the eye and need to the stomach has certainly adorned the eye of the sky with the kohl of light and spread a feast over the face of the earth.

There is a supreme miraculousness in the order of the universe

See, there is miraculousness in the organization of the universe; if to suppose the impossible all natural causes were agents that are able to do whatever they will,

They would, confessing their utter impotence in the face of this miraculousness, prostrate before it and declare: "All-Glorified are You! We have no power! Our Lord, You are the Eternal, All-Powerful One of Majesty!"

Everything is equal before the Divine Power

> Your creation and your resurrection are but as (the creation and resurrection of) a single soul. (31:28)

The Divine Power is essential to and inherent in the Divine Essence; impotence cannot access It.

There can be no degrees in Divine Power, nor can any impediment in any way obstruct It. Whether they be universal or particular, all things are the same in relation to It.

For everything is interconnected to and interdependent on everything else; one who cannot make everything can make nothing.

One who cannot hold the universe in his hand cannot create a particle

If one does not have a hand that is powerful enough to lift the earth, the suns, and the stars—those innumerable bodies—and string them in order like prayer-beads,

And place them on the head and breast of endless space, they cannot claim to create anything in the world; they have no right to claim to have invented anything.

Raising a species to life is the same as raising an individual to life

Just as revivifying a fly that has gone numb in the death-like sleep of winter is not difficult for the Divine Power,

Likewise, neither the death of the earth nor its resurrection will pose any difficulty for the Divine Power.

Nor will the raising to life of all beings with spirits present any greater problem.

Nature is Divine art

Nature is not the printer, it is something printed;

It is not the inscriber, but the inscription; it is not the doer or the agent, it is the recipient; it is not the source, but the pattern.

It is not the one who orders, it is the order; it is not the power, but the law; it is a set of laws that issue from the Divine Attribute of Will; it is not a reality that has a materialized self-existence.

The conscience recognizes God through its attraction

In the conscience there is an attraction, an infatuation; the conscience feels that it is constantly attracted by the pull of an attractive force.

If the All-Beautiful, Gracious One was to manifest Himself permanently without a veil, conscious beings would be overcome with ecstasy.

The consciousness—the human conscious nature—testifies decisively to a Necessarily Existent One, One of Majesty and Beauty and Grace;

The feeling of attraction is a testimony, and so too is the feeling of being attracted.

The innate disposition given by the Creator speaks the truth

A thing's innate disposition or God-given nature does not lie; whatever this innate disposition says is the truth. Given an inclination to grow, the tongue of the seed says: "I will sprout and yield fruit," and what it says is proven true.

The inclination toward life murmurs in the depths of the egg: "If God wills, I will be a chick." What it says is true.

If a handful of water intends to freeze inside an iron cannon-ball when it is cold enough,

The inclination to expand within it says: "Expand! I need more space." This command cannot be resisted.

Strong iron sets out to work, and does not prove it wrong; the water's truthfulness and honesty split the iron.

All these inclinations are Divine creational commands and each is a Divine decree. They are all Divine laws of creation and life, all manifestations of Will.

Divine Will directs all beings in this way: all inclinations conform to the commands of the Lord.

The Divine manifestation in the conscience is the same; the feeling of attraction and the feeling of being attracted are two pure "souls;"

They are two polished mirrors in which are reflected the eternal Beauty and the light of belief.

Prophethood is essential for humankind

The Divine Power, Which does not leave ants without a leader or bees without a queen

Surely would not leave humankind without a set of laws or a Prophet. The order of the universe self-evidently demands this.

The Ascension was for the angels what the splitting of the moon was for humankind

The angels saw in the Prophetic wonder of the Ascension a supreme sainthood within the undeniable Prophethood.

That shining person mounted *Buraq* (carrying him to heaven) and was like lightning; like the traveling moon, he saw the world of light throughout.

In the same way for humanity, which is scattered through this visible world, *And the moon split* (54:1) was an important, observable miracle;

So for the dwellers in the world of spirits, the Ascension, pointed out in, *All-Glorified is He, He took His servant for a journey by night...* (17:1) was the greatest miracle.

The proof of the affirmation of faith is within it

The affirmation of faith contains two sentences, each of which testifies to the other; one is an argument and proof for the other.

The first is the a priori argument for the second, and the second is the a posteriori argument for the first.

Life is a manifestation of unity

Life is a light of unity through which unity is manifested in this realm of multiplicity. Truly, a manifestation of unity unifies multiplicity, thus making it a unified entity.

Life causes a single thing to own all things together, while for a lifeless thing all things are non-existent.

The spirit is a law clothed in external existence

The spirit is a luminous law clothed in external existence and endowed with consciousness.

This spirit, which has a real, sensible existence, has become the brother, the companion, of that perceptible law.

Like established, constant natural laws, the spirit comes from the world of the Divine Command and the Attribute of Will.

The Power clothes it in a being with senses, attaches consciousness to its head, and makes an astral body the shell for that pearl.

If the Creator's Power were to clothe the laws operating in species in external existence, each would become a spirit;

If the spirit was stripped of external existence and consciousness, it would become an undying law.

Existence without life is like non-existence

Both light and life are the causes for beings to reveal themselves and be known. See, if there is no light of life,

Existence will be stained with non-existence; indeed, it is like non-existence. Even if it is the moon, it is a stranger and an orphan, unless it has life.

Thanks to life, an ant is greater than the earth

If you were to weigh an ant on the balance of existence, the universe to emerge from it could not be contained in our earth.

In my view, the earth is living. But if, according to what others suppose, you were to take the lifeless earth and place it in the other pan to the ant,

It would not amount to even half of the conscious head of the ant.

Christianity will follow Islam

Christianity will either become extinct or purified. It will surrender to Islam and give up arms.

It was fragmented repeatedly until finally Protestantism appeared, but it was unable to find there what was necessary to rectify it.

The veil was again rent, it fell into absolute misguidance. However, a part of it approached the affirmation of Divine Unity; in that it will find salvation.

It is preparing to be torn again. If it does not become extinct, Christianity will be purified and join Islam.

In this lies a mighty mystery to which the Pride of the Messengers alluded when he said: "Jesus will come and follow my Shari'a; he will be of my Community."

A partial or indirect view sees the impossible as possible

It is a well-known incident: a large group of people were scanning the horizon for the crescent moon to establish the beginning of the 'Iyd, but no one could see anything.

Then an aged old man swore that he had seen it. But what he had seen was a curved white eyelash.

The eyelash became his crescent moon. But how can a curved eyelash become the crescent moon? If you have understood our parable:

The motion of atoms has become the eyelash over your reason – a dark eyelash that blinds the materialist eye.

It cannot see the One Who has formed all species of beings, so misguidance comes upon you.

How can that motion replace the One Who has created and ordered the universe? It is a compounded impossibility to suppose the former to be the latter.

The Qur'an requires mirrors, not someone to act as a deputy

Rather than rational arguments, it is the sacredness of the source which encourages the mass of the Muslim Community and the common people to obey it and urges them to follow it.

Ninety per cent of the Shari'a is comprised of the obvious, indisputable matters and essentials of Religion, each of which is a diamond pillar.

The matters which are open to interpretation, controversial and secondary, only amount to ten per cent. One who has these ten gold pieces cannot own the ninety diamond pillars or put them in their purse, nor can they make them dependent on the gold pieces.

The source of the diamond pillars is the Qur'an and Hadith. The pillars are their property and should always be sought in them.

Books and interpretations of the Shari'a should be mirrors of the Qur'an or telescopes through which the Qur'an is examined. That sun of miraculous exposition does not need shadows or anyone to act on its behalf!

The falsifier of the truth adopts the false as true

Since by nature humans are noble, their purpose is to find the truth. However, sometimes falsehood comes to their hands, and supposing it to be the truth, they keep it in their breast pocket.

While digging out the truth, misguidance comes upon them involuntarily; supposing it to be the truth, they wear it on their head.

The mirrors of the Divine Power are numerous

The Power of the All-Majestic One has numerous mirrors. They open up windows, each more transparent and subtle than the other, all looking onto the World of Representations or Ideal Forms.

Various mirrors from water to air, air to ether, ether to representations or ideal forms, ideal forms to spirits, spirits to time, time to imagination, and from imagination to the mind, all represent the manifestations of God's acts. Turn your ear to the mirror of the air: a single word becomes millions!

The Pen of Power makes copies in an extraordinary way; this is the mystery of reproduction...

There are various sorts of representation

The image or reflection in a mirror is one of four sorts: it is either only the identity or the physical form of the thing reflected; or the identity together with the essential, living attributes; or both the identity and a ray from the thing's nature; or both the nature and the identity.

If you desire examples: a human being, the sun, the angel, and the word. The images of solid things in mirrors are moving dead forms.

The images of a luminous body in its reflections are living and connected to it; even if it is not the spirit itself or identical to it, they are none other than this.

They are each an expanded light. If the sun had been a living being, its heat would be its life, and its light, its consciousness—its image in the mirror has these qualities (i.e., it has both heat and light).

This explains the following mystery: Archangel Gabriel is both at the Lote-tree[185] and in the Prophet's Mosque in the form of Dihya[186] at the same instant—and who knows in how many other places!

Also, God knows how many places Azra'il can be present in simultaneously, taking the spirits of the dying.

At the same time, the Prophet appears to his Community both in the visions of the saints and in true dreams;

And on the Place of the Supreme Gathering on Judgment Day he will meet with all to intercede on their behalf.

The "substitutes" (abdal) of saints appear and are seen in numerous places at the same instant.

---

[185] The Lote-tree of the furthest limit (Sidratu'l-Muntaha in the Qur'an, 53:14); it signifies the boundary between the realm of Divinity and the realm of creation. (Tr.)

[186] Dihyatu'l-Kalbi was one of Prophet Muhammad's Companions. Archangel Gabriel sometimes came to the Prophet in his form. See, al-Bukhari, "Manaqib" 25; Muslim, "Iman" 271. (Tr.)

One qualified to make ijtihad may deduce a new law for himself, but he cannot be a law-giver

Anyone who has the competence to practice *ijtihad* may deduce new laws for himself in matters about which there are no explicit verdicts in the Qur'an or Sunna; these are binding on that person, but not on others.

He cannot make laws and call on the Muslim Community to obey them. His conclusions are regarded as belonging to the Shari'a, but they cannot be included in the Shari'a as being binding on all Muslims. He may be a mujtahid, but he cannot be a law-giver.

It is only the consensus of the majority of scholars which bears the stamp of the Shari'a. The first condition for calling on others to accept an idea is acceptance by the majority.

Otherwise, such a call is innovation and must be rejected; it is kept in the throat, and must not be uttered!

The light of reason comes from the heart

Unenlightened intellectuals should know this principle: an idea cannot be enlightened without the light of the heart.

As long as the ray of the mind has not been combined with the light of the heart, the result is darkness, oppression and ignorance. It is darkness dressed up in a false light.

Your eye has a white part, which resembles daytime, but it is blind and dark. But there is a pupil in it, which is dark like the night, but illuminated.

Without the pupil, that piece of flesh is not an eye, and you can see nothing. An eye without insight is also worth nothing.

So, if the dark pupil of the heart is not present in the white of thought, the contents of the mind will produce no knowledge or insight. There can be no reason or intellect without the heart.

The levels of knowledge in the mind are variable and can be confused

There are levels of knowledge in the mind that can be confused with one another and whose results are different. One first imagines something, then conceives of it, and clothes it in a form.

Afterwards, one reasons and reflects on this thing, then confirms it, and then has full conviction of it. Then they fully support it; then they become committed or devoted to it.

Your commitment is different, and so is your support, each of which results in a different state or attitude:

Steadfastness arises from commitment or devotion, while adherence comes from support or advocacy. Compliance proceeds from conviction and partiality from reasoning, while no ideas are formed at the level of conception.

If you remain at the level of imagination, the result will be sophistry. A beautiful, scenic description of falsehood and deceptive things will both injure and mislead simple minds.

Undigested knowledge should not be imparted to others

The true, scholarly guide is like a sheep, not a bird; they provide knowledge altruistically.

For the sheep gives its lamb digested food in the form of pure milk, whereas the bird gives its chick regurgitated food.

Destruction is easy, thus the weak are destructive

The existence of something depends on the existence of all its parts, while its non-existence is possible through the non-existence of one of its parts; thus, destruction is easy.

It is because of this that the impotent person never inclines to do or produce something positive or constructive that will show their power and capability; they act negatively, and are always destructive.

Force must serve right

If the principles of wisdom, laws of the state, precepts of right, and rules of force do not help or support one another,

They will neither be fruitful nor effective among the mass of the people. The marks or public symbols of the Shari'a will be neglected and fall into abeyance.

They will no longer be a point of support for people in their affairs, and people will no longer have confidence in or rely on them.

Sometimes opposites contain opposites

Sometimes opposites conceal their opposites within them. In the language of politics, the words are the opposites of their meanings.

Tyranny has donned the cap of justice. Treachery has found a cheap dress in patriotism. Jihad and war for God's sake have been labeled aggression and a violation of human rights. Enslavement to animal passions and the despotism of Satan have been called freedom.

Things have become their opposites, forms have been exchanged, names have been swapped, positions and ranks have changed places.

Politics based on self-interest is bestial

The politics of the present, which is based on self-interest, is a rapacious beast.

If you show love to a ravenous beast, you will not attract its compassion, but will rather sharpen its appetite.

Then it will turn on you and demand from you payment for the use of its claws and teeth.

Since human faculties have not been restricted in creation, their crimes are great

Unlike the animals, the faculties of human beings have not been restricted in creation; the good and evil that proceed from them know no limits.

If the selfishness that issues from one faculty and the egotism that proceeds from another are combined with haughtiness and obstinacy, such sins will be committed that no name has as of yet been found for them.

As these sins are proofs of the necessity of Hell, so too their penalty can only be Hell.

For example, in order to justify just one of his lies, a man desires, from his heart, the downfall of Islam.

The present time has shown that Hell is not unnecessary and Paradise is not cheap.

Sometimes good leads to evil

While in reality the merits of the elite should give rise to modesty and self-effacement in them, regrettably they have led to arrogance and oppression.

And while the destitution of the poor and the poverty of the common people should serve (as they do in reality) as means to arouse compassion and graciousness toward them, unfortunately they have now resulted in the abasement and servitude of the common people.

If honor and merit result from something, it is offered to the elite and leaders. But if vice and evil proceed from it, it is divided and distributed among the common people or employees and servants.

If a victorious tribe has won some honor, congratulations are offered to its Hasan Agha (the chief); but if some harm is obtained thenceforth, every curse is poured upon the members of the tribe. This is a sorry evil among humankind!

The absence of an objective strengthens egotism

If people have no goals to pursue, or if the main objective is forgotten or neglected, the minds turn to individual egos and revolve around them.

The ego thus becomes inflated, sometimes swelling with anger; it is not "pierced" or deflated so that it might become "we." Those who love themselves love no other.

A life of revolutions has sprung from the death of Zakah and a life of usury

The origin of all revolutions, all anarchy and corruption, the root and source of all evils, vices, and corrupt traits, can be summed up in two short phrases:

The first is: "I am full, so what is it to me if others die of hunger?" And the second: "You suffer so I may be comfortable. You work so that I may eat. Food is for me, laboring is for you."

There is one single cure for the lethal poison of the first word, which will sever it at the root and heal the situation:

That is the Zakah which is established by the Shari'a, a pillar of Islam. In the second word is a tree of Zaqqum; what will uproot it is the prohibition of usury and interest.

If humankind desires salvation and loves its life, it must impose Zakah and abolish usury and interest.

If humankind prefers life, it must put to death usury of every sort

The bond of human relation that extends from the elite to the common people has been severed. So from below (the lower social strata) arise the cries of revolution, the shouts for revenge, the screams of grievance and envy.

From above descend fires of tyranny and scorn, the thunder of arrogance, and the lightning of oppression.

What should arise from below are love, respect, and accord. And from above should descend compassion and assistance, kindness and consideration.

If humankind desires these, it should hold fast to the *Zakah* and abandon usury and interest.

The Qur'anic justice stands at the door of the world, saying to usury and interest: "No entry! You have no right to enter!" They should retreat from this door and disappear from the world.

Humankind has not heeded this command and has thus received a severe blow; people should heed this call now before receiving another, more severe blow.

Humankind has demolished slavery; it will demolish wage-earning as well

In a dream I said the less severe wars between nations and states make way for fiercer wars between the social classes.

For in previous eras, humankind did not approve of slavery and crushed it with its blood. Now it has become a wage-earner; at the moment humanity is putting up with this burden, but this too will be crushed.

Humankind has grown old, having passed through four stages (of social progress): savagery, nomadism, slavery, and colonialism; now we are in the fifth age, that of wage-earning, but this too is passing.

An unlawful way leads to the opposite of what was intended

The murderer cannot inherit (from the one whom he has murdered); this is a very significant principle: "Someone who follows an unlawful way (in Islam) to reach his goal generally attains the opposite of what they intended in retribution."

Love of (the second) Europe is not a lawful love in view of the Shari'a; it is a blind imitation and disagreeable friendliness. Its consequence and recompense is the tyrannical hostility of the beloved and its crimes.

The sinner condemned to loss will find, in the end, neither pleasure nor salvation.

There is a grain of truth in both the Jabriyya and the Mu'tazila

O seeker after truth! The past and calamities, and the future and sins are not the same in the view and consideration of the Shari'a.

The past and calamities are considered from the perspective of Divine Destiny; for this, the fitting word is that of the *Jabriyya*, (who refer every event to Destiny).

Human accountability is taken into consideration about the future and sins; for this, the fitting word is that of the Mu'tazila, (who deny the role of Destiny in human actions). The Mu'tazila and Jabriyya are reconciled here.

There is a grain of truth in both of these false schools. Each has a particular situation; falsehood arises from a generalization that goes beyond a particular situation.

Only the incapable seek solace in impotence and complaints

If you want life, do not cling to impotence for things which have no solution;

If you want ease of mind, do not have recourse to regretful complaints about things for which there are no solutions.

Sometimes little things have greater outcomes

There are some circumstances in which a little action raises the performer of the action to the highest of the high;

Then there are circumstances where a slight action sends its doer to the lowest of the low...

For some people a moment is a year

Some innate capacities develop in an instant, while others are gradual, unfolding little by little. Human nature contains both of these.

They depend on conditions, and change accordingly. Sometimes they develop gradually. Sometimes they are like gunpowder – dark, suddenly exploding into glowing fire.

Sometimes a look transforms coals into diamonds. Sometimes a touch can change a stone into elixir.

A single look from the Prophet transformed an ignorant nomad into an enlightened one of knowledge in an instant.

If you want a comparison: 'Umar before Islam, and 'Umar after Islam.

Compare the two: a seed and a tree. The seed instantaneously produced fruit. That look of Muhammad, the grace of the Prophet, upon him be peace and blessings,

Suddenly transformed the coal-like natures in the Arabian Peninsula into diamonds. He enlightened characters that were as black as gunpowder; they all became shining lights.

A lie is a word of unbelief

One grain of truth burns a million lies. A grain of reality destroys a castle of dreams. Truthfulness is a supreme principle, a shining jewel.

If speaking the truth may cause harm, silence can be preferred; but there is never a place for lies, even if they appear to have some use.

Whatever you say must be true, whatever judgment you give must be right, but you have no right to voice all that is true.

One should be well aware of this, and adopt it as one's principle: "Take what is clear and untroubled, leave what is turbid and distressing."

See the good side of things, so that you will have good thoughts. Know things to be good and think of them as good, so that you will find pleasure in life.

In life, hope and thinking well of things is life itself, while despair and thinking ill of others is the destroyer of happiness and killer of life.

In an assembly in the World of Representations or Ideal Forms

Comparisons between the Shari'a and modern civilization,
and between scientific genius and the guidance of the Shari'a

In a true dream on a Friday night at the beginning of the period of truce following World War I, I was asked by a supreme assembly in the World of Representations and Ideal Forms:

"What will emerge in the Muslim world following the defeat?" I replied, as the representative of the present age, and they listened to me:

From the times of its foundation, this State saw itself as duty-bound to sacrifice itself for the Islamic world and as the standard-bearer of the Caliphate,

And accordingly it undertook jihad, a collective religious obligation, to maintain Islamic independence and exalt the Word of God.

Over time, the calamity that has struck this State, this Muslim nation, will certainly bring prosperity and freedom to the Muslim world.

This present disaster will be compensated for in the future. One who loses three and gains three hundred in return makes no loss. As a zealous laborer, they change their present for a better future.

For this calamity has aroused compassion and Islamic solidarity and brotherhood, the yeast or catalyst of our lives, to an extraordinary degree; it has given a wonderful impetus to our brotherhood.

The present civilization, which is in fact meanness, will change form, and its system will be demolished; it is then that an Islamic civilization will emerge. Muslims will certainly be the first to enter it voluntarily.

If you want a comparison between the civilization of the Shari'a and the present one, closely examine the principles of each and consider their consequences:

The principles of present-day civilization are negative. Its foundations and values are five negative principles. Its machinery is based on these.

Its point of support and reliance is might or force rather than right, and the basic characteristic of force is aggression and hostility, from which treachery arises.

Its goal is, instead of virtue, the gratification of mean self-interest, the essential characteristic of which is conflict and rivalry, and the consequence of which is crime.

Its law of life is conflict rather than cooperation and mutual helping; the essential characteristic of conflict is contention and mutual repulsion; the consequence is poverty.

Its basic bond between peoples is racism or racial discrimination, which develops to the detriment of others; it is nourished and strengthened by the right of others being devoured.

Negative nationalism or racism paves the way for constant, terrible clashes, disastrous collisions; the result is destruction.

The fifth is this: the enchanting service of the present civilization excites lusts and passions, facilitating the gratification of animal desires; the consequence is dissipation.

The basic characteristic of lusts and passions is always this: they transform humans into beasts, changing their character; they deform them, perverting their humanity.

Most of these civilized people—if you were to turn them inside out—would appear as apes and foxes, snakes, bears, and swine. Their characters have appointed their forms. They appear to the imagination in their furs and skins!

By contrast, the Shari'a, is the balance of the earth. The mercy in the Shari'a comes from the heaven of the Qur'an. The principles of the Qur'anic civilization are positive. Its mechanism for happiness turns on five positive principles:

Its point of support and reliance is right instead of might and the unchanging characteristic of right is justice and balance, which give rise to salvation, security and well-being, removing wretchedness and villainy.

Its aim is virtue instead of self-interest and the basic character of virtue is love and mutual attraction. Happiness arises from these, and enmity disappears.

Its principle in life is cooperation instead of conflict and killing, and the essential characteristic of cooperation is unity and solidarity; these enliven the community.

In place of lust and passion, its form of service is guidance and the essential characteristic of guidance is progress and prosperity in a way that is befitting to humanity, as well as enlightenment and perfection in a way that is required by the spirit.

While racism and negative nationalism destroy the point of unity among the masses, the bonds the Shari‘a establishes between peoples are those of religion, citizenship, profession, and the brotherhood of belief.

The basic characteristics of these bonds are sincere brother/sisterhood, and general salvation, security and well-being. The Shari‘a only demands self-defense in the case of external attacks.

Now you have understood why Muslims have remained distant from the present civilization without adopting it.

Up to the present, Muslims have not entered this present civilization voluntarily, it has not suited them; rather, on them have been clamped the fetters of bondage.

While it should have been the cure for humankind, this civilization has become the poison. It has cast eighty per cent of the population into destitution and misery and given false happiness to ten per cent.

The remaining ten per cent has been left uneasy, stranded between the two. The profits that come from trade have gone to the tyrannical minority. But true happiness is the happiness shared by all, or at least salvation for the majority. The Qur'an, revealed as a mercy for humankind, only accepts civilization of the kind

That brings happiness to all, or at least to the majority. In the present civilization, passions are unrestricted, impulses and fancies too are free; this is an animal freedom.

Passions dominate people, impulses and fancies too are despotic; they have made unnecessary needs essential ones, and banished ease and relief.

While in primitive life a person was in need of four things, civilization has made them needy of a hundred, and impoverished them.

Lawful labor is insufficient to meet the cost. This has driven humanity towards fraud and the unlawful. It is due to this that civilization has corrupted the essence of morality.

It has given certain wealth and glitter to society and the human species, but it has made the individual immoral and indigent. There are numerous testimonies to this.

All of the savagery and crimes in former times and all the cruelty and treachery have been vomited by this malignant civilization all at once, and its stomach is still retching.[187]

The fact that the Islamic world is able to remain aloof is both meaningful and noteworthy. It has been reluctant to accept this civilization, and has acted coldly.

Truly, the distinguishing quality of the Divine light in the illustrious Shari'a is independence and self-sufficiency.

It is due to this quality that the light of guidance has never allowed the genius of Rome, the spirit of (European) civilization, to dominate it.

The guidance of the Shari'a cannot be combined with the philosophy of the latter, nor be grafted onto it, nor follow it.

The compassion and the dignity of belief to be found in the spirit of Islam, and the truths of the Shari'a which it has nourished—the Qur'an of miraculous exposition has been taken the truths of the Shari'a in its shining hand;

Each of these truths of the Shari'a is a Staff of Moses in that shining hand. In the future that sorcerer civilization will prostrate in wonderment before it.

Now, note this: there were two geniuses—Ancient Greece and Rome, those twins from a single stock. One was imaginative, the other materialist.

Like water and oil, they never combined. Such a phenomenon required time, civilization strove to do so and Christianity tried, but none has been able to combine them.

---

[187] That is, the civilization will vomit more terribly. It has vomited in the form of the two world wars in such a fashion that it has soiled the air, ground, and sea, staining them with blood.

Both preserved their partial independence. They have remained as if two spirits (in a single body); now they have changed their bodies; one has become German, the other French.

They have experienced a sort of reincarnation. O my dream-brother! This is what time has shown. Those twin geniuses have rejected any moves to combine them;

They are still not reconciled. Since they are twins, they are brothers and friends, companions in progress; but they have fought and never made peace.

How could it therefore be that the light of the Qur'an and the guidance of the Shari'a, when it has a completely different source, origin, and place of appearance, is reconciled with the genius of Rome, the spirit of modern civilization, and should join and combine with it?

That genius and this guidance – their origins are different: guidance descends from the heavens, genius emerges from the earth. Guidance works in the heart and genius works in the mind.

Genius works in the mind and confuses the heart. Guidance illuminates the spirit, making its seeds sprout and flourish; dark human nature is illuminated by it.

The capacity of guidance for perfection suddenly advances; it makes the carnal soul a docile servant; it gives zealous and endeavoring humans an angelic countenance.

As for genius, it focuses its attention primarily on the carnal soul and physical being; it comes into nature, making the soul an arable field and the carnal potentials develop and flourish;

It subjugates the spirit, causing the seeds to dry up; it displays satanic features in humankind. But guidance gives happiness to both lives—this and the next—and spreads light in both this world and the next, elevating humankind.

Genius, like Antichrist blind in one eye, sees only this life and this world; it is materialist and world-adoring. It turns humans into beasts.

Genius worships deaf nature and serves blind force. But guidance recognizes the conscious Art (manifested as nature) and turns to the wise Power (that gives existence to nature). Genius draws a veil of ingratitude over the earth while guidance scatters the light of thanks.

It is because of this that genius is deaf and blind, while guidance is hearing and seeing. In the view of genius, the bounties of the earth are ownerless booty;

It prompts the desire to usurp and steal them thanklessly, to savagely snap them off from nature.

In the view of guidance, the bounties scattered over the breast of the earth and the face of the universe are the fruits of Mercy; it sees a gracious hand beneath every bounty, and has kissed it in gratitude.

I cannot deny that there are numerous virtues in civilization, but they are neither the property of Christianity, nor the invention of Europe.

Nor are they the product of this century; they are the common property of humanity, produced as the result of the conjunction of thoughts and studies over time, from the laws of the revealed religions, and emerge out of innate need,

And particularly from the Islamic revolution brought about by the Shari'a of Muhammad. No one can claim ownership of these.

> The leader of the assembly from the World of Representations asked another question:

QUESTION: "Calamities are always the result of treachery but pave the way for reward. O man of the present century! Divine Destiny has dealt a blow and Divine Decree has passed sentence.

"What did you do so that both the Divine Decree and Destiny have so judged you – that the Divine Decree has sentenced you to this calamity and given you a beating?

"It is always the error of the majority which causes general disasters."

I said in reply:

ANSWER: Humankind's misguided thinking, Nimrod-like obstinacy, Pharaoh-like haughtiness grew and grew on the earth until they reached the heavens. Humanity also offended the sensitive mystery of creation.

It caused the shudders of the last war to pour down from the heavens like the plague and deluge; it caused a heavenly blow to be dealt to the infidel.

This means, the calamity was the calamity of all humankind. The common cause, inclusive of all humankind, was the misguided thinking that arose from materialism – bestial freedom, the despotism of carnal desires and fancies.

Our share in it resulted from our neglect and abandonment of the pillars of Islam. For the Creator the All-Exalted wanted one hour out of the twenty-four.

He ordered us, willed that we, for our good, assign one hour for the five daily Prayers. But out of laziness we gave them up, neglected them in heedlessness.

So we received the following punishment: He made us perform Prayers of a sort during these last five years through a constant, twenty-four hour drill and hardship, keeping us ceaselessly moving and striving.

He also demanded of us one month a year for fasting, but we pitied our carnal souls, so in atonement He compelled us to fast for five years.

He wanted us to pay as *Zakah* either a fortieth or a tenth of the property He gave us, but out of miserliness we did wrong: we mixed the unlawful with our property, and did not give the *Zakah* voluntarily.

So He had our accumulated *Zakah* taken from us, and saved us from what was unlawful in our property. The deed causes the punishment of its kind. The punishment is of the same as the deed.[188]

Good, righteous acts are of two sorts: one positive and voluntary, the other negative and enforced. All pains and calamities are good deeds, but they are negative and enforced. The *hadith* that tells us of this offers consolation.[189]

This sinful nation has made its ablutions in blood; it has repented with deeds. As an immediate reward, four million, a fifth of this nation, were

---

[188] I did not mention the *Hajj* in the dream, for neglect of the *Hajj* and its wisdom drew not calamity, but Divine Wrath, and the punishment it incurred was not atonement for our sins but an increase in our sins. It was the neglect of the elevated Islamic policy, which exists in the *Hajj* and brings unity of views through mutual acquaintance and cooperation through mutual assistance, and it was neglect of the vast social benefits contained in the *Hajj* which have prepared the ground for the enemy to employ millions of Muslims against Islam. Those were Indian Muslims! Thinking that he was their enemy, they killed their father (the Ottoman State), and now they are weeping beside his dead body. There are the Tatars and the Caucasian peoples! They understood that the one in whose killing they had collaborated with the enemy was their poor mother, but it was too late! They are weeping at her feet. These are the Arabs! They mistakenly killed their heroic brother, and now in their bewilderment they do not even know how to weep. These are the Africans! They killed their brother unknowingly, now they are lamenting. This is the Muslim world; it heedlessly helped the enemy kill its standard-bearing son, now it is pulling its hair out, groaning and lamenting. Instead of hastening to the *Hajj* eagerly, which is pure good, millions of Muslims have been made to make long journeys under the enemy flag, which is pure evil. Ponder on this and take heed!

[189] The Pride of humankind says: "In whatever circumstance a believer is, it is to his good. This is not so for anyone other than believers. For if something happy happens to him, he thanks God, and this is to his good. If some harm touches him, he remains patient, and this also is to his good." (*Muslim*, "Zuhd" 64; ad-Darimi, "Riqaq" 61.) (Tr.)

raised to the degree of sainthood through the rank of martyrdom or warring for God's sake; this wiped out their sin.

The elevated assembly from the World of Representations appreciated these words.

I woke up suddenly; rather, this was a meeting in true wakefulness before I went to sleep. In my view, wakefulness is a dream and a dream is a sort of wakefulness.

There I was the representative of this age, and here I am Said Nursi!

Rust-covered guidance is still a diamond

The guidance of Islam has rusted, while the genius of the present civilization has been gilded with desires and passions.

Even if a peerless diamond has rusted, it is always preferable to a gilded piece of glass. That diamond has been engraved with a heavenly inscription; the eyes of materialists do not see that peerless inscription; nor can they read it.

Materialists seek everything in matter; their intelligence is in their eyes, they are blind to whatever is spiritual, for bodily eyes are blind to that.

Ignorance takes a metaphor for a fact

If a metaphor falls from the hand of knowledge to that of ignorance, it is transformed into fact, and opens the door onto superstition.

During my childhood I saw an eclipse of the moon. I asked my mother, and she said: "A snake has swallowed it." I asked her: "Why is it visible, then?" She said: "The snakes there are semi-transparent."

A metaphor like this is perceived as a reality: At a Divine command, with the earth interposing between the points of intersection of the orbit of the moon and the sun, known as "the head" and "the tail," the moon is eclipsed.

The two hypothetical arcs that are formed and resemble two snakes were called "Tinninayn (two snakes)." The name was invented to explain an astronomical event figuratively and came to be taken to be in reality that with which it had been compared.

Exaggeration is implicit denigration

Whatever you describe, describe it as it really is. In my view, exaggerated praise is implicit denigration.

Seeing and showing someone or something as having more than what God has favored them with is, essentially, not a favor to them.

Fame is oppressive

Fame is a despot; it ascribes the property of others to the famous.

Of the witticisms attributed to the famous Nasreddin Hoja,[190] only its *zakah*, that is, one-fortieth or at best one-tenth, can belong to him.

The imaginary renown of Rustam-i Sistani plundered an age of the glories of Iran.

His legendary image plundered the heroism of others, and was combined with superstition, thus carrying Rustam beyond the limits of humanity.

Those who suppose the Religion and life to be separable are the cause of disaster

The mistake of the Young Turks[191] was that they did not know that our Religion is the basis of our life; they thought the nation and Islam were different from one another.

They imagined the present civilization would endure and dominate, and saw the happiness of life and prosperity as lying within it.

Now time has shown us that the system of civilization is corrupt and harmful;[192] unequivocal experience has taught us this:

The Religion is the very life of life, its light and its foundation. The revival of this nation is possible only through the revival of the Religion. Muslims have understood this.

In contrast to other cultures, our nation is able to progress to the extent that we adhere to our Religion. It has declined to the degree we neglected it.

This is a historical fact, which we have pretended to forget.

Death is not as terrifying as imagined

It is an incorrect, misguided supposition that makes death terrifying. Death is a change of clothes, or a change of places. It leads from the dungeon to garden.

---

[190] Molla Nasraddin or Nasreddin Hoja was a thirteenth-century Muslim figure who was famous and remembered for his wisdom, legendary wit, funny stories and anecdotes. (Tr.)

[191] The Young Turks were biased toward modern Western currents of thought and against the Ottoman administration. They struggled particularly against the government of Sultan Abdulhamid II. (Tr.)

[192] This refers to the oppressive, anti-religious civilization, which is moving towards its demise.

Whoever desires life should desire martyrdom. The Qur'an tells us that the martyrs are living. Martyrs, who do not experience the pangs of death, know and see themselves to be alive.[193]

But they find their new lives to be purer. They do not suppose that they have died. Note carefully the difference between them and the dead; it is as the following:

In a dream two persons are walking in a beautiful garden where there is every sort of delight. One knows it is only a dream and receives no pleasure from this.

It gives him no contentment; rather it fills him with regret. However, the other one knows that they are awake, and experiences true joy; this is real for them.

The dream is the shadow of the World of Representations, which is the shadow of the Intermediate Realm. It is due to this that their principles are like one another.

Politics is diabolical in people's minds; one should seek refuge in God from this

Modern politics sacrifices the minority for the comfort of the majority. Worse than this, the despotic minority sacrifices the majority of people for itself.

Qur'anic justice never sees the life of a single innocent person as being expendable; it never allows an individual's blood to be spilled, even for all humankind, let alone for the majority in a particular jurisdiction.

The verse, *He who kills a person unless it be (in legal punishment) for murder… will be as if he had killed all humankind* (5:32), lays two mighty principles before our eyes.

One is pure justice. This sublime principle is that just as the individual and the community are equal in relation to the Divine Power, the Divine Justice also sees no difference between them.

---

[193] The Qur'an declares: *And say not of those who are killed in God's cause: "They are dead." Rather they are alive, but you are not aware* (2:154). *Do not think at all of those killed in God's cause as dead. Rather, they are alive; with their Lord they have their sustenance, rejoicing in what God has granted them out of His bounty, and joyful in the glad tidings for those left behind who have not yet joined them, that (in the event of martyrdom) they will have no fear, nor will they grieve. They are joyful in the glad tidings of God's blessing and bounty (that He has prepared for the martyrs), and in (the promise) that God never leaves to waste the reward of the believers.* (3:169-171). (Tr.)

This is a permanent, established Divine and Prophetic principle and practice. An individual may sacrifice their rights themselves, but the law cannot sacrifice them, not even for all humankind.

The canceling of one's rights, or the spilling of one's blood, or the annulment of one's innocence is equal to the canceling of the rights of all of humanity, or the annulment of the innocence of all of humankind.

The second principle is this: if a self-centered person can murder an innocent person out of greed or passion, he may destroy the whole world if capable of that, should it be an obstacle to the fulfillment of his desires, and annihilate all humanity.

Weakness emboldens the enemy; God may try His servants, but they cannot try Him

O fearful, weak one! Your fear and weakness are futile and harmful to you; they embolden external influences and draw them toward you.

O you who suffer from doubts and delusions! A sure benefit should not be renounced for fear of potential harm. What you need is to take action; the outcome is with God.

One cannot interfere in God's concerns. He takes His servant to the arena of trial and says: "If you do that, I'll do this."

But the servant can never try God. If he says, "Should God give me success, I'll do this," he is transgressing his limits.

Satan said to Jesus: "Since it is He Who does everything, and His Destiny does not change, then throw yourself down off the mountain, and see what He will do with you."

Jesus replied: "O accursed one! God's servants cannot put Him to the test!"[194]

Islamic politics should proceed from Islam; politics should not be instrumental for others; partisanship causes hearts to be divided, not united

The politics of Istanbul at the present time resembles the Spanish flu, infecting people; indeed, it sometimes causes delirium.

---

[194] Ibnu'l-Jawzi, *Talbisu Iblis*, p. 344.

Political madness is the product of a Byzantine (i.e. deceitful and clandestine) mindset; politics does not go round and round by itself; rather it does so by means of an external orientation.

Europe hypnotizes politics and whispers in its ears. Thus, one can say a play is being staged here.

As the whisper comes from outside, if it is negative, it has, like individual letters, no value in itself; it is only beneficial when combined with others.

Our free will no longer has a part in it, so even if we are well-intentioned, our good intentions are of no use.

If the external whisper is positive, its value, like words in a sentence, is first for itself, and then, indirectly, for others.

The political divergences here go in opposite directions, and they have no point of intersection in the country; it is not possible for them to come together anywhere on the entire face of the wide earth.

Since this is so, those who take a positive, constructive way should be educated and follow knowledge. As the weak ones or the minority cannot guard the Qur'an, the powerful hand or the majority should guard it.

They should love and adhere to it, for the Religion cannot be used negatively or for a negative result. The 31-March Event[195] showed this.

It showed that even the least negative use of the Religion in the homeland yields a terrible result. Muslims came out of this as losers.

Do not overdo those things you like

The cure for one ailment may be harmful to another; what is an antidote for one becomes poison for another. If the cure is taken to excess, it causes illness and becomes fatal.

The eye of obstinacy perceives an angel as a devil

Obstinacy causes one to behave in this way: if a devil helps or supports one or their side, they hail them as "an angel" and call down blessings upon them.

But if they see an angel on the opposing side, they view them as a devil in the guise of an angel, and they call down curses on them out of enmity.

---

[195] The 31 March Event was a revolt which broke out on April 13, 1909 in Istanbul. Its real nature and reasons have not yet been revealed. It resulted in the dethroning of Sultan Abdulhamid II and the coming into power of the Unity and Progress Party. (Tr.)

The catalyst of the life of a community is sound and sincere solidarity

A society in which there is solidarity is an instrument that has been created to stir up the inactive; while a community in which there is malicious envy is an instrument created to pacify the active.

If there is not a sound or sincere unity in a community, it will weaken as its numbers increase through mere population growth. It is like the multiplication of fractions. The number grows less in proportion to how many times they have been multiplied.

Even if non-acceptance is your right, refutation is not

O seeker after truth! If something is related to you (particularly concerning a truth of belief or in the form of a *hadith* (Prophetic Tradition),

What falls upon you is to accept it, if there is a proof for its accuracy. If there is not, you may avoid its acceptance, which is a doubt.

The non-existence of a proof is an argument for your non-acceptance of it, whereas your claim of its non-existence means refutation and denial, which requires proof.

Something which cannot be established with proof cannot be claimed to be non-existent without proof.

Non-acceptance of something's existence is usually confused with the acceptance of its non-existence, though one is doubt and the other, denial. You have no right to denial.

It sometimes happens that there are many phrases related to the same incident and which are intended to convey the same meaning, or the meaning is something that has numerous indications or arguments.

If one or even ten of these are doubted or refuted, the existence of the narration and the intended meaning cannot thereby be refuted.

One should follow the majority of Muslims

O seeker after salvation and security! A *hadith* indicates that we should follow and keep the company of the majority of Muslims.[196]

The *Umayyads* were, in the beginning, not careful to follow the Religion, but after they joined the majority of the Muslim Community, they were eventually included among the *Ahlu's-Sunna wa'l-Jama'a*.

---

[196] *Muslim*, "'Imara" 59; at-Tirmidhi, "Fitan" 7; *Abu Dawud*, "Salah" 46.

The *Shi'a* were careful and steadfast in adherence to the Religion in the beginning, but a portion of them who were in the minority eventually formed the sect of *Rafidis*.

This is a significant, noteworthy reality.

After finding what is right, do not cause discord for the sake of something better

O seeker after truth! If there is consensus concerning what is good and true, and seeking what is better and truer causes disagreement and discord, then what is true is truer than what is truer, and what is good is better than what is better.

Islam is peace and reconciliation; It wants no dispute or hostility within

O World of Islam! Your life lies in unity, and if you want unity, your guiding principle should be the following:

You should adopt the principle, "This is true," rather than "This alone is true;" and "This is the best," rather than "This is what is exclusively good."

Every Muslim should say about their own school and way: "This is true; I do not interfere with others. Even if the others are good too, mine is the best."

They should not say: "This alone is true, the others are all false. Only mine is good, the others are all wrong and unpleasant."

The mindset of exclusiveness arises from self-love. It eventually becomes a disease and leads to dispute.

If the existence of numerous ills and cures is a rightful reality, right will also multiply. The variation of needs and foods is right, and right becomes diverse.

The multiplication of capacities and education is right, and this right will also multiply. A single substance is both poison and the antidote.

The truth is not fixed in the secondary matters of the Religion; it is relative and compounded according to the differences of temperament and circumstance.

The temperaments of those responsible for the conduct of such matters have a share in them, and they are concluded and formed accordingly.

The founders of the schools of law made judgments in non-specific terms, leaving the specification of the limits of their schools to the various temperaments that followed.

Bigoted attachment to a school causes the rulings of that school to be generalized, and partisanship arising from this leads to dispute.

The deep rifts between the classes of humanity before Islam, and the great distance between peoples and places demanded the existence of numerous Prophets at any one time, and a variety of Shari'as, and numerous sects.

Islam caused a revolution among humankind, and peoples drew closer to each other. The different Shari'as were summed up in a single Shari'a, and there was one Prophet.

But the levels of humankind were not the same, so the schools of law multiplied. If a single system of training and education were sufficient and proper for all, then the schools could unite.

There is great wisdom in the creation and combination of opposites: the sun and a minute particle are equal in the hand of Power

O brother with an alert heart! The Power manifests Itself in the combining of opposites. There is pain in pleasure, evil within good, ugliness within beauty, harm within benefit, trouble within bounties, fire within light... do you know why this is so?

It is thus, so that relative truths may be established and so there may be many things within a single thing, and numerous various incidents of existence become apparent.

Swift motion makes a point look like a line. The speed of spinning makes a point of light look like a luminous circle.

There must be relative truths so that seeds may sprout in this world. These constitute the clay of the universe, the bonds of its order, the connections among its inscriptions. These relative realities will become truths in the Hereafter.

The degrees of heat are due to the existence of cold. The degrees of beauty come about through the intervention of ugliness. The apparent cause becomes as if the ultimate cause or raison d'être.

Light is indebted to darkness, pleasure is indebted to pain; there is no consciousness of health without illness.

If there was no Paradise, perhaps Hell would not be torment. Hell cannot exist without extreme cold. If there were no extreme cold (besides its heat), Hell would not burn.

The Ever-Living Creator has demonstrated His Wisdom in the creation of opposites and His Majesty has become apparent.

That Everlasting All-Powerful One has displayed His Power in the combining of opposites, and His Grandeur has become manifest.

However, since the Divine Power is essential to and inherent in the Divine Essence, It can comprise no opposites and therefore impotence cannot intervene in It; there can be no degrees in It; nothing can be difficult for it.

The sun has become a niche for the light of His Power. The surface of the sea is a mirror to the light of that niche and the eyes of dewdrops are all tiny mirrors.

The sun, reflected by the broad surface of the sea, is also reflected by the drops on the wrinkles on its forehead. The tiny eye of the dewdrop also shines with it, like a star; they hold the same identity.

From the perspective of the sun, the dewdrop and the sea are the same; its power makes them equal. The pupil of the dewdrop's eye is a tiny sun.

The magnificent sun also is a tiny dewdrop; the pupil of its eye is a light received from the Sun of Power and it is the moon to that Power.

The heavens are an ocean; at a Breath of the All-Merciful, drops undulate in the wrinkles of its forehead, which are the stars and the suns.

The Power manifested Itself and scattered gleams on these drops. Every sun is a drop, every star a dewdrop;

Every gleam is a representation—that drop-like sun is a tiny reflection from this manifestation. It makes its polished glass a bulb for that gleam of manifestation, shinning like a pearl.

That dewdrop-like star has a place in its delicate eye for the gleam and the gleam becomes a lamp, with the filament as the eye— and its lamp is lit up.

Multiplicity manifests unity on either side of it

It is a manifestation of Divine Unity that the beginning and end of multiplicity are united at the same point, displaying the Divine Unity.

It is a manifestation of the Divine Power that the changeable power in the universe transforms unity into multiplicity;

Divine Power is distributed among particles and changes in nature, and it is from this that degrees or rays of gravity arise.

These rays are combined—the Maker makes them into a general gravity, which means multiplicity becomes unity.

If you have any merits or qualities, let them remain under the dust of concealment, so they may flourish

O one of renowned qualities! Do not be oppressive by exhibiting yourself; if you remain under the veil of concealment, you will be a source of favors and blessings for your brothers;

Also, you brothers will benefit from or have a share in your merits; it is even possible that every brother of yours will become like you—this will attract respect to each of them.

But if you emerge from concealment and exhibit yourself, although respected and magnanimous under it, you will become an oppressor in the open. There you were a sun, here you will overshadow others.

You will cause your brothers to lose respect. That means, self-manifestation and being distinguished individually are despotic attitudes.

If this is true of the manifestation of genuine qualities, what place remains for acquiring fame through lying artifice and hypocrisy? This is a profound mystery, and it is in accordance with this that the Divine Wisdom and the perfect order It has established

Draw the veil of concealment over an exceptional individual within their species, thus enhancing the value of the entire species and making it appreciable.

Examples for you: saints among humankind and the appointed hour within a lifetime are unknown, indefinite. Concealed within Friday is an hour when prayers are accepted.

Hidden in the month of Ramadan is the Night of Power and Destiny. Concealed among the All-Beautiful Names is the elixir of the Greatest Name.

It is their being undefined that creates the splendor in these examples —the splendor of the whole of humanity thanks to the saints among it, the whole day of Friday due to the hour when prayers are accepted, and the entire month of Ramadan due to the Night of Power and Destiny.

This beautiful mystery also is made manifest through being undefined and is established through concealment. For example:

There is a balance in the fact that the appointed hour being undefined: in whatever state you are, it always maintains the balance between the two pans of fear and hope, working for the next world and for this. And the imagined permanent existence imparts a pleasure to life.

For a life of twenty years with an unknown end is preferable to one of a thousand years with a known end. For after half of it which has passed, with every passing hour you are taking a new step towards the gallows.

Your suffering increases proportionately; there would be no imagined permanence which would afford you solace and you would find no peace.

It is mistaken to feel mercy or wrath greater than God's

One should not feel or show greater mercy than God's, nor should one feel wrath greater than that of God.

So leave matters to the All-Just, the All-Compassionate One, for excessive compassion causes pain and excessive wrath is wrongful and blameworthy.

Worldly recompense proves punishment in the Hereafter

Everyone has experienced this at least once in their lifetime and concludes: "That person has done that evil and has met with what they deserve." This is a principle in life.

This meaningful sentence is frequently expressed by people. The common point in evils of great variety is the very nature of evil.

This means, that an evil, by virtue of its very nature, is subjected to and requires punishment. Minor evils are punished here, while major ones are referred to the Hereafter.

The worldly recompense for evils is a proof of punishment in the Hereafter.

The ease of humankind is inversely proportionate to one's will and power; provision is a broad, gradually-assembled body

O humankind addicted to evildoing! Your free will and power have become the source and reason of your deprivation and troubles. Provision comes in proportion to weakness and impotence.

Once I saw an animal, which was pathetic, skin-and-bones. An able mother had given birth to it together with several others.

While itself could hardly find a morsel to eat, pleasant, nutritious sustenance flowed forth from its mother's teats; the Divine Power provided that sustenance.

That animate being was extremely weak and impotent while motionless in its mother's womb, but there too it received the best, perfect sustenance.

It came to the world while still weak and impotent, and its sustenance was good and relatively perfect.

It grew a little and began to feel it had a certain degree of will-power. It also began confronting troubles and difficulties, therefore parental compassion was still provided to help it.

But when it found itself to have some power along with will-power, it was set free and left to its own devices. Whatever it attempted to do of its own volition caused nothing but confusion.

When it had been unaware of volition, the mechanism of its body, accustomed to working with perfect regularity, caused no confusion, either in its home or in its town.

But when its will-power began to intervene, the order in its life was destroyed and its will-power left it defective. Therefore, we should always say:

"Our Lord! Do not leave us to our own devices in provision during our adulthood!"

And power should always say: "O my Lord! I have put my trust in You both at the beginning and end of everything in my life!"

In the sight of the Divine Power, the provision of an animate being has the same value as its life.

Just as the Power finds an "excuse" and gives that being its life, It also creates its provision and pours it out.

It is as if the Power works with a constant, intense effort, changing and transforming the world of death into that of life, and the dense into the transparent.

Just as It scatters the gleams of life, even into the lowliest of substances, It also sows and stores up providence in everything.

The dead atoms are set to move to meet with the light of life. Some form real bodies, while others form figurative ones.

Provision comes and is united with them. Provision is scattered wide and it is a broad body. In short, life has two bodies,

One is produced and composed, the other scattered. Provision and life are twins, having the same value in the sight of the Power.

It is the Power Which brings forth everything out of non-existence; Destiny arranges the first body in which it is clothed.

The Divine Favoring collects the provisions, the scattered body, and sends this creature to the existent being to be fed.

There is a difference between these two bodies: since life, the first body of the existing being, is a composition, it is visible in its totality.

Whereas provision is scattered and comes in a gradual process, so humankind worries about it. Unless the wrongful will-power of humankind intervenes, the rule is certainly true:

"There is no dying of hunger; a lack of provision does not cause death." There are many reserves deposited in the body, each of which is full.

Many things are deposited in the form of fat. But before this fat is used up, death comes. Therefore, the reason for death is not a lack of provision.

This sustenance is sufficient for a hundred days, but death can come in ten days.

Perhaps a disease arising from altering or abandoning routine nourishment came and caused death while there was still provision.

The lawful provision of carnivorous animals

There is an order and wisdom prevalent in everything; there is no room for chance, even though it appears to be thus due to our inability to comprehend this universal order which has been established by the Divine Wisdom.

Divine Wisdom has assigned as sustenance the numberless carcasses of wild animals for the flesh-eating ones in the animal kingdom.

It has invited these animals to eat these carcasses, so that they can both clean the surface of the earth and find their lawful provision.

So it is unlawful for them to kill a living one to eat in their way of their life. From elephants to vermin and insects,

Millions of beasts die every day, but none of their carcasses appear in the open. This is worth attention; consider the wisdom and the order of

How the originating Power and the profound Wisdom have made animals and humans needy of provision. They have put the halter of need and hunger on them.

They have put living beings in order through this halter, making them travel within the sphere of need, without allowing them to leave the order.

They both preserve the world from going into utter confusion and chaos and make need a springboard for progress in human life.

Wastefulness leads to dissipation, dissipation leads to poverty

My wasteful brother! Two morsels have the same amount and quality of nutrition, but one costs one kurush (cent), the other, ten;

They are also equal both before they enter the mouth and after they have passed down the throat. Only for a few seconds in the mouth do they give delight to the "intoxicated" sense of taste.

The only difference lies in their tastes, which is a cause of deception; the sense of taste is in fact a doorkeeper and inspector for the stomach.

But the deception causes its misuse. By only tipping the doorkeeper and gratifying it—giving a passing delight to the sense of taste,

One can confuse it in the fulfillment of its duty. Spending eleven kurush instead of one is a satanic habit.

It is one of the worst ways, one of the worst types of wastefulness: do not seek it.

The sense of taste is an informer; do not seduce it with pleasures

The Divine Lordship's Wisdom and Favoring have made, with the mouth and nose, two centers within you, which form a frontier post. They also have appointed correspondents.

In this microcosm—human being, God has made the blood-vessels telephones and the nerves telegraphs, appointing the telephones as assistants to the sense of smell (nose) and the telegraphs to the sense of taste (mouth or tongue).

Out of His Mercy, that True Provider has embedded instructions in all kinds of food: flavor, color, and smell.

Thus, these three attributes are proclamations, invitations, permits, and heralds from the All-Providing: those who are needy and desire food are attracted through them.

He has given the senses of taste, sight, and smell to the animals needy of provision as tools. He has also adorned food with various decorations.

He soothes desirous souls, and attracts the indifferent and idle by exciting them.

When the food enters the mouth, the sense of taste immediately sends telegraphs to every part of the body. The sense of smell telephones, informing us about the type of the food.

The senses and organs that are needy of provision act each according to their need and make the necessary preparations—they either admit or refuse.

Since the sense of taste is a telegrapher, charged with sending telegraphs by Divine Favoring, do not seduce it with pleasures.

For then it will forget what true appetite is; false appetite emerges and pesters it, bringing illnesses and addictions as penalties.

True pleasure springs from true appetite, true appetite from true need; this essential pleasure is sufficient for king and beggar alike, and makes both equal.

Also, while a *dirham* (cent) suffices for that pleasure and soothes the pain of both need and appetite, spending a dinar (dollar) is wastefulness and its value is reduced to that of a dirham.

Like intention, point of view may transform habitual actions into worship

Note this point! Just as through the intention (to lead a life that is pleasing to God), permissible habitual actions may become worship, so too according to the correct point of view, the physical sciences may become knowledge of God.

If you study and reflect, that is, if you look at things as signifying one other—their Maker—and in respect of the art they contain, you will utter: "How beautifully the Maker has made this, how well He has done it!" instead of "How beautiful it is."

If you look from this point of view at the universe, the gleams of purposes for its existence and of its perfection shining from the designing of the Eternal Designer, and the order and wisdom will illuminate your doubts;

And the sciences of the universe will become knowledge of God. But if you look at things as signifying themselves from the point of view of "nature," and from the point of view of "How have they come into being by themselves?"—

If you look thus at the universe, all of your scientific knowledge will be only ignorance. Ownerless truths become thus worthless in worthless hands. The testimonies to this are many.

Merely naming something is sometimes a reason to substitute full knowledge of it

Here is a light, but it darkens or is illuminated darkness—in the present way of thinking, it transforms simple ignorance into compound ignorance.

They give a glittering name to something that is unknown and think that by so doing they have attained full knowledge of it.

Comparing this to other unknown things, they suppose that they have explained them, whereas defining and explaining something means having a full picture of it.

Giving a mere name—the one who gives it is ignorant, and although it appears to the eye to be bright and attractive, its aspect that is connected to the thing named is dark:

It is possible neither to define nor explain with it; only the mind is deluded. Examples of this are many, such as:

General gravity, magnetic force, electric power, telepathy, vibration, and magnetism...

At this time, the Shari'a does not permit affluence

When pleasures call us, we should say: "*Sanki Yedim* (It is as if I have eaten it.)" For someone who made this a rule did not consume a mosque!

Formerly, most Muslims were not hungry, so ease and comfort were permissible to a certain extent.

Now, however, most have fallen hungry, and the Shari'a no longer permits a pleasurable life.

The livelihood of the mass of Muslims, of the majority of the innocents, is simple. So following them in their simple life is a thousand times preferable

To being like the extravagant minority, or the few profligates, in their luxurious lives.

Your pleasure lies in your pain and your pain in your pleasure

O one stricken by calamity!

Pains should urge you to this: You should welcome and smile at temporary pains rather than temporary pleasures.

Pains resemble bees: if you disturb them, they crowd around you, but if you remain indifferent to them, they scatter around to their work.

Whoever "turns back" to think of their past life, their heart or tongue will utter either a sigh of grief or a sigh of relief or words of praise and gratitude for God.

It is a hidden pain in the spirit that is translated by a sigh of grief, while the sigh of relief or the utterance of praise and gratitude for God informs us of a bounty and pleasure in the heart.

The memory of pleasures that remained in the past cause both the heart and the tongue to utter sighs of grief.

For, in the same way that the cessation of pain is pleasure, the cessation of pleasure is pain. Even thinking of or remembering the cessation of pleasure gives the spirit unceasing pain.

It is because of this that each of figurative loves—love for the opposite sex—is a collection of laments, arising from the pain caused by the fear of their cessation.

But the cessation of past pains leads both the heart and the tongue to utter sighs of relief and words of gratitude for God.

The disappearance of a day's pleasure is a perpetual pain, while the disappearance of a day's pain is a perpetual pleasure in the spirit.

The human conscience or consciousness always desires unending pleasure and bounty. This lies in love and knowledge of God, reflection, and spiritual perfection;

It also lies in spiritual gifts that pour into the heart, in gleams of the truth, and in the pursuit of true happiness. These are all possible through, and are based on, belief and certainty of belief in and knowledge of God.

Sometimes the absence of bounty is a bounty

Memory is a bounty, but forgetfulness is preferable for an amoral, heedless person at times of calamity.

Forgetfulness is also a bounty; it allows one to suffer the pains of only the present day but makes one forget accumulated sorrows.

There is a bounty in every calamity

O calamity-stricken one! Within the calamity is a bounty. Look closely and you will see it!

Just as in everything there is a degree of heat, so too in every calamity there is a degree of bounty. Consider a worse calamity and then see the extent of the bounty in the lesser one,

And offer abundant thanks to God. For if you are scared by exaggerating it, and you inflate it with complaints, it will grow.

And as it grows it will worsen. If you worry about it, it will double. Its image in your heart will turn into fact.

Calamity will learn from reality, then turn on you and start striking at your heart...

Do not appear important, or you will be degraded

O you with an inflated ego and conceited head! You should understand and consider this criterion: in human society, in the social structure of the human community, everyone has a window, known as status, through which to see and be seen.

If the window is higher than a person's height (stature or worth), they will, through pride, try to appear as tall (or taller). But if the window is lower than their height (their stature or the extent of their endeavors for God's sake and for people), they will bend and bow down out of modesty.

In the mature and perfected person, the measure of greatness is to know oneself as low-ranking. While in the defective person, the measure of low-ranking is to feign greatness.

If qualities change places, their natures change

One quality—in different places is sometimes a demon, sometimes an angel, sometimes virtuous, sometimes wicked—some examples are as follows:

If an attribute which is regarded as dignity or self-respect for the weak before the strong or powerful is found in the latter, it is pride and arrogance.

If an attribute that is regarded as modesty for the strong or powerful before the weak is found in the weak, it is self-abasement and hypocrisy.

In his office, the gravity of a person of authority is dignity, and his feeling of self-nothingness is self-abasement. But in his house, his feeling of self-nothingness is modesty and his gravity, arrogance.

Forbearance or tolerance on one's own account is good and public-spiritedness, and sacrifice (of one's own right) is also a good deed, a praiseworthy quality.

However, when done on behalf of others, one's tolerance is treachery, and one's sacrifice is a wicked attribute or act.

Entrusting the accomplishment of an affair to God before taking all the necessary measures and making all necessary arrangements is laziness, while leaving the desired outcome's realization to Him after doing all that should and can be done is reliance on Him as taught to us by the Shari'a.

Contentment with one's lot or with the results after having exerted one's efforts is praiseworthy contentment, and encourages further effort, reinvigorating one's energy.

But contentment with what one already has is not desirable contentment; rather, it is lack of the necessary endeavor. There are numerous other examples.

The Qur'an generally mentions good works and piety and righteousness without defining them. By leaving them undefined, it alludes to the defining importance of circumstances; its conciseness is in fact a detailed explanation and its silence, an expansive word.

"The truth prevails" is true both in itself and in respect of the consequences

Friend! A questioner once asked: "As 'The truth prevails' is the truth, why are the unbelievers triumphant over Muslims and force or might is triumphant over right?"

I replied: Consider these four points and your difficulty will be resolved. The first point is this. Every means to every truth and right may not be true and rightful at all times.

Similarly, not every means of every falsehood has to be false. The result is a means which (falsehood employs and) is true prevailing over a false means (which truth or right uses). In which case, a truth is overcome by falsehood. But this has occurred temporarily and indirectly, not essentially or permanently.

However, the final triumph is always that of the truth. (It should also not be forgotten that) force possesses a truth, and there is a purpose and meaning in its creation. The second point is this:

While it is obligatory that all attributes of all Muslims are Muslim, in reality this may not always be so.

Similarly, not all the attributes of all unbelievers have to be connected to unbelieving or arise from their unbelief.

In the same way, all the attributes of all sinful transgressors may not be sinful, nor do they need always arise from sinfulness.

This means that an unbeliever's Muslim attribute prevails over a Muslim's irreligious attribute. Indirectly and due to the means, the unbeliever can prevail over the believer.

Furthermore, in this world the right of life is all-embracing. Life—that meaningful manifestation of the universal Mercy—has an instance of wisdom, which unbelief cannot impede.

The third point is this: two of the All-Majestic One's Attributes of perfection give rise to two sets of laws. One is the Shari'a of life or of the creation and operation of the universe, which proceeds from the Attribute of Will;

And the other, the well-known Shari'a, which proceeds from the Attribute of Speech.

Just as the commands or laws of the well-known Shari'a are obeyed or disobeyed, so too do people obey or disobey the Shari'a of life.

The reward and punishment for the former is received mostly in the Hereafter, while the penalties and rewards of the latter are suffered mostly in this world.

For example, the reward of patience is success, while the penalty for laziness is privation; and the reward of labor is wealth.

The reward of steadfastness is triumph. The punishment of poison is illness and the reward of its antidote is health.

Sometimes the commands of both Shari'as are in force in a single thing; it has aspects pertaining to each.

That means, obedience to the rules of life is a truth, and obedience prevails, while disobedience to it is a false attitude.

If a truth has been the means to a falsehood, when it prevails it will be the true means to a falsehood. This is an example of truth being defeated by a falsehood owing to the means. It is not the defeat of the truth itself by falsehood.

In consequence, "The truth prevails" means: "The truth is triumphant essentially or in itself." Also, the end or consequence is intended.

The fourth point is this: a truth has remained in potential or it is powerless, or adulterated or contaminated. It needs to be developed or given fresh strength.

In order to improve and brighten it, falsehood is temporarily allowed to attack it, so that however much pure gold of truth is needed will emerge unadulterated.

Even if in the beginning falsehood is victorious in this world, it cannot win the war. *"The final (happy) outcome is in favor of the God-revering, pious,"* will strike it a blow!

So falsehood is defeated. The truth of "The truth prevails" inflicts punishment on it. See: the truth is triumphant.

Some social principles

If you want some principles for social life: justice which is not egalitarian is not justice.

The same age and status or social standing cause rivalry and conflict. Being complementary and congruous is the basis of solidarity.

An inferiority complex provokes arrogance. A weak character is the source of haughtiness. Impotence gives rise to opposition.

Curiosity is the teacher of knowledge. Need is the master and wheel of progress. Boredom and distress are the teachers of dissipation.

Thus, the source of dissipation is distress and boredom. As for distress, its mine is despair, pessimism, and evil-suspicion, as well as misguidance in thought, darkness in the heart, and misuse of the body.

Low civilization has destroyed respect toward women

When foolish men become womanish by following their fancies,
Rebellious women become masculine through impudence.

Low civilization has turned women into common goods and destroyed respect toward them.

The Shari'a of Islam mercifully says that it is (basically) their homes where women will enjoy true respect; in their homes, in family life, they are comfortable.

Cleanliness is their adornment, their magnificence lies in their good character, their gracious beauty is in their chastity, their true perfection lies in their compassion, and their children are their relaxation and entertainment.

In the face of so many means of corruption, one has to be as strong and unyielding as steel to remain uncorrupted.

If a beautiful woman enters a gathering of "brothers," ostentation and rivalry and envy and selfishness are aroused. Sleeping fancies and passions suddenly awaken.

Uncontrolled freedom for women has caused a sudden awakening and increase of vices in humankind.

Those small dead bodies called pictures, those smiling corpses, have an important and terrible role in the spirit of modern man becoming cross and ill-tempered.[197]

The prohibited statue is either petrified tyranny, or embodied hypocrisy, or solidified passion. Or it is a talisman that attracts these wicked spirits.

Tendency toward expansion which does not exist in the pious is a tendency to corruption and destruction

O you who are seeking *ijtihad* (new legislation) in Islam to broaden its limits! Consider your body: if the tendency toward its expansion comes from within, it leads to its expansion; but if it comes from without, then it tears your skin.

Similarly, a person sincerely confirms and completely complies with the essential and basic injunctions of Islam: the tendency toward expansion in such a person is a tendency toward perfection.

However, the same tendency in another who is outside the sphere of obedience to Islamic essentials and indifferent to them is a tendency toward corruption and destruction.

At this time, repeatedly afflicted by "storms" and "quakes," it is necessary not to open the door to new legislations, but rather to shut even the windows.

Those heedless and indifferent in belief and the practice of the Religion should not be indulged with dispensations; they should rather be warned strictly and aroused with heavier responsibilities and greater care.

The scope of Divine Power rejects intermediaries and helpers

For the All-Powerful One of Majesty, in relation to the scope of the control and operations of His Power, our sun is like a particle.

In order to have some glimpse of the vastness of the control and operations of His Power in a single realm of beings, take the gravity between two atoms, and then go and put it beside the gravity between the sun of suns and the Milky Way.

---

[197] Just as looking at the dead body of a woman with lust signifies an unparalleled vileness, so too looking desirously at the beautiful picture of a woman who is needy of compassion, which makes her similar to a corpse, extinguishes lofty feelings of spirit.

Bring an angel whose load is a snowflake to a sun-like angel who holds the sun; put a needle-fish beside a whale;

Then consider all at once the vast manifestation of the Eternal All-Powerful One of Majesty and the infinitely perfect "workmanship" in things, from the smallest to the greatest.

The things in circulation such as gravity, conductivity, permeability or pervasiveness, and laws—these are only names for the manifestations of His Power and the instances of His Wisdom;

They can and indeed have no other meaning or function. Think of them together and you will necessarily understand that claiming the existence of efficient or creative causes and means and attributing to Him helpers and partners is all false,

All is illusory and deluding in the face of that Power. Life is the perfection of existence; its rank is great and important. Therefore, I say: why should the earth, our world, not be an obedient, subservient entity, like a docile animal?

The Eternal Sovereign has numerous flying animals of this sort in the arena of space, and they are splendid and beautiful.

He has dispersed them through the garden of creation, and set them in continuous motion. The songs of those in space and the activities of these in the world are all words of glorification, acts of worship of the One Who has no beginning and end, the Eternal All-Wise.

Our earth resembles an animate being that displays signs of life. If, to suppose the impossible, it were reduced to the size of an egg,

It would most probably become a tiny micro-organism. If a micro-organism were enlarged to the size of the earth, most probably it would be just like the earth.

If the universe was reduced to the size of a human being, with its stars forming particles, it is possible it would become a conscious animal; reason does not deny this.

This means, the world with all its parts is a glorifying servant of the Ever-Living Creator, the Eternal All-Powerful One, obedient and subservient.

It is not necessary that a thing should be great in size in order to be great qualitatively, for a clock the size of a mustard-seed is more eloquent than a clock the size of Ayasofya (Hagia Sophia).

The creation of the fly is no less, indeed perhaps more, amazing than that of an imposing creature like the elephant.

If a Qur'an were to be written by the Pen of Power in atoms of ether on an atom from this world, in respect of the art it would contain, inversely proportional to its size,

It would be equal to a Qur'an written in the stars on the face of the heavens. The Eternal Inscriber's art is of the utmost beauty and perfection everywhere.

Everywhere it is thus. Everything being of the same degree of perfection proclaims the unity of the Pen and therefore the Divine Unity. Study carefully this most meaningful piece!

The angels are a community charged with the Shari'a of the creation and the operation of the universe

There are two Divine Shari'as (sets of laws), proceeding from two Divine Attributes; two kinds of humans are addressed, one being responsible for each:

The Shari'a of the creation and operation of the universe, which proceeds from the Attribute of Will, orders the circumstances and movements of the universe, the macro-human, which are not voluntary. It is the eternally determined system of the Lord, and it is what is wrongly termed "nature."

The Shari'a which proceeds from the attribute of Speech is the set of laws which orders the actions of humanity, the microcosm, which are voluntary.

The two Shari'as sometimes are in force in the same kind of beings—God's angels. They are a mighty community, a host of the All-Glorified One.

They are obedient servants and workers, who are responsible for the fulfillment of the first Shari'a; they are representatives, (representing the worship of the inanimate, plant, and animal kingdoms in the Court of God).

Some of them are worshipping servants of God, others are absorbed in knowledge and love of God, stationed near to Him around His Supreme Throne.

The angels are a community charged with the Shari'a of the creation and the operation of the universe

There are two Divine Shari'as (sets of laws), proceeding from two Divine Attributes; two kinds of humans are addressed, one being responsible for each:

The Shari'a of the creation and operation of the universe, which proceeds from the Attribute of Will, orders the circumstances and movements of the universe, the macro-human, which are not voluntary. It is the eternally determined system of the Lord, and it is what is wrongly termed "nature."

The Shari'a which proceeds from the attribute of Speech is the set of laws which orders the actions of humanity, the microcosm, which are voluntary.

The two Shari'as sometimes are in force in the same kind of beings— God's angels. They are a mighty community, a host of the All-Glorified One.

They are obedient servants and workers, who are responsible for the fulfillment of the first Shari'a; they are representatives, (representing the worship of the inanimate, plant, and animal kingdoms in the Court of God).

Some of them are worshipping servants of God, others are absorbed in knowledge and love of God, stationed near to Him around His Supreme Throne.

As matter is refined, life is intensified

Life is fundamental, basic; matter is dependent on and subordinate to it, and subsists through it. If you compare a microscopic organism with its five senses, and the human senses,

You will see that however much larger a human being is than the microscopic organism, his senses are inferior to the same degree.

The organism hears its brother's voice, sees its food. If it were enlarged to the size of a human being, its senses would be amazing, its life dazzling, and the sight of it like lightning flashing in the sky.

A person is not a living being composed of a dead mass, but a living human cell is composed of billions of living cells.

A human is like the large letters of *Ya Sin*, in which is inscribed *Suratu Ya-Sin*. *So Blessed and Supreme is God, the Creator Who creates in the best and most appropriate form!*

Materialism is a spiritual plague

Materialism is a spiritual plague. It has infected humanity with this terrible fever (WW1)—it has made it subject to Divine Wrath and punishment. Through insistent inculcation and imitation,

And in proportion to the growth of humankind's ability to criticize, this plague has become severer and spreads ever wider.

It is inculcated by science and imitated in the name of civilization.

Freedom has led to criticism, and misguidance has sprung from the pride civilization causes.

There is nothing idle in existence; an idle person works on account of non-existence

The most miserable, wretched, and distressed person is the one who is idle. For idleness is non-existence within existence, death within life.

Whereas exertion or working hard is the life of the body and the waking state of life!

Usury and interest are absolutely harmful to Islam

Usury causes idleness and extinguishes enthusiasm for work.

The profit of banks, which are the doors of usury and its containers, is always for the worst of humankind, the infidels.

Its profit for the infidels goes to the worst among them, that is, the oppressors.

The profit of the oppressors always goes to the worst among them; that is, the dissolute; it is absolutely harmful to the world of Islam.

The Shari'a does not require nor does it take responsibility for the continual prosperity of all humankind at all costs. For an infidel at war with Islam and Muslims does not deserve respect or legal protection.

The Qur'an defends itself and perpetuates its authority

I saw a man who was stricken by despair and sick with pessimism. He said: "The scholars have decreased in number, and this decrease in quantity causes a decrease in quality. I fear our Religion will die out one day."

I replied: So long as the universe is not extinguished, Islamic belief will not die out.

Also, so long as the public signs of Islam, the minarets of the Religion, the places of Divine worship, the teachings of the Shari'a—all like stakes firmly placed in the earth—so long as they are not extinguished, Islam will always shine.

The mosques are instructors, teaching those who frequent them through their very existence and nature. The public signs of Islam have all become teachers: through the tongue of their very existence and nature, they never fail or forget to inspire the believers.

All the signs are learned teachers, continually teaching the spirit of Islam to those who look on them, causing the world to last through the centuries.

The lights of Islam are as though embodied in its public signs; and the pure water of Islam is as if solidified in its places of worship, each of which is an embodied pillar of belief.

The injunctions of Islam are as though embodied within the public signs; the pillars of Islam are settled solidly in its domains—each is a diamond pillar, and through them the earth and sky are bound together.

In particular, the Qur'an of miraculous exposition is an orator; it has continually been delivering a pre-eternal discourse—no village, no place at all has remained within the Muslim lands

Which has not listened to its address, nor not heard its teaching. According to the meaning of *It is indeed We Who are its guardians and preservers* (15:9), to be a memorizer of the Qur'an is a very high station. To recite it is worship for humankind and jinn.

Its continual recitation both teaches and repeatedly reminds of the explicit, incontestable essentials of Islam; it also causes the theoretical matters to become so explicit that they require no further explanation.

These essentials of the Religion have ceased being theoretical matters and have become explicit, easily understood realities. To mention them is sufficient; to remind of them is enough. The Qur'an is constantly a healer (healing the wounds in the minds, hearts, and spirits).

Also, through the constant mentioning and reminding of Islam's essentials, and through the Islamic revival and social awareness they generate, the evidence for all these essentials is evidence for each.

Since social life began in Islam, an individual's belief is not restricted to the proofs particular to themselves, nor is their conviction or conscience based on them alone. Rather, such are also based on innumerable proofs that are located in the common heart of the community.

It is worth noting that as time passes it is difficult to abolish even a weak school of thought. So what about Islam, which is based on the two firm foundations—the Revelation and innate human disposition—and which has ruled so effectively for so many centuries!

With its firmly rooted principles, its profound works, it has cohered to half the globe, becoming a natural spirit. How can it be eclipsed, especially when it has just emerged from a temporary eclipse?

Regrettably, certain abusive infidels have engaged in falsehoods to attack the firm foundations of this lofty palace whenever they found the chance.

They try to shake Islam's foundations. But its principles cannot be attacked, or tampered with. Fall silent now, irreligion! That scoundrel is bankrupt. Enough now of this experiment of unbelief and lies!

The Islamic world's advance-post against the world of unbelief was this *Darulfünun.*[198] But due to our indifference and heedlessness, the snake-like enemy was able

To open up a breach behind the front; irreligion attacked and the nation was shaken. This advance-post, this Paradise-like "garden," illuminated by the spirit of Islam,

Should be the firmest, and most truly awakened, in respect of Islam, or it cannot be an institution referred to as the House of Sciences. It must not deceive Islam.

The seat of belief is the heart; the mind is where the light of belief is reflected

The mind is sometimes a warrior (fighting falsehoods), sometimes it is a broom (removing doubts); if the doubts of the mind do not enter the heart, then the faith and the conscience will not be shaken.

If, as some people suppose, belief is in the mind, many baseless possibilities (circulating about in the mind) can become ruthless enemies to the certainty that is based on experience, which is the spirit of belief.

Heart and conscience are the seats of belief. Intuition and inspiration are evidence for belief. There is another sense[199] which is a way to belief. Thought and intellect, or the mind, are the watchmen of belief.

---

[198] Darulfünun was the name of Istanbul University during the Ottoman period. This name literally means the House of Sciences. (Tr.)

[199] By another sense Said Nursi means the "senses" or points of reliance and seeking for help that are ingrained in the human conscience; he refers to this in many places of the *Risale-i Nur.* That is, every human feels the existence of points of reliance or support and seeking help, through which they seek a power to rely on and receive help from particularly in the face of calamities and helplessness. The existence of these senses or points shows the existence of an All-Knowing and Powerful One. (Tr.)

*Rather than instruction in theoretical matters, it is necessary
to remind people of Islam's explicit, incontestable essentials*

The essentials of the Religion, the explicit, incontestable matters of the Shari'a, are present in people's hearts; people will be made fully conscious of these if they are continually reminded of them.

The desired result is thus obtained. The Arabic language performs this reminder in a more sublime fashion.

Instruction in theoretical matters is not required in the sermon. Moreover, Arabic discourse is an imprint of unity on the united face of Islam.

*The Prophetic sayings (hadiths) say to the Qur'an's verses:
It is not possible to reach you!*

If you compare the Qur'anic verses and the hadiths, you will see clearly that even the most eloquent of humankind, the conveyor of the Revelation, could not attain the level of the Qur'an in eloquence.

The Qur'an does not resemble his sayings. That means that all the words issuing from Muhammad's tongue were not his.[200]

A concise explanation of the Qur'an's miraculousness

Once I had a dream: I was at the foot of Mount Ararat. The mountain suddenly exploded, scattering rocks the size of mountains all over the world and shaking it.

Then suddenly, a man appeared at my side. He told me: "Explain the aspects of the Qur'an's miraculousness known to you, concisely and precisely!"[201]

I thought of the dream's meaning while I was still in the dream and told myself: the explosion here symbolizes a revolution in humankind.

As a result of this, the guidance of the Criterion of truth and falsehood (the Qur'an) will be exalted everywhere, and will rule. And the time will come to explain its miraculousness!

[200] That is, apart from his own sayings (hadiths), Prophet Muhammad was also the conveyor of the Qur'an, revealed by God. (Tr.)

[201] By Volumes of books have been written on the inimitability of the Qur'an. What Said Nursi says here is a very brief summary. To a certain extent this was explained with examples in The Twenty-fifth Word. (Tr.)

I said to the questioner in reply: The Qur'an's miraculousness originates in seven universal sources or is composed of seven universal elements:

FIRST SOURCE: This is its brilliant manner of exposition that arises
from the fluency of its wording, the eloquence of its meanings, the originality of its concepts, the purity of its language, the beauty of its word-order,
and the uniqueness of its styles.

All these elements combined, its miraculousness manifests an amazing
embroidery of expressions, and an original linguistic art, thus its repetition
never wearies or bores.

SECOND (SOURCE OR) ELEMENT: Formed of the unseen principles
underlying cosmic events, and the unseen, mysterious Divine truths, and
the unseen realities contained in the heavens, and the events that have
become unseen behind the veil of the past, and the matters and events that
remain unseen behind the veil of the future,

The Qur'an is the tongue of the Unseen; it speaks with the visible, corporeal world, revealing some matters of the Unseen with subtle, profound
and symbolic expressions. It addresses humankind. This is another flash of
its miraculousness.

THIRD SOURCE: The Qur'an has an extraordinary comprehensiveness
in five aspects: in its wording, meanings, commands, and its knowledge,
and the balance in its aims.

Its wording: There are many diverse ways of expression and various
aspects in its wording, each being agreeable in the sight of eloquence, grammatically correct, and perfectly suitable for legislation.

Its meaning: The miraculousness of the Qu'ran's exposition at once
comprehends and contains the ways of all the saints, the illuminations of
those versed in knowledge of God, the schools of those following the Sufi
way, the ways of theologians, and the paths of the philosophers.

The extent and variety of what the Qur'an refers to, and the expanse
of its meanings: if you look through this window, you will see how broad
the arena is!

The scope of its commands: The wonderful Shari'a has issued from
the Qur'an; its pronouncements at the same time cover the principles necessary for happiness in both worlds, the means to salvation and security, the
relations of social life, the methods of education, and responsiveness to circumstantial realities.

The profundity of its knowledge: The Qur'an mentions or alludes to, at different levels, and with signs and indications, both the physical sciences and the Divine sciences; the Qur'an brings together all the paradisal gardens of all types of knowledge within the castles of its suras.

In **its aims and purposes**, the Qur'an has perfect balance and regular sequence, and it fully conforms to and agrees with the principles of the original Divine pattern and system of creation, and it has preserved the balance thereof.

See the magnificent comprehensiveness in the extensiveness of its words, the breadth of its meanings, the scope of its commands, the profundity of its knowledge, and the balance of its aims.

FOURTH (SOURCE OR) ELEMENT: The Qur'an bestows bounteous, luminous gifts and blessings on every age in accordance with its capacity of understanding and literary degree and on all classes of people in accordance with their capacities and abilities.

Its door is open to every era and every class within each. It is as if this Speech of the All-Merciful is freshly revealed at every instant, in every place.

The Qur'an grows younger as time grows older; its allusions and symbols become clearer and more manifest; that Divine Address rends the veil of nature and causes (ascribing creativity to nature and "natural" causes).

The light of Divine Unity in the Qur'an constantly bursts forth from every verse. It raises the veil of the visible, corporeal world from the Unseen. The loftiness of its address invites humans to be attentive.

The Qur'an is the tongue of the Unseen, speaking to the visible, corporeal world. From this source proceeds its extraordinary freshness, its being an all-encompassing ocean of meaning.

The Qur'an includes Divine condescension to human minds so that they may be familiar with it. The fluency of its styles in various forms makes it lovely to humans and jinn.

FIFTH SOURCE: The Qur'an relates all its narrative accounts and the events they contain with their essential points and presents these in an original, meaningful style as though observing the events at first hand.

Through these narrative accounts of the past events, the Qur'an warns humankind. It relates or tells about former peoples and their experiences, future people and what they will experience, the secrets of Hell and the Gardens of Paradise,

And the truths of the Unseen, mysteries of the visible, corporeal world, the Divine mysteries, and the bonds of creation and the universe. Its styles of narration give the impression that the Qur'an relates what it sees.

Neither time nor the facts discovered over time have refuted the truths of the Qur'an, nor does logic ever contradict them. As for the other revealed Books, which are revered by the world,

The Qur'an relates the points on which they agree in a confirmatory manner, and mentions the subjects on which they differ in a corrective style. All this knowledge and these arguments are related or conveyed by someone "unlettered:" this is a wonder of all times!

SIXTH (SOURCE OR) ELEMENT: The Qur'an was the founder of the Religion of Islam and comprises it. If you reflect on time and place, neither was the past capable of producing the like of Islam, nor is the future.

It is a heavenly rope that holds the earth in its annual and daily orbits, rotating it. It rides upon and weighs down the earth, not allowing it to rebel (against its duty).

SEVENTH SOURCE: The six lights pouring forth from these six sources exist one within the other, and it is from these that a beauty arises, and it is from that beauty an intuition, a luminous means of understanding, emanates.

This produces a pleasure that serves the comprehensive pleasure of its miraculousness, but our language is inadequate to describe this, the mind is also insufficient. That celestial star (of the pleasure in its eloquence) is seen, but cannot be held in the hand.

For thirteen centuries the Qur'an's enemies have desired to challenge it, while it has aroused in its friends a desire for imitation. This too is a proof of its miraculousness.

Millions of books have been written in Arabic as a result of these two intense desires, and have entered the library of existence.

If they are compared with the Qur'an, God's Revelation, if they are weighed on a balance, not only the learned scholar, but even the most common people, who only judge by their eyes and ears, will declare: "This one is heavenly; those are human!"

They will also conclude: "It does not resemble them, it is not of the same class. It is either lower than all of them—and this is self-evidently not true—or

"It is superior to all of them." During that long time from its revelation, the meanings of the Qur'an have always remained open to humankind; it has summoned to itself spirits and minds!

Humankind has employed these meanings, and has adopted them, but it still has not been able to oppose the Qur'an with its meanings; humanity will never be able to do this; now the time of testing has passed.

The Qur'an does not resemble other books; it cannot be compared to them. For due to Divine wisdom it was revealed part by part, over more than twenty years, in response to need and in miscellaneous parts.

The Qur'an was revealed on different occasions; to answer different and repeatedly asked questions, and to legislate judgments concerned with numerous and diverse occasions and circumstances. The times of its revelation were all different.

The conditions where the Qur'an was received and communicated were diverse and varied; the groups of those it was addressing were numerous and remote from one another; the targets of its guidance were numerous and of varying levels.

Based on these foundations, the Qur'an explains, teaches, answers, legislates, orders, forbids, advises, reminds, warns, praises, encourages, condemns, and restrains. Yet despite this, the Qur'an is perfect in eloquence, fluency, mutual proportion, and harmony. The sciences of rhetoric, eloquence, and fine arts testify to this.

The Qur'an has a unique characteristic; none of other forms of speech has it. If you listen to a speech, you will see the speaker (or writer) behind it, or you will find them within it: style is the mirror of the person who writes or speaks.

The Qur'an apparently points to the Prophet, its addressee, who is a veil before the Owner of the Speech. The Owner of the Speech is uniquely the Necessarily Existent Being, Whose words or discourses are infinite and innumerable.

He addresses all His uncountable addressees from eternity in the past to the eternity in the future; however, the Speech of the All-Eternal is only heard in embodied, finite speeches.

He could sum up all His discourse in a single manifestation of His Speech, if it had been possible for us to hear all His infinite words all at once,

Or if all His addressees had been a single ear formed of all the particles of the universe—then that universal ear, that universal light of belief, that inspiration in conscience,

Would have seen the representation of the All-Glorified's Speech behind or in infinite speeches or words in all Its majesty and grandeur.

This means that the variation in the styles of the Qur'an is because the Qur'an comprises God Almighty's condescension and manifestations of His Names and Attributes. This is seen by looking with belief behind His speech embodied in the Qur'an.

Every person can say, "In the world, which was built and is heated and lit up as my home, the sun, that eye of the heavens, smiles at me.

"If God had given it consciousness and speech, that delicate, beautiful entity of the heavens would speak to me and a mirror would be the means of communication with it."

The autonomy of mind gives every individual this right, so they can also say, "My Lord speaks to me from behind His speech, the Qur'an; I see an All-Merciful of Light with my belief."

All beings with spirits, even the whole universe, can say this all together, because there is no congestion or blockage when communicating with Him, (as one's benefiting from the sun does not prevent others from benefiting from it). No one can monopolize or restrict it. He is uncontained in time and space.

O dream-questioner! You asked for conciseness, so I have made an indication. If you want a detailed exposition, that is beyond my capability! A fly cannot watch and scan the sky.

For of its forty aspects of miraculousness, only one is the fluency of its word-order; this could not be explained fully in *Isharatu'l-I'jaz*.[202]

This nearly two hundred-page commentary of mine has been insufficient for that. Rather, I want a detailed exposition from you, as your spirit-inspirations are many.

The fanciful, lust-exciting, genius-impressing, earthly hand of Western literature cannot equal the healing, light-scattering, guiding, heavenly, eternal literature of the Qur'an

Anything pleasing to the elevated taste of the mature and perfected does not gratify childish fancies or dissolute natures.

---

[202] *Isharatu'l-I'jaz* is Said Nursi's commentary on *Suratu'l-Fatiha* (the Opening Chapter of the Qur'an) and the first 32 verses of *Suratu'l-Baqara*. It covers more than two hundred pages. It is a key to understanding and commenting on the Qur'an. (Tr.)

It does not entertain them. For this reason, one who has grown amid and been fed with base, dissolute, carnal and lusty pleasures will not know spiritual pleasure.

Looking within a perspective fashioned by and based on novels, the present literature, which has issued from Europe, will neither see nor experience the elevated subtleties or the majestic virtues of the Qur'an.

This literature cannot weigh up or measure the Qur'an by its own scales. There are three arenas in which literature revolves; it roams within their bounds:

Either love and sorrow, or heroism and valor, or a depiction of reality. The Europe-based literature does not seek the truth or acclaim right in heroism; rather, it instills a desire for power by applauding the cruelties of oppressors.

As regards sorrow and love, this literature is not aware of true love; it injects into the soul a lust-exciting thrill.

In the matter of the depiction of reality, it does not look on the universe as Divine art; it does not see it as a painting of the All-Merciful.

Rather, this literature approaches the Qur'an from the point of view of "self-existent nature" or naturalism, and depicts it thus; it cannot free itself from this limitation.

For this reason, what such literature inculcates is a false love of nature. It implants in the heart feelings associated with materialism, from which it cannot easily save itself.

Furthermore, that unmannerly literature is only a sedative and narcotic for the distress of the spirit which arises from the misguidance resulting from materialism; it can provide no remedy.

It has found a single remedy, and that is in novels and fiction. Books are animated corpses, movie pictures are moving corpses. The dead cannot give life!

And the theater—it feels no shame at these three sorts of its fiction resembling "reincarnated" ghosts from the vast grave known as the past.

It has put a false, lying tongue in humankind's mouth, attached a lustful eye to its face, clothed the world in a scarlet dress, and does not recognize pure beauty.

If literature indicates the sun, it puts in the reader's mind a beautiful blonde actress; but it apparently says: "Dissipation is bad; it is not fitting for humanity."

Literature indicates harmful consequences. But its depictions so incite dissipation that they make the mouth water and reason cannot maintain control.

They rouse appetite, excite desire, thus the emotions heed neither advice nor warnings. The literature of the Qur'an, however, stirs up no such desires;

It imparts love of and attachment to right, a passion for pure beauty and pleasure in it, and zeal to attain and establish the truth. It never deceives.

The Qur'an does not look at the universe from the point of view of "self-existent nature" or naturalism; it speaks of it as Divine art, as a painting of the All-Merciful. It does not confuse the mind.

It inculcates the light of knowledge of the Maker. It indicates His signs in all things. Both the literature of the Qur'an and that of the modern age can produce a touching pathos, but they do not resemble each other.

The literature born of Europe excites a pathetic sorrow that arises from a lack of friends, from being ownerless; this is not an elevated sorrow.

This literature is a despairing sadness inspired by a deaf nature and blind force. It knows and shows the world as a desolate wasteland, and not in any other way.

The literature depicts the world in this way, and it takes the sorrowful and places them, ownerless, among strangers, leaving them without hope.

Due to this emotional mood the literature has imbued them with, they gradually move to misguidance; thus the way is opened to atheism, from whence it is difficult to return. Perhaps they never will return.

As for Qur'anic literature, it produces a sorrow, but it is the sorrow of love, not of orphans. It arises from separation from friends, not from the lack of them.

Its view of the universe, in place of blind nature, is as conscious, merciful Divine art; it does not speak of "blind and deaf" nature.

Instead of blind force, the Qur'an describes the wise and gracious Divine Power. The universe, therefore, does not take on the form of a desolate wasteland.

Indeed, in the view of those with sacred sorrow to whom it is addressed, the Qur'an becomes a gathering of friends. On every side there is mutual love and responsiveness, which cause no distress.

There is friendliness at every corner, giving the sorrowful in that society a yearning sorrow, an elevated feeling, not a dejected grief.

Both give rise to eagerness. But through the eagerness that is provoked by alien literature, the carnal soul becomes excited, fanciful desires are stimulated; there is no joy to the spirit.

The Qur'an's eagerness, however, excites the spirit, spurring one on to lofty aims. It is for this reason that the Shari'a of Muhammad, upon him be peace and blessings, does not desire play nor pastime.

It has forbidden some (musical) instruments for amusement, and permitted others. That is to say, instruments that produce Qur'anic sorrow and eagerness are not harmful.

But if such music produces the despairing grief of the orphan or carnal excitement and eagerness, then the instrument is prohibited. It changes from person to person, not everyone is the same.

There are two viewpoints, one dark, the other illuminating

There are two viewpoints, and two kinds of investigation. One is increasingly illuminated and brightened, while the other is increasingly drowned in doubts, with the result that the mind is darkened.

For example: There is delightful, sweet water, flowing from a source. It flows in thousands of canals. Foul things may mix with it in some places.

A person sees the source, tastes the water, and understands that it is sweet. They conclude that the foulness is not from the source.

Whenever one passes by a canal or waterway, the smallest sign that the water is pure and sweet convinces them of its original sweetness and purity.

Only an otherwise decisive, substantial proof can contradict such a sign. Then the person says: "Some other substance has become mixed with this pure, sweet water."

This way of investigation strengthens belief, expands and exhilarates the heart, and develops and flourishes the truth. It is this splendid viewpoint that is encouraged by the Qur'an.

The other viewpoint is faulty and harmful. A foolish one walks with it around the canals unconsciously, instead of beginning from the source.

Their eyes are fixed on the ground; whenever they encounter a canal and see a doubtful sign that the water is bitter,

They doubt that the water is sweet. In order to judge that it is sweet, they seek a conclusive proof.

They desire to base the overwhelming result produced from a huge, pure source on one very insignificant sign.

Their doubt increases (as they encounter some insignificant foulness mixed with the water from the outside), and they begin to lose their former conviction, and become a target of groundless suspicions. The recompense of such a viewpoint is an increase in error.

Their intellect is defective, the principles they follow are flawed, and their capacity for understanding is narrow.

If they cannot reach the truth, they return and say: "This is not the truth," refuting and denying it.

There is a proverb among the Kurds: A bear stood under a vine, and not being able to reach the grapes, said, "Woe to these! They are foul and sour!"

Branches offer fruit in the name of Mercy

Apparently, the branches of the tree of creation extend the fruits of bounties to the hands of living beings on every side.

But in reality it is a Hand of Mercy, a Hand of Power, Which holds out to us these fruits on those branches.

You should kiss that Hand of Mercy in gratitude; you should thankfully proclaim the holiness of that Hand of Power.

An explanation of the three ways indicated at the end of Suratu'l-Fatiha

O brother full of aspirations! Taking your imagination with you, come with me. See, we are in a land, we look around. There is no one to see us.

A layer of black clouds has settled on the high mountains, which are like tent-posts. The clouds have also overshadowed the part of the earth where we are.

They form a solid ceiling over us, but some say its six sides are open and the sun is shining there. However, we are under the cloud and the darkness oppresses us.

The distress is suffocating; the lack of fresh air is killing us. Now three ways are open to us. One is an illuminated realm; I looked upon it once. I also came here once before; I have been to the third realm as well.

The first way extending before us is this: most people take it and it is the way through the world, inviting us to travel it.

See, we are on our way, going on foot. See the boiling sands of this desert, how they are scorching us with their anger, threatening us!

Look at the mountainous waves in that sea; they are furious with us too. Now thank God, we have reached the other side, we can see the sunlight.

But only we know the difficulties we have suffered. Alas! We have returned to this same wasteland, the dark ceiling of cloud hovering over us. What we need is a wonderful light-filled realm,

Which will brighten the eye of the heart; if you have the courage, we will enter this extremely risky way together to reach this destination.

Our second way: we will plunge through "nature," and pass to the other side. Or we will go trembling through a natural tunnel.

I traveled this way once before, full of entreaties and prayers, without feigning reluctance before God. But on that occasion I had with me a substance to smelt and rend "nature."

The Qur'an, the miraculous guide of the third way, gave it to me. Brother, stick close behind me, and have no fear!

See, here await tunnel-like caves and underground torrents. They will let us pass. Let neither nature nor these awesome lifeless beings frighten you in any way!

For behind its sour face the smiling Face of its All-Compassionate Owner—I perceived It through the light of that radium-like substance of the Qur'an.

How happy you are! Now we have come out into the light-filled world; see this graceful earth, this pleasant and lovely heaven.

Raise your head! See, this *Touba*-tree invites us—it grows high into the heavens, has rent the clouds, leaving them far below.

It is the Qur'an. It has spread its branches everywhere. We must hold onto this branch which is trailing down, so that it can raise us up.

One of the manifestations of that heavenly tree on earth is the Illustrious Shari'a. This means we ascend to this world of light in that way without difficulty; we will not be shaken by distress.

As we have gone wrong, we will now return to our former place and find the right way.

See, *our third way*! Over the mountains hovers a Royal Falcon, reciting the adhan to the whole world.

See, the supreme *muadhdhin* (the caller to Prayer), Muhammadu'l-Hashimi, upon him be peace and blessings, is calling humankind to the luminous world of light. He enjoins supplication and obligatory Prayers.

Look at those mountains of guidance! They have rent the clouds and have reached as high as the heavens. See those mountains of the Shari'a, how they have adorned the face and eye of the earth!

Now we must take off from here in lofty aspiration and endeavor. For the light and breeze are up there; the radiant face of grace is there. Ah, now here is the Uhud of Divine Unity[203], that mighty, beloved mountain.

Here is the Judi of Islam[204], that mountain of salvation and safety. Here is the Mountain of the Moon[205], which is the bright Qur'an; the "Nile," the pure water of life and mercy, flows from that sublime source. Take a drink of its sweet water!

> So Blessed and Supreme is God, the Creator Who creates in the best and most appropriate form! (33:14)
>
> And their final call is "All praise and gratitude are for God, the Lord of the worlds!" (10:10)

Friend! Now cast away your imagination and don your reason! The first two ways are those of "*those who have incurred Your wrath*" and "*those who are astray*."

Their perils are numerous. With these is perpetual winter, their whole year is winter. Only one out of a hundred is saved, like Plato and Socrates.

The third way is easy, and direct and straight. Weak and strong are equal. Everyone may take it. The easiest and safest is this: to be either a martyr or a "ghazi."[206]

---

[203] Mt. Uhud is a mountain in Madina, five kilometers north from the Prophet's Mosque. A fierce battle took place before it between the Muslim army and the Makkan polytheists during the Prophet's time, in 624. Once God's Messenger, upon him be peace and blessings, said: "Uhud – it loves us much and we love it much too." (al-Bukhari, "Fadailu'l-Madina" 6; Muslim, "Hajj" 462) (Tr.)

[204] Mt. Judi is the mountain where the Ark of the Prophet Noah settled following the Flood. See, the Qur'an, 11:44. (Tr.)

[205] The Mountains of the Moon are the mountain ranges in Ethiopia that were once believed to be the source of the White Nile. The writer likens belief, Islamic belief and life, and the Qur'an to certain mountains. (Tr.)

[206] "Ghazi" is an Arabic term which means one who has warred in God's cause. (Tr.)

Now we come to the conclusion: the first two ways are the path and school of scientific materialism and philosophy. As for the guidance of the Qur'an, the third way is its straight path; it will take us to our destination.

> O God! Guide us to the straight path. The path of those whom You have favored (with the blessing of guidance), not of those who have incurred Your wrath, nor of those who are astray.

All true pain is in misguidance, and all true pleasure in belief: a mighty truth dressed in imagination

Sensible fellow-traveler! O beloved friend! If you want to clearly perceive the differences between the luminous way of *the Straight Path* and *the dark path of those who have incurred God's wrath* and *those who are astray,*

Come, take your fancy and mount your imagination, together we will go into the darkness of non-existence. We will visit that vast grave, that city full of the dead.

An Eternal All-Powerful One took us out of the darkness of non-existence with His hand of Power, mounted us on existence, and sent us to this world, this city without pleasures.

Now we have come to the world of existence, this fearful desert. Our eyes have opened and we have looked in the six directions.

Firstly, we look before us seeking mercy and help, but tribulations and pain attack us like enemies. We take fright at this and retreat.

We look to left and right to the natural elements, seeking help. But we see their hearts are hard and merciless. They grind their teeth, looking at us angrily and threateningly. They heed neither plea nor plaint.

Like helpless creatures, we despairingly lift our gazes upwards. Seeking help, we look to the heavenly bodies, but see them to be threatening.

As though each was a bomb; having shot from of their housings they are speeding through space. But somehow they do not touch one another.

If one confused its way accidentally, this visible, corporeal world would be blown to pieces; God forbid! They move dependent on chance; no good can come of them.

In despair we turn back our gaze from that direction, overcome by painful bewilderment. We bow our heads, bent over our breasts; we look to ourselves, pondering and studying our own selves.

Now we hear the shouts of myriad needs coming from our wretched selves. The cries of thousands of desires issue forth. While hoping for solace, we take fright.

No good comes from that either. Seeking refuge, we consult our conscience or conscious nature; we look into it seeking a means and seeking help. Alas, again we are left unaided; we have to help our conscience or conscious nature.

For in it are thousands of aspirations, seething desires, wild emotions, all extending throughout the universe. We tremble with all of them, and cannot offer help.

Left unaided between existence and non-existence, these aspirations extend to eternity in the past on one side and eternity in the future on the other. They are so extensive. Even if the conscious nature were to swallow the world, it would still not be satisfied.

Whatever we have had recourse to on this painful path, we have encountered calamities. For the *paths of those who have incurred God's wrath* and *those who are astray* are thus. It is chance and misguidance which lead us on these paths.

It is we who have allowed chance and misguidance to lead us, and so we have fallen into our present state. We are in such a state that we have forgotten the beginning of existence and the end of the world, as well as the Maker and the resurrection of the dead.

We are in a state that is worse than Hell; it scorches more terribly and it crushes our spirits. We had recourse to these six directions, but the result was this state.

It is a merciless state, comprising fear and terror, impotence and trembling, alarm and isolation, being orphaned and despair.

Now we will take up fronts opposite each of the directions (from where we had sought mercy and help, only to fall into a merciless state) and try to repulse them. Firstly, we have recourse to our own strength, but alas! We are powerless, weak.

Secondly, we turn to our souls, hoping their needs can be silenced. But alas! We see that they cry out unceasingly.

Thirdly, we cry out for help, seeking a savior; but there is no one to hear and respond. We think everything is hostile, everything strange. Nothing consoles our hearts; nothing gives a sense of security or true pleasure.

Fourthly, the more we look at the celestial bodies, the more they fill us with fear and awe. A feeling of terrifying loneliness, which vexes the conscience, appears; it torments the mind and fills us with delusions.

Brother! That is the path of misguidance! On it we experienced all the darkness of unbelief. Come, now, my brother, we will turn again to non-existence.

Again we will come. This time our way is the Straight Path and the way of belief. Our guide and leader are Divine Grace and the Qur'an, the Falcon that flies over the centuries.

At one time, the Eternal Sovereign's Mercy and Grace willed our existence, His Power brought us forth, graciously mounting us on the law of His Will, completing us stage after stage.

Then It compassionately clothed us in the garment of existence, bestowing on us the rank of undertaking the Supreme Trust,[207] whose decorations are supplication and the obligatory Prayers.

All of these stages are mansions of bestowal on our long road. To make our journey easy, the Divine Destiny has inscribed a decree on the parchment of our foreheads;

Wherever we go, with whichever group we are guests, we are welcomed in truly brotherly fashion. We give of our belongings, and we receive from theirs: a delightful trade.

They nourish us, adorn us with gifts, then see us off on our way. Now at last we have come to the door of the world. We hear a noise.

See, we have arrived on the earth. We have set foot in the visible world. Here is a promenade and festival, organized by the All-Merciful for the clamorous habitation of humankind.

We know nothing at all, our guide and leader is the Will of the All-Merciful. Our delicate eyes are the deputy of this guide. We open our eyes and look around. Do we recall the former time from where we came?

We were strangers, orphans, we had many enemies. We did not know who our protector was. Now, with the light of belief, which is a strong pillar, we find in us a point of support and a point of help against those enemies.

Our protector, belief in God, repulses our enemies. It is the light of our spirits, the light of our lives, and the spirit of our spirits. Now our hearts are easy and we disregard the enemies, not even recognizing them as such.

---

[207] The Supreme Trust is the human selfhood or being human or human nature as the focus of the manifestations of God's Names that are manifested throughout the universe. (Tr.)

When on our former journey we consulted our conscious nature, we heard innumerable cries, laments, and complaints.

And so we were overcome by calamities. Now, our aspirations and desires, our capacity and senses, constantly desire eternity. But we did not know how to obtain it. We were ignorant of how to obtain it and our conscious nature lamented and cried.

However, all praise and gratitude be to God, this time we have found a point of help; it constantly gives life to our capacity and aspirations, making them take flight for eternity.

It shows them the way, and from that encouraging, mysterious point—belief in God—our capacity receives help, drinks the water of life, and races to its perfection.

The second pole of belief is affirmation of the Resurrection, the resurrection of the dead and eternal happiness. Belief is the pearl of this shell and the Qur'an is its proof. Human conscience is a mystery indicating it.

Now raise your head and take a look at the universe. Speak to it. On our former way how awesome it appeared. Now it is smiling on every side, gracefully winking and speaking.

Do you not see—our eyes have become like bees? They fly everywhere in the garden of the universe, around the multitude of flowers; each flower offers these bees delicious nectar.

Each flower also offers friendliness, solace, and love. Our eyes collect them and bring back the pollen of testimony. They make the most delicious honey flow forth.

As our gaze alights on the movements of the heavenly bodies—the stars, or suns—they give the Creator's wisdom in its hands. Learning important lessons and the manifestation of His Mercy, it takes flight.

It is as though the sun is speaking to us, saying: "My brothers and sisters! Do not feel lonely or frightened. You are welcome, how good of you to have come! This dwelling place is yours; I am but a candle-holder.

"I am like you, naught but a pure, absolutely obedient servant. Out of His utter mercy, the Unique and Eternally Besought One has made me a servant of light for you. Light and heat are from me, supplication and Prayer from you!"

Now look at the moon! And the stars and the seas; each says in its own tongue: "Welcome! It's good of you to have come! Do you not recognize us?"

Look through the mystery of cooperation, lend an ear to the signs of the order. Each says: "We are all servants, mirrors of the All-Majestic One's Mercy; do not worry, do not become weary or fearful of us!

"Let not the roars of the thunder and cries of events rouse in you fear or suspicion, for within them reverberate Divine recitations, glorifications, supplications, and entreaties.

"The All-Majestic One, Who sent you to us, holds their reins in His hands. The eye of belief reveals the signs of Mercy on their faces; each proclaims It."

O believer with a wakeful heart! Let our eyes rest a little; now in their place we will hand over our sensitive ears to the blessed hands of belief. We will send them to the world to listen to its delightful tune.

The voices and sounds that we thought were universal mourning and lamentations of death on our former way are in fact supplications and prayers, cries of glorification.

Listen to the murmuring of the air, the twittering of birds, the pattering of the rain, the splashing of the seas, the crashing of thunder, the crackling of stones; all are meaningful sounds of prayer and glorification.

The melodies of the air, the roars of the thunder, the strains of the waves are all recitations of Divine Grandeur. The chanting of the rain, the chirruping of the birds are all glorifications of Mercy—indications of truth is uttered in their languages.

The sounds of things are all sounds of existence: "I too exist," they say. The silent-seeming universe speaks uninterruptedly: "Do not suppose us to be lifeless, O chattering fellow!"

It is either the pleasure of bounty or the descent of mercy that makes the birds sing. With their different voices, their songs, they applaud mercy, alight on bounties, and take flight with thanks.

Implicitly they say: "Beings of the universe, O brothers and sisters! What fine conditions we live in; we are tenderly nourished, we are happy with our lot!" With beaks pointed to the heavens they send their cheerful songs through the air.

The universe is a lofty orchestra in its entirety; its recitations are heard through the light of belief. For wisdom rejects the existence of chance and the order in existence banishes any formation or event from being attributable to random coincidence.

Fellow-traveler! We are now leaving this world of representations, stepping down from the realm of images. We will stop in the field of reason, follow the ways we have traveled that lie before our eyes and compare them.

Our first, painful way is that of *those who have incurred God's wrath*, and *those who are astray*. It inflicts suffering on the conscience, in its innermost part; suffering and severe pain. Consciousness shows this; we traveled that way in opposition to our conscience.

We must be saved from it, we need to be—either the pain must be alleviated, or human feeling numbed—we cannot endure it otherwise, for our cries for help are not heeded.

Guidance is healing, but carnal tendencies and fancies block out the feelings. Submission to carnal tendencies and fancies requires solace, and solace requires forgetfulness, distraction, occupation, and entertainment

So that those elements of deception can fool the conscience and put the spirit to sleep, stopping it from feeling any pain. Otherwise, that grievous suffering scorches the conscience, the lamentation is unendurable and the anguish of despair cannot be borne.

This means, the farther one deviates from the Straight Path, the more one is stricken by this state, and the conscience cries out. Within every pleasure is a pain, which is a trace of this state.

This means that the glitter of civilization, which is a mixture of fancy, lust, amusement and dissipation, is a deceptive cure for the terrible distress that arises from misguidance; the glitter is a poisonous narcotic.

My dear friend! On our second way, that light-filled road, we perceived a state of mind in which life becomes a source of pleasure, and pain joy.

We understood that the second way imbues the spirit with a state that has various degrees according to the strength of belief. The body receives pleasure through the spirit and the spirit receives pleasure through the conscience.

An immediate pleasure is felt in the conscience; a spiritual paradise is present in the heart. Reflective thought opens up that pleasure only to increase it, while consciousness unveils secrets.

The more the heart is aroused, the more the conscience is stimulated and the spirit stirred, the greater the pleasure; fire is transformed into light and winter into summer.

The doors of paradises open up in the conscience and the world becomes a paradise. Within it our spirits take flight, soaring like falcons and kites, entreating, praying.

Dear fellow-traveler! Farewell for now. Let us offer a prayer together and then we will part to meet again!

O God! Guide us to the Straight Path. Amen.

The answer to the Anglican Church

Once a fierce, pitiless enemy of Islam, a political intriguer, a scheming deceiver who desired to show themselves as superior, in the guise of a priest, with the intention of denial,

At a grievous time, squeezing our throat with its claws, they asked us four things in a spiteful manner, wanting us to answer in six hundred words.

We should have responded by spitting in the face of such spitefulness, and by keeping silent in resentment in the face of their intrigue, and by giving a silencing, resounding answer to their denial.

However, I will not stoop to speak to that enmity, but will give the following answer to a truth-seeking one:

The truth-seeking one asked: "What is the religion which Muhammad brought?" I answered:

"It is contained in the Qur'an. The basic purposes of the Qur'an are the six pillars of belief and the five pillars of Islamic life."

His second question was: "What has it given to human thought and life?" I answered: "It has given unity to human thought and a straight direction to life. My witnesses to this are:

> Say: "He, (He is) God, (Who is) the Unique One of absolute Oneness" (112:1), and Pursue, then, what is exactly right as you are commanded (11:112).

He also asked: "How does it heal the present diseases of humanity?" I answered: "Through the ban on interest and usury, and the obligation of *Zakah*. My witnesses to this are:

> God deprives interest and usury of any blessing (2:176); God has made trading lawful and interest and usury unlawful (2:275); Establish the Prayer and pay the *Zakah* (the Prescribed Purifying Alms) (2:43).

Fourthly, he asked: "How does it view the tumults and revolutions in humanity?" I said in reply:

"Labor is essential, and wealth cannot be accumulated or held only in the hands of the rich and oppressors. My witnesses to this are:

> Man has only that for which he labors (53:39); Those who hoard up gold and silver and do not spend it in God's cause (to exalt His cause and help the poor and needy): give them the glad tidings of a painful punishment (9:34).

Index

A

Aaron (Prophet), 367, 368

'Abd al-Qadir al-Jilani, 233, 235, 252, 592, 700

'Abd al-Qahir al-Jurjani, 432, 462

abdal. See substitutes

ablution, 60, 290, 505

Abraham (Prophet), 5, 62, 229, 230, 382, 383, 436, 468, 550; miracles of, 273

Abu Bakr, 278, 391, 605

Abu Hanifa, 252

Abu Jahl, 278, 605

Adam (Prophet), xxxix, 259, 260, 273, 275, 404, 419, 439, 450, 529, 554, 557; time of, 86, 197, 423, 529, 552, 595, 669; children of, 261, 262, 264, 272, 321, 415; creation of, 415; miracle of, 272, 274

afterlife, ix, xv, xxxii, 110, 164, 363, 380, 455, 456, 527, 535, 537, 547, 549, 649, 658, 661

age of discretion, 138

Ahl al-Sunna wa al-Jama'a, 290, 291, 485, 507

Alawis, 432

alms, 185, 187, 286, 393; -giving 166, 392

America, 117, 189, 607

Americans, 20

angel, of inspiration, 288; of rain, 532

animal desires and appetites, 557, 559

Anti-Christ, 360, 363

appointed hour, 44, 101, 159, 165, 362, 658

Arabia, pre-Islamic, 157, 394, 452, 462; people of, 390

Arabic, xxxiv, 4, 10, 146, 157, 266, 304, 306, 388, 391, 402, 414, 432, 460, 462, 476, 486, 487, 492, 553, 554, 680, 682

Aristotle, 559, 563

ark (of Noah), 205, 398

Ascension (mi'raj), reality of, 583, 585, 586, 588; wisdom of, 592, 595, 596; fruits of, 601, 604

Ash'arites, 485

Astronomy, 286, 592

atheism, xxi, 189, 422, 462, 556, 557, 560, 604

atheists, xii, xxxvii, 160, 169, 188, 189, 190, 237, 596, 612, 624

Ayat al-Kursi, 150, 366

Azrail (Angel of Death), 308

B

backbiting, 367, 402

Barla, vii, xvii, 181, 184, 234, 237, 522

basmala (bismillah), xxviii, 6, 7, 9, 366, 417

Basra, 363

Bayazid al-Bistami, 252

Bayazid Mosque, 199

Be! and it is (command of), 63, 71, 96, 126, 214, 431, 568

belief, in the Creator, 382, 674; in God, xvi, xxxiii, 44, 49, 112, 117, 170, 305, 306, 320, 472, 579; in God's Messengers, 112; in the Hereafter

160, 161, 164, 186, 189, 190, 290, 381, 410, 413, 427, 485, 501, 511, 513

Mu'tazili school, 485, 561

Mu'tazilites, 290, 407, 459

mutual assistance, xxix, xxx, xxxvi, 148, 196, 315, 427, 560

mutual love and respect, 429, 656

mutual support, xxxvi, 315, 427, 432

N

Name, Greatest, 102, 108, 149, 150, 214, 216, 319, 321, 359, 360, 368, 389, 440, 585, 698; sacred Divine, 88, 100, 252, 344, 381, 594

nation of Abraham, 273

nationalism, xxix, 147, 426

natural forces, 559, 613

natural sciences, 417, 561

naturalism, 101, 169, 170, 359, 364, 412, 422, 455, 456, 557, 559, 560, 564, 617, 686, 689

naturalists, 101, 174, 532, 561, 565

nearness of two bows' length, 598, 599

nearness to God, 78, 510, 583

necessary cause, 486, 536, 538

necromancy, 270

neediness, 81, 249, 441, 697, 698

negative nationalism, 426

Neptune, 592

New Said, xxvii, 224, 341, 563

next life, 43, 159, 330, 548

next world, xxxiv, 252, 337

night and day, alternation of, 360, 436, 670

Night of Forgiveness, 366

Night of Power, xviii, 168, 362, 366, 527

nightingale, 224, 373, 374

Nile, 260, 264, 265, 420

Nimrod, 312, 406, 557

Noah (Prophet), 267, 398

nomads, 411, 419

North Pole, 364

Norway, 169

O

objective reasoning, 200, 291, 292, 451

observation, xvii, xxiii, xxviii, 21, 113, 174, 175, 307, 321, 322, 355, 357, 510, 531, 533, 537, 616, 659

old age, xxxii, 44, 59, 60, 130, 160, 223, 341, 652, 658

Omar Khayyam, 561

orderliness, 6, 7, 63, 77, 83, 88, 89, 92, 93, 94, 96, 105, 123, 126, 298, 299, 303, 308, 309, 314, 315, 375, 391, 404, 545, 566, 572, 621, 622, 688

organism, 97, 531, 545, 613, 614, 627

ostentation, xi, 429

Owner, All-Compassionate, 16; Eternal, 4; Majestic Owner of all existence, 98; Munificent, 147; of Majesty, 305; of Sovereignty, 150, 397; of the Day of Judgment, 62; of the universe, 322, 602; of treasuries, 79

P

parables, xxxix, 67, 74, 148, 157, 158, 197, 255, 295, 361, 409, 417, 632, 633

Paradise, blessings of, xxxiv, 486, 521; fruits of, 52, 401, 573; people of, 397, 549, 586, 592, 661, 662; pleasures of, 661; river of, 401

passion, 373, 477, 557, 560, 662

patience, xxxii, 45, 165, 166, 652, 657

Pen of Destiny, 83, 94, 488, 574

penitence, 450, 506, 700

People of the Book, 426

Peripatetics, 531

pessimism, xx, 561

Rafidites, 656

Ramadan (holy month of), xviii, 98, 186, 189, 199, 233, 362, 468, 563, 611

reality, of creation, 532; of things 157, 158, 197, 453, 454, 536, 694

realm, intermediate, 37, 163; permanent, 76, 80, 103; of eternity, 37, 114, 117; of happiness, 114, 129, 519; of requital, 82; of the Unseen, 68; of Wisdom, 125

Reckoning, 26, 91, 205, 488, 684

red blood corpuscle, 613, 617

reincarnation, 420

religion, of Islam, 466; of truth, 424; true, 49, 169, 620, 699; universal, 161

religions, xiii, xxiii, xxxii, 194, 427, 447, 531, 547, 699

religious, commandments, 269, 432, 510; innovations, 500; obligations, 163, 291, 481, 494; orders, 415, 510; scholars, xvi, 513, 531, 532, 533, 650

remembrance, 5, 247, 372, 674

renunciation, 513

repentance, xxxvi, 341, 449, 487

reproduction, 128, 311, 428, 573, 614, 660

researchers, 304

retaliation, 167

revolutions, 59, 74, 127, 243, 255, 299, 303, 330, 421, 427, 473, 509, 614, 631

reward, and punishment, 117; for religious acts, 365

rhetoric, 289, 414, 429, 430

Right Path, 290, 291, 559

righteous deeds, 425, 473, 649, 650, 651

righteousness, xxxv, 79, 112, 512, 550

Risala al-Hamidiya, 596

Risale-i Nur, v, xi, xiii, xv, xvii, xviii, xix, xx, xxi, xxii, xxiii, xxiv, xxv, 116, 159, 163, 164, 167, 168, 169, 170, 306, 461, 467, 470, 474, 475, 476, 477, 512, 579, 608, 626, 683

Romans, 424

Ruler, Just, 16, 102, 196, 269, 584, 585, 639; Majestic, 198, 395; Overwhelming, 196; Wise, 117, 588, 597, 668

Rumi, Mawlana Jalal al-Din, 236

Russia, 364

S

Sa'd al-Din al-Taftazani, 606

safety, 4, 16, 60

sages, 158, 412, 454, 638

Sahara Desert, 260

sainthood, 235, 357, 463, 507, 509, 511, 581, 582, 583, 586, 592, 600, 608, 640, 700

Sakkaki, 432, 462

salvation, xiv, 30, 53, 228, 432, 469, 470

Satan, vii, 30, 136, 199, 200, 201, 202, 203, 204, 205, 206, 259, 260, 261, 274, 288, 289, 290, 291, 292, 343, 407, 419, 420, 474, 476, 513, 527, 556, 645; tube of, 288

Satih, 596

Saturn, 286, 447

Sayed Sharif al-Jurjani, 635

scholars, purified, 79, 113, 116, 136, 322, 354, 389, 451, 457, 638, 673; saintly, 194, 356, 396, 639, 641; truth-seeking, 158, 160, 267, 320, 415, 453

schools, of conduct, 291; of philosophy and scientists, 425

science, of electricity, 171; of eloquence, 267, 431, 462, 471, 633; of medicine, 504

scientific thought, vi, 155, 456

scientism, vi, xiv, 145, 254, 429, 674

scientists, xv, xxviii, xxix, 101, 255, 268, 277, 369, 405, 411, 412, 422, 425, 547, 589, 595

Index of God's Names and Attributes

Lord, All-Compassionate, 334; All-Majestic
and Gracious and Munificent, 373;
All-Majestic, 310, 371; Exalted, 61; of
(all the) saints, 247; of Beauty and
Majesty, 344; of creation, xxxvii, 116,
554; of infinite Compassion and
Mercy, 86; of Majesty, 106; of
Perfection, 305; of the command Be!
and it is, 214; of the heavens and
Earth, i, 115, 172, 195, 370, 371, 500;
of the universe, 86, 115, 310, 581; of
the Worlds, 62, 86, 138, 149, 279,
323, 352, 367, 371, 389, 438, 439,
472, 575, 576, 584, 597, 598, 602,
605, 663; Majestic and Munificent,
373; Merciful, 109, 604; Munificent,
138, 373, 683, 691, 692; Sovereign
Lord of the universe, 86
Lordship, kingdom of God's, 198; seal of,
310; sphere of, 244, 586
All-Loving, 233, 354, 493, 630, 637, 639,
640, 643, 644, 692

M

All-Majestic, 8, 61, 89, 135, 151, 175,
180, 181, 182, 212, 213, 214, 215,
230, 234, 236, 264, 265, 271, 287,
308, 310, 313, 314, 319, 352, 371,
372, 373, 374, 375, 377, 383, 384,
448, 549, 591, 645, 677, 685, 688
All-Majestic One of Grace, 212, 215;
All-Majestic One of Perfection,
214; Majestic One of Splendor and
Glory, 82
Majesty, Supreme, 81, 616
Maker, xxxvii, 37, 77, 79, 80, 85, 89, 93,
95, 100, 104, 105, 115, 120, 130,
137, 138, 140, 147, 156, 172, 174,
181, 189, 198, 212, 217, 221, 222,

231, 236, 237, 238, 243, 244, 255,
287, 305, 308, 309, 312, 314, 317,
318, 327, 328, 345, 376, 399, 411,
412, 413, 416, 417, 418, 434, 455,
456, 459, 478, 491, 496, 518, 533,
534, 539, 540, 543, 549, 550, 554,
555, 556, 559, 565, 568, 571, 572,
573, 583, 587, 588, 590, 591, 593,
594, 597, 598, 599, 600, 602, 603,
604, 613, 615, 616, 617, 619, 620,
621, 622, 623, 625, 630, 631, 635,
639, 643, 644, 645, 646, 648, 652,
654, 659, 660, 668, 669, 670, 671,
672, 673, 675, 678, 681, 682, 683,
684, 685, 687, 689, 690, 691, 692,
693, 695, 698, 699; All-Beautiful,
243; All-Majestic, 230, 236, 287,
308, 314, 383, 384, 591, 688; All-
Munificent, 222, 683; All-Powerful,
77, 181, 626, 692; All-Seeing, 37;
All-Wise, i, 129, 212, 216, 221, 412,
413, 417, 518, 550, 572, 614, 642,
646, 653, 669, 670, 671, 672, 677,
681, 683, 685, 688, 692, 697;
Eternal, 92; Gracious, 137, 198, 583
All-Merciful, xxviii, 8, 10, 11, 37, 59, 62,
63, 80, 82, 87, 88, 90, 113, 137, 149,
170, 171, 234, 251, 252, 317, 318,
321, 329, 335, 340, 373, 374, 375,
388, 425, 442, 492, 493, 540, 590,
602, 603, 627, 630, 638, 639, 643,
644, 648, 649, 650, 651, 654, 655,
660, 677, 679, 686, 693, 700; All-
Merciful One of Infinite Beauty, 335;
All-Merciful One of Perfection, 63
Mercy, eternal, 113, 129; fruits of, 316;
gifts of, 82, 213; laws of, 268; robe of,
316; seal of, 8; treasure of, 81; treasury of, 236, 264, 317, 358, 437;
wealth of, 20